I Believe. Help My Unbelief!

I Believe. **Help My Unbelief!**
Christian Beliefs for a Religiously Pluralistic and Secular World

Veli-Matti Kärkkäinen

CASCADE *Books* • Eugene, Oregon

I BELIEVE. HELP MY UNBELIEF!
Christian Beliefs for a Religiously Pluralistic and Secular World

Copyright © 2024 Veli-Matti Kärkkäinen. All rights reserved. Except for brief quotations in critical publications or reviews, no part of this book may be reproduced in any manner without prior written permission from the publisher. Write: Permissions, Wipf and Stock Publishers, 199 W. 8th Ave., Suite 3, Eugene, OR 97401.

Cascade Books
An Imprint of Wipf and Stock Publishers
199 W. 8th Ave., Suite 3
Eugene, OR 97401

www.wipfandstock.com

PAPERBACK ISBN: 978-1-7252-7667-3
HARDCOVER ISBN: 978-1-7252-7668-0
EBOOK ISBN: 978-1-7252-7669-7

Cataloguing-in-Publication data:

Names: Kärkkäinen, Veli-Matti, author.

Title: I believe. Help my unbelief! : Christian beliefs for a religiously pluralistic and secular world / by Veli-Matti Kärkkäinen.

Description: Eugene, OR : Cascade Books, 2024 | Includes bibliographical references and index(es).

Identifiers: ISBN 978-1-7252-7667-3 (paperback) | ISBN 978-1-7252-7668-0 (hardcover) | ISBN 978-1-7252-7669-7 (ebook)

Subjects: LCSH: Christianity and other religions.

Classification: BR127 .K37 2024 (paperback) | BR127 .K37 (ebook)

VERSION NUMBER 07/25/24

Bible references, unless otherwise indicated, are from the Revised Standard Version of the Bible, copyright 1952 [2nd edition, 1971] by the Division of Christian Education of the National Council of the Churches of Christ in the United States of America. Used by permission. All rights reserved.

Christian creeds are from *The Creeds of Christendom*. Edited by Philip Schaff. 3 vols. New York: Harper & Brothers, 1877. 6th ed. Available at the Christian Classics Ethereal Library: http://www.ccel.org.

Roman Catholic documents, documents of Vatican II, papal encyclicals, and similar works are quoted from the official Vatican website: www.vatican.va.

Qur'anic references, unless otherwise indicated, are from *The Holy Qur'ān: A New English translation of Its Meanings* © 2008 Royal Aal al-Bayt Institute for Islamic Thought, Amman, Jordan. This version of the Qur'ān is also available online at http://altafsir.com.

Hadith texts are from the Hadith Collection website: http://www.hadithcollection.com/ (2009-).

Buddhist texts, unless otherwise indicated, are from "Tipitaka: The Pali Canon," edited by John T. Bullitt. Access to Insight, May 10, 2011 (http://www.accesstoinsight.org/tipitaka/index.html).

Bhagavad-Gita texts are from the translation by Ramanand Prasad, 1988. Available at http://www.columbia.edu/itc/religion/f2001/docs/bhagavad.pdf.

Rig Veda texts are from the translation by Ralph Griffith, 1896. Available at the Sacred Texts website: http://www.sacred-texts.com/hin/index.htm.

Upanishad texts are from *Sacred Books of the East* [SBE]. Translated by Max Müller. Vol 15. Oxford: Oxford University Press, 1884. Available at the Sacred Texts website: http://www.sacred-texts.com/hin/index.htm.

Contents

Preface | ix
List of Abbreviations | xi

Introduction | 1
1. Revelation: How Do We Get to Know God? | 7
2. God: If God Exists, What Is He Like? | 36
3. Creation: How Did Everything Come into Existence? | 77
4. Humanity: What Is the Human Being? | 110
5. Christology: Why Do We Need Jesus? | 155
6. Reconciliation: What Did Jesus Do for Our Salvation? | 197
7. Holy Spirit: What Is the Holy Spirit Doing in the World? | 218
8. Salvation: What Does It Really Mean to Be Saved? | 241
9. Church: For What Do We Need the Christian Community? | 287
10. Eschatology: What Will Happen at the End? | 356
    Epilogue | 415

Bibliography | 417
Author Index | 433
Subject Index | 437

Preface

It may not be an overstatement to claim that the book you are holding in your hands is totally unique. For while the presentation of key Christian doctrines and beliefs in itself is not of course a unique genre of literature, the way this primer introduces the basic tenets of faith is distinct in at least the following ways:

First, I know of no other book that also discusses the teachings of other living faith traditions—in this case, of four religions—alongside Christian ones. In this one, I introduce Jewish, Islamic, Buddhist, and Hindu "theologies" and put them in a sympathetic dialogue with Christian tradition. The added benefit of this is that besides Christianity, the reader also gains quite a lot of knowledge about these four faiths.

Second, this book is not limited to any particular Christian denomination, and indeed it also engages testimonies, insights, and spiritual advice from all over the globe and from teachers of diverse backgrounds, both female and male, Black, White, and Brown, as well as those who have quite different agendas. While sharing the common faith of the church, this diversity of voices and perspectives also highlights particular aspects of the rich and variegated Christian heritage.

Third, this book engages not only the living faith traditions but also sciences and the scientific worldview—for the simple and obvious reason that the most influential social and cultural force in the modern world is the discoveries and insights of natural sciences, whether those that explore the vast cosmos or those that study humanity. That the sciences are so influential is not only the case in the Global North (Europe and North America) but also in the Global South (Africa, Asia, and Latin America). In fact, both the biggest challenges to any religious faith and potentially the most fruitful opportunities for dialogue come from the scientific world.

Fourth, this book engages secular people's voices. Why? A growing number of men and women no longer subscribe to any religion. These "nones," as they are called, wish to live without a faith commitment in the traditional sense. In order not to exclude this growing section of humanity, a posture of attentive listening is important for current theology.

Finally, as expressed in its title, this book takes a questioning and open-minded approach to basic Christian doctrines and convictions. What this means is that such an open-minded and honest approach also critically and sympathetically investigates the foundational beliefs of Christian faith for their truthfulness and credibility. While I, as the author, do not want to hide my deep commitment to the faith of the church, neither do I want in this book to hide or minimize the many questions and problems related to my—and to any—faith tradition. Similar to the concerned father in the Gospel narrative who came to Jesus to seek help for his child, many of us in the beginning of the third millennium confess, "I believe—help me in my unbelief."

This text is based directly on my widely used 2019 academic textbook, *Christian Theology in the Pluralistic World: A Global Introduction*.[1] Yet in contrast to typical textbooks, this new one is conversational in style and does not tire the reader with documentation beyond direct references and the like.

As with the rest of my publications, I remain grateful to my school, Fuller Theological Seminary (in Pasadena, California) for providing professional editorial services (Ulrike Guthrie) and doctoral student-level research assistance (Mike Smith). While any mistakes or inaccuracies are my fault, without this indispensable aid the amount and weight of them would most probably be much bigger!

---

1. That textbook of over six hundred pages with its careful bibliographic documentation is based on a massive five-volume highly technical theological project titled *A Constructive Christian Theology for the Pluralistic World*, published by Eerdmans between 2013 and 2017: *Christ and Reconciliation* (2013), *Trinity and Revelation* (2014), *Creation and Humanity* (2015), *Spirit and Salvation* (2016), and *Community and Hope* (2017).

Abbreviations

OT   Old Testament

NT   New Testament

ANF   *The Ante-Nicene Fathers: Translations of the Writings of the Fathers down to AD 325.* Edited by Alexander Roberts and James Donaldson et al. 9 vols. Edinburgh, 1885–1897. Public domain; available at www.ccel.org.

NPNF¹   *A Select Library of the Nicene and Post-Nicene Fathers of the Christian Church.* 1st ser. 14 vols. Edited by Philip Schaff. Edinburgh, 1886–1890. Public domain; available at www.ccel.org.

NPNF²   *A Select Library of the Nicene and Post-Nicene Fathers of the Christian Church.* 2nd ser. 14 vols. Edited by Philip Schaff and Henry Wace. Edinburgh, 1890–1900. Public domain; available at www.ccel.org.

SBE   *Sacred Books of the East.* Translated by Max Müller. 50 vols. Oxford: Oxford University Press, 1879–1910. Available at www.sacred-texts.com.

Introduction

Why Bother with Beliefs—of Any Religion?

Faith or Knowledge?

Friends of Fouls?

MANY MODERN PEOPLE CONCEIVE of "faith" as the opposite of knowledge and facts. They routinely take faith to be a synonym for willingness to believe something that one does not necessarily know to be true. In some extreme cases, even if a believer knows that what she believes is not true, she still holds that opinion. Faith here is the opposite of fact. Such believers would likely say that while science tells us how things are in reality, religion encourages and consoles us, and does so with outdated beliefs that lack factual basis.

If this were true, I myself would not want to have anything much to do with religion. For even if religion did help me cope with life's obstacles, such religion would be—as the great nineteenth-century Russian atheist Karl Marx put it—"the opiate of the masses." Without a basis in reality, such religion would ultimately fail me, and fail badly.

Do I then think that faith and knowledge are to be equated with one another? No, I do not. But I, like many other Christian thinkers over two millennia, believe that beliefs could (and should!) have a reasonable basis for me to take them seriously. Or to put it another way, I think that while believing and knowing should be distinguished from one another, they should not be separated. A belief that is known to be irrational or absurd does not merit the nomenclature "belief." It is humbug. Whereas belief in, say, the resurrection of Jesus Christ from the dead, while hardly an uncontested conviction, may stand upon some historical and logical evidence. Even if such a belief is a counterintuitive claim, even if it might test our intellectual capacity, critical scrutiny may yield some solid evidence to undergird it.

I have found very helpful the epistemology (a branch of philosophy inquiring into the conditions and possibility of knowledge) of a former natural scientist turned philosopher, Michael Polanyi. He speaks of *Tacit Knowledge* (to cite the title of one of his well-known books). Tacit knowledge is a kind of anticipation, a hunch that a particular statement or fact or theory seems to be true. This kind of assumed knowledge "knows" before it really knows and just has to be tested and tried in the court of rational and life experience.

How Does Theology "Know"?

In this light it is instructive to note how the term "theology" came to be used in Christian circles beginning from early centuries. Far from being a Christian term in its origins, it was applied to three different branches of study and investigation. The first was the "mythical" theology of the poets concerning the deities and divine figures, who were often made in the image of humans with all kinds of rivalries, envy, and hatred among them. The second branch was called "political" theology, or theology of public life in the service of the emperor. This type of theology was (ab)used to consolidate and strengthen the power of the political elite. The third and final branch of study came to be called "natural" theology. Its ultimate goal was to investigate the true nature of deities—provided they even existed. Critical of fantasies of both the myths and power-play of the elites, natural theology wanted to know the truth about God and to seek to speak of God in a way in keeping with God's true nature. That was the "real" theology!

Early Christian tradition, while for a long time suspicious of adopting this pagan term "theology," reluctantly landed on it. In Christian circles, the term "theology" ultimately came to refer to Christian doctrines and beliefs derived from the Bible and from the developing Christian tradition.

From the beginning, Christian theologians were convinced that alongside—and perhaps we could say beyond—individual doctrines such as of the Trinity and of salvation, there is also an all-encompassing Christian vision of the world and God. In other words, there was the idea of a Christian interpretation of all that there is, including but not limited to human life.

If God is the creator of everything, as Christians do believe, then as the medieval Christian genius Thomas Aquinas would say, the object of theology is God *and* everything in relation to God precisely because God has created everything. In that spirit, one of the greatest recent theological minds, the late German Lutheran Wolfhart Pannenberg, has argued forcefully that theological work should not isolate itself by concerning itself merely with "spiritual" things (such as God, salvation, and prayer), but that it should also work hard with sciences that study God's creation, history that investigates the happenings of humanity, and so forth.

This kind of broad and comprehensive vision also guides my own theological work. As a result, as a part of laying out a Christian vision of the world, this primer discusses the insights of sciences, cultural studies, politics, and say, entertainment. It gives appropriate space to a careful dialogue with (natural and behavioral) sciences because sciences "rule" contemporary public life in the world of the third millennium. Particularly important is a careful consideration and exchange of ideas with sciences in relation to the doctrine of creation, the nature of human beings (theological anthropology), and eschatology, the doctrine of the last things.

While I wish to present a compelling account of Christian beliefs, I do not write this book as a hard-nosed apologist (a defender of faith) who wishes to convince the rest of the world of the rightness of Christian position. Rather, my approach is suggestive, inviting readers, whether Christians, atheists, agnostics, or of any other stripe, into a conversation. That said, no one lays out a vision of a particular religion or another ideology without having confidence in its explanatory power, and even its salvific power (in this case, of Christian faith).

Christian Beliefs in a Religiously Pluralistic and Secular World

How Radically the World around Us Is Changing!

Although theology in the third millennium continues the original task of explaining and seeking to make reasonable basic Christian beliefs, what is different from earlier times is the ever-complexifying environment in which Christian doctrine is worked out. This diversity relates to both the worldwide church itself and to the world in which the church ministers.

Did you know that the most typical Christian is not a well-educated White male from Europe or a White upper middle-class female from the US? No, the majority (currently more than 70 percent) of Christians are in the Global South (Africa, Asia, Latin America). By 2050, only about one-fifth of the world's three billion Christians will be non-Hispanic Whites. As a result, even in the US (and to a lesser degree in Europe) a typical Christian will increasingly be a younger, poorer, non-White person.

There is also a massive transformation of the church in terms of denominations. Whereas Roman Catholics continue to be the biggest church (at roughly 50 percent of all Christians), it is Pentecostals and Charismatics rather than the Reformed, Lutherans, United Methodists, or Baptists who form the second biggest category, about 25 percent.

In the world of the third millennium, unheard of cultural, social, economic, and gender diversity continues unabated. In the past, the church could safely assume that most people look alike, form a homogenous society, and tend to think alike. Not anymore. The world of this third millennium is extremely diverse and comes in many "colors" and "sounds."

This apparent diversity and complexity of the worldwide church and the world has brought to Christian vocabulary terms such as "global," "intercultural," and "contextual." Whereas the meaning of *global* is familiar to any English speaker, in theology it emphasizes an attempt to include a worldwide reach of testimonies and interpretations of Christian doctrines. In other words, when speaking of, say, Jesus and salvation, not only the views of elderly gray-haired Euro-American White male theologians are brought to the dialogue but also those of women, people of color, LGBTQ+, and younger folks. This makes the study and teaching of theology contextual: it seeks to speak in a way that is aware of its conditioning by the particular context or environment including gender, social class, race, and so forth.

Why Should Christian Theology Also Speak to Other Religions and the Secular World?

Furthermore, religions continue their growth despite the rumors of the coming secularization of the world. At the time of this writing in 2024, 6.6 billion people out of the world's 7.7 billion subscribe to a living faith tradition. Whereas Christianity is the largest religion with 2.4 billion adherents, Islam's current 1.6 billion number will outgrow Christianity by 2050, making it the religion with the most adherents. Currently there are a billion Hindus, mostly in the sub-continent of India, less than half of that number of Buddhists, and a tiny group of Jews.

What about the seculars or those with no faith ("nones")? As counterintuitive as it may sound to someone living in the Global North, the current secular 1.1 billion share of the world's population is getting a bit smaller rather than bigger when compared to religion's followers. Yet, secularism (and post-secularism, of which more in chapter 9) is a dominant force in the contemporary world and calls for a theological response as well.

One of the most dire liabilities of Christian theology has been its oblivion to other faith traditions. Theology has been taught, studied, and written as if the world has only one religion, as if some believe while others reject it, and without due attention to the great diversity of religious teachings and beliefs. Now we have slowly come to the conviction that a sustained dialogue is necessary not only for practical reasons such as building trust and helping communicate the gospel, but also because it is a *theological* mandate; that is, if the object of theology is God and everything God has created, then religions certainly belong to its domain. Therefore, this primer also engages the beliefs and teachings of other faith traditions (Jewish, Muslim, Buddhist, and Hindu).

This kind of dialogical way of doing theology—of listening to and learning from others while at the same time sympathetically critiquing the convictions of other faiths—may become an exercise in hospitality. It honors the otherness of the religious other and also makes space for an honest, genuine, and authentic sharing of one's convictions.

With these desiderata in mind, allow me to sketch out the big picture of this book.

The Plan and Nature of the Primer

This book's goal is to present a viable Christian vision of God and of the world—of everything—that God has created. While I treat Christian doctrines and beliefs in an innovative way, in subsequent chapters I follow this ancient and trusted order of topics:

- Revelation: How Do We Get to Know God?
- God: If God Exists, What Is He Like?
- Creation: How Did Everything Come Into Existence?
- Humanity: What Is the Human Being?
- Christology: Why Do We Need Jesus?
- Reconciliation: What Did Jesus Do for Our Salvation?
- Holy Spirit: What Is the Holy Spirit Doing in the World?
- Salvation: What Does It Really Mean to Be Saved?
- Church: For What Do We Need the Christian Community?
- Eschatology: What Will Happen at the End?

What makes the discussion of all of these topics new and novel is that alongside typical theological resources (biblical, historical-theological, and contemporary-theological, including global and contextual diversity), where relevant I include insights from sciences and other secular disciplines, and a continuing dialogue with other faiths. For a professor like me it is a tall order, but I will make every effort to keep the conversation non-technical and comprehensible.

1

Revelation

How Do We Get to Know God?

Why Do We Need Revelation—or Do We?

THERE IS VIRTUALLY NO living faith tradition without sacred books and without belief in their revelational capacity to tell us something essential about the Divine. Christianity is no exception to the rule. We Christians believe that the Triune God—Father, Son, and Spirit—has revealed God's own self to humans—not fully and exhaustively, as that is hardly possible for a finite human mind, but as much as is necessary for salvation and for finding the meaning of life.

In Christian tradition, the notion of revelation encompasses more than a mere book. As important as the Bible is, with the Old and New Testaments, the Christian doctrine of revelation, alongside writing and divine speaking, is also an *embodied* or *incarnational* event, the "Word was made flesh" (John 1:14 KJV).

Why do we need revelation? For two reasons. First, a finite human mind can never correctly imagine the nature and activities of an infinite God who, according to the biblical testimonies, is a mystery. As much as we humans may have correct ideas and intuitions of God, those ideas and intuitions are always only partial. Second, we believe that the human being, though created in God's image, has also fallen from grace. Therefore, there is also a defect of and deficit in human knowledge due to sin and corruption, not a total block but a defect and deficit. Hence, we humans need divine self-revelation.

Where might we find the divine revelation? What are its sources? Only after answering those questions can we define the uniquely Christian understanding of revelation as "triune-shaped," based on the joint work of the Father, Son, and Spirit. Throughout the book you will notice that I base every theological topic on and treat it from the perspective of the most distinguishing feature of our faith, the Trinity—and of course, the following chapter as a whole is an investigation into its many facets.

It is one thing to claim that divine revelation can be found in Christian faith. It is quite another to wonder whether it really is possible to believe in divine revelation in the modern world. I tackle this concern in all of its radical nature in the following discussion of various "models" or ways of understanding revelation in our contemporary world.

Thereafter, I scrutinize the all-important claim of Christian theology about the Bible as fully God's *and* a fully human word. What does such a claim mean? Is it believable? Another big, foundational question has to do with the location of the ultimate authority for Christians: Does it rest in the Bible alone, in the church's tradition, or in something or someone else?

The last major section of this chapter delves into the notions of revelation and sacred writings in four other faiths (Judaism, Islam, Hinduism, and Buddhism) and their relation to Christian notions of revelation. The better you know the basics of these faith traditions' views of revelation, the more you gain from comparative exercises throughout this book.

Where Can We Find Revelation?

In brief, divine revelation can be found in:

- general revelation, in
  - nature,
  - history, and
  - human being; and
- special revelation in Jesus Christ, in
  - the "Word made flesh," and
  - the Bible, the written Word.

Christian tradition believes that revelation is fully and most perfectly available in Jesus Christ, God among us, and derivatively, in the written Bible, the testimony to what God has accomplished for our salvation in Christ. The most well-known twentieth-century theologian, the late Karl Barth of

Switzerland, famously added the third layer to the special revelation—the church's preaching of the Word, of course derivative from the Bible.

Furthermore, the Christian Church has universally assumed that revelation also, though less completely, comes through other means, such as through nature, history, and human being.

If God is the creator and provider of all, as we Christians believe, then it is only logical to believe that behind and beyond the historical happenings—which, to be honest, often give the observer an impression of senseless events—can be seen the divine hand. Especially in the history of the people of Israel, God's chosen vehicle for spreading the message of salvation to all peoples, divine guidance and providence can be intuited in some sense or another. Perhaps even more clearly in nature—God's handiwork—the "vestiges of the Trinity" (St. Augustine) can be discerned—as the psalmist suggests:

> The heavens are telling the glory of God;
> and the firmament proclaims his handiwork.
>
> Day to day pours forth speech,
> and night to night declares knowledge. (Ps 19:1–2)
>
> Ever since the creation of the world his invisible nature, namely, his eternal power and deity, has been clearly perceived in the things that have been made. (Rom 1:20)

Furthermore, in the nature of the human being, created in the image of God, some real traces of the divinity can be observed. Even when fallen, the Maker's marks are still discernible. Again, let's listen to the psalmist's testimony:

> When I look at thy heavens, the work of thy fingers,
>   the moon and the stars which thou hast established;
> what is man that thou art mindful of him,
>   and the son of man that thou dost care for him?
> Yet thou hast made him little less than God,
>   and dost crown him with glory and honor. (Ps 8:3–5)

Echoing the same sentiment, the second-century church father St. Irenaeus concluded: "For by means of the creation itself, the Word reveals God the Creator; and by means of the world [does he declare] the Lord the Maker of the world; and by means of the formation [of man] the Artificer who formed him."[1] A number of other theologians throughout

---

1. Irenaeus, *Against Heresies*, 4.6.6, in *ANF* 01.

history endorsed the same: for the medieval master, Thomas Aquinas, the basic knowledge of God could be demonstrated from nature; he understood God's creation as a "preamble" to faith rather than it having to be the actual "article" of faith. Similarly, the Geneva Reformer Jean Calvin believed that "the Knowledge of God [is] Naturally Implanted in the Human Mind."[2] I could offer many other examples.

Over against the long history of people affirming the reality of general revelation, Barth famously reacted with utter rejection. Why? He was responding to his theology teachers who represented classical liberalism, a movement started in the nineteenth century that abandoned belief in divine revelation and substituted it with a this-worldly idea of "revelation" that was like enhanced human capacities to intuit religious insights—somewhat akin to an artist's creative skills. While Barth correctly opposed that radical departure from Christian tradition, he mistakenly took all references to general revelation as a form of human self-affirmation: that is, modern men and women no longer need revelation "from above." But that has never been the idea behind the Christian embrace of "natural" revelation, as that also comes from God, the Creator.

In fact, in contrast to Barth's fears, mainstream theology has always held that since the Almighty God is the only wellspring of all knowledge and intuitions about God, there is therefore no reason, nor need, to limit knowledge of God to what is unveiled to us through so-called special revelation. Furthermore, following the NT teaching, we can argue that the ultimate source even of general revelation is nowhere but in Christ, the agent, goal, and maintainer of creation. According to Paul (Col 1:15–17), Christ

> is the image of the invisible God, the first-born of all creation; for in him all things were created, in heaven and on earth . . . all things were created through him and for him. He is before all things, and in him all things hold together.

We can therefore say with full confidence that natural theology is *Christian* theology, just differently from special revelation.

Revelation Is Triune-Shaped

Whereas Barth struggled to understand the proper nature of general revelation, he saw most clearly what is the heart of the Christian claim for divine revelation when he spoke of "the life of God Himself turned to us,

---

2. The heading to Calvin, *Institutes*, 1.3.

the Word of God coming to us by the Holy Spirit, Jesus Christ."[3] This tells us that revelation in Christian understanding is not a sudden unveiling of mysterious secrets from the skies, as it were. Rather it is the loving Father's act of reaching out to persons created in his image, in the living presence of his Son, and in the power of the Spirit. This understanding is beautifully expressed in the Roman Catholic document *Dei Verbum* ("The Dogmatic Constitution of Divine Revelation"):

> In His goodness and wisdom God chose to reveal Himself and to make known to us the hidden purpose of His will (see Eph. 1:9) by which through Christ, the Word made flesh, man might in the Holy Spirit have access to the Father and come to share in the divine nature (see Eph. 2:18; 2 Peter 1:4). Through this revelation, therefore, the invisible God (see Col. 1:15; 1 Tim. 1:17) out of the abundance of His love speaks to men as friends (see Ex. 33:11; John 15:14-15) and lives among them (see Bar. 3:38), so that He may invite and take them into fellowship with Himself.[4]

This revelation is embodied in Christ, the Word made flesh. As St. Irenaeus so succinctly put it, "the Father is the invisible of the Son, but the Son the visible of the Father."[5] Jesus did not come to give us a lecture about a better life, though he taught invaluable lessons; nor did he merely come to inspire us, though his life, suffering, and self-sacrificial death do inspire. No: he came to be among us, and indeed to be one of us, and thereby to lead us to know the truth, walk the way, and access life. For, "no one comes to the Father, but by" him (John 14:6). Indeed, says Jesus, "He who has seen me has seen the Father" (John 14:9).

It is here that we see the distinctive nature of Christian revelation among religions as it is not "as in Islam, the revelation of a set of propositions, as though God were dictating laws or doctrines to be carefully written down. It is not, as in Hinduism, an inner experience of a supreme Self. . . . It is not, as in Buddhism, an experience of release from sorrow, desire, and attachment. . . . It is the unlimited Divine Life taking form in a particular human life. It is the realization of the Eternal in a particular historical individual."[6]

The knowledge and assurance of the access to the Father through the Son, recorded in the Holy Bible, is made alive and accessible through the power and presence of the Holy Spirit, "the Lord and Giver of Life, who

---

3. Barth, *Church Dogmatics*, I/2, 483.
4. Paul, *Dei Verbum*, para. 2.
5. Irenaeus, *Against Heresies*, 4.6.6, in *ANF* 01.
6. Ward, *Religion and Revelation*, 193.

proceedeth from the Father, who with the Father and the Son together is worshipped and glorified, who spake by the prophets" (Nicene-Constantinopolitan Creed).

So far, everything sounds relatively straightforward and intuitive. But there is a problem, or at least a challenge, here. Beginning from the time of the eighteenth-century Enlightenment, belief in supernatural divine revelation has been subjected to intense critique. Not that belief in such revelation has been abandoned as a result of that critique, only that people have raised serious critiques about its possibility.

Is It Still Possible to Believe in Divine Revelation in the Modern World?

"Traditional" and "Revised" Views of Revelation

Before delving into some details of how revelation has been conceived in the contemporary world among Christians, it might be helpful to draw a somewhat simplified contrast between what can be called "traditional" and "revised" theologies of revelation:

- "Traditional" theology says that God has graciously granted to humanity divine revelation which, while reflected also in nature, history, and human nature, is supremely manifested in God-made-flesh (Christ's incarnation) and inscribed in the Holy Bible. While only the most conservative believers consider Scripture to be inerrant in all that it states, most Christians consider the Bible to be infallible with regard to the message of salvation. Even after the advent of the critical principle of modernity (Enlightenment), it is still possible to consider Holy Scripture as divinely inspired and a fully reliable source of salvific knowledge of God.

- "Revised" theology says that rather than speaking of divinely given and unique revelation, as traditional theology does, it is best to imagine revelation as a heightened human awareness of sacred things. As valuable as the Bible is as a special vehicle of this human awareness and human religious experiences, it is neither divine in origin, nor free from errors and mistakes typical of human writings. Critical study of the Bible has shown its merely human nature.

Why this radical division between two camps? The secret is the Enlightenment, the radical intellectual transformation that began in the early eighteenth century, about which more in a moment. Before the emergence of the Enlightenment, the Bible's authority was simply assumed. Scripture was believed to be divine revelation and Scripture's divine inspiration was universally affirmed among all Christians. To this firm belief in divine revelation was attached (particularly in the Reformed tradition) insistence on the testimony of the Holy Spirit as revelation's source and guarantee, as in John Calvin's *Institutes of Christian Religion*: "The Testimony of the Spirit Necessary to Give Full Authority of Scripture."[7]

This takes us to the dramatic change at the time of the Enlightenment, the harbinger of modernity. Not merely rationality *per se* but the *independent* use of human reason, freed from all authorities, whether ecclesiastical or secular, became the hallmark of the Enlightenment. Linked with merging modern science with its unwarranted belief in the "omnipotence" of rational inquiry, the new application of human reason pushed toward replacing what were understood as ancient superstitions and outdated religious beliefs. Enlightenment philosophers objected to any notion of "supernatural" intervention of God. Instead of "revealed" religion (meaning religion based on the divinely inspired Scriptures), "natural" or "rational" religion came to the fore. British philosopher John Locke's book title *Reasonableness of Christianity* (1695) reflects this shift.

This radical transformation in the doctrine of revelation had reverberations on the rest of Christian theology and is often summarized as the collapse of the "Scripture principle." Briefly stated: this is the root cause of the division of theologies of revelation into two camps.

And the developments did not end there.

Is There Any Truthful Content to Revelation—or Is It Merely a Religious Experience?

Building creatively on the Enlightenment legacy, nineteenth-century classical liberalism (to be explained below), intuited revelation in an entirely new way. In keeping with the revised paradigm described above, inspiration, rather than being understood as a divine act "from above," was now understood as nothing more than the enhancement of natural human capacities for insights into religion. Imagine artistic work and its inspiration as a parallel. As deeply and overwhelmingly as an artist may be inspired, we don't make such inspiration a function of a supernatural divine intervention.

In order to understand this momentous shift, a brief look at the founder of liberalism—F. D. E. Schleiermacher—is in order. Counterintuitively, he located religion in human experience and "feeling." Note, however, that

---

7. Partial heading to Calvin, *Institutes*, 1.7.

the German term translated as "feeling" is much broader than the English term suggests. It refers to a primal, inner awareness of religious intuitions beyond human experiences of the world. Or, as Schleiermacher put it more technically: religion has the "feeling of absolute dependence," a deep sense of being dependent on something or someone beyond myself.

In that light, Schleiermacher interpreted all traditional doctrines as interpretations of, and responses to, this "feeling." With regard to the doctrine of Scripture and revelation, the effects of this interpretation are radical. Whereas traditional theology understood the Bible as divinely inspired authority, true and inerrant in its propositions, Schleiermacher's interpretation of the revelation of Scripture (any Scripture, including, say, Muslim and Hindu Scriptures) understood Scriptures being valuable and authentic expressions of humans' experiences of their dependence on the Ultimate, which Christianity, along with other theistic faiths, calls "God." Consider the story of the Israelites's crossing of the Red Sea recorded in Exodus 14. Rather than expressing interest in its factual, historical basis or its divinely conveyed revelatory word, Schleiermacher understood this narrative as Israelites's interpretation of their feeling of absolute dependence and dependence on God. You can easily imagine other biblical narratives, such as Jesus's miracle stories in the Gospels, through the same interpretive lens.

As creative as this Schleiermachean reinterpretation is, conservative critics were rightly shocked by the eclipse of the traditional belief in Scripture's divine revelation at the expense of a focus on the Bible as the record of shared religious human interpretations. No wonder that conservatives challenged this revised understanding. The Fundamentalist movements, which first gained prominence toward the end of the nineteenth century in the USA among conservative Reformed theologians connected with the newly founded Princeton Theological Seminary, presented the most robust attack against the Enlightenment paradigm and its heirs. Soon Fundamentalism became a powerful movement and gained support across Protestant denominations.

In sum: At the beginning of the twentieth century, the boundaries between "liberals" and "conservatives" were clearly marked and no unanimity was on the horizon. With this in mind, let us consider some ways in which believers in the twentieth century responded to this deep division with new ways of conceiving the meaning of divine revelation.

Revelation Today

The Conservative Defense of the Traditional View

Having registered the reasons why Fundamentalism sought to rebuff the revised view of revelation, whether by its rejection of divine inspiration (as among the Enlightenment thinkers) or by its affirmation of experience-based classical liberal model, it is useful to summarize Fundamentalists' tactics in more detail.

Fundamentalists' resistance to what they deem to be the liberal criticism and rejection of the traditional view of revelation shows a two-fold strategy: One tactic is an uncompromising insistence on the "inerrancy" of the Bible, meaning a belief that in its original manuscripts the Bible is free from all errors and mistakes, including even cosmological, historical, and other factual items. The main problem here is that we do not have any more original manuscripts (even though the later copies are reliable enough). A second, related tactic is understanding revelation primarily as "doctrine," namely a deposit of doctrines and teachings authoritative in themselves. This was a common understanding in Protestant orthodoxy following the Protestant Reformation and also in Catholic theology (until Vatican II in the 1960s). While of course hardly any Christian tradition denies the doctrinal importance of the Scripture, only a few continue to take the doctrinal deposit as the essence of Christianity, if not for other reasons then because the Bible obviously contains numerous diverse genres, from poetry to narrative, commandments to prayers and teachings, and so forth. Scripture is much more than doctrinal formulations.

Among conservatives who not only embraced the traditional understanding of divine revelation but who also became increasingly concerned about the reactionary, divisive, and at times isolationist Fundamentalist approach, a new movement emerged. It was later named Evangelicalism. Birthed in the English-speaking world on both sides of the Atlantic Ocean, "Evangelicalism" has become a major force. Here, the term *Evangelical* refers not only to those Protestants who adhere to the more orthodox version of Christianity as opposed to the liberal left wing, but also to those who want to distinguish themselves from followers of the Fundamentalist version of Christianity. It includes diverse denominations. Unlike the Fundamentalists, Evangelicals typically practice historical-critical study of the Bible while at the same time also affirming its divine inspiration and authority. Nor do Evangelicals find it useful to use the Fundamentalist rule of "inerrancy"; instead, they affirm the trustworthiness and reliability of the Bible, particularly with regard to its salvific power.

Revelation as "Testimony"

As he often did, Karl Barth made a proposal that sought to respond to both conservatives and liberals by retaining some parts and harshly critiquing other parts of their proposals. Hence, his approach is called "neo-orthodoxy" as it includes both "old" (orthodoxy) and "new" aspects.

The orthodox part of his proposal, in rejection of liberalism, insists on revelation's divine origin and authority. He famously argued that revelation came "directly from heaven." The *neo* part refers to his casting of revelation not as inerrant doctrine (as Fundamentalism did), but rather as a "testimony" or "witness." Thus for Barth and later neo-orthodox Christians, Scripture is not in itself revelation, but rather a witness to Jesus Christ, the true revelation. As a witness, the Scripture points always away from itself to its object, the Christ.

This turn to testimony has radical implications for Barth. Imagine a car accident. Those who witness it typically remember or share different recollections of the event, recollections that are often limited or biased. The same is true of the Bible. As a *human* witness to *divine* revelation, the Bible is far from inerrant. Famously, Barth argued that the Bible may basically contain any error or mistake—and that has in fact been the case! And yet, Scripture is the Word of God, derivative from the Word, Christ; as such, Scripture is just as fallible as human testimony! Furthermore, Barth opined that as a witness the Scripture is "dead" to the reader until the Holy Spirit brings it alive to them. Indeed, the Bible becomes God's Word "to the extent that God causes it to be His Word, to the extent that He speaks through it."[8]

Critics have rightly noted that as ingenious as Barth's reinterpretation of revelation might be, it needs to be corrected and balanced, particularly his one-sided emphasis on the fallibility of the Scripture as witness. To function as a reliable witness, the Scripture must get most things right—or the blind will be leading the blind!

Revelation as "History" and as "Promise"

While the dispute and division between conservatives and liberals—between the traditional and the revised views—continues into the third millennium, other attempts have emerged to conceptualize revelation in twentieth-century theology. Two of the most significant such attempts are revelation as "history" and as "promise." I begin with revelation as history.

---

8. Barth, *Church Dogmatics*, I/1, 114.

There are two ways to understand revelation as history. So-called "salvation history" proposed that without rejecting the traditional idea of God speaking, revelation comes to us mainly in terms of divine historical acts and events such as the liberation of Israel, Jesus's birth, life, death, and resurrection, and the pouring out of the Pentecostal Spirit. For the late Wolfhart Pannenberg, that was not enough: he went even further, surmising that not only salvific events but history at large is the arena for divine revelation. And this revelation is open to all who have eyes to see!

Whence this radical widening of the concept of revelation? From the central Christian belief that if God is the Creator of everything, then everything is related to the same God. As ambiguous as the historical happenings may look like, and even though their final meaning can be determined only in hindsight, they are revelatory in some real sense. While (the mature) Panneberg did not abandon belief in the function of revelation as the word, he also wanted to avoid mere subjective "fideism" (that is, based merely on human subjective religious interpretation). There need to be some "objective" criteria and manifestations of God's revelation, he insisted.

Of course, Pannenberg has been rightly critiqued for his unfounded optimism in human capacity to discern God's acts in the ambiguous maze of historical happenings. A closer alliance with the salvific historical school would have helped him find a better balance. Furthermore, many critics have suggested that a more robust appreciation of the Bible as the special revelation or word would be preferable. The lasting value of all this, however, is the widening of the domain of revelation.

Enter revelation as promise, another highly innovative model of revelation from another German, Jürgen Moltmann. Known as the architect of the "theology of hope" (of which more in the following chapter) with theology's gaze set into future, Moltmann considered the essential task of revelation to be to convey God's promises. He noted that the biblical narrative is a narrative of divine promises to Abram concerning the birth of the child, to Israel concerning exodus and entry into the promised land, to Jesus about resurrection, and so forth. In fact, the entire history of the people of God can be seen as the expectation of and walking toward the fulfillment of the promises. A central feature of promises is that often they happen against the odds, like the promise of a child to parents who are beyond the age of fertility, of freedom to people oppressed by a world power, and like the promise to the crucified one of being raised from the dead.

Moltmann's turn to promise as the framework for the Christian theology of revelation is useful as long as Scripture's role as the word is not thereby undermined as he has tended to do. There need to be criteria by which to judge which of the promises is to be trusted.

Yet another model of revelation—or perhaps more precisely another perspective on revelation—that has emerged in the contemporary world could be best named "liberation," that is, the attempt to highlight the many ways in which the Word of God helps set the captives free, open new opportunities, and advance human flourishing. And of course the opposite is also the case: by appealing to the Word of God, much harm has been done in terms of thwarting opportunities, binding men and women to various forms of bondage and imprisonment, and frustrating people's opportunities. Let us take a closer look at this vital current topic.

Revelation as "Liberation"

You might have heard of liberation theology—the theological movement or orientation that began to arise in the latter part of the twentieth century and now proliferates in many forms. As its name suggests, the main focus of the movement is to highlight the importance of freedom, liberation, and opportunities, particularly for minorities, the marginalized, and other vulnerable persons.

Liberation is a theme that has connections to a number of theological doctrines, not least to revelation. Consider the pioneering Black (African-American) theologian James H. Cone's lament: "Why is it that the idea of *liberation* (inseparable from the biblical view of revelation) is conspicuously absent in theological discussions about the knowledge of God?" (emphasis original).[9] That is a perceptive and pressing question, particularly at the beginning of the third millennium in a world plagued with all kinds of strife, conflict, inequality, and lack of opportunities for the masses. What might Scripture and revelation have to do with liberation?

Cone responds by asserting that he is "determined to speak a liberating word for and to African American Christians, using the theological resources" available.[10] This is in keeping with his overall vision of Christian theology as "a theology of liberation. It is *a rational study of the being of God in the world in light of the existential situation of an oppressed community, relating the forces of liberation to the essence of the gospel, which is Jesus Christ*" (emphasis original).[11]

While understandably not all theologians speak as robustly as Cone on the theme of liberation, it is also fair to say that the vision of liberation is part of the Gospel of Christ. Moltmann importantly speaks of "the biblical

---

9. Cone, *Black Theology of Liberation*, 44.
10. Cone, *Black Theology of Liberation*, xii.
11. Cone, *Black Theology of Liberation*, 1.

texts as furthering life" and of biblical interpretation that is sensitive to affirming and strengthening life and holism.[12] Recall Jesus's inaugural sermon in his home town synagogue following the water baptism and temptations in the desert (Luke 4:18–19):

> The Spirit of the Lord is upon me,
>
> because he has anointed me to preach good news to the poor.
>
> He has sent me to proclaim release to the captives
>
> and recovering of sight to the blind,
>
> to set at liberty those who are oppressed,
>
> to proclaim the acceptable year of the Lord.

Working for freedom and human flourishing is a theological mandate for the Judeo-Christian tradition. The Trinitarian revelation that comes to us as divine word and act, as promise that contains hope and knowledge, is meant not only for the life to come, for the "salvation of the soul." It also has everything to do with the realities of this earthly life.

Having now surveyed and assessed different models of revelation in contemporary theology, let us recall the earlier statement: that different models of revelation are not intended to be considered as total alternatives. Rather, they each have their own emphasis. Most theologians agree that both history and divine speaking matter; that while salvific events are more unambiguously revelatory, they take place in "secular history," as with (for example) the Israelites's journey toward the promised land. And, importantly, that whatever else the written Word—the Scripture—is, it is God's Word in Human Words, as the following section is titled. A number of key questions about the Scripture await our attention.

God's Word in Human Words—Human Words in God's Words

We have seen that until the Enlightenment people understood the inspiration of Scripture in terms of more or less direct divine influence on human writers and, similarly to Islam, as a virtual dictation of finished revelation received by the prophet. Behind this traditional understanding of revelation lies the assumption that revelation is a more or less timeless and changeless "product." Of course, the understanding was more nuanced than this, but you get the point. No wonder that this traditional view has been hotly contested. The way classical liberalism attempted to reorient the conception

---

12. Moltmann, *Experiences in Theology*, 148–50.

of revelation was to make inspiration not much more than the enhanced human capacity to gain insight into matters of religion.

So, how might we formulate a contemporary post-Enlightenment Christian view of the inspiration of Scripture? The way forward is not a return to a lost, idyllic, pre-Enlightenment mind-set. The value of sober criticism in service of a more reliable knowledge is an undeniable achievement of modernity. We employ critical faculties in all areas of human knowledge from medicine to technology and so forth, and their use in biblical criticism is entirely warranted.

A promising point of departure for a contemporary theology of inspiration is incarnation, the Word-made-flesh. Incarnation or embodiment means that the triune God, in the project of divine revelation, is fully embedded in human realities. That the infinite, almighty God became a finite human being tells us that fallible human minds are able to grasp and communicate divine things, mysteries beyond the human mind. In this light, rather than God dictating or mechanistically monitoring the exact words used to communicate revelation, it is better to think of inspiration in terms of divine-human synergy. Seen like this, rather than the humanity of the biblical writers being set aside, it is affirmed. On the other hand, because we are speaking of *divine* intervention, it is a matter of more than just giving eloquence to *human* experiences of religion, which would just be what classical liberalism dared to offer.

That the Divine Spirit was at work through finite means Vatican II's *Dei Verbum* expresses well: "Through divine revelation, God chose to show forth and communicate Himself and the eternal decisions of His will regarding the salvation of men."[13] Both the authors and the writings were inspired, Christian theology affirms. There is no need to debate whether the Spirit's work was limited to only one or the other. Moreover, in this act of divine inspiration, "God chose men and while employed by Him they made use of their powers and abilities, so that with Him acting in them and through them, they, as true authors, consigned to writing everything and only those things which He wanted."[14] It is a divine-human synergy.

Acknowledging the simultaneously divine and human form of Scripture also makes it possible to understand the breathtaking diversity of biblical genres and forms. Clearly, it was not the Almighty's plan, so to speak, to drop from the skies a legal document with precise wording, or a step-by-step manual brief enough to be grasped even by the feeble-minded. Not at

---

13. Paul, *Dei Verbum*, para. 6.
14. Paul, *Dei Verbum*, para. 11.

all. The Bible is a complex and challenging book to read and comprehend, even for academically trained theologians.

The mutual divine-human dynamic is also evident in the slow and incremental coming to existence of our present Christian scriptural canon. There was a lot of sorting out and human judgment involved in this process. Recall the beginning of Luke's Gospel, which tells us,

> Inasmuch as many have undertaken to compile a narrative of the things which have been accomplished among us, just as they were delivered to us by those who from the beginning were eyewitnesses and ministers of the word, it seemed good to me also, having followed all things closely for some time past, to write an orderly account. (1:1–3)

Clearly, the human acts of interpretation, memory, comparison between reliable and unreliable sources, and weighing of opinions were not set aside but rather used throughout the process. This is indeed what the two well-known NT texts, 2 Timothy 3:16 and 2 Peter 1:21, imply although often interpreted in a way that supports the more "mechanistic," direct understanding of revelation:

> All Scripture is inspired by God and profitable for teaching, for reproof, for correction, and for training in righteousness.

> [N]o prophecy ever came by the impulse of man, but men moved by the Holy Spirit spoke from God.

The expression "inspired" in the former passage (from Greek *theopneustos*, "breathed out by God") can be related to Adam receiving God's life-giving breath in Genesis 2:7. As Adam became a "living soul," so too do human writings, though "dead" in themselves, become the living Word of God as the result of divine inspiration. The Greek expression *pheromenoi* in the latter passage, referring to the influence ("moving") of human authors by the Holy Spirit, plays on the metaphor of being driven like a ship by the wind. Rather than human agency being taken away, as in a contemporary airplane's autopilot mode, the ship sailing under the "wind of the Holy Spirit" reaches its destination gradually and amidst many struggles.

To affirm the dual nature of Scripture as fully divine and fully human leads to the conclusion that while it is in Scripture (the Bible) that Christians believe they have the most authoritative revelation about what the Triune God wished to convey to us, because of the Bible's human nature there is no absolute equation between the Scripture and the Word of God. Nor should they be separated—for otherwise we would follow any leaders and prophets who on the basis of their mystical experiences or other means claim to have the authority of God's word.

Having established revelation in Scripture on the basis of the Word-made-flesh as a dynamic divine-human synergy, we will now reflect more deeply on what constitutes scriptural authority.

Scripture or Tradition or Church: What Is the Ultimate Authority?

Were you to take a poll of people on the street about where they think the ultimate authority of Christian faith and theology resides, you might find something like following:

- Protestants would vote for Scripture—and probably add: Scripture "alone."
- Roman Catholics's opinion would most likely say Scripture and tradition together—and add that for the faithful to read and interpret tradition correctly, the church's "magisterium," the teaching office, should be heeded.

Is this so? Yes. And no! It is more complicated than that. Even the (in)famous Reformation debates in the sixteenth century and beyond were far more complex. Indeed, the debate about the relationship between Scripture and tradition's authority actually emerged a few centuries prior to the Reformation, although it culminated there.

Before delving into the details, for the contemporary reader it might seem from all this that the notion of tradition suggests something frozen, unchanging, fixed. That, however, is not the case with the Spirit-led tradition among the people of God. In biblical and theological understanding, tradition is not a dead phenomenon. It is a living, dynamic, and hence, evolving process. And it is good to keep in mind that the term *tradition* refers both to the content, that which has been "traditioned" (carried over) from one generation of believers to the other, and to the process itself.

Now, to oversimplify a complex issue, it is fair to say that by the time of the Reformation, the following three positions had established themselves:

- that every truth necessary for salvation can be found in Scripture, and only therein;
- that the divine truth is found in both Scripture and the tradition of the church going back to the apostles; and

- that since the Holy Spirit abides permanently in the church, the church not only controls the interpretation of Scripture but may also add to revelation.

The Protestant Reformation's insistence on Scripture alone (Latin: *sola Scriptura*) spoke to this situation. That principle, however, was not meant to deny the role of tradition but rather to define the written, canonical Scripture as the ultimate norm of revelation. As often happens in fierce debates, so too in this one the participants tended to talk past each other. As a response to Protestant Reformers (Luther, Calvin, Zwingli, and others), the Roman Catholic Church (at the Council of Trent) considered it important to highlight the role of tradition, but so much so that it was in danger of undermining the proper role of the written Scripture.

It took a few hundred years for the Catholic Church to formulate a more balanced view. At the Second Vatican Council in the 1960s, they affirmed the most intimate relation between tradition and Scripture and insisted that they derive from the same source. Hence, in contemporary Roman Catholic understanding, "Sacred tradition and Sacred Scripture form one sacred deposit of the word of God, committed to the Church."[15] Further—and very importantly to Protestants—Vatican II regarded Scripture as the ultimate authority, yet of course never apart from tradition and the community.

On the other side, Protestants fortunately more clearly acknowledged the necessary role of tradition in the process of ensuring continuity between the first followers of Jesus and the use and role of Scripture throughout the centuries. Similarly, Protestants have more robustly rediscovered the important role of the church. Indeed, they acknowledge the mutual relationship between Scripture and church. On the one hand, we can say with certainty that there would be no Holy Scripture unless the followers of Jesus, the church, under the guidance of the Holy Spirit, were discerning the Divine Word in these writings and had ratified the Bible as the Scripture. On the other hand, it is clear that no church at all would have emerged apart from the life-giving Divine Word and Word-made-flesh.

One final task awaits us at the end of this chapter, namely a look at the various conceptions of revelation and nature, authority, and interpretation of Scriptures among some other faith traditions.

---

15. Paul, *Dei Verbum*, para. 10.

Revelation and Scripture among Religions

Why Turn to Other Faiths and Their Holy Writings

It is now obvious that in the American context—and even more so in most European settings—Christian faith can no longer be assumed to be the religion of the land. Both religious diversity and pervasive secularism have transformed the American and European cultures in dramatic ways. In the Global South, religious diversity is taken for granted and is a matter of fact in many areas; secularism is doing much more poorly there. That said, interfaith engagement has not occupied the minds of most theologians so far. Sheer lack of knowledge of religions usually nurtures not only misguided remarks about them but also negative attitudes.

Comparative work among religions faces huge challenges, not the least of them being the sheer volume of sacred Scriptures—illustrated by Max Müller's classic, *Sacred Books of the East*, published in fifty hefty volumes; yet even his "library" overlooks noteworthy portions of Scriptures from various parts of Asia. While most religions have either their canonical or otherwise-determined "primary" Scripture, they also have a huge secondary literature that typically is believed to be based on and to derive its (relative) authority from the primary revelation.

Whereas all religions have Scriptures, primary and secondary, their nature varies. Religions such as Judaism, Islam, and Christianity have a clearly defined and closed canon. In many others, most profoundly in Buddhism, especially in its Mahayana traditions, there is hardly any notion of a "closed canon." Hinduism lies somewhere in between, as I will show below.

Scriptures play different roles in the different religions. Whereas Judaism, Christianity, and Islam can rightly be called "religions of the book" because of the necessary and authoritative role played by the written canonical Scripture, in Hinduism the spoken word is primary. Furthermore, whereas almost all religions of the world regard their Scriptures as inspired and of divine origin, that is not the case in all their traditions. Buddhism, for example, has no concept of divine inspiration.

Finally, the nature and function of Scripture among different traditions vary greatly. The typical Muslim considers the Qur'anic revelation to be truly verbatim and to relate to all aspects of life. Typical contemporary Jews and Christians consider Scripture to be the ultimate authority, even though (apart from the Fundamentalists among them) they consider its principles and thoughts to be the inspired guide to faith and practice. For most Buddhists, Scripture's main role and authority lie in its capacity to convey Buddha's enlightenment and precepts. It is the Scripture's "object" rather than the Scripture as such that is highly venerated and authoritative. In Hinduism, Brahmins study Vedas as the divinely originated religious (and in many traditions, philosophical) authority, whereas for most Hindus, scriptural content comes in the form of folklore, rituals, artistic forms, and the general cultural environment in India.

With these caveats in mind, let us take a careful look at the four faith traditions' Scriptures and notions of revelation, beginning with the Hindu world, including a brief sympathetic-critical Christian assessment of each.

Hindu Scriptures and Authority in a Christian Perspective

The volume of Hindu sacred literature is vast, perhaps larger than that of any other living faith. That literature is commonly divided into two categories. First are the Vedas, which are called the *sruti* ("what is heard"), received directly by the *rishis* or "seers." These are the foundational, primary Scriptures honored by all Hindu traditions. Second are the *smrti* ("what is remembered"), which are considered to be humanly authored and come in the forms of epics, narratives, and folklore. Basically all forms of Hinduism consider the ancient Vedas as the Scripture par excellence. Indeed, it can be said that what keeps Hinduism together and allows it to be discussed as a unified—albeit extremely diversified—tradition is the common belief in the Vedas as foundational, authoritative, divine revelation.

Ironically, though, the Vedic literature is by and large unknown to most Hindus, apart from those in the higher castes (especially Brahmins). Instead, most Hindus get their scriptural teaching from various epics, religious folklore called the Puranas, among which the two most important and widely used are *Ramayana*, a story of Rama, depicted as an incarnation of Vishnu in later tradition, and *Mahabharata* ("Great Epic"), part of which is the *Bhagavad Gita*, the single most important writing of Scripture among all Hindus. The Hindu devotional literature (*bhakti*) is immense, and it appears in many languages. Furthermore, unlike in contemporary Christianity, Hindus often understand religious and religiously inspired art, such as music, dance, and paintings, as revelatory in nature.

The Vedas originated beginning around 1500 BCE. Each of the four collections (Rig Veda, Sama Veda, Yajur Veda, and Atharva Veda) has four parts:

- Samhitas, hymns to various deities
- Brahmanas, rules for Vedic rituals

- Aranyakas, "forest" discussions, symbolic and philosophical reflections on the rituals
- Upanishads, composed around 600 BCE or later, the most important ones being for the purposes of theological discourse

Theologies based on the Upanishads, called Vedanta,[16] embody much of Hinduism to the West; however, though philosophical in nature and based on the Vedas, this form of Hinduism is not necessarily the Hindu religion of common folks, even though it is by far the best known in the West. The Vedanta schools, also known as the "Later" (Uttara) Mimamsa, extensively and painstakingly engage the task of commenting on the Upanishads, in which they see the revelation of the Ultimate or Absolute, Brahman, as the main theme. Usually Vedanta theologians begin with and concentrate on attentive commentary of Brahma Sutra, including the careful consideration of the nature and works of the deities.

As highly venerated as is the Vedic literature (including the youngest Vedanta) among Hindus, there are no less severe hermeneutical (scriptural interpretation) debates and disputes about them than there are, for example, regarding their Christian counterparts. The following chapter on the doctrine of God highlights some of these important disputes.

What about the relation to the Christian doctrine of revelation? Both faith traditions build on scriptural authority. Virtually none of the Hindu schools deviate from scriptural authority. A contemporary Christian may mistakenly assume that with the rise of highly rational, philosophical views of the divine developed among Vedanta traditions, the authority of the (last part of) the Vedas is replaced with a typical post-Enlightenment historical-critical attitude. Nothing could be more off the mark. Despite all their rational powers, even the philosophically oriented Vedanta scholars build solidly on the divine revelation. Indeed, so central to Hinduism as a religious tradition was the affirmation of Vedic authority—at least in principle—that those who did not subscribe to it (such as adherents of Buddhism and Jainism, early deviations from Hinduism) were considered heretical. The post-Enlightenment Christian theological rejection of all notions of authority not only in the Christian religion but also, by implication, among other faiths, does not exist in Hinduism.

Because of their divine origin and eternal nature, Hindus understand the Vedas to be infallible, free from all error. All orthodox Hindu traditions adhere to a strong doctrine of verbal revelation. Materially, they affirm a

---

16. Vedanta is merely one of the six main schools or traditions of Hinduism. The six orthodox traditions are Nyaya, Vaisesika, Samkhya, Yoga, Purva Mimamsa, and Vedanta.

similar kind of doctrine regarding the infallibility of sacred Scripture as do classical Christianity and Judaism, as well as Islam. This qualifies the alleged openness of Hinduism to other faiths. That said, counterintuitively for the Christian, in the Hindu understandings of "inspiration" (to use the Christian vocabulary) there is nothing particularly miraculous. The seers' reception of the Vedic revelation as oral speech originating in eternity was a matter of "the progressive purifying of consciousness through the disciplines of yoga, [which] had simply removed the mental obstructions to the revelation of the Divine Word."[17] On the other hand, there is nothing in Hinduism like the long struggle of the prophets and other biblical authors with God in real historical events or the notion of progressive revelation, developing and becoming clarified incrementally over the course of history.

What then is the main function of Scripture for Hindus? It is important to know that the word *veda* derives from the Sanskrit root *vid*, "to know." Yet the knowledge in mind here is neither the Western Enlightenment-based "objective" knowledge nor even necessarily the biblical idea of wisdom or knowledge whose goal is the "fear of the Lord." For Hindus, the aim of knowledge has everything to do with the ultimate goal of the "salvific" vision of liberation (*moksa*) behind which is "ignorance," the true insight. Even the Upanishads, the most philosophically oriented part of each Veda, do not seek detached abstract knowledge but rather have as their main goal liberation from ignorance. This is markedly different from Christian Scripture's ultimate goal to lead persons into salvific knowledge of and personal fellowship with the personal triune God, who has revealed himself in the Word become flesh.

Perhaps the most radical difference between the Judeo-Christian faith and Hinduism is that the latter is not deeply anchored in historical events.

Does Buddhism Know Divine Revelation?

Virtually every introduction to Buddhism is bound to begin with a question as to whether it is a religion rather than an ethical system. This is because, when separating from the mother faith Hinduism, it wanted to reorient its focus from devotion to deities to pursuit of final liberation based on one's own resources. While not atheistic in the modern sense, Gautama Buddha made an effort to help his followers shift the attention from "above," as it were, to "below." The following chapter on the doctrine of God will consider this issue in a more sustained way.

17. Coward, *Sacred Word*, 106.

In the meantime, the following conclusion seems warranted. While it is true that "Buddhism is, in one sense, a religion without revelation; there is no active communication from a God in most forms of Buddhism," it is also true that "there is certainly an authoritative teaching in Buddhism, derived from the enlightened insight of Gautama."[18] In this sense, it is ironic that Buddhism has produced one of the largest volume of sacred texts, and has done so in various languages.

It makes sense to speak of Scripture in Buddhism as long as one acknowledges its distinctive role in this tradition. While the Buddhist Scripture is focused on the founder, the Gautama, who became Buddha as a result of enlightenment, unlike in Christianity the founder has nothing to do with "salvation." Gautama is not a savior but rather an example to be followed and emulated in the pursuit of enlightenment.

Following the approximately forty-five-year teaching career of Buddha, each of the early schools developed rich scriptural collections; unfortunately, only the Pali-language Tipitaka ("Three Baskets") was preserved, and it is the "canonical" Scripture of the oldest and most traditional Theravada school. After Buddha's death, in 486 BCE the First Buddhist Council established criteria and procedures for the memorization of Buddha's words. Only after about five hundred years was the canonical collection put into writing.

Sutta Pitaka contains mainly doctrinal discourses, some of them relating to earlier lives of Buddha. A separate, huge collection about former incarnations of Buddha, *Jataka* relates to the same topic. While noncanonical, this is a highly popular collection, and samples of it circulate widely among Buddhist laypeople. The second "basket" of Tipitaka is the Vinaya Pitaka, which is about monastic rules and discipline. The third, Abhidhamma Pitaka, is the most systematic form of Buddhist thought and beliefs.

Alongside the Tipitaka, there are a number of other significant writings such as that of the fifth-century CE Buddhist teacher Buddhaghosa's *Visuddhimagga*, "The Path to Purification," a highly significant guide particularly to religious practices among the Theravadans. Most of these writings are not accessible for ordinary Buddhists. Instead, a small portion from the canonical text, called *Dhammapada*, is close to what we may call the "Buddhist Bible," a slim anthology of verses summarizing the core teachings of Buddhism.

Around the beginning of the Common Era with the birth of the Mahayana school, a rich reservoir of Scriptures as well as a competing hermeneutics emerged. Similarly to the founding school, this new one claimed

---

18. Ward, *Religion and Revelation*, 58.

to build on Buddha's own teaching—in this echoing the mentality of some Christian "back to the Bible" restorationist movements. It claimed that Buddha's initial, programmatic sermon "The Turning of the Wheel," believed to be hidden for a while, was rediscovered in its most authentic form—again, a development not unknown in other religious traditions.

Soon Mahayana literature began to be disseminated throughout Asia, and as early as the second century CE, texts started to be translated into Chinese. A couple of hundred years later, the Tibetan collection of sacred writings was developed with the birth of the third major school, Vajyarana, aka Tantric Buddhism. The highly influential "Perfection of Wisdom," an essential Mahayana teaching about Bodhisattvas (the Enlightened Ones) and the principle of "emptiness" (*sunyata*) can be found in both languages. Shorter versions continue to play a determinative role today. The Diamond Sutra and the Heart Sutra are the best-known parts of the Sanskrit language "canon."

Importantly, there is no ratified, closed "canon" for Mahayana, whereas some kind of canonical status in Theravada can be assigned to Tipitaka; hence, one cannot really speak of a fixed pan-Buddhist canon.

What is the status and role of Scriptures in Buddhism? There is an interesting dynamic—some might say, internal tension—at work here:

> On the one hand, those [sacred] texts have themselves been the objects of the utmost veneration; and life, limb, and more have been sacrificed to ensure their unaltered preservation and correct understanding. At the same time, Buddhism avers that the sacred text has, in and of itself, no particular value. Its worth depends entirely on what is done with it, and at best, the sacred text is never more than an aid that must be abandoned by each individual at a certain point on his journey toward the Buddhist goal of enlightenment.[19]

This twofold, dynamic attitude toward the Scripture is best illustrated in the famous "Discourse on the Great Decease" (Digha Nikaya 16),[20] which recounts the death of Gautama. On the one hand, it urges the disciple Ananda to be the "island" and "refuge" to himself, and on the other hand, it tells him that the Dhamma is the lamp and refuge (16.2.33)! Unlike in the Judeo-Christian canon, in Buddhist texts one never sees the explanation "Thus said Buddha"—even though the oldest canon claims to preserve Gautama's teachings. Consequently, scriptural "authority" is not based on believing

19. Ray, "Buddhism," 148.
20. This discourse is also known by the names "Last Days of the Buddha" and "The Great Discourse on the Total Unbinding."

certain doctrines (although, of course, there are doctrines). Rather, the main function and authority of Scripture is to serve as an aid to accessing Buddha's experience of the enlightenment. Yet another difference from the Judeo-Christian tradition is that, similarly to Hinduism, there is little or no concern for the historicity of narratives and scriptural records and there is a lack of any notion of divine inspiration.

Despite all the differences highlighted between Buddhist and Christian attitudes toward the Scripture, some similarities can be discerned between the Christian understanding of Christ as the Word and the Buddhist view of the nature of a revealed word. Samyutta Nikaya (22.87) says: "He who sees Dhamma . . . sees me; he who sees me sees Dhamma. Truly seeing Dhamma, one sees me; seeing me one sees Dhamma." At the same time, they differ radically, not only because of Buddhism's ambivalence about theistic notions, but also because of its approach to Scripture and "revelation," as expounded above. One has to be careful not to overvalue apparent similarities.

The Holy Bible and Holy Qur'an

In no other religion is Scripture more central than in Islam. Unlike Hinduism and Buddhism, in which the canon is either vast or barely defined, Islam has a clearly defined canon, the Qur'an. Linked to later exposition and expansion of the Qur'anic materials, there is also a vast Hadith tradition that consists of the sayings of the Prophet and other sages. The sayings and actions of Muhammad narrated in the Hadith Muslims believe to be inspired, but not revealed. By the ninth century, as many as 600,000 Hadiths had been recorded, which were then condensed to about 25,000. By far the most important is the Hadith of Bukkhari; significant also are the Hadiths of Muslim, of Sunan Abu-Dawud, and of Malik's Muwatta.

Understandably, Islamic tradition has also produced commentaries. Sunni exegesis during the first Islamic centuries in particular became famous for its meticulous and time-consuming work. Along with the mainline Sunni and Shi'ite schools, the mystical Sufi schools have produced an amazingly diverse devotional and mystical literary and poetic treasury.

It is highly significant that the Qur'an does not do away with earlier revelations, Jewish and Christian. Rather, it considers itself to be their fulfillment and correction. That said, Islam also includes the determined insistence on the Qur'an's supremacy and finality. Sura 5:44–48 makes this clear by presenting the Jewish Torah and the Christian NT as stepping-stones to the final revelation given in the Qur'an. It is in light of the Qur'an that the value of other revelations is assessed.

Similarly to the Hindu view of the Vedas, most Muslims consider the Qur'an to be the eternal speech or words of God. Again, like Hinduism, oral Scripture is the primary mode. It is interesting that the term *Qur'an* in Arabic means both "recitation" and "reading," thus embracing both oral and written aspects. But unlike in Hinduism, whose *rishis* (seers) merely passively "hear" the eternal speech in the Vedas, the prophet Muhammad is more than just a passive recipient. Hence, the usual nomenclature of the "messenger" probably underplays the role of the Prophet.

Unlike the Bible, in which most of the divine speech comes in human words and in many literary forms, often embedded in the struggles of human life and in the events of history, "[i]n the Qur'an, Muhammad receives a direct, fully composed revelation from God, which he then recites to others."[21] The belief that the revelation of the Qur'an came to Muhammad directly from God does not mean that it came all at one time and in the form of dictation, as it were. According to 17:106, "We have revealed it by [successive] revelation." Hadith traditions give vivid accounts of various ways in which the reception of revelation took place, including through dramatic emotional states, without the struggles having any influence on the revelation.

All Islamic movements regard the Arabic Qur'an as the direct, authoritative speech of God (42:7), and thus find translations to be not fully revelational. In fact, reciting in Arabic is the divine revelation in its fullest sense. The form of Arabic used in the Qur'an is of the tribe of Quraysh, that of Muhammad. Interestingly, stylistically it is identical with none of the known bodies of Arabic. Even the Arabic of the Hadith is different from that of the Qur'an.

Muhammad's role as the human conduit of revelation directly from Allah is critical and unique. An ancient tradition holds that the Qur'an is but a copy of a "Guarded Tablet" in heaven (85:22). As a result, the Qur'anic view of Scripture is strongly propositional. A strict view of the infallibility of the Qur'anic revelation and words is affirmed by all orthodox Muslim traditions. According to 2:2, "That Book, in it there is no doubt" (see also 5:15–16; 5:48). In this respect, a surprising and ironic situation exists between the two cousin faiths:

> In many respects, the conservative Christian view of the Bible as infallible and as inspired word for word is closer to how Muslims view the Qur'an than to the liberal Christian view of the

---

21. Coward, *Sacred Word*, 82.

Bible as a potentially fallible, human response to experience of the divine. On the Muslim right, the Bible is regarded as so corrupt that it no longer has any value. On the Christian left, an attempt is made to understand how the Qur'an can be accepted as "revelation." One difficulty is that Christians who deconstruct the Bible are likely to transfer this approach to the Qur'an as well, which is unacceptable, even to more liberal Muslims. Yet despite each side's view of the Other's Scripture, Christians and Muslims from both the "right" and "left" cite from the Other's Scripture to support their views.[22]

A radical difference from Christian tradition is that its original language, Arabic, is also its only "revelatory" language. A foundational similarity is that the Qur'an defines its main and ultimate goal as the salvation of humankind. It also often refers to itself as the guide (2:185; 14:1; among others).

Not surprisingly, the Islamic tradition has paid close attention to careful and authoritative exegesis (*tafsir*) of the Qur'an. Indeed, because the Qur'an lays the foundation for and regulates all aspects of life and society, more is at stake in the hermeneutics of Scripture in Islam than with most other traditions. The main difference between the Sunni and Shi'ite schools is that the latter regards the imams as also inspired (and perhaps even infallible), a claim strongly rejected by the Sunni.

A negative counterpart to *tafsir* is *tahrif*, usually translated as "alteration." At its most basic level, it refers to Christian (and other) misreadings of Islamic Scriptures, beginning from problems of textual variants, all the way to the charges of deliberate alterations of the text. Furthermore, it can also simply mean a misguided interpretation of the texts. Interestingly, the current *tahrif* criticism of the Bible skillfully—and selectively—uses the insights of (Christian) historical-critical study in rebutting the truthfulness and reliability of the text.

Among all differences and similarities between Christian and Islamic theology of revelation none is probably more important than this: It is not the prophet but rather the book that is the closest parallel to Christ. Islam is not based on Muhammad, who is merely a human being (though the first one among the ranks of the Prophet), but rather on the Qur'an and Allah. Hence, it is in Christ's role as the living Word of God in relation to the divine revelation of the Qur'an that the deepest commonalities are to be investigated. Vincent Cornell has appropriately noted that whereas Jesus in Christian tradition is the "Word made flesh," the Qur'an in Islam

---

22. Bennet, *Understanding Christian-Muslim Relations*, 16.

is the divine word "inlibrate."[23] There are surprisingly deep similarities among the accounts in the Qur'an of the power of its word, OT claims about the word of the Lord, and NT statements about Christ as the creative word. Consider Q 59:21: "Had We sent down this Qur'an upon a mountain, you would have surely seen it humbled, rent asunder by the fear of God." The Islamic tradition speaks of the living words of the Qur'an in terms of destruction, healing, tranquility, and so forth.

The First and the Second Testaments: Jewish Theology of Revelation

Similarly to Christian faith but differently from the rest, in the Jewish religion the process of reception of revelation is fully embedded in historical events and living tradition. While divine in its origin, the revelation is given and received in the matrix of human life at personal, tribal, national, and international levels. Unlike in Hinduism and closer to Buddhism, the main focus of Jewish revelation is on ethical and moral obedience. This is not to deny the importance of moral precepts in other living faiths. Rather, it is to say that in them the connection between moral conduct and belief in God is not established in the integral way it is in Judaism—and of course, by implication, in Christianity.

For the classic Jewish faith, revelation is propositional in nature. According to ancient tradition—although not supported by recent Jewish historical academic study—Moses basically received the law by divine "dictation" of detailed lists of commands, exhortations, laws, and practices.

The center of the Jewish canon, Tanakh (an acronym formed from the first letters of the three sections of Scripture: Torah, Nevi'im, and Ketuvim), is Torah ("teaching," "instruction"), the "Five Books of Moses." The two other parts of the canon, albeit not as sacred, are Nevi'im (prophetic books) and Ketuvim ("Writings"). Importantly, what the Christian Bible names "historical books" (Joshua, Judges, 1–2 Samuel, 1–2 Kings) are prophetic here. Since Yahweh is the Lord of history, the modern separation of "secular" and "sacred" history is a foreign idea. While Judaism divided into many groups, all of them held Torah as the canonical Scripture but had varying views concerning the value of extrascriptural tradition.

---

23. Cornell, "Listening to God," 37. Cornell agrees with this description of the Qur'an so long as it is understood as a "living voice for Muslims" as opposed to "musty tomes consulted by bearded scholars who maintain the 'dead hand' of inherited tradition."

If "prophetic Judaism" (the Judaism until the beginning of the common era) brought about the Hebrew Bible as we have it now, then "rabbinic" Judaism produced the huge and varied collections of the so-called oral Torah; the nomenclature "oral," of course, has to be taken in a qualified sense here. Think of oral Torah as the needed commentary and further exposition of the details of laws present in the written Torah.

This large oral Torah is classified under the general categories of *halakah* (ritual and legal practices and traditions) and *Haggadah* (with its focus on homiletics, ethics, exegesis, and theology). The first major such work that also became foundational to the oral Torah is the *Mishnah*, compiled in the second century CE. Over several centuries, huge collections of Talmudic tractates—the most important of which are the Babylonian and Palestinian—emerged as commentaries on the Mishnah. While not canonical in the sense of the written Torah, oral Torah is irreplaceable in that it helps make the written Torah living and applicable to ever-new situations. Hence the importance of midrash, the meticulous examination of the written text to find its right and true meaning.

Rabbinic Judaism became the dominant form of the religion following the devastation caused by the destruction of the Second Temple in 70 CE and with it the loss of land. The Pharisees, the mainstream of rabbinic Judaism, became the custodians of developing tradition. Through painstaking study of the Law (Torah) and the rest of the canon, they uncovered meanings not apparent on a cursory reading.

In medieval times, revisionist movements arose, such as Karaism, which questioned and basically rejected the rabbinic notion of Jewish tradition, and mystical-esoteric Kabbalism, which, unlike Karaism, did not reject either rabbinic tradition or the oral Torah, but rather filled it with new meanings, often highly speculative and imaginative.

As important as prophetic and rabbinic Judaism is to that religion, in the contemporary world there are a number of non-orthodox movements, from the Reform movements of the mid-nineteenth century to various liberal schools of our twenty-first-century era. While all these movements, in some sense or another, consider Torah to be the canonical Scripture, they disagree widely about how to deal with the rules (*mitzvoth*) of Torah in the contemporary world.

What about the domain of Jewish revelation? Is it only tribal (concerning one nation, one people) or also universal? It seems as if, on the one hand, it is particular, as the laws and promises are meant for Israel, the Jewish people. On the other hand, it is also the case that—and this applies by extension to Christianity—it is clearly universal in that it speaks of Yahweh as the creator and the God of all men and women and the whole of creation.

When it comes to the relation of the two peoples of God who share the same Torah as their Scripture, we have to note the sad and long track record of Christian anti-Semitism. As early as the second century CE, there were Christian teachers such as Marcion who wanted the Christian church to reject the OT as canonical Scripture. While some promising mutual connections have been attempted occasionally throughout the common history, only beginning in the twentieth century has sustained work toward mending the relations taken place. More of that in what follows.

The consideration of the theology of revelation takes us naturally to the doctrine of God, the topic of the next chapter.

2

God

If God Exists, What Is He Like?

"I Believe in God." Really?

WHILE RELIGION OR RELIGIOUS feelings might not be too hard for an enlightened person of the third millennium to tolerate, for many people belief in God—Almighty, All-Knowing, All-Present, and full of love—sounds like a stretch. Can we even know that God truly exists? Are there any proofs?

Let's set aside for a moment the question of the proofs of God's existence and for the sake of the argument suppose that God does exist. Then the question becomes what kind of God the God of the Bible might be, and whether that God is in any ways different from, or similar to, the conceptions of deities in other religions. How to discern the right and true God? Furthermore, for us living in the contemporary world a burning question has to do with the existence of evil and suffering in the world that God is alleged to have created.

This lengthy chapter combines two intertwined discussions. As a way of orienting the reader to the first main section of the chapter, I establish the conditions for speaking of God in a contemporary culture plagued with secularism and various kinds of atheistic rebuttals. Relatedly, I will consider whether there are any "proofs" that show evidence of God.

Thereafter, a closer look at what the Bible is telling us about God is in order, followed by inquiry into whether, and in what ways, this God may be related to the world God has created—for if we do the first without the second, we end up being "deists," those who believe in God's existence but assume that God has left the world to its own devices.

The second main section will address the thorny question of the meaning of the doctrine of the Trinity, undoubtedly the most distinctive Christian belief. No wonder that this seemingly complex doctrine has given rise to many and various interpretations, several of them generally deemed heretical, that is, deviating from the norm. To consider them and the reasons they were rejected may help us tremendously to learn more about the correct ways of understanding the topic.

That discussion leads to the question of trying to understand more closely the nature and distinctive characteristics of God, at least to the extent that we as finite human persons can understand; this exercise is known in tradition as "divine attributes." Under the rubric "God of Hospitality, Belonging, and Peace," I will investigate the liberative, uplifting, and reconciling power of God in the world plagued with violence, exclusivism, and juxtaposition.

Similarly to how I treat all other topics throughout the book, in this chapter I compare the Christian conception of the divine with those of four other living faith traditions.

We begin by considering the conditions of belief in God in this secular world of ours. At first blush, it looks as if god-talk is not easily introduced in this kind of environment.

Can We Even Begin to Talk about God in Our Secular World?

The Many Faces of Secularism and Its Attack on Belief in God

Things were different in the past. In ancient cultures, including the biblical ones, the existence of God was not doubted, but taken for granted. The problem lay elsewhere, namely in deciding *which* God to follow, meaning establishing which god is the most powerful. In this light, it is interesting to recall that, because of their reluctance to bow before the Emperor, deemed to be divine, the earliest Christians were accused of atheism!

In a world ruled by sciences and technology, questions both about God's existence and about the very meaningfulness of talk about God have taken a front seat. No wonder, God-talk in many European and North American contexts is being bluntly ignored! It is different in the Global South, say in Africa and many locations in Asia, where it is a ready topic of conversation even among strangers.

So, we have entered the era of secularism—or have we? You may recall that in the 1960s the "prophets of secularism" declared with confidence that

Christianity, alongside other religions, would simply disappear altogether as science and "civilization" march onward. Known as the "secularization thesis," it follows the long and honored line of modern atheism going back to the great pioneers of the nineteenth century, such as Karl Marx, Ludwig Feuerbach, Sigmund Freud, and many others. Most recently, the so-called New Atheists have revived this thesis, as I will discuss below.

But before passing judgment, consider that the answer to the question above, namely whether we have entered the age of secularism, is both "yes" and "no"! As far as religion's loss of power over secular institutions such as universities, schools, and politics is concerned, the secularization thesis appears to be accurate for the most part. Generally speaking, religion has indeed lost its firm grip on society and culture in the Global North and in some locations in the Global South. In fact, the situation is far more complex. In contrast to the popular notion that the current world is becoming less religious, the opposite has happened: never before have there been so many adherents of living faiths! Moreover, it is not the "liberals" among religious adherents but rather Fundamentalists and conservatives who are becoming more and more dominant—meaning that traditional belief in God(s) and teaching of religions is becoming stronger, as loud and all-embracing as the voice of the secularists and atheists in the mass media and academia might be!

This means that secularism is a highly complex phenomenon, and it has everything to do with whether belief in God will continue into the third millennium. This is the subject of the Canadian philosopher Charles Taylor's brilliant and lengthy analysis of the many forms of secularism in *A Secular Age*.[1] While he grants the validity of the secularization thesis in one respect, namely the retreat of religion from the public sphere (what Taylor identifies as Type 1) and the decline in belief and practice (Type 2), he also challenges and discredits that thesis by introducing yet another type of secularism—namely a shift in the conditions and nature of belief in God. For this type of secularism has not necessarily abandoned all notions of God. Rather, on the one hand in this type of secularism belief in God has become a matter of personal choice: you may choose to believe or not. On the other hand—and this introduces the concept of "postsecularism"—men and women may still follow religious rituals and rites, even belief in transcendence (that there is something "beyond" or "above" this visible, material reality), but they "believe" differently. They do not believe like the church or established religion might want them to do. They choose their own ways of believing.

---

1. Taylor, *Secular Age*.

This means that both religions and multifaceted secularism are coexisting in the third millennium!

What about atheism?

Atheistic Rebuttals of Faith in God

When did atheism begin? Is it a recent development in world history, perhaps an offshoot of the Enlightenment? But then what about the heroes of the ancient world, such as Socrates, the ancient philosopher? He was known as an "atheist"—though nowadays that term would no longer describe him. As a dissenting thinker, he did not deny the existence of god(s) (as would modern atheism). Rather, he wished to shift people's focus from the cult of local gods to become independent thinkers.

Atheism in the modern sense did not emerge until the aftermath of the Enlightenment. The heyday of the first powerful wave of atheism was in the nineteenth century. Sometimes called the "last real atheist," Friedrich Nietzsche learned from Charles Darwin that the human mind is little more than an expression of nature, and hence mental events such as ethical reasoning and artistic imagination are nothing but "natural" physical processes. If so, he surmised, then religion has no basis in reality, let alone in "real" deities. Yet unlike typical atheists, Nietzsche was not content with merely denying the existence of God—which he of course did vehemently. His project was to "kill" God as presented forcefully in his widely circulated work of 1882/87, *Gay Science (The Joyful Wisdom)*.

Another great nineteenth-century atheist, Ludwig Feuerbach, famously argued that faith in God is but a human projection of the God-figure into the skies, as it were. In other words, God-talk is nothing but wishful projection. Not only is that projection not real, it is also dangerous, he said, as it diverts people from engaging in this world. Off such religion, people had to be cured to become rational adults!

Karl Marx picked up Feuerbach's ideas with the intention of creating a new materialist vision to make a difference in this world. Like Feuerbach, he considered religion harmful and dangerous, "the opiate of the masses," and therefore deemed it necessary to excavate religion from the human mind in order for sanity and happiness to return. The same "religion as harmful disease or deception" argument was one that Sigmund Freud advanced. He joined the project seeking to cure minds of what he perceived to be a sickness.

How valid and legitimate are these standard modern atheistic rebuttals of faith in God? Differently from their alleged claims, these criticisms are not based on neutral sciences but are rather speculations and "educated guesses." They are worldview choices rather than inferences based on hard facts of science and, in that sense, are quite like philosophical and theological convictions. Furthermore, even at their best, they are lopsided and lack nuance. Against every misuse of religion, numerous positive and constructive examples of religion's effects can certainly be found.

What about the New Atheists?

The most recent decisive attempt to get rid of religion and faith in God is often named New Atheism. Building on but also going beyond the work of the great nineteenth-century predecessors, New Atheists excel in trying to cure-people-from-the-sickness-of-religion. Among them, most well-known to the public are the two Oxford scholars, ethologist Richard Dawkins and chemist Peter Atkins, as well as the British American popular science writer Christopher Hitchens.[2]

We can summarize these atheists' claims as follows. First, after the advent of modern science, particularly the evolutionary sciences and physical cosmology, any appeal to belief in God has no basis in reality. Evolutionism has replaced not only faith in God but also the doctrine of creation. Second, and related to the first claim, New Atheists insist that faith and reason are totally opposite to each other and belong to alternative realms. Consequently they contend that religion lacks any basis in reason, contrasting this with their confidence in the indubitable truthfulness and validity of atheism. Third, they say, not only is atheism true, but unlike religion it is capable of providing a healthy worldview. Fourth, unlike religions that are conceived to be dogmatic and intolerant, atheism and secularism by definition are tolerant and hospitable. Fifth, atheism helps defeat religious education, which at its worst is nothing but child abuse. Sixth and finally, new atheists are firmly convinced that there is an integral and necessary link between violence and faith in God.

What to make of these claims? While not without merit, these arguments nonetheless suffer from many failures and deficiencies. Alongside fallacies similar to earlier generations of atheists' arguments, let me mention at least the following:[3]

---

2. For a representative widely read work in this genre, see, e.g., Dawkins, *Blind Watchmaker*.

3. This list is indebted to the writings of Alister E. McGrath, for example *Dawkins' God*.)

First, belief in science as the platform capable of explaining "everything" in the world—at times called scientism—is hardly a self-evident premise. As important as science may be, it can explain only so much. There are huge areas of life and the cosmos about which even the exact sciences cannot provide any kind of final explanation, such as why there is something as opposed to nothing.

Second, the claim that after the advent of Darwinism no legitimate place is left for God grossly ignores the simple fact that mainstream contemporary Christian theology does not see Darwinism as its opponent or as an alternative to the Christian doctrine of God. In fact, as I will discuss in some detail in the next chapter, the idea of evolution of the cosmos at large and of its inhabitants is not necessarily a contradiction to theological intuitions. Only Fundamentalist theologians oppose the scientific account of the origins of the world and humanity—and thereby provide fodder for atheists' misguided claims.

Third, the argument that faith is an attitude that lacks any rational basis has already been laid to rest at the beginning of this book. And it clearly conflicts with the fact that among the most well-respected scientists and intellectuals in every age a large number have been confessing Christians. Similarly, the rest of the atheist rebuttals of faith, including alleged violence as a necessary result of faith, is an utterly unnuanced statement and I will rebut it in what follows.

Turning from defense to a more constructive posture, let us consider what kind of marks or indicators of God might be found in God's creation.

Can We Find God's Footprints in the World?

Common sense and Christian intuition have long posited the existence of God on the basis of the created order, including the human person. On this basis, early in Christian theology—and, indeed, much earlier in the philosophies of antiquity—an understandable effort emerged to somehow "prove" the existence of the Creator. This effort is not limited to Christian theology alone; we see it in other Abrahamic faiths and also in Asiatic faiths, though it appears somewhat differently there.

But what do we "prove" when we seek to provide evidence for God's existence? It is helpful and even crucial to recall that before the Enlightenment theology and theologians did not consider the divine footprints or traces in the world in an apologetic sense, that is, as an attempt to prove God's existence by force of logic. Rather, they took for granted the existence of God and then made an effort to show that God-talk is reasonable and meaningful; precisely this the Enlightenment denied.

One of the most famous ways of seeking to prove God's existence in Christian philosophy comes from the medieval master Anselm of Canterbury. Often referred to as the ontological argument (ontology being a branch of philosophy that inquires into the nature of being or the existence of things), Anselm framed his argument like this:

> Even the Fool, then, is forced to agree that something-than-which-nothing-greater-can-be-thought exists in the mind, since he understands this when he hears it, and whatever is understood is in the mind. And surely that-than-which-a-greater-cannot-be-thought cannot exist in the mind alone. For if it exists solely in the mind, it can be thought to exist in reality also, which is greater.[4]

But what about the validity of Anselm's claim that God is something "than which nothing greater can be conceived"? It helps the inquirer to imagine God as something that completely transcends all the limitations of created beings. That is its benefit. The argument's liability is also quite intuitive, as Immanuel Kant, the great philosopher of modern times most famously pointed out: it is far from self-evident that the real existence of a thing or being is necessary on the basis of an *idea* of an existence. Or to put it another way: Isn't it possible to imagine a planet bigger than any planet we already know?

Proofs for the existence of God, therefore, might seem to be on firmer ground if we shift our attention from abstract logical thinking to the world itself, the creation. This so-called cosmological proof another medieval master, Thomas Aquinas, famously presented. Among his many attempts to the same effect, the most well-known is the set of five proofs presented in his *Summa theologiae*: the proofs from motion, causality, contingency, grades of perfection, and purpose. Take the first one. It makes complete sense to imagine that a movement of a thing has to be caused by someone (or something) else, the "first mover." That first mover (God) must be the source and origin of the movement. The same with causality: How can there be an effect without a cause? And so forth. Behind these five ways and similar other ones is the intuition that through our experience of the world that God created we can know something of the Creator.

Turning our attention to the created reality opens the way for yet another useful consideration in terms of whether God's footprints can be found. Let's call it anthropological proof as it begins from the human being

---

4. Anselm of Canterbury, *Proslogion*, 87.

and from the fact that to be open to and inquire into the realities beyond the visible world seems to be part of human nature. This is what the sociologist of religion Peter Berger named "a rumor of angels."[5] Indeed, even in environments in which faith in God has been suppressed and believers have been oppressed, the persistence of intuiting something beyond the physical has not ceased, as the history of modern atheist countries such as former Soviet Union and current China evinces. For such reasons some theologians speak of the "incurable religiosity" of men and women.

But what, if anything, does this anthropological observation prove? Not necessarily the existence of God, because the atheist may rightly note that this persistence of a sense of transcendence is merely human projection. Recall Feuerbach, Freud, and Marx's arguments above. Hence, if carelessly used this alleged evidence may instead strengthen the atheist rebuttal of God. What this anthropological point of view is doing—and this is very important for theology and faith—is to make talk about God "natural" and therefore rational. Faith in God is not something superimposed onto the human mind as atheism claims; rather, it is something that fits the structure of human beings as the image of God.

A related argument to the anthropological proof is what is traditionally called the "moral argument." It simply states that the moral compass within the human person—call it conscience or something else—seems to point to its divine source or at least to a source beyond humanity. In its most sophisticated form, Immanuel Kant developed this intuitive argument in his *Critique of Practical Reason*. He was impressed by "the moral law within" as much as he was by "the starry heavens above."[6] Kant intuited that this moral law pushes us toward the highest level of morality and that it judges us when we fail. In short, it is difficult to posit a "foundation" for morality apart from God.

Having clarified the conditions for and rebuttals of God-talk and God's existence, we now move on to consider the actual doctrine of God as it has been conceived in Christian tradition and contemporary theology. We begin by taking a quick look at the Bible, whose main theme is who God is and what God does.

---

5. Berger, *Rumor of Angels*.
6. Kant, *Critique of Practical Reason*, 256.

What Does the Bible Tell Us about God?

The One God Is Known by Many Names

When inquiring into who God is and what God does, we should keep in mind that the Bible is not a collection of ready-made doctrines; rather, it is a compilation of testimonies, metaphors, pictures, hymns, and stories about God and about real life encounters with God.

The most foundational and uncompromising biblical teaching about God is known as *monotheism*, from two Greek words, *monos* meaning "one," and *theos* meaning "God." It is summarized in Israel's famous "confession of faith" (often called the *Shema*): "Hear, O Israel: The Lord our God is one Lord" (Deut 6:4). This made Israel's faith unique among neighboring nations that each worshiped many deities.

One of the principal ways in which we get to know God in Scripture is through naming the divine names. Unlike in our current culture—but similar to many cultures of the Global South—in the ancient world being named and particularly giving someone a new name (like Israel to Jacob or Peter to Simon) was a powerful event.

Along with the general name *Elohim*, rendered "God" in most English translations, the uniquely Israelite tetragrammaton YHWH (usually transliterated "Yahweh" or "Jehovah" and translated "Lord" in English Bibles) are the first two names to be introduced to the reader of the OT. The latter name relates to the special covenant between Israel and God. There is thus both universality (*Elohim*) and particularity (YHWH), a dynamic that characterizes the rest of the biblical narrative of God.

You may recall the narrative in Exodus 3 in which God, in response to Moses's query regarding the identity of the One speaking from the burning bush, gives the mysterious and open-ended response: "I am who I am" (v. 14)! The revelation of this name is as much a matter of veiling—as is appropriate for an infinite God who is beyond all human conceptions. That said, there is also a large reservoir of names and designations of God which are specific and speak to specific needs and helps, including:

- *El Elyon,* "God Most High" (Gen 14:18–22)
- *El Roï,* "God of seeing" (Gen 16:13).
- *Yhwh yireh,* "The Lord will provide" (Gen 22:14)
- *El Bethel,* "God of Bethel" (Gen 35:7)
- *El Shaddai,* "God Almighty" (Gen 17:1)

- *Yahweh Sabaoth,* "Lord of hosts," apparently signifying military power (1 Sam 1:11)

We Get to Know God by What God Does

Along with naming, another key way in which the OT narrative presents God is by testifying to God's works and deeds. Creation is the first act of God. The very first line of our Bible states: "In the beginning God created the heavens and the earth." No wonder the power and wisdom of the One who is capable of creation is often extolled:

> The Lord by wisdom founded the earth;
>> by understanding he established the heavens;
> by his knowledge the deeps broke forth,
>> and the clouds drop down the dew. (Prov 3:19–20)

The biblical canon describes God's creative act in a number of delightful, creative ways. Walter Brueggemann reminds us that: "Yhwh designs and shapes like a potter, begets like a father, travails like a mother, makes like a craftworker, creates like an artist, stretches like a sheikh, and commands like a king. . . . Together these images suggest the precision, purposefulness, pleasure, pain, care, effort, sovereignty and effectiveness of the creator's work."[7]

The Bible portrays God as the one who promises. Indeed, as Moltmann reminded us in the previous chapter, a way to conceive the essence of revelation in the Bible is through the category of promise. For not only does God promise, God is also the One who guides and provides: "And you shall remember all the way which the Lord your God has led you these forty years in the wilderness" (Deut 8:2). Biblical narratives attribute both the exit (or exodus) out of Egypt and the entrance into the promised land to God's faithfulness to the promises and divine provision.

Many other divine acts could be added to the list; the ones mentioned above suffice to shed light on who God is. The many metaphors that are another hallmark of the biblical theology of God likewise allude to God's nature and essence. Brueggemann divides divine metaphors into two categories:[8] the metaphors of "governance" include God as judge, king, warrior, and father. These metaphors are also interconnected: "Yahweh as warrior is the one who, as a judge committed to a rule of law, acts

---

7 Goldingay and Payne, *Critical and Exegetical Commentary*, 40.
8 Brueggemann, *Theology of the Old Testament*, chap. 6.

to stabilize, maintain, or implement that rule, over which the king will preside."[9] The second category includes the metaphors of "sustenance" such as God as artist, healer, gardener, vinedresser, mother, and shepherd. Drawn from various everyday life contexts, each and every picture speaks to different needs and provisions in human life and the life of the world. God is there for his creatures and creation.

What about the NT? What else do we learn about God there? Surprisingly, not much, but certainly the following crucial things.

God of the Old Testament Is the Father of Jesus Christ

The Father of Jesus Christ is none other than "the God of Abraham, and the God of Isaac, and the God of Jacob" (Matt 22:32), the Yahweh of Israel. However, the NT does offer some fresh understandings about God, which the following three categories summarize:

- The Trinitarian nature of God (to be discussed below)
- The Kingdom of God/The God of the Kingdom
- The fatherhood of God

Whereas the idea of the fatherhood of God is not unknown in the OT—just think of the delightfully intimate picture in Hosea 11 of Yahweh teaching Israel, his son, to walk—nor is it a major theme. Things change with the coming of Jesus, the Son. Indeed, at the heart of Jesus's message is his talk about the Father, intimacy with him, obedience to him, and the desire to serve the coming of his kingdom. Indeed, the only prayer Jesus taught us is directed to the Father!

Particularly striking is Jesus's use of the intimate, family-related way of addressing God as Father—*abba* (whether by a child or a grown up). Jesus not only addressed God as *abba*, including in his utmost distress in Gethsemane (Mark 14:36); he also taught his disciples to do so. But whereas he teaches them to address God as "our Father" (Matt 6:9), Jesus alone uses the expression "my Father" (Matt 7:21; 10:32; among others). What is important here is that Jesus wanted to share the filial relationship with his followers.

With regard to the third NT innovation about our picture of God, namely, that related to the kingdom, something similar to the innovation of a father relationship is going on. Although the idea of the kingdom is of course known in the OT, only in the NT does it become the very center of

---

9 Brueggemann, *Theology of the Old Testament*, 241.

Jesus's preaching and ministry. Indeed, in Jesus's preaching and teaching, including numerous parables, everything is about the kingdom of God, and hence, about the God of the kingdom.

God Is Not Absent from the World!

God Nearby and God Far Off

A crucial question for all believers has to do with whether the God of the Bible is a distant, far off God, or—as depicted in Jesus's teaching—an intimate, familiar God. It is fair to say that in the Bible as a whole God is on the one hand spoken of as the absolutely majestic, transcendent, "incomprehensible," and "hidden" God—as in the expression from Isaiah 45:15: "Truly, thou art a God who hidest thyself." Hence the rhetorical question in Jeremiah 23:23, "Am I a God at hand, says the Lord, and not a God afar off?" On the other hand, this same God is so close to his creatures that there is no place in the whole cosmos to which they can flee from his presence:

> Thou knowest when I sit down and when I rise up;
>> thou discernest my thoughts from afar.
>
> Thou searchest out my path and my lying down,
>> and art acquainted with all my ways.
>
> ... Thou dost beset me behind and before,
>> and layest thy hand upon me.
>
> ... Whither shall I go from thy Spirit?
>> Or whither shall I flee from thy presence?
>
> If I ascend to heaven, thou art there!
>
> If I make my bed in Sheol, thou art there! (Ps 139:2–3, 5, 7–8)

In a masterful way, Paul's famous speech at the Areopagus (Acts 17) puts these two dimensions of God's nearness and God's hiddenness in a dynamic and mutual relationship:

> The God who made the world and everything in it, being Lord of heaven and earth, does not live in shrines made by man, nor is he served by human hands, as though he needed anything, since he himself gives to all men life and breath and everything. And he made from one every nation of men to live on all the face of the earth, having determined allotted periods and the boundaries of their habitation, that they should seek God,

in the hope that they might feel after him and find him. Yet he is not far from each one of us, for

"In him we live and move and have our being";

as even some of your poets have said,

"For we are indeed his offspring." (vv. 24–28)

In light of this dynamic teaching of Scripture, Christian theology has struggled to find a dynamic balance between the two claims: that God is near *and* that God is far off. In general we can say that quite early on in Christian history a tendency to safeguard God's absolute freedom by emphasizing his distance, incomprehensibility, and mysterious nature tended to take priority. Theologians came up with a term to express this development, namely "classical theism." Classical theism highlighted the distinction—although of course not the absence—from the world of God, and as a result the way in which theology came to speak of God often smacked of abstract, sterile, and spirituality removed from the everyday.

Critics of classical theism paint a picture of God who is distant and rigid at the expense of the dynamic and living narrative of the Bible. The God of classical theism, they claim, is like an "Unmoved Mover" who, while enjoying his own perfect fullness of being, is distanced from the world and unaffected by the happenings of history. An example is the witty book title of the late Canadian Baptist Clark Pinnock, *Most Moved Mover*.

Though these criticisms might be exaggerations, and even caricatures, they convey the legitimate concern of not letting abstract speculations blur the profile of the living God of the Bible. As an alternative, or to be more precise, as a way to balance and challenge classical theism, contemporary theologians invented the term "panentheism." What does it mean?

"In Him We Live and Move and Have Our Being"

The term "panentheism" may sound dangerous to the Christian's ear, for it sounds like "pantheism," a word familiar to us from everyday language. Pantheism refers to the belief that God and world are totally equated with one another. To put it crudely, this would mean that God is world and world is God. This view is strictly against Christian faith.

But don't confuse pan*en*theism with pantheism. For panentheism refers to a close, intimate, and mutual relationship between God and the world, but in a way that maintains the absolute uniqueness of God. While God is in the world, deeply intertwined with its happenings as its Creator and Sustainer, and while the world is in some sense in God, yet God is much, much "bigger" than the world. And while God responds to and is "moved" by the world, God is not dependent on the world for God's glory and eternal bliss. The world is totally dependent on God, including all creatures, great and small.

Echoing panentheistic intimations, many contemporary theologians remind us that despite all his power and majesty, the Bible also depicts the living God as a compassionate, cosuffering, and sympathetic Father—and Mother! This theme Moltmann develops particularly dramatically in his highly acclaimed book *The Crucified God*, the author having himself undergone the experience of being a prisoner of war in World War II, with all the losses and fears imaginable. Similarly, a growing number of contemporary female theologians have found in panentheism a way to underline values such as intimacy, connection, and responsiveness. Not that any of these is uniquely a female value, but that we male theologians are indebted to our sisters for having reminded us of these important aspects of biblical faith.

Having discussed some key topics in the Christian understanding of God, it is now time for us to tackle the most distinctive—and most challenging to understand—feature in the doctrine of God, namely the divine Trinity. That will occupy the rest of the chapter and also take us back to considering from another perspective the work of God in the world and God's relationship with the world.

Why Do We Need the Trinity—or Do We?

Look in the World to Find the Trinitarian God!

In the words of the Orthodox Bishop Kallistos Ware, "[T]he doctrine of the Trinity is not just one possible way of thinking about God. It is the only way. The one God of the Christian church cannot be conceived except as Trinity."[10] And the same with another theological giant, the Reformed Barth: "The doctrine of the Trinity is what basically distinguishes the Christian doctrine of God as Christian."[11] That said, for most Christians this doctrine sounds outdated and complex. So, do we "need" the doctrine of the Trinity?

One of the reasons why Christian tradition has at times failed to comprehend the full significance of the Trinity has to do with the way the doctrine came to be formulated. In the course of history, the doctrine was often divorced from the larger "economy" of divine works (creation,

---

10. Ware, "Holy Trinity," 107. He is approvingly explaining the thought of Gregory of Nazianzus.

11. Barth, *Church Dogmatics*, I/1, 301.

salvation, sanctification) and came to be based on somewhat abstract speculations into the inner life of God, as it were. As a result, a feeling arose in the minds of the faithful that if the doctrine is so complicated and complex, perhaps it is not for every believer!

Contemporary theology has been attempting to overcome this liability with its turn toward the economic "from below" approach to God. This turn was brilliantly heralded by the twentieth century's most important Roman Catholic theologian, Karl Rahner. Let me quote his somewhat technical "rule" and then explain it in plain terms: "*The 'economic' Trinity is the 'immanent' Trinity and the 'immanent' Trinity is the 'economic' Trinity.*"[12] The term "economic" Trinity simply refers to all that God has done and is doing in the world, like creation and providence. The term "immanent" refers to God's own inner life, the eternal loving relationship among Father, Son, and Spirit. Now, Rahner is saying that access to any knowledge of God moves up, so to speak, from the observation of God's work in creation, providence, reconciliation, and consummation ("economic"), to the life of God itself ("immanent"). Whatever can be known of God by the limited, finite human mind is based on the economy of salvation rather than on God's inner life. Yet we can trust that this knowledge of God, however limited and occasional, is reliable because God, as faithful Creator and Savior, is the same in God's own life (the immanent Trinity) as in God's works in the world (the economic Trinity).

How do we know that this gateway to understanding the doctrine of the Trinity is the correct and feasible one? Incarnation is the answer—the fact that the Triune God has become one of us in the Word-made-flesh. By looking at Jesus (John 14:6), we get to know the Father! This is different from all other faith traditions: only in Christianity has God, the Infinite, become one among God's creatures!

Where Does the Bible Teach the Doctrine of the Trinity?

How many times does the term "trinity" appear in the Bible? Never. Not even once! If that's the case, isn't it a non-biblical, later development? Not really. For while the term itself never appears in the Bible, the *idea* of the one God as the Father, Son, and Spirit is everywhere in the NT. As soon as you begin to read the NT, beginning from the Gospel of Matthew, talk about Father, Son, and Spirit is everywhere. How different from the OT! No wonder it took some time for Christian theology to make sense of the pervasive plurality in the talk about one God. Ultimately, after a few centuries,

---

12. Rahner, *Trinity*, 22, italics original.

the *doctrinal* description was ratified and in that sense—but only in that sense—is the *doctrine* a later development. That said, it was necessitated by the plurality of ways referring to the one God of the OT.

A number of NT passages speak of God in terms of Father and Son alone, no mention of the Spirit yet. Just read the Gospel of John! Technically, that would be "binitarianism," belief in one God as two (persons). The critical stage in moving from a binitarian to a trinitarian understanding of God had to do with the growing insistence on the Spirit as an integral member in the life and work of the one God. The God who raised the Son from the dead by the power of the Spirit (Rom 1:4) will raise believers from the dead as well (8:11). Just recall the baptism of Jesus in Jordan, a narrative told in all four Gospels. The oldest one, Mark, puts it this way (1:10–11):

> And when he came up out of the water, immediately he saw the heavens opened and the Spirit descending upon him like a dove; and a voice came from heaven, "Thou art my beloved Son; with thee I am well pleased." (1:10–11)

Here the Father and the Son and the Spirit are at work simultaneously. Even though the Bible text does not provide us a key to how to understand their mutual relationship and "rank," clearly the one God is depicted as three. These and numerous other passages throughout the NT were the reason why the early theologians and church leaders deemed it necessary to come up with an explanation, what in hindsight we call the doctrine of the Trinity. On the way there, a number of interpretations and suggestions arose that were ultimately deemed heretical or at least wanting.

Righting the Heretical Views

Early Challenges to What Became the Correct Doctrine

The first (two-part) problem facing the early theologians was simple and profound. First, under what conditions would it be feasible to call God the human being Jesus of Nazareth? Second, if that is even possible, what about monotheism, belief in one God? After all, as you already know by now, the Father of Jesus Christ—the Christians' God—is the Yahweh of the OT.

One common-sense solution sounded appealing: What if we consider God the Father as the sole possessor of divinity in its absolute sense and make Jesus (and later the Spirit) a partaker of the divine nature and activities but not entirely a God? The name given in hindsight to this heresy was *monarchianism*. It comes from two Greek terms that mean "sole sovereignty" and simply indicate that among the three persons of the Trinity only the Father was absolutely, totally God, the two others less so. To make things more complicated, there were at least two versions of this heresy.

Known by the name "dynamic" monarchianism, some clever theologians proposed that God's sole deity can be maintained if what happens with Jesus of Nazareth is understood in terms of him being dynamically empowered by the Father. This empowerment certainly made Jesus higher than any other human being, but it did not make him God. In other words, God's power (Greek, *dynamis* of which the nomenclature "dynamic") made Jesus *almost* God—but not entirely. Thus, the Father's uniqueness (sole sovereignty) was secured.

Another version of the heresy, known as "modalistic" Monarchianism, took another route and sought to defend God's sole sovereignty by regarding the "Son" (and later, the "Spirit"), not as a distinct person in the godhead but merely as an alternative name or "mode" of the same God. In other words: when we say that the Father created the world and the Son reconciled it, we are using these two titles (Father, Son) only as alternative ways of speaking of the one God; we are not speaking of real distinctions. Another clever tactic in itself!

Why did the church find these two versions of the same heresy problematic? The main reason was biblical. Early defenders of orthodoxy (meaning: the correct doctrine) went back to narratives such as Jesus's baptism cited above. How can you support modalism when hearing about the Father's voice to Jesus, the Son, upon whose head was seen the Holy Spirit in the form of a dove? As much as the early teachers opposed tritheism (belief in three separate deities), they could not make any sense of Gospel stories such as Jesus's baptism if Modalists were right about their view. Concerning the other version, dynamic Monarchianism, among several other viewpoints, early theologians rightly argued that no amount of empowerment or gifting can make one God. It only makes one an exceptional person. And if Jesus was not God, then our salvation is in jeopardy as only God is able to save whereas the finite human being, even the best one, is himself or herself in need of salvation.

As soon as both versions of Monarchianism were defeated, an even more serious heretical proposal emerged in the early centuries, called Arianism, after an elder by the name Arius in one of the main centers of Christian learning at the time in Alexandria. Arianism revived the Monarchian type of desire to make the Son, Jesus of Nazareth, almost—but not absolutely—God in order to defend absolute monotheism, as Arianism saw it. The details of this heresy, similarly defeated on the basis of biblical, pastoral, and theological reasons, I consider in the chapter on Christology, as it relates directly to the status of Jesus the Son.

So, What Do We Mean When We Speak of the Trinity?

Instead of delving into other heretical views, I close this section by identifying the positive, constructive implications of the Christian trinitarian confession of the one God.

To say that one God exists as Father, Son, and Spirit is to speak of fellowship, the personal communion of the three. The biblical way of speaking of communion is to describe God as love (1 John 4:16). The one and only God in three divine persons—Father, Son, and Spirit—lives in and from eternal loving communion. They are all equal, just differently. Love is relationship; it is communion. As the late Catholic feminist C. M. LaCugna put it: "God, too, lives from and for another: God the Father gives birth to the Son, breathes forth the Spirit, elects the creature from before all time. . . . God's rule is accomplished by saving and healing love."[13]

The reference to the divine love takes us to the next important topic, namely to the question of what kind of God is the God of the Bible. Traditionally this topic is known as "divine attributes."

What God Is Like: The Divine Attributes

The many characteristics of God came to be known as divine attributes (or at times as divine perfections). While in classical theological manuals one may find highly speculative and fine-tuned classifications and treatises, it is more useful for us to follow the "economic" approach.

Here is one way to classify some of the main attributes building on the well-known, biblically based notion of God as eternal and as love:

> Eternal God as
> > Holy
> > Faithful
> > All-Wise, -Powerful, and -Present
>
> Loving God as
> > Compassionate
> > Good

---

13. LaCugna, *God for Us*, 383.

Merciful

Just and Righteous

Eternal God

What does it mean to call God "eternal"? Though it is obviously related to "time," we typically find it even more of a conundrum. Eternity (about which more in chapter 10) is not only the opposite to time but also its fulfillment, bringing to perfection all that is imperfect in our world. Whereas our life here and now is conditioned by the past, present, and future, in eternity the sequence of time does not apply and it represents all for which we long. Hence, calling God eternal is a finite human way of saying that in God all characteristics we find limited and imperfect in humanity and the rest of the creation are absolutely perfect.

The same is true of the first attribute in our list under God's eternity, namely holiness. God is absolutely holy, pure, and blameless. There is in God no defect, no sin, no imperfection in morality and ethics. A useful way to try to understand what this kind of absolute holiness may mean is to refer to the classic philosophical concept of "infinity."[14] Against common sense, infinity has two features. First, it distinguishes and separates itself from all that is finite. Second, it also includes and embraces the finite, otherwise it would end up not being infinite—encountering a borderline between itself and the finite. Only that kind of infinity that both distinguishes and includes finite can be truly infinite. That is a way to speak of God's holiness. On the one hand, it is distinct and separated from all that is unholy, sinful, and imperfect. On the other hand, as evident in the self-sacrifice of Jesus on the cross, God's holiness also includes and embraces all that is sinful. Think of Paul's statement in 2 Corinthians 5:21: "For our sake he made him to be sin who knew no sin, so that in him we might become the righteousness of God." By becoming sin, the total opposite of holiness, the Triune God also abolished all that is unholy! In other words, the holiness of God "enters the profane world, penetrates it, and makes it holy."[15]

Highlighting faithfulness and constancy is an important aspect of God's eternity. Theological tradition uses a strange term, that of divine "aseity." It means that God has his existence in himself without anything else. God is not subject to the process of decay to which humans and the rest of creation and cosmos are subject (Ps 102:26–27). In other words, God is constant. Relatedly, God is also ever-faithful, and in that sense it can be

---

14. Pannenberg, *Systematic Theology*, 1:397–401.
15. Pannenberg, *Systemaic Theology*, 1: 400.

said that in "the Father of lights ... there is no variation or shadow due to change" (Jas 1:17). God remains constant and faithful. But this does not mean that God is ever a distant, "emotionless" observer of world events. No: as discussed, God is a loving and caring Father or Mother who responds to his or her creatures and is ever-faithful and reliable. His "mood" does not change from day to day, as happens with us humans.

In theological treatises, the reader may find other descriptions of God that highlight God's eternity and infinity. They usually begin with the strange word "omni-," like God's omnipresence, omniscience, and omnipotence. The first part of the terms simply means "all-," as in all-powerful. Let us take a closer look at them.

The biblical conviction that God is ever-present in his creation (Jer 23:24) and absolutely transcends even "heaven and the highest heaven" (1 Kgs 8:27), is another theological way of saying "eternity." A useful way to speak of the presence of God everywhere and always in creation is in terms of the divine Spirit. Through his Spirit—the energy that brings about all creatures and also upholds them everywhere—God is intimately involved with all things. At the same time, this divine Spirit is also infinite, that is, transcendent. This helps avoid the danger of pantheism. Eternal God can never be contained by creation. Simply stated: God is both present everywhere and also transcends everything.

God's knowledge or omniscience, widely attested in Scripture, is related to God's presence in creation in that all things are present to God at all times. "When we speak of God's knowledge we mean that nothing in all his creation escapes him. All things are present to him and are kept by him in his presence,"[16] as Psalm 139 affirms.

Similarly related to God's eternity is the attribute of omnipotence (Job 42:2; Isa 45:7; Jer 32:17; Rom 1:20; etc.). It manifests itself particularly in the context of creation, in that God "gives life to the dead and calls into existence the things that do not exist" (Rom 4:17). Omnipresence and omnipotence are closely related to each other. As Pannenberg brilliantly puts it: "[W]hereas God's eternity means that all things are always present *to him*, the stress in his omnipresence is that he is present *to all things at the place of their existence*" (emphasis original). Consequently: "As all things are present to God in his eternity, and he is present to them, so he has power over all things. His omnipresence for its part is full of the dynamic of his Spirit."[17] That said, God's omnipotence, in contrast to that of the world's tyrants, is loving, caring, and kind. It always looks for the best of God's creation and

---

16. Pannenberg, *Systematic Theology*, 1:379–80.
17. Pannenberg, *Systematic Theology*, 1:410, 415 respectively.

creatures. This builds a bridge to the other set of God's characteristics—those under the rubric of the God of love.

The God of Love

The most well-known and for most Christians undoubtedly the most significant biblical statement is simple and profound: "God is love" (1 John 4:8, 16). In other words, love is the basic essence of God. As with everything else in the Christian understanding of God, the Trinity comes to our aid here. The idea of God as love finds its theological basis in the Trinitarian doctrine. Father, Son, and Spirit love each other eternally. Nozomu Miyahira, a Japanese theologian, calls this deep inner-Trinitarian love "concord" or "betweenness" among the Father, Son, and Spirit. It expresses itself in mutual knowledge, trust, and glorification.[18]

With the same love as that shared between Father, Son, and Spirit, the Triune God loves us and the world. The sending of the Son to the world for its salvation manifested the fatherly and motherly love in a most profound way (John 3:16). Jesus also made available this shared loving relationship to those who loved him (John 14:21; 15:9; 17:23). Indeed, nothing can separate them from God's love (Rom 8:31–39). An essential feature of the divine love is self-giving, donated to us through the Holy Spirit. This is what Paul says in Romans 5:5: "God's love has been poured into our hearts through the Holy Spirit which has been given to us."

Here, I focus on some important "attributes of the divine love" to highlight and extol its greatness: compassion, goodness, grace, righteousness, and patience.

A Loving and Compassionate God

Contemporary theology often—appropriately—laments that as much as Christian tradition has talked about God's loving compassion, it has also tended to restrict its meaning, fearing that speaking too tenderly of love and caring may begin to compromise divine omnipotence and majesty. This concern is all fine and understandable, but it may also lead to an understanding of God who is too distant and separated from the world that the same God has created. After all, the God of the Bible is a compassionate Father and Mother. Hence, it is both justified and also uplifting to speak

---

18. Miyahira, *Towards a Theology*, 181–82.

robustly about the tender and caring love of the Triune God. In fact, compassion literally means "to suffer with."

With the affirmation of divine compassion, contemporary theology puts in perspective two classical concepts drawn from ancient philosophy and culture, "immutability" and "impassibility." Whereas the former means that God does not change for any reason, the latter means that, therefore, God is unable to suffer. Why? The logic goes something like this: If there is change in God, then it has to be a change either for the better, in which case God is better tomorrow than today, or for the worse, in which case God is better today than God is tomorrow. The main problem with this abstract reasoning is that it is, well, *abstract*! A more useful way is to consult the Bible narrative for passages that describe the loving, passionate, and caring Father or Mother as deeply concerned about the well-being and suffering of men and women.

Alongside many female theologians, liberationists, and others, Moltmann reminds us: "[A] God who cannot suffer is poorer than any man. For a God who is incapable of suffering is a being who cannot be involved.... But the one who cannot suffer cannot love either. So he is also a loveless being."[19] Some Korean theologians speak of the same with the term *han*, "a feeling of acute pain and sorrow in one's guts and bowels."[20] Not only Jesus's death on the cross but also his whole life "bespeaks of the han of God for the children of the poor.... Jesus's suffering for three hours on the cross was one thing; his many years' suffering . . . was a profound source of Jesus's han."[21]

A Good and Gracious God

Closely related to God's loving compassion is God's goodness, a key theme in the Bible and one often expressed in terms of the love of the covenant-faithful God. No wonder this attribute is a reason for constant praise and thankfulness!

> Praise the LORD!
> O give thanks to the LORD, for he is good;
>   for his steadfast love endures for ever!
> (Ps 106:1; see also 107:1; 118:1).

19. Moltmann, *Crucified God*, 222.

20. Quoted in Joh, *Heart of the Cross*, xxi. Joh mistakenly attributes this quote to Han Wan Sang, whereas it actually comes from Younghak Hyun and can be found in Hyun, "Three Talks on Minjung Theology," 7, 36.

21. Park, *Wounded Heart of God*, 125.

As the fountain of goodness, the heavenly Father responds to his children not only when they ask him (Matt 7:11) but also regardless of merit (20:15), whether they are bad or good (5:45). Theological tradition reminds us that goodness is not only a feature of God's nature but that, somewhat technically put, God is good "necessarily." What does this mean? Simply that God cannot but be good. According to Thomas Aquinas, "God is the highest good," unable to "bear any mingling with evil."[22]

Not so fast, some critics may scream! The goodness of God is far from an established fact, they say—and for obvious reasons. There is simply too much pain, suffering, and injustice in the world. How even to begin to speak of goodness given this rampant evil and suffering? Without in any way trying to get around this most urgent question, suffice it to mention that I will return to this topic in some detail in the final chapter on eschatology.

A God of Righteousness and Patience

Moving to the topic of righteousness—under the rubric of God's love—might seem to be a deviation. For common sense would connect righteousness with the holiness and judgment of God rather than with love. So why am I connecting righteousness with divine love here? The key lies in the biblical link with covenant righteousness. This is exactly what lies behind the Pauline statement: "This was to show God's righteousness, because in his divine forbearance he had passed over former sins; it was to prove at the present time that he himself is righteous and that he justifies him who has faith in Jesus" (Rom 3:25-26). For the apostle, God's faithfulness to his covenant, in tandem with divine forbearance, is the highest expression of his righteousness.

It is understandable that Christian theology has been in danger of losing the biblical covenant-based notion of God's righteousness as it has too often conceived of it primarily in penal and judicial terms. In fact the Reformer Martin Luther's groundbreaking insight was that, rather than penal justice, God's righteousness is salvific righteousness that makes believers righteous and restores their relationship with God.

At the same time, to rediscover fully the biblical notion of the righteousness of God as part of God's love, its "practical" implications in relation to liberation and justice must be affirmed in a more robust way. According to the black theologian James Cone, "It is important to note . . . that the righteousness of God is not an abstract quality in the being of God, as with Greek philosophy. It is rather God's active involvement in

---

22. Aquinas, *Summa contra Gentiles*, 1.95.3-4.

history, making right what human beings have made wrong."[23] In other words, those who have experienced God's righteousness as salvation are called to put into practice the same covenant-faithfulness and love toward the neighbor, near and distant. The next section "Divine Hospitality" develops that topic further.

Linked with righteousness is divine patience. To appreciate it, we must remind ourselves of the freedom and independence the Creator has granted to us creatures. Rather than forcing us creatures to live in union with their Creator, loving God makes space for our independence—and then, notwithstanding our continued rebellion, pursues us for our salvation. Patience is an expression of love that both affirms the independence of the creatures and makes every effort to establish communion. That is what a caring and wise parent does! Not for nothing, in several OT passages that list Yahweh's attributes, patience is mentioned along with righteousness, mercy, and grace (Exod 34:6; Pss 86:15; 103:8; and 145:8).

Alongside these many characteristics of the Triune God, in contemporary theology some other divine attributes are linked with particular issues pertinent in our world. To those we turn next.

God of Hospitality, Belonging, and Peace

Hospitality in a World of Indifference

In an important study titled *Hospitable God*, George Newlands and Allen Smith set the tone and theme for this section: "Though we may not find the word 'hospitable' on every page of the doctrinal tradition about God, we suggest that hospitality provides a summative term which may express eloquently affirmations and concerns which lie at the heart of the Christian gospel."[24] Hospitality is a familiar term to us. It speaks of welcoming, opening up ourselves and our homes to the stranger, giving and receiving gifts, cultivating fellowship, and belonging.

At the heart of hospitality is a turning toward others, the neighbor, particularly to those who may not deserve such a graceful act. In the triune God, this overflowing hospitality is fully manifested. As Luther put it powerfully, "Rather than seeking its own good, the love of God flows forth and bestows good."[25] God's love seeks that which is worthless in itself and donates not only gifts but one's self, as was discussed above.

---

23. Cone, *Black Theology of Liberation*, 2.
24. Newlands and Smith, *Hospitable God*, 22.
25. Luther, Heidelberg Disputation, thesis 28, in *Luther's Works*, 31:57.

Just imagine what would happen if, following feminist theologian Letty M. Russell, we embodied "hospitality as the practice of God's welcome . . . in our actions . . . bringing justice and healing to our world in crisis"?[26] Too often, I fear, Christians (as well as followers of other religions) are instead perceived as those who constantly make a separation between "us" and the "others." Authentic hospitality, while not a call to give up one's own identity—in Christian parlance, one's genuine faith commitment to Christ—also makes room for the otherness of the other persons. Take, for example, the problem of Islamophobia: rather than being a necessary result of sincere commitment to Christian faith, it can also be a function of a person's sense of ethnic and religious superiority and fear of difference. A hospitable interfaith attitude, by contrast, is willing to continue the painstaking negotiation between one's own dearest beliefs and those of the followers of other faith traditions.

The God of the Bible "shows no partiality" (see Acts 10:34). Hospitality means opening up one's arms to others, as Jesus did on the cross, nailed to the tree between two criminals.

Above we learned that at the center of the Christian confession of the Trinity is communion, fellowship, and belonging. Trinity speaks of God as the dynamic, living, engaging community of the three. It speaks of relationality, belonging, and inclusion. In our world of isolation, suspicion, hatred, and indifference, the good news of the Triune God as the symbol and embodiment of belonging and communion resonates.

Peace in a World of Violence

Alongside indifference and isolation, our current world is also plagued with violence and hatred, including wars and genocides. Not only that, but religions may also contribute to this juxtaposition between people and peoples. Hence, we have provocative book titles such as Mark Juergensmeyer's *Terror in the Mind of God: The Global Rise of Religious Violence*.

What is the Christian response? Is it true that religions at large and Christian faith in particular may cause violence and wars? Sadly, we have to admit "yes." It has happened in the past and is common even today. Recall the medieval Crusades, or the long-term conflicts in the British Isles between Catholics and Protestants, for example. Indeed, violence is a part of every faith tradition's history. At the same time, violence is unfortunately not limited to religions alone; it is also part of the record of atheistic and other secular ideologies' legacies. Recall, for example, the

---

26. Russell, *Just Hospitality*, 2.

70 million purported victims of communist regimes, among them a large number of believers of various faiths.

Two implications follow: First, while all too common among religions, violence is not a distinctively religious phenomenon. Second, it is consequently possible to envision religions that advocate peace and coexistence rather than war and juxtaposition. Indeed, it seems justified to conclude that "religion does some harm and some good, but most people, faced with the evidence, will probably agree that it does a great deal more good than harm."[27]

Now immediately a question emerges regarding the scriptural texts that seem to endorse God's violence—and they are many and well-known. Wouldn't those passages alone make any defense of the innocence of the God of the Bible meaningless? On this complex question, the following responses might be useful. First, in every society in the ancient world, violence has been and remains rampant and horrible. All living faiths' holy Scriptures and ancient texts share that feature; the Bible is no exception. Second, Christian theology of revelation builds on progressive revelation: God takes people at the level they are at and patiently, over the centuries, shapes them. To that progressive revelation also belong nuancing, balancing, and finally forbidding the right to violence. Third, the full revelation in Jesus Christ tells us that violence has been superseded and replaced with unconditional love and embrace. In the sacrificial death of his Son, God has put an end to violence.

To the principle of hospitality belongs also the consideration of the way we speak of God. Let us take a closer look at it.

How Might We Speak of God in an Inclusive Way?

The issue of what might be the appropriate way to do God-talk is pertinent to the third millennium, particularly in terms of language. Although this problem was not tackled much in the past, in our current culture it is pressing. The liability of the traditional way of speaking of God is the one-sided dominance of male pronouns and ways of expression. It is as if God were male and as a result, women and girls were either excluded or, at its best, marginalized.

What to do about this issue? What might be the best way to work toward an inclusive way of speaking of God? We can discern at least three main tactics. They all have their advocates; I recommend the third one:

---

27. Ward, *Is Religion Dangerous*, 7.

- Replace traditional naming with the new form,
- Stick with the traditional form of naming, or
- Use both of these tactics in a balanced manner.

The assumption that traditional God-language is not only hopelessly sexist but also supportive of oppressive structures motivates efforts to replace all traditional (meaning predominantly masculine) talk of God with something else. Metaphorical God-talk is the solution because God, as a mysterious unknown, makes sticking with only one particular name or nomenclature seem unwarranted. A whole new repertoire of descriptions of God is available, such as Source, Word, and Spirit; Creator, Liberator, and Comforter; Creator, Redeemer, and Sanctifier; and so forth. A gender-free way of addressing the triune God would avoid the problems related to traditional discourse. The extreme opposite to this tactic is to consider the biblically based terms—Father, Son, and Spirit—as "proper names." They are not, of course, subject to be changed at will. Proper names are irreplaceable, so the argument goes.

The mediating position acknowledges on the one hand the limitations of the traditional sexist and patriarchal nature of God-talk. On the other hand, while not treating Father and Son as proper names, it honors them for the sake of their biblical roots and long traditional usage. Hence, this tactic continues using Father, Son, and Spirit alongside other names such as Creator, Redeemer, and Sanctifier. Furthermore, it seeks to help redeem traditional naming such as Father from its alleged necessary exclusive meaning by noting that the infinite God, as opposed to finite human beings, can never be defined along gender boundaries. It is also argued that the negative linking of father or masculine language with abuse, power play, and marginalizing women is only a human phenomenon; they do not apply to Heavenly Father at all! Finally, this approach notes that there are occasional maternal and feminine designations of God in the Bible and specifically in Christian tradition. In sum: this mediating position seems to me to be the most promising.

Is the God of the Bible the Only True God?

Not All Christians Think Alike about Other Faith Traditions' Conceptions of God(s)

The last part of this lengthy chapter attempts a dialogue about the deity with four other faith traditions. While basically all religions (perhaps with the exception of Taoism and original Theravada Buddhism) have conceptions of the deity or deities, understandably they do not agree on the nature and work of those deities. In a religiously pluralistic world, a careful look at the differences and similarities is in order.

But even before that, a brief look at divergences of opinions among various Christian traditions is important for more nuanced interfaith work. Like any other faith tradition, there are significant internal differences in Christianity with regard to how best to account for other faith traditions' ideas of god(s) and whether Christians should regard their own as superior to others. This exercise is technically called theology of religions.

Theologians have devised a simple typology to highlight the distinctive features of differing opinions about the theology of religions:

- "Exclusivism" teaches not only that salvation is to be found only in Christ, the one and only Savior, but also that the person to be saved must hear the gospel preached and give a personal response to it through the Word (and sacraments).
- "Pluralism" means that no religion has the final and ultimate word about God, but that all different faiths are more or less equal paths to truth and salvation. It insists that there is some kind of "rough parity" between religions.
- "Inclusivism" is the most complex response, according to which salvation can be found only in Christ (in agreement with exclusivism), but it says further that many people in other faiths who never had a meaningful encounter with the Christian gospel may still be saved because of the universal salvific effects of Christ.

We can say with only some exaggeration that by and large the Christian Church until modern times took for granted the first, exclusivist, position. Even though already during the era of the church fathers there emerged a hope that at least some "pagans" with no opportunity to hear the Gospel might be saved—similarly to infants who passed away before the age of accountability or persons without the needed intellectual and moral powers—in the main, the exclusivist view was rarely challenged. It still is the hallmark of the majority of Christians, other than Roman Catholics, particularly those on the more conservative side.

Before taking a more careful look at the opposite stance—pluralism—I note briefly the third one, often named inclusivism. This one is much more complicated to understand than the other two. While its roots go deeply into Christian history, as a stated doctrine it was not formulated until the 1960s at the highly influential Roman Catholic Church's Second Vatican Council (briefly: Vatican II). Its genius lies in its attempt to negotiate between the two extreme positions. With exclusivists (and in rebuttal of pluralists), inclusivists understand Christ as the only Savior. In contrast to exclusivists, inclusivists believe that under two conditions masses of people in other faiths can or might attain salvation in Christ even if, through no fault of their own, they have not had an opportunity to hear the Gospel. The conditions are: first, that these people sincerely seek in their own religions the truth of Christ and the Christian Gospel, the "fulfillment" of all religious aspirations; and, second, make an effort to live in keeping with the moral precepts stipulated by their own religion. From a Catholic viewpoint, such people are already turning toward the God of the Bible without being aware of it or calling it such. But is this merely salvation by works, a typical Protestant may ask? No, because these people will only be saved by Christ's salvific work that the Holy Spirit is able to convey to those people mysteriously, in ways known only to God. Furthermore, the Catholic teaching makes very clear that only in the (Catholic) Church is the fullness of salvation to be found, and therefore mission and evangelism continue to be the Christian mandate. In this light, it is easy to see that despite ill-versed Protestants's judgment to the contrary, the world's largest Roman Catholic Church has not embraced religious pluralism at all—if pluralism means compromising Christ's uniqueness as the Savior and the church as the summit of salvation.

We turn now to the pluralistic option, as its appeal is growing rapidly among Protestants, Anglicans, and some others outside the Catholic (and Eastern Orthodox) Church.

Do All Religions Lead to the Same End Goal?

Echoing the common sense idea on the street that no particular religion is unique and that all religions are more or less equally valid, religious pluralism assumes that all religions are more or less the same, notwithstanding apparent differences in some outward manifestations, such as habits and times of prayer or the nature of holy Scripture. Ultimately they are all equally (much or little) true and salvific. Hence, no religion has the prerogative to consider its own God/gods as unique or exclusive, say pluralists. As a result, pluralists would say that Jesus Christ is only one way, but not the only way, to God. This is often called "theo-centrism" (from *theos*, God.)

The most well-known advocate of first-generation pluralism is the late British-American John Hick. Having left behind the conservative Christian confession of his youth, he initiated what he called a Copernican revolution. Analogously to what happened in the transition from the Ptolemaic, earth-centered astronomy to the Copernican, sun-centered one, Hick compared religions to planets that revolve, he said, around one and the same "sun," God—or the "Ultimate Reality," as he later came to call it in order to make his model even more open-ended. Religions are merely human interpretations of the one and same divine reality. Rather than divinely revealed truths about God, religions are but human conceptualizations, visions, and experiences, he said. Hence, all religions—all of which are more or less exclusivistic by nature—are called to soften their own identity and acknowledge the commonality of the religious experience and belief. A related and very critical asset in Hick's turn to pluralism is his understanding of religious and theological language as metaphorical (or mythical). Hence, rather than being propositional and factual, statements such as "Christ rose from the dead" are to be understood in an elusive and nonliteral manner.[28]

What about Hick's view of the Trinity? He does not engage the topic in any detail, and instead simply states that there is no way to follow that ancient doctrinal statement because it would only strengthen exclusivism even further. Reluctance to consider Jesus (or the Spirit) as divine alone would make that belief obsolete.

Critics have been quick to point to a number of problems in Hick's pluralism, including the following: First, it seems as if Hick is no neutral critical observer of religions but rather a founder of a new kind of "religion" that is similar to no existing one. Second, rather than a beacon of tolerance and openness, Hick's demand for the followers of other religions to give up their deepest convictions about the uniqueness of their views smacks of imperialism and of a sense of one's own superiority. Third, most contemporary scholars of religions hardly support uncritically Hick's foundational assumption of the common essence of religions; a good case can be made for deep and critical differences.

Take, for example, Asia, and specifically India, a highly multireligious environment, and its growing sense of religious tolerance but increased and intensified political and social intolerance. Add to that a keen sense of the mysterious, and there seems to be room for negotiating any religion's ultimate truth claims. Stanley J. Samartha believes that the finite, and thus, relative nature of human mind does not allow any religious community to have exclusive or unique knowledge. He seeks to compromise claims to exclusivity.[29]

Critics of Samartha and the like note that to speak of God as mystery is nothing new in Christian tradition (just think of the long mystical

---

28. Hick, *God and the Universe of Faiths*.
29. Samartha, *Courage for Dialogue*, 152–53.

tradition) and that it was not a means of denying the uniqueness of God but was rather a warning to the limited human mind not to claim to be able to attain too much knowledge of God. Likewise, familiar in the Christian tradition is the desire to "soften" the rational claims of theology and make room for aesthetic and mystical elements. But it has not been used in tradition to compromise the salvific role of the triune God.

Now we are ready to place the trinitarian God of the Christian religion among other world religions.

How Would the Triune God Fare among the Deities of Other Religions?

How even to begin the enormous task of comparison between various religious traditions' ideas of and beliefs in gods? Any such attempt faces immense and complex challenges. We have to be careful not to deny the distinctive features of each tradition in our search for potential commonalities. Highlighting real differences is an equally important task in any comparative work.

With this caveat in mind, let us begin with the Abrahamic cousin faith, Islam, before considering Buddhist and Hindu views. In this particular topic I include no separate focused investigation of Jewish tradition because of the obvious family relationship between the mother and child religion, although I will bring some key Jewish ideas to the dialogue with Islam.

Allah and the Father of Jesus Christ

Muslims Are Strictly Monotheistic

Although all Abrahamic faiths are monotheistic, Islam seeks to be most radically so. Affirmed everywhere in Islamic theology, the short sura 112 of the Qur'an puts it succinctly, taking notice also of the fallacy of the Christian confession of the Trinity:

> Say: "He is God, One.
> God, the Self-Sufficient, Besought of all.
> He neither begot, nor was begotten.
> Nor is there anyone equal to Him."

Hence the basic Muslim confession of *shahada*: "There is no god but God, and Muhammad is the apostle of God."

An essential aspect of the divine unity is Allah's distinction from all else. The common statement "God is great" (*Allah akbar*) means not only that but also implies that "God is greater" than anything else. Hence, the biggest sin is *shirk*, or associating anything with Allah. Importantly, *shirk* literally means "ingratitude." In other words, "there is only one divine Creator who should be thanked and praised; no other being is to be given the thanks due only to God."[30] In that light it is understandable that, unlike modern forms of Christianity, the Muslim faith encompasses all of life, whether secular or sacred. The five pillars of Islam (profession of faith, prayers, almsgiving, fasting, and pilgrimage) shape all of life.

Similarly to Christianity but in even more intensified form, the Muslim theology of God includes the built-in dynamic between the absolute transcendence of God because of his incomparability and uniqueness on the one hand and, on the other, his presence and rulership in the world, which is a call for total obedience. God is sovereign; all reality is totally dependent on Allah.

Now the term *allah* predates the time of Muhammad. It did not originate in the context of moon worship in Arabia (even though the crescent became Islam's symbol and even though moon worship was known in that area). Instead, the term derives from Aramaic and Syriac words for God. In that light, it is fully understandable that even among Christians in Arabic-speaking areas, the term *Allah* is the designation for God. Visitors to Christian services in the Muslim heartland notice this immediately.

One of the most well-known ways in Islamic theology to imagine God is by listing the Ninety-Nine Beautiful Names of God; while not to be found in the Qur'an as such, various kinds of listings of the attributes of Allah can be found in Scripture.

As is true also of God in the Bible, the Qur'an occasionally uses anthropomorphic (human-like) metaphors of Allah, such as the "face of God" (Q 2:115) or the "hand(s) of God" (48:10; 5:64), although in general Islam is very cautious about picturing Allah. While there is hardly a classified typology of attributes in Islamic traditions, representative is the listing of thirteen attributes mentioned in sura 59:22–24: "He is God, than Whom there is no other god, Knower of the unseen and the visible. He is the Compassionate, the Merciful . . . the King, the Holy, the Peace, the Securer, the Guardian, the Mighty, the Compeller, the Exalted . . . the Creator, the Maker, the Shaper."

---

30. Carman, *Majesty and Meekness*, 323.

Do Muslims and Christians Worship the Same God?

So, do Muslims and Christians worship the same God or not? This question is not new to either tradition. As early as the seventh-to-eighth Christian century churchman John of Damascus, who had firsthand knowledge of the Muslim faith and once worked in Muslim administration, delved deeply into this question in the last chapter of his treatise *On Heresies*. Even though he considered Muslims "idol worshipers," John seemed to assume that both traditions worship one and the same God. Or consider the fifteenth-century Catholic cardinal Nicholas of Cusa who, following the ransacking of the holy city of Constantinople in 1453, sought to achieve in his *On the Harmonious Peace of Religions* a "harmony among religions" and "perpetual peace." At the same time, he also critically judged Islam's errors! Even Martin Luther, with his well-known and deep suspicions toward Muslims (and Jews), assumed that "all who are outside this Christian church, whether heathen, Turks [Muslims], Jews, or false Christians and hypocrites . . . believe in and worship only the one, true God."[31]

The key issue has to do with divine unity and the Trinity. In keeping with the stress on the unity, the Qur'anic teaching categorically rejects any notion of the threeness of God, and likewise rejects Jesus's deity (4:171; 5:72–76), an occasion of gravest *shirk*. It is good to remember that the charge of tritheism (belief in three deities) was leveled against the Christian faith long before Islam. In the fourth century, Gregory of Nyssa had to pen an important rebuttal titled, *On "Not Three Gods."* A foundational reason for the strict rebuttal of the Christian doctrine of the Trinity is the sheer absurdity of the idea of God having a child by a woman, a view foreign also to Christianity! Often behind the Muslim charge of *shirk* is an inadequate or even heretical (in the Christian estimation) view of who Jesus Christ is, for example that he was a highly elevated divine figure but not equal to God; of course Christians categorically reject that view as well.

These rebuttals against the Christian trinitarian conception of the one God are well known and they should be considered carefully. Yet there are also important similarities between Christianity and Islam. Very importantly, both traditions speak of God in universal rather than "tribal" terms. Similarly to the Bible, the Qur'anic message "is a message for all people: all people should become Muslims, for God is the sovereign God of all people."[32] Part of the universalizing tendency is the important promise in sura 42:15: "God is our Lord and your Lord. Our deeds concern

---

31. Luther, *Large Catechism*, part 2 ("The Creed"), art. 3, line 66.
32. Vroom, *No Other Gods*, 104.

us and your deeds concern you. There is no argument between us and you. God will bring us together, and to Him is the [final] destination." Hence, the reason why Muslim theology can unequivocally affirm both the identity of the God of Islam and the God of Christianity has to do with the principle of continuity—in terms of fulfillment—between the divine revelations given first to the Jews, then to Christians, and finally, in completed form, to Islam (2:136; 6:83–89; 29:46).

An important asset to Christian theology for reflecting on the relation of Allah to the God of the Bible is its relation to Judaism. Hardly any Christians would deny that Yahweh and the Father of Jesus Christ are one and the same God. Yet Jews no less adamantly oppose the Trinitarian confession of faith. This simply means that Christian tradition is able to confess belief in and worship of one God, even when significant differences exist in the understanding of the nature of that God. To confess one God does not require an identical understanding of the nature of God.

Hindu Deities and the God of the Bible

Foundational Differences

Moving from Abrahamic faiths to Hinduism is a huge, huge step. The differences between Abrahamic and Asiatic faith traditions are many and well known, but often the issues are blurred by the existence of popular and (to a large extent) misleading (or at least, inaccurate) alleged divergences:

- Whereas Christianity has a personal God, Hinduism has an impersonal god.
- Whereas Christianity is monotheistic, Hinduism is polytheistic.
- Whereas in Christianity the Divine can take the form of humanity, in Hinduism the deity remains transcendently distant; and so forth.

As with any popular stereotypes, they are just that: *stereotypes*. But there are important, foundational differences that have to be brought to the table for comparative purposes:

- Whereas for Christianity (and Islam) the doctrinal understanding of God is binding and normative, Hinduism lacks that. As long as one is not going against the authority of the Vedas, the oldest Scriptures, one is allowed a lot of leeway.

- While by far the majority of Hindu adherents embrace some kind of personal deity, theologically speaking, beyond the personal notion, there is still the "true" impersonal deity.
- Deep differences in worldview and epistemology also often complicate the task of comparison: Asiatic cultures are by and large cyclical, whereas Abrahamic are linear, and so forth.

Many Gods or One God?

The oldest Vedas, particularly Rig Veda, list a number of deities or *devas* (this term denoting "divine being" rather than god in the current sense of the word). Among them, Indra, the cosmic power, while a fairly late arrival in Vedic religion, plays the central role. Other important figures include Agni, the deity of fire, associated particularly with sacrifices; the lovely Savitri, "Mother Earth"; Aditi; and a host of others.

A critical move toward embracing one major notion of the deity amid the bewildering diversity of *devas* began in classical Hinduism, as represented by the last part of the Vedas, the Upanishads. The well-known answer (in Brihadaranyaka Upanishad, 3.9.1, 9) in response to the question of how many gods there are altogether, drawn from a Vedic text, is 330,000, which then boils down to one, and this one god is Brahman. The many gods are "only the various powers of them." Ultimately, there is one ultimate divine, Brahman, represented by a number of individual deities.

So, how many gods are there in Hinduism? Here we come to the most important *theo*logical affirmation in theistic Hinduism: *atman* is Brahman (4.4.5 and 25). Whereas Brahman is the ultimate notion of the divine, *atman* is the ultimate reality about us. While everything else in the world, including everything in us, changes, *atman* does not. Though it is routinely translated as "soul," in no way is that individually driven Western concept a good way to communicate the meaning of the Sanskrit word.

Most typically, three deities are seen as the major manifestations of Brahman: Brahma (not to be confused with Brahman), the "creator" god; Vishnu, the "preserver" god; and Shiva, the "destroyer," or better, "consummator," god. The distant Brahman comes to be known and worshiped in any of these deities or their associates known as *isa* or *isvara*, the "Lord" or Bhagavan, the Exalted One.

Typically, the "Lord," be it Vishnu or Shiva—since by and large the worship of Brahma almost completely vanished a long time ago—becomes a more or less exclusive title in popular piety, although theologically either one and both of them manifest Brahman. Hence, we have the proliferation of Hindu denominations, among which the most important are Shaivism (followers of Shiva) and Vaishnavism (followers of Vishnu), with an ever-increasing number of sub-sects. Either related to the main deities or separate from them, local and tribal deities, both male and female, and cults of worship dedicated to them, fill India.

While it is of course true that the Hindu conception of Brahman as the ultimate reality leans toward an impersonal notion unlike the personal God of Semitic faiths, it is also true that Hinduism is quite familiar with personal conceptions of deities. Not only does the personal deity come to the fore in the hugely popular and widespread folk piety based on the great religious epics discussed in the previous chapter, but even in the later stages of the Upanishads personal notions begin to emerge in various forms.

What is distinctive about Hindu deities is the prominent place of female deities. Usually Shiva and Vishnu are accompanied by their wives, Parvati and Sri (Lakshmi). The prominent female deity is known as Sakti, "power," or Devi, the "Divine Mother." Sometimes Sakti is described as exercising the same powers as Vishnu and Shiva.

How Is God Related to the World?

Here you have a chance to engage in some serious intellectual gymnastics. If you find this subsection to be a bit complicated, it's because it is! (Just skip to the next section if you get stuck!)

Here is the main issue: From the Brahman-*atman* relationship derives the single most widely debated and complex issue in Hindu theology and philosophy, namely how exactly we should envision the relationship between the two. To use Christian terminology, it is about the relationship between God and world. Among the many Vedanta schools with differing nuances, the positions of two are most well-known. Let's take a look them.

Whereas the ninth-century teacher Sankara's strict *advaita* (nondualism, literally "no two") allows no real distinction between God and the world, the eleventh-century Ramanuja's "qualified" nondualism negotiates it delicately without endorsing dualism. These differences come to the fore in the debates of authoritative commentaries on *Vedanta-Sutras*, a key Upanishadic writing.

Why is Sankara so strict in his nondualism? For him, the major fallacy behind distinction is *avidya*, "nescience," which is incapable of distinguishing between relative and absolute being. A familiar illustration is imagining a rope to be a snake. They only appear similar! As long as one lives under this misguided assumption of *avidya*, one must continue in the cycle of samsara, leading to rebirth and to reaping the law of karma, the law of cause and effect. The correct insight into the total and absolute unity of God and world will bring about one's ultimate release, leading to "nirvanic" extinction. Sankara is deeply intellectual in orientation, and it appears that knowledge rather than, say, devotion or ethics, is the key to the true knowledge of God in this interpretive tradition.

What then is Brahman according to Sankara? The Brahman "is all-knowing and endowed with all powers, whose essential nature is eternal purity, intelligence, and freedom."[33] Clearly, there are parallels here with Abrahamic traditions with their conceptions of God as the omniscient and omnipotent Absolute Being. At the same time, Sankara's God, somewhat differently from that of Ramanuja, leans strongly toward an impersonal and pantheistic notion, yet it does so in a more complex way. Sankara makes an important distinction between two aspects of the Divine, namely *nirguna* and *saguna* Brahman. Whereas the former is without any qualities and thus beyond human grasping, the latter has qualities and is thus known. In light of that distinction, in Sankara's impersonal monism, the worship of the *isvara* type of personal deity can be tolerated but of course is known by "wise" persons to be a false impression!

It is here that, a few centuries later, Ramanuja comes to challenge Sankara with his own "qualified" monism in which "*brahman*, who is identical with īśvara . . . is none other than Visnu. Creation is the body of *brahman* but not without qualification."[34] His way of speaking of the world as the body of God has parallels in some contemporary panentheistic Christian conceptions. An important related idea is that of "infinity": "God contains all finite realities, both good and evil, but also transcends them. God is with and without form. . . . [God] is separate from all beings yet united with all beings."[35] In saying this, Ramanuja categorically rejects Sankara's *nirguna-saguna* distinction for, in his deeply theistic interpretation of Vedanta tradition, he conceives of *isvara* as having an infinite number of supreme and auspicious qualities. That kind of Divine can be worshiped and praised, unlike Sankara's Divine. This affirmation of the supreme Brahman as personal Lord makes it possible to embrace and encourage (rather than simply to tolerate as a false belief, as Sankara would have it) *bhakti*, devotional tradition, the mainline form of theistic Hinduism among the masses. Ramanuja's thought also considers salvation as a collaboration between divine grace, human effort, and loving surrender to God. All in all, it is easy to see that in many ways Ramanuja's qualified monism reflects

33. Sankara, *Vedanta-Sutras*, 1.1; *SBE* 34:14.
34. Klostermaier, *Survey of Hinduism*, 359.
35. Carman, *Majesty and Meekness*, 146.

theological and devotional aspects closer to the Abrahamic and particularly the Christian tradition than those of Sankara.

(Did you manage to stay with me through that? If so, congratulations. And if not, let's pick up the story here! We are returning to more familiar territory now.) What about the Trinity? I have not yet mentioned it explicitly in engaging Hindu theology of deities.

The Trinitarian God and the One Absolute Divine

The obvious starting point to consider any Trinitarian parallels in Hinduism is the above-mentioned "trinity" of classical deities—Brahma, Vishnu, and Siva—named Trimurti. As promising as it might sound to Christian ears, this trinity has never been widely popular in Hinduism, although a strand of Hindu piety developed cultic rites to honor the threeness. Recall that for most Hindus, different gods (these three or any others) are ultimately the expression of the One—an observation that in principle should be highly compatible with the Christian confession of one God in three persons. An important reason why Trimurti did not excite too many Hindu believers has to do with the virtual disappearance of the cult of Brahma, leaving only two major gods, Vishnu and Siva. Furthermore, even when the three Hindu deities are not conceived of as three gods but rather as manifestations of one, Hindus still routinely consider one of them supreme.

For some, a more promising bridge may be found in the ancient concept of *saccidananda*, three words run together meaning "being," "intelligence," and "bliss." Consider this statement by Brahmabandhab Upadhyay, a famous nineteenth-century Hindu convert to Catholicism:

> I adore the *Sat* (Being), *Cit* (Intelligence), and *Ananda* (Bliss), ... the Father, Begetter, the Highest Lord, unbegotten, the rootless principle of the tree of existence . . . the increate, infinite Logos or Word, supremely great, the Image of the Father . . . [and] the one who proceeds from the union of *Sat* and *Cit*, the blessed Spirit (breath), intense bliss.[36]

Other Hindu converts and reformers have similarly shown more interest in this parallel than in the three deities discussed above. To put these and many other explorations in perspective, the Jesuit Hindu expert F. X. Clooney summarizes in a way worth repeating and affirming:

> That the record is mixed should not surprise us. We know that the rich, deep Christian tradition of trinitarian theology, so

36. Cited in Clooney, "Trinity and Hinduism," 317.

nuanced and difficult, did not come together easily or suddenly in the earliest Church; rather, it took centuries to put together right insights into the three persons of God. . . . [Similarly] it was very hard indeed to explain in India the fine points of trinitarian thought, and as a result many did not see a great difference between Christian ideas of God and Hindu ideas.[37]

What about the other major Asian religion, Buddhism, with regard to the God-question?

Are There Any God(s) in Buddhism?

Mutual Dialogue Is Only Now Beginning

Except for a few occasional contacts during the sixth to the eighth centuries, unlike with Judaism and Islam, Christian and Buddhist traditions did not have much mutual engagement until the nineteenth century—and even then the beginning was slow. By and large, Christian assessment of Buddhism was plagued by both ignorance and negative judgments leading to typical caricatures, such as that Buddhism is atheistic (or idolatrous, as some peoples mistakenly believed Buddhists adored images of the dead Gautama). Christians also routinely considered the Buddhist worldview nihilistic because of the doctrine of *sunyata* ("emptiness") and life-denying because of the principle of *dukkha* ("suffering").

In fact, this mutual dialogue faces significant challenges. To begin with, people routinely ask whether Buddhism is a religion in the same sense as are other living faiths. The reason is that Buddhism separated itself from the parent religion, Hinduism, because for Gautama Buddha and his first followers Hinduism appeared to neglect moral-ethical pursuit with its sole focus on deities and things transcendent. Particularly the original Theravada Buddhism still seeks to be faithful to that vision, notwithstanding its acknowledgment of the existence of deities.

Even in the currently mainstream movement of Mahayana, notwithstanding strong theistic orientations particularly in folk spirituality, believers do not regard deities and gods as "saviors" in the same sense as in Abrahamic faiths. Even Buddha is not a Savior but rather the one whose teaching and example help the interested followers to find the right path. On the other hand, all Buddhist denominations search for some kind of "ultimate reality," even if not god in the traditional sense.

---

37. Clooney, "Trinity and Hinduism," 320.

If Buddha Is Not "God," Is He Any Form of Ultimate Reality?

Not only is Buddha not a savior, he is also not the "ultimate reality." Furthermore, in contrast to the parent religion, Hinduism, Buddhism strictly rejects the idea of Brahman and *atman* as the ultimate answer. That said, Buddhists do not abandon the search for the/an ultimate reality, and it is a part of the mainstream Mahayana tradition in particular.

Most scholars of Buddhism agree that its foundational idea of *sunyata* ("emptiness") is the most likely Ultimate Reality for Buddhists—although not the only one. But for this discussion, it suffices to consider only this main proposal.

According to the leading (academic) teacher of Mahayana Buddhism in the West, Masao Abe of Japan, "The ultimate reality . . . is neither Being nor God, but Sunyata."[38] Notoriously difficult to translate and even harder to understand, *sunyata* literally means "(absolute) nothingness." However, it is not an "empty nothingness." But what does that mean? Allow me to use Abe's quite abstract and technical description: *sunyata* is only "empty" in terms of being "entirely unobjectifiable, unconceptualizable, and unattainable by reason or will."[39]

The Japanese Master's attempt to define *sunyata* is aligned with what might be the single most important classic formulation in the "catechism" of *The Heart Sutra*:

> Form is Emptiness, Emptiness is form. Emptiness does not differ from form, and form does not differ from Emptiness. . . . [I]n Emptyness [sic] there is no form, no feeling, no recognition, no volitions, no consciousness; no eye, no ear, no nose, no tongue, no body, no mind . . . no ignorance and no extinction of ignorance . . . no aging and death and no extinction of aging and death; likewise there is no Suffering, Origin, Cessation or Path, no wisdom-knowledge, no attainment and non-attainment.[40]

Furthermore and importantly, "Sunyata should not be conceived of somewhere *outside* one's self-existence, nor somewhere *inside* one's self-existence" (emphasis original).[41] So, what, if anything, can be said of its potential convergences in relation to the Christian tradition's doctrine of God?

---

38. Abe, "Kentoic God," 50.

39. Abe, "Kenotic God," 50.

40. Heart Sutra (no translator given, n.p.; available at http://www.sacred-texts.com/bud/tib/hrt.htm).

41. Abe, "Kenotic God," 51.

The Christian God and the Buddhist "Ultimate Reality" in Perspective

What would Christian interlocutors think of the concept of *sunyata* as the Ultimate Reality in relation to their own faith? Responses have tended to be cautiously skeptical. The reasons for this are many and obvious, such as that *sunyata* seems not to be transcendent in the sense that a theistic notion of god or Ultimate Reality is usually envisioned. Related to this, Christians seem to intuit that, if there is a notion of the divine in Buddhism, this virtually equates reality and the divine—which is nothing but pantheism! Indeed, Buddhist experts themselves seem to confirm that assumption, including that the borderline between the personal and the impersonal (so crucial to Abrahamic faiths) is blurred: "God *is* each and every thing," and in this "completely kenotic God, personality and impersonality are paradoxically identical."[42]

After a careful dialogue with the Buddhist teachings about ultimate reality, in my own research a few years ago I came to this conclusion and recommendation, that "[F]irst, unlike any *monotheistic* tradition, Buddhism is happy with a plurality of answers to 'one question' without suppressing the diversity; second, [that] unlike any *theistic* tradition, Buddhism, even in its major Mahayana forms, makes every effort to resist the tendency to rely on gods (even if their existence and role in the world thereby need not be denied after modern Western anti-theistic ideology); and third, that therefore, Buddhism and Christianity represent deeply and radically different paths to liberation/salvation. Wouldn't that kind of tentative conclusion serve an authentic, hospitable dialogue better than a forced, I fear, one-sided (!) '*con*-sensus'?" (emphasis original).[43]

Be that as it may, it takes continued and painstaking dialogue and exchange of ideas between Christian and Buddhist traditions to come to a deeper and wider understanding of the crucial issue (at least to Christians) about the issue of God and Ultimate Reality.

---

42. Abe, "Kenotic God," 40, 41.

43. Kärkkäinen, *Trinity and Revelation*, 415.

3

Creation

How Did Everything Come into Existence?

Does Theology Really Have Anything Useful to Say about the Origins of the World?

OF ALL THE CHRISTIAN doctrines, perhaps the most contested one for the secular person—as well as for numerous Christians—and the one most often left for theologians to explain is that of the origins and workings of the cosmos. While people in the church may still speak of the theology of creation, meaning that God has created the world in six days, very few if any educated people, so the argument goes, really believe it. Theology should stay away from the conversation—if for no other reason than to save itself from a public embarrassment. Science is the discipline that tells us how things are in the cosmos. Religion and faith have their own limited domains of knowledge and experience, and, some say, help us cope with the troubles of everyday life and aspirations for the sweet by and by.

But is that a valid argument? Hardly! We might say on the one hand that no credible religious account of how this vast cosmos and its life forms came into being can afford to turn a blind eye to what the sciences have been able to uncover. But on the other hand we might also say that no scientific explanation is able to provide answers to the questions of why and by what agency the cosmos has emerged and functions in such an orderly manner. For now at least it is left to philosophy and religion to seek meaningful answers to these existential questions.

With that in mind, this chapter delves into the following interrelated topics: The first brief section elaborates why and how theology, including other religions, should be engaged in a conversation with sciences. Then follows a robustly Christian *theological* account of creation. According to trinitarian logic, the bringing into existence of the vast cosmos is the result of the joint work of the Father, Son, and Spirit. As an interfaith counterpart, then follow reflections on "creation" narratives of four other faiths, which will be engaged further throughout the rest of the chapter.

A lengthier section on what the natural sciences are discovering about these origins follows, also with an eye toward theological implications. This discussion tackles fascinating issues such as whether we know the secret to the emergence of life or what is the meaning of time and space or how Darwinism is received among religions.

Related to this, another lengthier section focuses on the ways the Creator God is preserving and guiding the world. This treatment likewise engages deeply with the natural sciences and their idea of the world as self-sustaining and self-regulating, without any need, nor even "room," for divine agency.

The chapter ends with an inquiry into the theological and religious resources to consider the suffering and pollution of nature and environment as well as help enhance its flourishing and well-being—a burning issue for the third millennium.

Religions Meet Sciences

Why Should Theology Care about Sciences?

So, why should theology be engaged in conversation with sciences? Here's the simple reason:

If God is the Creator of everything—like literally "everything," the vast cosmos—then for theology to exclude consideration of creation would be like turning a blind eye to a Supreme Artist's finest work! As much as the explanations and approaches to nature/creation between scientists and theologians may differ, they both study and reflect on one and the same reality—a reality that, according to the Christian vision, is created and sustained by God.

Therefore, let us first pause for a moment and consider the benefits and liabilities of differing theological approaches to the question of whether and in what ways theology should engage sciences. As a shorthand, I refer to these approaches as:

- Theology in Continuity with Science

- Science in Continuity with Theology
- Theology and Science as Separate Realms
- Theology and Science as Mutually Interactive

In the first category, nineteenth-century classical liberalism is an apt example. It made a programmatic separation between "nature," the domain of facts, and "history," the domain of human values. While the former was for the natural sciences to study, the latter, with its search for meaning rather than naked facts, was for the attention of the humanities, particularly philosophy, the arts, history, and theology. What should we think about such tactics? While the separation does not arouse conflict, it nonetheless inhibits theology from engaging "serious" public discourse about the origins and workings of the world. It pushes the church into a cultural corner and hinders theology from speaking to public issues.

The second category is rooted in the pre-Enlightenment worldview in which theology was seen as the queen of the sciences. As long as the Scripture principle stayed intact, the authority of Scripture surpassed that of the sciences and philosophy. On the contemporary scene, the Fundamentalist movement known as creationism, with its advocacy of an anti-evolutionary scientific paradigm as an alternative to mainline natural sciences, represents this category. It is based on literal interpretation of the biblical message, including matters of science, and a search for archaeological/paleontological "evidence" in support of a young earth theory. The obvious problem with this approach is that it lacks scientific credibility and hence even at its best remains a purely religious affair.

The third category is most notoriously represented by Karl Barth and neo-orthodoxy with its fideistic (based on faith alone) elevation of divine revelation as the arbiter of all matters of knowledge and its rejection of "natural theology." It ends up endorsing more or less the same kind of separation between nature and history as classical liberalism and it rejects dialogue with the sciences. The third category's main liability, similar to that of the second category, is the failure of theology to have a public voice and also to make its own contribution to the sciences.

If these three attitudes toward the theology-science relationship have limitations, what might a more constructive attitude look like? The orientation I recommend is the "Mutual Interaction of Theology and Science."[1] It is in keeping with Vatican II's statement (*Gaudium et Spes* para. 36) that "earthly matters and the concerns of faith derive from the same God" and hence in principle cannot violate each other. A number of theologians, some

1. Adapted from the subtitle of Russell, *Cosmology*.

of them having the highest academic training in both natural sciences and in theology, represent the same kind of mindset—namely of theology being willing both to learn from the results and insights of the natural sciences and at the same time to do the work ignored by scientists (as far as they stick with their own principle of not transgressing the borderlines of sciences), namely of raising questions of why, whence, and by "whom" or "what" everything emerged. This more constructive attitude believes that theology should not merely serve as science's religious interpreter, but should also challenge and contribute to science's quest.

What about Other Religions: Do They Engage the Sciences?

Religions' attitudes about sciences and their explanations about the origins of the cosmos vary quite dramatically. Jewish religion is the most positive about this issue. No other ethnicity can boast so many leading scientists throughout history and in the contemporary world than the Jewish—from Galileo to Einstein. And yet, the Jews entered the modern scientific field relatively late, no earlier than at the beginning of the twentieth century. Apart from some of the most conservative Jews, even rabbis usually adhere to scientific explanations and do not necessarily see a discrepancy, nor conflict, between science and their religious understandings. In this, the religious teachers are following in the footsteps of key medieval philosophers such as Moses Maimonides, who was an intellectual giant of his time. As in the mainline Christian tradition, Jews largely embrace the natural sciences, including evolutionary theory.

The situation is dramatically different in Islam. By and large, there is strong resistance in Islam toward scientific explanations about creation and creatures, particularly with regard to the evolutionary sciences. Historically this is a counterintuitive stance in light of the fact that, unlike in Judaism, among the Muslims there was once a "golden age" of scientific and philosophical excellence. That said, it is also ironically true that current Western scientific academia and Christian theology are indebted to Islamic scholars for their translation and introduction of once leading philosophical and scientific writings of those like Aristotle and others. Similar to the Jews, modern science came to Islamic lands only beginning in the nineteenth century. For that and other reasons, scientific education is in the process of catching up; leading Muslim scholars lament the status of scientific education at large in most Muslim lands. Virtually none of the main producers of modern science is a Muslim.

CREATION

Unlike in the West, in Islamic contexts the link between religion and science is tight, so much so that, according to the Algerian astrophysicist Nidhal Guessoum, even current textbooks are hardly much more than "a branch of Qur'anic exegesis." Unlike the Christian tradition (and more recently, the Jewish tradition), the religion-science dialogue is still a marginal phenomenon among Muslims. Generally speaking, the majority of Muslims reject science because of its alleged opposition to revelation. On the other hand, Muslims often uncritically embrace the technocratic practical results of Western science in pursuit of equality with Western nations as regards power and competence. Similarly to Christian Fundamentalists, there is also an effort to build a distinctively "Islamic science" based on the authority of the Holy Qur'an and Hadith. Only a small (but slowly growing) group of Islamic scholars and a few religious leaders are seeking to negotiate between the legitimacy and necessity of contemporary scientific principles and methods while at the same time critiquing the metaphysical, ethical, and religious implications of the scientific paradigm.

What about Asiatic faiths? In contrast to the post-Enlightenment Western ideals of total objectivity and objectification of nature, the traditional Hindu vision has integrated scientific pursuit with the religious and ritualistic domain. In Asiatic faiths, religion and science are deeply intertwined. Consider this: "India is the one and only country in the world that simultaneously launches satellites to explore space *and* teaches astrology as a Vedic science in its colleges and universities" (emphasis original). Since 2001, astrology has indeed been taught as a scientific subject in Indian colleges and universities.[2] On the other hand, beginning in the mid-nineteenth century, a vast and wide intellectual renaissance started in India that resulted in its current great scientific pursuit; that was also an era in which a European-style educational system was introduced (related to the British-led colonial project). For these reasons, it is understandable that assessments of and attitudes toward modern science have varied among Hindus. A way to classify them is a three-fold typology:

- the "critical traditionalists," who believe that Indian foundations can be redeemed even if some important aspects of the West are incorporated;
- the "modernists," who wish to adapt to the European lifestyle; and
- the "critical modernists," who envision a creative synthesis of the two.

---

2. Nanda, "Vedic Science and Hindu Nationalism," 30.

Furthermore, not unlike some Muslims, a group of Hindu scientists has attempted to develop a credible "Hindu science" (also called a "Vedic science") paradigm. Not surprisingly, this project has been critiqued by both the scientific community and some Hindu thinkers.

Modern Buddhism's relation to Western science is not entirely different from that of Hinduism. Its claims about science emerged in a polemical manner as Buddhists worked hard to convince Westerners, including Christians, that their scientific understanding is not superstition but rather a rational, sound account of reality. The Buddhologist José Ignacio Cabezón suggests a typology similar to ones devised by Christian theologians.

The first model, "Conflict/Ambivalence" with its negative attitude toward science, may be related to Western science's general hostility toward religion. It represents a fairly marginal phenomenon among Buddhists.

By and large, the Buddhist attitude can be called "Compatibility/Identity." This model can manifest itself either in terms of similarity between Buddhism and science or in the idea that "Buddhism *is* science" (emphasis original) and that therefore Buddhism and science are more or less identical. As in all other faith traditions, there is a growing body of contemporary (mostly popular) literature written by Buddhists around the world concerning the astonishing compatibility between, say, quantum mechanics and compassion or emptiness and relativity theory.

The final category is "Complementarity" which, as a middle position, seeks to negotiate both similarities (unlike the first option) and differences (unlike the second option). Buddhism complements the atheistic materials with the inclusion of the mental/spiritual/"inner." Whereas sciences rely only on rational, conceptual, and analytic methods, Buddhism also draws on intuition, meditation, and "inner" resources.[3]

Now, back to the Christian theological understanding of creation.

Creation as the Work of the Triune God

"Triune" Creation

Recall that Christian faith and theology are "triune" in its shape and form. As a result, the trinitarian God's works in the world are also triune in nature. This lesson the fourth-century church father from the East, Basil the Great, expressed beautifully when he wrote: "And in the creation bethink thee first,

---

3. Cabezón, "Buddhism and Science," 41–56.

I pray thee, of the original cause of all things that are made, the Father; of the creative cause, the Son; of the perfecting cause, the Spirit."[4]

If the Father is the "original cause" of all things, then why was there a creation? In fact, even for philosophers such as the atheist Jean-Paul Sartre the existence of something as opposed to nothingness was the ultimate question, as he first masterfully articulated in his 1943 *Being and Nothingness*. The Christian answer to why there was a creation is simple and profound: by and for the sake of divine love. Expressed theologically: with the same love that the Father loves the Son in the Spirit, the world is "loved" into being.

If that is the case, then what is the role of Christ, the second person of the Trinity? Christ is the "agent," the mediator of creation—as the NT suggests in many places (John 1:1–14; Col 1:15–17; Heb 1:2–3). This makes possible the distinction, albeit not the separation, between creation and the Creator who is uncreated—or else pantheism follows.

> [F]or in him all things were created, in heaven and on earth, visible and invisible, whether thrones or dominions or principalities or authorities—all things were created through him and for him. He is before all things, and in him all things hold together. (Col 1:16–17)

The role of the Spirit is about life-giving power, which makes everything alive. At the same time, the Spirit of God is the unifying link between the Creator and the universe as well as between God and human beings. You may recall that at Creation, the Spirit of God "was moving over the face of the waters" (Gen 1:2). This very same divine energy also sustains all life in the cosmos (Ps 104:29–30):

> When thou hidest thy face, they are dismayed;
> when thou takest away their breath, they die
> and return to their dust.
> When thou sendest forth thy Spirit, they are created;
> and thou renewest the face of the ground.

It is significant that the term we translated as both "breath" and "Spirit" is the same in the original Hebrew. God's "breath" gives "breath" to all creatures and created things—and in its absence they all immediately wither.

Having briefly described the distinctive yet interrelated roles of Father, Son, and Spirit in the work of creation, let us probe more deeply

---

4. Basil, *On the Holy Spirit* (*De Spiritu Sanctu*), 16.38, in *NPNF*[2] 08.

into the wisdom and power of the Creator in bringing about this amazing work of creation.

A Sovereign Creator and an Immensely Valuable Creation

The main goal of the first biblical account of creation in Genesis 1—which is, indeed, a tightly structured and ordered liturgical text, as illustrated in its hymnic form—is not to teach biology and cosmology but to combat the many creation narratives of the surrounding pagan nations, such as the Babylonian creation myths, *Enuma Elish*. That widely known epic conceives "creation" as a battle between Marduk, the principal god, and another god figure, Tiamat. Whereas in Babylon the heavens and the earth emerge out of the fatal fight between the gods, in Israel creation is the function of the sovereignty of God bringing about an orderly and good world. By the power of the divine word (and spirit), everything comes into being. God's power also subdues astral entities, such as sun and moon and the gigantic living beings of the deep seas. The particular Hebrew term used to highlight the Creator's sovereignty is *bara* (Gen 1:1), "to create," a term used in the OT exclusively of divine creation.

As a free gift of love, the coming into existence of the vast cosmos is not a necessary act of God. Before ages, the loving and sovereign Creator decided to bring about the world. This is to affirm God's freedom as opposed to God acting under necessity.

Because a free gift and act of God, creation in Christian understanding has an innate, intrinsic value. The atheist Ludwig Feuerbach completely missed this when he insisted that: "Nature, the world, has no value, no interest for Christians. The Christian thinks only of himself and the salvation of his soul."[5]

According to the first creation story, the goodness and value of creation help us affirm also the goodness and value of materiality (physicality). In the Judeo-Christian worldview, the material is not evil and "dirty" as in Gnosticism, an ancient heresy conceiving the world dualistically in spiritual = good, material = bad terms. No: Everything created is good. With the focus on physicality as an integral aspect of God's creation, early theology successfully attacked the pagan idea of the eternity of matter. Thereby early theologians helped reaffirm the relative value and goodness of all created reality.

---

5. Feuerbach, *Essence of Christianity*, 282, emphasis removed.

God Cares Deeply for and Caters to Creation

In its well-meaning defense of the absolute freedom and power of God, the Creator, early theology often ended up conceiving of God as so transcendent and aloof from the world that it sidelined the equally important value of intimacy with creation. Contemporary theology has helped us negotiate the God-world relation in more dynamic and mutual ways. In the words of theologian Mayra Rivera, "God is irreducibly Other, always *beyond* our grasp. But not beyond our touch" (emphasis original).[6]

In fact, a number of female theologians have rightly insisted on the delicate balance between affirming the Sovereign Creator's absolute freedom and powers on the one hand, and the same loving and caring Creator's desire for engagement and intimacy on the other. The Catholic feminist theologian Anne M. Clifford summarizes this balance succinctly: "God exists in everything. Paradoxically, God is never really distant from creation, although creatures, since they are unlike God in nature, are necessarily distant from God."[7]

Before continuing to discuss the many facets of the contemporary Christian understanding of the theology of creation, including the topic of evolution, let us take a look at the theologies and myths of beginnings and "creation" in some other faith traditions.

How Do Other Faiths Imagine the Coming into Existence of the World?

First, the "Big Picture"

The comparison among faith traditions regarding any topic is a daunting challenge! Creation is no exception. One of the continuing obstacles is a growing list of misconceptions, usually based on one's own imagination rather than on a careful scrutiny of other traditions. These include the common assumption that whereas the Asiatic religions are cosmocentric, the three Abrahamic faiths are anthropocentric, interested mainly in humanity. The fallacy of this assumption is simply this: Asiatic faiths do not have a developed vision of final consummation for the cosmos, as their focus is on the hope for the individual person, whereas to the Judeo-Christian "endtime" vision belongs a hope for the whole wide cosmos.

---

6. Rivera, *Touch of Transcendence*, 2.
7. Clifford, "Creation," 218.

The chief differences between Abrahamic and Asiatic traditions have to do with the meaning of history, the intentionality of creation, and the moral dimension. Whereas for Asiatic religions, particularly Hinduism, reality is an "appearance," for Judeo-Christian and Islamic traditions, it is where "salvation history" takes place. Whereas for Buddhism there is no "reason" for the emergence of the cosmos (certainly no divine cause), and whereas for Hinduism creation is a "side effect" (or *lila*, "play"), Jews, Christians, and Muslims believe in an "intentional creation."[8] God creates the world for a purpose. The ensuing discussion will delve deeper into these big questions.

Abrahamic Traditions' Shared Beliefs

Even if some differences exist among Jewish, Christian, and Islamic theologies of creation—to be mentioned below—in their basic outline they are similar enough to be put under one and the same umbrella. All three traditions believe in God, the almighty Creator, who has brought into existence the cosmos and sustains and guides its life from the beginning to the end. Everything derives from and is dependent on God.

The same Creator also guides the creation with the help of the laws of creation he has put in place (Q 30:30). There are divine purposes present in creation. While God and world can never be separated, neither can they be equated. God is infinite; cosmos and creatures are finite.

Since the Christian theology of creation is based on the OT, there is no need to delve here into a distinctively Jewish theology of creation. Suffice it to note that the major difference has to do with the Trinitarian interpretation of the work of creation by the one God in Christian tradition.

Similarly to the Bible, the Qur'an describes God as the Creator in the absolute sense, that is, as the One who brought into existence that which did not exist "before": "When nothing had yet come into existence, there was the One, the First (*al-Awwal*)," the ineffable one, incomparable,[9] who never perishes (Q 55:26–27).

Interestingly enough, the Qur'an speaks of the created order as *muslim*. The idea behind the term (which means submission) is that one who submits to God avoids disintegration. Creation follows ("submits" to) the laws set up by the Creator. The Qur'an testifies, "to God prostrate whoever

---

8. Soskice, "*Creatio Ex Nihilo*," 29. Soskice quotes "intentional creation" from David B. Burrell, 'Freedom and Creation in the Abrahamic Traditions', International Philosophical Quarterly 40 (June 2000) 161–71, at 167 (this from her footnote).

9. Iqbal, "In the Beginning," 62.

is in the heavens and whoever is in the earth, together with the sun and the moon, and the stars and the mountains, and the trees and the animals, as well as many of mankind" (Q 22:18). Terminological difference notwithstanding, this is not far from the Judeo-Christian idea of God's creation as an orderly, harmonious cosmos praising God, the Creator and serving the purpose the Creator has set for it.

Similarity can also be found in the shared idea that, as a result, created realities are considered "signs" revealing the Creator (Q 30:22). Hence, the study of nature may draw us nearer to God (41:53).

Markedly different conceptions of the nature and origins of the cosmos come to the fore with the shift to Asiatic faiths.

Buddhists on Origins

A foundational difference from Abrahamic faiths is that none of the Buddhist traditions consider the Divine as the "Creator." This applies even to Mahayana traditions, which show much more pronounced interest in deities. In that sense, Buddhism is a "naturalist" philosophy closer to contemporary scientific materialism but with the crucial difference that even in its nontheistic orientation it is the spiritual/mental dimension that is primary. Buddhism, even Theravada, is not atheistic.

Buddha himself had no interest in speculations about the origins of the universe, and as is well known, he often warned his followers about not getting into such speculations, as they are useless in the pursuit of the ultimate release. That said, it is ironic that Buddhist cosmology is rich, variegated, and highly sophisticated.

There is no absolute "origin" or "creation" in Buddhism. According to Lotus Sutra, the "catechism" of the Mahayana tradition, the cosmos was "not derived from an intelligent cause," nor does it have any purpose (Lotus Sutra 5.80).[10] Rather, the cosmos is everlasting and without beginning (Lotus Sutra 13.19).[11] Instead, all Buddhist schools agree with the central concept of the "dependent origination." The famous scriptural passage on this reads thus:

"When this is, that is."

"From the arising of this comes the arising of that."

---

10. Trans. Kern [1884]; *SBE* 21, available at https://sacred-texts.com/bud/index.htm.

11. Trans. Kern [1884]; *SBE* 21, available at https://sacred-texts.com/bud/index.htm.

"When this isn't, that isn't."

"From the cessation of this comes the cessation of that."

(Samyutta Nikaya 12.61)

In other words, according to the principle of effect, everything emerges in an interrelated manner through various sequences, finally consummating in ultimate liberation. Everything is in a continuous process of change. Buddhism teaches that the world passes through cycles of evolution and dissolution, *ad infinitum*, similarly to Hinduism.

Cosmologies of Origins among the Hindus

Similarly to Buddhism, Hinduism does not have a doctrine of *creation*. Another similarity is Hinduism's unusually rich treasure of religious cosmologies. Notwithstanding the lack of a doctrine of "creation" strictly speaking, the Bhagavad-Gita speaks amply of the Deity as the creator and sustainer of the world (Gitas 7; 13). Despite this, it contains no teaching about a onetime creation "from nothing."

A distinctive Hindu teaching in various scriptural traditions affirms that God and "nature" (the world) are the same. The description of "creation" in Brihadaranyaka Upanishad (1.4) is a case in point: Brahman first made himself split into two, bringing about male and female; out of female came cow and bull, out of them mare and ass, and so forth. Out of his body parts, further things were created. No wonder the cosmos is sometimes compared to a cosmic being, a living organism.

What is more similar to the Semitic faiths is that "Hindu Scriptures attest to the belief that the creation, maintenance, and annihilation of the cosmos is completely up to the Supreme Will."[12] Bhagavad Gita puts it in a way that closely resembles the NT statement about Christ (Rev 1:8): "I am also the beginning, the middle, and the end also of all beings" (Bhagavad Gita 10.20). What is radically different from the Abrahamic traditions is that all Hindu scriptural traditions also affirm rebirth and a cyclical worldview: hence, "creation" does not mean the absolute beginning, as in the Semitic traditions.

In the previous chapter, we looked at the debates on the God-world relationship (to use the Christian terminology) between various Vedanta schools and their interpretation of the Upanishads. While all affirm

---

12. Dwivedi, "Dharmic Ecology," 6.

non-duality, differences in formulation do exist. (You may want to review that section before proceeding.)

Creation in Evolution: Theology and Sciences in Mutual Interaction

How the Radically Changed Worldview Has Totally Transformed Our View of the World

Our first task is to register the changes in worldview stemming from Modernity beginning in the seventeenth century and the immensely radical new view of the world as the result of the invention of twentieth-century scientific theories.

Whereas previously the cosmos had been conceived of as (at least almost) eternal, steady, and solid, from the beginning of the twentieth century all that changed. We now conceive of the cosmos as highly dynamic, "lively," and evolving. This is due to the introduction of Einstein's theories of relativity, and subsequently the birth and ongoing development of quantum theories.

Whereas Albert Einstein's 1905 special relativity theory linked space and time together in a space-time continuum and thereby made all points of observation relative rather than absolute, the 1916 general relativity theory included gravity. Radically revising the Newtonian theory, in which space and time were understood to be some kind of separate backgrounds or "containers" in which matter moved, Einstein established space-time as a four-dimensional manifold (three space and one time dimension) that "can stretch, warp, and vibrate."[13] Furthermore, whereas Newton's 1680s theory of gravity applied only to bodies at rest or moving slowly ("slow," that is, in relation to the speed of light), Einstein's theory applied to bodies in all conditions. That is because gravitation was thought of no longer in terms of a "field" but rather as a distortion of space and time. As the physicist John Wheeler's famous dictum puts it: "Matter tells space how to curve" and "[s]pace tells matter how to move."[14] Think of the surface of a balloon with colored spots while it is being blown up: it is not that the spots are moving (even though they are) but that the surface of the balloon is expanding. Talk about a dynamic worldview! And add to it the radical new insights coming from quantum theories beginning in the 1920s.

---

13. Spitzer, *New Proofs*, 15.
14. Misner et al., *Gravitation*, 5.

Quantum theory has helped overcome once and for all the naive mechanism and full determinism that were often assumed in the older paradigm. Not only at the smallest, subatomic level (where quantum theory primarily functions), but also at the macro level, nature reveals surprises, irregularities, and unpredictability—notwithstanding the amazing regularity of its processes. Still, the laws of nature are in place and natural phenomena are (relatively speaking) deterministic, otherwise no scientific observations would be possible. What the unpredictability means is that determinism is not ironclad and that—at least according to the major (Copenhagian) interpretation of quantum theory—natural processes and events are probabilistic in nature.

In other words, there is some "happenstance" in the otherwise highly ordered workings of nature. These indications of indeterminacy are well known, such as the wave/particle duality (that is, light appears both as wave and as particle) and the incapacity to measure both the momentum and position of the particle.[15] Or consider the highly counterintuitive quantum "entanglement" (Bell's theorem), according to which, without any "real" reason, the measurement of two chance events—imagine the measurement of the spin of two electrons when they travel as a result of the decay of an atom—shows definite nonlocal correlation; that is, while it cannot be said that these two chance events really influence each other, they are to a certain extent inseparable.

Add to these the whole new field of chaos theory, which shows that, while causality (rightly understood) is of course not to be set aside, the more developed the processes, the less *mechanistically* causal they are—even if they are basically deterministic! Consider the famous "butterfly effect": the slightest change to climate in one part of the world, when amplified, may cause a huge storm on the other side of the globe!

In this kind of "open universe," dynamic and evolving, new things and processes emerge. Indeed, the term "emergence" is a key to understanding our world. It means "that new and unpredictable phenomena are naturally produced by interactions in nature" and that while dependent on what is already there, they also manifest something new and innovative.

---

15. The famous "superposition" principle, roughly speaking, says that a particle can be said to be both "here" and "there," not of course simultaneously but probabilistically, that is, we can never know for sure. Consider also other celebrated quantum examples of indeterminism and counterintuitiveness, namely, the "double-split experiment"; that is, imagine a beam of electrons shot through a metal plate with two narrow slits; the results clearly imply that these particles have behaved more like waves as they appear to have entered both slits!

These newly emerged phenomena, in turn, may give birth to yet more new things![16]

With all this in mind, we are ready to take a brief look at the way in which contemporary cosmology and other natural sciences envision the origins and workings of this vast universe.

"The Big Bang": How Everything Started and Got Going

As much as modern cosmology is a scientific enterprise, in contrast to its speculative mode during history, it also faces daunting challenges. Its object is the whole universe—and therefore, in a real sense of the word, even itself—that is, those who study cosmology! It also deals with issues such as the beginnings and origins of existence, about which typical empirical (experience and measurement-based) study can hardly be done. That said, we can trust and rely on the amazing work done by some of the most brilliant minds in the world. Moreover, that cosmology (similarly to any good scientific work) continuously fine-tunes and at times corrects its findings, is a testimony to its reliability!

While many questions about the origins of the cosmos are still being debated or call for further investigation, it is safe to say that the big bang theory is the standard, established position, and that it has huge experimental support. It is significant that the big bang theory was originally proposed in the 1920s by the Roman Catholic priest-physicist Georges Lemaître (although the name was applied to his finding only in hindsight). Based on Einstein's relativity theories and later quantum theories, briefly explained above, the standard big bang model argues that the cosmos came into being about 13.8 billion years ago from a singularity of zero size and infinite density (usually marked as $t = 0$ in which t denotes time), and has since expanded to its current form.[17] Overly simplified: by observing and understanding the galaxies flying apart as indications of the universe's ongoing expansion, the big bang theory simply looks back in time to the point at which the expansion started; finally you come to the "beginning point."

Since the Hubble telescope's discovery in the 1920s, we know that the galaxies are receding from us, and therefore that the cosmos is expanding.[18] Important evidence for this expansion and the big bang came from the

---

16. Clayton, *Mind and Emergence*, vi.
17. NASA, "What Is the Big Bang," n.p.
18. NASA, "Discoveries," n.p.

discovery in the 1960s of the microwave background radiation that is believed to be an echo of the original big bang.[19]

A highly important recent refinement to the original model is the so-called "inflation period." Immediately after the big bang, during the extremely short period of time (the so-called Planck time, or 10^{-43} seconds, the shortest measure of time), dramatic developments occurred.[20] What is strange and counterintuitive is that contemporary science is not able to explain what happened during that immensely short period immediately following the bang, since no known laws of nature apply to it. Nonetheless, we have established that something so dramatic happened that at the moment not only do we not know what it really is, but that it also messes up, so to speak, any complete reconciliation between the theory of relativity and quantum mechanics—as foundational and reliable as they are in themselves! No wonder many brilliant minds are still looking for a "theory of everything" that would be able to explain both the smallest (the domain of the quantum theories) and the biggest things (relativity theories).

Although this big bang theory is still the standard foundation of all scientific cosmologies, revisions and challenges to it are ongoing. Here, I mention only one among many because that one has direct implications for theology. The renowned late British scientist Stephen Hawking and his American colleague James Hartle revised the earlier view of the big bang, shifting from an assumption of an initial singularity to a boundary-less scenario that still presupposes the "beginning" (and thus, the finite nature of the universe with regard to the beginning), although no beginning in time (no singularity). Its difference from the standard model is easily depicted with the following illustration: imagine a piece of wood in the shape of a cone. In the standard model there is a sharp edge. In the no-boundary model the edge is rounded off, smooth; hence, there is no singularity, no beginning in time. From there, Hawking also draws what I think is an unwarranted metaphysical conclusion: "'The boundary condition of the universe is that it has no boundary.' The universe would be completely self-contained and not affected by anything outside itself. It would neither be created nor destroyed. It would just BE."[21]

We will come back to Hawking's careless "theological" conclusion! Beyond the question of the existence of God, the Hawking-Hartle theory makes the question of the "beginnings" even more urgent. What about the famous creation *ex nihilo* (out of nothing) clause?

19. Howell and Dobrijevic, "What Is the Cosmic Microwave Background," n.p.
20. NASA, "What Is the Inflation Theory," n.p.
21. Hawking, *Brief History of Time*, 141.

Creation Out of Nothing

A common assumption among pagan philosophies was that if God is eternal, then creation is as well. And there were some early Christian theologians who also wondered whether, on the basis of God's eternity, the world is also eternal; that view, however, was rebutted pretty quickly.

St. Augustine got it right: rather than creation taking place in time, time itself comes into being in creation; time is created! Over the centuries, this became the "canonical" view in Christianity. Similarly, Jewish religion rejected the eternity of the world because of its incompatibility with scriptural teaching. Yet interestingly, some medieval Islamic scholars were open to the eternity of the cosmos.

If the universe is not eternal, then there has to be some kind of beginning. But what does that mean? As the Hawking-Hartle proposal suggests, the "beginning" might not be as simple as we think it is. Are we talking about the beginning *of* time; beginning *in* time; or the beginning as in "origin," the ultimate "source" or "cause" of everything?

The main theological argument in all three Abrahamic faiths is that the world is neither self-generating nor self-sufficient. God, the Wise and Almighty, has brought it into existence out of nothing. Hence, the world is dependent or contingent on God (see, for example, Qur'an 7:54). This is a major difference from Asiatic faiths.

In Jewish tradition, however, the *doctrine* of *ex nihilo* took a long time to be established. Why? The reason is that Genesis 1:1–2 can be interpreted in terms of God working with "something" already in existence and not necessarily as *ex nihilo*. The rest of the biblical teaching, however, eventually won the day, favoring creation "out of nothing."

The *ex nihilo* conviction of course helped reject the Platonic notion of the eternity of matter and the idea of the divine architect fashioning the cosmos out of materials already available.

So, how would *ex nihilo* relate to scientific theories of origin?

The Big Bang and the Theological Doctrine of Creation Out of Nothing

Indeed, it is no wonder that theologians—many of whom might at first have been startled by the big bang theory—soon came to welcome it as an idea compatible with the biblical teaching on "in the beginning." Often cited is Pope Pius XII's embrace of the big bang theory, which is all the more astonishing in light of his resistance to how evolutionary theory applies to humanity! In fact, "if the universe began in time through the act of a Creator, from our vantage point it would look something like the Big Bang that cosmologists are now talking about." Just be mindful of this caveat: "What one cannot say is, first, that the Christian doctrine of creation 'supports' the Big Bang model, or second, that the Big Bang model 'supports' the Christian doctrine of creation."[22]

But what about the Hawking-Hartle proposal denying a beginning of time? Would it cause problems for theology? Hawking himself believed this to be the case, drawing the unwarranted conclusion that in the absence of beginning *in time*, no Creator is needed. But obviously his conclusion is faulty (and is not strictly science). The doctrine of creation in no way restricts divine activity to bringing about (in the beginning) the universe. For the doctrine of creation is also about continuing creation and providence. The relation of the "beginning" to time matters little or nothing—although Augustine's idea of time being created makes much sense.

But what is time? And space? Let us take a closer look at both.

Time and Space in Creation

While the meaning of "time" has long prompted speculation, not least among Christian thinkers, the question became much more complicated in the aftermath of Einstein's theories of relativity. And when you add "space" to the equation, all the more so! Complex matter simplified: in our current scientific worldview neither time nor space has the kind of "absolute" existence it had in classical physics. They are deeply intertwined, as briefly explained above in the discussion on relativity. Hence, the use of the somewhat awkward phrase, the space-time continuum.

So, what is time? While Augustine correctly made time a created entity, he also entertained a couple of common mistaken ideas: that if time has its origin in God, then God somehow must exist "outside" time and that, as a consequence, God's eternity is something "timeless" or just unending time. A theologically more correct vision is to conceive of God as deeply engaged in time and history as opposed to an aloof deity "outside" time. At the same time, God is not a "prisoner" to earthly time and its limit—particularly the necessary sequence of time from the past, to present, to future. God, while deeply engaged, also transcends time. Just consider incarnation: it tells us that God exists in space-time—but as the almighty Creator, God can certainly not be contained by it. God is both "in" and "outside" it simultaneously!

22. McMullin, "How Should Cosmology Relate," 39.

Also, rather than marking the "end" of time (timelessness) or merely unendingly long time, eternity is the source of earthly time and will bring it to fulfillment, as chapter 10 on eschatology will explain.

What about space? Suffice it to say this much: whereas in the past space has been conceived either as a "receptacle" or as a "container" of all objects (leading to Newton's "absolute space" idea), or as "relational," the quality of material objects that are related to each other, relativity theories stripped off the separate existence of space. There is a space-time continuum, integrated with matter and energy. Theologically speaking, similarly to time, we should imagine God both "in" (his own space) and "outside," to ensure immanence and transcendence.

Having examined the issues of the "beginnings" of the universe and its space-time, we now focus on the "beginnings" of life-forms. The much-discussed notion of the "anthropic principle" builds that bridge. If time and space are challenging concepts, how much more so "life" and its meaning!

It Looks as If the Cosmos Was Waiting for Us to Appear!

All life in the universe is basically made of three components: protons, neutrons, and electrons. But what is astonishing is that, contrary to what was believed, the universe overall is not made mainly of this "baryonic matter," as it came to be called. On the contrary, most of the universe is something "dark," namely, "dark matter" (23 percent) and "dark energy" (72 percent), which leaves only a few percent for the "stuff" of which life is made. While much is still unknown about both dark matter (a form of matter so dense that it neither emits nor absorbs any light and therefore cannot be detected) and particularly dark energy, the latter is important in helping explain the 1998 discovery that the expansion of the universe is speeding up.[23]

As mysterious as life still is to us, it is astonishing how extremely "fine-tuned" the cosmos is in order to bring about creative processes, particularly life. The values of the universal (physical) constants controlling the interrelationships between space, time, and energy in the universe seem to be perfectly calibrated to enable life.[24] Indeed, it would appear to be much more likely for these conditions for life to be absent. Even the smallest imaginable changes block not only the emergence of life but basically everything else as well!

This fine-tuning is also the condition for the emergence of humanity, the highest known life-form. Recall the physicist Freeman Dyson's

23. NASA, "What Is the Universe Made Of," n.p.
24. See further, Schombert, "Anthropic Principle," n.p.

oft-cited comment that "[t]he more I examine the universe and study the details of its architecture, the more evidence I find that the universe in some sense must have known that we were coming."[25] This is the famous "anthropic principle."[26]

Not only Christian theologians but also our Abrahamic counterparts have noted the significance of the anthropological principle. They often invoke the Qur'anic passage from 21:16: "Not for (idle) sport did We create the heavens and the earth and all that is between!"[27] The fine-tuning argument can also be found in Jewish theology. In contrast, it seems that Buddhist cosmology is prone to dismiss the entire argument because of its rejection of both creation and Creator. Most likely the same applies to Hindu cosmology.

So far we have talked about religious responses to fine-tuning. Naturalists and atheists disagree. Whereas for theists, it speaks of the Creator, for atheists and naturalists fine-tuning is either accidental or, thanks to "multiverse" theory (the existence of infinitely many parallel universes), inevitable as one of the possibilities. Be that as it may, science alone cannot resolve the issue; it is ultimately a theological and metaphysical one.

Whatever the religious interpretation, the fine-tuning principle points to the emergence of life on our planet.

But What Is Life and from Where Did It Come?

Creation is striking not only because of its unbelievably rich diversity—more than two million species of plants and animals have been identified, and many more are awaiting discovery—but also because of the sheer fact of its multiplicity; yet all organisms are related by common ancestry. Not only to the religious imagination but even to science, the emergence and nature of life is a mystery without explanation, a mystery heightened by the fact that "the universe is *essentially* lifeless" (emphasis original).[28] As a scientific field, "origin-of-life" studies, which look at the emergence of life on Earth in the wider context of cosmic evolution, is a fairly recent enterprise.

Organic life has emerged extremely slowly on our planet. After the advent of the most elementary forms of bacterial life, it took over two billion years for higher forms to develop. What is the theological response to this? Theology's task is neither to compete with the scientific account,

---

25. Dyson, *Disturbing the Universe*, 250.
26. Schombert, "Anthropic Principle," n.p.
27. Trans. Abdullah Yusuf Ali, at www.altafsir.com.
28. Haught, *Is Nature Enough*, 57.

which relies on principles of randomness (and regularity of nature), nor to seek an alternative explanation as to *how* the logistics of the emergence and diversification of life-forms took place. Instead, theology's task is to inquire into the metaphysical implications and conditions.

The Creator who in the first place established the natural laws that govern the evolution and sustenance of the vast cosmos seems to be utterly patient with letting those regularities—combined with accidents—produce ever-more sophisticated life reaching up to the highest form of life that we know, namely, consciousness. Even though we know with a high degree of accuracy what kinds of biological and chemical processes, in addition to metabolism and the capacity to reproduce, are the essential conditions for living beings in contrast to physical objects, we are far from knowing the ultimate answer.

A significant step that may take us closer to the mystery of life is the highlighting of the capacity to carry information (just think of DNA). Information, truly, stands at the heart of contemporary inquiry into what life is and whence it comes. Theologically we can state that God is not only the original creator but also the one who continuously creates and acts in the world. In that sense, creativity and the emergence of new forms seems to be a built-in feature of the world.

So far, I have taken scientific evolutionary theory for granted. And that, of course, raises the question of that theory's compatibility with theology. If there ever was an arena for theology-science warfare, here we have it. Let us take a deeper look at the issue.

So, What Should We Think of Darwinism?

How Christians relate to the evolutionary theory of Darwin has run the gamut, from cautious acceptance in the beginning years, to vehement opposition subsequently by many, and finally to its embrace by mainline Christianity in its theistic form—notwithstanding continuing opposition among the conservative churches (particularly in the United States but also elsewhere). Particularly challenging has been the application of the evolutionary scheme to the evolution of humanity.

Against popular misconceptions, the idea of evolution of the created reality is neither a novel idea stemming from modern science nor something that is either religious or antireligious at core. Consider the first creation story in Genesis chapter 1. It presents creation in terms of a sequence of events and forms, even when its presentation understandably differs in details from contemporary science.

Although Charles Darwin was not the original modern inventor of what we now call evolutionary theory, he became its most eloquent public disseminator. The key ideas of his 1859 *Origin of Species by Means of Natural Selection* are well known:

- random variations among species;
- the struggle for life due to the exponential increase of populations;
- the best chance of survival for those with the most useful variations; and
- the passing on of the most useful traits to the next generation by possessors of those traits.

Darwin himself was no atheist; neither did he consider his theory to deny the idea of the Creator God. While a desire to avoid conflict with religious authorities might have sparked his remarks in the second edition of *The Origin of Species* on the "grandeur in this view of life, with its several powers, having been originally breathed by the Creator into a few forms or into one,"[29] they also point to the possibility of a theistic interpretation of evolutionary ideas. No wonder, particularly in the American context, that evolutionism was cast in a theistic framework from the beginning and was not at first greatly resisted by the churches. Rather, it was Darwin's interpreters' atheistic, cosmically oriented interpretation of evolutionary theory that helped emerging evolutionary theory take a decidedly antireligious turn.

Darwin's subsequent main work, *The Descent of Man in Relation to Sex* (1871), was likely to rouse more resistance from religious circles. In hindsight, it is somewhat ironic that while the resistance to Darwinism soon intensified in the United States, after a fairly smooth embrace of evolutionism, the opposite was the case on the continent and the British Isles.

While it would be a fatal mistake for Christian theology to oppose evolutionary theory in principle, we should also be mindful of the abuses of the theory. Indeed, evolutionism has emerged as "a secular religion."[30] Social Darwinism has been used as a means of shaping economic and sociopolitical programs deeply antagonistic to the values of human dignity and the equality of all. Most drastically, in the hands of Nazis, some communists, and other tyrants, traces of evolutionism have funded cruelty and violence. That said, theologically we can conclude that contemporary evolutionary theory, rather than being an enemy of a theistic

---

29. Darwin, *Origin of the Species*, 243.

30. Purcell, *From Big Bang*, 115–18. Purcell takes the phrase "secular religion" from Ruse, *Evolution-Creation Struggle*, 212–13.

view of creation, "has given theology an opportunity to see God's ongoing creative activity not merely in the preservation of a fixed order but in the constant bringing forth of things that are new."[31]

What about other faiths?

Evolutionary Theory among Religions

Among Jews, a basically similar kind of development has taken place as happened among Christian communities. The leading rabbis of the nineteenth century, along with most traditional communities in the United States, vehemently opposed evolutionism, while some others saw it as compatible with Jewish faith. Mainline Jewish theology nowadays sees no conflict with the theistic interpretation of evolution, including human evolution. Indeed, significantly more Jews in the United States accept evolution than do Christians.

Islam has the greatest difficulty in finding a constructive way to deal with evolutionism. So fierce is the opposition that it is not uncommon to find fatwas (more-or-less binding legal-religious rulings) on it. What is striking in Muslim countries is that not only a large majority of the general public but also university students and professors strongly and consistently oppose evolution, particularly human evolution. Even among American Muslims, fewer than half accept evolution. The most important reason for their opposition is the question of the origins of humanity.

Among the main Asiatic faith traditions, evolutionary theory has caused hardly any concern. Regarding Buddhism, there are a number of reasons for this. First, Gautama considered questions of origins to be secondary and marginal. Second, as discussed above, an evolutionary view (though not in its modern form) can be discerned in at least some key Buddhist scriptural accounts. Third, the idea of no-self and impermanence leans toward evolvement and evolution. The Hindu traditions similarly consider the origins and development of the whole of reality in terms of evolution and a common ancestry. Moreover, for Hindus, even the gods may assume animal features.

The next big topic to discuss in this chapter has to do with the way the same Creator who has created the cosmos also provides for it. Traditionally this is named the doctrine of providence.

---

31. Pannenberg, *Systematic Theology*, 2:119.

The Ways the Creator God Is Guiding and Providing for the Life of the World

God Is Not Absent from the World God Has Created

Every theist or person who believes in God—at least in Abrahamic traditions—celebrates the ways in which the Creator of the world is also the One who cares for it and caters to its needs and processes. The term *providence* refers to God's intentional, loving care, maintenance, and guiding of the cosmos. The theme is so prevalent in the Bible that it is useless even to begin to compile a list of passages. As St. Augustine put it succinctly, "But the universe will pass away in the twinkling of an eye if God withdraws His ruling hand."[32]

Theological tradition has made the commonsense distinction between "general" providence, the all-embracing maintenance of the world's order and life, and "special" providence, which encompasses redemptive and saving acts of God as well as particular divine "interventions" related to prayers and miracles. Another useful way of speaking of divine providence includes three interrelated categories:

- preservation (proper): that God keeps in existence and maintains the world;
- concursus: that God graciously invites the creatures to collaborate in the maintenance work; and
- governance: that God lovingly guides the world toward the desired end goal, showing his faithfulness to creation.

That said, the modern person faces a number of challenges to trusting divine providence, particularly righteous governance. Just think of the two world wars, the Jewish Holocaust, and innumerable other worldwide crises, from poverty and hunger to natural catastrophes. They all question God's goodness. Ultimately, it is only with the eye of faith that God's provision can be discerned in a world plagued with suffering, injustice, cruelty, and other problems.

---

32. Augustine, *Literal Meaning of Genesis*, 4.12.22 (trans. Taylor, 1:117).

Do the Sciences Leave Room for God's Continuing Action in the World?

So far so good! Until the rise of modern science and the radically transformed view of the world, divine providence seemed to be accepted unquestioningly. Things have changed since. Here's the problem: with the emergence of modern science, it seemed there was no need for God to intervene in the world process after having created the world and having caused it to follow its laws. The establishment of the principle of inertia—the object's tendency to stay in the existing state or motion until an outside force causes a change—further helped consolidate a purely naturalistic, mechanistic explanation of the world. When combined with atheism, naturalism made God as provider obsolete.

Add to this evolutionary theory with its focus on chance and you will see the profound challenge to theological explanations with reference to God. In brief: "Physical science, it appears, leaves no place for divine action" precisely because it seems like laws of nature as regular processes help maintain and guide the world.[33]

Not surprisingly, theologians reacted in more than one way to this seemingly devastating criticism of divine providence. Conservatives continued the affirmation of divine acts without concern for science, and liberals virtually abandoned any factual notion of divine acts, conceiving them to be merely subjective responses to religious influence; that is, it only seems to the believer that prayers are answered (for example), although factually they are not!

So, is there a way to redeem and reaffirm the proper role of divine providence? Many theologians, including those with either training or expertise in the natural sciences, believe that there is. Let me introduce to you what I think is the most promising way to do so. (And please bear with the cumbersome terminology as I do so!)

Theologian-scientist Robert J. Russell, with the help of scholars such as philosopher-theologian Nancey Murphy and many others, has proposed an awkward but very promising nomenclature—"Non-interventionist Objective Divine Action" or NIODA. What a mouthful! What are they talking about? Let me try to explain. First, the background.

As said, modern science seemed to block any intelligent notion of the need for God to take care of the "business" of the world. The reason was simply this: any intervention by God into the affairs of the world that the same God had designed to follow its regular laws and processes seemed

---

33. Clayton, "Impossible Possibility," 249.

to be nothing less than an intrusion. A tempting—but very problematic—theological response is that which says that God "intervenes" only when no other recourse is present. The problem is that would create the "God-of-the-gaps" in which the only room left for God is that which cannot (yet) be explained by human reason.

By and large, only two options were left for theologians facing the challenge from sciences. The first one is to argue that God's "interventions" are not really true and factual but rather our—the believers'—feelings and subjective assurances of God's presence and working? Call this the "subjective" divine action, something that only happens in the believer's head, so to speak. Its counterpart is "objective" action, which truly allows God to participate in the affairs of the world, even at times "miraculously"—but not only in order to avoid the God-of-the-gaps fallacy.

Now we are ready to unpack the monster acronym NIODA. It claims that God's continuing actions and world could—and should—be seen as "objective" but still not constitute an "intervention." This is, to repeat, "non-intervention" and "objective" divine action. How to explain this? Through the trinitarian doctrine, similarly to creation itself and God's other work. Through and in Spirit, God is pervasively present in the world, from the tiniest to the greatest processes and happenings. Hence, his is not an intervention but a continuing, pervasive, all-embracing divine presence and activity. This is the theological side of the explanation. But what about the sciences? Do they allow such an explanation?

Whereas in the beginning of the modern scientific enterprise it was believed that the world works entirely mechanistically, as if it were a machine, the relativity and particularly quantum theories have provided a more complicated picture of world happenings. While the world is extremely regular in its processes and happenings—as evident, for example, in the fine-tuning of values discussed above or in the daily rising and setting of the sun, or the seasonal cycle of nature's processes—it is not absolutely deterministic. This is the claim of the mainstream interpretation of quantum theory (the so-called Copenhagian interpretation). We can only know the world's processes with high probability. Recall the counterintuitive superposition principle: when knowing an object, say an electron's position, its momentum is not known for sure and vice versa. And, due to the utter complexity of the world, according to chaos theory—which presupposes basically deterministic processes—the absolute measurement of values is not possible. Just think of weather forecasting and the famous "butterfly effect."

Yes, It Is Possible to Affirm Divine Providence Even in Light of Scientific Explanation

So, now back to theological explanation: the "opening" in the world processes explained above, as regular and fine-tuned (indeed almost deterministic) as it may be, leaves room for the Triune God to act. Creator God is not coming into the world from outside, as it were. No: "All things are present to him and are kept by him in his presence,"[34] as Psalm 139 (7–10) classically affirms:

> Whither shall I go from thy Spirit?
> Or whither shall I flee from thy presence?
> If I ascend to heaven, thou art there!
> If I make my bed in Sheol, thou art there!
> If I take the wings of the morning
> and dwell in the uttermost parts of the sea,
> even there thy hand shall lead me,
> and thy right hand shall hold me.

In this sense, though using totally different terminology, the (re-)establishment of the possibility of divine providence and action is but restating that the Triune God who indwells creation from its biggest to its tiniest entity cares and guides.

In sum: it is meaningful to speak of providence as divine presence, maintenance, and guidance in the world, that the same Creator has made extremely regular in processes and happenings but not ironclad deterministic. But what about miracles? Can we go as far as to speak of God's "objective" actions, without an intervention, even when those actions seem to exceed natural events?

What about Miracles?

Since the Enlightenment, it has been difficult for the modern person to affirm the possibility of the miraculous. As alleged divine "interventions," they would be but violations of the laws of nature. The term "miracle" itself is linked with the "supernatural," an anathema to science.

Not so fast! The meaning of the term "miracle" is more complex than what common sense tells us. Its meaning has changed quite dramatically over the course of time, most particularly during the Enlightenment. For

---

34. Pannenberg, *Systematic Theology*, 1:380.

early theology, the supernatural-natural distinction did not exist if by it was meant, as in modernity, the distinction between two realms, that of God and that of the sciences, respectively. All of reality was governed by God. What they called miracle was an event for which they did not know the explanation, but it was not contrary to nature.

In theological usage, the term "supernatural" did not become common until medieval times, when it came to mean something like "going above" [the Latin term *super*] the order of nature, such as in healing the sick. Even then, something supernatural was not considered to be against nature. What made people consider an event to be miraculous in that era was not that it went *against* nature, but that "it surpasse[d] the faculty of nature,"[35] and hence is God's work, hidden to human understanding.

Things changed dramatically in modernity. As soon as people understood nature to be running on its own powers like a machine, miracles came to be perceived as violations of nature's laws. But that view of the world has been definitively left behind—and the nature of God's providential action in the world was defined as non-interventionist. These developments help us tremendously in thinking more accurately about the miraculous. And for those who believe that "God, a supernatural being, has caused, and continues to cause, the whole universe to exist . . . how plausible it is, then, to say that such a God will refuse to operate in the world in particular ways."[36] In other words, if you believe in the "Big Spirit," the Almighty God, the Creator of the universe, it seems a much simpler matter to believe in "small spiritual" events such as healing taking place!

Before moving to the next chapter, the last big topic to consider the creation and nature of the human being has to do with nature's suffering and its potential for flourishing. I begin with nature's suffering.

Suffering—and Flourishing—of Nature and the Environment

Why Is There Suffering in Nature?

Although the mystery of evil is likely to remain that—a *mystery*—any theistic faith has to account for the presence of evil in light of God's goodness. The problem is particularly pressing for Abrahamic faiths that insist on God's fairness, love, and goodness. Rampant suffering and acts of evil in the world, in relation both to humanity (moral evil) and to nature

---

35. Aquinas, *Summa Theologica*, 1.105.7.
36. Ward, "Personhood," 155.

(natural evil), not only constitute a major atheistic challenge concerning the existence of God; suffering also poses the question of what kind of God there is, if indeed there is one.

Traditionally, the topics of suffering and evil have been discussed under the rubric of theodicy (that is, how to justify the goodness and power of God vis-à-vis rampant evil and suffering in God's creation), and its focus has been almost exclusively on pain and suffering in human life, largely ignoring nature's suffering. In our times, it is pressing that we take into consideration both nature's and humanity's suffering and prospects for well-being. The next chapter on humanity will pick up human flourishing, and the final chapter, on eschatology, will tackle the theodicy question.

A particularly vexing problem is that of animals' and nonhuman living organisms' suffering, since it is not easy to find a reason for it. While Christian tradition has not totally ignored nonhuman suffering, it has typically linked the latter's suffering with what happens to humanity. Briefly put, Christian tradition says that suffering and death in the world were introduced following the perfect paradise state as a result of the fall of the first human couple. That explanation, however, is no longer scientifically credible, nor is it mandated biblically, as will be discussed in the following chapter. Also, one key reason that Christian tradition overlooks animal pain is its subordinate and utilitarian view of animals, a stance hardly compatible with the intent of biblical theology.

What about plants (and other nonsentient entities)? Do they feel pain? At the time of this writing, science isn't speaking about this with a united voice. What we know is that plants seem to have some kind of biochemical injury mechanism and, for example, may release hormones that could indicate sensation. Perhaps we should find another term—because "pain" entails a nervous system—or use the term strictly analogically.

The wider framework for a theological consideration of suffering and pain in nature is the kind of world God has decided to create in which all created life is finite and necessarily subject to death and decay. To be born is to face death. In fact, entropy and suffering also seem to be instrumental to evolution and development. To put it another way: the emergence of complexity and intelligence requires a long process of "wastefulness." This insight seems to apply to both the biological world and to physics.

Because of the rampant suffering in nature, it is possible to argue that natural evils are an unintended by-product or consequence of God's free choice to create the kind of world in which we live, namely, an evolving world. Correctly understood, it can perhaps cautiously be said that God had "no choice" but to permit physical and biological natural evil in our kind of world, having in his freedom and love decided to bring about the world. But even that still leaves a number of important questions unanswered, particularly this one: granted that natural evil is necessary for this kind of world, one still wonders if *this much* natural evil is necessary.

Be that as it may, only with the turn to eschatological consummation can any long-standing hope be gained, a topic to be addressed in chapter 10. For now we turn to the topic of nature's suffering related at least partly to human action.

Are Asiatic Faiths "Green"?

The pollution of creation is a major and well-documented crisis threatening not only the well-being but even the *being* itself of our planet, so much so that "if current trends continue, we will not."[37] This raises the question of the role of religions in helping to overcome the impending eco-catastrophe. Happily, unlike in the past, most religions nowadays claim to be "green."

Although there is no denying religions' responsibility and guilt for the environment's pollution—just think of some Fundamentalist Christians' intentional neglect of the environment in hopes of an imminent eschatological consummation—the persistent criticism against a necessary link between natural disaster and religion is untenable. A related misconception is that whereas Abrahamic faiths are detrimental to the environment, Asiatic faiths by nature are "green." Before taking a closer look at that contention, let us recall something that critics of religions routinely ignore, namely the enormously devastating effects on nature by atheists, from the former Soviet Union to China and beyond. While this does not excuse religions, it does help to contextualize the question and the responsibility for the destruction.

Proponents of Buddhism's green stance routinely mention a number of the religion's features, from its alleged focus on nonhuman well being as opposed to Abrahamic faiths' focus on human well-being, to its interest in a this-worldly ethical pursuit rather than centering on other-wordly salvation, to Buddha's compassion toward all beings, and its nondualistic approach to the world in contrast to Judeo-Christian dualism. Are these rationales valid? Based not only on my own observations but rather on reports by Buddhist experts, I fear they are not. The most obvious reason has to do with the very "foundations" of Buddhism. Rather than the Christian vision of a new creation that encompasses the renewal of the whole of creation and all creatures, the Buddhist vision of seeking liberation from *dukkha* is deeply human-centered, individualistic, and perhaps even oblivious to nonhuman

---

37. Maguire, *Moral Core*, 13.

beings. Unlike in Abrahamic traditions in which nature has intrinsic value as the handiwork of a personal deity, in Buddhism and its cyclical view of time/history, nature is doomed to a repeated cycle of emergence and destruction *ad infinitum*. This hardly leaves much energy or vision for the protection of this vanishing world. All in all, these kinds of theological reasons that seem to obliterate or frustrate environmental pursuits and ethics among Buddhists are almost never mentioned in the popular promotional literature that hails the "greenness" of Buddhism. What about Hinduism, its mother-religion?

The significance of ecological attitudes among Hindus is immense in light of the huge environmental problems in India and surrounding areas. There is no doubt that, as in Buddhism, the cyclical worldview of Hinduism potentially leans toward being oblivious to the conservation of the earth. Furthermore, Hinduism's concept of the appearance nature of reality or the cosmos as *līlā* ("play," that is, as an unintended "by-product") similarly may cause the faithful to consider this earth a secondary, temporary dwelling place, a mere way-point to the "real world." Consider also these viewpoints: Can the strongly ascetic Hindu outlook in pursuit of one's own deliverance contribute to the communal and cosmic good? With regard to environmental care, what is the role of karma, the bondage to the world because of deeds in the past and present? What about the deeply *theologically* based and (originally) divinely sanctioned hierarchic nature of society (the caste system) when it comes to ecological concern?

What about Abrahamic Cousin Faiths' Attitudes Toward the Environment?

If Asiatic faiths' track record on the environment is mixed at best, what about the Abrahamic faiths? Taken as a whole, they contain a number of resources to facilitate the flourishing of nature. These include:

- the task of vice-regency given by God in all three traditions;
- the importance of history and time because of a linear rather than cyclical worldview; and
- the covenant spirituality of the Hebrew-Christian traditions that binds human beings to God, other humans, and nature.

Similarly to its sister faiths, the Jewish religion has acknowledged only recently the value of work on behalf of the environment. The reasons for this are many and understandable. The focus on the mere survival of the small dispersed nation of Israel, particularly in the Holocaust world, including continuing threats from the surrounding nations, has not made concern for the natural environment top of the Jewish agenda. Although secular Jewish eco-minded individuals have excelled in green activities beginning from the 1960s, the religious impetus for such activity came primarily from a few Jews in the United States. That said, such concern is hardly only a recent phenomenon. Consider the many nature-related blessings and prayers in the liturgy, many of them based on OT texts, including the annual feast of Sukkot, also known as the Feast of Tabernacles, during which people live in small huts for a week commemorating not only the forty years of survival in the desert but also nature and agriculture. Nowadays it is known as the "Jewish Environment Holiday."

When it comes to Islam, the US-based conservative Muslim intellectual S. H. Nasr has, on the one hand, harshly critiqued the technocratic use of nature in the modern West, and on the other, highlighted the spiritual and moral dimension of the ecological crisis. This is fully in keeping with mainline Islamic tradition, which ultimately attributes even the environmental crisis to "the loss of a relationship between humans, the natural realm, and Allah."[38] Islamic creation theology's foundational idea of creation as "sign" may have immense ecological ramifications, as it links all created beings to the Divine.

Having looked ever so briefly at Jewish and Islamic resources concerning the environment, let us wrap us by considering the Christian tradition.

Eco-Theological Resources in Christian Tradition

It is reasonable to assume that Christian theology is able to hold in dynamic tension both an attitude of reverent admiration for the beauty of creation in its endless diversity and creativity and a deepening concern for nature's vulnerability and suffering by current global economic-industrial rape. This reverence does not have to make nature an "idol," but rather an immensely valuable handiwork of God who in the act of creation deemed it "good."

What is very important for contemporary theology is that we consider carefully the meaning of the mandate in Genesis 1:26–27 to act as God's faithful vice-regents. The mandate does not justify abuse but rather is a call to responsible service on behalf of the good creation. Regretfully, the command to "subdue the earth" has too often been taken literally in Christian tradition.

Although there is the minor subsidiary "green" tradition in Christianity that includes mystics and saints for whom nature had intrinsic value

---

38. Chishti, "*Fiṭra*," 69–71.

and human dominion meant not abuse but stewardship and care of creatures, in the main Christian tradition has conceived of nature as having been made for humans and their benefit and, as a result, it has seen nature through a utilitarian lens.

The task of an ecological Christian theology is twofold: it has to clarify and help avoid ways of thinking and speaking of nature as creation that are detrimental to her survival and well-being, and it has to search for resources—theological insights, metaphors, approaches—that may help foster the flourishing and continuing shalom of God's creation. Particularly helpful in this enterprise has been highlighting the Spirit's work for continuous healing of creation, a topic that the chapter on pneumatology will address. Similarly, a careful negotiation of the dynamic between the value of creation in this era and the eschatological hope for final redemption and consummation (attempted in the last chapter) can potentially yield fruitful results.

4

Humanity

What Is the Human Being?

Speaking of Humanity in a Radically Changed Context

What if We Humans Are No Longer the Apex of Creation?

THE HUMAN PERSON AND humanity used to be considered to be the summit and apex of the world and creation—if for no other reason than having been created in the image of God. Now there are rumors—indeed, big rumors—that things might have changed and we have been downgraded, so to speak, to the same level as the rest of the creatures. Is that so? And does theology have anything to say on this topic?

There were good reasons why traditional Christian theology tended to emphasize the difference of humanity from the rest of creation rather than its continuity with it. Linking humanity too closely (so it seemed to the faithful) would have begun to erode her unique nature and position.

Be that as it may, a radical change in contemporary mindset, not least due to astonishing discoveries in the sciences including that our planet is not the center of reality, has caused a shift in humanity's place. Evolutionary theory and biology have definitively linked humans with the rest of creation. The neurosciences have revealed the astonishing bases of human decisions, emotions, and will in brain functions. Particularly challenging has been the application of the evolutionary scheme to humanity.

And it looks as if contemporary theology has not necessarily pushed against this radically changed perception of the world and the creatures in it. A growing number of theologians are speaking about continuity of humanity with the rest of creation, not only her difference. Biblical scholars remind us that this may not be a novel idea. The first two creation narratives in the OT (Gen 1 and 2) point to a dynamic mutuality among creatures. The emergence of a sequence of forms—or "generations of the heavens and the earth when they were created" (Gen 2:4)—culminating in the creation of humanity, makes the creation an interrelated web, a network. This is not to undermine the uniqueness of humanity in relation to God but rather to remind us of our indebtedness to all that God has created.

With these caveats in mind, let us delve deeper into what is technically called "theological anthropology." Obviously, this nomenclature refers to the placement of *anthropos* (human being) in relation to *theos* (God). Indeed, that is its meaning, as the goal and task of theological anthropology "is to set forth the Christian understanding of what it means to be human. Christian anthropology views the human person and humankind as a whole 'in relationship to God.'"[1] Traditionally and conveniently, it falls into two interrelated major parts, namely, humanity as the image of God, and the image of God in relation to (original) sin and the fall.

Theological anthropology has some good news for the Christian who wonders whether the uniqueness of humanity as the image of God can still be redeemed. Yes, it can, and such redemption does not necessitate, nor even encourage, the dismissal of scientific knowledge of us. Indeed, a sympathetic-critical engagement of sciences may strengthen our faith in God, the Creator.

Plan of the Chapter

This chapter falls in two major parts, following the two-fold division of the doctrine of humanity, namely the human being as the image of God and the human being as fallen and sinful. It ends with an extended discussion of human flourishing—and suffering.

The first part opens with an inquiry into the evolution of humanity in the long line of development, including what makes the human person unique. Thereafter, a detailed consideration of the meaning and implications of biblical and theological teaching on humanity as the image of God is in order, including the anchoring of human dignity and inviolability in God's creative work. This is followed by a careful look at the nature of human nature, in other words, of what are we made both in light of sciences, particularly neurosciences, and the teachings of religions, including Christian theology. A related crucial issue has to do with whether the human person really possesses the freedom to make choices or whether

---

1. Grenz, *Social God*, 23.

a person is predetermined; this is a question to both sciences and theology. To wrap up the first major part, I attempt to describe the visions of humanity and human nature among religions.

The second major part begins with a careful look at the meaning of the fall and sin in Christian tradition, including necessary revisions in contemporary theology due to a changed worldview and cultural contexts. This discussion also includes a careful engagement of sciences. Subsequently, the final section of the chapter on the question of "What's wrong with us?" focuses on four religions' teachings and insights.

In the end, the discussion of human flourishing and suffering engages a number of issues urgent in our contemporary world, including equality and justice, violence and war, work and economy, and migration and slavery. We glean ideas from biblical and theological resources to tackle these important current issues and also to converse with Judaism, Islam, Buddhism, and Hinduism.

The Uniqueness of Humanity from a Scientific Perspective

The Long Line of Development

The closest predecessors of modern *Homo sapiens* are the hominids.[2] The genetic evidence indicates that the oldest group of hominids goes back as far as 5 to 7 million years in history. The first known hominid species called australopithecines (from 4–5 million to 1.5 million years ago) walked on two feet and showed evidence of important growth in brain size.

About 2 million years ago the development of the hominids peaked, evinced by the further expansion of their brains and the gradual adoption of tools and of a dietary shift to include meat. About a million years ago, of several species of hominids only *Homo erectus* remained and started to expand from Africa where hominids were first located, to Europe and parts of Asia. About a half-million years ago, an even more developed form of *Homo erectus* appeared, called archaic *sapiens*.

In the transition to human beings (*Homo sapiens*), *Homo neanderthalensis* played the most significant role (400,000/200,000–45,000 years ago). Still, they were considerably different from us, for example lacking artistic capacities and having very limited intellectual skills. And, very importantly, despite their long existence, they made virtually no progress in the use of tools!

---

2. An amazing collection of current resources, easily accessible and scientifically reliable, is found at "Hominid."

HUMANITY

This brief tour through the ages reminds us that compared to the very long history of the hominids, we humans (*Homo sapiens*) are newcomers to the stage, having been around no more than about 50,000 to 150,000 years. According to a widely held scholarly interpretation, the most dramatic development, called the "creative explosion" or "cultural big bang," took place with the shift from the Middle to the Upper Paleolithic era 45,000 to 35,000 years ago: "it is during this time that human consciousness and intelligence emerged, and with it creative, artistic, and religious imagination."[3] Ian Tattersall and Jeffrey H. Schwartz, two leading American paleoanthropologists, summarize it well: "*Homo sapiens* is not simply an extrapolation or improvement of what went before it . . . our species is an entirely unprecedented entity in the world, however mundanely we may have come by our unusual attributes."[4] Hence, to speak of humans as "developed apes" does not make sense from the scientific perspective!

So, What Makes Us Unique?

What, then, are the defining, unique features of humanity in relation to other creatures? According to standard scientific consensus, these include features such as development in tool production, increased technological changes, use of ornaments, significant changes in economic and social organization, and so forth. Neuroscientists and psychologists add to the list the highly significant role of language and communication that facilitates even abstract ideas; the capacity to read another person's thoughts and feelings, as if getting under the neighbor's skin; vast capacities of memory; orientation to the future as opposed merely to survival mode in the now; and sensitive emotional and social skills. Let us mention a few more: the capacity to discern beauty and other aesthetic experiences; the importance of feelings such as falling in love or deep disappointment; the gift of imagination that "travels faster" than the speed of light; and, say, the sense of humor.

On top of these, and rooted in many of the items in the list, perhaps the capacity that makes men and women totally unique has to do with self-transcendence, that is, the power to step outside one's own mental space, so to speak, and consider one's own feelings, thoughts, fears, joys, and so forth. To illustrate with a familiar example: whereas the highest animals, say dogs, likely sense fear when facing danger and death, as far as we know, dogs are not capable of reflecting on that fear. In other words, it is an instinctual reaction. Human beings are capable not only of reflecting on, say,

---

3. Van Huyssteen, *Alone in the World*, 64.
4. Tattersall and Schwartz, *Extinct Humans*, 9.

fear, but of even being so overwhelmed and scared that they may even hurt themselves. As ironic and counterintuitive as it may sound, the possibility of suicide—known only among the humans—is a glaring manifestation of the capacity for self-transcendence!

A number of the features mentioned above are a part of the mysterious commodity of humanity called "consciousness." Human consciousness still remains a mystery to science! As much as some rudimentary forms of "consciousness" may be found in some animals, these are a far cry from human consciousness and lack the human mind's capacity for self-transcendence, that is, humans knowing that they know! Similarly, as much as higher animals may be able to "learn" to use—or imitate—words taught by humans, that skill has little to do with human symbolic behavior, including syntax and semantics.

But what about the genetic continuity between us and other creatures? Wouldn't that begin to erode our uniqueness in scientific perspective. It is true that since the discovery in the 1950s of the structure of DNA[5] and subsequent discoveries, genetics has become a massive enterprise in our society. Indeed, astonishingly, we know now that 98 to 99 percent of our genetic heritage is shared with chimpanzees. Does this mean that humans are only more advanced mammals? No. Genetic similarity explains only so much. Consider this: humans and dandelions share about 25 percent of their DNA, and humans and daffodils even more.[6] Hence, the genetic similarity between humans and chimpanzees is not what matters, but rather, "just how strange we are compared to all other living species on this earth."[7]

To all that we have to add a truly essential contribution to human uniqueness not present in even the highest animals: culture. At the threshold of the appearance of modern human beings (about 50,000 to 75,000 years ago), anatomy and behavior parted ways. Whereas until then they progressed in tandem, thereafter behavioral and cultural change began to accelerate in a dramatic way. The all-important role of culture to human evolvement, while at times ignored, should be duly credited in making us who we are.

Because human behavior is guided by rationality, not merely by instincts and drives (as is the case with infants), its evolution is not

---

5. Of course, DNA itself was known much earlier, beginning from the end of the nineteenth century. But its amazing importance and some key features have been discovered toward the end of the second millennium. Reliable accessible guides to DNA include the following: "Deoxyribonucleic Acid"; "What Is DNA?"; and "DNA: Chemical Compound."

6. Marks, *What It Means*, 5, 28; see also 29–31.

7. Purcell, *From Big Bang*, 191.

determined by genes or even the environment. It is a complex and complicated process of dynamic factors. Cultural activities and capacities, including learning, reflection, and emotional attentiveness, all shape us significantly. The genetic and cultural information comes together in an absolutely unique way in *Homo sapiens*.

Language Makes the Difference

One of the defining features of human uniqueness whose importance cannot be underestimated has to do with our capacity to communicate. And of course, linguistic capacities are also essential elements of our cultural adaptation. While all higher animals communicate in some way or another, only humans use language.

This advanced use of language and communication is made possible by the extraordinary development of human brain capacity and the specific anatomy of the vocal tract. The crossing over the symbolic threshold around 75,000 years ago really makes us what is aptly called the "symbolic species."

How is this amazing communicative capacity possible? The human brain. Not only does the size of the brain matter (although its significance in human evolution should be duly noted), but also the specifics of the brain. At a weight of only three to four pounds in adults (with a man's brain being slightly heavier than a woman's), the brain contains 10 billion neurons communicating with each other through synapses that number about 10^{12}! What is amazing about brains is simply that although obviously physical (material), they give rise (or at least are necessary) to mental acts!

What really is remarkable about human language is that it makes possible humanity's openness to the future beyond physical and other limitations. Take imagination. Openness may also help explain the unbelievable drive for continuing innovation, improvement, and inventions in human culture—a feature unknown even among the hominids, let alone other animals. No wonder the difference between humans and other species is "not just a difference of degree. It is a difference in kind."[8]

So far we have discussed human uniqueness in scientific terms. Now biblical-theological resources join the conversation.

---

8. Tattersall, *World from Beginnings*, 101.

Humanity as the Image of God

Created in the Image of the Creator

Notwithstanding the scarcity of direct references to the concept of the image of God (*imago Dei* in Latin) in the biblical canon—after three occurrences in the beginning (Gen 1:26–27; 5:1; 9:6), the concept itself appears in only a couple of NT passages (1 Cor 11:7; Jas 3:9)—it has become an "umbrella" term. It provides a foundational account of the human person and humanity in relation to the Creator, other creatures, and the cosmos as a whole. That said, it is difficult, if not impossible, to nail down one specific meaning to the term in the Bible. Rather, its many meanings have given rise to different kinds of complementary interpretations throughout history.

In early theology, the so-called "structural" view was dominant—the idea that there is something within the structure of human beings that makes us the image of God, whether reason or will or something similar. By the time of the Reformation, the "relational" view came to be preferred. In relational interpretations, what is crucial about the image of God is humanity's placement in reference to God (and derivatively, other human beings).

Without necessarily leaving behind either one of these approaches, in modern times the "dynamic" view came to dominate. In that outlook, human beings are considered to be on the way to their final destination. The image of God is the divinely set destiny as much as a present reality. We are already the image of God, but we are also on the way to its fulfillment.

Importantly, not only each human person but also the whole of humanity exists as the image of God. This idea enforces and supports the equality of all human beings, including both sexes. In the early Christian centuries under cultures in which equality was a rare notion, this biblical teaching helped the church to affirm the equality and freedom of slaves, typically considered as lower level humans, as well as the sick, such as lepers, the outcasts of society. In fact, only the status of the image of God and "destiny of fellowship with God [confer] inviolability on human life in the person of each individual."[9] It means that "by virtue of our being destined for fellowship with God . . . no actual humiliation that might befall us can extinguish it."[10]

One of the helpful insights of modern interpretations is that not only reason and will, as important as they are, but also emotions and sociality are defining features of our creation in the image of our Creator. Relatedly, the image of God does not only, nor even primarily, refer to "soul" or mental aspects of the human but to all aspects of the human being, including

---

9. Pannenberg, *Systematic Theology*, 2:176.
10. Pannenberg, *Systematic Theology*, 2:177.

the body and embodiment. Recall that our eschatological hope is directed toward the resurrection of the body.

Speaking of our ultimate goal, the NT adds a significant note: the goal toward which we are growing and being transformed is none else but our Savior and Lord, the truly original and pure image of God, Christ Jesus (2 Cor 3:18). What a lofty and thrilling goal for us!

We Flourish in Relation to God and Others

Yet another useful insight in contemporary theology reminds us of the deeply relational aspect of humanity given that we have been created in the image of God, the trinitarian God. Trinity bespeaks relationality, community as established in chapter 2.

Understanding the *imago* as based in our relatedness to God is the only way to ensure that all human beings, regardless of their capacities—whether rational, emotional, relational, or other—exist in the state of the image of God. Otherwise, for example, the intellectually disabled could not be. Even when it comes to relationality, its basis has to be God relating to the human being, rather than the measure of the human person's capacity to relate. There are people who do not have the capacity to reciprocate relationality.

That we are placed before God means that the ultimate goal of humanity is to seek and honor God as the Creator and also to live in communion with other people God has created in his image. Since not only each human person but also humanity as a whole exists in the image of God, then human destiny cannot be achieved alone.

This universal nature of the image of God is further deepened by the conviction that not even the fall and sin could erase it. While certainly tarnishing the likeness to God, even after the fall the human being is addressed as the image of God (Gen 5:1; 9:6).

Yet another important implication of the relatedness to the Creator is the mandate and responsibility to serve as God's vice-regents. The God-given task to name the creatures is an aspect of this calling (Gen 2:19–20). In the ancient world—as in some cultures in our day—naming means exercising power and authority.

Relatedness also has much to say to gender relations. According to the Bible, both male and female exist equally in the image of God. Sexual distinction belongs to the essential and formative nature of human creation. Sexuality, then, is deeply social in nature. It is now generally agreed that the designation of woman as "helper" (Gen 2:18) is not a way of making the female subordinate or the servant of man; the use of the Hebrew term (*'ezer*) in the biblical narrative does not warrant that.

Christian theology has traveled a long road to establish the full equality of women and men. The denigrating sayings about women by leading theologians throughout the ages are well known and have to be corrected. Regretfully, the same applies not only to other Abrahamic faith traditions but also to other religions. The problem of what is often named as "complementarianism" is that it makes one-half of humanity the receiver, the other half the giver. More theologically sound is that real differences between male and female, obvious as they are, "will not be accepted as warrants for social systems which grant men in general authority and power over women in general."[11] In keeping with that is Moltmann's comment that the lasting theological meaning of having been created as male and female is that "to be human means being sexually differentiated *and* sharing a common humanity; both are equally primary."[12]

Let me add an important afterthought here: that human beings are uniquely endowed and uniquely placed in relation to God is not meant to disassociate us from the rest of creation even if they do not have the same status. Indeed, as the most highly developed creatures, humans have the biggest responsibility to be mindful of their deep links with the rest of the life of the cosmos and the well-being of the planet in which they find their dwelling place.

Before delving further into the nature of human nature, in other words, what are we made of, so to speak, let us take a detour and explore the interesting question about whether the image of God talk has any correspondences among our Abrahamic sister faiths.

What about Our Abrahamic Sister Faiths?

Whereas the explicit image of God talk applies only to Judeo-Christian tradition, the foundational placement of humanity in relation to God is an invaluable shared treasure among all three faiths. Understandably Islam totally eschews the concept "the image of God" in order to avoid the *shirk*, a blasphemous linking of God with anything created. But as the ensuing discussion details, the idea of relatedness to God is nonetheless central to Islam.

Whereas the Qurʾan lacks any direct statement about the image of God, in the Hadith there are such renderings: "Allah, the Exalted and

---

11. Cahill, *Sex, Gender, and Christian Ethics*, 1–2.
12. Moltmann, *God in Creation*, 222.

Glorious, created Adam in His own image" (Sahih Muslim 40, para. 6809). The closest the Qur'an comes to affirm the idea is the well-known passage of 30:30: "So set your purpose for religion, as a *hanīf*[13]—a nature given by God, upon which He originated mankind." Here the term *fitrah* is used of [human] "nature." It is clearly akin to the image in Christian-Jewish vocabulary. Other similarities with the biblical account include the making of the human being of clay (Q 23:12-14). Not only that, but the Spirit of God also breathes into the one made of clay, and therefore even the angels prostrate themselves before him (15:26-30).

The technical term *fitrah*, used of human nature—"an inborn natural predisposition which cannot change, and which exists at birth in all human beings"[14]—has a number of interrelated meanings, including moral intuitions and religious instinct. According to a well-known Hadith statement,

> Everyone is born according to his true nature.... There is none born but is created to his true nature (Islam). It is his parents who make him a Jew or a Christian or a Magian quite as beasts produce their young with their limbs perfect.... The nature made by Allah in which He has created men there is no altering of Allah's creation; that is the right religion. (Sahih Muslim 33, para. 6423)[15]

On the basis of this teaching, in Muslim tradition *fitrah* is universal, not limited to Muslims alone, and is an immutable feature of humanity. Very closely resembling the Christian idea of the innate knowledge of God, it "is the faculty, which He has created in mankind, of knowing Allah." As a result, belief in Allah (the confession of *tawhid*) is "natural" to human beings. Therefore, Islam is at times called *din al-fitrah*, the religion of human nature, that is, religion that is in keeping with natural human instincts and inclinations, a claim shared by Christian theologians regarding their own tradition.

Not surprisingly, similar to Christianity, cousin faiths affirm the dignity of humanity in relation to God, the Creator. Suffice it to mention this Hadith saying: "When any one of you fights with his brother, he should avoid his face for Allah created Adam in His own image" (Sahih Muslim 32, para. 6325).

---

13. The exact meaning of the term is somewhat unclear (hence left without English rendering here). A number of times it refers to "faith" (of Abraham) and also has the connotation of a nonpolytheistic faith. See Jeffery, *Foreign Vocabulary*, 112.

14. Mohamed, *Fitrah*, 13.

15. The last sentence is a citation from Q 30:30.

Furthermore, a common theme for all three traditions is the idea of humanity as God's viceroy on earth. In Islam, the idea of vice-regency is typically described in terms of *caliph*. According to Qur'an 2:30, when God announced to the angels, "I am appointing on earth a viceregent," they demurred and wondered whether God knew the risks involved because of the frailty of human nature! In response the Lord taught them how to name the creatures, and that was a cause of marvel among the angelic beings. By extension, some key figures in the Qur'an such as Noah and David can be considered to act in the manner of a caliph (viceregent).

Of What Are We Made? The Nature of Human Nature

How Do Religions Conceive of Our Nature?

It is fair to say that despite deep differences in visions of human nature, virtually all religions agree that humanity is more than merely material and physical; they affirm a spiritual view, however each religion might define it.

At one end of religions, there is the view that only the spiritual dimension of humanity matters, not the bodily dimension, nor individuality in any sense (such as in Hinduism's *advaita* Vedanta of Sankara). Thus, the whole point of the spiritual quest is to overcome the illusion of dualism between the "spirit" and everything else. While the other major Hindu Vedanta school allows for some form of duality (the qualified nonduality of Ramanuja), its basic view of humanity is not that different.

While radically different in many ways, the main schools of Buddhism, with their denial of the persistence of "self," envision "salvation" in terms of transcending embodiment and thus also individuality. In that sense, they come closer to Hindu than Abrahamic traditions' view.

Things are different among the Semitic faiths. Despite internal differences, all three envision human nature as "embodied soul" or "spirited body." In other words, essential to human nature is both the embodied, physical side and the mental, spiritual side. Particularly in Jewish-Christian traditions, embodiment/materiality is an essential part of human nature, either because of a "this-worldly" eschatology (Judaism) or because of life in the resurrected body in the new creation (Christianity), themes to be discussed in the final chapter. Abrahamic faiths also make human existence finite and thus not immortal. Everything created is finite; only God, the Immortal, is infinite (1 Tim 6:16).

Despite differences in emphasis regarding the ways in which the physical (material) and the non-physical, non-material (spiritual and mental) relate to each other and whether they both belong to the ultimate constitution of human nature, all religions are largely dualistic. This means that, differently from most scientific and many philosophical conceptions, which are "monist" materialistically, that is, the understanding that we are ultimately only made of one "stuff," the physical, religions as well as the religious faithful typically envision the human to be constituted of both the physical *and* the non-physical.

That said, a growing trend in Christian theology is to avoid such dualism, which separates or even too robustly distinguishes the physical from the mental/spiritual. In short, this trend is toward a strongly integral or integrated view of human nature, even if nuances still exist.

What Does the Bible Tell about Our Nature?

From early on, Christian tradition faced two kinds of legacies—legacies that in many ways were opposite to each other. On the one hand, from pagan philosophies in the Greco-Roman world including such luminaries as Plato, Christianity inherited a deep body-soul dualism, which resulted in the denigration of the body and material, ultimately understanding the body as a prison of the immortal soul. As a result, Christians welcomed death, understanding it to separate the two and release the soul from its bodily imprisonment. Happily, from Plato's pupil Aristotle the church inherited a more nuanced and less separatist view of human nature, in which the soul is the "form" (or actuality) of the body. This means that soul cannot normally exist without the body and vice versa. This so-called hylomorphic view was at its most dominant in the work of the medieval theological scholar Thomas Aquinas. On the other hand, particularly from the OT but also somewhat less unambiguously from the NT, early Christianity inherited a view of human nature we might call "mutual conditioning" or "integrated duality." In short, the church moved away from the separatist dualistic view of human nature and toward Thomas's hylomorphic understanding of the human.

Readers of the OT find in it a diversity of ways of speaking of the human person, including references to body, spirit, soul, life, and so forth. All these are more vague ways of trying to grasp human nature from complementary points of views. Very importantly, we now know that even the key term once often translated as "soul" (Hebrew *nephes*) actually more accurately means "life" or "living [being]." Hence, the famous Genesis 2:7 verse should be rendered like this: God having breathed the spirit of life into Adam, Adam became a "living being" (rather than "soul" in its everyday meaning of something merely spiritual or mental as opposed to physical and bodily).

Even in the NT, in which—following the habit of the times—dualistic terminology is pervasive, manifold ways of speaking of human nature follows the OT's elusive pattern. Just think of the familiar passage from Hebrews 4:12 that speaks of the "sword" of the Word of God "piercing to the division of soul and spirit, of joints and marrow, and discerning the thoughts and intentions of the heart." Many such pluriform, complex expressions can be found in Scripture implying that no systematic definition is meant to be offered! Rather, all various aspects of human nature belong together and can be referred to in complementary ways. Here is a clue to contemporary (to us) theology to underline the importance of an integrated, integral account of human nature.

Holistic, Integrated Human Nature—A Contemporary Christian Vision

What is the main concern about an extreme, dualistic account of human nature? It locates the image of God and human uniqueness in the soul rather than in the human person as a whole, something not found in the Bible. Besides, strong dualisms of this sort tend to elevate reason above other features of human nature, as if emotions, embodiment, mental capacities, sociality, and so forth are not equally (but differently) important. What results is often a downplaying of the body, emotions, and passions. Jürgen Moltmann rightly wonders: "If the body does not belong to the *imago Dei*, how can the body become 'a temple of the Holy Spirit'?"[16]

At the same time, the reasons why scientific and philosophical materialist monisms cannot do the work of Christian (and religious) anthropologies is the need to insist that there is "more" to human life and dignity than just the material. This "more" also seems necessary for the affirmation of morality and ethics. A merely physically based reality cannot make moral judgments. Finally, to remind everybody of the afterlife, theology and faith resist materialist monism.

It is worthwhile to retain these invaluable lessons from chastened dualisms while at the same time resisting the extreme and harmful dualistic accounts of human nature. The sciences that study human behavior and human nature can help us here. While of course scientific results in themselves do not support religion or philosophy, a Christian interpretation may find them pointing to a deeply integrated view of the nature of human nature.

16. Moltmann, *God in Creation*, 239.

This integrated nature of human nature also raises the old and oft-debated question about human freedom: Do we really choose what we do and how we act? Or, is our behavior predetermined—in which case the freedom of will is but an illusion? Here, it is useful to consult some philosophical, scientific, and theological resources.

Human Nature and Freedom in Light of Contemporary Sciences

The Deep Connection with Brain Events and Human Mind

Astonishingly, as recently as the late eighteenth century the deeply integrated connection between the physical and mental had not yet been discovered in scientific work. It took some dramatic events—such as the oft-referenced case of Phineas Gage—to awaken the sciences and society to this insight. In 1848, an explosion caused a tamping iron to pierce the skull of this twenty-five-year-old New England railroad worker. The iron exited through the top of his skull, leaving his personality profoundly changed. With no visible effects of this traumatic injury beyond obvious scars, this once-stable person was now emotionally and socially bankrupt. The obvious lesson from this poor rail worker's incident is simply that brains and neurons have much to do with emotions, sociality, and thoughts. There is no lack of more recent such reports, thanks especially to new electro-magnetic imaging techniques.

In fact, rapid developments in psychology and neurosciences have yielded an amazing array of information about the incredible connections between the brain and human behavior. It has been shown that certain brain systems are linked with particular mental and physical activities, such as language capacities, types of memory functions, and error detection and compensation. Highly interesting to me, for example, is the phenomenon of blind sight. People blind due to brain damage can still detect objects without being able to "see" them. Not only are behavioral, cognitive, and emotional functioning and activities linked with the brain, there is also an integral connection between neuronal processes in the brain and decision making in ethical and moral domains. And even more: a tight link has been detected between such neuronal processes and religious activities such as prayer, meditation, and speaking in tongues.

What are the implications for theology of this close linking of neural/brain events and human behavior/mind? A particularly important issue is whether the mental is not only a "real" property but can also exercise causal influence downward. Can our beliefs, desires, intentions, and plans have real influence in a world that, according to the sciences, operates along the regularities of natural laws, including brain activities and processes? Theologians face mounting opposition from advocates of various theories concerning brain and mind/mental connections, including:

- the "brain/mind identity theory": that mental events are but neuronal events, and vice versa
- "psychosocial parallelism": that physical events are caused by physical causes and mental events by mental causes
- "epiphenomenalism": that mental life is nothing but a by-product of brain processes
- "eliminativism": which bluntly rejects that mental events are real in the first place

All these theories of the mind-body relationship not only challenge theologians but also—if shown to be true—fatally defeat commonsense (and necessary) intuitions of the reality of mental life and its effects. In particular, the existence of consciousness poses an urgent question. This is the famous zombie question: Is a being that behaves like the rest of us but has no consciousness a human?

The basic problem with these and some other related theories, into which we cannot delve further here, has to do with "reductionism," that is, that mental capacities are nothing but physical events. Both philosophically and theologically, a strong case can be made against the above-mentioned "identity" theories (that the mental is but the physical). The existence and function of free will is at least to some extent a powerful reason against them. It is also a common-sense conviction that the mental (human choices and determination) are causal; they make the human person do something—and therefore, the human person is held responsible. (Otherwise child molesters, thieves, or murderers could excuse their evil deeds by appealing to their lack of any mental powers.) We also know that alongside this physical base, our contexts—including our culture, human relationships, learning and training, and similar domains—significantly shape our human behavior and mental life. Human behavior is intentional and purposeful and is able to assess the results and conditions.

Still, a question may remain in the doubter's mind. What about "hard" neuroscientific study? Hasn't it finally defeated all illusions of human freedom, that is, the freedom to choose? Aren't our choices ultimately the result of brain events?

Neurosciences Hardly Defeat Human Freedom!

The word is out there that neuroscience has resolved an issue that had so far been reflected on only philosophically and theologically. Some people go so far as to say that current science has made all talk about free will obsolete and wrong: "Free will is an illusion."[17]

So, what exactly is neuroscience saying about volition, freedom, and free will? In the early 1980s, the neuroscientist Benjamin Libet and his colleagues conducted the now classic experiment using EEG (electroencephalography) to measure the brain's electrical activity to study the antecedents of voluntary action, that is, what happens in a brain just before one "chooses" to act voluntarily. Subjects were asked to flex their finger or wrist spontaneously, at their choosing. The result was that some milliseconds before flexing, signals could be discerned in the vertex (the midline of the skull). This basic observation with repeated patterns and refinements led to this highly counterintuitive sequence: brain event, to be followed by the intention to act, resulting in action. In other words, it seems as if it is not the mind (free will) but rather the brain (the physical "mindless" base) that ultimately influences human behavior. Is that so?

Contrary to these artificially designed experiments, philosophers and theologians consider human action and choices in a wider network of influences and factors. Real "action" is part of a large network of factors, including language, social relationships, beliefs and convictions, as well as education and training, including the person's own shaping of their life as a result of the pursuit of the good. Human freedom also entails decisions not to act if there are reasons to do so. Rather than paying attention to fleeting, millisecond-long mental events, in real voluntary action we should speak of a mental *state* that consists of awareness, knowledge, reflection, emotions, imagination, and other mental events—by a fully embodied person, in the network of one's community/communities, life experiences, and so forth. Practicing human life is a lifelong project, and is essentially just that: a *practice*. Human behavior, morality, and the good life are a matter of patient character formation, practicing of virtues, and formation of habits in constant interaction with other people and communities. There are good reasons for men and women, created in the image of God, to assume the freedom to choose and bear its responsibilities.

In sum: As closely as brain and human mind are connected with each other, there is no credible evidence to suggest that human freedom to choose and thus, responsibility, might have been eliminated. If so, what

---

17. Harris, *Free Will*, 5; emphasis removed.

about human freedom and responsibility in relation to God: Would divine foreknowledge and omniscience rule them out?

Divine Foreknowledge and Human Freedom

Is There Room for Genuine Human Choices?

The problem of the possibility and conditions of human freedom arises as soon as one makes the theological claim that all that happens is not only foreknown by God but also divinely determined. St. Augustine, who is well known for emphasizing divine omnipotence, and even "double predestination" (that is, that some are chosen by God for salvation and others to damnation) was confronted by his interlocutor Evodius who wondered "how God can have foreknowledge of everything in the future, and yet we do not sin by necessity." Evodius is stuck between a rock and a hard place because "[it] would be an irreligious and completely insane attack on God's foreknowledge to say that something could happen otherwise than as God foreknew."[18]

In many ways the simplest and most commonsensical solution to our problem is what theologians call the "simple foreknowledge view." Originally devised by the medieval master Thomas Aquinas, it assumes that because God is a "simple" being (that is, there is no composition such as that between essence and existence), God's "act of understanding must be His essence."[19] Since God's knowledge of everything is simple, there is no room for contingency (at least ultimately): if God's knowledge never changes, we must more or less assume divine determinism. Later on, the Reformer Calvin, gleaning from Augustine, advocated a very robust account of divine sovereignty and a thin account of human freedom, thus essentially continuing the Thomistic tradition.

If all this is so, then what about human freedom? Here philosophers have made an important distinction between "incompatibilism," that is, that divine determinism and human freedom are not compatible with each other, and "compatibilism," its opposite, arguing that, yes, they are in fact compatible. Augustinian-Calvinist determinism can only resort to compatibilism although, as far as I understand, how that is possible seems to be left without a sophisticated explanation.

One sixth-century theologian who sought to provide at least some kind of explanation of how the simple foreknowledge view might work

18. Augustine, *On Free Choice*, 3.2.
19. Aquinas, *Systematic Theology*, 1.14.4.

was Boethius. He offered the so-called "eternity solution," which says that because God is timeless (or "eternal"), the question of who/what decides or has decided certain events in a particular human being's life does not arise, for there is no interval between moments of time. Apart from the difficulty with that concept of time (and eternity), there are other theological and logical reasons to reject the eternity view it espouses.

Are There Any Solutions in Sight?

The sixteenth-century Spanish Jesuit Luis de Molina made an innovative proposal that tries to hold in tension divine sovereignty and human freedom. He sought to reconcile two claims long thought to be incompatible, namely, that God is the all-knowing governor of the universe and that individual freedom can prevail only in a universe free of absolute determinism. The Molinist concept of "middle knowledge" holds that God knows (though he has no control over) truths about how any individual would freely choose to act in any situation. Given such knowledge and then creating such a world, God can be truly providential while leaving his creatures genuinely free.

In this way, Molinism goes further than compatibilism, which merely holds together divine determinism and human freedom without explanation. For Molinism seeks to explain *how* God knows the contingent future. Whereas "natural knowledge" is the knowledge of necessary truths (and all logical possibilities), and "free knowledge" encompasses the actual world as it is, "middle knowledge" is the knowledge of the "counterfactuals" of all feasible worlds, that is, what humans might do in any given context. The promise of the proposal is that it makes it possible to be "an incompatibilist about causal determinism and human freedom (in the relevant sense), but a compatibilist about God's omniscience (foreknowledge) and such freedom."[20]

Far from being a resolved issue, even contemporary theologians continue to wrestle with the problem of human freedom and divine foreknowledge. An interesting attempt comes from the movement named "Open Theism" and its "free will" theory. It seeks to reconcile divine foreknowledge and human freedom by seriously redefining foreknowledge. It says that while "omniscient," God can only know those future events that are possible to be known, but not those that are so contingent on human choices (or nature's events) that it does not yet make sense to speak of their knowledge.

---

20. Fischer, "Putting Molinism in Its Place," 209 (not Fischer's own opinion).

The price paid, namely, of compromising—or at least of significantly redefining—divine omnipresence, causes concern to many theologians.

It seems to many that foreknowledge is necessary for God's proper governance (providence) of the world, including foreseeing the future—even though not necessarily in the spirit of Augustinian-Calvinist determinism in which God's foreknowledge secures the future by knowing and *determining* his decrees. In that sense, Molinism is still an appealing option to many theologians. Its "twin pillars" are then a belief in the traditional notion of providence (the idea that everything that happens is "specifically" intended or else permitted by God) and libertarianism, the existence of freedom of the will. That said, not only open theism and other options but also Molinism has faced critique, particularly with regard to the concept of counterfactuals (the complicated philosophical questions that go beyond the level of this primer).

Humanity and Human Nature in Religions' Teachings

The Embodied Ensouled Human Being: The Jewish Vision

As counterintuitive as it may sound at first, particularly in the older portions of the OT, the Jewish idea of the human resembles what we nowadays call materialism, in that they did not have a developed conception of afterlife and that the expectation of God's blessings was focused on earthly matters. Noteworthy is also the liberal borrowing from pagan sources later in OT history, including regarding the preexistence of soul. The Platonic influence reached its zenith in the most well-known ancient philosopher, the first-century AD Philo of Alexandria.

Later in tradition, the eleventh-century Spaniard Solomon Ibn Gabirol (aka Avicebron) creatively engaged the Hellenistic (and also to some extent Islamic) tradition and contributed significantly to understandings of self, soul, and personal identity. His *Fountain of Life* suggests a novel form of "materialism" in which, except for God, all substances, whether spiritual or physical, are composed of matter and form. The human soul (like that of the angels) is a kind of "spiritual matter." Avicebron's hylomorphism is thus a creative combination of Aristotelianism and Platonism; as in Plato, the soul acts something like the captain of the ship. The leading medieval Jewish philosopher, Moses Maimonides, set the tradition firmly in the Aristotelian camp and greatly influenced Christian scholarship. On the one hand, Maimonides built on the Hebrew Scriptures's emphasis on the integral relationship between body and soul, and on the other hand, he continued the religious/philosophical tradition of allowing the soul some kind of independence, particularly after death.

According to the twentieth-century Russian-born American rabbi Samuel S. Cohon, "The Jewish conception of human nature reaches its fullest expression in the belief that man is endowed with a divine soul." The immortal soul (immortality given by God) in the rabbinic teaching is "the life-principle and innermost self of man, [which] reveals and praises God, the abiding principle, the life and mind of the world."[21] Judaism thus operates dualistically, making a distinction between the material and immaterial (spirit, soul) without in any way implying any moral dualism of good and evil, as is the case in Platonism. This is in keeping with the normative rabbinic view of human nature regarding the human person as body and soul, the former linking with the earth, the latter with heaven. While closely related to the body, the soul is also independent and continues after death. That said, Jewish dualism is thoroughly holistic and integral in contrast to ancient pagan dualism(s).

The Christian commentator may note several things about Jewish anthropology. First, the OT anthropology majors in a holistic, embodied view of human nature with due acknowledgment of community and the link with earlier generations. Second, this is in keeping with not only the OT but also the Jewish emphasis on "salvation" in this life, with much less stress than Christian tradition has on future eschatology. Third, like its Christian counterpart, Jewish anthropology was heavily shaped throughout history by influences from philosophical and religious traditions. In sum: it seems to me that a highly integrated hylomorphist account of humanity with the acknowledgment of soul and belief in the resurrection of the body is an important current Jewish view. This laid the foundation for Christian anthropology as well.

The Human Being as Body and Soul: The Islamic Vision

Although the general Islamic view of humanity is realistic, acknowledging many limitations and failures of human nature (Q 4:28; 10:12; 14:34; 16:4; 17:11; 33:72; 70:19; etc.), the particular principle of *fitrah* discussed above elevates the human person to a unique place among the creatures. A number of sayings point to this divinely given status, for example, "Verily We created man in the best of forms" (Q 95:4; also 40:64). Humanity's status also appears in her inviolable dignity and invitation to serve as Allah's viceroy, discussed above.

---

21. Cohon, *Jewish Theology*, 346.

The Qur'anic creation accounts contain several references to humans having been presented to angels before they were created and having been assigned the lofty status of God's viceregents (2:30). God's blessings and providence have been lavished upon humanity (7:10; 31:20; 17:70). The reason why the Qur'an (unlike Hadith) dares not use the Jewish-Christian expression of the image of God is to safeguard the utter transcendence of Allah (42:11). That said, the Qur'an teaches that the Creator is "nearer to [the human] than his jugular vein" (50:16). After all, the Spirit of God has also breathed into the clay-formed human being (15:26–29).

Islamic anthropology is deeply dualistic. The Qur'an and subsequent Islamic theology speak everywhere of the soul as distinct from body. In keeping with Abrahamic faiths, the normative Islamic tradition rejects the eternity and preexistence of the soul.

Aristotle became the guiding philosophical influence in Muslim anthropology. That said, Avicenna (Ibn Sina) and Averroes, the leading medieval scholars, were dualist; body and soul are separate substances, and personality is located in the soul and has total independence from the body. In that sense, they did not follow Aristotelian (and its Christian Thomistic version of) hylomorphism.

The twelfth century, during which a number of Islamic, Jewish, and Greek (Plato, Aristotle) works were translated and disseminated, was a fertile time for interfaith debates about the soul-body problem. Thomas Aquinas and Mulla Sadra, another Muslim authority, were united in criticizing the Neoplatonically based body-soul dualisms in which the body is a mere instrument in the employ of the soul. They advanced a hylomorphic account. Unlike Avicenna, Sadra worked toward a highly integrated body-soul connection.

Generally speaking, current Muslim theology continues affirming traditional body-soul dualism, and only a few individual revisionist scholars have dared to tackle issues such as whether, in light of scientific knowledge, there is a soul. As evident from this brief discussion, basic theological intuitions about humanity are very similar to the Christian tradition; the only major exception has to do with the doctrine of sin and the fall, discussed below.

The Many Hindu Visions of Humanity

Hinduism in general envisions the human being, *jiva*, "the living being" (sometimes also translated as "soul"), in terms of three bodies, namely a physical ("gross") body, a subtle body, and a causal body. The causal body is a kind of "blueprint" that causes the human being to be what it is. The "subtle" body is the "mental" part of human nature with mind, intellect, activity of sense organs, vital energy, and so forth. As long as the human being falsely assumes separate individuality because of *avidya*, "ignorance," and has not yet grasped the insight of the identity of *atman* with Brahman, the subtle body represents continuity in the process of transmigration (meaning that at death the physical body is left behind and decays). To understand this foundational Hindu idea better, recall the distinctive conception of the world and reality: in Hindu cosmology and imagination it is typical to speak of the "appearance" of reality—meaning that the visible world is merely an appearance of the "real" world of the spirit, and thus that ultimately everything is *atman*, that is, Brahman). This of course does not mean that the world therefore does not exist, of course it does, albeit only as appearance. This appearance nature of reality can easily mislead men and women to cling to what is *maya*, transitory and impermanent. In contrast with Abrahamic faiths with their emphasis on embodiment and the importance of historical happenings, Hindu movements consider only the world of the spirit to be real.

In light of the appearance nature of reality, it is understandable that foundational to a Hindu understanding of humanity and human nature is the sharp distinction between the *real* self and the *empirical* self that lives in the phenomenal world. Whereas the latter is made of "stuff" such as earth, water, and light, and includes the "subtle body" of vitality (breath, mind, intelligence), it is not the "real" me, contrary to common intuitions. The real self is the *atman*, the eternal and formless, indeed the Brahman ("Spirit," "God," the Divine). Of course this does not mean that "I" do not exist at all; even appearances, or dreams, or illusions exist in some sense. What the mainline Hindu philosophy is saying is that I do not exist "ultimately" or "really." To grasp this truth is the key to release.

Here we return again to the famous internal divisions among the Vedanta theologies, namely Sankara's strictly non-dualistic *advaita* and Ramanuja's qualified non-dualism. Related to it, Vaishnava traditions, based on the teachings of the Bhagavad Gita, teach the eternity of each individual self: "There was never a time when I [or] you . . . did not exist; nor shall we ever cease to exist in the future" (Bhagavad Gita 2.12). Such sayings are understood to refer to the existence of an infinite number of selves, with no beginning and no end. This interpretation differs from that of *advaita*, according to which only the Absolute Self exists and all other "selves" are but appearances thereof. Not only that but the Vaishnavites also believe that the souls are created by God, the Absolute Soul, and are to serve the Lord (Krishna or similar). In this sense, there is some commonality between how the souls are related to Krishna, the major avatar of Vishnu, and how individuals are related to Christ in Christian tradition. Somewhat similarly, Krishna is both unchanging and changing in nature and considers devotees dear to him. While devotion to Krishna seems to require a continued personal life and some form of embodiment, even the Vaishnava view rejects the idea that the self is to be identified with the material body.

Notwithstanding a wide variety of views among Hindus, it seems to me that Hindu anthropology is deeply dualistic. Consider this summative statement by the late Swami Adiswarananda: "According to Hinduism, man is essentially a soul that uses its body and mind as instruments to gain experience."[22] Part of this teaching is the separation between the apparent and real self as well as the eternity of the "soul." Clearly, these tenets are in deep conflict with all current notions of the natural sciences. Furthermore, it seems that the *advaita* view cannot be reconciled with Abrahamic theistic belief due to its ultimate conflation of the divine and the human (known as pantheism in Abrahamic traditions). Finally, the Christian anthropology that resists extreme body-soul dualism and lifts up the importance of embodiment and sociality is definitely contra any attempt to divide human nature between the apparent and the real, and to consider the bodily only as the temporary "tool" of the eternal spirit.

"No-Soul"—The Buddhist Vision

Three foundational and broad Buddhist principles govern talk about human nature:

- *dukkha*
- interdependent origination
- "no-self"

The first two I have explained in the chapter on creation. Interdependent origination (or causal interdependence), we recall, relates not only to the physical but also to other dimensions of reality, including the human.

Not only humans but everything else is impersonal or selfless (*anatta*, "no-self"). "What we call a 'being,' an 'individual,' or 'I,' according to Buddhist philosophy, is merely a combination of ever-changing physical and mental forces or energies . . . "[23] There is no "self" or "soul" that is permanent. Calling the person a "self" is an elusive, conventional way of

22. Adiswarananda, "Hinduism," para. 5.
23. Rahula, *What the Buddha Taught*, 20.

referring to that fleeting combination of elements. To be liberated from the illusion of being permanent and hence clinging to something requires the "salvific" insight into the true nature of reality (meaning release from samsara, the cycle of rebirths).

How would a Christian respond to the Buddhist teaching of no-soul? Keith Ward rightly notes that "from a theistic viewpoint, it will seem to be false that there is no enduring Self and that there is no permanent and noncontingent reality—for God is precisely such a reality." In that sense, "the whole Buddhist world-view and discipline leads away from theism."[24] Indeed, in the absence of self, it is impossible—at least for the Western mind—to imagine "who" is the one who clings to life due to desire, suffers from the effects of karma, and particularly comes to the enlightening realization (if it ever happens) that the saṃsaric cycle is now overcome. This also has to do with what seems to me a deep and wide difference of orientation between Semitic faiths and Theravada Buddhism, namely, the notion of individuality and the individual's relation to others. Furthermore, it seems impossible to think of ways to affirm the dignity of human personhood if there is nothing "permanent."

It is often assumed that the Buddhist notion of humanity is pessimistic and gloomy. But it is not. Instead, it is realistic. As is well known, Gautama gave a long litany of things in life that are enjoyable and should be enjoyed, from economic security to wealth to happiness on account of living a good life. Indeed, says Rahula, "a true Buddhist is the happiest of beings" because he or she has no fears or anxieties.[25]

What about the Buddhist notion of human nature in terms of body-soul/physical-spiritual distinctions? On the one hand, the Buddhist view of humanity is deeply holistic and resists dualisms. In keeping with Buddhist cosmology's principles of interrelatedness, all "five constituents" that comprise this cosmology interrelate and collaborate. On the other hand, ultimately the spiritual quest moves away from embodiment, and in that sense a perennial dualism is present. What about the soul? Although it is not difficult to establish the usage of the term "soul" in Buddhist thought, it is difficult to determine its meaning in relation to the typical terminology in Abrahamic faiths and Western philosophical traditions.

Having discussed the main topics related to the Christian understanding of humanity as the image of God, including a sympathetic-critical conversation with the sciences and some living faith traditions, it is now time to move on to the second major part of theological anthropology,

24. Ward, *Religion and Revelation*, 166.
25. Rahula, *What the Buddha Taught*, 27.

namely what is wrong with us. Traditionally, this question is known under the nomenclature of sin and fall.

What's Wrong with Us? Sin and "Fall"

Are We Still Obliged to Speak of Sin?

Although the sinfulness of humanity, as Richard Niebuhr succinctly put it, is "one of the best attested and empirically verified facts of human existence,"[26] nowadays even ministers and theologians have a hard time addressing this issue. One reason for the discomfort has to do with the radically changed view of the emergence and evolution of humanity after the entrance of scientific explanations.

That said, notwithstanding many disagreements among the Christian traditions concerning the importance of "fall" and "original sin," there is no denying the simple fact that while "no religious vision has ever esteemed humankind more highly than the Christian vision," no other tradition has also "judged it more severely."[27] In other words, as many challenges as we may have in the third millennium to speak of the "logistics" of what has gone awry and why with humanity, the fact that we are sinners is in no doubt in Christian understanding.

We begin by taking a look at the church's understanding of sin and fall in Bible and history.

What Does the Bible Say about Sin?

The Bible says a great deal about sin—in both testaments. A worthwhile Bible study for a church group would be to explore the richness of biblical terminology for sin in its symbols, metaphors, pictures, stories, and testimonies.

Let me prime the pump with these examples. It is significant that the most typical terms for sin in the OT (*chata*) and NT (*hamartano*) mean something like "missing the mark," that is, not meeting the standard set by God. Another key term could be translated in English as "transgression," implying direct violation of divine commands. Other common designations include rebellion, treachery, perversion, ignorance, error,

---

26. Niebuhr, "Sin," 349.
27. Jewett with Shuster, *Who We Are*, 57.

inattention, restlessness, evil, trouble, and so forth. Even this short listing gives you an idea of the multifaceted notion of sin.

Although the Bible contains no attempt to systematize or organize teaching about sin, the following list highlights some of its basic dimensions portrayed in the biblical narrative:[28]

- Sin as violation of God's law or disobedience
- Sin as breaking the covenant
- Sin as willful and prideful rebellion against God
- Sin as idolatry
- Sin as unbelief
- Sin as selfishness
- Sin as sloth or apathy

Notwithstanding the frequent references to sin, the OT gives little reason for the presence of sin in human life. In fact, even the NT, apart from some well-known Pauline references, is silent about its origins. Although in Pauline theology (recall that Adam and the Genesis narrative are mentioned nowhere in the Gospels) the universality of sin is traced back to Adam (Rom 5:12), Paul does not speak of inheritance of sin in any of the technical senses in which tradition came to speak of it but instead attributes individuals' suffering to their sins.

Eastern Orthodox theology followed that tradition in understanding the example and sin of Adam as representing the whole of humanity instead of linking this notion to the idea of inheritance of sin from generation to generation merely by function of having been born into the human family.

Radically Differing Visions of Sin and Fall in Christian Tradition

Notwithstanding conviction of sinfulness, in various times and various contexts, quite different kinds of interpretations emerged. Importantly, patristic theology (the theology of the first Christian centuries) did not have a developed doctrine of sin other than a deep intuition of the fallen and sinful nature of humanity. Freedom and responsibility were high values to early theologians in a culture plagued with fatalism, the idea that everything happens by fate. In fact, rather than sin and guilt, in that era the redemptive and reconciliatory work of Christ was at the forefront.

---

28 Adapted from Garrett, *Systematic Theology*, 1:455–62.

Among Latin-speaking Christians (the predecessors of the Christian West: Roman Catholics, Protestants, Anglicans, and others, in distinction to the Greek-speaking Orthodox Christians), beginning from the end of the fourth century a clearly defined doctrine of sin and the "logistics" of the fall were hammered out. An impetus came from reaction to Pelagianism, a heretical movement initiated by Pelagius, an allegedly British monk, whose understanding of sin was very thin alongside the confidence in human capacity to live pleasing to God relying on human powers.

St. Augustine was the central theologian even with regard to this doctrine. He emphasized the seriousness of the fall by contrasting it with the alleged perfect blessedness of life in the original paradise, making Adam virtually a perfect being before the fall. Pride, said Augustine, was the reason for the fall, which resulted in "concupiscence" (a strong desire and inclination to sin) and death. Western writers also deemed it necessary to establish in a rigid way the theory of the transmission of sin, and this eventually led to the Augustinian notion of hereditary transmission (that is, just by virtue of having been born into the human family, the infant is already under the influence and guilt of sin). In sum: the fall "from grace" was complete and disastrous—but that is human beings' fault, not God's.

The way Augustine and after him the Christian West explained the logic of the transmission of sin was this: when Adam sinned, we participated in it. The faulty Latin Vulgate translation of Romans 5:12 supported this interpretation; it translated the Greek *eph ho* as "in whom," signaling that we all participate in Adam's guilt. By virtue of sexual intercourse, the sin is transmitted to the next generation, even in the case of baptized parents—an interpretation that the Eastern Greek-speaking church consistently rejected.

Understandably this Augustinian doctrine, though confirmed as the church's official teaching in the Christian West, had a hard time winning the day. Some kind of compromise between it and the mild forms of Pelagianism often became the established opinion at the grassroots level.

It is instructive to note that the Greek-speaking Christian East took a decidedly different route to explain what is wrong with us. It regarded the human person as mortal even before the fall, and hence death *per se* could not be seen as punishment for the fall. Even more, human nature was good by virtue of existing as the image of God, and free will was not destroyed, only impeded, by the fall. Hence, sin was rooted in human freedom. The East followed the Hebrew mindset with no idea of the Christian West's understanding of original sin.

According to Eastern theology, we do not inherit sin but rather its consequences when we sin, its corruption rather than guilt alone. While Eastern theology affirmed the universality of sin, it often described it in terms of woundedness or sickness. As did early tradition, Eastern theology denied that infants were born in sin. Because of freedom of will, a "return" to the state of grace is possible at all times, although after the fall moral and other weaknesses in us abound. The Christian East followed St. Irenaeus (the Western theologian born of Greek parents who wrote in Greek), who had already established the powerful vision of Adam and Eve as yet immature "children" undergoing growth and development toward perfection. That is a drastically different vision of the fall from the Christian West's gloomy picture.

Rather than looking back so much, the Christian East looks into the future, the ultimate goal of perfection (deification, that is, union with God). Furthermore, although the Greek fathers trace sinfulness back to Adam, they do not teach that "we participate in Adam's actual guilt, i.e. his moral culpability, nor [do they] exclude the possibility of men living entirely without sin."[29]

Back to the Christian West and later developments. With some modifications (particularly by Thomas Aquinas), this Augustinian-driven account of the origin and influence of sin became dominant in the Christian West in Catholic, Anglican, and Protestant traditions (with further modifications in each of these theologies). The important Thomistic tweaking, still programmatic in the Catholic Church, notes the difference between "natural" capacities, such as reason and will, and "supernatural" gifts, namely faith, hope, and love. Whereas the former were merely tainted by the fall, the latter can be had only by virtue of divine grace. The fall hence entails privation of original righteousness. This is a less radical account of the effects of the fall than the account in Lutheran and Calvinist traditions, although both depend on Augustine. If possible, Calvin even intensified the Augustinian interpretation, speaking of "natural depravity which we bring, from our mother's womb, though it brings not forth immediately its own fruits, is yet sin before God, and deserves his vengeance."[30]

What about the revisions in modern theology?

How Do We Think of Sin and Fall in Contemporary Theology?

In the aftermath of the Enlightenment and the rise of the critical principle, dramatic intellectual transformations took place. No wonder that for scientific and cultural reasons modern theology rejected a number of traditional beliefs about sin by allying itself with a theistic evolutionary

29. Kelly, *Early Christian Doctrines*, 347–48.
30. Calvin, *Commentary on the Epistle*, 5:12 (n.p.).

view of the development of humanity. Schleiermacher's interpretation is illustrative. For him, rather than a dramatic fall from grace, instead the fall was an event that arrested our God-consciousness and has little or nothing to do with traditional belief in universal sinfulness transmitted from generation to generation. While much closer to normative Christian tradition, neither does the Danish theologian Søren Kierkegaard's identification of despair as the main problem of humanity concur with tradition. Such a despair-focused view of sin can easily be interpreted as nothing more than existential feeling and sadness.

If we consider these thin accounts of sin to say too little about the nature and influences of sin, what might be some guiding principles for theologians in search of a thicker interpretation—yet also with the needed corrective to traditional corollaries? How would theology after the advent of evolutionary theory and a radically changed account of the origins of the cosmos formulate the problem of what is wrong with us?

Only in light of the dignity of humanity by virtue of the *imago Dei* can we meaningfully speak of the fall and sin. That, however, does not mean a return to the idyllic idea of a perfect original state, not only because the biblical narrative does not mandate it but also because it is scientifically untenable. Also, several feminists have wondered, for example, whether making pride the main source of the fall is too male-driven an interpretation and whether it may hide human liabilities more familiar to the female gender, such as dependence, negation of self, and undermining one's own capacity.

While sensitive to these kinds of cultural and scientific changes, theologians should not make sin merely a human issue. For sin, as deeply as it relates to human persons at personal and collective levels, is also a God-ward phenomenon. It is violation against the commands of holy God. In the words of David's penitential Psalm (51:4):

> Against thee [God], thee only, have I sinned,
>   and done that which is evil in thy sight,
> so that thou art justified in thy sentence
>   and blameless in thy judgment.

At the same time, a theology of sin should keep hold of the goodness of human nature as God's creation and so avoid making sin in some sense (a necessary) part of human nature. It does not really take sin to make an authentic human being! Sin is not part of human nature; it is an intrusion. Nor should theology link sin with the natural, beautiful, and good enjoyments of earthly life.

For if sin and judgment of it are somehow being transmitted "naturally"—and even biologically—then humans can hardly be held responsible for their sinful actions. Hence, sin cannot be regarded as a fate that comes upon human beings as an alien power against which they are helpless.

Whatever tactic we choose to try to explain the effects of the fall, it is essential for theology to continue affirming key intuitions of original sin in tradition while correcting its time-bound problematic notions in tradition:

- human beings are sinful before they commit a sinful act notwithstanding the fact, mentioned above, that guilt will be imputed only in light of personal responsibility;
- sin, therefore, is located at a deeper level than any individual act;
- the universality of sin is the presupposition for the universality of redemption in Christ; and
- sinfulness is something bigger than each individual person because humanity forms one family.

To highlight the last point: the traditional and primarily individualized account of sin should be corrected and balanced with communal, structural, social, and relational interpretations, in so doing extending the meaning of sin beyond the personal. Women theologians and others importantly remind us of structural sin's contexts, such as those related to sociopolitical, economic, and gender-related oppression, environmental sins, and many global and local wrongs. Peruvian liberation theologian Gustavo Gutiérrez reminds us that "sin, the breach with God, is not something that occurs only within some intimate sanctuary of the heart. It 'always' translates into interpersonal relationships . . . hence is the ultimate root of all injustice and oppression—as well as of the social confrontations and conflicts of concrete history."[31] For the African American theologian Garth Kasimu Baker-Fletcher, sin "means becoming aware of the ways in which Afrikans [sic] (male and female, rich and poor) are engulfed in a demonic system of whiteness/Euro-domination/oppression that has colonized both their bodies and their innermost thoughts, desires, and feelings."[32]

What about the origins of sin, i.e., the meaning of the fall, in light of current evolutionary scientific explanation?

---

31. Gutiérrez, *Power of the Poor*, 147.
32. Baker-Fletcher, *Xodus*, 86. Baker-Fletcher seems to use "Afrikans" deliberately.

Evolution and the Origins of Sin

Current knowledge of human development clearly conflicts with the traditional view that all humans descended from one couple. It is estimated that a minimum of about 10,000 members are needed for a vibrant human community to begin to sustain itself. What about the idea of the perfect estate, the cornerstone of the traditional idea of original sin? Happily for theologians, a plain reading of Genesis 3 hardly leads to the idea of the perfect state. Nor does the biblical narrative teach that as a result of disobedience, human nature was changed; it merely states that the first humans were banished from the garden.

Long before the emergence of the questions posed by modern science, beginning with the church fathers, biblical expositors have been aware of many problems with the literal understanding of Genesis 2–4, including the fact that while Genesis 2–3 speaks of a couple (Adam and Eve), Genesis 4 refers to a larger population of humans. While traditional exegesis understood Genesis 3 as actual history (etiology), most contemporary scholars consider it in some way to be a description of the state of humanity, perhaps a universal symbol of the whole of humanity and/or history of every person. All these interpretations are in keeping with the name "Adam," which means humanity or human person in general.

One promising way to consider the biblical fall narrative is to take Adam and Eve as representatives of a collective of the "last" hominids in their transition to modern *sapiens* in terms of the capacity to exercise free will and self-consciousness, as well as deeper self-awareness, including a new awareness of God. Perhaps these "first" humans, while becoming aware of God and God's requirements, "more often than not rejected them. One could even imagine that this awareness was particularly clear, uncluttered by the spiritual darkness that eventually clouded the minds of the human race because of its turning away from God."[33] But this does not have to follow tradition in meaning perfect knowledge, nor perfect innocence, let alone immortality. On the contrary, the first humans were subject to temptations, the desire to turn away from the "voice" of the Lord, inclinations they had inherited from their evolutionary past, including vulnerability to all kinds of perversions, violence, abuse, self-centeredness, and the like. Analogous to the way humanity inherits all other traits and capacities in a genetic-cultural matrix, spiritual darkness and bondage, including the associated violence, can be said to be spread throughout generations.

---

33. Collins, "Evolution and Original Sin," 470.

This proposal seems to be in keeping with Paul's teaching in Romans 1, which, unlike chapter 5, has been curiously absent from the discussion. It looks as if 1:18–32 is meant to present Paul's "fall" narrative. Without any theory of how or when, Paul simply states that human persons, who knew God through the divine presence and traces in nature, turned away from following God and thus were given to darkness and perverted behavior.

What about Romans 5:15–19, which seems to assume a literal interpretation of Adam as "one man" (repeated several times)? First, it is clear that Paul (and even Jesus) shared the (then) commonly held beliefs about the biblical narrative, including Adam's historicity. But upholding this common, time-bound notion is not necessarily the same as needing to teach this idea as indispensable to the doctrine. Just think of the doctrine of creation in the Bible; the fact that it assumes ancient cosmology and six days of work is not its primary message to us.

Second, when this passage is placed in the wider context of the Epistle to the Romans, it is clear that "Paul does not *begin* with Adam and move *to* Christ" (emphasis original)[34] and his salvific work, as Peter Enns rightly notes. Hence, the wider context in Romans highlights the sinfulness and plight of humanity in need of salvation rather than being fixated on historical-etiological concerns about Adam.

Third, even if Paul assumes the individuality of Adam, he contrasts Adam with the Last Adam and thus treats both as corporate representatives.

Now, to wrap up this chapter, it is time to engage other faith traditions' views of what's wrong with us, another opportunity for us to learn.

Human Misery in the Vision of Religions

Sin and Fall in Other Abrahamic Traditions

As much as the Semitic faiths share in common, it might come as a surprise to know that they share no unified conception of human misery. Jewish and Muslim theologies insist on human freedom to choose and on responsibility for the choice. That said, all these sister faiths place the discussion of sin in relation to God and, derivatively, in the human domain. All of them, though in somewhat different ways, consider the "origin" of sinfulness in humanity's deviation from the Creator. Not surprisingly, all three scriptural traditions therefore share the common narrative of the fall and its consequences, even though their interpretations differ quite dramatically from one another. In

---

34. Enns, *Evolution of Adam*, 82.

many ways, Jewish and Muslim interpretations share more in common with each other than Christian interpretations do with them.

Jewish theologians rightly acknowledge that in the Genesis 3 story there is "no doctrine of the fall of the race through Adam, of the moral corruption of human nature, or of the hereditary transmission of the sinful bias."[35] Adam plays no role in the rest of the OT story. Jewish tradition also rejects his immortality before the fall.

Instead of original sin, the Jewish (rabbinic) tradition speaks of two tendencies or urges in every human being, namely, *yetzer ha tov* and *yetzer ha ra'*, urges for good and for evil, respectively. Even though the "inclination" to evil in itself is not evil, it is a matter of which of the two is the guiding force in life. Hence, the main term for repentance from evil is *teshuvav*, literally [to] turn. Every human being is engaged in the constant fight between the two urges.

This is not to undermine the seriousness of the sinful tendency. Just think of how radically Genesis speaks of the wide diffusion of moral evil (4; 6:5–12; 8:21; 9:20–27; 11:1–9). According to the biblical testimonies, human wickedness is great, and even the imaginations of the heart are evil (Gen 6:5; 8:21). In other words, the evil urge is present at birth. But each person is responsible for sinful behavior; such responsibility is not inherited. Although the evil inclination plagues the human person, it does not rob the person of all moral integrity, nor cause lostness (as in Christian tradition). It is of utmost importance for Judaism to affirm human nature's freedom from depravity and innate evil, despite its serious inclination toward evil. Second Baruch (19:3; 48:42–47; 54:15, 19; 59:2) teaches that even after Adam's sin that brought about death, each new generation has to choose its own path.

Both Jewish and Christian traditional ways of reading the Genesis narrative have undergone radical revisions as a result of the scientific advances concerning human evolution. At the same time, for the continuing dialogue to be meaningful, we need to acknowledge the differences between *theological* interpretations of the effects and the "source" of human sinfulness.

The Islamic tradition never envisioned Adam and Eve in terms of perfect paradise imagery as in Christian tradition. Its account of humanity is realistic, as illustrated in Qur'an 95:4–6: "Verily We created man in the best of forms. Then, We reduced him to the lowest of the low, except those who believe and perform righteous deeds, for they shall have an unfailing reward." In a number of places the Qur'an speaks of weaknesses, frailties, and liabilities of humanity (4:28; 10:12; 14:34; 16:4; 17:11; 33:72; 70:19;

---

35. Cohon, *Essays in Jewish Theology*, 220.

96:6; 103:2). That said, according to mainline Muslim teaching, human nature is, generally speaking, good—or, at least, it is not sinful and corrupted as in Christian teaching.

Although Islamic tradition, similarly to others, has had internal negotiations particularly with regard to the presence (or lack) of evil inclinations, the normal Islamic theology assumes a more or less neutral view that takes the beginning of human life as a blank slate, thus emphasizing the role of free will—not unlike Christian Pelagianism.

That the Qur'an does not acknowledge the doctrine of original sin or the idea of moral depravity at birth does not mean that the concept of the "fall" is not part of the Muslim tradition. The fall narrative can of course be found in the Qur'an—indeed, in three related narratives. But its implications (like Judaism's) are different from those of Christian theology. In the (chronologically) earliest narrative (20:115-27), after Adam became forgetful of the covenant, God invited all angels to prostrate themselves before him, and they did—all except for Satan (named Iblis), who then promised to take Adam and Eve to the tree of immortality and knowledge. They ate the fruit, became ashamed, and tried covering themselves with leaves. "And Adam disobeyed his Lord and so he erred" (v. 121). God called Adam again and advised him to leave the garden that had now become an "enemy" (obviously because Satan was said to be there, v. 117). God promised to guide the human, or else blindness would follow for the one who previously was able to see. The punishment of blindness would be revealed on the day of resurrection, and even more severe forms of punishment might follow. The (chronologically) later account in 2:30-38 repeats the Genesis 3 story very closely, with only a few significant deviations. The third major passage, 7:10-25, speaks of the disobedient nature of Adam in starker terms and also mentions Adam and Eve's exit from the garden in more definitive terms (v. 27). Furthermore, all the accounts speak of enmity and distress as a result of the disobedience for which Adam himself (rather than Satan or Eve) is mainly responsible (albeit tempted and lured by Satan).

What is totally missing in Islamic theology of sin is the idea of transmission of "original sin" from one generation to another and its punitive effect on one's progeny. Adam himself (along with Eve and Satan) is blamed for disobedience, not later generations. Importantly, unlike the Christian tradition, the Qur'anic narrative does not link the fall with lostness.

The Human Condition According to the Asiatic Faiths

I begin with Buddhism, in which Gautama once used the simile of cloth to illustrate the difference between the pure mind and the defiled mind. The impure cloth absorbs all bad into its fabric, the result of which is "an unhappy destination [in a future existence]," whereas a happy future awaits the pure minded (Majjhima Nikaya 7).[36] Particularly dangerous, so Buddha teaches, is the appeal of sensuality in its many forms (Majjhima Nikaya 13).[37] With right knowledge and true effort, one can however attain purification from all defilement. Even though the devotee considers the example of the Buddha, finds teaching in Dhamma, and has the community of *sangha*, the person is their own savior.

Following the *dukkha* principle, there is the persistent force of craving (*tanha*), which not only clings to life in general but is also accompanied with greed, hatred, and delusion. Although that craving and passion may be intense, behind the human misery (*dukkha*) is the yearning to cling to what is merely fleeting, decaying, impermanent. That is the main problem for humans.

Whence this (evil) craving? As with all other topics, Buddha declined to speculate, and instead focused on defeating such evil cravings with the help of moral pursuit and right insight. (That there are mythical stories of the origins of craving in the Pali Canon does not change the main orientation theologically.) From the Christian perspective, the only understanding these two traditions have in common is of the universal human condition as something requiring liberation, insight, or salvation.

Moving to the Hindu world: the beginning point for the generic consideration of "sin"—human misery—is the notion of dharma. Dharma represents the positive standard against which all deviations must be compared. It refers to one's "duty," the correct way of life, and regards all activities and spheres of life. Its opposite is *adharma*. Somewhat similarly to Buddhism, Hindu traditions have developed detailed lists of vices to avoid, including delusion, greed, and anger, the roots of all vices.

Not unlike most religious traditions, Hinduism makes a distinction between greater and lesser sins. The most grievous offense is the killing of Brahmin, which is unforgivable and prompts the death penalty. Other examples of a great sin include drinking intoxicating beverages and stealing. In principle, all great sins are unpardonable, with no possibility for atonement.

---

36. The title of this section of the Majjhima Nikaya is "Vatthumpama Sutta: The Simile of the Cloth."

37. The title of this section of the Majjhima Nikaya is "Maha-dukkhakkhandha Sutta: The Great Mass of Stress."

For lesser sins, penance and atonement may be available. In keeping with the caste system, killing a person of a lower caste might be a less severe crime than slaughtering a cow! Although there is some commonality with the Abrahamic faiths' conception of sin, the difference is also deep. Whereas sin is ultimately transgression against God, *adharma* is basically a deviation from the "impersonal" law of the cosmos known as reality.

Adharma is appropriately considered in the wider context of the Hindu philosophy of human "bondage" to *avidya* or "ignorance." Ignorance makes one cling to *maya*, "fiction," and thus makes one subject to the effects of karma, leading one to be reborn over and over again. Only with the removal of this "ignorance" can the soul's essential nature as pure spirit be restored.

Living faith traditions not only envision human misery and liberation from it but also imagine what constitutes a good life. Let's call it human flourishing and pick up the conversation begun in chapter 3 on the flourishing of nature.

Human Flourishing—and Suffering— in Theological Perspective

The Beauty and Ugliness of Flourishing Human Life

We human beings live our lives in the quotidian, the routines of the everyday life. To this quotidian life belong various kinds of hurdles, riddles, and unresolved problems. Part of our creaturely, finite life also entails physical limitations, the most dramatic of which is the ultimate disintegration of our bodies over the years.

Likewise, to human life belong sickness and disability, none of which takes away from human dignity and value. This is because humanity's status as the image of God in terms of being related to God saves theology from anchoring human dignity in the possession of a quality or commodity. One's relation to the Creator is not affected in the least by one's disabilities, not even intellectual ones. Even if the disabled person is not able to relate to God due to intellectual or emotional deficits, God is able to relate to him or her.

In our contemporary fast-paced society, health easily becomes an idol, or at least idealized; just consider the World Health Organization's definition of health as "a state of complete physical, mental and social well-being and not merely the absence of disease or infirmity."[38] Secular definitions

---

38. From the preamble to the Constitution of the World Health Organization as adopted by the International Health Conference, New York, June 19–July 22, 1946

consider health and human flourishing in terms of functionality—meaning that the opposite of health is "dysfunction." Theologically we must resist this kind of attitude because, "Only what can stand up to both health *and* sickness, and ultimately to living *and* dying, can count as a valid definition of what it means to be human" (emphasis original).[39] This is of course not to deny that a healthy life is preferred to a sick one, nor is it a superficial way to glorify suffering. It is simply a *theo*logically driven way to save life from standards external to created life in the kind of finite world in which God has placed us. (Nor is this to thwart the promise of healing that was part of Jesus's ministry and mandate to his followers, an important theological topic to be studied in detail in chapter 8 on salvation.)

A theology of human flourishing entails a proper theology of disability, a topic notoriously difficult for all religious traditions and cultures to consider well. Notwithstanding some exceptions, into the twentieth century, prejudices, omissions, and negative attitudes prevailed. Hence, an essential task for contemporary theology is to correct and redirect these attitudes toward a "redemptive theology of disability."[40] A related new challenge to Christian churches, as well as to other faith traditions, is to stand for and unwaveringly affirm the full humanity and dignity of HIV/AIDS patients, a problem easily forgotten now that some modest medical advances are in use and development.

Human flourishing at the personal and communal level can only happen fully in tandem with efforts toward equality, justice, and liberation of all. Let us begin by looking at resources in other faiths. How do such resources promote liberation, or do they?

Are Religions Helpful in the Work toward Liberation?

The three Abrahamic traditions share not only the idea of the inviolable dignity of human nature because of humans' relation to God, but also the equality of both sexes and all races. The fact these traditions have not always upheld these ideals—and more often than not, have acted quite explicitly contrary to these beliefs—does not nullify this foundational belief.

While the Qur'an does not recognize the historically later concept of "race," it affirms the equality of all, albeit using different terminology: "And of His signs is the creation of the heavens and the earth and the differences

---

(Official Records of the World Health Organization, no. 2, 100), entered into force on April 7, 1948.

39. Moltmann, *God in Creation*, 273.
40. Yong, *Theology and Down Syndrome*, 42.

of your tongues and your colours. Surely in that there are signs for all peoples" (30:22; similarly also 49:13). The term "sign" here speaks of creation as pointing to God, as discussed above. No wonder all humanity shares the same divine destiny (4:124). Even gender does not count as a criterion of superiority. In Islam, women are as human as men. They are not evaluated on the basis of their gender, but on the basis of their faith and character. That said, authoritative Islamic tradition also includes well-known teachings that contradict these Qur'anic teachings and are used as bases for the submission of women. It is the task of prophetic Muslim theology to negotiate this tension for the sake of liberation.

In Buddhist faith, there is a deeply entrenched irony with regard to its liberative potential. On the one hand, comparable to the Judeo-Christian Ten Commandments and Jesus's Sermon on the Mount, Buddhism lists its key ethical principles and actions—the Eight-Fold Path—at the center of its faith. On the other hand, particularly Theravada's nontheistic human-centered view of salvation and the principle of kamma ([karma] according to which one reaps what one has sown and others should not be quick to interfere) clearly point toward isolationism rather than social activism. A related ambiguity about the tradition is that although Gautama was by and large a pacifist, the Buddhist category of soldiers emerged claiming that true detachment (the main aim of all Buddhist practices) had freed them to fight without any anxiety about either their own lives or the lives of others. As in other faith traditions, so in some Buddhist traditions attempts to rediscover and creatively reinterpret tradition to fund work for liberation have emerged in modern times.

In India, the divinely sanctioned caste system (notwithstanding its official abolition in the twentieth century) constitutes a major challenge to Hinduism's liberative potential, particularly because of its violent and unjust exclusion of masses of people. The caste system goes back to the hierarchical division of society into four classes (*varna*)[41] based on Eternal Dharma as taught in the Scriptures. Below the four classes (with their innumerable subclasses) is the bottom caste, the "Untouchables," known by the self-designation of the Dalit, which means the "oppressed, the ground down." Since it is allegedly divinely sanctioned, the caste system is essentially a *theological problem*. Notwithstanding some important reform efforts that began in the nineteenth century, the structures of inequality profoundly shape the life of Hindus living in India and some related areas.

---

41. The four classes are Brahmans, Kshatriyas, Vaishyas, and Shudras. Etymologically referring to "color," *varna* was related to different skin colors.

What capacity does Christian theology have to resist dehumanization and related attacks against the value of human life?

Christian Resources toward Equity, Justice, and Fairness

Human history is full of examples of desecration of human life, too many to begin to list—and the most horrific ones in the modern world are in atheistic societies from China to the former Soviet Union and beyond, as well as in "Christian" nations such as (Nazi) Germany. Yet dehumanization refers not only to genocide and other such horrific crimes; it can also refer to ethnicity, race, and immigration. Dehumanization takes many forms; it often likens people to animals in pejorative ways. It may present women (or children or even men) as mere sexual objects in pornography and commercials.

Judeo-Christian theological tradition stands firmly against all dehumanization and makes every effort to reclaim the immense value of each human being created in the image of God. Few Christians are aware that leading patristic teachers built on the scriptural traditions to find a theological basis for affirming the equality of all human beings, created in the image of God. They established freedom of religion on the same basis. This was quite unheard of at the time. Beyond that, even prior to the establishment of Christendom in the fourth century when the church became officially ratified and supported by the state, the church also stood against war, abortion, and infanticide, as well as torment, killing, and shedding of blood (like in the gladiatorial arenas). Although this biblically based vision was seriously frustrated by Christendom and its grab for earthly power, even during the darkest times there were faithful witnesses. In that light, modern critics who have expressed deep doubts about Christianity's capacity to uphold human dignity are mistaken. At the same time, Judeo-Christian tradition insists that no amount of humiliation, torture, blaming, degradation, or other inhumane treatment can remove the humanity of a human being. Based on God's work of creation, the dignity remains, whatever.

In our complex world, theology continues to remind us that human dignity based on the image of God allows no separation due to race or skin color. All human races share a common origin. Racial differences are minute and form no basis for ranking people groups. The theological grounding of human dignity also critiques and resists ethnocentrism—the belief in the supremacy and unique value of one's own group. Racism builds on ethnocentrism and is often coupled with violence and harassment. When coupled with colonialism and slavery, as has happened with blacks and the First Nations of America, among others, racism means making human beings a commodity, as illustrated particularly horribly in the apartheid system of South Africa. In South Korea the *minjung*, the "masses," were treated not only as nameless and faceless but also as persons without rights and dignity. In India, the Dalit similarly have been the objects of harsh racist and dehumanizing actions. And so forth.

Theology's response to all forms of racism, whether explicit or subtle, is an unwavering *no*. For the human being, having been created in the image of God, racist attitudes toward another person or group is a twofold sin: first in that the perpetrator commits a sin against another human being, and second in that the perpetrator arrogantly denies the permanent value of the Creator's work of humanity. Furthermore, by being racist the perpetrator is dividing one united humanity into two classes, those who are fully human, and those who are only partially human.

What about Violence and War?

Do Religions Really Incite Conflicts?

Even a cursory look at the statistics makes for sorrowful reading concerning the pervasiveness of violence, including toward children, youth, women, and other particularly vulnerable persons. Although faith in God *per se* is not a cause of violence (as discussed in chapter 2), there is no denying that violent acts are often prompted by religious motifs.

The greatest challenge to all Abrahamic faiths in this regard is the concept of holy war. In Judaism, holy war has important limits: war must be carried out as ordered by and meant for the glory of Yahweh, and victory is understood to be won not by human force of arms but rather by the power of Yahweh. Very problematic is the concept of *herem*, total annihilation of enemies and their goods (the Amalekites being the prime example in the OT). Whereas current liberal Jews consider *herem* to be merely a theological principle implying total devotion to God, religious Zionists apply the principle to Palestinians and other nearby Arabs. Similar to Christian hermeneutics, mainstream Jewish scholarship considers this a matter of development of revelation in Scripture. In marked contrast to the OT, the Talmud notably by and large supports peace and active peacemaking, without, however, advocating pacifism.

For Islam, the key violence-related challenges are not only holy war but also the way in which *jihad* is interpreted, whether as "the greater jihad" (a personal struggle over spiritual obstacles and temptations) or as "lesser jihad" (a call to a holy war). Like the OT, the Qur'an sets out fairly unambiguous rules for just war, including holy war:

- after seeking spiritual guidance from Allah, war should be resorted to only as the last means;
- *jihad* should be led by an imam or at least a Muslim leader; and
- the enemies should be given an opportunity to accept Islam first—or if they are followers of another Abrahamic faith, merely Islamic political rule with a special tax and *zakat* or almsgiving.

A number of diverse contemporary Muslim reformers have spoken up on behalf of the nonviolent way. Similarly, some revisionist scholars and clergymen have advocated for a pluralistic, tolerant, and democratic Islamic theory of society.

To an outsider, Hinduism offers a highly complicated case with regard to violence. Well known is the term *ahimsa* ("noninjury," "nonviolence"). As in other traditions, the scriptural texts exhibit a confused approach to violence, both condoning and restricting it. What seems to be clear is that war is deeply embedded in the Hindu system, as one of the four main castes of people consists of soldiers. It is the dharma of the Kshatriya, the soldiers, to carry on with that profession. Indeed, in the most famous scriptural Hindu epic (Bhagavad Gita), Arjuna consults Krishna, one of the many avatars of Vishnu, about whether he should refrain from fighting in a battle against the group that includes his relatives. Arjuna is told he should fight because he is a soldier, and failing to do so would mean failing the dharma. From a Christian perspective, all arguments in favor of violence are deeply problematic, notwithstanding the presence of the "just war" concept.

Not only is the popular picture of Buddhism as a peaceful and pacifist religion unnuanced, but Buddhist history knows the use of violence. Even more, some of its key concepts, such as karma and rebirth, have been used to legitimate violence—the former in terms of justifying all kinds of diseases and ills as "judgment," and the latter as a way of helping ease an evil person's karmic effects by ending life. The main historical figure, King Asoka of the third century BCE, who was instrumental in the early spread of the religion, helped convert masses as part of his military conquests, a project similar to Christian Crusades. In the contemporary world, Buddhist nationalisms and fundamentalisms (similarly to Hindu and Muslim movements) are well known among scholars. In other words, regrettably, even the followers of the Lotus flower have resorted to violence, including even His Holiness the Dalai Lama, who earlier in his career approved the use of violence against the true enemies of the people.

HUMANITY

What about a Christian take on violence?

Christian Faith Has the Potential to Defeat Violence and Cruelty

Since this important question about what Christianity says about violence is discussed in this book in relation to a number of Christian doctrines— God (Chap. 2), the cross and atonement (Chap. 6), eschatological judgment (Chap.10), and the church's peace-building efforts (Chap. 9)— a brief statement suffices here.

In the Christian worldview, neither the world nor faith in God is based on violence but rather on love and hospitality. This can be seen even in the Judeo-Christian creation stories in which the Creator God is not fighting other deities or powers, but rather brings about the world out of sheer love. Theology of creation based on the divine pronouncement of the goodness of creation (Gen 1:31) refuses to ontologize violence, war, and conflict, that is, it refuses to make violence a necessary part.

Acting on the basis of hospitality rather than violence, Christians should therefore be guided by the spirit of openness, inclusion, and welcoming the other. They can either "embrace"—receive the other with outstretched arms—or "exclude," go with these evil dispositions and acts, and be unwilling to make space for the other.[42] The will to embrace is based on and derives from the self-donation of the triune God that reaches its zenith on the cross.

Yet another arena of human flourishing has to do with work, economics, and finances—particularly in the globalized world.

Whether Theology Has Anything to Say about Work, Economy, and Migration

Work as Gift and Challenge

While theologians have devoted numerous books and studies to matters such as the sacraments, which take place during a short session on Sunday, only a handful of studies have been devoted to work, which occupies men and women throughout the week. Related issues such as the effects of globalization and global markets, the growing gulf between the haves and the have-nots, increasing migration, and new forms of slavery likewise call for theological reflection.

---

42. Volf, *Exclusion and Embrace*, 30.

Why do we work? Is it merely an effect of the fall (Gen 3:17–19)? Or is it a main way to achieve human happiness, as classical economic theory surmised (Adam Smith)? Or, perhaps, as the Reformers taught us, work is a Christian vocation. Be that as it may, Christian theology is both realistic (Gen 3) and appreciative, unlike the depreciating attitude prevalent in the ancient world. Early theology made work respectable (often referring to Adam's example in paradise; Gen 2:15). On the basis of biblical injunctions (1 Thess 4:11; 2 Thess 3:10), various writers—and the church—affirmed the necessity of working. Often they connected it with the doctrine of sanctification and a belief that new life in Christ would manifest its fruit in everyday labor and lifestyle.

Miroslav Volf's important study *Work in the Spirit* reminds us that if work is related to the divine purpose of creation that points to new creation, then work gains its ultimate meaning from the anticipation of God's new future. While judged, creation will not be fully annihilated with the coming of God's new creation, but rather will be preserved and brought to perfection. That affirms the goodness and intrinsic value of human work as part of the divine "cultural" mandate. Human work is thus a form of cooperation with the Creator (Gen 1:26–27).[43]

At the same time, we should not idealize work. It is appropriate to consider this essential human theme through a theological lens. Theologians also do well to recall the harsh, complicated, and tiring circumstances and conditions under which work is often done—along with the rest of our lives in its daily ordinariness.

In Search of Equity and Fairness in Economy and Opportunities

What about the evil economic and political structures that plague and oppress men and women, especially the poor and marginalized? Or "culture industries" that promote consumption, backed by massive advertising and marketing? Do theologians have any theological insights on those?

From a theological point of view, theologians and believers in general widely support the following three conditions concerning the minimum set of conditions for a fair economic system:

- freedom and dignity of individuals: our value is not measured by our work or possessions;
- satisfaction of the basic needs of all people, with special reference to the weak: a fair society makes every effort to make sure that the

---

43. Volf, *Work in the Spirit*, 76–102.

- protection and flourishing of nature: as important as effectiveness of production may be for the rapidly growing global population, neglecting the needs of the environment can only result in utter disaster.

These conditions are based on creation theology's stewardship principle, the inviolability of each human person as the image of God, and the communion of human persons with the rest of creation, as well as on the greatest commandment, namely to love the neighbor as one loves oneself. Whereas they do not dictate details of economic systems or planning, they do guide the thinking and work of Christians in charge.

Rather than the hegemony of desires in a consumption society, theology recommends "Sabbath Economics: The Theology of Enough."[44] Rather than glorifying abundance, Jesus's "downward economic mobility" is the guide: "Apparently unemployed, he seems to have been sustained by the generosity of others (Luke 8:3), homeless, having 'nowhere to lay his head' (Matt 8:20; par. Luke 9:58)."[45] Less is more in economics and finances!

A Christian response to economic matters might also be framed as an "economy of grace."[46] Despite the many similarities between the market system and Christian ethics, such as the value of work and industry, personal and communal responsibility, as well as demand for fairness, there are a number of differences, such as competition, greed, and maximization of foreign profit. While both views of economy understand the human being as a creature of desire, "Christian anthropology imagines the end of the human being as praise of God; the market system views the end of the human being as maximized utility." Whereas the market calls for unending pursuit of the satisfaction of desire, in the Christian vision, true "enjoyment" can only be had in God and "in participation in the abundance of God's communion through God's grace."[47] Whereas the market system constantly creates new desires, theology knows that only in relationship with God and the neighbor can fulfillment be found.

Finally, faithfully acknowledging their debt to the Creator, the church is supposed to stand on the side of those who are oppressed and marginalized—not only to feed the hungry and offer a cup of water to the thirsty

---

44. Browning, "Sabbath Reflections," n.p.
45. Kelsey, *Eccentric Existence*, 1:629.
46. Meeks, "Economy of Grace," 196–214.
47. Meeks, "Economy of Grace," 205.

individual, but also to stand up against injustice systemically. The discussion of ecclesiology (chapter 9) will deepen this topic.

Migrants, Slaves, and Other Displaced Persons Are Under the Special Care of God

One surprising phenomenon in the contemporary world is the return of the nomadic lifestyle, long known throughout history, including in biblical times. Yet the sociologist Zygmunt Bauman famously distinguished between "tourists" and "vagabonds." Whereas the former travel because they can, the latter are on the move because they don't have a choice. Vagabonds are useless to global markets, as they don't make good consumers; they are the outcasts, the marginalized, but they form the majority of the world and are growing rapidly.[48] In this "new world" where entire masses are "disposable people,"[49] slavery has not been eradicated. Part of the wider slavery problem is the increase in labor and sex trafficking, which includes children and the underaged, and a high number of female victims.

The victims of economically and politically forced migration and all forms of slavery and trafficking not only lack human value but even minimal living conditions—and almost all of them are landless. For the typical person in the contemporary Global North, landlessness may not sound like a problem because even land is made a commodity. However, land is a deeply personal, communal, cultural, and religious issue. It has to do with identity, belonging, and self-worth.

Do you know that half of the over 200 million migrants in the world are Christians, and that a number of them suffer from other forms of dehumanization as well? Of course that is not the only reason to act, but that alone should suffice. Christian theology's continuing upholding of the dignity and equality of all human beings created in the image of God loses credibility if the most vulnerable and marginalized are not on its radar screen. There is also an opportunity for interfaith collaboration. Much promise can be found in the emerging ecumenical field of migrant theologies and initiatives.

---

48. Bauman, *Globalization*, chap. 4.
49. Bales, *Disposable People*.

5

Christology

Why Do We Need Jesus?

Introduction: In Search of the "Real" Jesus Christ!

Who Is Jesus Christ and What Has He Done for Us?

CHRISTOLOGY, THE STUDY OF the doctrine of Jesus Christ, has long been divided into two interrelated parts, namely the "person" of Christ, i.e., who he is, and the "work" of Christ, i.e., what his salvific achievement for us is. While his personhood and work cannot be clearly separated, this distinction does help us get our minds around this wide and comprehensive theological topic. Whereas this current chapter focuses on his personhood, the following chapter highlights the main teachings about the work of salvation, traditionally considered under the heading "atonement."

Biblical testimonies and later theological wisdom remind us that the usual way we get to know who Christ is, is after we have encountered and come to know Jesus personally and have received gifts of salvation or healing from him. Think of the incident at the beginning of the fifth chapter of the Gospel of John. The paralyzed man came to "know" Jesus only through his salvific works of healing and forgiveness; yet even without knowing much about Jesus, he nonetheless went out to proclaim good news about him (v. 15). Not for nothing, Philip Melanchton, Luther's right hand in the Reformation, stated: "to know Christ is to know his benefits."[1]

While the study and discussion of Christology has occupied church teachers and leaders from the beginning of the theology's history—just think

---

1. Melanchthon, *Loci Communas Theologici*, 21.

of the many fine-tuned debates resolved at ecumenical councils of the first centuries—a dramatic shift happened with the eighteenth-century Enlightenment. Given the rise of the critical principle of modernity, it comes as no surprise that the "foundations" of Christology also came under critical scrutiny. Classical tenets of faith, including Christ's preexistence, virginal conception, miraculous works, salvific work of the cross, resurrection from the dead, and ascension were either radically revised or outright rejected. While of course the masses of the faithful and most ministers continued affirming the faith of the church, the Enlightenment criticism slowly gained more strongholds, particularly in the academic world.

In the aftermath of the Enlightenment, a typical way of identifying approaches to the study of Christology came to be called "From Above" and "From Below." Whereas the former, typical of earlier tradition, began its study of Christology by considering the lofty titles and status given to Jesus Christ in the biblical testimonies, titles such as the Son of God and Savior, the latter approached Jesus from the ground up, so to speak, by investigating carefully all the historical evidence and documentation to ensure the validity of the basis of faith. Whereas modern critical scholarship naturally prioritized the From Below "method" that focused on the earthly Jesus of Nazareth, traditionally oriented scholarship took the From Above approach as its basis. That said, the implications of these methodological choices are more complex than that. Among the critical From Below advocates there were some who ended up affirming what can be called "high Christology," the endorsement of (at least most) of the tenets of classical Christology, such as Christ's deity and resurrection. The late Pannenberg is a prime example.

Which method is the correct or the preferred one? Common sense tells us that the distinction between the two approaches is not either/or but rather both/and; they are clearly complementary. The obvious danger of the From Above view, divorced from the history of Jesus, is the violation of the biblical insistence on Jesus, the human person, as the way to the knowledge of God (John 14:6). The danger of a one-sided From Below approach is that it can at best reveal an interesting religious teacher, but one without any theological significance. The famous Quest of the Historical Jesus project that started in the early nineteenth century and has been followed since with many new quests represents the culmination of this development. The whole project of the Quest(s) is to scrutinize and critically filter all available historical documentation about Jesus of Nazareth.[2]

---

2. For overviews of the pre-twentieth and twentieth century quests, see respectively parts 1 and 2 of Dickson, "Quest for the Historical Jesus."

In most of the recent study of Christology, something very important has been rediscovered, thanks to it delving more deeply into cultural and religious history: namely Jesus's own historical and religious background, that is, Jewish faith and Jewish culture. It is almost embarrassing how little attention was paid to this crucial context of Christology in the past. This divested theology of an integrally Jewish messianic dimension. Fortunately, contemporary Jesus research conducted by biblical scholars has shown remarkable interest in the Jewishness of Jesus. Among theologians, a good example is Jürgen Moltmann's subtitle for his acclaimed Christology monograph—*Christology in Messianic Dimensions*—in which he discusses in detail "Jewish messianology."[3]

"Jesus Christ on the Way"

Alongside the interest in the Jewishness of Jesus, we can learn something else exciting from Moltmann's *The Way of Jesus Christ*. His discussion of Christological topics follows Jesus Christ "in the forward movement of God's history with the world,"[4] by considering carefully the major "moves" on the Messiah's road, from his birth, to earthly ministry, to cross, to resurrection, to current cosmic role, to the return of Christ. This is different from the traditional way of outlining the discussion, which typically moves from one dogmatic topic to another—the divinity, humanity, and two natures of Christ, for example. While there is absolutely nothing wrong with the way the tradition structured the conversation, by its very nature the Christology "on the way" is closer to the dynamic biblical Christology, based as it is on the gospel story. In the Gospels of the NT, we have no fewer than four iterations of the narrative about Jesus on the way!

Understandably, liberation Christologies and Christologies from the Global South and elsewhere are drawn to this dynamic approach and its grassroots orientation to the biblical story of Jesus. With good reason, Womanists (Black female theologians) glean from "deeds of the historical Jesus and not the idealized Christ, in keeping with the liberative traditions of the religious community."[5] Not for nothing, the black male theologian James H. Cone critiques the classical Christology of the creeds for neglecting the grounding of the "christological arguments in the concrete history of Jesus of Nazareth," as a result of which too "little is said about the significance of

---

3. Moltmann, *Way of Jesus Christ*, xv.
4. Moltmann, *Way of Jesus Christ*, xiii.
5. Terrell, *Power in the Blood*, 108.

his ministry to the poor as a definition of his person."[6] These are helpful comments as a preface to the study of Christology.

Of course, these new "turns" and emphases do not make contemporary Christology any less interested in the continuing retrieval of the significance and implications of classical topics of the "two-nature" Christology of ancient creeds. Rather, they enrich and make more comprehensive this exciting and foundational Christian topic.

The Plan of the Chapter

The plan of this chapter is as follows: After a careful look at the diverse and rich NT presentation of Jesus Christ, his life and ministry of teaching, preaching, healing, exorcism, and reaching out to the marginalized, a guided tour across some exciting global and contextual interpretation of Christology follows.

Following this, we will delve into some details of the many historical debates and disputes about key issues in Christology, both those of early centuries, which resulted in the hammering out of creedal statements, and the radical revisions of the Enlightenment. For the sake of a proper contemporary (to us) understanding of who Jesus Christ is, these historical debates are of much more than antiquarian interest.

The next hefty section is one of the more demanding—but also rewarding—portions of the book as we tackle almost all of the church's central doctrinal teachings related to Jesus Christ, including his preexistence, virginal conception, incarnation (and how to see Christ as fully human and fully divine), his sinlessness, as well as his resurrection. It is a tall order but it is a task certainly worth our time and energy.

The final two sections of the chapter concern the urgent issue of religious pluralism. They first consider various Christian approaches to the diversity of faiths, and then delve into four living faiths' conceptions of Jesus.

---

6. Cone, *God of the Oppressed*, 107.

How Rich and Diverse the Biblical Narratives of Christology Are!

The Prism of the Gospels' Testimonies to Christ[7]

As you might expect, the Bible itself contains no systematic theological or doctrinal explanation of Jesus the Christ. Instead, there are a number of testimonies, stories, witness reports, metaphors, and other quite open-ended and diverse narratives. Importantly, the teachings of Jesus recorded in the NT come to us in the form of parables, stories drawn from everyday life, and occasional lessons; his salvific, liberative, and miraculous deeds of course also convey invaluable lessons.

An indication of the diversity and richness of the NT testimonies is the existence of several complementary silhouettes of Christ. Instead of one summary story, there are no less than four Gospel narratives. Consider these well-known emphases in the narrative of the four Gospels:

- The Suffering Servant in Mark
- The King of the Jews in Matthew
- The Friend of All in Luke
- The Word of Life in John

The narrative in the Gospel of Mark, routinely taken as the oldest, is fast-paced. It begins with the appearance of John the Baptist, the forerunner of Christ, and climaxes in the fatal encounter between Jesus and the religious and political leaders of Israel. The narrative plot presents Jesus as the Messiah, the Son of God, whose destiny is to suffer, die, rise from the dead, and return as the glorious Son of Man.

Because Matthew's audience is Jewish, his Gospel account opens with the Davidic genealogy. Jesus's infancy narratives (chapters 1–2) not only identify Jesus as the Son of David, they also establish the link with the whole history of Israel going back to generations of forefathers. Everywhere, the Gospel highlights the fulfillment of the OT prophecies and frequently cites Scripture. Central to Matthew's narrative are the five great speeches of Jesus: the Sermon on the Mount (chapters 5–7), the sending of the Twelve (chapter 10), the parables (chapter 13), and speeches on the church (chapter 18) and on eschatology (chapters 24–25).

Whereas Mark is a fast-paced narrative and Matthew a Jewish portrait of Israel's Messiah, "Luke's Gospel has functioned like a warehouse of scenes

---

7 This section borrows liberally from Kärkkäinen, *Christology*, chap. 1.

and stories from which favorites might be drawn, whether in discussions of the virginal conception or of everyday ethics, whether by preachers or theologians or artists."[8] Luke's special concern and interest is for the poor, widows, children, and other marginalized persons.

The first three Gospels in our NT are called "synoptic" Gospels, literally (from the Greek) "looking in the same direction." By contrast, the Gospel of John comes from a different world altogether! Consider these differences: rather than Galilee, in John Judea is the center of Jesus's ministry. Rather than one year, the ministry of Jesus in John seems to last about three years. Furthermore, there are no exorcisms, the number of healings is meager, and the miraculous acts are called "signs," signifying their symbolic importance and spiritual lessons. In contrast to the many found in the Synoptic Gospels, amazingly, there are no parables in John. Instead, John's Jesus delivers seven "I am" oracles, harking back to the OT's "I am" statement of Yahweh in Exodus 3:14. Highly distinctive is also the Gospels's Prologue, in which the Word—Christ—is linked with God and indeed named as God, the Creator and the Light. Many other distinctive features can be found in what is believed to be the youngest Gospel, including the long Farewell Speech(es) in chapters 13 to 17.

And that is to mention only the first part of the NT. What about the diversity and richness of the Pauline letters and other sections? Yet even this brief survey suffices to remind us of how much there is to learn about Jesus the Christ, who is given so many varied titles in the biblical narrative, including Christ (Messiah, from the Hebrew term "Anointed"), Son of God, Son of Man, Lord, Son of David, and Word (from Greek *Logos*).

In light of this rich diversity of the NT teaching of, and testimonies to, Jesus the Christ, let us pause to consider the theological meaning of the focus of the Gospel stories, namely Jesus's earthly life and ministry. A surprise is awaiting us here!

Why Does Jesus's Earthly Ministry Carry So Much Theological Weight for Us?

Surprisingly—and counterintuitively—theology at large has more or less forgotten or marginalized the theological and pastoral significance of Jesus's earthly life and ministry. Even if there are remarks on, say, miracles, their goal has been apologetic rather than theological; that is, they have been used to defend Christian faith and belief in the miraculous against its detractors. The lion's share of discussions in theological books and

---

8 Green, "Luke, Gospel of," 540.

sermons is usually devoted to the events to do with the cross and resurrection. This all happens in the wider context of discussions of Jesus's divinity, humanity, and unity with God.

Why am I raising this issue? Let me refer to Moltmann. In reference to ancient creeds, say the Apostles' Creed, which we recite regularly in liturgical churches, Moltmann asks what is there between "born of the Virgin Mary" and "suffered under Pontius Pilate"? His response: only a comma![9] Why does that matter? Because for the Gospel writers, the "comma" occupied by far the biggest space in their narrative. Consider the first Gospel: After the stories of the virginal conception in chapter 1, Matthew takes until around chapter 26 to tell the story of Jesus's passion, death on the cross, and resurrection. In other words, to the first witnesses to Jesus, the earthly life of Jesus mattered. And so the teachings, healings, exorcisms, pronouncements of forgiveness, table fellowship, and prophetic acts dominate the account.

In light of the creeds' lack of focus on the earthly life and ministry of Jesus, Moltmann suggests an amendment, an addition to the creed. Following the clause: "and born of the virgin Mary," he suggests adding:

> Baptized by John the Baptist,
> filled with the Holy Spirit:
> to preach the kingdom of God to the poor,
> to heal the sick,
> to receive those who have been cast out,
> to revive Israel for the salvation of the nations, and
> to have mercy upon all people.[10]
>
> [to be followed by: "He suffered under Pontius Pilate."]

Imagine how this kind of "addition" would nurture, enrich, and stimulate our spirituality! (I know, of course that the creeds are not up for annual review, nor that Moltmann is really suggesting we do that!)

To highlight the theological importance of Jesus's earthly ministry, let us recall that Jesus initiated his public ministry in the context of the baptism of John the Baptist. By submitting himself to baptism, Jesus identified himself with the covenant people, the ones in need of the baptism of repentance. At the same time, Jesus's baptism can be seen as anticipating the "baptism" of suffering and death (Mark 10:38), thus also pointing to the cross and resurrection. In other words, by submitting to the baptism of repentance, the One

---

9. Moltmann, *Way of Jesus Christ*, 150.
10. Moltmann, *Way of Jesus Christ*, 150.

who did not need to repent did so for others—as was the case also with the rest of his ministry, culminating in his suffering and death on the cross.

An itinerant preacher and healer, Jesus was on the way most of the time; his route took him to towns and the countryside, homes and synagogues. Occasionally he also visited pagan areas. Jesus broke national, religious, cultural, and sexual barriers by associating with people not usually involved with a Jewish rabbi. He assumed authority over the precepts of Torah, Sabbath, and the temple, all foundations of the allegedly exclusive nature of salvation (for the "covenant people"). Particularly his involvement with the "sinners," including through table fellowship (Matt 9:10–13 and par.), became a radical challenge to the religious establishment. The poor (Luke 4:18) and the children (Mark 10:13–16) were especially dear to Jesus. These are all powerful theological lessons for us concerning the countercultural and counter-religious nature of Jesus's ministry.

Feminists, Womanists, and other female theologians have rightly reminded us that in his ministry and behavior "the femaleness of the social and religiously outcast who respond to him has social symbolic significance as a witness against . . . patriarchal privilege."[11] According to Womanist theologian Jacquelyn Grant, by reading the biblical narrative about Christ, who was inclusive in his love toward women and other marginalized people in society, black women found a Jesus they could claim, and whose claim for them affirms their dignity and self-respect.[12]

Totally different from the later modernist and "liberal" interpretations, in which Jesus appears to be a kind, ethical teacher who cultivates the inner life of individuals and communities, the Jesus of the Synoptic Gospels announced both a personal and a public message. The announcement was about the kingdom of God that "was a warning of imminent catastrophe, a summons to an immediate change of heart and direction of life, an invitation to a new way of being Israel."[13] Although public and "naked," his teaching came mostly in the form of the parables, which of course are open to more than one interpretation.

Not surprisingly, Jesus's ethical teaching and nonviolence have elicited positive responses among various religions. In the words of Jewish historian Joseph Klausner, "there is not one ethical concept in the Gospels which cannot be traced back to Moses and the prophets."[14] Although the

---

11. Ruether, *Sexism and God-Talk*, 137.
12. Grant, "Womanist Theology," 346–47.
13. Wright, *Jesus and the Victory of God*, 172.
14. Lapide, *Israelis, Jews, and Jesus*, 6, quoting from Klausner, *Jesus of Nazareth*, without page reference.

Qur'an (19:32) readily acknowledges Jesus's compassionate nature—and considers him to be one of the "prophets"—his role as teacher is marginal in the Qur'an. Indeed, what the Qur'an emphasizes is that God teaches Jesus "the Scripture, and wisdom, and the Torah, and the Gospel" (5:110). Alongside compassion, Buddhists value Jesus's teaching, particularly the Beatitudes, the admonition to love one's enemy, the admonition to repay evil with kindness, and the emphasis on charity and equanimity. That said, what is repulsive to all Buddhist views is Jesus's emphasis on the kingdom and eschatological rule of God. This rejection is true also of the other three religions engaged here.

The Miracle-Man and the Exorcist

Besides being a preacher and teacher, Jesus was also an itinerant "miracle-worker," a healer, and an exorcist. Whereas premodern theology took the miraculous acts as proof of the divinity of Jesus of Nazareth, the Enlightenment mindset bluntly rejected their factual and historical nature. At its best, classical liberalism took the miracles as "myths" elicited by the powerful encounter with Jesus; it said that even if they never happened, they were still of great value in pointing to the influence of Jesus on his followers. Both of these paradigms are problematic theologically. Unlike the precritical interpretation, the key NT passages that speak of incarnation and divinity do not resort to miracles as their support. And unlike the reductionistic modernist rejection of the miraculous, contemporary worldviews allow us to accept the possibility of the miraculous, as I discussed in the previous chapter.

Fortunately, with the spread of Christianity to the Global South, the modernist refusal to grant the possibility of the miraculous has faced a major challenge. Among the several titles appropriate for Jesus Christ in African cultures is the Healer. Health means not only lack of sickness but also well-being in a holistic sense. Sickness is a result not only of physical symptoms but also of spiritual causes. Unlike their counterparts in the West, African Christians reject both the secularist worldview and missionaries' Western conceptions of reality and the spiritual. "Orthodoxy" has left Christians helpless in real life, and so an alternative theology has been necessary that relates to the whole range of needs, including the spiritual but not limited to abstract, otherworldly spiritual needs. Indeed, for many African Christologists, healing is the central feature of the life and ministry of Jesus Christ. A parallel can be found between the Gospel figure of Jesus as the itinerant healer and the traditional African medicine man. Both practice a holistic form of healing on the physical, mental, and social—and even the environmental—levels. Of all Christian traditions, Pentecostalism and later charismatic movements have particularly focused on the role of Jesus Christ as the healer.

What is the theological meaning of the mighty deeds of Jesus? They indicate God's approval of the ministry of Jesus. Rather than being done by Beelzebub, the mighty deeds are the function of the Spirit of God (Mark 3:20-30). Similarly to the parables, the mighty deeds, including exorcisms, point to the coming of the kingdom of God: "But if it is by the Spirit of God that I cast out demons, then the kingdom of God has come upon you" (Matt 12:28).

The healing ministry of Jesus is a robust statement about the all-inclusiveness of God's salvation; it includes the physical and emotional as well as the spiritual. Healings also were signs of profound sympathy, of cosuffering (Matt 14:14). Finally, healings and other mighty deeds anticipate eschatological fullness. (For a theology of healing, see chapter 8.)

What about other religions? What is their take on Jesus's miraculous works? Miracles are of course known among many religions. What makes Islam unique is that, on the one hand, the Qur'an does not chronicle any specific miracle performed by Muhammad, since the miracle of the Qur'an itself—as the Word of God—is by far the biggest and most important miracle. On the other hand, the Qur'an recounts several miracles of Jesus, such as healing the leper and raising people from the dead. The Qur'an also tells of miracles such as shaping a living bird out of clay based on the apocryphal gospels (5:110). A remarkable miracle is the table sent down from heaven spread with food as the divine proof of Jesus's truthfulness as the spokesperson for God and divine providence (5:112-15). That said, Jesus's miracles do not make him divine; indeed, miracles belong to the repertoire of many prophets, and they attest to their authenticity.

Understandably, most Hindus similarly have no quandaries with miracles reported as being performed by Jesus. When it comes to Buddhism, Mahayana traditions are particularly familiar with miraculous stories of Gautama Buddha and other enlightened ones. However, similarly to Islam, what is radically different among Buddhist thinkers is the interpretation of the meaning of miracles. The capacity to perform miracles points to the fact that Jesus was an extraordinary individual, but that capacity itself does not indicate a person's deity or link with the kingdom of God, as outlined above.

Separately from numerous miracles recounted in the OT, Jewish appraisal of the NT claims to Jesus's miracles is more complicated. They are routinely considered to be "magic," often with the OT-based suspicion about an effort to establish one's credentials on the basis of miracles since, as Deuteronomy 13 reminds us, a (messianic) pretender may excel in miraculous acts and yet lead astray the people of God.

How Rich and Diverse Are the Global and Contextual Narratives of Christology?

For countless Christians in the Global South, faith in Christ used to mean a necessary and uncritical renunciation of their previous culture and beliefs. That was a gross negligence of the fact that "Jesus was in Africa even before the rise of Christianity," as his family found a hiding place in Egypt and one of the first converts was Ethiopian, among other early allusions to that Continent.[15] Recall also that a number of early theologians such as Tertullian, Cyprian, and Augustine were North Africans.

Asian and African contexts attempt a distinctive approach to appropriating Jesus Christ's local and contextual meaning by employing the culturally relevant ancestry terminology and imagery. The Roman Catholic Charles Nyamiti's widely acclaimed book *Christ as Our Ancestor* (1984) is one of the trailblazers in this regard. Ancestors mediate between humans and the divine, and they occupy a sacred status. They remind us of the close link between the living and the dead. It does not take too much imagination to see some thematic parallels with Jesus Christ here.

For Liberation theologians of various stripes, Jesus's countercultural ministry has served as a great inspiration. The Roman Catholic Peruvian Gustavo Gutiérrez rightly insists that the turn to liberation, rather than being an optional move, is "a question *about the very meaning of Christianity and about the mission of the Church*" (emphasis original).[16] In fact, the most recent Jesus research has highlighted the social, political, and ideological importance of Jesus's radical egalitarianism. In keeping with this, liberationists in various global contexts, such as Latin America, have rightly argued that Christ's presence is to be found among the poor, not in an exclusive sense (maintaining that Christ is present *only* in the poor) but in an inclusive way, stating that Christ is present *at least* among the poor and the outcasts. Recall that Jesus himself was poor. A significant majority of the "common people" of the world are poor and marginalized, such as the Dalits (casteless) of India and the *minjung* ("masses of people") of Korea.

Female theologians, such as the feminist Rosemary Radford Ruether, come to the study of Christology with the question about the equality of men

---

15. Wessels, *Images of Jesus*, 98–99, here 98.
16. Gutiérrez, *Theology of Liberation*, xi.

and women. Her now classic question, "Can a Male Saviour Save Women?"[17] remains worth pondering. It is clear that female images are needed to both challenge and correct overly literalist and patriarchal ways of speaking of the Divine and so to introduce alternative symbols and metaphors of the divine, or "discourses of emancipatory transformation."[18]

In this context, the difficult question arises: What about the fact that in the Bible Jesus is male? The theological response is this: From a historical and cultural point of view, the biblical portrait of Jesus as male is fully understandable. That cultural milieu affirmed the predominance of the masculine sex; all religions' "founders" and holy persons were men. Yet despite divine incarnation in a Jewish male, Logos understood as the universal principle of reality is of course beyond gender. Had the incarnation occurred in the form of the female gender, the corresponding problem would have been how to include the male sex. Hence, replacing male-dominated talk about the divinity with female-dominated talk is counterproductive. It would sharpen rather than help resolve the issue of lack of inclusivity.

Another great concern among many contemporary theologians has to do with the question of race. James Cone points out that since the Christ of the dominant forms of Christianity is presented as a white Christ tailored to the values of modern white society, there is a need for a black Christ: "If Jesus Christ is to have any meaning for us, he must leave the security of the suburbs by joining blacks in their condition. What need have we for a white Jesus when we are not white but black?"[19] This is an important question and demands a careful theological-pastoral response. It is clear that Jesus of Nazareth does not represent the "pure" European-American Caucasian male. Rather, Jesus was a Middle Easterner and most probably much darker than is usually depicted in devotional paintings. As the second person of the Trinity, this fully human person transcends and puts in perspective the parameters that define our human life.

Contemporary theologians are also reminding us that the figure of Christ has been used both by Christian and by secular authorities in a way that has supported and facilitated colonialist enterprises. At the end of the fifteenth century, when South America was (re)discovered under the leadership of Christopher ("The Christ-Bearer") Columbus and taken over by the *conquistadors* (Spanish soldiers), the Spanish introduced the figure of Christ to the first nations of the continent. The Christ they presented to the Indios represented the side of the powerful and the ruler. This was followed

---

17. The subtitle to chap. 4 of Ruether, *To Change the World*.
18. Johnson, *She Who Is*, 5.
19. Cone, *Black Theology of Liberation*, 111.

by enormous suffering among the masses due to colonialism—colonialism that was clearly linked with Christ's legacy. Not only in Latin America but also in many parts of Asia, "it was largely colonization and evangelization in tandem that brought and propagated the western understanding of Jesus," foreign to the culture and hostile to its customs and beliefs.[20] The shadow of the "European Jesus" superimposed by the colonialists of the past centuries is a continuous challenge to Asian theologians as they are in the process of rediscovering the "Asian faces of Jesus"[21]—and this in the midst of religious plurality and rampant poverty.

These few examples from the tapestry of global and contextual Christologies remind Christians everywhere to take seriously the importance of the context in which we live and its needs and promises. They remind us that all of our interpretations of who Jesus Christ is and what he has done for us are subject to our limited and "perspectival" point of view. They also inspire us to learn more from the Other. This same observation also applies to the history of the Christological doctrine, our next topic. On the basis of bibical diversity and richness of testimonies to Christ, it was frankly inescapable that a diversity of interpretations of beliefs about the Christ would emerge. Let us take a closer look at them.

A Guided Tour of the Right and Wrong Views Concerning Christ

Why Should We Be Interested in Christological Debates of the Past—or Shouldn't We?

Let me test your theological sensibilities—or your patience!—with this list of strange and awkward terms: homoousios, hypostatic union, Ebionitism, Arianism, Nestorianism, Chalcedon. What do they tell you? Or are they merely hocus-pocus? For the trained theologian, these and many related terms have to do with an important chapter in Christian theology, one that has to do with various either heretical or "orthodox" (that is, correct) views about Christ, for example, the ways in which his two natures, the divine and the human, relate to each other. But what, if anything, do they communicate to the rest of the faithful, those who are not trained theologians? Are they merely of antiquarian interest? A curiosity? Certainly, one does not have to know the meanings of these strange words to be able to place one's faith in Jesus Christ. Not at all. But for the one who wishes to know what is the nature and meaning of the

20. de Mesa, "Making Salvation Concrete," 2.
21. Sugirtharajah, *Asian Faces of Jesus*.

Christ in which he or she believes, a brief historical detour might be much more meaningful and useful than expected.

So, let us embark on a journey to revisit briefly the many debates that Christian ministers, teachers, and leaders of the first centuries had to endure in order to come to a more defined understanding of their faith. While the Bible was their ultimate authority in all matters of faith, it hardly provided them—or us—with systematic, definitive doctrines. Rather, the multiplicity of testimonies, metaphors, teachings, and testimonies in the sacred Scripture mandated a careful scrutiny between right and wrong teachings. As a result of this centuries-long process, an orthodox view about Jesus Christ and his work slowly and painfully emerged—and they tested it against the scriptural teaching repeatedly.

How to Explain the Presence of God in Jesus

Somewhat counterintuitively, a key debate present in the NT was not so much about whether Christ was divine but rather about whether Christians could fully affirm Christ's humanity—so much so that in the Johannine community belief in Christ's humanity became the criterion for true orthodoxy (1 John 4:2–3). In other words, Jesus's incarnation and humanity matters a lot.

As time went by, the question of the deity of Christ also became a burning issue. That is particularly understandable given the Jewish culture of the first disciples. Having been trained in the strict monotheism of Israel, even the suggestion of another deity alongside Yahweh, the only, true God, smacked of heresy, even blasphemy. And yet that was the message of the early Christians, most of them Jewish: as a result of the raising from the dead of the Messiah by the power of the Holy Spirit, Jesus was confirmed to be divine (Rom 1:3–4).

In the second century, early church fathers took it for granted that Christ was human. This is not to ignore some heretical groups that denied or contested his true humanity, the Ebionites (from a Hebrew term meaning "the poor ones"), primarily a Jewish sect that regarded Jesus merely as an ordinary human being and docetists (from the Greek word *dokeō*, "to seem" or "to appear"), according to which Christ was completely divine but his humanity was merely an appearance. But they were fairly easily defeated. Docetism had a divine Savior who had no real connection with humanity. Ebionitism had only a human, moral example but no divine Savior.

The first major attempt to express in precise language the NT's dual emphasis on Christ as both a human being and a divine figure came to be known as Logos Christology. The second-century apologist Justin Martyr and others who sought to establish a correlation with Greek philosophy and Judaism gleaned the idea of logos ("word," or wisdom, or learning) from the prologue to the Gospel of John: "In the beginning was the Word [logos] . . ." The term was also already known among pagans, as in Greek philosophy it referred to something solid amid constant change. Furthermore, the idea of the divine "word" also had a solid OT background (the Hebrew term *dabar*). Justin Martyr argued that the same logos that was known by pagan philosophers and was also present in the OT had now appeared in the person of Jesus of Nazareth. And in a revolutionary way, the Gospel of John teaches that in Jesus Christ the logos became flesh (1:14). This was totally unheard of! Consider the statement of the leading second/third-century Eastern church father Origen, who said that in the incarnation the human soul of Christ was united with the Logos, as in this illustration: "If, then, a mass of iron be kept constantly in the fire, receiving the heat through all its pores and veins, and the fire being continuous and the iron never removed from it, it become wholly converted into the latter."[22] In keeping with the NT teaching, Origen also taught that the Father had begotten the Son by an eternal act; therefore, Christ existed from eternity.

If that is true, what then of the unique status of the Father in relation to the Son? Would the Father's absolute deity be compromised by the Son's?

How to Negotiate the Deity of the Son in Relation to the Deity of the Father

This task led to a group of views soon to be deemed heretical and known by the term "monarchianism," which means "sole sovereignty" of the Father in relation to the Son (and later, the Holy Spirit). Among many variations, two versions of monarchianism are relevant for us: dynamic and modalistic monarchianism. In their emphasis on the absolute uniqueness and unity of God, the proponents of these terms argued that either the status of the Son is lower than that of the Father (dynamic) or that the three "persons" of the Father, Son, Spirit do not really signify any real distinctions but rather refer to one and the same person (modalistic).

Dynamic monarchianism sought to preserve the "sole sovereignty" of the Father based on the idea that God was dynamically present in Jesus, thus making Jesus higher than any other human being but not yet God. Whether at baptism or resurrection (or perhaps at the moment of virgin birth), God's power (Greek *dynamis*) made Jesus *almost* God but not

22. Origen, First Principles (*De Principiis*) 2.6.6 in *ANF* 04.

equal to the Father, by which the Father's uniqueness was secured. This view was condemned by the church.

In modalistic monarchianism, the three persons of the Trinity are not self-subsistent "persons" but rather "modes" or "names" of the same God; in other words, they do not signify any real distinctions. They are like three "facades" of the one and same God, with a different one presented depending on the occasion. Even this version of monarchianism was deemed heretical. Why? If not for other reasons, then on the basis of the biblical teaching. Consider the account of Jesus's baptism, during which the Father spoke to his Son and the Spirit descended on the Son. Isn't that a direct death blow against any assumption of the lack of distinctions in the one, undivided godhead?

But even the correct position—the one rejecting both forms of Monarchianism—had to struggle with this obvious question: If Christ is divine but is not the Father, are there not two Gods? Tertullian, one of the ablest early Christian theologians from North Africa, sought to clarify this problem with a series of metaphors: "For the root and the tree are distinctly two things, but correlatively joined; the fountain and the river are also two forms, but indivisible; so likewise the sun and the ray are two forms, but coherent ones. Everything which proceeds from something else must needs be second to that from which it proceeds, without being on that account separated."[23] By analogies such as these, Tertullian and others believed they had clarified the NT distinction between Father and Son without leading to belief in two gods. But of course these metaphors taken from everyday life, similar to Jesus's teachings in parables, have to be handled with care in order to let them make the main point—and then, stop there, in order to avoid misunderstandings.

The most well-known attempt to negotiate the deity of the Son in relation to that of the Father in a way that ended up being heretical is known as Arianism.

What If the Son Is Almost as Divine as the Father?

As soon as Christian theology had combated monarchianism, it faced an even more challenging problem: Arianism, named after Arius, a priest of Alexandria. According to his opponents (on whose reports we have to depend here), Arius and Arianism taught that God the Father is absolutely unique and transcendent, and God's essence (the Greek term *ousia* means both "essence" and "substance") cannot be shared by another, not even the

---

23. Tertullian, *Against Praxeas* 8 in *ANF* 03..

Son. Consequently, the distinction between Father and Son was one of substance (*ousia*); if they were of the same (divine) substance, there would be two gods. Rather than sharing the same "essence" with the Father, the Son is the first and unique creation of God. A saying attributed to Arius emphasizes his main thesis about the origin of Christ: "There was [a time] when he was not." That would of course make the Son a creature rather than a preexistent god.

Why this obviously heretical solution? Whatever the ultimate motive, besides protecting the uniqueness of the Father and thus monotheism, pagan culture's rejection of the idea of God suffering might have energized Arianism; if the one who was crucified was not fully God, the problem of divine suffering would not arise.

The ablest opponent of Arianism and the defender of the full deity of Christ was the Eastern father Athanasius of Alexandria. He argued that not only our theology but also our salvation would be put in jeopardy if Christ were not fully divine. Only God can save, whereas a creature—even the highest creature—is in need of being saved. Thus, if Jesus were not God incarnate, he would not be able to save us. Furthermore, Athanasius reminded the heretics that Christ had been worshipped in the church, an act that would result in blasphemy if the object of the worship were other than God. No wonder that Arianism came to be rejected and that the correct view specified in the 381 AD Nicene-Constantinopolitan creed was worded as follows:

> We believe . . . in one Lord Jesus Christ, the Son of God, begotten of the Father [the only-begotten; that is, of the essence of the Father, God of God], Light of Light, very God of very God, begotten, not made, being of one substance [*homoousios*] with the Father.[24]

The statement that Christ was "not made" but rather was "of one substance" with the Father summarized the defeat of Arianism. While some related issues continued to be debated, the main thrust of this critical heresy was now put to rest.

But new challenges and versions of heresies were bound to emerge as soon as Christ's deity was established. The obvious question has to do with the way the deity of the Son may relate to his humanity, a tenet of faith unequivocally confirmed. Let us take a closer look at this conundrum.

---

24. Schaff, *Creeds of Christendom*, 1:28–29.

If Christ Is Divine, How Then Does That Relate to His Humanity?

There are at least two ways in which the reconciliation between Christ's "two natures" (as they came to be called) could go wrong—and it did! On the one hand, the two natures could become so separated from each other that their integral union would be compromised, making any talk about one divine "person" in two natures virtually impossible. This was the attempted solution of the heretical Nestorianism. On the other hand, the emphasis could be laid on the primacy of one nature (the divine) over the other (the human) to such an extent that Christ's true humanity would be called into question, a heresy titled Apollinarism.[25]

Behind these two tactics were different cultural milieus, at times named two "Christological schools." Although both of them originate in the Christian East, namely in Antioch of Syria and Alexandria of Egypt, over centuries they also prompted a wider split between the Greek-speaking Eastern (Orthodox) Church and the Latin-speaking Western Church. While the mainstream Alexandrian and Antiochean Christologies were both deemed orthodox (in the sense of "correct doctrine," not in terms of the later Orthodox denomination), they were also liable to particular kinds of excesses, culminating in the heretical solutions named above.

Here is a brief and simple profile of each of the two theological schools of thought: Alexandrian Christology emphasized the divine nature of Christ—to ensure the possibility of the human person being united with the divine Savior. While never ignoring humanity, at times it seemed like this was a kind of "one-nature" approach. In contrast, the Antiochean school sought to hold together the divine and human natures, paying more attention to the theological significance of human nature than their Alexandrian counterparts. Hence, not only the divinity, but also Christ's earthly life and obedience played a more important role.

Now, with this in mind, one can easily imagine how some Alexandrians might end up endorsing Apollinarism's one-sided focus on divine nature at the expense of the human. Commensurately, for Antiocheans the danger of separating the two natures remained a liability.

For Apollinarius of Laodicea (from whom the heresy got its name), the road to the heretical understanding went something like this. Christ, the divine Word (*Logos*), assuming human nature in its entirety by becoming incarnated seemed to imply that the weaknesses of human nature were contaminating the divine nature. And if that were the case, then the sinlessness of Christ would be compromised. To avoid this unacceptable view,

---

25. There were several versions of "one-nature" (or "miaphysite," from the Greek "one nature") heresies, including Eutychianism. We will skip them here.

Apollinarius suggested that if a real human mind in Jesus were replaced by a purely divine mind, one obviously immune to any sinful tendencies, that would solve the issue. As his opponents rightly noted, the problem with this move was that it renders the human nature of Christ incomplete. One of the greatest Eastern theologians from Cappadocia, Gregory of Nazianzen, concluded that it would effectively lead to compromising of Jesus's role as Savior because the saving incarnation would assume only part of humanity; that kind of a Christ could not identify fully with humans.

What about the Antiochean heresy? To simplify an incredibly complex issue, here's how Nestorian heresy emerged in relation to a practical pastoral issue. For Nestorius, patriarch of Constantinople of the fifth century, the widely used term Mother of God (Greek *theotokos*, literally "God-bearing") in regard to Mary, erroneously communicated that God has a mother—in other words, that a woman had given birth to God. Hence, if used, it should be complemented with the expression of Mary as "human bearing" (*anthropotokos*)—or, to try to get around the whole issue, as "Christ-bearing (*Christotokos*). The reasoning behind this move was simply that instead of bearing God, Mary bore humanity; in short, she was a sort of instrument of divinity.

Alexandrians, however, given their focus on divinity, were not convinced by this argument and continued to use the ancient title of *theotokos*. It was often coupled with another ancient concept of "communication of attributes," which played a significant role in various doctrinal contexts throughout history. With regard to Jesus's two natures, the expression means that what pertains to one nature also pertains to the other. In other words, because we can say that Mary bore the human baby Jesus, we can also at the same time say that Mary bore the divine person Christ. What, then, made Nestorius's doctrine unorthodox? Historical and conceptual problems aside, his Alexandrian opponents simply charged him with believing that Jesus had two natures joined only in a purely moral union but not in a real way. Altlhough Nestorius repudiated this interpretation, the accusation stuck and the church officially condemned the idea as a heresy.

Now, after all these challenges and errors (as well as some others not discussed here), what in fact became the right doctrine—orthodoxy?

This Is What (Most) Christians Believe about Jesus Christ

Whereas participants at the Council of Nicea in 325 AD initially hammered out the groundbreaking basic outline of beliefs concerning the Triune God and particularly Christology, resulting in the Nicene-Constantinopolitan

Creed of 381 AD, the Council of Chalcedon in 451 AD defined the final details (for the time being). The Council attempted to solve the Christological debates in a way that both Alexandrians and Antiochians could embrace, while at the same time continuing to refute the heretical views.

The main thrust of Chalcedon holds that, provided Jesus Christ was both truly divine and truly human, the precise manner in which this is articulated or explored is not of fundamental importance as long as commonly condemned heresies are excluded. On the one hand, Chalcedon functioned as a signpost pointing in the right direction, and on the other hand, it was a fence separating orthodoxy and heresy. Here is what it says about Christology:

> We, then, following the holy Fathers, all with one consent, teach men to confess one and the same Son, our Lord Jesus Christ, the same perfect in Godhead and also perfect in manhood; truly God and truly man, of a reasonable [rational] soul and body; consubstantial [coessential] with the Father according to the Godhead, and consubstantial with us according to the Manhood; in all things like unto us, without sin; begotten before all ages of the Father according to the Godhead, and in these latter days, for us and for our salvation, born of the Virgin Mary, the Mother of God, according to the Manhood; one and the same Christ, Son, Lord, Only-begotten, to be acknowledged in two natures, *inconfusedly, unchangeably, indivisibly, inseparably*; the distinction of natures being by no means taken away by the union, but rather the property of each nature being preserved, and concurring in one Person and one Subsistence, not parted or divided into two persons, but one and the same Son, and only begotten, God the Word, the Lord Jesus Christ, as the prophets from the beginning [have declared] concerning him, and the Lord Jesus Christ himself has taught us, and the Creed of the holy Fathers has handed down to us.[26]

Chalcedon takes great pains in affirming, on the one hand, the true humanity and deity of Jesus Christ and, on the other hand, both the unity and duality of this God-man. These affirmations could only be defined negatively with the help of four terms: "inconfusedly, unchangeably, indivisibly, inseparably." The two "natures" in one person are not to be separated or conflated; in other words, divinity and humanity cannot be a mixture, for that would entail a "third nature."

---

26. Schaff, *Creeds of Christendom*, 2:62–63; emphasis original.

Theological tradition presupposed that in the NT both divine and human attributes are predicated of only one subject, Christ (the divine Word, Logos), as seems to be the case in passages such as Acts 3:15 and John 17:5, among others. Logos, the divine Word, is the "subject" of the Incarnate One, traditionally expressed with the help of the term "hypostatic union." The divinity and humanity of Jesus Christ inhere or mutually indwell each other, without separation, and without mingling of the two natures.

This much was said to define the orthodox or correct belief. Much had to be left unsaid in order not to exclude but the communally condemned heretical views. Understandably, even Chalcedon is more like a milestone than an end station. Many details continued to be discussed and fine-tuned throughout history, even to this day.

Having examined established creedal orthodoxy and its meaning for us, we are ready to tackle a number of key Christological doctrines before beginning the interfaith work. This gives us an opportunity to delve into a number of doctrines whose content is empty and undefined for most Christians.

A Guided Tour through Central Christological Doctrines

On the Basis of the Resurrection from the Dead, We Know Who Jesus Christ Is!

We begin our consideration of Christological doctrines with the most foundational and most critical question, namely whether there is a way to know that Jesus Christ is what he claimed to be—the Son of God. The shorthand response to this crucial question is "through his resurrection from the dead." Yes, that is the ultimate answer. According to Paul, Jesus was "designated Son of God in power according to the Spirit of holiness by his resurrection from the dead" (Rom 1:4). The significance of the resurrection for Christology lies in the fact that not only the title "Son of God" but basically all Christological titles used in the early church stem from the Easter event, including the title "Lord" (*kyrios*). Paul also argues that the resurrection justified Jesus's work of salvation (Rom 4:25).

In Christian tradition, several other ideas have been proposed to establish the deity of Jesus, such as his sinlessness, that he taught "with authority" (Mark 1:22, 27), his death on the cross, and Jesus's own claims to messiahship. While important in themselves, none of these proposals has the capacity to constitute his deity. Even though human history knows no persons without sin, finding one wouldn't necessarily make that person a god, any more than the most insightful and wonderful teaching would. Jewish history identifies a number of self-made messiahs who made all kinds of claims without any basis in history or personality. Death on the cross is not a unique event in human history; at its best, crucifixion could have made Jesus a (failed) self-made messiah (as was the case with a host of figures in the Jewish milieu), or an innocent martyr.

We are thus left with resurrection as the most appropriate candidate for establishing Jesus's deity. When combined with his own claims of having been sent by his Father and the Father's promise of raising him up on the third day, resurrection can be seen as the divine vindication. That came on the day of Easter, and the early church interpreted it as such (Acts 13:30, among other passages). Karl Barth agreed: "[T]he resurrection of Jesus Christ is the great verdict of God, the fulfilment and proclamation of God's decision concerning the event of the cross."[27]

It is significant that the biblical idea of resurrection is without parallel in other religions. Even though other religions have their myths of gods rising and dying, those represent different genres and motifs. No wonder the gentile audience found the claim to resurrection incredible (Acts 17:32). Even in the OT and Judaism, the resurrection of one single person, including the Messiah, before the resurrection of everyone and everything at the end is totally unknown. Radically revising Jewish hopes, early Christianity saw in the resurrection of Jesus the beginning of the end times, which the faithful believed would culminate in the resurrection of all (1 Cor 15:20–28).

On the same basis, the raising from the dead, we can also affirm Jesus Christ's full humanity as the "Word made flesh," yet without sin (a tenet of faith that we will study further below). Resurrection was divine confirmation for this claim of having identified totally with humanity.

The reference to resurrection as the vindication of Jesus Christ raises a further question of its historical validity. For if the claim about the resurrection from the dead could be shown to be a fabrication or an outright lie, its function as the confirmation of Christ's divinity falters right away. No wonder that since the Enlightenment the affirmation of resurrection as a historical event in terms of bodily resurrection has been hotly contested.

Critics claim that what theology considers to be reliable first-hand testimonies to the truthfulness of resurrection are actually merely subjective experiences, even mere wishes, of the disciples. But this argument forgets that there are at least two kinds of "hard" evidence that point toward the truthfulness of the disciples' reports. One is the empty tomb. As much as the opponents of Jesus who killed him also opposed his claims

---

27. Barth, *Church Dogmatics*, IV/1, 308.

that he would rise up from the tomb on the third day, when it happened they did not dismiss the actual emptiness of the tomb. The other weighty evidence is the presence in the NT of a great number of contemporary eye-witnesses to whom Jesus had appeared after the resurrection. The opponents did not rebut those testimonies, although of course they harshly rejected the implications of the testimonies, namely that Jesus had thereby shown to be who he claimed to be.

In sum: belief in the physical resurrection of Jesus from the dead is not necessarily a matter of faith totally apart from historical investigation and rational reasoning. That said, we need to acknowledge the limits of historical inquiry alone. No amount of historical evidence or logical reasoning is meant to establish certainty beyond questioning.

"The Word Became Flesh": Incarnation

The doctrine of the incarnation and the corollary doctrines of preexistence and virgin birth are all different ways of speaking about the unique relation between Jesus's divine origin and his human existence. The NT widely testifies to incarnation (John 1:14; 14:7; Rom 8:3; 1 Cor 8:6; Gal 4:4-6; Phil 2:6-8; Col 1:15-17; 1 John 4:2). And incarnation and preexistence are mutually related teachings. If the former is affirmed without the latter, adoptionism follows, that is the idea that at some point of Jesus's life he was "made" what he is. Preexistence tells us that the Word-became-flesh is divine, has existed for eternity. Similarly, any talk about the *Christian* view of incarnation without the presupposition of the deity of Christ—which would lead, as in the Gnostic Gospel of Philip, to the affirmation of every human person's divinity—results in an impasse.

Thomas Aquinas raises an interesting question, namely whether it was fitting for the divine to become a human being (*Summa theologiae* 3.1.1). He lists a number of potential objections, such as that the divine has been without flesh from eternity, that the infinite difference between the divine and human makes it impossible for the divine to be "contained" in a human life, and so forth. Yet, in the end Aquinas finds it fitting for perfect goodness to communicate itself for the sake of others. Along the same lines we can add that since human nature is good (being God's handiwork), therefore it is fitting for God to assume it—as he was without sin, unlike anyone among us. In fact, early theology had already established a link between incarnation and creation, as is profoundly evident, for example, in Athanasius's *On the Incarnation of the Word*:

> For this purpose, then, the incorporeal and incorruptible and immaterial Word of God comes to our realm, howbeit he was not far from us before. For no part of Creation is left void of Him: He has filled all things everywhere, remaining present with His own Father. (8.1)

But why incarnation? Theological tradition has given two answers. The first and most obvious answer is that human sin and disobedience necessitated the incarnation of the Son; this question was profoundly addressed by medieval theologian Anselm of Canterbury in his classic study *Cur Deus Homo?* (Why did God become human?). This is also the commonsense view. The second answer is that "God intended the incarnation of the Son of God from eternity. His intention was formed together with the idea of the world" in terms of preparation for the coming of the Son to humanity.[28] In other words, even without the problem of the fall and sin, God the Creator would have desired to be united with men and women whom he had, after all, created in God's image. Negotiating these two answers does not, of course, necessarily demand two alternatives. Moltmann makes a brilliant suggestion: Rather than incarnation's "reason" (as in the first answer), the fall is its "occasion."[29] Here, Athanasius is a great example. Whereas he underscores the importance of linking incarnation with creation, he also speaks everywhere of human lostness and humans' need for the Savior to come and die and be raised from death for their salvation.

The incarnation is not a passing moment in the divine life. If it were, the event would be closer to ancient mythologies in which deities change into human beings (and possibly also back into deities). As the Athanasian Creed says, the incarnation happened "not by conversion of the Godhead into flesh, but by taking of that manhood into God."[30] In that sense we can speak of "permanent incarnation."

As soon as we affirm incarnation, we also raise the question of how to understand the unique, one-time event in which one "Person," Christ, exists in two "natures," divine and human.

How to Make Sense of Two "Natures" in One "Person"

Another way of framing our question is this: How do we even begin to speak of the coming together of the infinite (divinity) and finite (humanity)

---

28. Moltmann, *Trinity and the Kingdom*, 114.
29. Moltmann, *Trinity and the Kingdom*, 115.
30. In Brannan, *Historic Creed and Confessions*, n.p.

in one and the same person? A case-study, long reflected upon in Christian history—indeed, beginning from the early centuries—has to do with miracles assuming divinity and suffering implying humanity. One intuitive (though theologically suspicious and wanting) suggestion is to attribute miracles to the divine nature and suffering to the human nature. The obvious problem is that it seems to endanger the unity of the one person and can be interpreted in a way that supports Nestorian heresy.

A useful beginning point is to note that we should always avoid abstract and formal speculations when speaking of the unique coming together of two natures in one person in Jesus Christ and focus on this particular, unrepeatable event. The NT narrative can then be taken as the main guide. The two key passages in the NT on which the Chalcedonian incarnational Christology is anchored—Philippians 2:5-11 and John 1:14—contain hardly any abstract description of the divine Logos suddenly descending on the specific man, Jesus of Nazareth. Paul's point is that the historical person Jesus refused to clutch his divine prerogatives and instead chose the path of the obedient servant, all the way to death on the cross. His exaltation by the Father was the result of his obedient life as a whole. Jesus's entire life mattered, not, for example, only the virginal conception that tradition often highlighted as the key to understanding incarnation.

What about John? In speaking of the preexistent Word (Logos) becoming flesh, John "appeals to eyewitnesses who observed our Lord's earthly life. On the basis of personal observations of Jesus's life (not his birth), these persons bear testimony to the incarnation" (John 1:14). In that sense, the confession "the Word became flesh," rather than being a presupposition, is the conclusion of Jesus's person on the basis of his entire history.[31] Recall what we discussed above, namely the importance of the entire earthly life and ministry of Jesus. Hence, the commonsense intuition stemming from patristic theology of locating the main significance of incarnation in the miraculous birth of Christ says too little. This will become even clearer as we delve more deeply into the meaning of Christ's self-emptying in his incarnation.

This concrete rather than abstract or speculative way of speaking of the God-Man also comes to the fore in regards to Jesus's "self-emptying."

What Does *Self-Emptying* Mean?

The NT writers speak audaciously of the humanity and self-emptying of Jesus Christ. The mention in Hebrews of the shaping of Jesus's character in

---

31. Grenz, *Theology for the Community*, 310.

order for him to be "a merciful and faithful high priest" (Heb 2:17) sounds daring, for it could be interpreted as divesting Jesus of part of his divinity! Or think of the statement that, having been made "perfect through suffering" (2:10), he "became the source of eternal salvation to all who obey him" (5:9)! This narrative and testimonial approach of the NT, relating to the whole life of Jesus, is really the key to a proper understanding of the incarnation and related topics.

Hence, Christ's "self-emptying" (aka *kenosis* from Greek; Phil 2:7), is neither a renouncing nor even a temporarily turning off of the use of divine powers—which, when taken to its logical end, would lead to the heretical denial of the full divinity of the incarnated Son; rather, his *kenosis* is the voluntary submission of the earthly Jesus to his Father's will (John 5:19, 30, 36, and the passages from Hebrews above). Unlike the first Adam, the will of the new Adam corresponded completely to the will of God.

As a result, after much debate, theology came to affirm the presence of both human and divine will as opposed to the heretical "one-will" claim. This was yet another way of endorsing the full humanity of the incarnated one.

We should also note that this voluntary self-emptying from any divine prerogative for the sake of our salvation that culminates in Jesus's sorrowful suffering and death on the cross is not something that is contrary to the divine nature or deity of the Son. Barth understands that, "in this condescension, He is the eternal Son of the eternal Father."[32] In other words, Jesus's self-emptying, his making himself dependent on the will and love of his Father, is in keeping both with the true divinity of the Son as revealed to us and with the true humanity as created by God. Dependency, contingency, and reference to the other characterize human nature; these elements of human nature Jesus's humanity models for us most purely and innocently.

This voluntary subordination to his Father's will often comes to the fore in the NT narrative with regard to the Spirit. Jesus attributed his power to the Spirit given him by his Father (Matt 12:28; Luke 4:18; 11:20). Understood like this, the earthly Jesus was dependent on the Spirit for his ministry, teaching, and miracles, as well as for overcoming temptations. But can this Spirit-dependent earthly and human Jesus also be totally sinless?

Can a True Human Person Be Totally Sinless?

The sinlessness of Jesus is based on NT statements such as Hebrews 4:15 that "in every respect [he] has been tempted as we are, yet without sin"

---

32. Barth, *Church Dogmatics*, IV/1, 130.

(so also 7:26; 9:14; 2 Cor 5:21; 1 Pet 2:22; 1 John 3:5). The creeds affirm the same. The thicker account of Jesus's sinlessness came to be expressed technically as "not able to sin," which says more than the thinner expression "able not to sin." Whereas the latter could be said of the mere human person who never sinned, only the human person who was simultaneously also fully divine could be "not able to sin."

Early theologians were well aware that along with the affirmation of sinlessness also came the affirmation of the different nature of Jesus's humanity from our empirical nature. Yet that is seen not as threatening but rather as facilitating the redemptive work of Jesus Christ. The basis for the affirmation of sinlessness, apart from biblical references, was evident in Jesus's total obedience and moral perfection, as well as in his union with God.

In the aftermath of the Enlightenment, as one might assume, sinlessness came to be either rejected or simply dismissed. For religious pluralists (about whom more below), sinlessness would have raised Jesus to a totally unique status in relation to other savior figures, and therefore had to be rejected. Unrelated to the Enlightenment criticism, a few influential theologians have simply not found a way to sever sinlessness from the Word's total identification with sinful flesh.

How, then, was theology able to continue establishing the sinlessness of this one Person? Recall that neither Jesus's foes, nor his friends, charged him with any sin. Some opponents' cheap charges about issues such as gluttony and association with sinners—or even the most serious of all in the Jewish context, blasphemy—are just that: *cheap* charges with no evidence to support them. That said, ultimately the affirmation of sinlessness has to be—again—an inference from the resurrection that confirmed his claims to deity and true humanity. Mere sinlessness does not of course make the human person divine; but God, by definition, cannot sin.

Theological consideration of the possibility of reconciling the doctrine of sinlessness and the full humanity of Jesus has to keep in mind the nature of the original human nature. True humanity as the image of God does not of course entail sinfulness. It is our fallen humanity that is corrupted. Indeed, rather than asking first how a pure, sinless humanity of Jesus Christ can represent humanity, we have to wonder how our fallen humanity can still be said to represent humanity!

To say that Jesus was fully engaged in the human predicament, yet sinless, is to acknowledge that as human he was deeply affected by the effects of the fallen world, without himself participating in sinful acts. He shared our lot in the fallen and sinful world, full of pain, suffering, and injustice.

What about temptations? Whereas Christian tradition has struggled to understand the authenticity of temptations alongside affirmation of his sinless nature, the Gospels make the temptations a matter of Jesus's relation to the Father. All three temptations raise the question, "If you are the Son of God . . . " So temptations are about obedience. Beyond that, the difference between Jesus and us is that temptations in humans originate from within the fallen nature (Jas 1:14), whereas in Jesus's case, they originate from outside. Yet that did not weaken their appeal, particularly when, as in the desert, he faced hunger after forty days.

Going back to the "not able to sin" clause: doesn't it compromise his authentic human freedom? Doesn't it make sinlessness "necessary" for him? Recall the rejection of the "one-will" view in favor of "two wills," meaning that Jesus had a true human will. On top of that, recall that authentic freedom does not require the possibility of sin—or else God would not be free! As Augustine argued, "the will that cannot sin at all is more free than the will that can either sin or not sin."[33] The freedom of Jesus Christ was not predetermined, semiautomatic submission, but rather true freedom *in God*. Freedom essentially is a relational concept; misuse of freedom—sinning—means breaking our relationship with God.

In sum: however one negotiates sinlessness theologically, one has to steer a radical middle path between two considerations: Jesus's humanity cannot be so different from ours that in his incarnation and innocent suffering our fallen human nature was not assumed and healed. For otherwise our salvation would be in jeopardy. On the other hand, his human nature, by being in "hypostatic union" with the divine, has to be unique enough to mark him as the Son of God.

"He Came Down from Heaven": Preexistence

In Christian tradition, affirmed in the Nicene-Constantinopolitan Creed, the doctrine of preexistence means that the second person of the Trinity, the eternal Son of God, became human in Jesus of Nazareth. Of course tradition doesn't teach that the man Jesus existed in any real sense before the incarnation, but that God the Son existed prior to the incarnation. Not surprisingly, it took early Christian theology some time to formulate its view of the nature of preexistence due to the vacillation between a purely ideal preexistence, as existing in the mind of God, and "real" ("personal") preexistence. Preexistence and incarnation belong together and mutually presuppose each other.

Again not surprisingly contemporary scholarship has cast serious doubts on the doctrine's biblical support. The standard opinion is that

---

33. Paraphrased in Pannenberg, *Systematic Theology*, 2:258n287.

preexistence can only be found developed in John, whereas Pauline and other NT traditions contain at the most only ambiguous references. In rebuttal, it seems evident that preexistence is present in various NT traditions (1 Cor 8:6; Gal 4:4; Phil 2:6-8; Col 1:15-17: Heb 1:2; among others).

The revisionist view of twentieth-century British bishop J. A. T. Robinson is a good example of a "thin" account of preexistence. For him, Christ in incarnation "completely embodied what was from the beginning the meaning and purpose of God's self-expression."[34] It is quite difficult to say what exactly he means with that. Understandably, for religious pluralists the whole idea of preexistence is problematic in suggesting a totally unique person.

The main problem with the rejection or radical revision of preexistence is that it compromises Christ's divinity, making him a creature rather than God. As a result, ultimately, the whole doctrine of the Trinity is at stake.

What about Virgin Birth?

By now it is hardly news that virgin birth, alongside resurrection and preexistence, has not been a favorite topic of modernity! It is not helped by the well-known fact that there are only a couple of direct references to virgin birth in the NT (Matt 1:18-25; Luke 1:26-38). Yet, belief in the supernatural virginal conception of Jesus soon became a universally held view in early Christian theology, including creedal traditions, and it has continued since. Tradition says that the Holy Spirit conceived Jesus supernaturally in the Virgin Mary, apart from normal sexual intercourse. Put in the wider context of religions, Islam strongly affirms the importance of Jesus's virgin birth. But of course Islam rejects Jesus's deity.

Not until the rise of the quest of the historical Jesus in modernity was there a widespread rejection or radical reinterpretation of the traditional belief in the virgin birth. Much of contemporary mainline NT scholarship does not regard the virgin birth as a historical event but rather as a "theological" or symbolic one, for example, in terms of total human surrender to God of the human being as embodied in Mary's attitude.

Not surprisingly, conservative segments of the church reacted vehemently to this idea of the virgin birth not being a historical reality. The Fundamentalist movement listed belief in the virgin birth (understood in the traditional sense) among the "five fundamentals" to be affirmed and believed. While not Fundamentalist, no other contemporary theologian has stressed

---

34. Robinson, *Human Face of God*, 179.

the theological importance of the virgin birth as much as Karl Barth: "The mystery of the revelation of God in Jesus Christ consists in the fact that the eternal Word of God chose, sanctified and assumed human nature and existence into oneness with Himself, in order thus, as very God and very man, to become the Word of reconciliation spoken by God to man."[35]

Even though the NT does not make a direct link between virgin birth and preexistence, early in Christian theology that link came to be established. It taught that it was Logos, the preexistent Word of God, that was conceived in the Virgin Mary. Some other ideas related to virginal conceptions are more problematic, namely that excluding the father's (Joseph) role was necessary to ensure sinlessness, as the effects of the fall come mainly from the father, and that virginal conception saves Jesus from the effects of the sinful sexual intercourse of parents.

These are mistaken opinions. Not only Orthodox Christians and Roman Catholics but also Protestants should honor Mary appropriately as the "mother of God," for she plays a unique role in salvation history. This has nothing to do with the mistaken Mary-cult, virtual worshipping of Jesus's mother in some forms of folk piety.

So far, while delving briefly into interfaith engagements, we have engaged mainly Christian (and Jewish) traditions. The last two lengthier sections of this chapter open windows onto other religions and theological responses to Jesus Christ among Christian religious pluralists and among other faith traditions.

Christological Challenges from Religious Pluralists

Revisionist Interpretations of the Incarnation

Whereas until the Enlightenment incarnation was understood as a one-time, unique event, after it some leading philosophers and theologians began to envision it in terms of a collective divine presence, perhaps even one that reached the whole of humanity. A critical tool in this radical revision was the concept of "myth" in light of which incarnation—similarly to, say, resurrection or virginal conception—was not any kind of historical-factual event but rather a metaphor or an elusive idea. The above-mentioned Bishop Robinson's view of incarnation as "a breakthrough of cosmic consciousness" in his *Human Face of God*[36] continued the same elusive line of interpretation. In other words, not only one person—Jesus

---

35. Barth, *Church Dogmatics*, I/2, 124.
36. Robinson, *Human Face of God*, 204.

Christ—was incarnated, but rather many, or even all, human beings bear this robust divine presence. Of course such an interpretation dilutes the notion of the uniqueness of Jesus Christ.

The leading religious pluralist of our times, the late John Hick, not only builds on this legacy but also sharpens it. Having left behind the doctrine of the Trinity, he unabashedly represents "low Christology," in which Jesus's "incarnation" means nothing more than a difference in degree of God-consciousness. Incarnation should be taken seriously but not literally, not as a historical fact he said in *The Metaphor of God Incarnate: Christology in a Pluralistic Age*. He suggested that for the sake of religious tolerance the basic claims of the creedal Christological tenets of faith be abandoned. What really matters, says Robinson, is the earthly Jesus's ethical teaching and example, not much unlike with classical liberalism of modernity.

Not surprisingly, critics have challenged him severely (not repeating criticisms against Hick presented in chapter 2). First, his universal rather than particular historical notion of incarnation is against biblical and creedal traditions. Second, Hick's system makes all talk about Trinity nonsensical, as Christ is not divine in the first place. Third, his "turn" to metaphorical and mythical language blocks the way to a solid historical-critical study of Jesus traditions. Fourth, only a few are ready to acknowledge that Hick's radically revisionist account of Jesus the Christ is any more "neutral" or objective than is the interpretation of those who are time-wise and culturally much closer to Jesus, particularly his earliest followers. In sum, any denial of Jesus Christ's incarnation as a particular, unique, nonrepeatable event severely undercuts Christian orthodoxy.

This takes us to the deeper consideration of the uniqueness of Christ among the religions. Is there any place for it? And if so, how do we continue to establish it for our own times?

In What Ways Christ Is Unique—or Is He?

For religious pluralists, the theocentric approach is the key: rather than Jesus as the only way to God, they suggest that a general notion of God is at the center of Christianity and Jesus is only one way to God. Jesus Christ is "unique" in that he is an authoritative revelation of God, but there may be other savior figures among other religions. Yet this is hardly a convincing argument, as theocentric Christology contradicts the biblical insistence on Jesus as the only way to God. Note also that against the wishes of its advocates, its value for a robust dialogue is also limited, as it does not allow the representatives on the Christian side to present their own views in an authentic and open way.

No wonder that other ways of affirming uniqueness have been attempted. The Roman Catholic pluralist Paul F. Knitter has suggested that we turn instead to religio-theological considerations, to the work of liberation and environmental care as the key to speaking of Jesus in the pluralistic world. This "eco-liberationist" pluralism, "a globally responsible, correlational dialogue among religions,"[37] values the power of any given religion to facilitate and inspire work for social and ecological improvement. Jesus's uniqueness would be measured with this yard stick rather than with doctrine.

Critical commentators liberally admit that calling religions to work together for the betterment of this planet and life on it is something all religions should support. But they rightly wonder why this renders void the value of doctrinal discussions and comparisons? After all, it cannot be assumed that all religions agree even on what is justice and equity. These are complicated ethical-theological topics. And most important for this particular topic: Any talk about Jesus's "uniqueness" in this matrix would be practically meaningless.

Whereas discussion among Christian theologians (of religions) is bound to continue, it would be most profitable if it were to move beyond this tradition's boundaries and engage specific insights, teachings, and visions of other faiths. This will occupy us for the rest of this chapter.

Jesus Christ among Religions

The Jewish Messiah and the Christian Messiah: How Do They Relate to Each Other?

"When one asks the basic question of what separates Jews and Christians from each other, the unavoidable answer is: a Jew," says the Jewish NT scholar Pinchas Lapide.[38] One of the ironies of history is that for eighteen hundred years or more, Jewish theologians by and large ignored Christian claims that Jesus is the Messiah, and their perceptions of Jesus were very negative. A case in point is the most important early Jewish source on Christ, *Toldot Yeshu* (from the fifth or sixth century), which radically alters the Gospel narratives and in general advances a highly polemical and mocking presentation. For example, it attributes Jesus's miracles to sorcery or other similarly forbidden sources.

---

37. Section title in Knitter, *One Earth, Many Religions*, 15.
38. Lapide, *Resurrection of Jesus*, 30.

The rabbinical writings contain a definite and direct rebuttal of the claim to the divine Sonship of Jesus, "a blasphemy against the Jewish understanding of God." The Christian doctrines of the incarnation, atonement through the cross, and of course the Trinity, among others, "remained alien to normative Judaism and taboo to the rabbis."[39] Yet resistance to the historical figure of Jesus of Nazareth was less the target. Of greater concern to Judaism was so-called Pauline Christology and the subsequent patristic and creedal tradition.

In the aftermath of the Enlightenment, and with the newly opening opportunities for Jews to participate in wider European society, interest in Jesus emerged among Jews, partly to help justify Judaism as a religion. Moses Mendelssohn painted a picture of Jesus as a thoroughly Jewish religious figure, so much so that, "closely examined, everything is in complete agreement not only with Scripture, but also with the [Jewish] tradition."[40] At the same time, a goal of the Jewish search for the Jewish Jesus was to develop "a counterhistory of the prevailing Christian theological version of Christianity's origins and influence."[41]

On the Christian side, unrelated to Jewish-Christian relations, recent decades have seen an unprecedented interest in the Jewishness of Jesus, beginning with the first generation of the "New Perspective (on Paul)" in the 1970s. And as I mentioned at the beginning of the chapter, theologians such as Moltmann have in recent decades highlighted the same theme.

This interest among Christians in Jesus the Jew, late as it is, is a welcome move in light of the deep and wide anti-Semitic heritage of the church. Just consider the destruction of Jerusalem by the gentiles in 70 CE; that alone should have led Christians to reach out to their suffering Jewish brothers and sisters in sympathy and love—yet it did not! Anti-Semitism has an appalling and long track record in Christian tradition.

While anti-Semitism in all of its forms has to be condemned and rejected, I note that—against some influential theologians' opinion to the contrary—there is nothing inherently anti-Semitic about Christianity's Christology. This is not to contest or ignore the critique, at times harsh, of Jewish faith and people in the NT. Whereas before the destruction of Jerusalem in 70 CE we find very little documentation attributing the death of Jesus to Jews, in the later Christian writings the tone becomes harsher, and crucifixion is attributed to the Jews alone. A particularly harsh critique of the Jews is in Matthew 23, but it is not necessarily different from

---

39. Lapide, *Israelis, Jews, and Jesus*, 76–77.
40. In Heschel, "Jewish Views of Jesus," 151.
41. Heschel, "Jewish Views of Jesus," 152.

or untypical of the harsh criticism of one Jewish group by another Jewish group at the time. Even when the Jewish people as a whole are addressed, usually the target of the Christians' criticism is that religious or political leadership is deviating from the will of God.

Understandably, the question of the Messiah both connects and deeply divides these two faiths. Although too often left unacknowledged, the Christian Messiah is after all a Jewish Messiah. Why then the Jewish rejection? The main reason a typical Jew cannot acknowledge the arrival of the Messiah is simply that nothing has changed in the world; indeed, everything in the conditions of this world seems to speak against the arrival of the Messiah. This is a hard question to Christians.

Without downplaying and certainly without dismissing this profound difference in understanding of what the coming of the Messiah and the ensuing redemption mean, Moltmann poses the "gentile" question to the Jews: "[E]ven *before* the world has been redeemed so as to become the direct and universal rule of God, can God already have a chosen people, chosen moreover *for the purpose of this redemption*?" (emphasis original).[42]

Be that as it may, Christian Christology must resist any notion of imperialism, whatever form it may take. The Messiah confessed in Christian theology is the crucified one "who heals through his wounds and is victorious through his sufferings . . . the Lamb of God, not yet the Lion of Judah."[43] This kind of "theology of the cross" makes it possible for Christian theology to tolerate and appreciate the Jewish "no" rather than assuming that God has abandoned the people of Israel because of their reluctance to acknowledge the Messiah (Rom 9–11).

A dialogue about Messiah and other corollary Christological issues between Christians and Jews is meaningful only if there is mutual trust to allow both parties to represent their positions faithfully. The challenge to the Jewish faith is to stop "constructing Jewish conceptions of Jesus . . . and try to confront Christian claims about him as we [Jews] actually hear them from Christians." That said, it is also important for Christian theologians to acknowledge that the Jews have the right and prerogative to conceive of Jesus within their own faith before they take a look at him through a Christian lens.[44] Jews also have a right to comment on Christian doctrine of Christ. Such comments are opportunities for Christians to learn more about their own faith. What about Islam and Christ?

---

42. Moltmann, *Way of Jesus Christ*, 30.
43. Moltmann, *Way of Jesus Christ*, 32.
44. Kogan, *Opening the Covenant*, 112.

Why Does Jesus Play Such a Big Role in Islam? And Does Islam Reach an Impasse about Christ?

The Roman Catholic Second Vatican Council's document *Nostra Aetate* (Declaration on the Relation of the Church to Non-Christian Religions) sums up the general Muslim perception of Jesus: "Though they do not acknowledge Jesus as God, they revere Him as a prophet. They also honor Mary, His virgin Mother; at times they even call on her with devotion" (para. 3). Did you happen to know that in the Qur'an alone there are roughly one hundred references or allusions to Jesus and his mother Mary (with two entire suras—3 and 19—devoted to her). Furthermore, numerous references to Jesus appear in later literature.

Jesus stands in the long line of prophets, beginning with Noah and reaching all the way to Jesus. Indeed, Jesus is second only to the Prophet himself. His virgin birth is affirmed, as are his miracles, as discussed above. His teaching is appreciated, though with some reservations, as also discussed.

Amazingly, "Islam is the only religion other than Christianity that *requires* its adherents to commit to a position on the identity of Jesus" (emphasis original)![45] No wonder that Islamic tradition considers Jesus to be "Muslim." It is not difficult to find books with titles such as *The Muslim Jesus*.[46] Curiously, Christian perceptions about Muhammad have been much more critical than Muslims's concerning Jesus!

That said, Jesus is also a very divisive figure, and ambiguity about him has characterized Muslim-Christian exchange from the beginning. The Christian polemical side has leveled strong complaints against alleged distortions and mistakes in Muslim interpretation of Jesus. A significant portion of Muslim references to Jesus are based on Christian legends and Gospels not included in the NT, such as the Gospel of Barnabas, whose influence even today is immense in anti-Christian polemics.

Among Muslims, there is a strict and absolute rebuttal of Jesus's divinity. The claim to deity is the greatest sin, that of "association" (with Allah), the *shirk*. The handful of direct references to the Christian claim of Jesus as the Son of God and his divinity in the Qur'an are bluntly denied (4:171; 9:30; 19:35). Similarly denied is the idea of Allah having a son (2:116; 4:171; 17:111; 39:4; 72:3); a related reason is that there being a son would require Allah to have had a consort (6:101).

---

45. Barker, "Muslim Perceptions of Jesus," 83.
46. Khalidi, *Muslim Jesus*.

Even the fact that Jesus is a miracle-worker in the Qur'an, unlike Muhammad, does not imply that he should be thought of as higher than the Prophet of Islam; the miracles wrought by Jesus are similar to those performed by Moses and other such forerunners of Muhammad. In other words, the most the miracles can do for Jesus is confirm his prophetic status; they cannot confirm his divinity. Even the fact that Jesus is described as sinless in Hadith and legendary tradition—whereas it is not quite certain if Muhammad is—does not make Jesus superior. Furthermore, the highly celebrated title in Judeo-Christian tradition, Messiah, which surprisingly is applied only to Jesus in the Qur'an (e.g., 4:171) has no divine connotation. And going even further: that in the same verse, Jesus is named the "Word" and "a spirit from Him [Allah]" similarly lacks any allusions to deity.

The categorical rejection of the deity of Jesus Christ also signifies the categorical denial of the doctrine of incarnation. Muslim scholars argue that incarnation is in contradiction not only to the Qur'an but also to the Bible! While quoting Qur'anic passages that refute Jesus's divinity (e.g., 5:72, 73) Muslims also employ Qur'anic passages that speak of the mere humanity of Jesus (e.g., 5:75). As for the Bible, Muslim scholars devote considerable attention to the sayings that speak of Jesus's humanity, such as his being the son of David and Abraham (Matt 1:1) and that he ate, drank, slept, traveled, rode a donkey, suffered, and died. Similarly, his need to pray, his temptations, and so forth for Muslims indicate humanity rather than divinity. Jesus's physical conception and birth as part of the doctrine of incarnation Muslims understand as incompatible with both Christian and Muslim teachings.

On top of theological rebuttals of incarnation stands the violation against *tawḥid*, the oneness of God, a death blow against the Christian doctrine of the Trinity. *Tawḥid* was seen by Muslims as taught not only by the Qur'an but also in the Bible (Deut 6:4). A related concern among Muslim commentators is the incompatibility of incarnation with God's transcendence. The idea of God becoming flesh violates Muslim sensibilities concerning the principles of God's glory and greatness.

Although Jesus Christ and Muhammad share a similar status of not being divine in Islamic understanding, in the comparative work between Islam and Christianity, Christ's counterpart is not Muhammad but rather the Word of God! Why is that? For many reasons. First, even though Christ is named a "prophet" in the Qur'an, it is Muhammad who is the "seal of the prophets" and thus occupies a unique role. Second, unlike Christian faith, which is determined by belief in Christ, Islam is not based on Muhammad but rather on the Qur'an and Allah. Christ as the living Word of God in the

Christian view and the divine revelation in the Qur'an in Islamic understanding is the more appropriate comparison.

This is not to say that no comparison between the two founding religious figures, Jesus and Muhammad, should therefore be attempted. In fact, particularly in the Hadith collections a number of sayings seek to clarify the relation between the two men. Among them is the important, oft-quoted, and highly respectful statement by Muhammad of Jesus: "Prophets are brothers in faith, having different mothers. Their religion is, however, one and there is no Apostle between us (between me and Jesus Christ)."[47] We know historically that Muhammad's own relation to Christianity and Christian tradition in general, especially in the early phases of his career, was fairly positive and constructive.

In terms of the continuing and widening mutual engagement between these two sister faiths, similarly to what I mentioned in regards to the Jewish sister faith, Christians do well to engage from a humble and hospitable place. That posture also makes possible mutual learning and even self-criticism. Useful to both parties is the veteran comparative theologian Hans Küng's piece of advice: "If we on the Christian side make an effort to reevaluate Muhammad on the basis of Islamic sources, especially the Qur'an, we also hope that for their part the Muslims will eventually be prepared to move toward *a reevaluation of Jesus of Nazareth on the basis of historical sources* (namely, the Gospels) as many Jews have already been doing."[48]

Moving now to Asia, we will encounter in Buddhist and Hindu estimations of Jesus Christ much stranger territory.

Jesus and Buddha: Strangers or Comrades?

Unlike the relationship with Islam, the interaction between Jesus traditions and Buddhist traditions has not been wide and deep until the twentieth century. In Europe and North America, best known are the many Mahayana traditions that represent the majority "vehicle" of Buddhism, as opposed to the original Theravada.

Even though Gautama Buddha, like the founder of Islam, is not considered divine but rather the first one to have discovered the secret to enlightenment, many parallels between him and Jesus of Nazareth make good comparisons, notwithstanding the scarcity of details about the Shayamuni's (Gautama's) life, including:

---

47. Sahih Muslim, *Kitāb al-Fadā' il*, bk. 30, para. 5836, quoted in Leirvik, *Images of Jesus Christ*, 38.
48. Küng, "Christian Response," 111.

- miraculous elements attached to the birth of both founders; including cosmic signs and phenomena, as well as ominous threat;
- that both faced temptations, one in the forest, the other in the desert;
- that both became itinerant preachers and teachers and were considered miracle-workers; and
- that both were men of prayer and meditation.

From the Buddhist perspective, there are also key differences. Particularly in Theravada tradition, given the fact that Buddha taught no fewer than forty-five years, the teaching ministry of Jesus, comprising only three years at most, does not easily gain respect. Even with their fairly kind assessments, Buddhists present occasional criticisms—such as the illicit status of Mary and the coming of Jesus at such a late moment of history.

A foundational difference between the two faiths, as the Buddhist Rita M. Gross puts it, is that Christianity locates the "truth in the messenger, whereas Buddhism tends to focus on the message." This is linked with the fact that Christian tradition has a tendency "to personify the ultimate while Buddhists tend toward nonpersonal metaphors about ultimate reality."[49]

Similar to Islam's, understandably Buddhism's biggest obstacle is the Christian claim of Jesus's divinity and corollary creedal beliefs. Despite all their appreciation of Jesus's ethical life, ministry, and teaching, this is the key stumbling block, as the leading Tibetan Buddhist scholar and practitioner José Ignacio Cabezón notes: "The problem lies not in the claim that Jesus is the incarnation or manifestation of a deity. What I find objectionable is (a) the Christian characterization of the deity whose incarnation Jesus is said to be, and (b) the claim that Jesus is unique in being an incarnation."[50]

Behind the Buddhist refusal to grant a salvific role to Jesus lie a number of doctrinal presuppositions. In Buddhist thought, every sentient person is responsible for his or her destiny. The idea that the salvation of men and women would be dependent on any historical event, let alone such as the cross, is totally foreign to Buddhism. After all, says Buddhists, mere belief or doctrine cannot save the human person; only effort toward enlightenment can lead to it.

That the idea of incarnation in itself is not a problem for Buddhists is based on the belief prevalent among all Mahayana Buddhists that the universe is populated by enlightened beings who, having attained the buddhahood, have the capacity to incarnate for the welfare of others. That said, to consider Jesus as incarnate on the basis of his extraordinary teaching, miracles, and

49. Gross, "Meditating on Jesus," 44.
50. Cabezón, "Buddhist Views of Jesus," 21.

CHRISTOLOGY

ethical life is not to say that therefore he "possessed the quality of maximal greatness (enlightenment), that is, that he was a buddha."[51]

In many respects, Jesus might be better compared with a Boddhisattva, a Buddha-in-the-making, who for the sake of others is willing to suffer and postpone his own enlightenment (as happens in Mahayana traditions). In the (Japanese and Chinese) Pure Land tradition, Jesus can be similarly respected as a Boddhisattva, a compassionate being who helps others, a manifestation of Amitabha. Even then there is no ultimacy to the role of Jesus after the Christian tradition. Yet wider differences separate the Theravada tradition and Christian interpretation of Jesus, as Theravada does not emphasize the idea of the ones having experienced enlightenment postponing their final release for the benefit of others.

But what about the fact that anyone who knows Buddhism in its everyday manifestation—even in the Theravada form—knows how highly Buddha is venerated and how significant a role he plays in the structure of that religion? Consider these two well-known examples. Buddha makes an identification with Dhamma (the doctrine, teaching): "He who sees Dhamma . . . sees me; he who sees me sees Dhamma" (Samyutta Nikaya 22.87). Doesn't this resemble in some important ways the Johannine Jesus's words about the unity between him and the Father (John 10:30)? Indeed, Buddhist tradition speaks of the kind of "visible Dhamma" in terms of the life of the person who has freed himself or herself totally from hatred, delusion, and greed. Or consider the story of Brahman Dona in the Pali Canon who, having discovered Buddha's footprints goes to Buddha filled with amazement and awe to ask about their origin. Buddha explains that they belong neither to a *deva* (celestial being) nor to a spirit nor even to a human being, since all those forms of existence still are stuck within the bounds of samsara leading to rebirths. Instead, Buddha has transcended all that—and that's what makes him *Buddha*!

With regard to these kinds of observations, the Mahayanas remind us of their foundational doctrine of "buddhahoods" or "three bodies" (*trikaya* in Pali), which sheds more light on the complexity of Buddha's role. He is:

- "Transformation Body," the earthly Buddha, a transient and illusionary form of existence;
- "Enjoyment Body," the form of existence for the sake of others; and
- "Dhamma Body," the ultimate form of existence that indeed is no longer a "form" of existence but is formless. In other words, the last

---

51. Cabezón, "Buddhist Views of Jesus," 21–22, here 22.

"body" transcends the form and laws of existence. It is inconceivable and ineffable.

Much comparative work is required to come to a more precise understanding of the implications of this key Mahayana concept. All that can be said at this point is that the major difference is its vision of multiple Boddhisattvas (Enlightened Ones) vis-à-vis the Christian focus on a single savior.

Christ and Avatars in Hindu-Christian Engagement

Although it is likely that there was a Christian presence in India as early as the first century, no evidence of Hindu perceptions of Jesus survives; we have to wait until the seventeenth century for that. What makes the mutual dialogue between Hindus and Christians both promising and challenging is that there are few, if any, doctrinal boundaries that are exclusively Hindu or required of followers to belong.

Importantly, beginning from the end of the nineteenth century, a new wave of interpretations of Christ emerged, interpretations deeply rooted in the religious (Hindu) soil of Asia. This wave was known as the Indian Renaissance or neo-Hindu reform, and the titles of Raimundo Panikkar's *Unknown Christ of Hinduism* and M. M. Thomas's *Acknowledged Christ of the Indian Renaissance* reflect that. The contemporary Indian theologian Stanley J. Samartha's *Hindu Response to the Unbound Christ* reminds us that while many Indians attached themselves to the person of Jesus Christ—who reflects the features of Hindu avatars (incarnations of Hindu gods such as the famous Krishna or Vishnu)—they also detached that person from the institutional church.

Some strands of Hinduism, such as the Hare Krishna movement, consider Jesus to be a guru. Hare Krishna focuses on love and devotion rather than on doctrine, particularly toward Krishna, the avatar of Vishnu. The ultimate goal of this pursuit is active love and desire for God. Avatars, divine embodiments, empowered with divine *shakti* (power), help revive the devotion to God. Jesus is one of those divinely empowered incarnations.

If this is possible, *The Gospel of Sri Ramakrishna*, written by the great nineteenth-century Bengalese guru Ramakrishna Paramahansa, granted high status to Jesus. He even claimed to have had a number of mystical encounters with Jesus. His most famous disciple, Swami Vivekananda—best known for his influential speech at the first World's Parliament of Religions in Chicago (1893) and as the founder of Vedanta Societies—wrote the highly laudatory preface to the (unfinished) Bengali translation of Thomas à Kempis's *Imitation of Christ*.

Several Hindu writers were excited by the social teachings of Christ but did not make a personal commitment to him. An example is Swami Vivekananda of the Ramakrishna order who elevated Jesus to the company of the highly revered figures of Buddha and Krishna, the incarnation of Vishnu. Mahatma Gandhi's Jesus is well known as an ethical teacher, reflecting the same principles that guided his own pacifistic fight for the liberation of the Indian people, namely, *satyagraha* (the search for truth) and *ahimsa* (nonviolence). There are also Hindus who have become Christians but insist they have remained Hindus, of whom the best known is Brahmabandhab Upadhyaya. His spirituality is based on an intimate experience of the person of Jesus the Son of God, who became both his guru and his friend. For him, whether or not Jesus was divine is not the point.

By and large, Hindu perceptions of Jesus are positive. This is similar to Buddhist views and different from a number of Jewish and Islamic views. In general, Hindu perceptions of Jesus, including twentieth-century ones, can be described in this way: "(1) Jesus is a rational teacher of universal values; (2) Jesus is an incarnation of God among other incarnations; and (3) Jesus is a spiritual teacher. These positions are not, of course, mutually exclusive."[52]

Among the Hindu commentators are those who consider Jesus of Nazareth a mere human teacher, albeit a highly respected and honored one. These interpreters of Christ also reject belief in Jesus being the incarnation of God. Materially these interpretations echo many of the views of classical liberalism. There are also people like Keshub Chunder Sen who, replacing the doctrine of the Trinity with the Biunity of Father and Spirit, fall short of regarding Jesus as the divine incarnation, his "Divine Humanity."[53] Reminiscent of classical liberalism and early Christian pluralism is also the fairly typical "difference of meaning between *Jesus* and *Christ*. Jesus is the name of a little human body in which the vast Christ Consciousness was born. Although the Christ Consciousness manifested in the body of Jesus, it cannot be limited to one human form" (emphasis original).[54] In this framework, "Christ" does not mean a particular individual but rather a collective or perhaps even cosmic consciousness.

In sum, it is perhaps fair to claim that most contemporary Hindu interpreters of Jesus are willing to grant divine status to Jesus Christ, somewhat parallel to Krishna, the avatar of Vishnu. At the same time, important qualifications and clarifications are in order. It is a commonplace in Hindu thought to believe that some dimension of the human being is divine. The

---

52. Flood, "Jesus in Hinduism," 202.

53. Editors's (Barker and Gregg, *Jesus beyond Christianity*) explanation as an introduction to Sen, "Lectures in India," 165–66, here 165.

54. Yogananda, *Man's Eternal Quest*, 297.

possibility of realization of the divine lies within the reach of any human being; however, in most cases that does not happen. Jesus is one of those who did realize the divine in himself, and as such (say Hindus) his importance lies in his role as the symbol of the potential of the realization of the divine in the human person. From that perspective, even the cross may be appropriated as the form of an ultimate self-sacrifice, although it has nothing to do with atonement for sins in the Christian sense.

Now, from the point of view of Hinduism, what about the role and work of divine embodiments or avatars? Do they resemble Christ as divine incarnation? As background let me remind you that in classical Hinduism the one Brahman in its "manifested" form is known as the Hindu Trimurti, namely, Brahma (the "Creator God"), Vishnu (the "Preserver God"), and Shiva (the "Destroyer God" [or "Completer God"]). As it is Vishnu's task to make sure the universe and its order will not be destroyed in an undue manner, Vishnu intervenes in the affairs of the world through various forms of avatar. This "descent," as the word avatar literally means, can be thought of as "incarnation." Consider the oft-cited passage in Bhagavad Gita (4.7–8), which renders it as follows:

> Whenever there is a decline of Dharma and the rise of Adharma, O Arjuna, then I manifest (or incarnate) Myself. I incarnate from time to time for protecting the good, for transforming the wicked, and for establishing Dharma, the world order.

In that the purpose of the "coming down" of God is the establishment of dhamma, the right order, "righteousness" has only marginally to do with the Christian notion of atonement and salvation (although in Christian tradition, the return of Christ at the End will usher in justice and peace).

Hindu mythology includes numerous accounts of incarnations. Among those, an established doctrine widely shared by various Hindu strands is ten incarnations of Vishnu beginning as a fish and then a tortoise, and continuing all the way to Rama and Krishna, the two most cherished avatars of all, and finally to the Buddha.[55] Furthermore, unlike Christian tradition, it is customary for Hindu thought to conceive of avatars in degrees, from a partial to a fuller to a fullest measure of incarnation. This is in direct contrast to the traditional Christian view of incarnation. So, also, is the idea of multiple "descents" of the divine.

The following chapter continues Jesus story but with a focus on his work as the Savior.

---

55. Sharma, *Classic Hindu Thought*, 6–7, 82–86.

6

Reconciliation

What Did Jesus Do for Our Salvation?

Continuing the Jesus Story with a Special Focus on His Salvific Work for Us

YOU MAY RECALL FROM the previous chapter the two-fold division of the doctrine of Christology, namely: Who is the person of Jesus Christ? And what is his salvific work for us? Here we focus on the latter, known traditionally under the rubric of "atonement." Whereas Christ, the Savior, is of course the center of any discussion of atonement, at the same time, in keeping with the trinitarian nature of all Christian theology and faith, Father and Spirit are also intimately involved, as we will see below.

Similarly to what was discussed in the previous chapter about the need to look at the whole history of Jesus Christ, not only one aspect of it, the doctrine of atonement seeks to frame the conversation in comprehensive terms. As Moltmann puts it succinctly: "In the theological sense, salvation is whole salvation and the salvation of the whole, or it is not God's salvation; for God is 'the all-determining reality.'"[1] All aspects of our lives—the spiritual, mental, physical, social, intellectual, and so forth are in need of the healing and saving touch of the Triune God. God, the Creator, is not only interested in the salvation of our souls in eternity, as much as that is the ultimate goal; salvation begins here and touches all aspects of our lives.

We begin by taking a careful look at the ways in which the Bible highlights the many aspects of Christ's atonement, and then take some

---

1. Moltmann, *Way of Jesus Christ*, 45.

lessons from the many ways in which the church and theology developed these ideas in the so-called "atonement theories."

An important current question about the suffering and death on the cross relates to the question of violence in the world. So we consider that carefully next. All of that prepares us to reflect on the many facets and gifts of the salvific work of the Triune God for our salvation, including the role of the church in bringing about reconciliation in the world.

That reflection will naturally lead into the last section of the chapter, which picks up the interfaith engagement from the end of the previous chapter, only this time centering on the question of "salvation."

What Does the Bible Tell Us about the Salvific Suffering and Death of Christ?

As important as are the last days of Jesus on the earth, days culminating in his suffering, death, resurrection, and ascension, in all four Gospels the work of reconciliation encompasses all of Jesus's life and all of his ministry with its teaching, healing, exorcism, declaration of forgiveness, and caring, particularly for the weak and the marginalized. The rest of the NT expands on the salvific meaning of this all-encompassing and salvific Christ "event."

What is most distinctive about the biblical teaching on atonement is its use of numerous metaphors, symbols, and images, all intended to highlight atonement's many dimensions and benefits. Some of the metaphors are drawn from the OT world, and others from various sources familiar to the cultures of the times. They include the court of law (e.g., justification), the world of commerce (e.g., redemption), personal and communal relationships (e.g., reconciliation), cult and worship (e.g., sacrifice), as well as the battleground (e.g., triumph over evil).

The culmination of suffering in the death on the cross did not come as a surprise: it was not only announced beforehand (Mark 8:31–38), but there was a clear divine plan and determination behind it (Matt 16:21; Mark 8:31; Luke 9:22; etc.). In the Gospel of Mark, Jesus speaks of giving "his life as a ransom for many" (Mark 10:45) and pouring out his "blood of the covenant . . . for many" (14:24). The term "ransom," one of the numerous metaphors, refers to the ideas of deliverance and release. It is drawn from the Roman slave trade and the hopes of the OT people of God who lived under foreign tyrannies. The metaphor of covenant blood is connected with Yahweh's faithful acts in saving, freeing, and protecting his people on the basis of covenants often sealed with blood (as in Gen 15).

RECONCILIATION

It was left to Pauline traditions to offer a rich and variegated depiction of the many dimensions of the saving significance of Jesus's work for us. Often Paul mixes a number of metaphors in one passage. Consider 2 Corinthians 5:14—6:2 (which you may want to read in your Bible before continuing). It is a grand example of the conflation of metaphors. While "reconciliation"—bringing together two distanced parties (as also in Rom 5:10–11; Eph 2:16; Col 1:20)—towers here as the main metaphor, other metaphors in the passage include "substitution," "representation," "forgiveness," "sin offering," "(cosmic) renewal," "righteousness," and divine "favor." Similar rich and multifaceted descriptions can be found for example in Galatians 3:10–14, with images such as "cursing" (of the one hang on the tree), justification, redemption, and blessing. Or think of images drawn from the battlefield, cosmic or earthly, as in Colossians 2:15, which speak of the defeat of powers.

The reason why the Gospel and the Acts authored by St. Luke are so important is that they claim to represent authentic samples of the missionary preaching of the early church encompassing both Petrine and Pauline ministries. Alongside the cross, both have a strong focus on the resurrection and ascension, as well as on the pouring out and power of the Holy Spirit. For Luke, the Pentecostal pouring out of the Spirit on all flesh (Acts 2) marks the beginning of the last days. The crucified Messiah has now been made the risen and ascended Lord (2:36) who brings about forgiveness and restoration to the people of God (5:30–31). Healings as a foretaste of a holistic salvation and promises of the coming eschatological fulfillment are an integral part of the early church's preaching (Acts 3:1—4:22).

If it is possible, the extensive Johannine traditions depict an even more distinctive approach to atonement with their great rhetorical devices, such as speaking of the cross in terms of "lifting up" (John 3:14–15; 8:28) and glorification of the Son of Man (13:32). These writings join familiar OT metaphors of the sacrificial lamb (1:29) with metaphors of water and cleansing (13:10–11; 15:3), which also relate to pneumatological aspects of salvation (4:13–15; 7:37–39). John's epistles are fond of images of "light" and "purification" (1 John 1:5–7; 2:9; 3:3), forgiveness (1:8–9), and sacrifice for sins (2:2; 3:5). The book of Revelation uses several OT images in the cosmic context, including the victorious Lamb (Rev 5:5–10).

The book of Hebrews is fully embedded in the OT imagery of the temple, priesthood, sacrifices, and covenant. First Peter, while conversant with images of salvation such as the hope for the eschatological inheritance (1 Pet 1:3–5, 13), emphasizes what later theology calls the "moral example" view, meaning the invitation to imitate the suffering and cross of Christ (2:12, 19, 21–25; 3:14–17).

In sum: no single metaphor can capture the fullness of salvation; many metaphors are needed. This is the overarching message of our brief Bible study!

The Many Ways Atonement Has Been Illustrated

The Healing Touch of the Savior—and the Snatching Away from the Devil

Given the great detail and skill with which the Church Fathers handled the complex questions of the Trinity and Christ's "two-natures," it is curious that they did not attempt to explain the precise meaning of the atonement. While the life, suffering, death, and resurrection of Jesus appeared often in their teachings, surprisingly they had very few, if any, significant debates and disputes about this most central issue of faith.

For the first millennium of Christian history, the so-called "Christ the Champion" (Latin *Christus Victor*) metaphor was the most typical way of conceiving atonement. Its central idea is of the victory gained over sin through the incarnation, of the defeat of the powers that resisted, and of the healing, redemption, and liberation that the Triune God achieved through the Son.

What is known under the "recapitulation" version of *Christus Victor* metaphors originated from the teaching of Irenaeus, the second-century bishop of Lyons, born to Greek-speaking parents, and thus also highly regarded in the Christian East. Cosmic in its orientation, highlighting particularly the blessings of Christ's incarnation, this approach understood mortality rather than sinfulness as the ultimate power to be defeated. Behind this interpretation is an understanding of the fall as an unfortunate accident, natural to humanity-in-childhood, and typical of the East, rather than as a tragic fall from grace as the Western Church later formulated it. The incarnation then means that Christ "recapitulates" (or reviews) in himself all the stages of human life, including those that belong to our state as sinners—not only individual human lives, but even the whole "history of humankind" and indeed of the creation. Irenaeus taught that Christ by his incarnation and human life reverses the course on which Adam by his sin started to lead humanity. Christ communicates immortality to those who are united to him by faith and effects a transformation in their lives. Each step of recapitulation of human history brings healing and a saving touch.

The other version of the *Christus Victor* model employed the imagery of "ransom" and has its secular background in the act of releasing slaves through payment. The fourth-century Eastern Bishop Gregory of Nyssa created his famous—or rather, infamous—image of God paying the ransom by deceiving the devil with the trickery of a fishhook. Hidden under human nature, said Gregory, was Christ's deity, which the devil devoured as bait and in so doing participated in destroying his own power. Immediately following the hook allegory, Gregory interpreted Christ's work also in terms of "healing touch," a metaphor similar in many ways to Irenaeus's allegory.

Meeting God's Righteous Demands and Being Saved from Guilt and Condemnation

Whereas healing touch and release from captivity to enslaving powers were the dominant images of atonement during the first millennium, in the Christian West the slow development of atonement theology came to highlight much more robustly both issues of God's righteous demands as the judge and the need for humanity to escape the fear of damnation and condemnation. The stark Augustinian concept of original sin discussed in chapter 4 points to those themes.

The famed eleventh-century British Bishop, Anselm of Canterbury, is known for "satisfaction" theory. His *Cur Deus Homo?* (Why God became Human) offers logical and theological reasoning for the necessity of the incarnation. Medieval feudal society, with its hierarchy and desire for harmony, regarded sin as a disruptive factor. In this worldview, rather than being a debt to the devil, sin is the failure to render to God his due, a blockage to the free flow of divinely intended happiness for humanity. Since the just God is not able to forgive sin without payment for the lost honor, satisfaction is needed—satisfaction proportional to the seriousness of the violation. Satisfaction can be paid only by God via the God-man through his voluntary death, which was not occasioned by his own need but was rather a voluntary self-offering as payment on our behalf. This innocent life, suffering, and death of the incarnate Son provided satisfaction and God's righteousness and justice was maintained.

Anselm's contemporary, Peter Abelard, disagreed with him. Abelard insisted that God indeed has the right of ownership to humans and that it is perfectly appropriate for God to forgive without any "satisfaction," if God so wishes. Hence, rather than satisfaction or sacrifice, Jesus's suffering and death are a compelling example to follow. Jesus embodies God's sacrificial love. Thus, we have the nomenclature the "Moral Example View." Abelard's quite thin theology of sin and the fall made this possible, somewhat akin to the Christian East.

Yet not surprisingly, instead of Abelard's view, the Anselmian interpretation became the dominant view in the West. Thomas Aquinas helped consolidate the satisfaction view in the context of the Western Church's emphasis on sacrifice and the debt of sin. The Protestant Reformers, particularly the Reformed side, continued in the line of the Anselmian view, even if some like Luther also had a high regard for *Christus Victor*.

The Reformers' view is often labeled the "Penal Substitution" view, which hints at its Anselmian basis and the need for a sacrificial-expiatory death on the cross as a way to deal with condemned humanity's lot because of sin. In Reformed theology and particularly in the ensuing conservative and Fundamentalistic Christianity at the turn of the twentieth century, the endorsement of the penal substitution often became the test of orthodoxy. Charles Hodge, a leading and highly influential Reformed theologian in the USA, argued that it is axiomatic that forgiveness requires "satisfaction," and that can be had only through "punishment" in terms of Christ's "sacrifice."[2] Karl Barth, while in many ways diverging from his Reformed tradition, in his massive discussion of the topic of atonement under the telling heading "The Judge Judged in Our Place," unabashedly defended the substitutionary nature of atonement as Christ becomes the sin-bearer and the condemned.[3]

Before going further, yet another detour is in order, once again to underline the richness of atonement theology. As much as Abelard's moral example view became marginal in many ways, later movements and thinkers embraced his type of interpretation (though not always in reference to him). Dissatisfied with Anselmian and Reformational theories, the Enlightenment thinkers understandably found much to commend in the moral example view. It fit well with Immanuel Kant's idea of Jesus as the moral ideal rather than the crucified one. Liberal Protestants, similarly, considered this interpretation appealing.

Now, after this brief survey, a question arises: Which of these atonement theories is the correct one? What are their strengths and potential weaknesses?

The Gains and Liabilities of Traditional "Atonement Theories"

The recapitulation view helps theology make an integral connection between incarnation, life, death, resurrection, and ascension—in other words, with the whole history of Jesus. It is a big gain in light of everything we have talked about so far. It also reminds us of the obvious insight that as dramatic

---

2. Hodge, *Systematic Theology*, 2:480–54.
3. Barth, *Church Dogmatics*, IV/1, 211–82.

a problem as sin is, mortality is the ultimate problem. What really counts is that both in life (as "recapitulated" by the Incarnate Savior) and in death (conquered by his death and glorious resurrection) we will be healed and saved. Hence, I strongly recommend that all Christians notwithstanding their denomination or locality become more familiar with this "classic view," as it is also called at times (alongside the "ransom" version of Gregory and others). Speaking of the latter, I think we shouldn't be put off by the infamous "tricking the devil" rhetorical device. The more substantial challenge to this version is the mistaken view of the rights of the devil. While the NT puts the fallen "world" (*kosmos*) under the power of Satan (1 John 5:19), that in itself does not imply that Satan "possesses" the world. Even talk about "debt" or being indebted to the devil is not helpful; if sin accrues a debt, it is rather a debt the creature owes to the Creator.

That said, the ransom theory rightly highlights the need for personal, communal, and cosmic release from under the powers that both resist the will of God and claim authority over creatures and the creation as a whole. By implication, the hope for freedom from all sorts of powers, including sociopolitical or sexist ones as in liberation theologies, is grounded in the history of salvation rather than in a utopia.

While not often highlighted, the Anselmian way of explaining the atonement agrees in important ways with the classic view, particularly the recapitulation version, in its integral linking of atonement to incarnation. Even if the Anselmian theory shifts the focus from incarnation to the "payment of satisfaction," its foundational instincts lean into a more comprehensive view of the salvific history of Jesus.

Where we have to be careful with the Anselmian satisfaction model is to acknowledge its deeply contextual nature. For while it spoke directly to the issues of its times (the medieval hierarchical society in which it was one's duty to pay honor to one's superiors), its applicability in our modern world is far less obvious. Not to say that it is out of date, but that its main intuitions have to be "translated" for our own contemporary contexts.

Highlighting (God's) honor rather than (human) guilt in itself is legitimate since in many parts of the world, ancient and contemporary, honor is a central cultural category. However, the liability of Anselm's way of conceiving of divine honor is that it seems to operate with a formal, abstract principle. Biblical theology operates according to covenant-based, relational, and personalistic notions of the divine honor. This helps us distinguish between the abstract, juridical notion of justice in medieval society, which lays the background for the Anselmian model, and the notion of justice in terms of living rightly and in keeping with the committed, grace-based covenant relationships of the Bible. Those who hold the Anselmian viewpoint do well to see the work of salvation as stemming not so much from God's offended honor as from the unbounded love of the Creator for the creatures gone astray. According to the biblical witness, God is the subject of reconciliation (2 Cor 5:18–20) rather than the "object" of satisfaction.

Going beyond this, but building also on the satisfaction model, the penal substitutionary version highlights the theme of guilt, which leads to punishment and thus the need for a sacrifice. While no one reading the Bible should do away with sacrifice and related rites of shedding blood, we also have to listen carefully to the legitimate critique against this model's one-sided employment, including:

- its view of justice, which focuses too much on penalty and satisfaction as well as God's wrath;
- that it is laden with the guilt- and penitence-oriented ethos of the later medieval/Reformation culture, which begs the question of the role of divine love and mercy;
- that it may mistakenly set the Son and Father over against one another, and at the same time leave no role for the Spirit in the trinitarian work of atonement;
- that it tends to suffer from over-individualism and ignorance of communal, sociopolitical, and cosmic dimensions of salvation;
- that while it does not ignore the incarnation, the whole history of Jesus may be undermined by its focus on the satisfaction on the cross;
- that it may at times lack ethical incentive with its robustly negative view of human nature and its total incapacity to respond to God's initiative of salvation; and
- that it is concerning that in recent decades among many conservative Protestant churches, this model has been made the primary test of orthodoxy. This is against the observation that at no times has the church had only one theory of atonement and that none of the creeds rule on the details of the issue.

In defense of the penal substitution view of atonement, there is no denying the presence of punishment and even retaliation in the NT (see Rom 2:6–11; Matt 13:42, 50; and throughout the book of Revelation). That said, the emphasis in salvation is not so much on retaliation as it is on rescue and repair.

We can glean important lessons from moral example theory, too. There is certainly good biblical support for it. As long as we do not ignore the fall and sin—and, as a result, forgiveness and reconciliation—this model can also help balance some liabilities of the satisfaction and penal-substitution views listed above.

In short, we need the whole diversity of the above theories of atonement to capture the richness of the gift of salvation. While guilt is part of the human problem, guilt is not all that plagues humanity. Furthermore, guilt is not only about personal life: it also relates to communal and other structural sins. Mortality and decay as well as bondage and slavery to powers—as the classic view contends—are problems too. Forgiveness and renewal of life, rather than merely an abstract satisfaction or another kind of divine transaction, should be the focus when speaking of guilt, repentance, and forgiveness.

Are Suffering and Violence Necessary for Salvation?

There is no denying the horrific violence and even torture that Jesus experienced in his suffering and death on the cross. No wonder modern critics of Christianity have found this fertile soil to highlight the horror of violence. Similarly, a growing number of "insider" critics, namely Christian theologians themselves, have weighed in on this issue. Rather than ignoring them, the church and theology would do well to listen carefully to them.

Particularly liable to criticism are satisfaction and penal-substitution models, but they are not the only ones. Even the classic theories endorse the biblical story of suffering and death, as does also the moral example view. Here is a summary of the most typical attacks on Jesus's suffering and death:

First, many people find it unacceptable to assume a God in need of, or as an agent of, violence. Such people would say that the satisfaction (and by inference, penal-satisfaction) model perverts the picture of a loving, merciful God by producing a "sadomasochistic theology and practice based on the idea of an 'offended' God who can only be mollified through the payment of innocent blood."[4] Second, it is a commonplace to note that violence fosters violence and thus should be abandoned. Third, a number of female theologians have encountered satisfaction-based models as means of legitimizing and perhaps even endorsing female suffering and patriarchy. There are those who go so far as to link the suffering and cross to child abuse!

---

4. Ruether, *Introducing Redemption*, 100.

How have Christian scholars responded to all such claims? It might be appealing simply to deny the presence of violence in the biblical story of atonement. That, however, is a misjudgment; yes, there are violent, indeed, very violent elements in the Passion Story. A more appropriate place to begin might be to remind us that Jesus's sacrifice is the ultimate and last one, once and for all (Heb 7:27). No more instances of sacrifice or shedding of blood are needed (9:14; 10:14). Not only Jesus's death on the cross but also his life and ministry speak for the cessation and overcoming of the cycle of violence. According to Miroslav Volf, "the Crucified Messiah" absorbs aggression and so stops violence. Ultimately, Christ's cross is an act of embrace of his opponents. The death of Christ means atonement for sins. It also makes it possible for human beings to embrace enemies.[5]

Regarding criticisms presented above: While the charge against the "sadomasochistic" God hardly deserves a serious theological response, behind the rhetoric there is a serious lack of a proper trinitarian framework. Too easily traditional models of atonement yield a picture of the suffering Son in the hands of the just and demanding Father. The corrective can be found in a solid Trinitarian communion theology based on mutual love, respect, and joint work rather than domination and abuse. We should never use voluntary suffering on behalf of others (embodied most purely in the Savior of the Cross) as a pretext for encouraging those already marginalized and suffering to endure unjust treatment, let alone do so silently.

Furthermore, we have to be able to make a distinction between violence *per se* and necessary harm with a view toward a higher good. Thus, a medical doctor's amputation of a patient's leg to save his or her life is not violence. Killing, hitting, abusing, or speaking badly of my neighbor or a stranger is always and without question violence. Very importantly, while humans have no right to violence (perhaps, apart from civil disobedience and "just war"), God has the right. Taking his cue from the vision of Revelation 19, Volf concludes: "*The end of the world is not violence, but a nonviolent embrace without end.* . . . The world to come is ruled by the one who on the cross took violence upon himself in order to conquer the enmity and embrace the enemy. The Lamb's rule is legitimized not by the 'sword' but by its 'wounds'" (emphasis original).[6]

Now we are in a place to attempt a more comprehensive and wider account of the wonderful work of atonement given to us by the Triune God. Afterwards we will look at Jewish, Muslim, Hindu, and Buddhist ideas of salvation.

---

5. Volf, *Exclusion and Embrace*, 290–95.
6. Volf, *Exclusion and Embrace*, 300–301.

Putting It All Together: A Comprehensive View of Atonement

The "Actors" of Atonement: Father, Son, and Spirit

Having emphasized throughout this book the trinitarian shape of our faith, let us pause for a moment to remind us of the cooperation between the three. Recall the Pauline saying that "God was in Christ reconciling the world to Himself" (2 Cor 5:19 NASB). Christ's voluntary suffering for us is not so much a "substitute" as it is the divinely appointed means of total identification with and representation of humanity. When we see atonement as the unified work of the triune God, it becomes evident that "God does not love us because Christ died for us, but that Christ died for us because God loves us, and his sacrifice is an expression of this love. The cross of Christ was not given by man to change God, but given by God to change man."[7]

The Spirit's role comes to the fore particularly in the raising up from the dead of Jesus. The Father raised his Son from the dead through the power of the life-giving work of the Spirit (Rom 1:4; 8:11). In doing so, the work of the Spirit brought to culmination the work of salvation.

We'll say more about the Spirit's distinctive role in atonement as we talk about resurrection below.

"The Crucified God": God in Christ Suffers with and for Us

The biblical story about the Suffering Messiah is a powerful statement about what kind of God we have: God who did not eschew suffering. Rather, God is a cosufferer. No other contemporary theologian has underscored this more clearly than Moltmann, who boldly considers "the cross of Christ as the foundation and criticism of Christian theology."[8] In the preface to *The Crucified God*, he claims that "whatever can stand before the face of the crucified Christ is true Christian theology. What cannot stand there must disappear."[9]

The cross tells us that God makes suffering his own and so overcomes it. The Son suffers the pain of being cut off from the life of the Father, and the Father suffers the pain of giving up his Son. By doing so,

---

7. Culpepper, *Interpreting the Atonement*, 131.
8. Subtitle to Moltmann, *Crucified God*.
9. Moltmann, *Crucified God*, x.

God "also accepts and adopts [suffering] himself, making it part of his own eternal life."[10]

Jesus's physical sufferings were real. Yet even more painful was the rejection, first by his own people and then ultimately by his Father.

> To suffer and to be rejected are not identical. Suffering can be celebrated and admired. It can arouse compassion. But to be rejected takes away the dignity from suffering and makes it dishonourable suffering. To suffer and be rejected signify the cross.[11]

Christ's sufferings had both an active and a passive side. On the one hand, they were voluntary, not imposed by others (as is the case in domestic violence or wartime rape). On the other hand, Christ represents the victim rather than the perpetrator. Christ, the Suffering Servant, also resisted power structures, abuse of the weak, and any instrumental treatment of the other. Suffering and pain are reprehensible and objectionable not only to women or other minorities but to all of us. They are not to be glorified.

The Cruel Plan of the Humans and the Saving Plan of God

In the eyes of his own people and the people of the occupying Roman Empire, Jesus was put to death as a messianic pretender and blasphemer, allegedly having violated the law and tradition and usurped the status of God. In fact, he was regarded as a rebel. From the perspective of the society of his times, "Jesus's death on the cross is best viewed as what that event concretely was, an imperial execution."[12] From the perspective of the eternal plan and love of God, Jesus's suffering and death ultimately brought about the divinely appointed blessings and salvation for the world.

The Roman Catholic Aloysius Pieris of Sri Lanka reminds us that Jesus's "double baptism" took place in the context of "true local churches of Asia . . . [having] been baptized in the Jordan of Asian religions and the Calvary of Asian poverty." The powerful crucified him on "a cross that the money-polluted religiosity of his day planted on Calvary with the aid of a colonial power (Luke 23:1–23)."[13] Whatever political and religious reasons and motives there were behind the murder of Jesus, ultimately it was a part of the divine plan.

---

10. Moltmann, *Trinity and the Kingdom*, 119.
11. Moltmann, *Crucified God*, 55.
12. Taylor, *Executed God*, xiv.
13. Pieris, *Asian Theology of Liberation*, 50, 49 respectively.

The Korean-born theologian Andrew Sung Park looks at the meaning of the cross through the lens of the key Korean cultural concept of *han*, which denotes suffering and pain, "a sense of unresolved resentment against injustices suffered, a sense of helplessness, . . . a feeling of acute pain and sorrow in one's guts and bowels."[14] Incarnation and crucifixion speak to the theme of *han*: "The all-powerful God was crucified. The cross is the symbol of God's han which makes known God's own vulnerability to human sin. . . . The cry of the wounded heart of God on the cross reverberates throughout the whole of history."[15]

The Father Raised the Son from the Dead through the Power of the Spirit

Resurrection is an integral part of the salvific work of the triune God: The Father raised his Son from death through the power of the Spirit (Rom 1:3-4). As the eternal bond of love, the life-giving Spirit broke through the power of death and manifested new life in the bodily resurrection of the crucified One.

Protestants speak a lot about the cross, but in our talk resurrection and particularly the ensuing ascension to the right hand of the Father do not feature nearly as much. Things were different with the early church. The Apostles in their preaching linked the cross intimately with the resurrection and ascension (Acts 3:14-15; see also 2:23-24; 4:10; 5:30; 10:39-40; Rom 6:3-11; 8:34; 1 Peter 1:19-21; 3:18, 21-22). In fact, resurrection is the seal of our salvation, as Christ "was put to death for our trespasses and raised for our justification" (Rom 4:25). It is evidence of God's vindication of the condemned and executed Jesus. Or else, our salvation would have been in jeopardy.

It is highly significant that Acts also links the cross to forgiveness and physical healing. The apostles proclaimed the gospel of healing on the basis of the resurrection and ascension of Christ, followed by the pouring out of the Holy Spirit: "And his [Jesus'] name, by faith in his name, has made this man strong whom you see and know; and the faith which is through Jesus has given the man this perfect health in the presence of you all" (3:16; so also 4:8-12).

---

14. Quoted in Joh, *Heart of the Cross*, xxi. Joh mistakenly attributes this quote to Han Wan Sang, whereas it actually comes from Younghak Hyun and can be found in Hyun, "Three Talks on Minjung Theology," 7, 36.

15. Park, *Wounded Heart of God*, 123.

In the NT theology, Christ's resurrection has a reference to the future, to the eschatological consummation of God's eternal plans, not only to the future of our own hope for resurrection, but even beyond, to the future of this world and creation. In Moltmann's words, in his resurrection we see "not the eternity of heaven, but the future of the very earth on which his cross stands." Even more, "It sees in him the future of the very humanity for which he died."[16]

This future hope empowers us for work toward the betterment of this world, while waiting for the final consummation. As the African American ethicist Garth Kasimu Baker-Fletcher rightly notes, resurrection hope brings "release of our inner captive so that we might rise to new life as self-affirming Afrikans."[17]

The Risen Christ Is Now Sitting at the Right Hand of the Father

If there is any topic that remains marginal in contemporary theology, it is the doctrine of the ascension of Christ, notwithstanding its NT evidence. This is different from the early church in whose proclamation not only atonement and resurrection but also ascension played a critical role. Alongside Luke-Acts (Luke 24:50–53; Acts 1:9–11; 2:32–36; 5:30–32), ascension is also mentioned quite frequently elsewhere (Eph 4:8–10; Phil 2:6–9; 3:20; 1 Tim 3:16; Heb 2:9; 12:2; 1 Pet 3:22).

The early theologians of the church understood this biblical teaching to speak about "cosmic Christology" that is, establishing the Risen and Ascended One in a wide cosmic framework, sitting at the place of world government.

Following the NT witness (John 15:26; 16:7; Acts 1:4–11; 2:1–4; Eph 4:7–10), patristic theology also forged an integral link between ascension and the pouring out of the Holy Spirit at the day of Pentecost. That event also ushered in the Christian Church!

Throughout history, Eastern Orthodox tradition has faithfully appreciated ascension, and in so doing has reminded the rest of the church that by ascending into his glory Christ completed the work of our redemption.

In sum: ascension highlights the significance of Christ's being lifted up to the right hand of the Father in terms of the completion of salvation and having been made the cosmic ruler in anticipation of the final consummation of God's salvific purposes.

---

16. Moltmann, *Theology of Hope*, 21.
17. Baker-Fletcher, *Xodus*, 88. Quoted in Weaver, *Nonviolent Atonement*, 117.

How Does the Christian Theology of Atonement Relate to Other Faiths?

Is it Even Relevant to Speak of "Atonement" among Religions?

Similarly to some other topics, we have to be careful not to impose Christian concepts uncritically onto other faith traditions and simply assume that they do the proper work. That said, any comparison between two or more faith traditions can only happen with the help of vocabulary that is familiar from one's own tradition. Furthermore, although no other faith tradition conceives of salvation as the result of the violent death and resurrection of the innocent mediator, that does not mean that these traditions therefore lack their own ways of negotiating "salvation," say, or "release." They just have their own particular ways of thinking of the "resolution."

With these caveats and principles in mind, let us cautiously and in a hospitable manner attempt a comparison between Christian and other faith traditions, approaching the task from the perspective of Christian theology of atonement—and keeping in mind the comparative work we did in the previous chapter on Christology.

The Irony of the Similarity and Dissimilarity in the Judeo-Christian Tradition

Through his announcement of the imminence of God's righteous rule dawning in his own ministry, "Jesus came to move the covenant people to conversion to its God."[18] Importantly for the Christians, even the fact that Jesus's own people were not willing to receive him as the Messiah did not thwart God's saving purposes. Ironically and counterintuitively, it was only after being rejected by his own people that Jesus's death on the cross made him the "Savior of the nations."[19] In light of Israel's resistance to Christian interpretation of the story of the Jewish Jesus of Nazareth, it is notable that in *The Star of Redemption* the influential Jewish philosopher of religion Franz Rosenzweig affirmed the role of the Christian church in the preaching of the gospel to the gentiles. He is not the only Jewish theologian to have taken this stance. But the few who have are exceptions to the rule.

The same dilemma that was already present in the NT times still continues: Israel has not acknowledged Jesus of Nazareth as her Messiah. While not denying that "salvation is from the Jews" (John 4:22), the

18. Pannenberg, *Systematic Theology*, 2:311.
19. Pannenberg, *Systematic Theology*, 2:312.

Christian Church is compelled to proclaim even to Jewish brothers and sisters that Jesus is "the way, and the truth, and the life; [and that] no one comes to the Father, but by" him (John 14:6).

So what, for Jews, is the basic problem with the Christian claim that the Jewish Messiah, Jesus of Nazareth, has achieved the work of atonement for his own people and indeed for the whole world? The basic theological difference is that rather than through a vicarious sacrifice, the normal way for a Jew to be saved is simply by following the Torah, the divinely given law. As discussed in chapter 4 on theological anthropology, Jewish theology does not hold to the Christian tradition's view that the fall necessitates some kind of divine initiative, such as the death on the cross. Furthermore, as likewise discussed previously, the otherworldly goal of salvation in the afterlife is not as central either in the OT or in later forms of Judaism as it is in Christian tradition.

In that light, it is remarkable that it was on the basis of Hebrew Scriptures such as Isaiah 53:4–6 that Christian theology came to interpret the vicarious suffering of the Messiah. In other words, "the sacrificial concept of Jesus's death was not developed in response to gentile ideas but, rather, as a Jewish conception of the righteous one who reconciles us to God by his sacrifice of suffering and death."[20]

How, then, would Jewish tradition interpret such key NT statements as "Behold, the Lamb of God, who takes away the sin of the world!" (John 1:29)? The standard Jewish response has nothing to do with atoning for sins in the Christian sense—although Jews may gain insight into the meaning of the phrase through the lens of the biblical notions of purity and impurity, sacrificial offices and systems, as well as the temple. Of course, reference to the Lamb who takes away sin is based on the slaughtering of lambs for the expiation of sins. But even then, for Jewish theology that is not *the* way of salvation, meaning apart from following the way of the Torah. There is also this dramatic difference when it comes to the sacrificial system: whereas in Jewish faith the high priest conducts the sacrificial act, in Christian faith Jesus is the sacrifice, the sacrificial Lamb.

Not that the Jewish faith has no place for substitutionary suffering for others: of course it does! Think of both the "Suffering Servant" of the book of Isaiah (52:13—53:12) and righteous martyrs, such as during the Maccabean era before Christ. Still, the way in which Christians interpret the self-sacrifice of Jesus to be final is markedly different from the continuing sacrificial cult administered by the priesthood in Judaism. Not only the finality of the sacrifice of Jesus but also its universality marks it

---

20. Lyden, "Atonement in Judaism," 51.

as different from the understanding of the Jewish tradition. Jesus's sacrifice, even though it is the work of the triune God, is contingent on his person, a claim without parallel in Judaism and a stumbling block to its monotheism. For in Judaism the role of the Messiah is to serve as the agent of reconciliation, but not as the one who reconciles, for in Jewish understanding only Yahweh can reconcile.

Finally, a foundational difference has to do with the object of the sacrifice and who offers it. Whereas in Judaism people offer the sacrifice to Yahweh, in Christian theology (2 Cor 5:19) it is God who reconciles the world to himself.

The Jewish theologian Michael S. Kogan succinctly states the dynamic tension facing Christian theology with its belief in Christ as the Messiah as needing "to be faithful to the New Testament command to witness for Christ to all peoples and to convert all nations, while, at the same time, affirming the ongoing validity of the covenant between God and Israel via Abraham and Moses."[21] At the center of this tension lies the obvious but important fact that "historically Christianity has been theologically exclusive and humanistically universal, while Judaism has been theologically universal and humanistically exclusive." Christian theological exclusivism, however, is qualified by the equally important conviction that Christ died for all and that therefore all people from all nations can be beneficiaries of this salvific work.[22]

Progress on this foundational issue poses a challenge to both parties. For if Jews want Christians to affirm the continuing validity of the covenant after the coming of Jesus Christ, then (as Kogan aptly states) Jews have to ask themselves: "Are Jews ready and willing to affirm that God, the God of Israel and of all humanity, was involved in the life of Jesus, in the founding of the Christian faith, in its growth and spread across much of the world, and in its central place in the hearts of hundreds of millions of their fellow beings?" Kogan answers *yes* to this question, and suggests that his fellow Jews who do not are no more "enlightened than those Christians who still refuse to affirm the Jews's ongoing spiritual validity as a religious people."[23]

The irony of the similarity and dissimilarity between Jewish and Christian views of salvation is bound to continue! What about the younger Abrahamic counterpart?

---

21. Kogan, *Opening the Covenant*, xii.
22. Kogan, *Opening the Covenant*, xii–xiii.
23. Kogan, *Opening the Covenant*, xiii; see also 13.

The Cross Really Is the Stumbling Block to Muslims

There is a sharp difference between Christianity and Islam in terms of both the source and the means of salvation: "The cross stands between Islam and Christianity. Dialogue cannot remove its scandal, and in due course a Muslim who might come to believe in Jesus has to face it."[24] One of the many reasons the suffering Messiah does not appeal to Muslims is that the image of the suffering and crucified Messiah is reprehensible to Islam, virtually implying that God failed.

Indeed, the single most important dividing issue between Islam and Christian faith is the interpretation of the crucifixion. The Qur'anic explanation for the crucifixion (and incidentally the only explicit reference to it) in 4:157–59 reads as follows:

> (157) And for their saying, "We slew the Messiah, Jesus son of Mary, the Messenger of God." And yet they did not slay him nor did they crucify him, but he was given the resemblance [or: "but a semblance was made to them"].[25] And those who disagree concerning him are surely in doubt regarding him. They do not have any knowledge of him, only the pursuit of conjecture; and they did not slay him for certain.
>
> (158) Nay, God raised him up to Him. God is ever Mighty, Wise.
>
> (159) And there is not one of the People of the Scripture but will assuredly believe in him before his death; and on the Day of Resurrection he will be a witness against them.

The most common Muslim interpretation of the crucifixion is that Jesus of Nazareth did not die on the cross but that a substitute took his place. As to the identity of the substitute, a number of candidates are listed, usually headed by Simon of Cyrene or Judas Iscariot. Instead of dying on the cross, such interpretations say, Allah took Jesus up to heaven to await his return to earth at the eschaton (to be discussed in chapter 10 on eschatology).

Two key observations from the text are particularly important for our purposes: the meaning of "God raised him up to him" (v. 158) and of "a semblance was made" (v. 157). The former has to do with what really happened to Jesus if he was not put to death on the cross. The latter relates to the question of who, instead of Jesus, was crucified. The main Christian counterargument

---

24. Bebawi, "Atonement and Mercy," 185.
25. Translation of Robinson, *Christ in Islam*, 106.

is that the Qur'an is inconsistent, on the one hand, in affirming the death of Jesus (3:55; 19:33) and, on the other hand, in denying it (4:157).

In sum: the whole of Muslim theology unanimously "denies the expiatory sacrifice of Christ on the Cross as a ransom for sinful humanity."[26] Nor would such a sacrificial, atoning death be needed. For, similarly to Judaism, Muslim theology lacks a doctrine of the fall and sinfulness after Christian tradition.

No wonder that attacks against the Christian teaching of the crucifixion have played a significant role in Muslim anti-Christian polemics and continue to do so, as illustrated in the widely influential pamphlet by the Indian-South African Muslim thinker Ahmed Deedat, entitled *Crucifixion or Cruci-fiction?*

Is There Any "Salvation" or "Savior" in Buddhism?

We have learned already that Buddhism has no Savior in the Christian sense. Instead, each individual is responsible for their own destiny. One is one's own refuge, and no one else—not even Buddha—can save a person from the law of kamma. Buddhists simply "balk at the idea that any deity is capable of granting salvation to others simply through an act of will."[27] These categorical statements are true even in some Mahayana traditions that refer to a "savior," as will be mentioned below.

Even though the specific instance of Christ's death on the cross for our salvation is totally unknown in Buddhism, the generic idea of redemptive or "vicarious" suffering on behalf of others is not. Think of the well-known story in Thai (Theravada) Buddhism about the sixteenth-century self-sacrifice of Queen Srisuriyothai to save her people from the threat of the king of Burma. But this has little, if anything, to do with the Christian type of atonement.

What Buddhism does embrace is the idea of a guide and example to help a person reach his or her blessed destiny. In Mahayana, the enlightened Boddhisattva—unlike the *Arahat* of Theravada, who has stepped into nirvana—is willing to postpone his own entrance into the *nibbana* to help others reach the goal.

What about Pure Land Buddhism? Is the path outlined by this Buddhist tradition compatible with the Christian view of salvation? No, it is not, although the two have remarkable commonalities, unlike any other major form of Buddhism. In Pure Land Buddhism, the main savior figure is

26. Ayoub, "Towards an Islamic Christology," 94.
27. Cabezón, "Buddhist Views of Jesus," 23.

Boddhisattva Dharmakara, who, through the rigorous and pure practice of forty-eight vows, reached enlightenment and became Amitabha Buddha. He opened the path of salvation in primordial times by establishing the Western Pure Land and made it possible for all sentient beings reborn in that land to reach enlightenment, or "salvation." Given his reservations about all human religiosity, it is telling that Karl Barth felt deep sympathies for the Pure Land tradition, the existence of which he said was "a providential disposition" parallel to Reformed Christianity based on the logic of grace.[28]

What about Hinduism?

Similar to Buddhism, atonement through a vicarious death by another person is not a part of Hinduism, not even in the main theistic traditions. Though Hindus may be willing to listen to the Christian message to glean guidance and inspiration from Jesus, they absolutely do not attribute any atoning power to him.

In other words, the biblical idea of Jesus as the Lamb of God (John 1:29) sacrificed for the sins of the world is foreign to all strands of Hinduism. That said, as mentioned earlier, the idea of self-sacrifice for the sake of others and their well-being is very much part of Hindu thought. The sacrificial lamb imagery can only make sense if it is understood in its "cosmological"—we could probably also say metaphorical—sense and if it is linked with the basic Vedic principle of *rita* (right order). This multifaceted term denotes cosmic order as well as moral order and, in relation to sacrifices, also the right order of sacrifices. Sacrifices offered to gods were the basic means of securing order in ancient Hinduism. Indeed, in Rig Veda, "sacrifice" is identified as "the world's centre" (1.164.35). The NT and early Christian atonement theories include perspectives that are related to these kinds of cosmic ramifications of the cross. However, in Christian tradition they are integrally related to the biblical narrative of the triune God breaking the power of evil and resistance to divine purposes in Christ, and in so doing reconciling everything in heaven and earth with God.

Christian theology has to do with forgiveness. While that is not a totally foreign idea to Hinduism, it is not a central one. The *Bhagavad Gita* (18.66) enjoins the faithful person: "Setting aside all noble deeds, just surrender completely to the will of God (with firm faith and loving contemplation). I shall liberate you from all sins (or bonds of Karma). Do not grieve." To understand this statement appropriately, one has to take the Hindu view of what "sin" is, namely, "that which keeps the mind attached to sense

---

28. Barth, *Church Dogmatics*, I/2, 342–45, here 342.

perception and objects of the senses. Such attachment produces restlessness, which clouds perception of the soul."[29]

That said, the idea of grace properly understood is not unknown in Hinduism, particularly in Vaishnavism (a Vishnu-god-based theistic religion) and as taught particularly in the *Bhagavad Gita*. We will study that topic carefully in chapter 8, on salvation.

Whereas Christian tradition emphasizes "the God who is offering salvation," Hinduism, even Vaishnavism, and particularly Saivism (Siva-god based) and other traditions, all emphasize "the effort of the individual seeking salvation."[30] Put otherwise: "In the Christian doctrine of Grace . . . we confront an act of God," whereas in the Hindu view, liberation is a matter of human initiative and accomplishment.[31]

---

29. Cited in Bharat, "Hindu Perspectives on Jesus," 256.
30. Kulandran, *Grace in Christianity*, 245.
31. Kulandran, *Grace in Christianity*, 242.

7

Holy Spirit

What Is the Spirit Doing in the World?

The Growing Excitement about the Spirit and Her Work

NOW THAT WE HAVE had a chance to investigate in more detail the person and work of two members of the Trinity—the Father and creation and the Son and atonement—it is appropriate to turn our attention to the third, the Holy Spirit. And even if the two-fold template of "person" and "work" is not so readily applied to Spirit, there is some precedent for thinking of pneumatology, the doctrine of the Spirit (from Greek *pneuma*, "spirit" or "wind"), in terms of who the Spirit is and what the Spirit is doing in the world and about salvation.

Studying pneumatology in the beginning of the third millennium is a most exciting and inspiring task as we have witnessed an unprecedented increase in interest in the Holy Spirit. Some theologians even speak about a "pneumatological renaissance." This resurgence of interest is happening not only in academic theology but also among the churches and individual Christians.

The massive and dramatic shift of the Christian Church from the Global North to the Global South has helped raise interest in the Spirit and spirits, as many of the cultures in the South are more spirit[ually] sensitive and open. The huge growth in Pentecostal-Charismatic movements has also been a significant reason for this, and these movements have brought the Spirit-experience to ordinary Christians, not only to theologians and ministers. This charismatic enthusiasm is not limited to the Pentecostal movement alone. In Africa, now the most "Christianized" continent in terms of membership, even the Roman Catholic Church has now opened its doors to fresh expressions of Spirit/spirituality.

The renewed interest in pneumatology has also brought to light the profound cultural-religious differences between past and present, and between global locations. Whereas before the Enlightenment era all cultures and religions considered talk about spirituality, spirits, and the Spirit (of God) to be "natural," the contemporary European-American secular mindset—and, ironically, much of university-based academic theology—considers spirit talk "supernatural" and fanciful.

Human history has always taken for granted that beyond the visible, physical causes of events there are spirits, even divine spirits, in fact the spirit world. Although the Enlightenment challenged this state of affairs with its turn to merely physical, materialist explanations, particularly among the educated elites in the Global North, the reality of the spirit world is still taken for granted and even embraced in the Global South—and in many quarters of the North.

A growing number of Christians are seeking a more robust and comprehensive account of the Spirit and spirituality. This quest is heralded by Moltmann's vision of a new king of pneumatology:

> On the one hand, it must comprehend human beings in their total being, soul and body . . . person and sociality, society and social institutions. On the other hand it must also embrace the wholeness of the community of creation, which is shared by human beings, the earth, and all other created beings and things.[1]

This search for a holistic and comprehensive pneumatology is of course in keeping with what is happening overall in current theology, for example in the understanding of Christian salvation as encompassing all spheres of life and cosmos. In other words, the Spirit is no longer "restricted" to personal piety and the life of the church and its activities, given the extent to which Christian and ecclesial life is dependent on the Spirit; the Spirit's domain now also includes that which used to be regarded as strictly secular. This chapter provides many examples of this widening sphere.

This development is also in keeping with the multifaceted and diverse metaphors, symbols, and teachings available in the Bible. The images the Bible employs are taken from the material, animal, and personal world. These appeal to imagination, not only to analytic thinking. The basic terms used in the OT—the Hebrew term *ruach*—and in the NT—the Greek term *pneuma*—have a similar ambiguity: "breath," "air," and "wind." Other

---

1. Moltmann, *Spirit of Life*, 37.

metaphors used of the Spirit are fire, dove, and *Paraclete*, the "Advocate" or "Counselor." Thus, when studying pneumatology, we should remind ourselves that at all times, the Spirit "blows where it wills" (John 3:8).

The structure of this chapter follows its underlying assumption that the work of the Spirit occurs in mutually related concentric circles, as it were, beginning from the most comprehensive and "universal" sphere. We are asking questions such as these:

- Who is the Holy Spirit and what is Spirit's place in Trinity?
- What is the Spirit doing in creation?
- What is the role of the Spirit in the cosmos?
- Can we find the Spirit among the religions beyond Christianity?

Subsequently, in chapter 8 we will consider the question:

- What is the Spirit doing in salvation?

And in chapter 9 we will tackle yet another central issue, namely:

- What is the Spirit doing in the Church (including through charismatic gifts and endowments)?

Who Is the Spirit and What Is Spirit's Place in Trinity?

Why Did it Take So Long Time for the Doctrine of the Spirit to Develop?

While it took time for Trinity and Christology to be framed doctrinally, the development of pneumatological doctrine progressed even more slowly and painstakingly. That said, "Long before the Spirit was a theme of doctrine, He was a fact in the experience of the community."[2] Or before theology, there was spirituality, in the words of the Indian ecumenist Stanley J. Samartha:

> To most Christians the Holy Spirit is associated not so much with doctrine as with life. It is in the unwrapping of the gift of God in Jesus Christ that the Spirit becomes alive in the hearts and minds of Christians. The Spirit inwardly nourishes the new life in Christ and guides the community of believers in their acts of witness and service in the world.[3]

2. Schweizer, "Pneuma," 6:396.
3. Samartha, "Holy Spirit," 250.

An indication of the slow doctrinal grasp of this in the early centuries is the occasional confusion between the "Spirit" and "Word" (Son). We see an example of this in the famed second-century apologist Justin Martyr's claim that "it is wrong, therefore, to understand the Spirit and the power of God as anything else than the Word, who is also the first-born of God."[4] In his era, it was not uncommon to talk about the threeness in terms of God, Word, and Wisdom.

Because the full complexity of the deity had not yet been established, at times the Spirit was ranked as the "third" member in the godhead.

Why did this doctrine develop so slowly? For many reasons. Both in biblical traditions and in people's minds, the Spirit is a more subtle and a less concrete phenomenon than the Son and the Father. It is far easier to find everyday metaphors and symbols for Father and Son. Along with this elusive nature and "shyness" of the Spirit is also the biblical perception that the Holy Spirit never draws attention to herself but rather turns our attention to the Son and through the Son to the Father.

Similarly to Trinity and Christology, much of the energy behind the development of pneumatological doctrine came from the threat and challenge of heretical views, including those of the so-called "Fighters of the Spirit" and other similar ones. These heretics were not willing to give the same divine status to the Spirit as to the Son. Like Arian heresy in Christology, these heretics rejected the full equality of the Spirit with the Father and the Son—including that the Spirit was created! A powerful rebuttal came from Greek-speaking theologians, including the first major pneumatological treatise by Basil the Great, fittingly titled *On the Holy Spirit*.

In the Latin-speaking church, Saint Augustine's decisive establishment of the deity of the Spirit was a final step in the slow progression to doctrinal clarity. Although all members of the Trinity are holy, what makes the third person unique is that the "Holy Spirit is a certain unutterable communion of the Father and the Son."[5] In other words, "He is the Spirit of the Father and Son, as the substantial and consubstantial love of both."[6] More daring than the Cappadocians, Augustine felt comfortable calling the Holy Spirit "Very God, Equal with the Father and the Son."[7]

Around the same time, the authoritative formulation of the Spirit was finally ratified in the creedal statements. Whereas the statement of

---

4. Justin Martyr, *First Apology*, 33, in *ANF* 1; also Tertullian, *Against Praxeas*, 7, 8, in *ANF* 1

  5. Augustine, *On the Trinity*, 5.11.12, in *NPNF*[1] 03.

  6. Augustine, *Tractates on John*, 105.3, in *NPNF*[1] 07.

  7. Augustine, *On the Trinity*, the preamble to 1.6; also 1.6.13 in *NPNF*[1] 03.

the Council of Nicea (325) was very brief—"And [we believe] in the Holy Ghost"—the Nicene-Constantinopolitan Creed (381) officially confirmed the consubstantiality of the Spirit: "And [we believe] in the Holy Ghost, the Lord and Giver-of-Life, who proceedeth from the Father, who with the Father and the Son together is worshipped and glorified, who spake by the prophets."

Spirit and Son Work in Tandem

The Spirit's role in the Trinity is integrally related not only to the Father but also to the Son. This brings us to what theologians have come to call "Spirit Christology"—or "Christological pneumatology"—meaning that although they are distinct, Christ and the Spirit's work cannot be separated.

How do we know this? Because the Bible tells us so! The integral, mutually conditioned relationship between the two is evident everywhere in the Gospels and is also assumed in the rest of the NT as we see in the following passages:

- Jesus's birth and its announcement (Matt 1:18–25; Luke 1:35)
- his baptism (Matt 3:16; Mark 1:10; Luke 3:22; John 1:32–33)
- his testing in the wilderness (Matt 4:1; Mark 1:12; Luke 4:1)
- his anointing (Luke 4:18–21)
- his ministry with healings, exorcisms, and other miracles (Matt 12:28; Luke 4:18; 11:20)
- his rising from the dead by his Father in the power of the Spirit (Rom 1:4), so much so that he "became a life-giving spirit" (1 Cor 15:45)

Importantly, the roots of Spirit Christology go deep into the OT; recall that *Messiah* literally means "the Anointed One." Particularly in the prophetic literature, the messianic figure appears as anointed and empowered by the Spirit of God (Isa 11:1–9; 42:1–4).

Having now established the deity of the Holy Spirit in the context of the Christian doctrine of the Trinity, we highlight the manifold work of the Spirit of God in the world in various contexts and in manifold ways.

What Is the Spirit Doing in Creation?

The Life-Giving Spirit

In his exposition of the creation narrative in Genesis (1:2), Luther paints this most delightful and poetic picture of the Spirit's work in creation:

> The Father creates heaven and earth out of nothing through the Son ... the Word. Over these the Holy Spirit broods. As a hen broods her eggs, keeping them warm in order to hatch her chicks, and, as it were, to bring them to life through heat, so Scripture says that the Holy Spirit brooded, as it were, on the waters to bring to life those substances which were to be quickened and adorned. For it is the office of the Holy Spirit to make alive.[8]

Indeed, the Spirit's role as the omnipresent divine energy which brings and sustains all life (Gen 1:2; Ps 104:29–30) makes the world both alive and lively. To quote the eco-feminist Elizabeth Johnson:

> Of all the activities that theology attributes to the Spirit, the most significant is this: the Spirit is the creative origin of all life. In the words of the Nicene Creed, the Spirit is *vivificantem*, vivifier or life-giver.... The Spirit is the unceasing, dynamic flow of divine power that sustains the universe, bringing forth life.[9]

Such statements place the ministry, role, and work of the Spirit in a robust cosmic framework. The Spirit is everywhere in the world that the triune God has brought about. Nothing escapes the omnipresent, omnipotent, and omniscient Creative Spirit. Moltmann has therefore appropriately reminded us that a turn to the Spirit allows us to "discover God *in* all the beings he has created and to find his life-giving Spirit *in* the community of creation that they share" (emphasis original).[10]

You may recall that in the very beginning of the Bible, God's Spirit is described as "moving over the face of the waters" (Gen 1:2), "breathing" life (2:7) into creatures. The Psalmist says the same in his own way:

> By the word of the LORD the heavens were made,
> and all their host by the breath [*ruach*] of his mouth. (Ps 33:6)
>
> ... when you [God] take away their breath, they die

---

8. Luther, *Lectures on Genesis 1–5*, in *Luther's Works*, 1:9..
9. Johnson, *Women, Earth, and Creator Spirit*, 42.
10. Moltmann, *God in Creation*, xi.

and return to their dust.

When you send forth your spirit [*ruach*], they are created;
and you renew the face of the ground. (Ps 104:30 NRSV)

The Korean-born theologian Jung Young Lee writes lyrically of "[c]loth as a metaphor of the Spirit [that] protects and sustains all things on earth. Unlike the shield, a masculine metaphor of protection, it is closely associated with a feminine image in Asia. Women weave cloth and use it for the protection and decoration of the body."[11]

On Whether We Dare to Speak about the "Green" Spirit of God

While Christian tradition has, for good reasons, been keen not to compromise the Spirit's sovereign transcendence and distinction from creation, it is also appropriate and useful to speak reverently of the Spirit in "earthly" and embodied terms. American religious scholar Eugene F. Rogers Jr. notes that, "The Spirit, who in classical Christian discourse 'pours out on all flesh,' had, in modern discourse, floated free of bodies altogether."[12] As a result, "the Spirit ha[s] grown dull because [it is] unembodied."[13]

The most profound theological statement against divorcing the divine Spirit from creation and the physical is the Incarnation, an event of divine embodiment. This is because: "If we wish to understand the OT word *ruach*, we must forget the word 'spirit,' which belongs to Western culture."[14] Unlike in Greek, Latin, and contemporary Western languages in which spirit is taken as an antithesis to the bodily and material, in the OT, as explained above, the basic term *ruach* means strong wind or tempest.

What can be called "ecological" or green pneumatology has made this a leading theme. One of its ablest trailblazers, M. I. Wallace, confesses: "I believe that hope for a renewed earth is best founded on belief in God as Earth Spirit, the compassionate, all-encompassing divine force within the biosphere who inhabits earth community and continually works to maintain the integrity of all forms of life."[15] This is in keeping with what St. Athanasius said in the fifth century: "For no part of Creation is left void of Him: He has filled all things everywhere, remaining present with His own Father."[16]

---

11. Lee, *Trinity in Asian Perspective*, 104.
12. Rogers, *After the Spirit*, 1.
13. Rogers, *After the Spirit*, 3.
14. Moltmann, *Spirit of Life*, 40.
15. Wallace, *Finding God*, 6.
16. Athanasius, *On the Incarnation of the Word*, 8.1, in *NPNF*[2] 04.

This is not to dilute or compromise the radical distinction between the uncreated, infinite God and the finite creation. Nor is it to separate the Creator from creation. For though "God is irreducibly Other, always *beyond* our grasp[, God is] not beyond our touch" (emphasis original).[17] This careful distinction yet intimate linking of the Spirit with creation also helps in preserving the earth, a theme discussed above (chapter 3).

That the third member of the Trinity, the life-giving and life-sustaining energy, is present in creation is one thing. That the Spirit present in the cosmos vis-à-vis alleged spiritual powers and entities is quite another.

What Is the Role of the Spirit in the Cosmos and Among the Spiritual "Powers"?

Can We Still Talk about Spiritual Powers and Angels?

If the Divine Spirit is omnipresent in God's creation, then even those realities that biblical and Christian terminology identifies as "powers" and angels and demons are related to pneumatology. In fact, both the Bible and early theology understood these spiritual realities as *realities* rather than merely superstitious fantasies. At the same time, notwithstanding occasional overenthusiasm, St. Origen reminds us, "Regarding the devil and his angels, and the opposing influences, the teaching of the Church has laid down that these beings exist indeed; but what they are, or how they exist, it has not explained with sufficient clearness."[18] One of the reasons might have been the surrounding pagan cultures' particular interest in them.

As mentioned, the worldview of the ancients was not only open to notions of supernatural forces, but considered such forces to be entirely "natural." The world was filled with spirits, spiritual powers, "spiritual warfare," and similar experiences and intuitions. Just consider the cosmology of the NT, whether Jesus's own ministry or the worldview of the Apocalypse, and you get the picture. The cosmos was "spirited."

Building on this rich biblical reservoir, beginning with the fathers, Christian tradition developed a rich and creative angelology. This culminated in the highly speculative ideas of medieval theology, the most well-known of which is the medieval nine-layered cosmic vision in *The Celestial Hierarchy* of Pseudo-Dionysius the Areopagite. Although less speculative than that, even medieval masters such as Aquinas devoted huge intellectual effort to detailed scrutiny of angelology. That said, by

---

17. Rivera, *Touch of Transcendence*, 2.
18. Origen, *First Principles* (*De Principiis*), preface, 6, in *ANF* 04.

and large Christian tradition has followed Calvin's "rule of modesty and soberness"[19] when speaking of angels.

Challenges from the Scientific Worldview and Materialism

In contrast with such tradition, not surprisingly modern thinkers either rejected or marginalized belief in spiritual beings—and indeed almost everything that did not cohere with "natural religion," religion in keeping with modern reason. Yet the majority of ordinary people believe in spiritual realities—at least if public polls such as the 2008 Pew survey can be trusted.[20] In postmodern times, we are experiencing a resurgence of interest in angels and spiritual experiences.

With that in mind, can or should contemporary theology still speak of the powers in light of the radical differences between the modern worldview's denial, ancient people's assumption, and some religious movements' overenthusiasm of everything "spiritual"? The basic challenge is the predominant worldview of modernity, which can be called "naturalism," that is all that there is, is nature, nothing "beyond" or "above." It is a flat view of the cosmos, one that has no room for transcendence (meaning anything beyond the physical or material). A related challenge from modernity is the difficulty for the scientific mind—used to thinking of world processes as following (more or less) deterministic laws of nature—to envision something as counterintuitive as divine action (providence). The main theological counterargument is that naturalism or materialism is far from being a scientific result or finding, and more like an ideology or a worldview. Hence, it can hardly prevent theology—any more than can religions-at-large or philosophy or other humanities—of assuming the truth of spiritual reality. As a result, in keeping with chapter 3's establishment of the possibility of real ("objective") divine action or providence, there is no good reason to rule out either divine agency in the world or belief in angels, demons, and other spiritual powers.

In sum: we contemporary theologians should pay more attention to the virtual universality of belief in spirits and spiritual powers throughout global Christianity, as well as among followers of other religious traditions. Those testimonies and experiences we would do well to incorporate into our theological reasoning. That said, theology should also exercise appropriate critical judgment and not jump onto every bandwagon trumpeting alleged spiritual powers and actions!

19. Calvin, *Institutes*, 1.14.4.
20. Pew Research Center, "Summary of Key Findings," 11-12.

What about the Bible? What does it say about our topic?

What Does the Bible Say about Angels and Demons?

Biblical testimonies to angels and spiritual powers abound—with the curious exception of the creation narratives of Genesis 1–2. Particularly significant is the naming of heavenly, angelic forces as "spirits" (Greek *pneumata*) (Heb 1:14; 12:9; Rev 1:4; etc.), including "ministering" spirits (Heb 1:14).

According to the Bible, all spiritual beings are created beings. The NT teaches that they are not only created in Christ (Col 1:16) but also subjected to his Lordship (2:15). By subordinating the role of both good and evil angels and powers to God, the Bible avoids dualism. Even the role of Satan, which evolved gradually over the course of history, is that of a subordinate, and in some cases even of a servant of God, as in the beginning of Job. This clear and uncompromising distinction between God and other spiritual beings is an essential part of Jewish-Christian faith and helps keep them in appropriate perspective.

Angels are mentioned in numerous biblical passages. Their appearance is typically in important revelatory and salvific and at times judgmental events and processes, where their role is to be God's messengers and aides. The most curious among these beings is the "Angel of the Lord" (for example in Gen 16:7–13), a semi-divine figure widely understood by Christians as a prototype of the preexistent Christ.

The appearance of demons, which are always evil spiritual beings, is depicted here and there in the OT, including in accounts of cosmic conflict and chaos (Job 3:8; 38:8–11; Pss 29:3–4; 89:9–10; Isa 51:9–11). In the Synoptic Gospels, Jesus's encounters with evil spirits are quite frequent and, alongside healing, casting out, and silencing the demonic, are an important sign of the kingdom of God.

Notwithstanding this plethora of references, the Bible curiously provides precious few details about the angels and spiritual forces, including the question of at which point angelic beings emerged, although the tradition assumes that they are "older" than humans. Nor does the Bible really teach us what prompted the distinction between good and bad angels, although it clearly affirms the existence of evil angels (Matt 25:41; 2 Pet 2:4; Jude 1:6; Rev 12:9). The Christian tradition's assumption about the angelic fall (including of Satan) is based on only a couple of obscure passages (Isa 14:12–14; Ezek 28:12–19), and is merely that—an *assumption*.

Nor does the biblical witness give us a definitive answer about whether angels, good and evil, are personal in nature, though it often treats them in a way that suggests a nonpersonal nature: seven spirits or lampstands, torches, stars, and so forth (Rev 1:4–20). The mention of four winds (Rev 7:1; cf. Heb 1:7) is a reference to cosmic forces, including heavenly "hosts," and stars (Isa 40:26). Importantly, the NT also uses terms such as "principalities," "powers," and "thrones" (Rom 8:38–39; 1 Cor 15:24; Eph 1:21; 1 Pet 3:22).

Yet at times the text suggests these entities' personal nature, for example by speaking of their intelligence and will (1 Kgs 22:19–21; Dan 10:5–21; Matt 4:3–11; Mark 5:6–13).

Be that as it may, both the biblical and the historical-theological teaching and imagination of the church envisions a great variety of spiritual powers and "beings." Furthermore, like good angels, evil and demonic beings can be envisioned under many categories, from the archetypal primeval chaos, to destructive powers, to "domination systems" (social, historical, political, economic, religious, and so on), to regional and geographic entities, and even "anticelestially as fallen angels."[21]

What about current theology? To many people's surprise, beginning in the middle of the twentieth century an interest in both benevolent and malevolent powers has resurfaced.

What Can We Say Theologically about Powers, Both Good and Evil?

Karl Barth devoted a surprising amount of space to angelology in his multivolume *Church Dogmatics*. The best way to steer a middle path between overenthusiasm and modernist rebuttal, he thought, was to stick with biblical teaching. The Bible presents angels as God's ambassadors, "ministering spirits" (as in Heb 1:14). As representatives of heaven, they appear in critical moments of salvation history, including at the birth and death of Jesus.

But a couple of Barth's claims have been disputed. First, his claim that the Bible is not interested at all in angels' nature cannot be true because any talk about their function and place in salvation history in itself reveals something about their nature. The second contested claim is that in contrast to earlier theology, Barth categorically refused to talk about demons as fallen angels; he insisted that there are only good angels. Whatever demonic forces there might be in the cosmos, they are related to an ambiguous and elusive concept of "nothingness" (German *das Nichtige*), a domain of utmost resistance to God. The problem is that we have no idea to what extent this abstract notion explains anything—and certainly to say there are no demonic forces seems to contradict many biblical allusions and testimonies.

---

21. Yong, *Spirit of Creation*, 218–19.

An example of a modern reinterpretation of spiritual powers relates them less to spiritual fights and battles and more to structures and powerful influences in wider society and life at large. This tactics amounts to denying their "spiritual" reality altogether and speaking only of political, social, economic, and other powers that resist good life, equality, and peace. This Walter Wink developed in great detail in his famous trilogy on "the Powers."[22]

A possible way to talk about angels and powers at the beginning of the third millennium is to take as our starting point the traditional belief in a spiritual reality while at the same time challenging and expanding it toward the wider social and institutional sphere. *Christ and the Powers*, the small but significant book by the Dutch Reformed theologian Hendrikus Berkhof, does precisely this. Speaking of powers as structures that undergird all human and societal life, Berkhof envisions them as providing cohesion and preserving society from disintegration. These structures or systems can be social units such as the family or tribe, but also religious or other ideological beliefs. Stanley J. Grenz's "structures of existence" continues this interpretation; he envisions these structures or power as "those larger, suprahuman aspects or dimensions of reality which form the inescapable context for human life and which therefore condition individual and corporate human existence."[23]

Following this both/and approach, Grenz emphasizes that although the structures have no independent reality apart from humankind, they also transcend humanity and lie beyond human control. As such they are "quasi-independent" and "quasi-personal." Here comes the link to the biblical, and particularly the Pauline, way of speaking of principalities and powers, which make no strict correlation between the structures of existence and biblical talk about angels and spirits. Because originally the structures were meant to facilitate human life, God created them as good entities. However, they can be abused and manipulated for evil—and they often are. As structures of cohesion, "by holding the world together, they hold it away from God, not close to Him."[24] As a result, "[t]hrough the diabolical misuse of structures, evil realities bring humans into structural bondage," including slavery to powers and demand for uncompromising loyalty. The structures thus become channels or vehicles for evil, though still under the Lordship of Christ.[25] Ultimately, through the reconciling power of Christ and the coming of God's kingdom, the structures will conform under Christ.

---

22. For a summary, see Wink, *Powers That Be*.
23. Grenz, *Theology for the Community*, 228.
24. Berkhof, *Christ and the Powers*, 24.
25. Grenz, *Theology for the Community*, 233–35, here 233.

What Do Other Faiths Have to Say about Spiritual Powers?

Although belief in angels, demons, and spiritual beings among secular Jews (a majority of whom reside in the United States) is mixed, over half of them no longer affirm the traditional belief; among religious Jews, that belief is still widely held, and to them spiritual powers have a definite place in the scriptural tradition.

The OT Testament term *malak* (messenger) can be used of both divine and human agents; only the context determines the meaning. A special category is the "angel of Yahweh" (Gen 19 among others), at times identifiable with God himself. Somewhat similarly to Christian medieval theology, the most creative reflection on spiritual beings emerged in the mystical Jewish Kabbalah.

The appearance of demons or evil spiritual beings in the OT is infrequent, particularly in the postexilic period, although there are accounts of cosmic conflict and chaos (Job 3:8; 38:8–11; Pss 29:3–4; 89:9–10; Isa 51:9–11) throughout the canon. Unlike Asiatic and other pagan traditions, biblical tradition always subordinates the role of both good and evil angels to Yahweh, and thus avoids dualism. Even the role of Satan, which gradually evolved through history, is that of a subordinate—in some cases, even of a servant of Yahweh's, Job being a fine example. This clear and uncompromising distinction between God and other spiritual beings carried over to Christian tradition beginning with the church fathers' writings.

Of the three Abrahamic faiths, it is in Islam that angels and spiritual beings play the most significant role, whether in scriptural tradition or in (folk) piety. Belief in angels is one of the key tenets of Islam, and to deny them is to reject the Word of God. There is a well-known narrative in Scripture about angels' creation prior to that of humans and about Allah's consultation with them before creating humans (Q 38:71–72).

Somewhat similarly to the OT, the Qur'an provides various kinds of artistic portraits of angels (such as having hands and two, three, or four wings; 6:93; 35:1) and describes them ministering through various tasks of service and messaging, including intercession (53:26). A further similarity is an allusion to the hierarchy of angels, Gabriel being the most prominent, and Michael the second. The most important angelic task is that given to Gabriel as the messenger from whom Muhammad receives the divine revelation. No wonder highly sophisticated angelologies were constructed by leading Islamic philosophers and theologians.

A special class of heavenly beings, the jinn—hugely important in folk Islam—are mentioned often in the Qur'an. They are made of fire, whereas humans are made of clay. They are endowed with freedom of the will, and there is ambiguity about whether they are evil or good; mostly they are understood to be evil. Jinn are believed to interact in various ways with humanity. In folk religion, they are frequently invoked for magical and miraculous purposes. Spiritual healers often address the jinn as part of their rituals.

What about the role and nature of angelic beings and powers in Asiatic faith traditions? The issue is more complex than in monotheistic traditions. Particularly in Hinduism, it is often difficult to make a clear distinction between deities and non-divine spiritual beings. In contrast to Abrahamic traditions, even the main deities such as Vishnu get entangled in numerous ways in the lives and workings of less-than-divine beings. Furthermore, not all demons are necessarily evil.

The Hindu belief in reincarnation blurs any absolute distinction between human and "superhuman" angelic or demonic beings. To make the issue more complicated, even *devas* (the godlike or divine beings) are subject to reincarnation. Nor is it impossible for humans to be reincarnated as *devas*. Because of the complex, multimillennial history of religious and cultural beliefs, it is no wonder that there is a rich diversity of beliefs and traditions and rituals related to either invoking good spirits or trying to cast away evil spirits.

Buddhist traditions have wide and rich demonological traditions with many local colors. Somewhat similar to the temptations of Jesus on the eve of his public ministry, in early Buddhist tradition Mara, the arch-devil, along with his three daughters, Rati (Desire), Raga (Pleasure), and Tanha (Restlessness), sought to dissuade Gautama from achieving enlightenment. Although early on the Theravada tradition (against its initial intentions, one may argue) began to develop quite sophisticated visions of spiritual beings, that development was even more massive in the various Mahayana traditions and their extremely rich folk piety.

This brief discussion of "other spirits" in four living faiths reveals that there is a remarkable consistency concerning the place of spiritual beings across different traditions, both monotheistic, polytheistic, and "non"-theistic (Theravada). Similarly, belief in spiritual beings seems not to be limited to any cultural or geographical location or to any specific racial group. It is also clear that the basic structure and orientation of the religion, whether strictly monotheistic or not, determines the place of the powers vis-à-vis the Ultimate Reality. In Abrahamic faiths, they are strictly under the lordship of God. Furthermore, it seems that a division into evil and good forces is a basic human religious intuition even when the boundary line may be variously (or at times ambiguously) drawn. Finally, it is clear that all major faith traditions assume the belief in the influence of the spirits on the affairs of humans and the world. It is curious that what is now considered the normative opinion in post-Enlightenment academia in the West—that spirits are but an archaic, outdated, and mistaken imaginary fantasy—is historically a new and novel view.

In recent years, an interesting question has arisen in certain quarters of the Christian Church regarding acts such as "spiritual warfare," exorcism, and other ways of encountering the demonic spirits. While in no way a new phenomenon, the Pentecostal-Charismatic movements, including those within established churches such as the Catholic Church, have given it particular visibility in our times.

How Can We Think Theologically about Exorcism and "Spiritual Warfare"?

Not only demons and evil spirits but also the rituals and techniques of exorcism were quite common in the ancient world, and are common also in contemporary living faiths, including the biblical narrative.

We can discern the theological meaning of exorcisms and healings by looking at them in the wider context of Jesus's ministry and person. Such events are signs of the power and approval of God at work in his life. The practices of exorcism and casting out devils continued in the early church, along with healings and other miraculous acts, and were an integral part of the church's regular activity of prayer, liturgy, sacraments, and missionary outreach (Acts 5:16; 8:7; 13:6–12; 16:16–18). Even a few mass exorcisms are recounted, such as the one in Ephesus (Acts 19:11–12).

Arbitrarily determining these narratives to be mere fables while considering Jesus's and the early church's teaching and pronouncement of forgiveness as authentic is hardly a "neutral" scholarly judgment. Behind it is a deeply skewed modernist epistemology that has a hard time exercising self-criticism against its own unspoken presuppositions.

Assuming the possibility of demonic activity, what kind of theological-pastoral guidelines might be available? According to the Pentecostal theologian Amos Yong, who is deeply engaged in the religion-science and interfaith dialogues, resistance to demonic forces may take many forms, including "prayer, fasting, the charisms, spiritual warfare in its various guises, as well as through the methods of exorcism deployed by Jesus himself." He elaborates:

> If the traditional rite of exorcism was designed to expel evil and destructive spiritual realities from the lives of people, then contemporary rites expose and unmask the privative and perverted

nothingness of demonic realities. Exorcisms thus can function at various levels:

- personally, resulting in healing of fractured self-identities (e.g., in terms of Jungian theory);
- socially, resulting in reconciliation between people (i.e., in terms of the enactment of spiritual warfare against greed); [and]
- politically, resulting in shalom that includes justice (namely, in terms of undermining territorial spirits).[26]

At the same time, theology's task is to subject the habits of exorcisms and spiritual warfare to critical analysis. This critical task relates particularly to a fairly new phenomenon that is variously called a "power encounter" or "spiritual mapping" or refers to "territorial spirits" and "spiritual strongholds," and the like. In (semi)popular literature that advocates an uncritical and at times sensational way of resisting the demonic, it is common to identify spiritual warfare at various levels: at the "ground level," referencing influences of the evil in individuals; at the "occult level," referring to defeating false ideologies such as Satanism, New Age, or Masonry; and at the "strategic level," at which one counters "high ranking principalities and powers as . . . demonic entities [that] are assigned to geographical territories and social networks . . . also referred to as territorial spirits."[27] Advocates of such ideas make the theme of spiritual warfare central to their preaching, teaching, missionary strategizing, and their general ethos of the Christian life.

Unfortunately there is no solid critical scholarly literature by the advocates of this kind of "spiritual warfare," and therefore it is very difficult to offer a fair and comprehensive theological assessment of their ideas. The foundational challenge I have for advocates of such ideas is this: Why would they wish to apply contemporary critical methods of investigation in medicine, law, sociology, and, say, agriculture, but not in religion and theology? Because of lack of critical scholarship, there tends to be a deep-seated dualistic mentality in the rhetoric and defense of this kind of spiritual warfare. Consider their uncritical and alarmingly mistaken listing of "enemies," which includes "Eastern religions" (identified as Satanism!). Or relatedly consider the spiritualizing tendency that sees "spirits" behind abortion, homosexuality, and certain spiritual practices. Apart from the lack of support for such

---

26. Yong, *Spirit of Creation*, 223.
27. Wagner and Greenwood, "Strategic-Level Deliverance Model," 179.

ideas in biblical sources and tradition, this spiritualizing also undercuts a thoughtful ethical-moral consideration of such themes.

And yet the fact that this paradigm should be rejected theologically and pastorally need not prompt critical scholars to throw out the baby with the bathwater. The need for this dynamic balance also relates to the topic of the next section: discerning the Spirit of God among the spirits and truth claims of other religious traditions. As the Indian theologian Joseph Pathrapankal states, the Spirit is "the foundational reality which makes [it] possible for the humans to exercise their religious sense and elevate their self to the realm of the divine."[28] No wonder, then, that part of the cosmic orientation of all traditional and most contemporary cultures in the Global South involves the deep and wide sense of spirits and spiritualities in religions.

Can We Find the "Spirit(s)" in Other Religions?

Ruah ha-Kodesh: The Holy Spirit in Judaism

Because Christians share with Jews the bulk of the former's sacred Scriptures, no separate study of OT pneumatologies is needed here. That the *Shekinah*, the divine immanence of Yahweh, rather than "Holy Spirit," is at the center of the vast rabbinic literature is understandable in light of the need to avoid too close a connection with the NT and emerging Christian theology of the Spirit. Furthermore, there is the well-known, but also widely debated, rabbinic claim for God's Spirit having left Israel (during the "Intertestamental Period," to use older Christian terminology). That said, interest in the Spirit was not lost altogether. Based on the scriptural teachings, the rabbinic literature considers *Ruah ha-Kodesh*, "holy spirit" or "spirit of holiness," to be the divinely given power of prophecy and leadership.

Similarly to Christianity, pneumatology in Judaism has undergone significant revisions and transformations, including diverse medieval movements. The Zoharic literature, compiled in the late thirteenth century, represents a culmination of the mystical Kabbalistic traditions and a response to Christian teachings of the Holy Spirit.[29] Its focus is on mystical spiritual experience and union with God. As in rabbinic literature, the Holy Spirit is identified with the *Shekinah*. It accompanies the people of God and represents the powerful divine immanence in the world, including guidance of the people of God. Something curious about the pneumatology of *Zohar* is not the existence of evil spirits or "nonholy spirit," but

28. Pathrapankal, "Editorial," 299.
29. For an overview of Zoharic literature, see Jewish Virtual Library, "Kabbalah."

that it "posits secondary 'holy spirits,' that derive from the *Shechinah* and other emanation-related holy spirits."[30] In the *Zohar*'s understanding, even angels can be called holy spirits.

If we jump to the turn of the twentieth century, it is interesting to note the influence of the Enlightenment and modernity. The title of Hermann Cohen's important book says it all: *Religion of Reason Out of the Sources of Judaism*. The book's focus is almost entirely on ethical-moral rather than traditional religious-spiritual themes. Regarding the Holy Spirit, the only "religious" meaning relates to holiness, all else is generic spirit-talk of modernity. And Cohen is not the only representative of this secularly and philosophically driven abstract approach to the Spirit.

A markedly different approach is the pneumatology of the contemporary American rabbi Rachel Timoner. Her 2011 book entitled *Breath of Life* closely resembles current Christian pneumatologies. Unlike her predecessors, Timoner links *ruach* with "life-giving breath, a simple wind, and the spirit that animates creation."[31] In a particularly holistic fashion she also forges a link with redemption, a move missing in tradition. In keeping with Christian pneumatologists, Rabbi Timoner also discusses topics such as "embodied spirit"[32] and the deep interconnection and relationality between the physical and mental/spiritual, personal and communal, human and the rest of creation, and so forth.

There is no need to mention Christian theology's deep and wide indebtedness to the OT teaching and later rabbinic and other materials. For the far-reaching reorientations in contemporary Christian pneumatologies that have dramatically widened the sphere and ministry of the Holy Spirit are partially rediscoveries of the OT teaching on *ruach Yahweh*. Whereas the doctrine of the Trinity is a major block between the two traditions, neither one disputes that the Spirit of Yahweh is equivalent to the NT Spirit of God.

The other Abrahamic faith's conception of the Spirit bears significantly less similarity to Christian pneumatology, and it is to this that we now turn.

Ruh Allah: Islamic Testimonies to the Spirit

The basic Qur'anic term *ruh* is, of course, a Semitic cognate with shared meanings of breath, wind, and air. The twenty Qur'anic references to *ruh* can be divided into four "sense-groups."[33] The first group relates to the sayings

---

30. Gertel, "Holy Spirit in the Zohar," 88.
31. Timoner, *Breath of Life*, xviii.
32. Timoner, *Breath of Life*, 17–19.
33. O'Shaughnessy, *Development*, 15–51.

about the angels and the spirit (97:4). Here the Spirit is (semi)personified. The second sense-group concerns the sharing of Allah's spirit with humans. Here, the Qur'an makes a definite shift from a (semi)personal agent to an impersonal breath, as in Genesis 2:7. Interestingly, this breathing relates only to Adam (Q 15:29; 32:9; 38:72) and Jesus (4:171), including the passages in which Mary's virginal conception is mentioned (4:171; 21:91; 66:12). What is the meaning of the Qur'anic saying that Jesus is a spirit from Allah? Neither divinity, nor trinity, as the same sura hastens to add: "So believe in God and His messengers, and do not say, 'Three'" (4:171).

The third sense-group of *ruh* sayings in the Qur'an is the least understood: "Say: 'The Spirit is of the command [*amr*] of my Lord'" (17:85; also 16:2; 40:15; 42:52). The exact meaning of *amr* is disputed: does it mean "command" or "affair" or something else entirely?

The fourth and final sense-group relates to the important theme of "Holy Spirit," the "Spirit of Holiness." The occurrences of this use emerge at the end of the Prophet's ministry, as he also became better informed on Christian faith and the role of Jesus. Three times it is linked with Jesus in terms of Allah "strengthening" or "confirming" him (2:87, 253; 5:110); other instances refer to other faithful persons being likewise strengthened with a spirit from Allah (58:22).

Going beyond the Scripture, grassroots-level enthusiasm over spiritual experience, similar to that of other faiths, appears from early on in Islamic mystical Sufism and related movements. It seems reasonable to assume that the rapid and steady growth of Sufism and such spiritualist movements is explained at least partly by the full embrace of the spiritual experiences and manifestations. No wonder that throughout the years people have enthusiastically acknowledge and claimed "power encounters" and miraculous acts to lie behind many conversions.

From a theological perspective, Sufism's virtual identification of the Spirit of Holiness/Holy Spirit with God himself is particularly important, and is an idea that tests the limits of strict monotheism. While doctrinally suspect, Sufi mysticism focuses on love and spiritual unity as well as on spiritual experiences. It is said of Husayn ibn Mansur Al-Hallajah, a famous ninth-century Sufi mystic, that he "was so full of the Holy Spirit that he could no longer distinguish himself from God," an abomination to the establishment, leading to his crucifixion in 922.[34]

In terms of the relation of these religions' understandings of Spirit to Christian pneumatologies, it is easy to discern many commonalities including the Spirit's close relationship to Jesus, including in the virginal conception; its

---

34. Kritzeck, "Holy Spirit in Islam," 110.

relationship to the Word of God; the ministry of strengthening the faithful; and so forth. At the same time, one must be careful not to interpret common theological terms such as "spirit" and "word" without taking into consideration the deep underlying theological differences.

An interesting interfaith debate has to do with how to translate and interpret the identity of the Johannine metaphor of the Holy Spirit—Paraclete. There is a long and extensive tradition, particularly in folk Islam, of identifying the Paraclete with Muhammad. The dispute goes back to the interpretation of Qur'an 61:6: "And when Jesus son of Mary said, 'O Children of Israel I am indeed God's messenger to you, confirming what is before me of the Torah and bringing good tidings of a messenger who will come after me, whose name is Ahmad.' Yet when he brought them, they said, 'This is manifest sorcery!'" The *parakletos* ("Counselor") of John 16:7 is equated with *Ahmad* of Qur'an 61:6 (in many English renderings, the "Praised One"). In Islamic tradition a version of Muhammad's name is Ahmad. There are, however, a number of problems with this identification, the most obvious one being that there is absolutely no textual evidence for it in Greek manuscripts of the NT. Furthermore, it is doubtful that Muhammad himself would have endorsed this interpretation.

Atman and Hindu Conceptions of the Spirit(ual)

Despite their astonishing diversity, all Hindu traditions are united in their belief in the Spirit(ual) as the ultimate reality. What is much more challenging is how to define and express precisely in Hindu terms what Christian faith means by "God is spirit" (John 4:24). The reasons for this difficulty are many, including that the demarcation lines in Hinduism between "personal" god/deity, spiritual powers, and energies, including those in nature, are fluid and open-ended. Note also that Hindu philosophy has a number of words that could be translated something like "spirit," the most obvious ones being *atman*, *antaryamin*, and *shakti*.

Be that as it may, any inquiry into the "pneumatology" of Hinduism must begin with the most foundational statement in Vedic Upanishadic texts: "that Self [*Atman*] is indeed Brahman" (Brihadaranyaka Upanishad 4.4.5). a topic already addressed in various chapters above. As the ultimate reality, Brahman is beyond all qualities, definitions, and limits; to use Western philosophical terminology, Brahman is absolutely infinite. Still the question persists: How exactly is this related to pneumatology within this framework? Are there any parallels with Abrahamic faiths?

In light of the deep spirituality of Indian cultures and religions, it comes as no surprise that Indian Christian theologians have shown remarkable interest in the Holy Spirit, considering it particularly through the lens of Indian spiritualities. This search for potential correlations between the two "pneumatologies" has employed two kinds of tactics. One focuses on the concept of "spirit" *per se*; the other places the Spirit in the Trinitarian context and looks for any links.

As a representative of the first category, we may look at the alleged connection between the concept of *shakti* and God's Spirit. *Shakti* refers to extraordinary power and energy, not limited to the workings of humans but also related to some deities, particularly Durga and Kali, the prominent female deities. Even more important with regard to parallels with the Holy Spirit is the belief in *shakti* as the energy of creation, sometimes known as the "Universal Creator."[35] For the Catholic theologian Raimundo Panikkar, this was a key insight: from the Hindu perspective, the Spirit can be described as the "Divine *śakti* penetrating everything and manifesting God, disclosing him in his immanence and being present in all his manifestations."[36]

More work has been done on the second category, namely spirit in relation to Trinity. Having investigated Trinitarian parallels in chapter 2, here let it suffice to highlight the Spirit's role therein. In reference to the ancient concept of *saccidananda* ("being," "wisdom," "bliss") discussed in the chapter on Trinity, some Indian theologians have seen parallels between *Ananda* (bliss) and the Holy Spirit, the bringer of joy and blessedness. While this Hindu interpretation cannot be reconciled with Christianity for obvious reasons such as its lack of "personhood," as a *Hindu* interpretation it deserves attention. But as said before, the "cash value" of attempts to find a parallel between Christian Trinity and Hindu Trimurti is meager, at least in light of investigations undertaken to date. Nevertheless, continuing these dialogical exercises is necessary and useful.

Is There Any(thing) Spirit(ual) in Buddhism?

If this is possible, the search for correlates between the Christian Holy Spirit and conceptions of the Spirit(ual) in Buddhist traditions is an even more complicated task, beginning with (Theravada's) intentional avoidance of deities. That said, Buddhist "theology" and cosmology are still foundationally idealist, that is, based on the primacy of the Spirit(ual) rather than the natural (materialist). Having discussed the issue of an ultimate reality (in

35. Kumar, "Indian Appreciation," 29.
36. Panikkar, *Unknown Christ of Hinduism*, 57.

chapter 2), here we need merely mention that the only viable candidate for comparison would be *sunyata* (emptiness).

But could we really discern any kind of meaningful parallelism between *sunyata* and *pneuma*? The Christian comparative pneumatologist Amos Yong assumes some commonality between them but fails to specify what precisely. However, Yong rightly mentions at the outset that "[i]n the Buddhist case *shunyata* functions in a non-theistic context," and therefore he finds it useful to relate it to the spiritual aspects in human person and creation at large rather than more narrowly in relation to the Holy Spirit alone.[37] While some other avenues of comparison have been explored, the results and materials are too scant to be speculated upon here.

Having now briefly surveyed the conceptions of the Spirit(ual) in four other traditions, a fitting ending to this section is to inquire into criteria for discerning the Holy Spirit among religions at large.

How Best to Discern the Holy Spirit among Religions?

The obvious place to begin such a search is of course in Christian Scripture. But the dilemma here is that the discernment of spirits in the biblical canon is set in a different context than this multifaith contemporary world of ours. In Scripture, the discernment has to do with the encounters with false prophets and finding God's will among competing claims. Furthermore, what is important is the discernment regarding issues of spirituality and morality, particularly in the post-biblical church. That said, important here is the NT's contribution in terms of the charismatic gift of the "distinguish[ing] between spirits" (1 Cor 12:10).

Since there are "no simple phenomenological criteria by which we can test the presence of the Holy Spirit,"[38] ultimately, such discernment requires a theological and spiritual process of judgment and assessment. For this, Christology is the most important criterion, for "every spirit which does not confess Jesus is not of God" (1 John 4:3). As Lesslie Newbigin used to say, "The work of the Spirit does not lead past, or beyond, or away from Jesus."[39] Alongside Christ, the appeal to ethical and moral criteria is also important and is in keeping with what I noted above.

Important is to keep in mind at all times that our task is discerning and not controlling the Spirit of God. "To ask [whether or how the Holy Spirit is at work in the world] is to remind the church that the Spirit is

37. Yong, *Pneumatology*, 59; Yong follows a similar tactic in *Cosmic Breath*.
38. Hiebert, "Discerning the Work," 151.
39. Newbigin, *Light Has Come*, 216-17.

not under our control and that it may even challenge us to repent and reform."[40] As a work in progress, discernment is not only provisional but also communal and deeply ecumenical in nature; ultimately, it calls for engagement beyond faith traditions.

In sum: Alongside the cautious exercise of the gift of discernment, the community applies the Christological criterion and takes into account moral and ethical implications as well as the law of love, as with every Christian decision.

This brief discussion of the person and work of the Holy Spirit is fortunately not all this book has to say about pneumatology. Alongside many references to the Spirit in relation to revelation, Trinity, creation, and Christ, a central theme in chapter 8 on salvation is pneumatology, namely in reference to the communication of salvific gifts. Chapter 9 on the church likewise contributes significantly to our understanding of the work of the Spirit, and the final chapter (10) on eschatology highlights the diverse and rich ministry of the Holy Spirit.

---

40. Bergen, "Holy Spirit," 84.

8

Salvation
What Does It Really Mean to Be Saved?

How Can One Speak of "So Great a Salvation"?

A PROMINENT THEME IN our theological discussion has been the manifold and rich salvific gift that the Triune God has achieved for us by sending his Son to save the world in the power of the Spirit. A vast array of metaphors, symbols, and testimonies are needed even to begin to paint the picture of what the unknown author of Hebrews (2:3) names "such a great salvation."

Whereas in chapter 6 we delved into the details of "atonement," and specifically the incarnation, life, ministry, suffering, death, and resurrection of Jesus Christ for us and for our salvation, building on that foundation this eighth chapter inquiries into the many salvific gifts the Holy Spirit is conveying to us. In theological tradition this is known as the "order of salvation" (Latin *ordo salutis*).

What does the "order" of salvation mean? It is simply shorthand for theologians' attempts to make sense of the diversity and richness of the "stages" or "dimensions" of the reception of salvation wrought by the Triune God. Biblical passages such as Romans 8:28–30 provide inspiration for such efforts:

> We know that in everything God works for good with those who love him, who are called according to his purpose. For those whom he foreknew he also predestined to be conformed to the image of his Son, in order that he might be the first-born among many brethren. And those whom he predestined he also

called; and those whom he called he also justified; and those whom he justified he also glorified.

Although the entire Trinity participates in the communication of this precious salvific gift to humans, the Holy Spirit plays a particularly prominent role, as is evident in typical definitions: "The ordo salutis describes the process by which the work of salvation, wrought in Christ, is subjectively realized in the hearts and lives of sinners. It aims at describing . . . the various movements of the Holy Spirit in the application of the work of redemption."[1] Terms and topics such as the following appear in theological presentations on the *ordo salutis*, and they all highlight a particular aspect of the gift of salvation:

- election: the ways God has chosen and elected us for attaining salvation (at times coupled with the term *God's foreknowledge*);
- calling: the ways God seeks the lost and is drawing them to salvation;
- repentance: the ways we respond to the call of the Gospel in turning away from evil ways and toward God;
- forgiveness: the ways God in his mercy and grace provides us pardon and an opportunity to begin again;
- faith: the trust placed on the Savior through which one acknowledges one's own incapacity to save oneself and willingness to receive the gift of salvation as gift;
- justification: the result of being accepted by God by grace through faith;
- regeneration or new birth: being born as the child of God as a result of forgiveness and justification-union: new birth, regeneration unites the believer with the Triune God through the Spirit;
- sanctification: the process of growing in new life and into the likeness of the Son of God, our Savior and brother; and finally
- glorification: the end goal of the process of salvation reaching the ultimate destiny in God's presence in eternity and in communion with other saints.

Not all theological traditions use the same terms as this, and their order may vary. Those are details beyond our interest here. Suffice it to say that these are somewhat elusive ways of speaking of the many dimensions of God's salvific gifts. At the same time, it is exciting to see the expansion of the order of salvation in terms of widening the scope of salvific

---

1. Berkhof, *Systematic Theology*, 415–16, emphasis removed.

gifts. For our discussion, particularly significant are the two interrelated topics of charismatic empowerment and divine healing, whether physical or mental. While in no way the commodity of any particular Christian tradition, the rise of Pentecostal-Charismatic Christianity has naturally helped bring them into the center of attention, among more traditional topics such as election and justification.

After a more general look at the visions and metaphors of "salvation" in Judaism, Islam, Buddhism, and Hinduism, this chapter will consider the following aspects of the order of salvation, including frequent brief references to other faiths:

- election and calling ("The Divine Favor and Invitation for Eternal Fellowship");
- conversion and repentance, and forgiveness of sins ("(Re-)Turning to God—and to the Neighbor");
- forgiveness ("Pardoning and Remembering Rightly");
- justification, sanctification, and deification, including union ("One with God: Rightwising, Renewal, and Integrity of Life");
- charismatic empowerment and healing ("Healing, Restoration, and Empowerment"); and finally
- glorification and perseverance of the saints ("The Faithfulness of God and the End of Human Yearning").

But first, a consideration of other faiths!

What Kinds of Visions of "Salvation" Can Be Found in Other Religions?

Redemption and Submission in Abrahamic Faiths

Jewish Way: Redemption through Following Torah

Notwithstanding marked differences among the Semitic faiths in regard to human misery (as discussed in chapter 4), all three faiths place humanity before God. Though somewhat differently, they all consider the "origin" of sinfulness to lie in humanity's deviation from the Creator. These are all important common themes and convictions. That said, quite dramatic differences can also be found within the Abrahamic family.

We saw in chapter 4 that in Judaism the human person is tasked to choose and follow good inclinations rather than evil, and that therefore in Hebrew the principal term for repentance from evil is *teshuvav*, literally "turning" (to God). Rather than "salvation," Jewish theology typically speaks of "redemption," which appears well over a hundred times in the OT; its key idea has to do with deliverance. While not limited to national deliverance, the idea is present in most Jewish traditions even beyond Zionism, the modern movement advocating the importance of Jewishness and the state of Israel as independent.

What about faith and belief? Counterintuitively, in the Jewish "Bible there are no articles of faith or dogmas in the Christian or Islamic sense of the terms." Rather than being an invitation to believe (in an intellectual sense), the biblical call is for faithfulness. The reason for the absence of catechism (in the Christian sense) is the emphasis on conduct and ethics. That is not to deny the presence of theological reflection and doctrines in later Judaism. Yet those came about largely because of apologetic need and external pressure.[2] The Shema (Deut 6:4) is of course the basis and foundation of Jewish faith. Yet monotheism is more than a belief; it is the central thrust of Jewish (and Islamic) faith tradition.

Rightly or wrongly, Jewish theology considers the Christian version of redemption to focus on the spiritual. This also has to do with the radically different messianic theology of Jews, as discussed in chapter 5 on Christology. For the Jews, the arrival of the Messiah means the reconciliation and radical reversal of affairs in the world. Recall also that in contrast to the Christian tradition, the Jewish concept of redemption has nothing to do with a vicarious atonement. For Jews, following the Torah *is* the way of salvation. The central teaching of Torah is about covenant, and that calls for faithfulness and obedience.

What about contemporary Jewish theology? Notwithstanding great diversity, this much can be said: "In modern Jewish thought redemption has been viewed as referring to the eventual triumph of good over evil, to the striving of individuals to self-fulfillment, to the achievement of social reforms, and also in terms of the reestablishment of a sovereign Jewish state."[3] This is in keeping with the this-worldly orientation of Jewish theology that derives from the OT.

Islamic Way: Submission and Obedience

Enter Islam. Ignorance of the right path and unwillingness to submit to Allah are the main salvific needs in Islam. Redemption is not a divine gift

---

2. Abrahams, "Belief," 3:290–91.
3. Graetz, "Redemption," 17:154–55, here 154.

but rather a result of right choice. Unlike in Christian theology, in Islamic theology wrong choices cannot be atoned.

This is not to deny the presence of grace and mercy in Islam, as is evident in the Qur'an's repeated idea of Allah as merciful (24:21). That mercy, however, does not translate into an idea of "justification by faith." Everything is about submitting to the will of Allah, particularly by observing the Five Pillars (confession of faith, alms, prayers, fasting, and pilgrimage). Access to Paradise will be granted as a "reward for what they used to do" (56:24).

In sum: "salvation" in Islam simply entails submission to Allah. But the fact that salvation ultimately depends on whether or not one wishes to submit does not mean that believing is marginalized. One cannot submit if one persists in ignorance of the revealed will of God. Belief goes hand in hand with repentance (3:16-17; 19:60) and "righteous deeds" (good works) (4:57).

While deliverance from sin does not have to be excluded from the Islamic vision of salvation, deliverance from eternal punishment, often depicted as the "fire" of hell, seems to be the main focus. What about "assurance of salvation"? Although Qur'anic promises to those who believe and do good deeds seem reassuring, there are also warnings throughout not to fall away (4:13-14; 6:82). Although one may lose salvation, every believer can also trust Allah's "guidance" (an almost technical term in the Qur'an referring to divine help for believers, as in 4:51; 6:157; 17:84; 28:49; 67:22; and so forth).

Like other faith traditions' mystical movements, Sufism focuses on personal devotion and repentance. Union with God—theologically a most scandalous idea in light of normal Muslim teaching—comes to the forefront. It is to this we turn next.

The Human Condition and Release in Asiatic Traditions

Moksa: *Release, in Hindu Vision(s)*

Describing what "salvation" entails in Hinduism is quite difficult, not only because there are hardly any binding doctrinal tenets in this religion, but also because of Hinduism's amazing diversity and countless local variations. What is safe to say is that the standard for what is right and true among all Hindu movements is dharma, the "duty," the correct way of life. Its opposite is *adharma*. It is not only or primarily about deeds and behavior but belongs to the wider context in Hindu philosophy of human "bondage" to *avidya*, "ignorance." Ignorance makes one cling to *maya*, "fiction," and thus makes one subject to the effects of karma, leading to repeated rebirths. Only with the removal of this "ignorance" can the soul's essential nature as pure spirit be restored. To summarize, in most Hindu traditions, release from ignorance is the key, and that leads to ultimate "liberation" or *moksa*.

Beyond this broad picture, three major orientations are routinely mentioned: one focuses on devotion (*bhakti*), a second one on knowledge (*jnana*), and a third on effort (or work, *karma*). They are complementary (Bhagavad Gita 2.47–48).

For the masses, the devotional theistic Vaishnavism (or Vishnuvism, after the main deity Vishnu) is the way of salvation: "But, to those who worship Me as the personal God, renouncing all actions to Me; setting Me as their supreme goal, and meditating on Me with single minded devotion; I swiftly become their savior." A hugely popular figure of devotion is Krishna, the most important *avatar* of Vishnu (discussed in chapter 5 on Christology). Only the strict *advaita* of Sankara rejects or, at its best, tolerates *bhakti*; most other traditions are open to it. It is also in these *bhakti* traditions that the concept of grace is found most prominently. Consider this oft-quoted verse of the Bhagavad Gita (18.58), the "Bible" of the common folks: "When your mind becomes fixed on Me, you shall overcome all difficulties by My grace" (see also 18:62).

Among the philosophically minded elite, particularly within the strict *advaita* of Sankara, the knowledge-based way is to pursue release from ignorance. The third path, the works-driven one, holds a most fundamental position and is not necessarily an alternative to the other two. It is connected with liberation because liberation consists in the complete freedom from karma and from all its consequences. Each person, possessing divine nature, can attain liberation by the person's own moral choices and good deeds. In the twentieth century, the most well-known advocate of this path has been Mahatma Gandhi, who also, typical of a general trend, combined it with *bhakti* and regarded the Bhagavad Gita highly.

Enlightenment: Buddhist Visions of Liberation

Based on earlier discussions in the book, we can summarize briefly: the chain of kamma (karma) due to ignorance can only be broken through enlightenment, a result of right insight. Even Buddha is not a savior but rather an example to follow. Although many movements (of Mahayana particularly) acknowledge the concept of grace and (divine) assistance in search of liberation, ultimately liberation is dependent on one's own effort.

"Enlightenment"—or insight—is the soteriological term that Buddhism favors. Following the teachings of Buddha as expressed in the Noble Eightfold Path, as well as emulating his experience, paves the way to release from false attachment, including the error of considering one's self permanent. Mahayana in particular has also developed a growing tradition of spiritual exercises in pursuit of liberative insight.

The most distinctive vision of liberation can be found in the Mahayana Pure Land tradition developed by Shinran (1173–1263), which, as discussed, is deeply theistic and envisions a kind of savior. But that movement is an exception to the Buddhist rule of everyone being one's own savior.

Now that we have introduced the broad visions of salvation and liberation of four other living traditions, it is time to delve into key Christian soteriological topics. In each case, where relevant in light of the self-understanding of other faiths, I will attempt a sympathetic and critical dialogue.

The Divine Favor and Invitation for Eternal Fellowship (Election, Calling)

Why Is the Doctrine of Election So Complex and Widely Debated?

As important a role as the idea of divine election has played throughout history, including through fierce disputes about it, until Augustine (of the fourth and fifth century) there was very little specific interest in patristic theology in formulating a theory of election. While the fathers were convinced of divine election, their concerns were different from those of later tradition in which the individual person's salvation or damnation became the burning issue. For patristic thinkers, particularly in the Christian East, pagan fatalism (the idea that blind fate determines everything) loomed large. A related factor is that it took until Augustine's time to have an established doctrine of original sin in the Christian West. Generally speaking, the Church Fathers universally believed in the freedom of the will—without of course denying sinfulness *per se*.

A critical milestone was the famed controversy between Augustine and Pelagius, the latter allegedly a British monk and a strict moralist. As discussed in chapter 4, Pelagius rejected the Augustinian (and later Christian West's) idea of the serious weakness of the will because of the fall. Instead, he maintained that men and women are able to choose between good and evil. In response to what many consider justified criticism, Augustine further consolidated his view by emphasizing the sovereignty of

God and the unconditionality of divine election in eternity. This led to what is called "double predestination," the view that people are destined for condemnation unless they are rescued from it by God's sovereign choice. Although Pelagianism died hard, the Augustinian view prevailed. The idea came to its fullest fruition much later, in the sixteenth century, in John Calvin's Reformed tradition as well as in Anglicanism.

Not surprisingly, the Arminians vehemently resisted the Augustinian-Calvinist interpretation for, despite fully acknowledging human sinfulness and humans' incapacity to save themselves, they considered it necessary to make some room for real human response. While not going as far as the Christian East—which continued affirming the relative freedom of human will and hence responsibility—the Arminians rejected the idea of double predestination and the total lack of the power of will to choose.

The Reformation debate between Luther and the Catholic humanist Erasmus is likewise highly instructive. Whereas Luther argued that the human will is totally unable to take any initiative toward salvation "before God"—although men and women can choose rightly in earthly matters, "before other human beings"—Erasmus found in the same biblical materials potential evidence for an authentic human response to grace. But even Luther did not go so far as to embrace the doctrine of double predestination.

What can be named "milder predestinarianism"[4] became the mainstream opinion in the Christian West. This affirmed election to salvation, but not reprobation. Again, the Eastern Church was not part of these historical debates.

In the twentieth century, the Reformed theologian Karl Barth wanted to turn the tables, rejecting double predestination and shifting the focus from the election of human beings to that of Christ who, Barth said, was a Mediator who was both the "Electing God" and the "Elected Man." Christ, insisted Barth, is the only one who was elected, and in him all persons as Christ has gone through the rejection of the sinners at the cross and the vindication of all in resurrection. As a result, no longer will anyone be rejected. Assessments regarding Barth's proposal vary. What concerns critics particularly is that there hardly is any biblical basis for making Christ the "object" of election. Barth's proposal also suffers from the dangers of universalism, the idea that all will be saved at the end (a topic to be discussed in the final chapter).

---

4. So named by Jewett, *Election and Predestination*, 7.

In Search of a More Satisfactory Account of Election

Although no final resolution on this matter has been reached, contemporary theologians have proposed a number of alternative approaches. Yet rather than speculate about the "mind of God," it seems better to take our lead from the doctrine of revelation, discussed in chapter 1:

> In His goodness and wisdom God chose to reveal Himself and to make known to us the hidden purpose of His will (see Eph. 1:9) by which through Christ, the Word made flesh, man might in the Holy Spirit have access to the Father and come to share in the divine nature (see Eph. 2:18; 2 Peter 1:4). Through this revelation, therefore, the invisible God (see Col. 1:15; 1 Tim. 1:17) out of the abundance of His love speaks to men as friends (see Ex. 33:11; John 15:14-15) and lives among them (see Bar. 3:38), so that He may invite and take them into fellowship with Himself.[5]

This profound statement assures us that out of abundant love and having revealed himself in the Son, the Father through the Spirit is actively and passionately seeking fellowship with us. This anchors election in history, and its context is the spiritual community. Theological tradition should have borne this in mind rather than—as happened in the Augustinian-driven theology—both locating divine election in eternity, apart from and unrelated to historical happenings and choices of human beings, and focusing it on individuals.

A correction is needed, as in fact the biblical narrative itself instructs us. In the OT, persons such as Abraham and David are elected for the sake of the community and the mission of Yahweh to the nations. In other words, election is intertwined with the idea of calling and sending out for God's mission, as can be seen in the case of Abraham (Gen 12:2-3).

In the NT, men and women are called to salvation for which they have been foreordained; indeed, one has a hard time finding programmatic statements about "double predestination" when it comes to our eternal destiny. Consider Ephesians 1:4-14. Having mentioned that God "chose us in him [Christ] before the foundation of the world," the text says that the goal of being chosen is "that we should be holy and blameless before him." The text then continues highlighting the salvific gifts in Christ, culminating in the Spirit. The conclusion is that "since God wills the salvation of all, offers it to all, and holds those to be without excuse who reject it, his predestination must be based on his foreknowledge of who will and

---

5. Paul, *Dei Verbum*, para. 2.

who will not accept the grace offered in Christ."[6] Along with the earliest patristic theology, this view dominates the entire Eastern Orthodox tradition and is basically similar to that of Arminianism.

Election is based on God's "unbounded generosity." "The God we love and trust is not One to be satisfied until there is a healing of the nations and an innumerable host of redeemed people around his throne (Rev 7:9; 21:24–26; 22:2–6)." This attitude speaks of hospitality, a "hermeneutic of hopefulness"[7] as opposed to the "fewness doctrine," according to which only a small number of people will be saved.[8]

On the other hand, should the human person refuse the invitation, the Creator honors the (relative) human freedom graciously granted by that same Creator. Eliminating all human choice—on the basis of eternal divine determination done before time and unrelated to human choices—seems a strange and perverted way of appreciating the fatherly love of the Creator God. Could we think of the heavenly Father as any "worse" than an earthly father? This personal-relational aspect is lost in the Augustinian-Calvinist scheme. What it rightly emphasizes is the sovereignty and grace of God in salvation. It skips over the possibility for relationality in the way it formulates the idea of God's graciousness and power in terms of the human person's total incapacity and passivity.

What about other religions? Do they know election? Is there freedom of choice?

Other Religions on Choice, Freedom, and Determinism

Sister Abrahamic Traditions

There is a curious dynamic here: On the one hand, "the essential presupposition of most major religions is that humans are born with freedom of choice."[9] On the other hand, most of the religions at the same time embrace the idea of divine election or divine determinism of some sort.

The most peculiar and formative doctrine of election is found in Judaism. The idea of "chosen people" defines her identity going back to Abraham, in light of the covenant between Yahweh and his people. Deuteronomy 7:6 summarizes election: "For you are a people holy to the LORD your God; the LORD your God has chosen you to be a people for his own

---

6. Jewett, *Election and Predestination*, 68.
7. Pinnock, *Wideness in God's Mercy*, 19–20.
8. Pinnock, *Wideness in God's Mercy*, 13.
9. Marcoulesco, "Free Will and Determinism," 3200.

possession, out of all the peoples that are on the face of the earth" (see also 14:2). Election is based solely on Yahweh's love and purposes. It happens despite the unworthiness of the elected one. The selection or election of the few is for the sake of the people and her mission to other nations rather than for the benefit of the few.

What about freedom of the will? Differently from some Christian and Islamic versions of robust predeterminism, Jewish tradition does not interpret divine action in a way that would frustrate the exercise of human free will and consequently responsibility. According to Moses Maimonides's oft-cited statement, "[M]an does what is in his power to do, by his nature, his choice, and his will; and his action is not due to any faculty created for the purpose." Not only that, but "[a]ll species of irrational animals likewise move by their own free will."[10]

In Islam, election does not play the same crucial role as in Judaism. Islamic theology emphasizes the election of several key persons, such as Noah, Abraham, and prophets. Understandably the greatest stress is on the election of the Prophet, Muhammad, and the community established by him (*ummah*). The Qur'an teaches that while other nations might have known God, only Muslims know Allah intimately and are rightly related to God (37:40; 38:40).

A dominant principle of Qur'anic teaching has to do with human responsibility, the shorthand for which is obedience (submission) to Allah. Indeed, there are hundreds of such Qur'anic texts. That said, other important Qur'anic passages seem to deny any notion of human freedom of choice. Consider 35:8: "Indeed God leads astray whomever He will and guides whomever He will" (also 8:17-18). Hence, similarly to Christian theology, fierce debates continue to be fought in Islamic philosophy and theology. Modernist Muslim commentators argue that, notwithstanding diversity, the Qur'an endorses the concept of human freedom in choosing one's belief and human responsibility for human actions. God has foreknowledge of human actions, but this divine knowledge does not compel humans to commit sin.

In sum: all Abrahamic faiths robustly affirm humans' relative yet genuine freedom of the will and our consequent moral and religious responsibility.

---

10. Maimonides, *Guide for the Perplexed*, 3.17; 285.

Asiatic Traditions

But what about Asiatic traditions? The following statement helps put in perspective Abrahamic and Asiatic traditions' views on free will and election:

> The main traditions of Hinduism and Buddhism do not posit a personal deity with an omnipotent will, and thus the polarity of free will and predestination in relation to the salvation of souls has not been so prominent as in Judaism, Christianity, and Islam. The doctrine of *karman* can constitute a kind of determinism whereby an individual's lot in life is determined by his behavior in past lives, but the doctrine can also imply that a soul is in charge of its future destiny; its modern proponents therefore sometimes consider the doctrine to imply freedom more than fatalism.[11]

From the perspective of the Abrahamic faiths, it is not readily evident how to negotiate freedom and determinism in relation to *karma*, an ironclad principle. The freedom principle comes to the fore particularly in the ancient concept of *svaraj* (self-ruling), which Mahatma Gandhi took as the basis for his social activism. The Hindu expert Klaus Klostermaier notes that "Karma does not cancel free will and genuinely free decisions; nor do free will and one's own decisions neutralize karma."[12] Be that as it may, a whole spectrum of interpretations is found in diverse Hindu traditions.

Talk about divine election is even more marginal to Buddhists than to Hindus. This is not to deny the possibility of an idea of divine favor or election among some theistically driven Mahayana movements; it is rather a summary statement about Buddhist doctrine at large.

Buddhist Scriptures add to the complexity. Because of causal relations and the interdependence of the world as well as the denial of the existence of "soul," there seems to be very little room in Buddhism for personal choice, even responsibility. On the other hand, because there is no god to depend on, the human person is left totally on their own in the pursuit of "salvation." Following the Buddhist "middle way," a fitting conclusion says something like this: "[T]he Buddha rejected the philosophical extremes of both determinism and indeterminism and discouraged his followers from embracing any view that might undermine their inspiration to devote themselves to an ethical life in the pursuit of liberation."[13]

---

11. Wallace, "Free Will and Predestination," 3204.
12. Klostermaier, *Survey of Hinduism*, 176.
13. Wallace, "Buddhist View of Free Will," 231.

Now that we have looked at the divine initiative in salvation, it is natural to move to the human response under the classic rubrics of conversion, repentance, and forgiveness of sins.

(Re-)Turning to God—and to the Neighbor (Conversion, Repentance)

"Repent... and Turn Again"

The traditional theological *ordo salutis* includes "repentance" as an aspect of conversion, specifically the way to turn away from sin, with regret and remorse as accompanying conditions for turning to Christ in faith. Similarly to forgiveness, the personal acts of repentance and conversion are also integrally related to sacraments, particularly to the sacrament of reconciliation (penance) and to the Eucharist. In all Abrahamic faiths, conversion also relates to the neighbor.

Biblical references to repentance and conversion abound. In fact, the very first public announcement of Jesus in Mark's Gospel has to do with repentance (1:15). Like the main term denoting conversion in the OT, *shuv*, the NT *epistrephō* means "to turn (around)." The religious usage of these terms entails turning away from evil and disobedience to serving God, as evident for example in Acts 3:19–20 from which the heading above derives.

We may assume this commonly, but actually the Bible rarely connects conversion to a change in one's religion; instead, it is a call for the people of Israel to (re-)turn to God. This is of course not to negate the possibility of changing religion in our contemporary pluralistic world, but rather to remind us of the central place of conversion in the life of the people of God.

What was the main target of conversion and repentance in Jesus's message? Did he address mainly individuals or the whole people of God? They should not be taken as alternatives: Jesus's focus was on the individual. This is a marked shift from the OT prophets' focus, which was mainly on entire nations and their leaders.

Theologically speaking, "[c]onversion is a work of the Holy Spirit, involving the mystery of divine initiative and human response at the same time. It is a restoration of relationship between us and God which involves a reordering of relationships with others."[14] This holistic vision of conversion raises the question of whether conversion is primarily a one-time event or a longer process.

---

14. Langmead, "Transformed Relationships," 10.

What Can Revivalistic Evangelism Learn from a Theology of Conversion?

Conversion has been a main goal in revivalism throughout history, and continues to be so today. Understandably, it has also been criticized as an overly eager method to win converts, and for its "one time fix" mentality. How do revivalistic spirituality and evangelism go hand in hand with the biblical-theological idea of conversion?

Clearly, in the NT conversion is both an event and a process, not merely a one-time experience. When its process-nature is taken into consideration, the typical complaints against revivalism—that its message is thin, its follow-up is weak, it tends to triumphalism, and it neglects previous religious experiences of the people—can be overcome. On the other hand, those who understand conversion only as a gradual and lifelong process could learn something from revivalism's challenge of individuals toward making a conscious decision of faith. The Anabaptist ethicist Erin Dufault-Hunter's expression of "conversion to thick faith [that] envelops all aspects of a person's life," illustrates this.[15]

In light of the perceived liabilities of the revivalistic traditions' view of conversion, some leading advocates are working toward redefining conversion:

> Older revivalism assumed that conversion was punctiliar, that the focus of a converted life was religious activities, in anticipation of a life "in heaven" that would come after death, and that this "conversion" was essentially an interior, personal, and subjective transaction. Revivalists had little appreciation of the place of the sacraments or the intellect in spiritual life. For the revivalists, the church has only one agenda: to obtain conversions; to be successful, congregations should have plenty of growth by conversion.[16]

To that litany can be added revivalists' use of fear of death as a motive for conversion, As a way of correction, a new paradigm for understanding conversion is emerging in which

- heart and mind will be integrated;
- body and mind will be integrated;
- individual and communal aspects will be noted;

---

15. Dufault-Hunter, *Transformative Power of Faith*, x.
16. Smith, *Transforming Conversion*, ix; for details, see 1–16.

- human will and divine initiative will be put in a dialectical and mutual relationship;
- conversion will be seen as both an "arrival" and a "beginning";
- the sacraments will be incorporated into conversion;
- the transmission of Christian faith from one generation to another will not be dismissed; and
- the hope for the world to come and a this-worldly focus will be put in a dialectical relationship.[17]

The maturation of the revivalist tradition, as clearly evident in this revised account of conversion, has considerable ecumenical potential. Such a revised account of conversion may also help the more traditional ecclesiastical families to rediscover in their daily practice the importance of conversion.

What about conversion studied from a human perspective?

Is Conversion Merely Manipulation of the Mind?

The rise of new religious movements in recent decades has elicited interest among researchers of conversion. The 1902 book *Varieties of Religious Experience* by American pragmatist William James famously defined the *experience* of conversion in terms of a transformed self-perception related to religious ideas and realities. For James, the content of these ideas was secondary; what mattered primarily was a new kind of attitude and direction for life.

A much more thoroughgoing dismissal of the *content* of the experience of conversion came from nineteenth-century atheism, followed by current neo-atheism. Their assumption is that not only is there no content behind religious conversion, but also that whatever there is, is harmful and even violent. Not infrequently, in sociology (of religion) the convert appears not only as an object of proselytizing activity but even as a victim of it. Conversion may be attributed, for example, to overwhelming emotional states. Part of this tendency is the result of the alleged link between religious conversion with social and economic deprivation.

Although the theologian has no need to deny that in some cases conversion can be explained with the help of these models, many—and indeed probably most—seemingly healthy, rational, and well-to-do people undergo and sustain a religious conversion experience. Similar critique can be targeted against the neuropsychological and neurocognitive study of

17. Smith, *Transforming Conversion*, 17–18.

conversion that has tended to explain conversion with the help of abnormal experiences such as seizures and epilepsy. Although, for example, the relationship between epilepsy and heightened religious activity and mystical experiences can be established statistically, it would be absurd to make all conversions a merely neuronal act. Why?

First, because all these varied disciplinary approaches to the study of conversion tend to be reductionist in that they focus solely on phenomenology or experience or alleged sociological reasons such as deprivation. Second, because the main theological lacuna has to do with the dismissal of the content of belief. More conducive to theological intuitions is the emerging study of conversion in "neurotheology" or "spiritual neuroscience," which, on the one hand, takes seriously the neurological basis of all human experiences but, on the other hand, does not necessarily reduce conversion experience to the physical basis. It rather allows the human being to be reshaped over the years.

Finally, perhaps the most pressing question about conversion in our religiously pluralistic world is this: Is it legitimate to try to convert others?

Is Conversion Unethical and Unjustified in the Pluralistic World?

Any talk about "conversion" elicits a number of debates about its meaning and suitability for our current religiously pluralistic context. Such talk also has a loaded history; it has been linked with proselytism (a forced or otherwise unethical converting of other people), colonialization, and similar dubious or even outright unethical activities.

Not surprisingly, postcolonial theorists have approached the topic with great suspicion, as "conversion to a world religion, such as Islam or Christianity, is interpreted as a part of the 'colonization of the mind and spirits' of the dominated peoples."[18] Some feminist theorists have asked whether there is a "power play" behind at least some conversions. And so forth.

Particularly in two geographical and cultural areas—Africa and India—discussions of conversion have received a lot of attention. The main challenge to African Christianity has been the question of how to conceive of conversion in a way that would not mean abandoning one's cultural heritage and identity, as well as power and privilege. In India, the continuing heated discussions around conversion also have everything to do with proselytism and the question of the legitimacy of evangelization.

Contemporary theology has to take very seriously all these challenges concerning the ideological, power-play driven, and otherwise destructive

18. Rambo and Farhadian, "Conversion," 1971.

SALVATION

potential implications of conversion. That said, there is no justification for saying that every experience of conversion is by default harmful and counterproductive even if sound ethical and moral principles are followed, every human person's freedom of choice is followed, and evangelism is conducted in the spirit of Christian love. The next chapter tackles this topic under the rubric of proselytism.

"Pardoning and Remembering Rightly" (Forgiveness)

Why Is Forgiveness Such a Crucial Topic for Us?

All Abrahamic faiths affirm that the source of forgiveness is God; in Christian theology, that affirmation is based on the atoning work of the triune God. In recent years forgiveness has also caught the attention of behavioral and social scientists, who have undertaken massive research projects. At the same time, a flood of "self-help" books on forgiveness has been published. All this is to say that both within and outside the church, forgiveness is both a pivotal and a timely topic at the moment.

Similarly to conversion and repentance, forgiveness played a crucial role in the ministry of Jesus of Nazareth (Matt 12:31–32) and that of his followers (Luke 24:47; Acts 2:38). The creeds also speak of forgiveness.

The theme is also prevalent in the OT, including in a number of narratives about human forgiveness (e.g., Joseph and his brothers; Gen 45–46). Although turning to God (repentance) is required (2 Kgs 17:13–14; Jer 3:11–24), the later prophets also emphasized that what really matters is the right attitude rather than the mechanical following of cultic practices (Amos 5:21–25; Isa 1:11–17; Hos 6:6). In sum: the horizontal and vertical dimensions are intertwined, in the midst of all the ambiguities of dramatic human stories.

In the Gospels, the two main words used to convey the idea of forgiveness are *aphiemi* ("let go, cancel, remit, leave") and *aphesis* ("release, pardon, cancellation"), whereas Paul expresses the idea using words such as "justification," "reconciliation," and "redemption." Often the *idea* of forgiveness may be present in the Bible even if the word is missing (as in the parable of the prodigal son).

Two issues strike the reader of the Gospel stories of forgiveness (whether or not that word appears): First, Jesus's teaching on forgiveness is often notable in its generosity. Particularly important is table fellowship with "sinners," a way of saying that even those outside God's covenant with Israel belong to the people. It seems that repentance is often presented in the Gospels as the response *to* forgiveness rather than the condition *for* it.

But second, even a cursory reading of the Gospels reveals that both John the Baptist (Mark 1:4) and Jesus also link forgiveness with repentance (implied in 1:15); the same mandate is given by the risen Lord to the disciples (Luke 24:46–47), and the early church carries on with this tradition (Acts 2:38; 5:31; 8:22; 26:18). How these two aspects can be negotiated is an important task for us to ponder.

Are There Any Conditions for Forgiveness?

Christian tradition does not speak with a unanimous voice about the unconditionality of forgiveness. Historically, from the early centuries repentance came to be linked with the more or less technically defined rite of penitence, linked with the demand for satisfaction as the prerequisite for forgiving. A related and important development was the emerging distinction between sins forgiven at baptism and those committed after baptism. So, what would be a proper theological response?

Theologically, it seems justified to argue that repentance should not be made a prerequisite of forgiveness: "God unilaterally makes forgiveness possible by offering forgiveness 'while we were yet sinners' (Rom 5:8)."[19] Here is a difference between Jewish and Christian theologies of forgiveness. Although Judaism is of course familiar with divine forgiveness, it is normally conditional upon repentance and restitution, as well as the forgiving of others. With Jesus comes "judgment of *grace*," which not only condemns sin and wrongdoings but also gives the energy and capability to re-turn to God and others in repentance and acknowledgment of one's faults.[20]

That said, the affirmation of unconditionality is not an abandonment of repentance. On the contrary, repentance (and restitution) become(s) the necessary *consequence(s)* of the reception of divine forgiveness. Furthermore, Jesus's message made a radical shift in the whole idea of repentance: rather than intended only for some, repentance was for everybody, including the "poor" and the marginalized; that is, Jesus called both the perpetrators and the victims to repentance. This is because forgiveness always has in view not only reconciliation but also transformation and change. This principle of unconditional forgiveness should also guide our understanding of forgiveness between human persons.

---

19. Couenhoven, "Forgiveness and Restoration," 165.
20. Jones, *Embodying Forgiveness*, 136, 145–50.

"As We Also Have Forgiven Our Debtors"

Forgiven people are called to imitate that act of hospitality. In forgiving, humans mediate the gift of forgiveness they have themselves received. "Failure to offer forgiveness indicates a devaluation of God's forgiveness."[21] To put it another way: withholding forgiveness would mean the exclusion of another person and would be tantamount to excluding God.

Following theologian Miroslav Volf, we may locate forgiving in the context of two opposing movements: embrace and exclusion. Exclusion may happen in many ways, including elimination (as in ethnic cleansing), assimilation (when acceptance is based on the demand to be like us), domination, and abandonment.[22] Embrace, by contrast, is based on "the mutuality of the self-giving love in the Trinity," "the outstretched arms of Christ on the cross for the 'godless,'" the welcoming by the father of the prodigal son.[23] This "will to embrace" includes both opening oneself and drawing near to the other, and making space for the otherness of the other.

We forgive the other not for our own sake, but as a manifestation of our love for our neighbor. For their part, victims decide "no longer to hold the injury they have suffered against their offender."[24] This gift has the potential to set the violator free from the guilt and grip of the wrongful act. However, the act of gift giving is costly. Indeed, forgiving means being willing to pay the price for the neighbor, even the one who has sinned against us.

To assert that forgiveness is done out of love for the neighbor is not to deny the potential benefits to the forgiver; it is rather to make the benefits to oneself secondary. This principle goes counter to the trend and emphasis in much of contemporary popular self-help literature and behavioral sciences concerning the therapeutic value of forgiveness and its benefits to the forgiver.

If the ultimate goal of the act of forgiveness is the well-being and restoration of the neighbor, it means that the act of forgiveness looks not only to the past but also to the future. The orientation to the future is what is so vital about God's forgiveness.

---

21. McLellan, "Justice, Forgiveness, and Reconciliation," 13.
22. Volf, *Exclusion and Embrace*, 74–75.
23. Volf, *Exclusion and Embrace*, 29.
24. Terry, "Forgiveness of Sins," 13.

"Forgive and Forget" or "Forgive and Remember"?

A long tradition of philosophical and theological reflection on forgiveness has linked it with resentment. In this view, forgiveness primarily means a process of overcoming resentment, the feeling of anger caused by having been the object of wrongdoing. A version of this view is that forgiveness is supposed to free the wronged person from all forms of negative feelings, even disappointment. Often this is linked with demands that the wronged person suspend even their critical judgments of the offender.

The resentment theory is contrary to Jesus's teaching that invites us not only to "turn the other cheek" and embrace the offender in forgiveness, but also to expose the wrong act for the sake of justice and to allow the wrongdoer to find reconciliation in accepting guilt and receiving forgiveness. Here Christian tradition seems to follow Aristotle's oft-cited rule, according to which a truly moral person is "angry at the right things and with the right people, and, further, as he ought, when he ought, and as long as he ought."[25]

Why is this important? Because restoration cannot happen without the wrongdoing being exposed and judged. As Moltmann aptly puts it, forgiveness is about "the new life to which [God] desires to awaken the guilty."[26] To that act may also belong a protest, even an emotional protest. But what about unconditional forgiveness such as we talked about above? It raises questions like the following: What about justice? Shouldn't an authentic act of forgiveness be able to erase from the offended person's mind all negative feelings?

Much of earlier self-help literature took for granted that an authentic act of forgiveness also helps erase the painful and negative memories of the offender's acts from the victim's mind. Hence, book titles such as *Forgive and Forget*.[27] By contrast, theology claims that for authentic forgiveness and healing to happen, it is essential that we remember *rightly*[28] the pain of the wrongdoings against us. For this establishes the truth. Acknowledging and recalling the wrong act is in fact a moral obligation, for without it justice and righteousness cannot be established. Furthermore, it is also required for the healing and restoration of the victim. But not remembering is also required for the offender to be restored. Mere forgetting is often

---

25. Aristotle, *Nicomachean Ethics*, 2.5, 1125b32–1776.
26. Moltmann, *In the End*, 75; cited in Ledgerwood, "Hope of Forgiveness," 14.
27. Smedes, *Forgive and Forget*.
28. Volf, *End of Memory*, 11–16.

nothing more than a way of repressing negative memories, leaving the victim feeling enmity and hatred.

Instead, by right remembering the victim lets the offender know the moral wrongdoing they have committed and so helps that person seek forgiveness and reconciliation. "If your brother sins against you, go and tell him his fault, between you and him alone. If he listens to you, you have gained your brother" (Matt 18:15). At times, help from other trusted persons and the Christian community is needed for this to happen (vv. 16–20). But this condemnation of the wrongful act should not be confused with retribution or vengeance. For forgiveness is the refusal to press charges against the violator. Instead, it offers a way to reconciliation, even if the victim has the right to press charges.

By the same token, for the violator to receive forgiveness entails first accepting condemnation, and this is why the reception may sometimes be too difficult for a person to do. The person who says *no* to forgiveness that is offered is in reality saying that he or she has not done anything wrong. To the art of remembering rightly also belongs the capacity to make a distinction between violator as *violator* and as a human person. Perhaps apart from some extreme cases of violence and abuse (such as the mass murders by Hitler and other mass murderers), the victim should avoid reducing the violator to the violation.

Only in a qualified sense does forgiveness, after all, mean "forgetting." The ultimate goal of the one forgiving has to be imitating God, who does not remember our sins anymore (Jer 31:34; Heb 8:12; 10:17).

Before continuing, let us take another important detour into other religions with regard to the two latest topics of conversion and repentance as well as forgiveness.

Conversion, Repentance, and Forgiveness among Religions

Let's Begin with the More Familiar Turf, Our Abrahamic Cousins

Jewish Insights and Experiences

In the OT, the terms denoting conversion, literally "to turn" or "to return," are frequent and many. Often they are set in the context of the age of the Messiah and the coming judgment. The Christian message of repentance and forgiveness in the ministries of John the Baptist and Jesus builds on these same themes in light of Jesus's coming.

Among the Israelites, forgiveness became all the more important as the elected people continued sinning and eventually were doomed to exile. The availability of God's forgiveness, particularly in post-exilic Israel, the Israelites understood as confirmation of their election and covenant. Even more widely, "the conception could involve the prophetic notion of restoration as well as the conversion of pagans."[29]

Although God is the ultimate source of forgiveness, obedience to Torah based on the covenant is the emphasis in the OT. What about the role of sacrifices? According to a key text of the Mishnah (Yoma 8:8–9), the sin offering atones for all unintentional sins, but intentional sins require repentance and returning to God—even though full atonement may come only at death or through the Day of Atonement (provided that the sinner refrains from further intentional sins). Jacob Neusner concludes that although the "sinner should be, and is punished . . . sin is not indelible. If the sinner repents the sin, atones, and attains reconciliation with God, the sin is wiped off the record, the sinner forgiven, the sinner's successors blameless." Forgiveness entails repentance because without it the rule of justice is violated as repentance "defines the key to the moral life."[30]

Similar to revival movements, mystically oriented Jewish movements such as Hasidism have focused much on repentance and forgiveness as a way to ensure the genuine nature of spiritual life. The Kabbalistic tradition's emphasis on repentance as the way of rectification (*tikkun*) is in the same category.

Similar to other Abrahamic faiths, Jewish tradition also highlights the importance of forgiveness in relation to the neighbor. Divine forgiveness cannot be had if an intentional violation against the neighbor has been committed and there is not yet reconciliation.

Islamic Insights and Experiences

Similar to the OT, the earliest Qur'anic passages were not calling people to convert to a new religion. Rather, the Meccans were called to "worship the Lord of this House [Ka'ba]" (Q 106:3).[31] Only later, with rising opposition from worshipers of local deities, was a decisive break announced and the confession became, "There is no god except God" (37:35).

Because the Qur'an teaches that "[t]here is no compulsion in religion" (2:256), conversion should be a matter of one's choice. This is not to

29. Aune, "Repentance," 7757.
30. Neusner, "Repentance in Judaism," 60, 61–62, respectively.
31. The Ka'ba is the center of the holy place in Mecca.

deny—similar to Christian history—that there have been forced conversions, but those have to be considered anomalies rather than the norm. What is strictly forbidden, however, is conversion to another religion, an apostasy potentially resulting in punishment by death.

Conversion to Islam entails confession of two simple but necessary convictions: that Allah is the only god and that Muhammad is the prophet of God—(a confession usually recited in Arabic and followed by "the greater ablution" of the whole body. Part of the conversion process is an ongoing mind-set of penitence and contrition, although there are no mandatory formal rites or rituals. Ritual prayers and *zakat*, "almsgiving" (9:5, 11); and submission (*islam*) to God (39:54) accompany the internal process of remorse and repentance.

Recall that Muhammad declared himself to be the Prophet of repentance. In the Qur'an, and particularly in the later Hadith tradition, repentance plays an important role. Among several terms denoting repentance and remorse, the key scriptural term, akin to Hebrew, is *tawbah* (3:90; 4:17; 40:3), meaning not only "to return" but also "to return frequently." While forgiveness is based on God's grace, clearly human initiative is needed: "Indeed God does not alter the state of a people unless they have altered the state of their souls" (13:11).

Similarly to Jewish mysticism, continuous repentance is particularly important in Sufi mysticism, for the latter is deeply concerned about repentance and conversion in its desire for deepening spiritual life. The normative medieval theologian al-Ghazali, who also gleans from Sufi mysticism, names repentance as the starting point for followers of the spiritual path, and therefore insists "it must be put first in the Quarter of Salvation."[32]

What about its conditions? Repentance requires a true change of heart. A prideful and arrogant attitude blocks forgiveness. That said, similar to Judeo-Christian tradition, "God's mercy takes precedence over God's wrath."[33] Yet—again like other Abrahamic traditions—Islamic theology has to be able to maintain God's justice in all of that.

As in the other Abrahamic traditions, forgiveness in Islam encompasses both divine and human forgiveness. In keeping with Judeo-Christian teaching, before praying to God one must be reconciled with one's neighbor. Forgiveness thus calls for a change of heart toward the violator without excluding the need to expose and judge the wrong act.

---

32. al-Ghazali, *Al-Ghazzali on Repentance*, 29–30.
33. Davary, "Forgiveness in Islam," 135.

What about Our Asiatic Counterparts?

Hindu Perspectives

Rather than conversion, what counts in Hinduism is a religious experience, spiritual "realization," and conduct. Rather than "deliverance from sin," conversion is "progressive enlightenment in which the ignorance and desire that keep us trapped in our human dilemma are expelled."[34] With this view, Hinduism rejects the Abrahamic traditions' call for conversion.

Notwithstanding the hesitancy against conversion, Hinduism knows not only the reconversion of lapsed faithful but also active missionary efforts to convert "pagans." This was certainly the case in the third to fifth centuries during the establishment of Hindu rajas in South India to replace Buddhism. More recently, Hare Krishna and a number of less well-known revival movements in the West have sought new converts.

What about repentance? Notwithstanding a radically different theological context from Abrahamic faiths, both in classical Vedic religion and in theistic (particularly *bhakti*) traditions, repentance is present. The seriousness of sin is certainly present, although, unlike the classical Christian interpretation, there is not an "original sin" but rather a form of contamination and defilement. Related to the key Vedic concept of *rita*, the cosmic and moral order, sin in Hinduism ultimately has to do with violation of this cosmic order, the guarantee of peace, harmony, and blessings. This accrues "debt" that must be paid in order to regain balance.

Somewhat like Christian tradition, some Vedic traditions make a distinction between unintentional and intentional sins: whereas the former can be cleansed with the help of reciting proper Vedic passages, the latter can only be rectified by restitution. The most serious offenses can be "burned off" only in the process of numerous reincarnations, including temporary time spent in various hells. In Hinduism, the reconciliation of the most serious offenses may also entail various kinds of vows, a practice echoing the rationale of merits to be earned in the process of penance (rite of reconciliation) in Roman Catholic tradition.

Although atonement by the deity is not an unknown idea in Vedic religion, the emphasis by and large is still on "self-atonement." The situation is different with *bhakti* spirituality: grace and divine forgiveness are in the forefront as taught in the Bhagavad Gita (18.66): "Setting aside all noble deeds, just surrender completely to the will of God (with firm faith and loving contemplation). I shall liberate you from all sins (or bonds of Karma). Do not grieve." Various opportunities and ways to forgiveness are

---

34. Hiebert, "Conversion," 11.

offered in these traditions, from pilgrimage to a sacred site, and bathing in the sacred river Ganges, to being tutored by the guru (who is believed to bear sins as well), and so forth. Particularly important is the recitation of Sanskrit hymns and divine names.

Similar to the Abrahamic traditions, there are Hindu teachings about the need to extend forgiveness also to fellow humans. Rig Veda (5.85.7) contains the plea to Varuṇa: "If we have sinned against the man who loves us, have ever wronged a brother, friend, or comrade, The neighbour ever with us, or a stranger, O Varuṇa, remove from us the trespass."[35]

Buddhist Perspectives

As in Hinduism, Buddhist traditions display an ambiguity concerning conversion. On the one hand, it looks as though beginning with Gautama's enlightenment experience, a radical break with the past is the norm; on the other hand, it can also be argued that (apart from some exceptions such as conversion by force) the people who joined the movement rarely experienced any sense of radical crisis. One way to reconcile this apparent tension is to argue that only when the religious seeker made the decisive choice to break off from the "world" and become a Theravadin (an ascetic), was the break a crisis. That said, a significant number of disciples who joined Gautama already belonged to other religious movements.

As a general rule, it can be said that (perhaps with the exception of Pure Land) forgiveness is not linked to divine pardon that ensures entrance to eternal blessedness. Gods play little (or virtually no) role in conversion, repentance, and forgiveness. Furthermore, "the early Buddhist doctrine of kamma allows for mitigation, though not eradication, of the consequences of actions under some circumstances";[36] however, the kind of expiation of sins present in Hindu traditions discussed above is not present. At the forefront in the Buddhist tradition are the "practices of self-examination, feelings of remorse, the renunciation of unwholesome patterns of life, and the possibility of radical moral change."[37]

A more striking difference exists between Theravada and Mahayana Buddhism: whereas in the former the renunciation of the world ideally means devotion to full-time religious life with a view to personal salvation, including joining the community (*sangha*), the latter accepts the simple fact that for most of the masses this radical call is too much. Hence,

35. Trans. Griffith, 1896, available at www.sacred-texts.com/hin.
36. Attwood, "Did King Ajātasattu Confess," 279.
37. Eckel, "Buddhist Approach to Repentance," 122.

Mahayana with its theistic orientation offers the way of "salvation" somewhat similarly to forms of theistic Hinduism, that is, with devotion to the Ultimate Reality ("divinized" Buddha figure), and it encourages one to delay stepping into nirvana for the sake of helping others. In keeping with other faith traditions, all Buddhist traditions highlight the importance of forgiving other persons.

The next lengthy section takes up key Christian soteriological themes of justification, sanctification, and deification.

One with God: Justification, Deification, and Sanctification

What in the World Does "Divinization" Mean?

Instead of beginning with what is already familiar to most of us, namely justification by faith and sanctification, I begin by looking at the term for salvation in the Eastern Church, namely divinization or deification (from Greek *theosis*). In fact, this branch of the church uses a number of distinctive terms and metaphors for salvation, beyond that of divinization, some of them also familiar to the Christian West, such as participation and union. Wait: am I saying that Orthodox Churches believe that we humans can become God? Isn't that pantheism, the equation of the divine with the created—like, God is in everything and everything is in God? No, that is not the case!

The Eastern Church got her favorite idea of salvation as deification from the Bible rather than from pagan sources. The key texts for this are 2 Peter 1:4, which speaks of becoming "partakers of the divine nature" and Psalm 82:6, as quoted by Jesus in John 10:34: "I said, you are gods." The Petrine passage highlights the key idea of release from the corruption and mortality caused by the evil desires of the world. These are, of course, not the only such passages: there are many more in which the teaching about the union or oneness with God is found, including Exodus 34:30; John 17:21-23; 2 Corinthians 8:9; and 1 John 3:2; 4:12.

Several Church Fathers spoke to the same effect. The most well-known are Irenaeus's description of Jesus as "the Word of God, our Lord Jesus Christ, who did through his transcendent love, become what we are, that He might bring us to be even what He is Himself,"[38] and Athanasius's statement, "He [Christ] was made man that we might be made God."[39]

---

38. Irenaeus, *Against Heresies*, 5, preface in *ANF* 01
39. Athanasius, *On the Incarnation of the Word*, 54.3 in *NPNF*[2] 04.

A millennium later the fourteenth-century theologian Gregory of Palamas helped establish conclusively the main theological ramifications of the doctrine. The key aspects of his teaching are:

- the creation of the human being in the image of God;
- the incarnation of the Word (Logos) of God; and
- the human being's communion with God in the Holy Spirit.

Palamas also taught that the distinction between God's essence and God's "energies" makes it possible to say that deification means participating in divine energies but not in the divine essence as such. He thus avoids pantheism, the equation of God with the world. God still remains God, and humans remain human, though participating in the divine.

We have seen that Eastern theology does not focus so much on guilt as the main problem of humanity as it does on mortality. Nor does it juxtapose divine grace (and initiative) with human freedom (and responsibility). Instead, it speaks of divine-human "synergy" or cooperation. Although God is much "bigger," God graciously invites men and women to respond joyously and energetically.

Having now surveyed the Christian East's exciting soteriological vision (to which we will return below), let us focus in more detail on the Christian West.

Putting "Justification by Faith" in Perspective

In the Christian West, justification by faith has become an umbrella concept that covers virtually all aspects of the salvific relationship to God. Although that usage cannot be established biblically, as the Bible portrays the concept of justification/righteousness only as one of the many metaphors of salvation, it is legitimate to employ "big concepts" in order to make sense of rich diversity. Theologians and churches only have to keep in mind the fact that by doing so they should not make this chosen "window" onto salvation the test of orthodoxy, as has at times happened. Consider that in the church and theology of the Christian East, the term justification is virtually unknown!

Patristic writers did not express the doctrine of salvation using the term *justification*, even though that word does appear. One of the reasons for this is that Pauline theology—which says quite a lot about that topic—did not yet play the *central* role that it would in later theology. That only became the case at the turn of the fifth century with Augustine. But his take on justification was different from that of the Reformation teachers, particularly in that for him justification did not refer only to the "declaration" of the sinner as righteous ("forensic justification") but also to the act of making the sinner righteous (sanctification, or "effective justification"). Only at the time of the Protestant Reformation did the distinction between forensic and effective justification become programmatic.

To Luther's credit, it has to be said that he categorically rejected his previous Catholic teacher Gabriel Biel's slogan that "God does not deny grace to the one who does everything in his or her power." This essentially meant "do your best and then God takes care of the rest," an idea that may easily lead into despair, for the question of when I, the sinner, have done "enough" to merit God's gracious intervention, is always open. It was all the more important to reject this principle at the time because of the prevalent gross misuse of the theology of salvation in the Catholic Church through the sale of indulgences—as if paying money to be absolved of one's sins was the same as God forgiving them. While originally meant to act as the sign of commitment to authentic repentance and reparation of serious sins, the indulgences in time became a way for anyone who was willing and capable of paying to buy forgiveness—and for the church a way to finance its grand (building) projects.

That said, it is useful to ask why Reformation thinkers distinguished between and at times even almost separated the two aspects of justification rather than linking them together per Augustine and the earlier tradition. They had solid theological reasons, chief among them the need to resist any notion of "works-righteousness." Related is the pastoral concern not to drive weak Christians into despair with questions like: "If I do not recognize any spiritual fruit in my life, am I even justified?" In fact, this very dilemma had led the young Luther, a former monk, into despair as he spent hours and hours each day confessing in meticulous detail all his possible sins, both big and small. In hindsight, we can say that whereas the Protestant Reformers erred on the side of "safety" (by protecting Christians from those kinds of experiences of despair and unhealthy soul-searching), the Catholics, in keeping with tradition, wanted to remind believers of the need to cultivate spirituality and progress in holiness, in keeping with Jesus's advice of judging the tree by its fruit.

No wonder that the Catholic Church, Luther's former community, reacted critically to Protestants at the Council of Trent in the mid sixteenth century. The Catholics reminded the Protestants that although faith is necessary for justification, without love even faith does not suffice. In other words, following the teaching of James 2 in the NT, Trent argued that there needs to be fruit evident in Christian life. Mere declaration of faith is insufficient; without fruit, one's faith might be dead.

Notwithstanding its polemics, Protestants would have done well to heed Catholics's call to hold together the two aspects of justification: declaring righteous and making righteous (sanctification). Furthermore, the Council of Trent's highlighting of the role of the freedom of the will, as limited as it may be, could have been interpreted as conditioned by grace rather than as an affirmation of human independence.

The Renewal of Life: Push toward Revising the Protestant Doctrine of Justification

Theologically, how then would we assess the Reformation doctrine of justification by faith? In my assessment, as a Lutheran Minister of the Word and Sacrament, a main liability of the Protestant Reformation was its incapacity to negotiate constructively the relationship between the divine initiative (divine election and calling) and human response (repentance, conversion, and faith). More often than not, Protestant mainstream Christianity results in nominal Christians, in which people baptized as infants—or as believers in some Protestant denominations—do not feel the need to cultivate spiritual life, including regular attendance at church services, the Christian education of children, and so forth. The conviction that having been declared justified regardless of one's quality of life while expressing the deepest message of grace rediscovered at Reformation and pastoral sensitivity easily turns into an excuse for "cheap grace" (Dietrich Bonhoeffer). We will take up this issue below in the context of sanctification.

In this light, the teaching of Martin Luther himself may offer some help, for it is somewhat different from the official confessional writings of the Lutheran Church drafted mainly after his passing and so by others than himself. Luther's own view of justification did not typically operate with a programmatic distinction between forensic and effective justification. Instead, for him the crux of justification was the idea of Christ moving to live within the believer through the Holy Spirit. The Latin slogan *in ipsa fide Christus adest*, "in the faith itself Christ is present," summarizes this union with Christ approach. While both "just and sinner simultaneously" (Latin: *simul iustus et peccator*), and in need of daily repentance and return to Christ's grace, the Christian begins to be transformed into Christ's image who lives in his or her heart. In fact, in that the Christian begins to do the kinds of good and loving works Christ did, a Christian can be called *christ* (lower case).

Similarly, the teaching of Luther's younger colleague, Calvin, the founder of Reformed Protestantism, came closer to basic intuitions of

Augustine and the later Roman Catholic tradition in highlighting as the goal the renewal of life and not only the "forensic" declaration of the sinner. Calvin begins the discussion of soteriology in the third part of his main theological work, *Institutes of Christian Religion*, by first speaking of union with Christ: "so long as we are without Christ and separated from him, nothing which he suffered and did for the salvation of the human race is of the least benefit to us. To communicate to us the blessings which he received from the Father, he must become ours and dwell in us."[40] In this way, he intertwines justification and sanctification in order to refute the charge of "cheap grace" and complaints about a lack of emphasis on good works as the fruit of salvation.

An even more robust push toward a more integral relationship between justification and sanctification came from the third wing of the Reformation (alongside the Protestant and Roman Catholic), namely from the so-called Radical Reformers, including Anabaptists (later Mennonites), and the emerging Free Churches led by the Baptists. While these embraced the Protestant doctrine of justification by faith, they also made many complaints about the lack of due emphasis on good works and neighborly love. Like James of the NT, Balthasar Hubmaier, the early Anabaptist, declared: "Mere faith alone is not sufficient for salvation . . . for a true faith can never exist without deeds of love."[41]

Although Calvin connected sanctification and justification tightly through the concept of union, and although he expressed grave concerns about the liability of the Protestant doctrine of justification's lapse into complacency, that was not enough for the post-Reformation Pietist movement and other renewal movements. Regeneration rather than (forensic) declaration became the chief aspect in the soteriology of such renewal movements. Regeneration was understood as a dynamic event and—unlike external forensic acquittal—an act that brought about inner change. It pointed to new life, holiness, sanctification. Whereas forensic justification is a one-time event, and is the same for all, holiness is a matter of growth and progress, a typical Orthodox and Catholic idea.

The theology of the former Anglican, John Wesley, took a radical turn in pursuing renewal and change of life in the justified person. Like his Pietist and Puritan forebears, Wesley faced the dilemma of wanting to hold on to the forensic Protestant understanding of justification, including the distinction between justification and sanctification, while also understanding justification as regeneration—an inner change. Sanctification marks

---

40. Calvin, *Institutes*, 3.1.1.
41. Cited in McClendon, *Doctrine*, 117.

the "last and highest state" of this progress. Wesley at times even used the daring word "perfection" to mark the highest level of progress in spiritual life. Although—despite others' misunderstandings—perfection for him did not entail perfect sinlessness, it definitely set Wesley's vision of soteriology outside the Protestant mainstream. It held tightly to Jesus's admonition to "be perfect, as your heavenly Father is perfect" (Matt 5:48).

As suspicious as the desire for perfection may sound to mainstream Protestant and Anglican ears, Wesley's vision actually aligns itself well with the deep and wide Christian tradition. The pursuit of perfection was evident early on, among the Church Fathers, both in the East and in the West. It is not a coincidence that Wesley read and helped translate some of the key texts of the Eastern fathers.

These important historical developments help us understand and appreciate in a fresh way the richness of God's salvific gift, whether called justification, sanctification, deification, or something else. With those historical developments in mind, I turn now to some very promising findings and insights in our own time.

Exciting Current Convergences

Have you ever heard the following kinds of questions and claims?

- Whereas Protestants and Anglicans affirm justification by faith, Roman Catholics say justification is through one's good works.
- Whereas Methodists, Holiness movements, and many Free Churches pursue sanctification, for mainline Protestants and Anglicans to be saved, being a church member suffices.

As the following discussion shows clearly, these observations are one-sided at best and misleading at worst. To put them in proper perspective, let us first look at the promising conversations and consensus between the Roman Catholics and Protestants in their pursuit of a joint understanding of justification.

You might have heard about the "Joint Declaration on the Doctrine of Justification" (1999)[42] between Roman Catholics and Lutherans, later endorsed also by Methodists, Anglicans, and the Reformed. While not without critics on both sides of the dialogue—let alone numerous misunderstandings among church folks mainly due to ignorance of the

---

42. Available at Lutheran World Federation and the Catholic Church, "Joint Declaration."

details—the process was successful in showing that despite continuing differences, a convergence could be found and earlier condemnations nullified as regards the doctrine of justification.

Even though both Catholic and Lutheran emphases and qualifications are not lost in the process, a summary of the main mutual agreement goes something like this:

- not by works but solely on the basis of God's grace and in union with Christ, through faith sinners are forgiven and made righteous even though the fight against sin and the pursuit of renewal remain daily tasks;
- renewed persons bring forth good works, and they can be confident that the just and faithful God will see to their final salvation;
- in sum: there was a consensus about grace of God as the basis of salvation, justification by faith as both declaration and inner change, as well as good deeds as natural fruit of the justified life.

The "Joint Declaration" was thus an amazingly significant milestone in itself as it helped to rectify long-standing and persistent misunderstandings on both sides.

Another important conversation had to do with Protestant and Orthodox visions of salvation. Notwithstanding definitive differences in the understanding of sin, freedom of will, and related issues mentioned before, there is hope for better mutual understanding and that people on different sides will learn from each other. Luther's own understanding of salvation can be expressed not only in terms of the doctrine of justification, but also as *theōsis* and that the idea of justification as "Christ present in faith" means a real participation in God (union) through the indwelling of Christ in the heart of the believer through the Spirit. On some rare occasions the Reformer even went so far as to say: "[I]t is true that a man helped by grace is more than a man; indeed, the grace of God gives him the form of God and deifies him, so that even the Scriptures call him 'God' and God's son."[43] In other words, there are important convergences even between the Christian East and the West.

A Common Search for Life-Affirming Holiness

There are, moreover, promising biblical and theological discoveries in current theology regarding a deeper and wider understanding of sanctification

---

43. Luther, "Sermons at Leipzig and Erfurt, 1519; 1521," in *Luther's Works*, 51:58.

and holiness. The biblical tradition approaches the question of salvation from the perspective of the likeness of God's people to God. For this to happen, a change has to take place in the human person. Of course, this may entail a change of status, such as if somebody who has committed a crime is being pardoned. This, however, is not the main thrust of the biblical data. Protestants should learn from Luther's teaching on Christ present in faith through the Spirit, making the believer a "christ," although perfection can only be had in the eschaton. They would also benefit from Wesley's insight that sanctification, rather than an optional second moment, so to speak, is "the inevitable consequence of justification."[44] In other words, sanctification and justification have to be kept integrally related to each other.

Although the pursuit of holiness and likeness with God should be made a daily affair, talk about "perfection" has to be qualified. A useful reminder here is the wisdom of the aforementioned Lutheran slogan *simul iustus et peccator*, "at once righteous and sinner"—or *peccator in re et iustus in spe*, "a sinner in fact, righteous in hope."[45]

In a biblical understanding, holiness implies not escape from the world, nor isolationism—although, rightly understood, the basic meaning is separation from all that is not holy, in other words, all that is not in keeping with the integrity of God. Nor is biblical holiness a kind of "elitist 'privatizing' of spiritual experience" that leads to "detachment from both the community of faith and the service to the world." That kind of escapist holiness is only "attained at the expense of the more pressing task of serving Christ in the world."[46] While turning away from that which is not pleasing to God, holiness is life-affirming and invites the believer to assume a God-like posture, meaning one that pursues the values and love embodied in Jesus and in his teaching. That kind of holiness is "something 'contagious,' that is, humans and things become holy from contact with the holy God."[47]

Although human effort is necessary, ultimately this kind of growth—both natural and spiritual—is a matter of the divine Spirit. As in justification, of which divine righteousness is the source, in sanctification God's holiness is the basis. Sanctification and deification occur when we are fully one with God through Christ in the Spirit.

Protestants need to work toward a better balance of two mutually conditioned aspects of sanctification, namely "dying to oneself" (Latin *mortificatio sui*) and "being made live in the Spirit" (*vivificatio in Spiritu*). The

---

44. Moltmann, *Spirit of Life*, 165.
45. Moltmann, *Spirit of Life*, 164.
46. Fergusson, "Reclaiming the Doctrine," 380.
47. Chan, "Sanctification," 789.

former has tended to dominate Western traditions, which have been deeply influenced by the penitential culture of the medieval and Reformation period and its overly negative anthropology. For the Eastern Church and for Wesleyan movements, finding this balance is easier because of a more robust pneumatological orientation and an idea of sin not so much as a transgression to be atoned for as a sickness to be healed.

Ultimately, holiness and sanctification mean "rediscovering *the sanctity of life* and *the divine mystery of creation*, and defending them from life's manipulation, the secularization of nature, and the destruction of the world through human violence" (emphasis original).[48] Recall the etymology of the term "holy" in various Western languages: "entire, healthy, unhurt, complete, and 'belonging especially' to someone."[49] Likewise, a holy life is a "whole" life.

A cure against individualism and elitism is the NT observation that it is not an individual "saint"—separate from the community—but rather every Christian, even one in the beginning states (or even temporarily backslidden), who is called holy. After all it is the plural "saints" that typically appear in the biblical testimonies!

What else may the salvific gift of the Triune God include? Not only spiritual goods, as important as they are, but also empowerment and healing for life on earth, here and now. This is the focus of the following section.

Healing, Restoration, and Empowerment

How Did Theology Overlook the Importance of Healing and Charismatic Empowerment?

Healings are well known among all religious traditions. In our current era, there is also a growing interest in healing, restoration, and integrity of life in various medical disciplines. And, of course, healings feature prominently in the Bible. The NT Gospels narrate numerous healings and miraculous cures, and the Synoptic Gospels add to the picture acts of deliverance and exorcisms. Jesus used various "methods" to heal, from touch, to laying on of hands, to healing from a distance, to more curious things such as the use of saliva (Mark 7:33; 8:23; John 9:6).

In fact, Jesus of Nazareth was an itinerant healer and exorcist, and his followers were sent out not only to preach and teach but also to heal and deliver from under oppressive powers. In the book of Acts, healings

---

48. Moltmann, *Spirit of Life*, 171.
49. Moltmann, *Spirit of Life*, 175.

and exorcism continued as an integral part of the church's regular activity of prayer, liturgy, sacraments, and missionary outreach. Throughout Christian history healing in various forms has continued, including also the establishment of hospitals and sanatoriums. Importantly, the Eastern Orthodox bishop George M. Nalunnakkal of India says that not only is "the theme of healing . . . central to the theology, and particularly the soteriology, of almost all churches," but it is so central that "[i]n Orthodox theology, 'healing' is almost a synonym for 'salvation.'"[50] With the spread of Christianity to the Global South, the significance of a holistic view of salvation in Christian theology has been rediscovered.

In light of all that, a deep irony and profound omission in academic theology surface: although no major Christian tradition at any historical period has denied the healing and empowering capacity of the Creator God, no major doctrinal/systematic presentation has included the topic of healing in the *ordo salutis*. With the exception of an important discussion of healings, exorcisms, and charismatic effects in Moltmann's celebrated *Spirit of Life* (chapter 9) and my *Spirit of Salvation* (chapter 12), one searches in vain for that category in any noteworthy doctrinal manuals, unless they are written by Pentecostals and charismatics.

What might be the reasons for this omission of the topic of healing and charismatic empowerment in theology? Two factors appear to be determinative. First, academic theology's uncritical embrace of the naturalistic (materialist) epistemology of the contemporary scientific worldview, rooted in the Enlightenment, has closed our minds to something as "supernatural" as healing and exorcism. Second, known by the term "cessationism," some theological movements throughout history have concluded that while healings could happen—and did happen during the first centuries of Christian history—their time and validity ended when the biblical canon was ratified.

Having already critiqued and overcome the naive naturalist epistemological standpoint that refuses to grant the possibility of real divine action, and hence of healings and restoration, we now focus on the cessationist argument. It is deeply embedded in some Christian traditions, particularly traditional Protestantism and current conservative Reformed churches. Its roots, however, go back to patristic theology, particularly Augustine (although before the Reformation, cessationism was rarely an officially formulated and strict doctrinal standpoint). Theological cessationism readily affirms the presence and reality of miracles in the biblical world and until the time of the closing of the Christian canon by the end of the fourth

---

50. Nalunnakkal, "Come Holy Spirit," 17, 18 respectively.

century; after that, miracles ceased, its proponents argue. Once the written Word of God (the Bible) came to function as the spiritual norm, no miraculous charismatic experiences were needed as divine confirmation, as they had been before the canon was established.

There are two forms of theological cessationism, which can be named the "soft" and the "hard-core" views. Whereas the former does not categorically reject the possibility of miraculous events now, practically they are rendered nonexistent not only because they are not needed but also because they seem not to take place anymore. The "hard-core" version categorically denies the existence of all miraculous events after the apostolic era and judges all claims to their existence to be counterfeit, as Fundamentalist Reformed theologian B. B. Warfield argues in *The Counterfeit Miracles* (1918). What is highly ironic about cessationism is that though its proponents offer no biblical reasons to support it, they are Fundamentalist scriptural "inerrantists." In fact the NT data says nothing about an end to charismatic gifts.

While rejecting cessationism, theologians should not resist the great benefits of the Enlightenment or its critical principles. Rather, it is the uncritical, naive use of modernist criticism that we should leave behind. A sound, self-critical, and open-minded use of critical principle is necessary in all areas of life in the contemporary world. That in itself does not make our worldview "flat" in terms of, say, materialism (or naturalism)—that is, the idea that all that there is, is the material. Nor does the resistance to cessationism lead into the theologically—and logically—suspicious claim that only Christians in certain global locations, for example in Africa, are by default open to the miraculous while others are not. Whereas in "spirited" cultures such as in Africa and Asia, people get turned on more easily by miracles and extraordinary happenings, Christian claims for healing, exorcism, charisms, and other spiritual happenings are not limited to certain locations!

What Might a Sound and Healthy Theology of Healing Look Like?

The Many and Diverse Ways of Healing and Empowerment

The healing ministry of Jesus is a robust statement about the all-inclusive nature of God's salvation; it includes the physical and emotional as well as the spiritual. Healings and exorcisms were also signs of profound sympathy, or of "cosuffering" (Matt 14:14). Jesus's bodily contact with people considered "untouchable," such as the woman with bleeding (Mark 5:24–34), helped overcome the belief that women's bodies are dirty.

In keeping with the manifold ways of Jesus's ministry, healing and restoration have taken many forms in the church. Some Christian traditions hold a predominantly sacramentally oriented approach, as is the case in Eastern Orthodoxy, Roman Catholicism, and Anglicanism. In other communities, the charismatic gifts and hope for instantaneous healing are more typical, as in Pentecostal/charismatic movements.

The Czech Reformed theologian Pavel Hejzlar has discerned "two paradigms for divine healing." The "healing evangelists" expect an instantaneous recovery to occur as the normal response, and often the charismatically endowed healer is the instrument. The "pastoral healers" likewise believe in a rapid restoration of health, but they are open to both the gradual and the instantaneous work of God; the healer's role is less pronounced and may also include a group of Christians over a period of time.[51] This difference in orientation is of course not either/or but both/and. Furthermore, in recent years, collaboration between health professionals and Christian ministers has emerged.

Correcting a Couple of Popular Theological Misconceptions about Healing

On the way to providing some principles of a sound and constructive theology of healing, it is important to rectify two widespread and well-meaning but ultimately harmful misunderstandings. Like most such ideas, they are based on half-truths, and as such they are misleading. Let's begin with the popular statement that there is "healing in the atonement." What are we to think of it?

Without doubt, Christian theology affirms the close link between the atonement and healing based on the OT testimonies (Isa 53:4–5) and their creative use in the NT (Matt 8:17; 1 Pet 2:24). But how exactly are the two—atonement and healing—linked theologically? It is instructive to see how Matthew (8:17) applies Isaiah 53:4–5 to Jesus's healing ministry: "He took our infirmities and bore our diseases." There is no reference to the cross here any more than in 1 Peter's use of the Isaiah's passage. Both in the context of the epistle as a whole and in the immediate context, it appears that Jesus's suffering provides encouragement for Christians to follow Jesus in suffering. Whereas in Matthew the link to (physical) healings is clearly presented, in Peter that connection is altogether missing. Thus, the first conclusion is that the link between healing and atonement can be affirmed only at a general level, that is, in light of Christian salvation

---

51. Hejzlar, *Two Paradigms for Divine Healing.*

stemming from the atoning and reconciling work of Christ. But there is nothing "causal" or automatic there.

Furthermore, like salvation in general, healing "now" is a foretaste of the coming eschatological fulfillment based on the reconciling work of the triune God. Living as we do between the "already" of the coming kingdom and the "not yet" of its consummation, healings are signs of the final victory. But healing is not yet available in its wholeness and entirety. In sum: the claim of some healing evangelists that as surely as there is salvation in the atonement, there is also physical healing, is simply not true.

What about the other popular claim, which argues that whenever there is proper faith, healings happen, indeed, they must happen—or else, authentic faith is missing? What to think of this "faith-formula"—the teaching that true faith, which "claims" God's promises in terms of "positive confession," has an almost magical power to work miracles? Faith in that case is like a signed check to be cashed in! For many Christians who are waiting or hoping for healing or restoration, this kind of promise leads to endless examining of the quality of one's faith. It may also cause anxiety and pressure to perform.

The Gospels undeniably show an integral link between faith and healing. Jesus seemed to attribute some healings to faith (Matt 9:22; Mark 5:34; 10:52; Luke 8:48; 17:19; 18:42). At times Jesus rebuked people for lack of faith (Matt 14:31; 17:20). A closer look at the Gospels's data, however, yields a more complex and elusive link between the two. A number of healing incidents make no mention of faith (Mark 3:1-5; Luke 4:38-39; John 9:1-7). While in many instances the healed person's own faith played a role, there are also incidents in which Jesus commended the faith of other persons involved (Mark 2:1-12; Matt 9:1-8; Luke 5:17-26). Furthermore, whereas at times faith seems to precede healing (Mark 2:5; Matt 8:10; Luke 7:50), at other times faith emerges as a result of healing (Matt 11:4; John 12:37).

All this leads to the obvious conclusion that there is no automatic, let alone necessary, link between faith and healing. It is left to the hidden wisdom of God to determine that mysterious relationship. All we can say is that the Bible assigns promises to the exercise of faith, on the one hand, and that God cares for and supports those who, like the father in the Gospels, cried out to Jesus: "I believe; help my unbelief!" (Mark 9:24).

Some Principles for a Theologically and Pastorally Sound Healing Ministry

First, there is no "causal" relationship between the work of God and human response (faith). God's works are based on grace and compassion.

Second, when speaking of faith in relation to healing, we also have to insist on hope for God's continuing care amid sickness and suffering, and love for those who are not healed. We do well to remember that "God's power is as near to us in sickness and in death as it is in healing."[52]

Third, although there is no direct link between faith and healing, prayer for healing matters. As the American Lutheran OT scholar Frederick J. Gaiser puts it: "God does not become a God of love and healing because of our prayer. But our prayer opens us to the God of love, who desires our healing."[53]

Fourth, healing can be experienced at personal and communal levels in a variety of ways. Healing can be focused on a "healing evangelist" or "pastoral healer" paradigm; it can be instantaneous or gradual; it may be attributed mainly to prayer and spirituality or to medical expertise; it may be attained in a healing meeting or at a sacramental encounter.

Fifth, although sickness and healing are personal matters, the role of the faith community is not unimportant. James (5:13–16) recommends that a sick person contact the elders of the church for prayer and anointing with oil. In short, the healing ministry is an integral part of the church's daily life and ministry.

Sixth and finally, healings and deliverances ultimately point to the eschatological consummation. Healings are "signs" pointing toward fullness.

What about suffering in relation to healing? It is clear from the biblical teaching that both the pain of suffering and the hope for healing will coexist until the eschaton. While the acknowledgment of the presence of suffering should not become a pretext for not praying for divine healing, theological reflection on suffering, pain, and disability is an important part of a theology of restoration.

To widen the interfaith dimension, let us continue looking at the topics of this chapter in relation to other faiths.

Healing and Sickness among Religions

Both healings and sickness feature prominently among religions. All scriptural traditions deal with the problem of sickness and the possibility of restoration.

The three Abrahamic traditions speak of healing and well-being as a promise of God. The OT promises of Yahweh as healer are widely known. Indeed, in the Israelite faith both calamity and healing come from one

---

52. Blue, *Authority to Heal*, 49.
53. Gaiser, *Healing in the Bible*, 55.

and the same Lord (Deut 32:39). So deeply is healing instilled in Jewish tradition that a petition is recited in daily Jewish liturgy: "Heal us, O Lord, and we shall be healed."

According to the Qur'anic promise in 41:44, the divine word is "guidance and a healing" for believers but brings about deafness to the disobedient. God is the healer (26:80). The Hadith tradition continues and deepens this idea. According to the Prophet, "God has not sent down a disease without sending down a remedy for it."[54] Not surprisingly, all Islamic traditions also invite the faithful to pray for healing; it is particularly important in the mystical Sufi tradition. The folk healing tradition is pervasive in Islam.

What about Asian faiths? If there is a common denominator between widely divergent Asiatic faith traditions concerning insights into wellness, it has to do with harmony and balance. And all consider the human being's health to be part of a larger cosmic network.

Although all faith traditions locate sickness and health in a matrix of influences and factors, from religious to secular, in Hinduism the network of effects is unusually wide. It includes not only karma, the spiritual "cause-effect" chain, and other foundational theological themes such as "ignorance," as well as complicated rules and rites regarding ritual pollution and purity, but also caste and class, gender, and other such issues related to the sociocultural hierarchy. Briefly stated: the medical and religious are deeply intertwined. Some diseases are conceived to be the result of the anger of a god. Like other faith traditions, Hinduism also provides for deliverance from possession and demonic influence.

The question of the place of suffering and sickness in diverse Buddhist traditions is of course linked with the concept of *dukkha*. Another foundational concept, namely, the interrelatedness of everything in the cosmos, comes into play here: "Suffering is not unique to those who struggle with chronic disability or illness. The point is that even those who are physically healthy and materially wealthy nonetheless experience a chaotic, continually festering dissatisfaction."[55]

If the original Theravada tradition focused on "healing" in terms of spiritual healing, the theistically oriented Mahayana traditions imagine healing as both spiritual and physical. Not unlike other theistic traditions, Mahayana links healing directly to Buddha. Indeed, one of the most interesting developments in this regard is the emergence of the "Medicine Buddha," a hugely important object of worship and prayer in devotional movements throughout East Asia. An authoritative and widely used

---

54. Al-Baghawi, *Mishkat al-Masabih*, 3:945.
55. Schumm and Stoltzfus, "Chronic Illness and Disability," 164.

manual is *The Sutra of Medicine Buddha*.[56] No doubt this theistic version of healing in Buddhism echoes important themes not only in the Abrahamic but also in other theistic traditions.

Now back to the more familiar Christian environment and the question of the nature and role of charismatic empowerment and gifting in the order of salvation.

What Does "Baptism in the Holy Spirit" Mean?

Many Interpretations of Spirit Baptism

If possible, doctrinal theology's omission of the category of charismatic empowerment is even more striking than its omission of healing. The themes of Spirit baptism, charismatic empowerment, and gifting are simply altogether absent from presentations of the *ordo salutis*—with the exception of Pentecostal/charismatic ones.

Why should we be concerned about this category? There are at least three reasons. The first has to do with early Christian tradition. Both in the biblical and early Christian tradition, the charismatic element, at times named *Spirit baptism*, was integral to the process of Christian initiation. Second, the rise of Pentecostal/charismatic Christianity has again made Spirit baptism prominent. Third, a holistic view of salvation properly includes the dynamic element of gifting, inspiration, and empowerment.

What complicates the appreciation of Spirit baptism is not only academic theologians' general ignorance of the topic but also its many different interpretations among those who are familiar with it. While difference of opinions is nothing unusual with regards to theological doctrines, in this case the scarcity—indeed the almost total lack—of sound theological treatments (outside the Pentecostal-Charismatic constituencies) adds to the complexity.

For the sake of clarity, I divide the many interpretations of Spirit baptism into four broad categories. The first line of interpretation I call the "traditional soteriological view." Its main idea is that Spirit baptism is another name for everything that the Holy Spirit is doing in salvation in general. Examples of this kind of interpretation can be found both among Roman Catholic and Protestant theologians, of the past and present. Typically, a person's reception of the Spirit is linked with water baptism (in traditional churches normally as an infant). The implication of the traditional soteriological view is that if the term *Spirit baptism* were not used, nothing

---

56. Thanh and Leigh, *Sutra of the Medicine Buddha*.

would be lost, because it is just another way to speak of the Spirit's work in Christian initiation and life.

The second and most novel interpretation of Spirit baptism comes from the Pentecostal movement, which understands Spirit baptism as a necessary and distinct category in the *ordo salutis* which cannot be removed or replaced by something else. Most Pentecostal movements teach that Spirit baptism is distinct from and subsequent to conversion (or new birth). It happens "after" one has become a Christian. Whereas Spirit baptism happens only once in life, it is followed by daily fillings with the Spirit. The experience is something every Christian can (and should) have, and its main purpose is empowerment for witness and service (Acts 1:8). The most distinctive feature of the Pentecostal interpretation—although not universally taught by all Pentecostals—is the expectation that every believer experience *glossolalia* (speaking in tongues) as the "initial physical evidence." Whereas this "initial evidence" is a normative experience for all, many people may also receive the continuing gift of speaking in tongues and retain it throughout their Christian lives. In other words, some people make a distinction between the onetime "evidential" glossolalia patterned after several instances in the book of Acts (2:4–6; 10:46; 19:6) and a regular "prayer language" as mentioned in 1 Corinthians (12:28–30).

The third view, which I name "charismatic-sacramental," represents a radical middle way between the first two views. It forges an integral link between the sacramental water baptism in which the Holy Spirit is given to the baptized and the later experience of Spirit baptism as an occasion for the actualization and surfacing of the Spirit initially received in water baptism through a conscious charismatic experience. Similar to the Pentecostal interpretation, this charismatic-sacramental view expects the release of a charismatic gift, but unlike the Pentecostal view, it leaves open what kind of gift that might be. This general template is followed by the majority of theologians in the Roman Catholic charismatic movement and is also influential among some leading Anglican and Lutheran renewal movements.

Finally, the fourth interpretation, the "non-sacramental charismatic," is closely linked with both the second and the third in that it assumes the reception of charismatic gifts at Spirit-baptism but, differently from the Pentecostals (and in line with the "charismatic-sacramental"), it is not willing to limit these to glossolalia. Its difference from the "charismatic-sacramental" (in keeping with the Pentecostal) is the refusal to link baptism with the Spirit to any sacramental action, not even water baptism. Most neo-charismatics, say the Vineyard Churches, follow this line of interpretation, as do charismatics in other churches which are not sacramental in theology.

With these four main interpretations in mind, let us make some comparisons and attempt some useful guidelines.

Guidelines and Recommendations for the Theology of Spirit Baptism for All Churches

The first occurrence of the term "to baptize with the Spirit" (which can be found only as verb, never as noun) in the NT is Mark 1:7–8 in which Jesus, the one who is "mightier" than John the Baptist, is the Spirit-baptizer. It is Luke who is particularly interested in the Spirit's charismatic work. In a well-known gospel passage (Luke 7:18–23), Jesus clearly understands miraculous deeds as divine confirmation, and already earlier (4:18–19) had introduced his ministry as charismatic. The programmatic passage of Acts 1:8 then extends the promise of the Spirit's empowerment to the church and her mission as a whole:

> But you shall receive power when the Holy Spirit has come upon you; and you shall be my witnesses in Jerusalem and in all Judea and Samaria and to the end of the earth.

We are likewise indebted to Luke for the Pentecost event narrative, including the signs of tongues and fire (chapter 2).

Similarly, as conversant as Paul's theology is with a wide range of the Spirit's ministry, including the soteriological and ethical, it also highlights the Spirit's charismatic dimensions (1 Cor 12; 14; among others). The same template seems to have been at work during the first centuries of the Christian church, although after the patristic era and with the rise of infant baptism, the charismatic element began to lose prominence.

In light of this NT and patristic evidence, we can deem the traditional soteriological view way too limited because it simply says too little about empowerment. This is, of course, not to undermine or disparage—and certainly not to debunk—the authenticity of Christian initiation that lacks the charismatic and "experiential" element. But it is to remind us that a more holistic and integral vision of salvation can be had. The other two Spirit baptism interpretations are clearly superior in this regard. Each in its own way incorporates the charismatic element into a holistic vision of the *ordo salutis*.

The Pentecostal interpretation does this most robustly. Ironically, its separation of Spirit baptism from water baptism and Christian initiation is both its strength and its liability. The benefit of the separation lies in the legitimate reminder to us that there are no necessary biblical or theological (any more than pastoral) reasons to limit the charismatic breakthrough, even in its first occurrence, to water baptism. In this respect, the Pentecostal view agrees with the non-sacramental charismatic view. "The Spirit blows where it wills" (paraphrasing John 3:8). On the other hand, to separate it categorically in this way from the wider framework of Christian initiation is also a liability because in the NT, and particularly in the book of Acts, water baptism and Spirit baptism are clearly related. More importantly, the main fallacy of the Pentecostal interpretation is its insistence on one particular gift as the definitive one: namely, speaking in tongues. Not only is this not supported with the biblical data (notwithstanding several instances in the Book of Acts in which the pouring out of the Spirit and tongues are mentioned when the church transitioned into new spheres of evangelization and missionary work, as in 10:44–46), this interpretation also leads to a forced and stark division between two kinds of tongues, the tongues of Acts 2 intended for all believers in all ages, and the tongues spoken of in 1 Corinthians 12:30 according to which only some have that gift.

This takes me to the benefits of both the sacramental-charismatic and the nonsacramental-charismatic options. They both believe in the charismatic endowment with gifts (but not one particular gift) as a blessed surplus of Spirit baptism. As to which one of these two approaches to follow depends on one's wider church context. The nonsacramental is appealing to those Protestant traditions whose theology is not sacramental, such as the various kinds of Free Churches, some Reformed, some Methodists and Holiness movements, and so forth. The sacramental-charismatic approach is followed in older churches that have a sacramental theology.

Chapter 9 will explore in greater details the many charisms and forms of empowerment and endowment by the Spirit. The final topic in our consideration of the order of salvation has to do with the culmination of salvation.

The Faithfulness of God and the End of Human Yearning

Traditionally, the last "step" in the order of salvation is glorification, the ultimate consummation of salvation in God's blessed eternity. The classical biblical support for the doctrine of glorification comes from Romans 8:30: "those whom he justified he also glorified."

Confidence in the final consummation is expressed in the Reformed doctrine of "the perseverance of the saints to the end" that speaks to spiritual assurance based on God's faithfulness. The Lutheran version of perseverance is ecclesiologically founded. According to the Augsburg

Confession, "one holy Christian church will be and remain forever."[57] In other words: even if individual Christians, and if even leaders, fail, the church will remain. Notwithstanding differences in nuancing the doctrine of perseverance, Protestant theologians agreed on the following: "1. God the Father is faithful; he cannot deny himself (II Tim. 2.13). He never lets go of the person he has chosen. 2. God the Son prayed for those who are his 'that your faith might not fail' (Luke 22.32). 3. As advance payment and beginning of eternal life, the Holy Spirit remains with the people who are his to the end (*usque ad finem*). The Holy Spirit 'seals' God's children for the day of redemption."[58]

The Roman Catholic Church has been very hesitant to formulate a doctrine of perseverance, not because of a lack of God's faithfulness but out of fear that Christians will be led more or less automatically to assume salvation. The fear of self-assurance and overly optimistic trust in human steadfastness are what lie behind this attitude. While understandable, Catholics could also acknowledge that in its authentic form, the Protestants' endorsement of the assurance of salvation has nothing to do with human capacities and everything to do with God's faithfulness. In this sense, the Arminian party (as discussed in chapter 4) rightly resisted the ultra-Calvinistic TULIP formula of making the perseverance of saints a necessary condition.

We may safely conclude that as long as the locus of the doctrine of perseverance is anchored in God's faithfulness, it provides confident assurance to the believer. This does not mean that it is not possible for a Christian to fall away from grace but that, even in their darkest moments of life, men and women, as well as the whole church of Christ, may confidently rest in the assurance of God's fatherly love and care.

Christian tradition believes that the insatiable human yearning for fulfillment and happiness can be met only by the ultimate encounter with God that "glorification" seeks to conceptualize. In mystical experiences, there is already "an anticipation of the eschatological, immediate, and direct seeing of God 'face to face.'"[59] Although it is not a biblical term, the Roman Catholic tradition speaks of the consummation of salvation in terms of the "beatific vision," a dream of ultimate fulfillment of all human yearnings expressed in the Eastern traditions as the completion of deification. Having first concluded that no created good may bring ultimate and final happiness, Thomas Aquinas teaches that human yearning finds fulfillment in the

---

57. Augsburg Confession VII, in Tappert, *Book of Concord*, 32.
58. Moltmann, *Spirit of Life*, 156.
59. Moltmann, *Spirit of Life*, 205.

vision of God, indeed, in the "essence" of God as based on the scriptural promise in 1 John 3:2 ("we shall see him as he is").

In anticipation of the last two chapters of the book, I recall something I have already frequently highlighted in the discussion: that since the Christian hope of salvation is multifaceted and multilayered, it is more than my own personal salvation, let alone merely the "spiritual" salvation of the soul alone. It encompasses the whole human being and other human beings. Hence, the following ninth chapter on the doctrine of the church helps set this salvific hope in a wide and comprehensive communal context. And the final tenth chapter reminds us again that whereas the reception of the salvific gifts begins already on this earth, that reception will be consummated only in the coming of God's kingdom and the final personal, communal, and cosmic consummation of Triune God's eternal purposes.

9

Church

For What Do We Need the Christian Community?

Do We Really Need a Christian Community in Order to Exercise Our Faith?

"I LOVE THE CHURCH but cannot tolerate people" is more than just a snide remark. Aren't there already (too) many Christians who are fed up with the church and her continuing and ever-increasing problems and scandals? Do we really need more leadership scandals, painful divisions, child abuses, robbery of money, cases of nepotism, and so forth? In light of such problems, why is a faith that is between "Me and my Jesus" not sufficient? Isn't faith everybody's own private business?

Let me put it another way. In the recitation of the creed when we confess our belief in a church that is one, holy, catholic, and apostolic, are we deliberately ignoring the obvious reality? Instead of one, the church is deeply split; instead of holy, it is deeply sinful. And as for "catholic" and "apostolic," most Christians have no idea of what that means.

These kinds of questions, objections, and opinions are probably not unknown to you and these or similar ones might have emerged in your own mind as well. They will occupy us in this lengthier chapter on the doctrine of the church, what in theological jargon we call ecclesiology (from the Greek term *ecclesia*).

With so many questions in mind, it may come as a surprise to you that ecclesiology, unlike some other well-known Christian doctrines—say Christology and Trinity—did not emerge as a separate "chapter" in theology until around the time of Reformation. How so? Until then, there were only occasional disputes about the Christian community (some of which I revisit below) but no burning debates.

The reason why the Reformation brought the whole issue of the nature of the church to the fore had to do with deeply-seated disputes about what makes the true church. The Reformers, both mainstream (Lutherans, Reformed, and Anglicans) as well as radical (Anabaptists and later other Free Churches), vehemently questioned the "churchliness" of Rome given that it was plagued by a number of controversies such as fights about the papacy—and even the presence of more than one pope at the same time in a few instances—the moral laxity and corruption of the clergy, as well as the widespread abuse through the selling of indulgences. In the Reformers's eyes, the Catholic Church was rotten through and through and not capable of being repaired. On the other side, the Roman Catholic Church claimed to be the only legitimate successor to the first apostles and hence, to the Jesus-event that had first launched the church. Disputes between the two parties also had to do with the issue of the Bible and divine revelation (see chapter 1) and salvation (see chapter 7). The Eastern Orthodox Church for its part stayed uninvolved for now, having cut off contact with the Christian West.

So, that is from where the *doctrine* of the church, as we now know it, derives. Much has changed since then, and we are now facing a whole new matrix of challenges and opportunities. How are we to do ecclesiology in the third millennium? How are we to think about the church in our own times?

What Is Happening in the Church of the Third Millennium?

The Dramatically Transformed Context of the Global Church and Its Doctrine

At least four definitive and wide-ranging processes of change have taken place at the end of the second millennium, all of which thrust the Christian Church and her mission into a new and uncharted context:

- the globalization of the church;
- the denominational diversification of the church;
- the emergence of new kinds of ecclesial existence; and
- the importance of secularism and religious pluralism (as well as post-secularism).

Let us look at each in turn, beginning with the global spread of the Christian Church.

From its humble beginnings, the Christian Church has grown to be the world's largest religious community, with over 2.4 billion adherents, the majority of whom reside in the Global South. Africa is now the biggest "Christian" continent. Consequently, most church members in the near future—and already now—are not adult European-North American Caucasians but people of all ages, genders, and diverse ethnic backgrounds from across the globe. A typical Christian is young, poor, and most likely a female living in a city environment in Africa, Asia, or Latin America.

A defining feature of current globalization is the massive movement of peoples and people groups around the globe, as migrant churches and diaspora communities shape the life of the church. Currently, of the over 200 million migrants, about one-half are Christians, the majority of whom are in the United States and Europe. The next largest group is Muslims. Particularly visible are the Pentecostal/charismatic immigrant and diaspora communities, a significant number of whom are of African descent.

Alongside the globalization of the church, a massive transformation of the denominational structure is underway. Do you know which Christian denomination is the biggest one? It is Roman Catholic rather than any Protestant denomination. To date, half of all Christians are Roman Catholics. And can you guess which denomination is the next biggest? In fact, it is not one (historical) denomination, but rather a grouping of Christians under the elusive name of Pentecostals/charismatics, which constitute one-fourth of all Christians. If you add the over 50 percent of Catholics and about 25 percent of Pentecostals/charismatics, you have three-fourths of all Christians in the world. And recall, the majority are to be found in the Global South—and they are young, poor, female, and city-dwellers.

The rest of the members of the worldwide church, the last quarter, are Eastern Orthodox, Anglicans, mainline Protestants, and members of Free Churches. Among them, the Eastern Orthodox Church is the biggest, comprising about half of them. Which leaves quite a small slice of the cake of the Global Christian Church to mainline Protestants and Anglicans as well as "traditional" Free Churches. Consider this. I happen to be a minister in the (Evangelical) Lutheran Church (in America). The total population of the Lutheran World Federation is less than 80 million (plus a small number of Lutherans outside this global fellowship). Compare that to 2.4 billion (2.4 thousand million) Christians. My church is indeed a tiny minority!

But back to Pentecostal-Charismatics. That constituency calls for some explanation. It is common to divide it under three interrelated subcategories:

- (Classical) Pentecostal denominations such as the Assemblies of God, Foursquare Gospel, and Church of God in Christ, which owe their existence to the famous Azusa Street Revival in 1906: about 180 million members;
- Charismatic movements, Pentecostal-type spiritual movements within the established churches beginning in the 1960s (the largest of which is the Roman Catholic Charismatic Renewal, which compromises well over 100 million members): about 200 million members; and finally
- Neo-charismatic movements, including Vineyard Fellowship in the United States and African Initiated Churches, as well as countless independent churches and groups all over the world; usually even China's rapidly growing house-church movements are included here: over 300 million members.

The Mosaic of the American Ecclesiological Experiments

As a case study of this continuing diversification of the church, consider the United States, characterized by unprecedented denominational and ethnic diversity, originally going back to the pilgrimage of European immigrants from the old continent and now fostered by immigration and diaspora. Although the Catholic Church is today the biggest ecclesiastical player, large numbers of the first generations of new settlers also came from various types of Protestant and Anglican constituencies in which the nonconformists in particular often felt marginalized and oppressed. As a result, what Europeans would identify as "free-church ecclesiality" actually now forms the "mainline" American church reality. Among Protestants, Baptists of various stripes constitute the majority.

Alongside this historically unprecedented denominational plurality, the American experiment is also characterized by a deepening and widening multiculturalism. Among the several major American-based ethnic group families, none is growing as fast and proliferating as widely as the Hispanic American churches. The special challenge and asset of Hispanic communities in the United States are their ecumenical background in both Catholicism and Protestantism, lately also in Pentecostal/charismatic spiritualities. Most recently, churches and movements of Asian descent have been gaining significance with the mushrooming of diverse communities. Predominantly traditional in theological orientation, these churches reflect remarkable diversity and plurality. Before the Hispanics and Asians,

African American Christianity had already established its significant place in American religiosity. Black churches continue to grow, whether Episcopal or Evangelical or Pentecostal communities.

Emerging Communities and New Ways of Being the Church

Alongside this remarkable global and denominational diversity is the rise of a new and complex set of ecclesiastical developments linked with postmodern cultures. Book titles such as *ChurchNext* (2000) by Eddie Giggs and *The Liquid Church* (2002) by Pete Ward testify to this ecclesial "post-existence." A few decades ago, ecclesiologists spoke of the baby boomer generation. It was served with the so-called seeker-friendly suburban-based churches that catered to all kinds of needs of individuals and families. Subsequently, "purpose-driven" churches and the like caught our attention.

Most recently, these kinds of models, while still having an appeal with their own generation, are giving way to Gen X and other postmodern generations. Among them, a most exciting phenomenon ecclesiologically is known under the rubric of "emerging (or emergent) church" (USA)[1] and "fresh expressions of the church" (UK).[2] Highly active in virtual networks and ways of connecting, their ecclesiologies are fluid. Nor do they always meet in sanctuaries but may instead rent comedy clubs or pubs for their gatherings. Deeply missional in orientation with a focus on practices and everyday Christian service, they do not typically bother to delve into theological debates about ecclesiology, although many of their leaders may have a solid academic training in religion. The basic difference between the US-based emerging churches and the UK fresh expressions is that whereas the former is usually separatist, forming their own communities, most communities of the latter are birthed by and stay within the Church of England (and other mainline denominations).

What are some of the characteristics of these emerging churches? A wide survey reveals that they:

- identify with the life of Jesus and follow his teaching and example;
- transform the secular realm into the sacred by meeting, for example, in comedy clubs;
- live highly communal lives whether in person or in virtual reality;

---

1. For an overview of the emerging church in the USA, see "Emerging Church."
2. For an overview of the fresh expressions movement in the UK, see "Our Story."

- welcome the stranger, a person not a typical church-goer, or even a believer;
- serve with generosity;
- participate as producers, bringing to the church and services their own specific talents rather than merely sitting as an audience;
- be creative;
- lead as a body rather than according to the old pastor vs. congregation model; and
- take part in spiritual activities, whether ancient (such as liturgical) or new forms.[3]

What about Other Faiths—and Secularism?

To these three changes in the environment of the church—globalization, diversification, new ecclesial forms—one more critical factor has to be added, namely the ever-intensifying encounter with other living faiths as well as the many forms of growing secularisms (and post-secularisms).

Religions continue gaining more footholds all over the world. The implications to the church—and the *doctrine* of the church—are many and significant. The engagement in this book of four other religions with regard to each and every Christian doctrine is a response to this challenge.

Similarly, the challenges from secularism call for a careful consideration. It is a complex phenomenon, as will be discussed in more detail below in this chapter. Suffice it to mention here that while secularism continues to exercise huge influence over American and particularly European societies, it is also gaining a stronger footing in the Global South.

A Brief Orientation to This Lengthy Chapter

The chapter's first task goes to the heart of our topic by inquiring into the meaning of church and its distinctive "marks" as a unique community. This is followed by the key discovery in current theology concerning the church's missionary nature.

That discussion naturally leads to the issue of how to organize the community and its ministerial patterns and offices in order to best help the church succeed in her mission. Thereafter, a closer look at the nature and

3. Gibbs and Bolger, *Emerging Churches*, 45.

distinctive features of the ministry and ministers of the missional church is in order, including also the role of charismatic endowment and spiritual gifts in ministry. In the contemporary world, the question of the access to ministry by both men and women is a key issue as well. Following that, the spiritual life of the missional community in worship, liturgy, and prayer as well as in the celebration of the sacraments of water baptism and the eucharist (Lord's Supper) will be discussed in some detail.

The last two major topics delve into the questions of ecumenism and comparative theology. First, I consider the importance and means of pursuing and maintaining the unity of Christ's church on earth. To wrap up the chapter, the second lengthier section delves into the complex question of the relation of the church to Jewish, Muslim, Hindu, and Buddhist communities as well as to secular persons.

What Is the Church?[4]

The People of God, the Body of Christ, the Temple of the Spirit

Among the numerous metaphors and symbols in the Bible, over the centuries the following have gained particular importance:

- the people of God (1 Pet 2:9; Rev 5:9-10);
- the body of Christ (Eph 1:22-23; 1 Cor 12:27; Col 1:18); and
- the temple of the Spirit (Eph 2:19-22; 1 Pet 2:5).

Beginning with the last metaphor: as discussed in chapter 6, the Spirit not only works in one's personal life but also in the world and the community. Theologically speaking, the Spirit has a community-forming role, as is clearly evident on the day of Pentecost, at the founding of the church (Acts 2). Those who placed their faith in Christ, the Savior, God's Messiah, formed the community of the church in the power of the Spirit. Whereas the metaphor of the body of Christ is more familiar to us, the temple of the Spirit reminds us of the pneumatological importance of the church. As the "Spirit-ed" community, the church is charismatically endowed and empowered to accomplish her mission.

Particularly in Pauline theology, terminology calling the church the body of Christ abounds. Whereas in 1 Corinthians and Romans the *body* refers to the individual community, in Ephesians and Colossians it refers

---

4. This section, with minor amendments, is borrowed from Kärkkäinen, *Introduction to Ecclesiology*, 9-17.

to the whole church. The body metaphor for individual communities has to do with interrelated virtues and qualities of love, unity, and working for the common good (1 Cor 12–14). In relation to the whole church as the body, at the center are Christ's eternal purposes toward the reconciliation of all peoples and all of creation.

The third metaphor, peoplehood, is understandably based on divine election, a concept that of course has its roots in the election of the people of Israel in the OT (Gen 12:1–3). Divine election means both particularity and opening to the world. On the one hand, the chosen community has a unique relationship to God, notwithstanding the lack of superiority over other nations (Deut 7:7–9). On the other hand, on account of its election it has a missionary mandate to help other nations to know God (Isa 2:2–4; Mic 4:1–5). The peoplehood metaphor also highlights the inclusiveness and equality of all Christians as well as Israel, the first people of God.

Obviously, a trinitarian pattern is apparent here. No wonder that since the beginning theology has referred to the church as formed in the "image of the Trinity," parallel to the human being having been created in God's image. It reminds us that as the triune God is the eternal communion of Father, Son, and Spirit, so too the church as communion bespeaks belonging and unity.

This understanding is expressed with the help of an important NT term: *koinonia*, meaning "fellowship," "communion," or "community." Its many meanings and contexts in the NT remind us of the breadth and depth of the common sharing in the church with regard to both spiritual and mundane domains of life, including:

- fellowship with the triune God (1 Cor 1:9; 2 Cor 13:14; 1 John 1:3, 6);
- sharing in faith and the gospel (Rom 15:27; 1 Cor 9:23; 1 John 1:3, 7);
- sharing in the Eucharist (Acts 2:42; 1 Cor 10:16);
- partnering in common ministry (2 Cor 8:23; Phlm 17); and
- sharing in and contributing to economic and financial needs (Acts 2:44; Rom 15:26; 2 Cor 12:13; 1 Tim 6:18).

The Community in Service of the Coming of God's Kingdom

To the extent that the church is the image of the Triune God, it has everything to do with the coming of God's kingdom. The entire ministry and proclamation of Jesus Christ, the founder of the church, centered on the coming of the righteous rule of his Father in the power of the Holy

Spirit, the kingdom of God (Mark 1:15; cf. Matt 4:17; Luke 4:43–44). It had already arrived in his teaching, healings, exorcisms, and pronouncing of forgiveness, and culminated in his glorious resurrection from the dead on behalf of the world.

But the kingdom still awaits its final consummation. Between these two comings of Christ is the era of the church. Therefore, the church refers to the future of God, the eschatological consummation. In the words of Miroslav Volf, the NT "authors portray the church, which emerged after Christ's resurrection and the sending of the Spirit, as the anticipation of the eschatological gathering of the entire people of God."[5] Every gathering of the church references the final homecoming (Rev 21:1–4). The coming of the kingdom of God is not only the consummation of the church's highest hopes. Its scope is even wider and more comprehensive than that. Concurrent with the coming of God's kingdom will be the consummation of God's eternal plans regarding the entire cosmos.

Hence, it can be said that the church serves as the "sign" of the coming reign of God. The church in itself is not to be equated with God's rule. God's reign, his kingdom, is much broader than the church or even human society. The church is an anticipatory sign that points to the coming righteous rule of God in the eschaton.

The "Marks" of the Church

A cherished ancient way of describing the nature and goal of the church is to speak of the four "marks" of the church, as one, holy, catholic, and apostolic. This expression even found its way into the ancient creed. What do these terms mark?

These classical marks of the church were probably added to the creed somewhat haphazardly. Hence, rather than abstract definitions of the church, they are instead statements of faith or of hope. In fact, it is best to think of these marks as both gifts and tasks. On the one hand, they are gifts from God. We do not make the church one, holy, catholic, and apostolic; only God can do that. On the other hand, we see only too clearly that any church in the world, including our own, is far from having attained those markers. Hence, each description is also a matter of hope, which leads to action to move closer to attaining their realization. With these caveats in mind, let us take them one at a time.

---

5. Volf, *After Our Likeness*, 128.

The Church Is One

In light of the rampant divisions and splits, it really takes faith to confess that the church of Christ on earth is one. At the time of this writing, it is estimated that there are about 41,000 Christian denominations! Wow! No wonder that the NT so often exhorts us to foster unity and avoid further divisions (John 17:20–26; Acts 2:42; Rom 12:3–8; 1 Cor 1:10–30; Eph 4:1–6).

Although the unity of the church has been a spiritual and theological conviction from its beginning, we should not idealize the early church. Already in the NT era, divisions and strife emerged as soon as new communities mushroomed. Importantly, early in patristic theology deep concern for restoring unity emerged as well, as is evident in ecumenical tracts such as the early third-century *On the Unity of the Church* by Cyprian.

Recalling the gift/task distinction introduced above, the church's unity is a God-given gift because there is only one "head" with one "body" of Christ (Eph 4:15–16). At the same time, it is a grand task given to all Christians. Currently the ecumenical movement, both formal and informal, is engaged in this crucial work, which I discuss below.

The Church Is Holy

Similarly to unity, the holiness of the church is a challenging confession in light of the rampant sinfulness and corruption of churches and individual Christians. In fact, calling the church on earth holy sounds almost blasphemous, so many are its sins and abuses.

Not surprisingly, various tactics have been tried to ensure the church's holiness. One of them involves isolating the "holy members" from the rest. This goes all the way back to the (in)famous Donatist controversy in the patristic era. Whereas the rigorist Donatists started off from the premise of the purity of the church, Augustine's mainline party insisted on the primacy of love. Augustine also insisted on the church as a "mixed body" on this side of the eschaton, consisting of both holy and sinful members. The ultimate concern of the Augustinian party had to do with the unity of the body of Christ and the principle of love. The Donatists were overcome by the majority opinion. Yet another tactic makes a distinction between a church holy in itself and its sinful members; that is, it considers the *church* to be holy and its membership to be sinful. The obvious question arises, however: What is a church without Christians? Is it an abstract concept? An "invisible" nonearthly reality?

What, then, would be a theologically and pastorally appropriate way to envision a "holy" church of the creed despite the inevitable sinfulness of all its members? The starting point is the honest and bold acknowledgment of the sinfulness of the church. The church is simultaneously both sinful and holy. This means that the church derives its holiness not from the members—as Free Church ecclesiologies too often tend to imply—but from its Lord; nor does the church lose its holiness because of the presence of sin in the lives of men and women, as deplorable as that may be. That said, the idea of separation lies at the core of the biblical notion of holiness in both testaments—as Free Churches tirelessly remind older churches. Church members should turn away from all that is un- and anti-God(ly) and turn to the things of God. But notwithstanding the need for the human act of turning (away and toward), ultimately holiness is the work of the triune God.

The Church Is Catholic

The term *catholic* as one of the marks of the church does not denote a particular Christian tradition, the Roman Catholic Church. Instead, it is a theological expression that means "directed toward the whole" (literally in Greek), referring first of all to the whole church in distinction from local communities. The meaning of "fullness" and "perfection," that is, "lacking nothing," was later attached to catholicity, based on Ephesians 1:23. From this development, in polemical debates, the term catholic came to mean "orthodox."

In short, we today have to remember the original NT meaning of the term *catholic* (notwithstanding the lack of the term in the NT): it simply means the whole church, all local churches, which in themselves are fully churches insofar as they are in communion with other similar communities. Furthermore, although spatial extension, numerical quantity, and temporal continuity are not irrelevant to catholicity, they do not alone— or even primarily—constitute it. It is often and appropriately noted that the term *catholic* comes close to *ecumenical*, whose basic meaning, "pertaining to the whole inhabited world," came to denote (the search for) the wholeness, that is, oneness and unity, of the Christian Church.

The Church Is Apostolic

Although the adjective *apostolic* likewise never occurs in the Bible, the term *apostle* is a familiar NT term. Its meaning resembles that of an ambassador (for Christ). The term is not limited to the twelve disciples as is often popularly assumed. It can also refer to various persons and groups such as Paul himself, but also his opponents, the "false apostles" (2 Cor 11:13).

The original meaning of *apostolic* simply referred to a linkage with the apostles. Apostolicity, then, essentially involves continuity with the life and faith of the apostles and the apostolic church of the NT. It comes to manifestation in faith, worship, and mission. Whereas the Orthodox and Catholics base the apostolic succession in episcopacy, Reformed Christians highlight continuity with the apostolic Word.

The Church Not Only Has Mission—The Church Is Mission!

What Is "Mission"—and What Isn't?

Having now tentatively defined and described the meaning and nature of the church based on the NT witness and the important teaching in the early theology and creeds, it is time to seek to provide the most recent— and in my opinion, the most groundbreaking and most significant—current consensus about what the church is and what it does. Not that it is something new and novel in terms of having not been known before; not at all. Instead, what I mean is that in recent years all theological and ecclesiastical traditions have come to acknowledge the fact that the church on earth is at its core a sent community. In simple terms, and reflecting the above section heading: the church not only has a mission to do, it also exists as mission: it is missionary in its very nature.

For this programmatic turn to happen, the meaning of the ancient term *mission* has had to undergo several transformations. Whereas until the Reformation the (Latin) term *missio* denoted simply the "sending" of the Son by the Father, thereafter its meaning became related to the work toward the conversion by Catholics (spearheaded by the Jesuits) of non-Catholic Christians, until in modern times it adopted a meaning virtually synonymous with "foreign" mission. Only in recent decades has its basic meaning in theology and missiology become comprehensive and inclusive, referring to the basic nature of the church as a "sent" community.

Before getting into the many implications of the missional existence of the church, I have to address the all-important question about the alleged disastrously close link between mission and colonialism.

Colonialism as the Rupture and Corruption of Mission

The roots of colonialism—the desire to subjugate peoples and regions under the pretext of both economic-political and religious motives—is far older than the sad history of modern colonialism that ravaged Africa and Latin America, among other continents and countries. Although older than our faith, in Christian history its roots go back to as early as the fourth century when a once outlawed, occasionally persecuted Jewish-originated new cult called Christianity was made a "state-religion"—or, to be more precise: a religion favored by the state—thanks to Constantine the Great, the Emperor of Rome. This transition from the margins to the dominant position in its pagan society blurred the notion of the Christian community as the minority pilgrim on the way to heavenly city, caring and seeking for all who wanted to join in following Christ, the man of the cross. Though undoubtedly at times for noble reasons, the pursuit of earthly power and prestige to further God's kingdom supplanted the pursuit of love and humility.

The brutal use of power in "freeing" the promised land from Muslims during the Crusades is the ugly manifestation of such perversion, or likewise the conquest of South America in the sixteenth century by both the earthly sword and the sword of the Word of God, or the seventeenth-century forced "migration" of African slaves to the New World. Notable also is the church's silence in the face of the gross violence against the First Nations of North America, or the rampant racism against Blacks and other people of color in the USA, South Africa, and elsewhere. What shame and guilt such examples are for authentic mission!

Christendom (the exercise of the earthly power of the church ratified by the state) and colonialism share a common evil desire: the pursuit of power and earthly influence in order to subjugate and take advantage of the other. Sadly, colonialism is not limited to Western powers; the history of Asia also bears its legacy; just consider Japan's subjugation of Korea or the power of the Islamic Ottoman Empire with its sweeping brutal conquests.

Although it is crystal clear that the Christian church at large was involved with the colonial expansion of modern times and bears guilt for it, that should not lead to uncritical and unnuanced debunking of modern missions. In light of the newest missions histories, there is no doubt that missionaries also helped not only to establish and cultivate local languages ("mission as translation")[6] but also to empower local economies and cultures and prevent them from declining in order to advance colonialists' agendas. That same missionary translation also empowered indigenous resistance to colonialism.

---

6. Sanneh, *Translating the Message*.

While the colonial system represented a worldwide economic and military order, mission represented vindication for the vernacular.

In sum: while strongly and directly condemning all abuses of power and alignment with colonialism, the Christian Church has no reason to throw out the baby with the bathwater, namely mission done in obedience to God's command, in Christian love, care, and humility.

What Does the Missional Church Do?

The Many Facets and Aspects of the Work of the Church

Suppose that we were to do a poll on the street about what the church is supposed to be doing, in other words, about what its mission is. We would get diverse responses, most probably highlighting its spiritual, accompanied with diaconal and other services. This is all well and good. But surely we would also wish to add a more comprehensive and multidimensional menu for the missional church—as it serves the coming of God's righteous and loving rule in the eschatological consummation.

Besides the church's basic activities of

- liturgy, worship, and services, including caring for various age groups from infants to seniors, as well as other spirituality-enhancing activities such as prayer, Bible study, church music, and Christian education in terms of confirmation classes, Sunday school, and similar; and
- diaconal work of helping those in various social, economic, and other practical needs,

the missional church is also engaged robustly in the following kinds of works:

- mission as evangelism and common witness;
- mission as healing and restoration;
- mission as social justice and equality;
- mission as integrity and flourishing of nature;
- mission as reconciliation and peacebuilding;
- mission as seeking for the unity of Christ's church; and
- mission as dialogue and interfaith engagement.

Whereas liturgy and worship, including the sacraments, as well as ecumemical and interfaith challenge, will be discussed below, I turn first to other tasks on the list.

Not All Evangelism Is Proselytism!

Currently we are witnessing a widespread resurgence of evangelism, not only in younger churches but also in older churches, especially in the Catholic Church. Although a widely attested biblical term (*euangelion* and related words), "evangelism" (or "evangelization") in normal church usage was not rediscovered until the nineteenth century. In contemporary understanding, "it is at the heart of Christian mission to foster the multiplication of local congregations in every human community [as the] planting of the seed of the Gospel will bring forward a people gathered around the Word and sacraments and called to announce God's revealed purpose."[7] It is agreed that since the gospel is meant for every human person, everyone has the right to hear it. Evangelization should be done in a holistic manner and should follow the example of Jesus.

While engaging in evangelization, a number of pertinent, interrelated theological and practical issues and questions routinely arise:

- What is the justification for encouraging conversion? And does evangelism with that goal represent a perverted power play?
- What, if anything, is the difference between evangelistic persuasion with the aim of initiating a response, and proselytism?
- Under what conditions could Christians from various churches collaborate in giving a common witness?

Since conversion was already discussed in chapter 8, only the twin themes of proselytism and common witness are taken up here.

Proselytism has emerged as one of the most hotly debated topics between older, more established historic churches and younger churches with enthusiastic evangelizing activities. Routinely, Free Churches and other "newcomers" are labeled as proselytizers, and only recently have they been invited to mutual conversations about the topic.

But what is proselytism? Although "proselyte" originally meant a convert to Judaism and later, by derivation, a convert to any other religion, "'[p]roselytism' now refers to encouraging Christians who belong to one church to change their denominational allegiance to another, through ways and

---

7. WCC, *Mission and Evangelism*, 376.

means that contradict the spirit of Christian love, violate the freedom of the human person and diminish trust in the Christian witness of the church,'" and as such are "the corruption of witness." Some of the features of proselytism in contrast to authentic evangelism include

> [u]nfair criticism or caricaturing of the doctrines, beliefs and practices of another church without attempting to understand or enter into dialogue on those issues . . . [p]resenting one's church or confession as "the *true* church" and its teachings as "the *right* faith" and the only way to salvation . . . [o]ffering humanitarian aid or educational opportunities as an inducement to join another church, (emphasis original)

and similar unethical acts.[8]

While all churches should condemn and reject these kinds of proselytizing activities and attitudes, it is equally important not to confuse authentic evangelism and common witness with proselytism. For authentic Christian witness, including common witness, "is constructive: it enriches, challenges, strengthens and builds up solid Christian relationships and fellowship" instead of the proselytizing "counterwitness," which "brings about tensions, scandal and division, and is thus a destabilizing factor for the witness of the church of Christ in the world." Furthermore, as long as the person decides to move from one Christian community to another out of the person's own volition and freedom, charges of proselytism should not be leveled. Churches also agree that it is every Christian's privilege and the task to bear witness to Christ among all people, including other Christians, as long as it is done in Christ's love and with tact.[9]

Since the following tasks of the missional church have either been treated before or will be developed below, they will be lumped under the following rubric:

Mission as Healing, Justice, Nature-care, and Peace-building

As discussed in chapter 8, unlike proclamation and evangelism, healing—whether physical or mental—has not been the hallmark of Christian mission for a long time, nor does healing occupy any place in standard theological discussions. This is markedly different from the early church

---

8. All citations in this paragraph are from WCC, "Towards Common Witness," section II.

9 All citations in this paragraph are from WCC, "Towards Common Witness," section II.

and the long history of the church's life—let alone from the importance attached to healing, deliverance, and restoration among Pentecostals/charismatics and churches of the Global South across the ecumenical spectrum. Since this topic was discussed in detail in chapter 8, there is no need to repeat it here. Suffice it to emphasize that any missionary activity and presence worth its salt cannot afford to dismiss it.

The church's sociopolitical mandate has been taken up in the discussions of revelation, Trinity, and Christology, and will be revisited in the next chapter on eschatology. Hence, in what follows I merely link it tightly with the missional existence of the church.

The theological basis of the healing, flourishing, and integrity of creation is a key concern in contemporary theology and has been developed in the doctrine of creation (chapter 3) and pneumatology (chapter 7); I also revisit it in the following chapter on eschatology. So here an appeal will suffice: essential to the comprehensive missionary existence of the church is concern for God's creation.

I have previously discussed violence in the context of the doctrine of God (chapter 2) and of Christology (chapter 5). In condemning violence in all its illegitimate forms, the church is called to act as the herald and agent of peace-building and reconciliation. In fact the term *reconciliation* in this wider sense can be considered as the most inclusive concept denoting the various dimensions and aspects of salvation and hence, the vision of the missionary church. Here I sum it up in the words of the WCC document *Together towards Life*:

> God did not send the Son for the salvation of humanity alone or give us a partial salvation. Rather the gospel is the good news for every part of creation and every aspect of our life and society. It is therefore vital to recognize God's mission in a cosmic sense and to affirm all life, the whole *oikoumene*, as being interconnected in God's web of life.[10]

After this brief listing of the nature and tasks of the missional church, our next task is to consider who are the ministers of the missional church and the ways in which they are equipped and endowed for their many tasks. But before that, a quick look at the most typical ways churches have organized themselves and of their ministerial patterns is helpful.

---

10. WCC, *Together towards Life*, para. 4.

The Organization, Governance, and Ministerial Patterns of Various Churches[11]

Ministerial Patterns

Biblical scholarship has not been able to establish *the* scriptural model or ways of organizing the church. From the scattered NT examples, testimonies, and anecdotes, we can gather that there was no one uniform pattern of organization, even in the early church. It is important to acknowledge the improvised and fluid emergence of church structures in the NT and early Christianity. Along with simple needs in the church (as evinced in the selection of the first deacons in Acts 6), preserving the unity of and need to care for the fledgling communities seem to have been the major catalysts behind the appointment of leaders. It appears that the NT church functioned with two kinds of ministerial categories, namely:

- bishops and elders, often indistinguishable from each other; and
- deacons.

The office of the bishop (Greek *episkopos*), literally, "the one who oversees" (Acts 20:28; 1 Tim 3:1-2; Titus 1:7) has a history both in the Jewish temple overseer and in secular Greek office structures. The elder (*presbuteros*; Acts 20:17; 1 Tim 5:17-19; Titus 1:5; Jas 5:14) similarly comes from both Hebrew and Greek cultural backgrounds. At times, these two office designations seem to be used interchangeably (Acts 20:17-28; Titus 1:5-7). What is clear is that the essential task had to do with pastoral care and leadership.

The other main category goes by the name deacon (*diakonos*), which denoted waiting at table and helping, assisting. The first installation of deacons in the NT church in Acts 6 names charitable service as their main task. But importantly at least some of them also served through proclamation and evangelism (Acts 8). Indeed, early on in the church's life the deacon's task became assisting the bishop.

As early as the second century, this two-tiered structure gave way to the threefold ministry as the distinction between the bishop and pastor/priest established itself. Though we do not know how this process evolved, it is safe to assume that the latter office developed out of that of the *presbuteros*.

Importantly, the office of the bishop soon moved away from the life of the local community. The bishop came to be the leader of communities

---

11 This section, with minor modifications, is borrowed from Kärkkäinen, *Introduction to Ecclesiology*, 184-87.

in a certain area (synod). The central tasks given to the bishop included presiding over the liturgy (particularly the Eucharist), teaching, and governance. This kind of episcopal assignment has continued throughout history. The pastors/priests served under episcopal supervision and under the bishop's auspices in the sacramental ministry, as the bishop could obviously not preside at all individual baptisms and Eucharistic celebrations. The deacons functioned as the bishop's assistants as well as carrying out the church's social work. All that said, we do not yet have firm knowledge regarding the extent to which our contemporary conception of the bishop corresponds to the early episcopacy.

Although the three-tiered ministry structure has this ancient pedigree, it is doubtful whether it could—or should—be designated as normative for all Christian communities in the pluralistic and diverse world of ours. The flexibility of structures in the NT alone should make us cautious. What ultimately matters is the community's theological judgment regarding which structures in the given religio-cultural and societal context best facilitate missional ministry. The same can be said of the wider governance structures of the church.

Models of Governance

In a historical and contemporary perspective, it is typical to distinguish three different models of governance—each with nuances and differences of detail. First there is the episcopal model (not synonymous with the "Episcopal" church). In this model, the bishop stands at the top of the community and under him (usually) are pastors and deacons. All the bishops together form a college of bishops. The most robust episcopal tradition is the Roman Catholic Church, in which one of the bishops chosen from the college (of the cardinals, that is, the "senior" level bishops), namely the bishop of Rome, or pope, presides over the whole church and has a special status assigned to him (as explained in chapter 2 above). Whereas there is no pope in the Eastern Orthodox Church—as even the Bishop of Constantinople is only senior among his colleagues but not superior in the Roman sense—each of the patriarchates form episcopal communions headed by the most senior among them, and all patriarchates (ideally, though seldom in real life) are connected as equals. In the Anglican Church, the bishops, presided over by the Archbishop of Canterbury, are part of the ecclesial nature of the communion; hence, episcopacy is not optional.

In contrast to these three traditions, in the Lutheran Church episcopacy is optional, based on the conviction that as long as the "pure" Gospel is preached and the sacraments properly administered, everything else—like organization and church structures—can be designed and ordered in many different ways. As a result, there are Lutheran churches with bishops (usually with the archbishop, aka the presiding bishop, as the senior) and those with no bishops. The "thinnest" form of episcopal governance is common among those Methodist churches (such as The United Methodist Church) that are episcopal. Finally, there is a widespread use of the title "bishop" among churches such as black Pentecostals in the United States and various parts of Africa, as well as a number of Pentecostals of the former Eastern Europe. Theologically those churches are not episcopal and some of them have not always had bishops.

The second form of church governance is presbyterian. In that model, the leadership and authority resides in a group of elders, or presbyters, a model that recalls the Jewish synagogue life. In contrast to the episcopal model, there is no bishop, and hence there is only one level of ministers, notwithstanding administrative posts of supervision and leadership. The Presbyterian (Reformed) churches are the textbook example of this model.

In the third standard governance model called congregational, neither an individual leader such as a bishop, nor a college of elders, but the entire congregation is the seat and locus of authority. Typically, there is the idea of the autonomy of each local congregation even if, for the sake of collaboration, various kinds of ecclesiastical associations may be formed. Understandably, neither bishops nor levels of clergy are found in this model. Baptists, Congregationalists (a denomination), some Methodists, and non-episcopal Lutherans, among others, represent this governance type.

While there are other forms of governance, particularly among the Independents and the new emerging communities, the three above are the most well-known.

Missional Existence as the Charismatic-Diaconal Ministry

The Whole People of God as the Missional Minister

To the question of who serves as the minister in the missionary church, the foundational answer is: every church member, the people of God. Even though tasks vary and some persons are dedicated to a lifelong and full-time ministry, everyone is part of the common calling and vocation of the entire church. All are called and endowed for this common "priestly service" (1 Pet 2:9). This is currently a shared conviction among all Christian communities.

As is well-known, the famous slogan of the "priesthood of all believers" became a clarion call in Protestantism, particularly in Lutheranism. Luther's theology of ministry refused to grant any special status to ministers, even though he made necessary the ordained alongside the active laity. The only thing that distinguishes the pastors from others is their setting apart by the community for the community. Other Reformers, including Anabaptists, enthusiastically followed this lead. Roman Catholic theology continues to make a categorical distinction between the ordinary faithful and the priests as well as other religious (the monks and nuns); that said, they do affirm the shared ministry of all.

Assuming that all church members are ministers, what might be the main assets and resources for such a ministry? And, related to this, what is ministry in the first place? For it is a term widely used but seldom defined.

What Is "Diaconal-Charismatic" Ministry?

It is strange that the NT itself does not use any particular term equivalent to our English term "ministry." However, the following two terms come close. The first is "charism." For Paul (Rom 12; 1 Cor 12; 14; Eph 4) and others (1 Pet 4), a normal part of the church's worship and ministry is the exercise by the body of believers of various types of charisms or spiritual gifts. The second one is *diakonia*, "service"; this Greek term is most consistently translated as ministry (or service). Originally, it referred to the work of serving food and waiting on tables, work despised by all free Greek citizens. In Jesus's teaching and example, those tasks and such service focus on living for and serving others, even to the point of self-sacrifice.

These two words—charism and diaconal—help us define what church ministry is at its core: divinely gifted and endowed service in the power of the Spirit in a humble and unselfish manner. Think about how different that is from the alleged elite, power-laden, and high-profile ministries most of us can easily imagine.

This kind of service-oriented, Spirit-energized church "lives through the participation of its members, that is, the laity and the office holders, and is constituted through them by the Holy Spirit." This leads to what Miroslav Volf names a "polycentric community" model of the communion, with the participation, gifting, and responsibility of all instead of the traditional "bipolar" model in which those in office do the church work and the laity observes.[12]

---

12. Volf, *After Our Likeness*, 222–25, primary quote from 222.

In this model, ministries and offices of the church "only come into being by virtue of the common commissioning of the community itself." Those people are not separated or isolated from the community but rather render service among the people and on their behalf.[13] In keeping with NT testimonies and intuitions, any commission, charge, or ministry can

> be full-time or part time. They can be carried out by men and women, by the married and the unmarried, by the theologically trained and people without any theological training. They can be exercised by individuals and groups. None of these circumstances and aptitudes amount to a law.[14]

How all of this is planned, structured, facilitated, and empowered in each local church varies. But the idea of the whole church as the diaconal-charismatic minister is the ultimate guide and goal. For that to happen, let us delve deeper into the meaning, availability, and effects of charismatic endowment, a topic too often ignored in standard theology textbooks—if not for other reasons, then for the mistaken notion that such endowment is the commodity of only one type of church, namely Pentecostal and Charismatic.

What Is the Role of the Charisms in the Ministry?

Who are the Charismatics? Who might have charisms? Here I am not speaking of our contemporary context but rather the NT language: in the NT, each and every Christian and each and every church is charismatic, not only some. At least that was what Paul said.

The term "charism" (from the Greek stem *charis*, "grace") is used loosely in the NT with reference to various types of charismatic endowments, giftings, and capabilities. They range from the more extraordinary (miraculous works, words of wisdom, prophetic words) to the fairly "mundane" (teaching, exhortation, giving generously), and there is no fixed number of them.

Charisms are not only for individual believers, although of course they are that. They are first and foremost gifts and endowments for the whole church, in keeping with the focus on the whole church as the minister of the charismatic gifting and endowment of all.

Christian communities that have followed more closely the ministry patterns present in the Pastoral Epistles have tended to prefer order

---

13. Moltmann, *Church in the Power*, 302.
14. Moltmann, *Church in the Power*, 308.

over spontaneity, structures over improvisation, and the body of Christ metaphor over that of the temple of the Spirit. Those communities in the footsteps of the Pauline teaching for the Corinthian and Thessalonian congregations have sought an ongoing, fresh experience of the charisms and spiritual manifestations. Without pitting these NT traditions against each other, it is vital for the church of the third millennium to rediscover the charismatic structure of the church and its integral link with the diaconic structures of ministry.

The NT, particularly the Pauline literature, provides us with some important principles concerning the meaning and use of charisms. First and foremost, the charisms are distributed and delivered by the sovereign Spirit of God, "who apportions to each one individually as he wills" (1 Cor 12:11). At the same time, we are urged to "earnestly desire the higher gifts" (v. 31).

Second, charisms are not only exceptional and sensational phenomena—although there are also those, including glossolalia, powerful works, exorcisms, and healings (1 Cor 12 and 14; Acts 10:46; Mark 16:17)—but also everyday ministry energies and giftings, from giving and exhortation to helping and leading, from teaching and discernment of spirits to acts of mercy and administration (Rom 12:7-8; 1 Cor 12:8, 10; 1 Pet 4:10-11). Charisms are diverse and plural. There is no exclusive or exhaustive list of gifts anywhere in the NT; rather, we find various types of description, all open-ended in nature (Rom 12:6-8; 1 Cor 12:28-31; Eph 4:11-13; 1 Pet 4:10-11). The main goal of all of these various kinds of charisms is the common good of the church (1 Cor 12:7).

Third, there is a universal distribution of charisms, as every Christian is charismatic (Rom 12:6; 1 Cor 12:7; Eph 4:7; 1 Pet 4:10). No members are without charisms, although there might be some people—perhaps many—who have yet to discern and acknowledge them. Hence, the principle of "common responsibility" for the life of the church.

Having now highlighted the significance of the whole church as the main missional ministry, let us shift the focus toward that group of members called to be ministers in a special manner, so pastor, elders, bishops, deacons, and so forth. Rightly understood, we could call them "professional" ministers, many of them full-time, while others have part-time work as such.

Ordained Ministers in Service of the Whole Community

In light of the diversity and plurality of church structures, names of the offices, and organizational patterns, it comes as no surprise that even in the NT, there was never one fixed model; rather, the structures seem to have been improvisational and fluid in nature. Along with the simple need in the church (as evinced, for example, in the selection of the first deacons in Acts 6), the unity of and need to care for the fledgling communities seemed to have been the major catalyst for the appointment of leaders and designing of support structures.

That said, historically it is undisputed that as early as the second century the office of the bishop—and a fairly straightforward three-tiered ministry, with priests and deacons as assistants—emerged. The central tasks given to the bishop included presiding over the liturgy, particularly the Eucharist, teaching, and governing, and that assignment has continued throughout history. That said, we do not yet have a firm knowledge of the extent that our contemporary conception of the bishop corresponds to the early episcopacy. One important implication is the fact that not all churches currently have episcopacy should not be a problem—and that the term bishop may mean many things: how different is a Roman Catholic bishop from the bishop in the many Pentecostal Churches, for example. In sum: in light of the flexibility of church structures and patterns in the NT and early Christianity, we can surely welcome many kinds of current applications.

What is ordination? We know that it has had a long legacy even if its forms might have changed during the course of history. It is significant that even the Protestant Reformers with all their disdain for the gross abuses of the clergy in the Catholic church, including earthly privileges and riches, did not want to do away with the office of the ordained minister. They just wanted to restore it to its proper place, namely under the community and for the sake of the community it serves. Hence, ordination properly understood is a *"public reception of a charisma given by God and focused on the local church as a whole . . .* [and] *an act of the entire local church led by the Spirit of God"* (emphasis original).[15]

With this context in mind, we may summarize the following interrelated aspects and effects of ordination:

- reception of the gift of the Spirit (1 Tim 4:14; 2 Tim 1:6–7);
- public commissioning by the local church (Acts 13:3);
- acknowledgment of God's gifting and calling in the ordained person's life; and
- mutual commitment between the community and the ordained.

---

15. Volf, *After Our Likeness*, 249.

In sum: although the NT endorses no definite profile of ministry, it is clear about what it takes and means to be the holder of a church office: rather than being above or superior to the people of God, ministers are but cobelievers; and rather than being dignitaries to be served, they are servants willing to minister to others. All appeals to superiority over others are totally foreign to the biblical teaching (see Mark 9:33–35; 10:42–45; and parallels).

Can Both Women and Men Be Ordained into Ministry?

A burning issue for our own times is access to the ordained ministry by both sexes. In many churches, both in those that have resolved the issue toward inclusion and those with no such opening in view, heated and passionate debates have taken place. Orthodox and Catholic churches—alongside a number of the most conservative Protestant churches—do not allow female ordination, whereas Anglican and most mainline Protestant churches do.

The late American Reformed feminist theologian Letty Russell's celebrated *Church in the Round* uses the symbolism of the table to create new images of the church by employing the common cultural image of hospitality. The table represents inclusivity. An inclusive understanding of ministry takes it for granted that both the reception and the recognition of God's gifting for ministry apply to women and men alike. In patriarchal styles of leadership, authority is exercised by standing above in the place of power. Feminist styles of leadership draw their model from a partnership paradigm that is oriented toward community formation. An inclusive and hospitable vision of the communion helps us imagine an inclusive theology of ordination.

Why is there resistance to women's access to the office? Let us divide typical arguments into three broad categories:

- biblical-exegetical arguments focused on well-known NT passages seemingly barring women from ministry (1 Cor 14:34–35; 1 Tim 2:11–15);
- traditional-historical arguments related to beliefs about women's lack of access to ministry throughout history; and
- anthropological/gender-related assumptions based on conceptions of women's nature and role in Christian theological understanding.

What are the counterarguments in support of an inclusive view of ordination? Concerning the alleged biblical prohibitions, theologians have presented the following types of counterarguments and rebuttals that—if not all absolutely convincing—together seriously undermine the prohibitions' credibility as a whole and, indeed, have convinced the supporters of the inclusive view:

- arguments concerning the equality in Christ of both men and women (Gal 3:28);
- arguments concerning the gifts of the Spirit to both men and women (Joel 2:28–29; Acts 2:17–18);
- arguments concerning the hermeneutics of passages used to prohibit female ordination in the NT (particularly in 1 Cor 11 and 14, as well as 1 Tim 2), which have been successfully defeated with a number of counterarguments (which we cannot explore here);
- arguments regarding the presence of female leaders in the NT, such as Lydia (Acts 16:40), the four daughters of Philip (Acts 21:9), Priscilla (Acts 18:18; Rom 16:3), Euodia and Syntyche (Phil 4:2–3), among others;
- arguments that appeal to the precedent of twelve male apostles who lost their scholarly credibility long ago; some Catholic critics of their own church even acknowledge this; and
- arguments that note that the gender of Jesus is not a problem; rather, the way tradition uses Jesus's maleness to establish hierarchy, exclusivity, and power structures is the problem.

While undoubtedly these counterarguments are unlikely to change the opinion of some churches, there is no denying the direction in which the church is going, toward welcoming both women and men to Christ's ministry, as people called by God and empowered by the Spirit.

Our next task is to consider carefully the main aspects of the church's life and ministry, namely, first worship and liturgy, and second, the celebration of the sacraments of water baptism and the Eucharist/Lord's Supper.

Missional Existence as Worship and the Liturgy

Worship and Prayer at the Heart of the Church's Missional Existence[16]

The missional communion gathered around the gospel and sacraments constantly feeds, renews, and reinvigorates the church's spiritual life and missional fervor in regular prayer, reading of Scripture, and sacramental and liturgical participation. Vibrant, dynamic, and God-centered worship and liturgy also serve as the fountain of the ministry and mission of the sent community. Importantly, John Paul II's encyclical *Redemptoris Missio* (1990) reminds us that the same Spirit of God who is sending out the church to serve and minister to the world is also the energy behind "Missionary Spirituality,"[17] cultivated and sustained in regular prayer, reading of Scripture, and sacramental-liturgical participation. Similarly, the recent missionary document *Together Towards Life* highlights spirituality as the energy of mission: "Authentic Christian witness is not only in *what* we do in mission but *how* we live out our mission. The church in mission can only be sustained by spiritualities deeply rooted in the Trinity's communion of love."[18]

Nowhere else is this deep and wide connection between liturgy, sacramental life, and missionary orientation as evident as in the life of the first church described in the Acts of the Apostles (2:41–47), according to which that church's liturgical-sacramental life, filled with prayer and Bible study, helped launch this world-transforming mission with proclamation, healings, and deliverance to the ends of the earth:

> So those who received his word were baptized, and there were added that day about three thousand souls. And they devoted themselves to the apostles' teaching and fellowship, to the breaking of bread and the prayers. And fear came upon every soul; and many wonders and signs were done through the apostles. And all who believed were together and had all things in common; and they sold their possessions and goods and distributed them to all, as any had need. And day by day, attending the temple together and breaking bread in their homes, they partook of food with glad and generous hearts, praising God

---

16. This and the following subsection borrow directly from Kärkkäinen, *Introduction to Ecclesiology*, chap. 15.
17. Heading for chapter 8.
18. WCC, *Together Towards Life*, para. 29.

and having favor with all the people. And the Lord added to their number day by day those who were being saved.

Worship Here on Earth—and in Heaven

Formally defined, *worship* simply means "reverence offered a divine being or supernatural power."[19] In that sense, it is true that "worship is a universal human instinct, and people of other religions worship even though they are not Christians"—as evinced by all kinds of sacred rites, rituals, and ways of approaching the divine, as discussed above. That said, "there is something distinctive about Christian worship that arises out of a particular story—the story of God's saving work in Jesus Christ."[20] It is routinely and helpfully noted that the root of the English term *worship*, that is, "worth-ship," is a key to its meaning: to ascribe worth to the deity. The idea has a solid biblical background:

> Ascribe to the Lord, O heavenly beings,
>   ascribe to the Lord glory and strength.
> Ascribe to the Lord the glory of his name;
>   worship the Lord in holy array. (Ps 29:1–2)

Another way of putting this is to speak of glorifying or giving glory to God. Hence, "Amen! Blessing and glory and wisdom and thanksgiving and honor and power and might be to our God for ever and ever! Amen" (Rev 7:12).

In centuries gone by, worship was understood as "the enjoyment of God" revealed in the Scripture and manifested to us in the person of Jesus Christ in the power of the Spirit. Not for nothing does the beginning of the *Westminster Larger Catechism* (1647) tell Christians: "Man's chief and highest end is to glorify God, and fully to enjoy him forever."[21]

While it takes place here and now, worship also always references the future of God's consummating work. This link between the eschatological, the "heavenly," and earthly worship communions is beautifully depicted by the author of the book of Revelation to whom was shown "in heaven an open door" (Rev 4:1) to enter the 24/7 chain of worship and liturgy "round the throne" of the Lamb and elders (4:6). Revelation 5 draws from several prophetic sections of the OT (Ezek 1; Isa 6) with its vision of the

---

19. Merriam-Webster, "Worship," n.p.
20. O'Brien, *Christian Worship*, 15.
21. Orthodox Presbyterian Church, *Larger Catechism*, answer to question para. 1.

"scroll" (obviously signifying some kind of divine narrative of history) opened by the Lamb, who is worthy of glory and honor. The same heavenly direction is present in the worship vision in Hebrews 12. It describes worshipers of God who

> have come to Mount Zion and to the city of the living God, the heavenly Jerusalem, and to innumerable angels in festal gathering, and to the assembly of the first-born who are enrolled in heaven, and to a judge who is God of all, and to the spirits of just men made perfect, and to Jesus, the mediator of a new covenant, and to the sprinkled blood that speaks more graciously than the blood of Abel. (Heb 12:22–24)

Some Guiding Principles for Worship

Over the centuries, the church has developed a number of helpful guidelines to direct the church's liturgical life. Christian worship is:

- biblically based, including reading and meditating on Scripture;
- ideally a dialogical event in which, through the Word and Spirit, we speak to God and expect God to be speaking to us. An important way of talking to God is prayer;
- covenantal, in that in each gathering of the community Christians are reminded of and even receive a confirmation of God's gracious covenant on our behalf. In that respect, each worship event is an occasion for recommitment to God;
- trinitarian in nature and form;
- communal, the experience of the "communion of the saints";
- hospitable, welcoming all kinds of people regardless of race, gender, ethnicity, socioeconomic status, physical and mental ability, and other human barriers;
- in but not of the world, reflecting a particular location, culture, and setting, at the same time also challenging and enriching the particular location;
- a generous and excellent outpouring of ourselves before God. Worship should not be stingy;
- ideally, Christian worship is both expressive and formative. While authentically expressing the experiences, emotions, and ideas of the people—similar to what is described in the Psalms,

for example—worship should also shape, challenge, and stretch Christians and the community.[22]

An essential part of worship liturgy and worship is sacramental celebration, to which we turn next, first water baptism and then the Lord's Supper.

Missional Existence as Sacramental Celebration: Baptism and Eucharist/Lord's Supper

What Exactly Are the Sacraments—and the "Ordinances"?

While in Orthodox theology beginning from the seventeenth century the number of sacraments (often named "mysteries") is usually seven, throughout history there has been no defined or set number. The Roman Catholic Church acknowledges seven sacraments: baptism, confirmation, Eucharist, penance, anointing the sick, ordination, and matrimony. For Protestants, the number is two: baptism and Eucharist (although the Lutheran confessions also speak of "confession" as the third). Furthermore, although sacraments carry a fixed meaning (notwithstanding their number), in principle we could list a number of other acts that, if not sacraments, certainly have a strong sacramental sense to them, such as healings, acts of mercy, and the proclamation of the word.

With the exception of the (original) Quakers, even Free Churches, following Protestantism, practice sacraments; some Pentecostals and members of other churches also practice foot washing.[23] Instead of "sacrament," these communities often speak of "ordinances." Reacting vehemently against gross misuses of sacraments in the Catholic Church, Radical Reformers and their Baptist forebears chose to speak of "ordinances": baptism and the Lord's Supper were to be celebrated because they had been "ordained" by the Lord in the Bible. Rather than divine acts bringing about what they symbolized, for such communities ordinances were primarily a means of human response to God's command.

Notwithstanding differences in the scope of and meaning they attribute to the sacraments, all (Western) Christian traditions build on Augustine's teaching on the sacraments as "signs." He makes the needed thematic distinction between the "sign" and the thing signified. While not equated, they are closely and intimately related. This distinction has to be affirmed in a way

---

22. Steenwyk and Witvliet, *Worship Sourcebook*, 16–17.
23. Hunter, "Ordinances," 948–49.

that allows for the thing signified to be present already in a true anticipatory manner in the sign. (If this sounds complicated, it's because it is!)

Neither for Augustine, nor for the mainline Christian tradition, there was no downplaying the importance of faith and the Word of God. Speaking of baptism, Augustine said succinctly: "Take away the word, and the water is neither more nor less than water. The word is added to the element, and there results the Sacrament, as if itself also a kind of visible word."[24] Hence, it is not the ritual itself, it is a receiving and believing embrace that counts. With this tight linking of the sacrament with the Word of promise, we can say that "Christ's own presence at the Supper fulfills the promise contained in the words of institution."[25] With the Word and promise in mind—but only by so doing—what Saint Thomas defined as the core of the sacraments can be justly maintained, namely, that "they effect what they signify."[26]

So much can be—and should be—said even if the Protestant tradition at large eschews the (semi)automatic and technical *ex opere operato* formula. This Latin expression literally means "from the work done," meaning that the act of doing the sacrament, regardless of the disposition of the doer (the minister) or the object (the recipient) will convey its benefits. In Protestants's view, this interpretation led to gross misuse and lack of concern for proper disposition of the sacraments.

Baptism and Christian Initiation

Baptism as Sacrament and as "Ordinance"

Water baptism has been part of Christian initiation from the beginning. Orthodox, Catholic, Anglican, and Lutheran traditions uniformly understand baptism sacramentally; that is, linked with faith and the Word of God, it brings about what it promises: new birth.

In the Reformed family, there are well-known internal differences. For those who adhere to Zwinglian covenant theology, baptism indicates belonging to the people of God (somewhat similarly to the OT rite of circumcision). The Calvinist majority oscillates between Lutheran and Zwinglian understandings; while it does not consider the rite regenerative in the sense that the sacramental traditions do, it does consider it a "seal" of the covenant with God. As such, the sacrament is performed in anticipation of forthcoming faith.

24. Augustine, *Tractates on John*, 80.3, in *NPNF*[1] 07.
25. Pannenberg, *Systematic Theology*, 3:352.
26. Aquinas, *Summa Theologica*, 3.62.1.

Baptists, Anabaptists, and most all other Free Churches understand water baptism as an "ordinance," in other words, as an act ordained by Christ. Rather than a sacrament, it is a public response of a believer. Rather than infant baptism as in Catholic, Orthodox, Anglican, and Lutheran churches, Free Churches practice believers' ("adult") baptism by immersion.[27]

The Many Ways in Which the New Testament Speaks of the Efficacy of Water Baptism

Although baptism is not without pagan and Jewish antecedents, the NT establishes a distinctively Christian view of baptism with close links not only to the preparatory work of John the Baptist but also, and more importantly, to Jesus's own baptism (recorded in all four Gospels).

The Acts of the Apostles provides the most comprehensive baptismal data and examples of the first Christian baptisms (chaps. 2, 8, 9, 10, 16, 18, 19, 22). That initiation included hearing the gospel, repentance, faith, forgiveness of sin, and the reception of the Holy Spirit (at times with charismatic manifestations). Baptism follows immediately on conversion. All the baptized were at the age of responsibility. No information is given as to what kind of person performed baptism. Immersion was the normal baptismal mode. Baptism was done in the name of Jesus (although the church soon adopted the Trinitarian formula present in Matthew and elsewhere). Baptism is received from the community; one cannot baptize oneself. It is not repeated. Baptism is a gate to church membership.

In the Pauline and other NT epistles, the theology of baptism is depicted with the help of a number of images and metaphors:

- participation in the death and resurrection of Christ (Rom 6:3-5; Col 2:12);
- a washing away of sin (1 Cor 6:11); a new birth (John 3:5);
- an enlightenment by Christ (Eph 5:14);
- a re-clothing in Christ (Gal 3:27); and
- a renewal by the Spirit (Titus 3:5), and so forth.[28]

Baptism thus has both a human and a divine aspect; it is a gift of divine grace and an expression of human commitment.

---

27. Haitch, *From Exorcism to Ecstasy*, chap. 2.
28. WCC, *Baptism, Eucharist and Ministry*, Baptism Section 2.

When it comes to the spiritual effects of baptism, there are three types of orientations in the NT. Important passages link regeneration with baptism (John 3:5; 1 Pet 3:21; 1 Cor 12:13). Others seem to imply that what is decisive are repentance and faith, to be followed by baptism (Mark 16:16; Acts 2:38; 8:12, 13, 36; etc.). And finally, there are sayings in which repentance and faith without sacraments are linked with regeneration and new birth (Luke 24:47; Acts 4:4; 5:14; 11:21; etc.).

Two broad conclusions seem warranted from the NT data: First, in a number of passages baptism is depicted as effecting or "causing" salvation. That said, second, baptism happens in the context of hearing the gospel, of repentance, and of faith. That speaks to the importance of human response to God's doing. This dynamic divine-human aspect of baptism should be kept in mind when considering how to define the way a person becomes a Christian in relation to baptism.

The Rise of Infant Baptism: A Radical Change

Believers' baptism was the normal Christian way of baptizing, not only in the NT but for centuries thereafter. Even when infants', and at first older children's, baptism came alongside, it had to be justified against the original, normal mode, not vice versa, as older churches sometimes claim.

The (early) second-century church document containing a lot of pastoral-theological guidance, called the *Didache*, offers the first known description of baptismal practice:

- baptism was done in the triune name in "living" (or running) water (where available), and the candidates were expected to have fasted;
- before baptism, preparatory teaching was given; and
- eucharistic participation followed the baptism as well as instructions for ethics and Christian life.

Following earlier traditions, a three-year catechumenate for the sake of thorough instruction in faith before baptism became the norm. Anointing with oil and exorcism soon also became part of the rite.

With Augustine, things changed radically. While following the tradition prescribed above, having himself received water baptism as an adult after having personally confessed Christian faith, he introduced innovative teachings that emerged out of his painful encounters with the Donatists (mentioned earlier in this chapter) and Pelagians (discussed in chapter 4). He accused the former of rejecting Christian baptism and he consequently developed a thick theology of the sacrament in terms of its "indelible character"; he insisted that its efficacy is immune to the quality of the administrator or the recipient. Augustine also came to endorse infant baptism strongly, which of course fits this framework. The fight with the Pelagians further helped to consolidate the doctrine of original sin that required infant baptism.

On this basis, infant baptism began to rise. Undoubtedly, it is a new development in light of the NT and the earliest patristic theology. It emerged slowly and sporadically in various Christian locations, and its legitimacy had to be demonstrated and was sometimes rejected outright. This momentous shift began slowly from the end of the second century, and not earlier than the end of the fourth and beginning of the fifth, infant baptism had established itself as the main form of baptism. Ironically, instrumental in the slow rise of infant baptism were debates about baptism by heretics/schismatics and "clinical" or deathbed baptisms.

Notwithstanding the rise of infant baptism, believers' baptism as the dominant form of Christian baptism survived at least until the fourth century and continued as an alternative and legitimate form until at least the fifth (or even sixth) century.

Having now briefly recorded the winding history of the practice and theology of water baptism, let us focus on current theological-pastoral issues to do with this sacrament.

Faith and Baptism Belong Together. But How?

In keeping with the NT teaching in which faith normally precedes baptism and the act of baptism is a personal choice, all churches agree that baptism and faith belong together. Faith commitment should follow the baptized throughout life. Therefore, it is particularly important for parents and mentors of baptized infants to reminded them of the importance of personal commitment later in life, or else the goal and fruit of the sacrament may very well be lost.

That said, the relationship between baptism and human response is dynamic and mutual: the irreducible link with faith should be connected with the equally important link in the NT between baptism as "both God's gift and our human response to that gift."[29] In contrast to *wrongly* conceived and extreme ideas of the sacrament as a semi-mechanical *ex opere operato* or as a merely human act, the divine-human/human-divine nature of baptism helps steer a radical middle road. Ultimately, neither baptism nor faith "have their

29. WCC, *Baptism, Eucharist and Ministry*, Baptism Section 9, 8, respectively.

bases in themselves, but alike in the saving act of God in Christ." In short: "baptism comes from faith, and faith leads to baptism."[30]

The emphasis on the close link between personal faith and baptism brings to light the problems and liabilities of infant baptism. No wonder that the basic ecumenical argument is that believers' baptism should be adopted as the theological norm and standard when assessing various baptismal practices. The term "believers' baptism" refers not to the age of the candidate (although it is related to it) but rather to the baptismal act in which a candidate with personal faith requests to be baptized in accordance with the NT and early Christianity. But adopting believers' baptism as the theological standard does not have to lead to discrediting infant baptism. Rather, it helps those churches that continue this practice to evaluate such a practice's theological value in an ongoing way and one hopes to reconsider the adoption of both believers' and infant baptism models as legitimate. Rather than continuing the often frustrating and typically unfruitful dispute about infant versus believers' baptism, theologically trained persons would do well to embrace the scholarly consensus and begin to work toward a common understanding.

The adoption of believers' baptism as the theological norm raises the question of how to negotiate the presence of faith in the context of infant baptism. In support of infant baptism in the obvious absence of faith, ingenious tactics have been devised, but none of them is theologically—or *logically*—convincing. Both Augustine's justification of the vicarious faith of the infant (that is, parents or other believing adults believe for the child) in which, similarly to original sin, which comes from outside the child (from parents), the family members and the church bring faith on behalf of the yet-to-mature infant, and Luther's idea of "infant faith," are not only without biblical support but are also artificial and unconvincing.

Indeed, the general effort to find a "substitute" faith for that of the infant being baptized is not convincing. The reasons are many, not the least of which is the aforementioned lack of biblical support. Faith in the NT, as much as it is a divine gift communicated through the Holy Spirit, is also normally viewed as a personal choice that leads to commitment. In the NT, no one is baptized without the person's request or consent. This is not to deny the importance of the Christian family or of the church in cultivating the child's spiritual life. Nor is there any reason to expect an infant to display cognitive and volitional features of faith like those of a mature person. Yet those concessions have very little to do with baptismal practice. In contemporary culture, a further question arises as to whether

---

30. Küng, *Church*, 207.

baptizing infants may at least implicitly fail to honor each human person's integrity and inviolability.

Other typical arguments set forth in support of infant baptism are likewise unconvincing, including an appeal to the unconditionality of God's mercy. Were such unconditionality really the theological basis for infant baptism, it would necessarily lead to the conclusion that *all* infants, whether those of Christians or of non-Christians, should be baptized indiscriminately, which is a practice all churches condemn. Indeed, nowhere in the NT is the connection between unconditional grace and baptism established; rather, where the unconditionality of God's mercy comes to the fore is in Jesus's blessing of children—but that is unrelated to baptism (notwithstanding the text's uncritical use in its support).

Nor is the reference to Israelite circumcision finding its Christian counterpart in baptism successful. The origins of baptism in the NT point in completely different directions, including that John's baptism has no relation to circumcision but rather is linked with repentance—for the circumcised people! Not to mention that circumcision is part of Jewish religion, which is based on birthright, whereas Christian baptism is a public commitment of both Jews and gentiles willing to commit their lives for Christ and the church.

Finally, Augustine's appeal to infant faith because of the alleged "deadly" original sin falls short of having a sound theological basis. First of all, the church does not universally endorse the Augustinian doctrine of original sin, and even if it were to endorse it, nowhere in the NT is the sinfulness of humanity linked with baptism. As Pannenberg, a Lutheran theologian, categorically puts it: "The idea of the exclusion of unbaptized children from eternal salvation on the basis of the doctrine of original sin is not in keeping with the total witness of the NT."[31] If original sin were the reason for baptizing infants, surely the early church would have adopted that practice at the outset.

Suggestions for a Renewed Baptismal Theology and Practice for All Churches

All churches should make concentrated efforts to recognize the baptismal practices of other churches. Sacramental churches ought to give up the misguided insistence on infant baptism as the "default position," a position unfortunately too often coupled with harsh rejection of believers' baptism.

---

31. Pannenberg, *Systematic Theology*, 3:264.

That would help churches consider both infant and believers' baptism as parallel and legitimate practices.

Herein lies also a practical challenge—and an asset—to both baptismal traditions: whereas believer baptizers should seek to highlight more robustly that before baptism all children are already in the care and grace of God, infant baptizers should make every effort to stay away from indiscriminate baptisms and continuously encourage parents and guardians to work toward helping the growing young person to find personal faith. In this regard, we can learn much from the experiences of churches practicing both forms of baptism. The long-term ecumenical goal should be, on the one hand, a full mutual acknowledgment of both forms of baptism and, on the other hand, a gradual transition toward believers' baptism as the normal form of the beginning of Christian initiation.

The timing of baptism should be left to the parents. Consequently, those churches whose by-laws require the bringing of infants for baptism (such as the Lutheran church) should change this rule. It is somewhat ironic that in many secularized contexts of the Global North, particularly in Europe, an increasing number of parents already no longer baptize their children (even without any theological reason for or against).

All churches should consider again the original mode of baptism by immersion, as that "can vividly express the reality that in baptism the Christian participates in the death, burial and resurrection of Christ."[32] That practice is of course used widely in Eastern Christianity and is the norm for most churches practicing believers' baptism.

In the absence of and in place of infant baptism, a rite of blessing for infants and young children, ideally in the worship service setting, could be adopted as a standard practice, as is already the case for most believers' baptism communities. That would match the NT example of Jesus's blessing of children. Naming—"christening"—of the child could be related to the event, if so desired, but it is not necessary. If naming is done, then through teaching and preaching it should be made clear to the community witnessing the baptism that the act is much more than a mere cultural event.

Finally, what about confirmation, an important rite linked to baptism (whether viewed as a sacrament, as in Catholic and Orthodox churches, or merely as a "sacramental" act, as in Protestantism)? Ironically, there is hardly any NT evidence for what confirmation means today. Unless one keeps baptism and confirmation together, as the Eastern Church has always done, the delegating of the reception of the Spirit to a future rite is not justifiable. This is not to deny the important practical and pastoral function confirmation

---

32. WCC, *Baptism, Eucharist and Ministry*, Baptism Section 18.

has served over the centuries among Western churches, as it has provided an occasion for both catechesis for the baptized and public confession of faith. The focus here is its theological basis—which I suggest is questionable. Instead of confirmation classes, churches should make a focused effort to offer their youth Christian teaching, and the content of that teaching can glean much from hundreds of years of confirmation classes.

Eucharist/The Lord's Supper

Why Do We Celebrate the Eucharist?

A variety of meals described in the OT mark important events and acts of God in the life of the people of God. Jesus followed the same custom with the celebration of the last meal with his disciples, the event which also became the occasion for the institution of this sacred act for his followers throughout the ages that have followed. The early church continued the rite, and in the beginning practiced it as a daily ritual (Acts 2:42-46).

The term "eucharist" comes from the Greek word meaning thanksgiving: indeed, it is an occasion to give thanks to the Triune God for everything that God has done for our salvation. It is a memorial meal in which we remember the passion and resurrection, as the resurrected Christ himself instituted (1 Cor 11:23-25). As Jesus linked the celebration of the last meal to the coming of the kingdom (Matt 26:29), it points to the return of Christ (1 Cor 11:26). Thus, the Lord's Supper—the favorite term among most low church traditions—it is a profound event in which the church proclaims the death, resurrection, and return of Christ, the Lord of the Church (1 Cor 11:26).

Similar to water baptism, which issues a claim on the whole life of the baptized person, the Eucharist also binds the celebrant to the values of the Lord of the Supper, particularly reconciliation with God and others. "All kinds of injustice, racism, separation and lack of freedom are radically challenged when we share in the body and blood of Christ."[33]

Christ Is Present at the Celebration of the Sacred Meal

All churches agree that Christ is present in the celebration of the Eucharist on the basis of the NT teaching according to which he said "this is my body" and "my blood." What is debated is the mode of that presence.

---

33. WCC, *Baptism, Eucharist and Ministry*, Baptism Section 20.

Whereas Orthodox theology has refused to define in any conceptual way the nature of the presence, the Roman Catholic tradition has formulated it in terms of "transubstantiation," that is, the elements become Christ's body and blood by virtue of the words of institution. The Lutheran version is "consubstantiation" (Christ "under," "in," and "above" the elements), the idea that Christ is truly present but without the elements changing their essence. Among the Reformed churches, the Zwinglian version focuses on commemoration of Christ's work, whereas the Calvinist view oscillates between the Lutheran and Zwinglian understandings, affirming commemoration but insisting on Christ's presence through the Holy Spirit.

What is the point of holding onto these somewhat abstract and highly analytically defined nuances of interpretation? In my understanding, these are legitimate differences of opinion; what is of utmost importance is that the "real" and true presence of Christ is affirmed in one way or another in the celebration commemorating his saving work for us.

Let me try to explain the presence with the help of the ancient sacramental terminology. If this makes sense to you, good; if not, do not be concerned! In the celebration of the sacred meal we see the intimate relationship between the "sign" (bread and wine) and the "thing" (Christ's presence). In some real sense the sign *is* the thing—unlike typically when the sign indicates the clear distinction between it and the thing (as in a signpost that points to the destination away from it). At the Eucharist, "sign and thing are together, as when the sign indicates the presence of the thing signified."[34] My recommendation is that in order to avoid abstract speculation—and at times, the unnecessary confusion in the minds of the Christians—we do not go beyond this clear statement.

Similarly, I recommend that (in)famous disputes in the Protestant camp between the Reformed and Lutheran interpretations should not be allowed to become divisive. Whereas Lutheran theology insists robustly on Christ's real presence in the elements, the Reformed tradition instead speaks of a real *spiritual* presence through the Holy Spirit.[35] This should suffice.

What about the Pauline Warning about an "Unworthy Manner" of Celebration?

> Whoever, therefore, eats the bread or drinks the cup of the Lord in an unworthy manner will be guilty of profaning the body and blood of the Lord. (1 Cor 11:27)

---

34. Pannenberg, *Systematic Theology*, 3:299.
35. See Calvin, *Institutes*, 4.17.31.

Throughout history, this Pauline "unworthiness" ban on partaking of the Lord's Supper (1 Cor 11:27) has been conceived in terms of moral lapses and lack of holiness. Christians with weak, at times sick, consciences have stepped forward to the communion table with great trepidation—particularly in light of Paul's stern warning about possible catastrophic results (vv. 29–30): "For any one who eats and drinks without discerning the body eats and drinks judgment upon himself. That is why many of you are weak and ill, and some have died." What is going on here?

The wider context of 1 Corinthians helps us to locate the focus of Paul's concern: it has to do with the serious splits and divisions in the local community, related to leadership and attitudinal issues, as well as to the sharp gulf between the haves and have-nots. These divisions ruptured the unity at the table, the most profound symbol of the unity of the body. In short, the lack of care for others, the lack of care for unity, resulted in some finishing the meal before the others had even arrived (vv. 33–34); recall that, at the time, the Lord's Supper was a real meal, in a sense echoing the many sacred meals in the OT.

With this background in mind, we can establish what is the point of the Pauline warning. Although there is no reason to deny the importance of being attentive to one's moral and spiritual condition when approaching the Lord's Table, the need to "discern the body" (v. 29) had to do primarily with church unity. The celebrants are warned sternly not to split or divide the one church body. Hence, the advice about self-examination—"Let a man examine himself, and so eat of the bread and drink of the cup" (v. 28)—is less about scrutiny of one's own conscience as an individual person and more about paying attention to one's behavior and attitudes with regard to unity. Be that as it may, self-examination should in any case not result in the refusal to participate, but, on the contrary, precisely to joining the rest of the members of the church in eating and drinking!

That interpretation also urges us to continue pursuing the unity of the body of Christ. Each celebration of his meal is a powerful reminder to that effect. This reminder also builds the bridge to our next section, which focuses on the search for church unity, or ecumenical work.

Why Should We Be Concerned about the Unity of the Church?[36]

Striving for the Unity of the Church Is a Biblical Mandate

The simple response to the question of why we should be concerned about the unity of the church is that it is a clear and unambiguous biblical mandate and command. While its forms and strategies may vary, the basic task is not up for debate. "In brief, the New Testament does not speak of the church without, at the same time, speaking of its unity."[37]

Why speak of "ecumenism" rather than simply "unity"? While both terms are fine, the term *ecumenism* has established itself as the standard term and it has a long history. Ecumenism simply means the work and search for the unity of Christian churches. The term derives from the Greek word *oikoumene* (Luke 2:1; Acts 11:28), which means the whole inhabited world. Closely related to this word is the use of the term "ecumenical" with reference to ancient "ecumenical councils" such as that of Nicea (325) and the "ecumenical" patriarchate (of Constantinople).

The importance and urgency of the unity of the church is expressed most profoundly in the prayer of our Lord Jesus in John 17:20–21. He prayed for the unity of his followers based on the unity between the Father and Son, "so that the world may believe." This prayer tells us that the source of the unity of Christians is based on the unity of the Father, Son, and Spirit. The same prayer also highlights the integral relation between mission and ecumenism: the unity of the church, while essential in itself, is also needed for the sake of helping the world believe in Jesus.

Another key NT text is Ephesians 4:3–6, which urges Christians "to maintain the unity of the Spirit in the bond of peace" because

> There is one body and one Spirit, just as you were called to the one hope that belongs to your call, one Lord, one faith, one baptism, one God and Father of us all, who is above all and through all and in all.

This NT idea goes back to the vision of the oneness of the people of God in the OT based on the oneness of God (Deut 6:4). The importance of unity also comes to the fore in the term *koinonia*, discussed earlier in this chapter. Recall that it means sharing on spiritual, sacramental, social, emotional, and economic levels.

---

36. This section with only minor modifications borrows from Kärkkäinen, *Introduction to Ecclesiology*, chap. 17 (particularly from 223–27).

37. Meyer, *That All May Be One*, 8.

Notwithstanding differences among Christian communities regarding how best to work toward unity and what its implications for church life and self-understanding are, all Christian traditions agree that ultimately unity is based on the unity of the triune God, a deeply biblical conviction.

The Many Faces and Facets of Ecumenical Work

Striving for the unity of Christ's church in the world takes many diverse forms. Undoubtedly, the most important is the continuing prayer for unity, following Jesus's own example mentioned above. It is significant that in many churches' weekly liturgy and worship order this prayer is recited.

Without downplaying the importance of many formal processes and organizations (to be discussed below), perhaps the most far-reaching way of furthering unity, besides prayer, happens at the grassroots level in the encounters and exchanges between Christians of various churches. Getting to know a believer from another tradition, learning about his or her way of living out the Christian way, and having an opportunity to share about one's own helps build bridges and tear down dividing walls. Wise and insightful preaching and teaching in the church may greatly assist in all of this; by contrast, opinionated and disrespectful messages may do irrevocable damage between and among church members. Opportunities to participate in common witness, for example in city-wide evangelistic campaigns or in common service in terms of helping the poor and the needy in cooperation with other churches, is yet another effective grassroots way of doing ecumenism.

There are also other informal ecumenical contacts between leaders as well as laypeople at various levels that contribute significantly to unity. In other words, the term "ecumenical" has to be understood most inclusively and should in no way be limited to what might be called "official" or "formal" ecumenism.

What, Then, Is the Ecumenical Movement and What Does It Do?

Alongside the aforementioned types of foundational and groundbreaking informal work toward building unity in the Christian Church, a growing number of processes, organizations, and programs are happening at the more formal and organized level. There is broad agreement that beginning at the turn of the twentieth century, the rise of the ecumenical movement might be the most far-reaching development in the global church of Christ.

A number of initiatives and developments, including important ecclesiastical unions and agreements in Europe, North America, India, and elsewhere, prepared and facilitated the emergence of the ecumenical movement. The establishment of the World Council of Churches (WCC) in 1948 is undoubtedly the most visible sign of this process.

Very significant work is done in numerous bilateral (between two parties) and multilateral (among many parties) ecumenical dialogues. These continuing and often long-term processes help build trust, gather information about various churches' faith, eliminate prejudices, and provide insights for future convergence. As mentioned in chapter 8, the groundbreaking convergence in the doctrine of justification by faith between Roman Catholics and a number of Protestant church families is a fruit of such work.

Important work has also been done in various national ecumenical organizations, such as The National Council of Churches, USA, whose roots go back all the way to the Federal Council of the Churches of Christ in America, founded in 1898. National councils of churches work in close collaboration with the Faith and Order Council (1927), integrated into the WCC at its founding. Testifying to the close link between mission and ecumenism, a significant early twentieth-century push toward concerted efforts for unity came from the Edinburgh Missionary Conference, whose centennial was celebrated in Edinburgh in 2010.

But what is the WCC? And what is its task? It is important to know that WCC in itself is not a church but rather a "fellowship of churches," currently about 350 churches from all continents. While the biggest church, the Roman Catholic Church, does not belong to it, nor do most Free Churches and Independents, there is a lot of close cooperation across the organizational boundaries.

The WCC is simply "a fellowship of churches which confess the Lord Jesus Christ as God and Saviour according to the Scriptures, and therefore seek to fulfill together their common calling to the glory of the one God, Father, Son and Holy Spirit."[38] Its purpose is not to build a global "super-church," nor to standardize styles of worship, but rather to deepen the fellowship of Christian churches and communities so they may see in one another authentic expressions of the "one holy, catholic and apostolic church." This becomes the basis for joining in a common confession of the apostolic faith, cooperating in mission and human service endeavors and, where possible, sharing in the sacraments. All these acts of fellowship bear testimony to the foundational declaration of the WCC that the Lord Jesus Christ is "God and Saviour according to the Scriptures."

---

38. WCC, "What Is the World Council," n.p.

What Is the Ultimate Goal of Ecumenical Work?

What is the ultimate goal of the ecumenical movement, both informal and formal? It is "visible unity." What does that mean? The elimination of church traditions' boundaries, one big "world church," or something similar? No, not at all—despite the continued misunderstandings among churches and church leaders who repeat these already frequently debunked opinions. On the contrary—and here we come to the complexity and promise of the concept of the visible unity: On the one hand, "visible unity" as the ultimate goal is affirmed by almost all churches, except for a number of the most conservative and many Free Churches. On the other hand, no one knows what exactly "visible unity" means—although all churches agree that it is not the elimination of traditional boundaries, even less the building of one world church.

This much can be said safely of visible unity: while it of course includes "spiritual unity," meaning the shared consciousness among the Christians in various churches belonging to the invisible church on earth, the Body of Christ, that unity has to be manifested also in a visible and tangible manner. The lack of consensus about the meaning of "visible unity" results in the nature of unity being a continuing agenda and topic of discussions in the ecumenical conversations and work. At the same time, search for such unity should also find ways of affirming constructive and fruitful diversity. As the important ecumenical document *The Nature and Mission of the Church* puts it succinctly, "Authentic diversity in the life of communion must not be stifled: authentic unity must not be surrendered."[39]

Moreover, one development and process going on in the global church has everything to do with how unity may be realized: the constant and rapid emergence of new congregational models such as the Emerging/Emergent church and the rapid globalization of the church. The goal of seeking unity in the midst of these disparate, diverse, and organizationally disconnected movements of the globalizing church is a daunting challenge! All Christians, lay folks and leaders, have a role to play in this huge project. After all, ultimately the oneness of the church—similarly to her holiness, apostolicity, and catholicity—is God's gift and as such is a task for us!

From the work of reconciling differences among Christian Churches while pursuing the common shared hope, there is a natural transition to the last big topic of the chapter, namely the Christian Churches' role among other living faiths. While we have pursued the topic of interfaith comparison with regard to each and every doctrine (a task to be completed in the next

---

39. WCC, *Nature and Mission*, 2.C.62.

chapter on eschatology), here we focus on the conceptions of religious community, their life, and particularly their relation to the Christian Church. This includes also a brief look at the relation of the church to those who do not confess any particular faith, the seculars.

Christian Church in the Midst of Other Religious Communities —and the Seculars

Why Should We Be Concerned about Other Religious Communities?

The Theological Mandate of Engaging Other Faith Traditions

There are certainly many "practical" reasons for the church to engage the religious other, from establishing a pedagogical contact and preparing to witness to Christ in the matrix of religious convictions, to helping Christians live in a civil way with the other, and so alleviate conflicts. These reasons alone would suffice; on top of those, there are also weighty theological reasons, that is, reasons related to the way systematic theology is to be conducted.

Alongside the Great Commission (Matt 28:18–20) and the Great Commandment (22:37–39), Christian creation theology mandates us to reach out to all human brothers and sisters, seeking amenable relations, learning about their faith, and share our testimony about Christ. All men and women are destined for the same goal by the same God. This is put well in Vatican II's statement on other religions (*Nostra Aetate*, para. 1): "One is the community of all peoples, one their origin, for God made the whole human race to live over the face of the earth. One also is their final goal, God."

The mandate for relating hospitably to the other is grounded in these theological convictions. It seeks to cultivate inclusivism by welcoming testimonies, insights, and interpretations from different traditions and contexts, and so foster mutual dialogue. A hospitable posture honors the otherness of others as human beings created by the same God and reconciled by the same Lord as oneself. Hospitality also makes space for an honest, genuine, authentic sharing of one's convictions.

This hospitable, dialogue-seeking posture does not mean religious pluralism according to which all faiths lead to the same destiny and none of them has access to the ultimate truth (as discussed in chapter 2). The remedy to pluralisms, however, is not exclusivism—the idea that only church members with confession of faith in Christ and nobody else will be saved—but rather an attitude that takes delight in the potential of an encounter with the other without denying either party's distinctive features. That kind of engagement does not water down real differences in the way modernism typically does. Too easily, pluralisms tend to deny the self-definitions of particular religions.

But why does so much plurality and diversity exist among religions? Wouldn't it be easier if God had allowed only one religion? This is a difficult question. What helps me answer it is to acknowledge that "[f]or a religious person, to *accept* disagreement is to see it as within the providence of God"—even disagreement due to diversity of religious beliefs and convictions (emphasis original). Religions are not here without God's permission and allowance. That said, the continuing challenge for Christians and other monotheists is how to reconcile the existence of one's own deeply felt beliefs with different, often opposite, kinds of convictions.[40] There are no easy answers to this!

What Do the Trinity and Interfaith Engagement Have to Do with Each Other?

By now you have already become used to the statement that the Trinity is the distinctive Christian key to all topics in Christian life and theology. Yes, that is true, and it also applies to interfaith engagement. The foundational reason why this is so is that in the triune God there is both unity and plurality, communion and diversity. The Trinity as communion allows room for both genuine diversity (otherwise we could not talk about the Trinity) and unity (otherwise we could not talk about one God).

Borrowing from the biblical scholar Walter Brueggemann, we can make the term "other" a verb to remind us of the importance of seeing the religious other not as a counter-object but rather as a partner in "othering," which is "the risky, demanding, dynamic process of relating to one who is not us."[41] What matters is the capacity to listen to the distinctive testimony of the other, to wait patiently upon the other, and to make a safe space for him or her.

Calling it "The Holy Spirit's Invitation to Relational Engagement,"[42] the British Catholic Gavin D'Costa urges us to appreciate other religions as important for the Christian Church in that they help the church penetrate more deeply into the divine mystery and so also enrich its own spirituality and insight. While testifying to salvation in Christ, Trinitarian openness

---

40. Ward, *Religion and Community*, 25.
41. Brueggemann, *Covenanted Self*, 1.
42. Section title in D'Costa, *Meeting of Religions*, 109.

toward other religions fosters the acknowledgment of the gifts of God in them by virtue of the presence of the Spirit—as well as the critical discernment of these gifts by the power of the same Spirit.[43]

A true dialogue does not mean giving up one's truth claims but rather entails patient and painstaking investigation of real differences and similarities. The purpose of the dialogue is not necessarily to soften the differences among and between religions but rather to clarify similarities and differences as well as issues of potential convergence and impasse. The contemporary secular mindset often mistakenly confuses tolerance with lack of commitment to any belief or opinion. That is to misunderstand the meaning of the term "tolerance." Deriving from the Latin term meaning "to bear a burden," tolerance is needed when real differences are allowed.

Afraid of the power play, the secular mindset seeks to block the way to an authentic witness and proclamation and embraces only "neutral" dialogue. For a missionary faith, however, mission and dialogue, proclamation and interfaith engagement belong together and are not alternatives. Not only that, they also include common service, healing, and reconciliation.

Having now presented the theological mandate and clarified Christian theological guidelines for interfaith engagement, the next section considers the meaning and life of Jewish, Muslim, Hindu, and Buddhist religious communities and their relationship to the Christian Church. But before that, a short note on whether it makes sense to compare the "ecclesiologies" of diverse religions.

No Solitary Religions!

Although it would make only little sense use the distinctively Christian term of "ecclesiology," the doctrine of the church, in pan-religious terms, "it is part of the belief-structure of most religions that there should be a particular society which protects and sustains their basic values and beliefs, within which one may pursue the ideal human goal, as defined within the society."[44] That said, there are important differences: First, whereas the Abrahamic traditions are integrally communal, neither of the Asiatic faiths engaged here is; by the same token, the Asiatic faiths' visions of "salvation" focus neither on the whole of humanity nor on the reconciliation of the cosmos, as in Jewish-Christian traditions, but rather on personal "release." Second, whereas for Abrahamic traditions the religious community is rooted in God and divine election, in Asiatic faiths that is not the case. Third, whereas

43. D'Costa, *Meeting of Religions*, 115.
44. Ward, *Religion and Community*, 1.

the Asiatic faiths seek to renounce the world in pursuit of final release, the Christian faith seeks both to renounce "the world" and to penetrate it with the Gospel for the sake of God's kingdom.

Now, with each of the four religious traditions, in what follows I attempt three descriptions: first, to describe the nature of the religious community; second, to describe its liturgical and ritual life; and third, to describe its relation to other religious communities. Following these descriptions, the interfaith question will occupy the second part of the discussion for each one.

Jewish Synagogue and Christian Church

How Is One to Reconcile Separatism and Universalism?

Like her Abrahamic sister faiths, Judaism is communally oriented and community centered. But it is the only Abrahamic religion that originally was purely tribal and still continues to be ethnic. While beliefs, particularly uncompromising monotheism (Deut 6:4), came to be part of Jewishness early on, the basis of Jewish identity "is not a creed but a history: a strong sense of a common origin, a shared past and a shared destiny."[45] Indeed, one's Jewishness is not obliterated by the lack of faith or even a pronounced atheism—an unthinkable situation for a Muslim or Christian. One either is a Jew, by birth (of a Jewish mother), or one is not.

So far I have used the term "Jewish" in the established contemporary sense. However, totally differently from sister Abrahamic faiths (and Buddhism), the emergence and birth of the religion of Judaism are unique in that it happened in two distinct phases and over a millennium. "Israelite" community has Moses's legacy as the defining origin, as recounted in the Tanakh (the OT in Christian terminology). "Judaism" emerged beginning with the renewals led by Ezra following the Babylonian exile in the sixth century; its defining identity is shaped by the rabbinic tradition's Talmud. The emergence of the synagogue as the religious community in that phase is an important event. In what follows, however, I use "Israel" and "Judaism" interchangeably.

As discussed, Israel's distinctive identity is based on Yahweh's election of her as a "chosen people," based on covenant and its call for total devotion to Yahweh. Basically, separatism follows from this status, and at the same time from a claim for a specific territory, the Holy Land. Due to separatism, intermarriage has not been encouraged (as common as that

---

45. de Lange, *Introduction to Judaism*, 26.

has been in various eras), nor are conversions sought, although proselytism is possible under certain conditions.

Separatism and ethnic orientation, however, are only one part of Jewish identity. A strong trend in the OT is a missionary calling to bring other nations of the world to know the name of Yahweh and to be a vehicle of divine blessings (Gen 12:1–3). Although Israel's missional vocation is not similar to that of Islam and Christianity in terms of making concentrated efforts to reach nonbelievers, it is nonetheless embedded in Israel's identity in terms of expecting a universal end-time pilgrimage to Jerusalem to worship God (Isa 2:1–4; Mic 4:1–4).

A further defining feature of Jewish identity and her community is the continuing diaspora status beginning from the fall of Jerusalem in the sixth century BCE and continuing until the founding of Israel in 1948. The large majority of the Jewish community lives in diaspora outside the Holy Land, with the majority of them in the United States.

Jewish Spiritual Life and Worship

The origin of Jewish religious community, the synagogue, stems from the time of the sixth-century BCE crisis of losing the land and the temple, the beginning of (what became) rabbinic Judaism. The first synagogues were like ordinary houses, but the perception of holiness later led to the construction of fairly elaborate sacred buildings. Ten men are usually needed to establish a synagogue. Traditionally, women have been separated from men into a different space in the synagogue; in modern and contemporary times that varies.

Led by an elected council or official, a synagogue is autonomous, without any authoritative superstructure. Unlike in most Christian churches, but similar to Islam, no professional clergy is needed to lead prayers and worship in a synagogue. That said, in practice the rabbi, the religious leader and teacher since the founding of (rabbinic) Judaism, presides over the liturgy—but a rabbi's status should not be confused with that of a priest. Rabbis used to be only men; nowadays, in diaspora Judaism, many Reform movements endorse a gender-inclusive view.

Jewish (rabbinic) liturgy is founded around the Shema (Deut 6:4–9) and the related Eighteen Benedictions (or prayers, the *Amidah*[46]). Another ancient practice is the encouragement to recite one hundred prayers per day, covering all aspects of life and faith. The reading of Torah is an essential part of the worship. The contemporary Jewish diaspora, particularly

---

46. For an overview of Amidah, see Bloom, "What Is the Amidah?"

in the United States, has produced a wide variety of liturgical patterns and orientations.

Not unlike other religions, there is a religiously ordered pattern for both the Jewish person's life cycle and the life of the community, which follows the sacred calendar. What is unique is the centrality of weekly Sabbath, around which the weekly religious ritual is totally centered (beginning with the common Friday evening pre-Sabbath service).

What about Jewish Openness to Other Religions?

In light of the particularism and universalism discussed above, the question emerged: What about other religions? What is the Jewish take on religious plurality? As much as Yahweh's covenant with Israel calls for unreserved commitment, it also implies that the same God could covenant with other nations.

In other words, there is both particularity (separatism) and universalism (missionary calling). Consider Deuteronomy 32:8–9. No wonder Israel's relation to other religions has fluctuated over the centuries between exclusivism and inclusivism. The diversity of approaches has only intensified in contemporary times.

There are important theological reasons behind the wide-openness projected toward the religious other, particularly the "Talmudic position that embracing Judaism is not necessary for a Gentile's entering the world to come," for the simple reason that "God wants to give all people just rewards."[47] This is not to deny the presence of exclusivism, particularly toward Christians, but rather to appreciate the fact that despite Christians' (and others') horrible and inhumane treatment of Jews throughout the centuries and particularly in the twentieth century, there is this robust inclusivist impulse.

The Pain and Promise of Christian-Jewish Relations

What makes the encounter between Jews and Christians ironic and unique is that only after the Jewish people had rejected Jesus, the Messiah, did he become the Savior for all peoples. Along with these and related theological reasons, what has damaged relations between the two Abrahamic communities is supersessionism, which rejects the view that Israel continues to be the people of God, and its corollary, Christian anti-Semitism.

---

47. Shatz, "Jewish Perspective," 367.

It is against this sad and regrettable background—until modern times also including the lack of a thoughtful Jewish engagement of Christianity and the proliferation of caricatures and prejudices—that promising signs of a fruitful mutual dialogue are now beginning to appear.

As orientation to this complex discussion, it may be useful to outline briefly the main positions among Christian theologians with regard to this issue:[48]

- In the *supersessionist* (or traditional) view, the church as the "new people" replaces Israel and takes her place in the divine economy.
- *Dispensationalists* make a categorical distinction between God's dealings with the church and with Israel, and they expect a literal fulfillment of OT prophecies, including the rebuilding of the temple and its cult in the eschaton before the final consummation. Because this view is novel and therefore marginal in Christian theology, I do not engage it further.
- For the *revisionists*, there is ultimate redemption for both Israel and the church, and while for the latter it is through Christ, for the former it is not; indeed, the non-acceptance of Jesus as the Messiah for Israel is made a matter of obedience to God in this scheme.
- In *reunionism*, God's covenant with Israel will never be annulled but will be fulfilled through Christ, Israel's, and all peoples', Messiah; ultimately, both peoples of God, that of the OT and that of the New Testament, will be reunited and saved.

In support of the reunionist vision—and thus rejecting supersessionism—it seems clear in the biblical testimonies, first, that God's covenant with Israel is irrevocable (Amos 9:14-15; Rom 11:1, 29). Although for Paul the church embodied the true Israel (Rom 2:29; 9:6; Phil 3:3), this did not mean that God put Israel aside in accordance with the supersessionist scheme. Second, in the divine plan of salvation, Israel plays a unique role as the "light" to the nations (Isa 42:6; 49:6). That commission is not made void by Israel's disobedience. Third, in Jesus Christ, Israel's Messiah and the Savior of the whole world, the line of enmity between the chosen people and gentiles has been eradicated forever (Eph 2:12-22), hence making possible the coming eschatological reunion.

Taking for granted the inviolability of God's covenant in Romans 9-11, Paul holds that Israel is the "trunk" of God's tree, and that the church, as the newcomer, can be compared to its branches. In God's plan, the branches

---

48. Following, with minor modifications, Bloesch, *Last Things*, 43-46 and chap. 10.

could be united with the trunk (cf. 9:25)! This is a diametrically opposite approach to that of later Christian theology. At the same time, Paul is of course deeply troubled by Israel's unwillingness to embrace Christ as the Messiah, although he finds some consolation in the OT remnant theology. He is confident that Israel's current "hardening" is merely temporary and, ironically, that it is used by God to further God's plans for the salvation of the whole world (11:11). As a result, God's purposes will be fulfilled: "a hardening has come upon part of Israel, until the full number of the Gentiles come in, and so all Israel will be saved" (11:25–26). There is thus a common eschatological goal for both Israel and the church, and they are set in mutual, yet distinct, roles in relation to each other. All this means that the church should take a careful and self-critical look at herself as the people of God.

While holding to the continuation of God's covenant with Israel, the Christian church and theology also should exercise critical judgment in not identifying that status with the current secular state of Israel. Israel's political sins and wrongdoings, like those of her Arabic neighbors, should be subjected to the same kinds of ethical and theological judgments as are other nations' deeds.

The Unique Nature of the Christian Mission to the Jews

Unlike Judaism but like Islam, Christianity is an active missionary faith. We have to critique the revisionist view, which, while agreeing with much that has been said above, would oppose any notion of Jewish evangelization. Neither Paul nor the rest of the NT was advocating a "special path" for Israel in terms of the Jews not needing Jesus the Messiah. The one people of God will all be saved in and through Christ. Not only did Paul preach to both gentiles and Jews (Acts 9:15), but bringing the gospel of Christ to Israel took priority for him over other works of mission (Rom 1:16).

At the same time, the unique and special nature of Jewish evangelization and mission have to be noted. The gospel of Christ, even when rejected by Jews, is not calling the people of God into something "new" in the way gentiles are being called. After all, Jesus Christ is Israel's Messiah before he is the Savior of the world. Mission to the Jews should also include a contrite and repentant spirit and acknowledgment of guilt for the sins in which Christians have participated throughout history. At the same time, Christians should acknowledge their indebtedness to Israel for the message of salvation and for the Messiah.

These two broad theological principles help us better appreciate this continuing dynamic tension facing Christian theology, put well by a Jewish theologian: how "to be faithful to the NT command to witness for Christ to all peoples and to convert all nations, while, at the same time, affirming the ongoing validity of the covenant between God and Israel via Abraham and Moses." At the center of this tension lies the obvious but important fact that "[h]istorically Christianity has been theologically exclusive and humanistically universal, while Judaism has been theologically universal and humanistically exclusive."[49] Christian theological exclusivism, however, does not entail disqualifying others from salvation but—as the sympathetic Jewish observer further rightly notes—is funded by the conviction that Christ's salvific work is meant for the benefit of all.

Islamic Ummah and Christian Church

An Early Split with Dramatic Implications

Islam as a religion shares with Judaism and Christianity a deep communal orientation anchored in one God. The term for the community, *ummah*, appears in the Qur'an over sixty times, with diverse and varying meanings. The incipient universal vision of early Islam is evident in Qur'an 10:19: "Mankind was but one community; then they differed," obviously implying an original "single *ummah* with a single religion."[50]

There is a marked development in the relation of the *ummah* to the other during the Prophet's lifetime, beginning as inclusive of Muslims, Jews, and Christians, based on belief in one God, toward a narrower view limited basically to the followers of the Prophet. A definite limiting took place after his death, and that included a shift toward more sociopolitical and juridical aspects.

Alongside the early inclusivism, the idea of the superiority of this community was established with appeal to passages such as 3:110: "You are the best community brought forth to men, enjoining decency, and forbidding indecency, and believing in God." At times, however, a more hospitable interpretation could also include other God-fearing communities as exemplary.

Whereas all living faiths have experienced severe and continuing internal divisions, with Islam it happened early and established stark borderlines between two major traditions. This major division, between the Sunnis and Shi'ites, arose over the issue of the Prophet's successor after his death (632 CE). Abu Bakr, the father of the Prophet's beloved wife Aisha,

---

49. Kogan, *Opening the Covenant*, xii–xiii.
50. Wheeler, "Ummah," 9446.

was made the first leader (*amir*, "commander") by the majority, but that did not settle the matter, as the minority of the community preferred Ali, the husband of Muhammad's daughter Fatima, as their leader. Both theological and political issues were involved.

Whereas for the majority the leadership choice after the passing of the Prophet belonged to the *ummah* at large, for the rest it was a divine choice falling on Ali—with the ambiguous claim that he had divine endorsement as well as the Prophet's. The majority wanted to stay in the line of Mecca's dominant tribe, the Prophet's own tribe, Quraysh; whereas a minority received support from Medina. Full separation of the *ummah*, however, did not come about until after the brief leadership of Umar I and the longer office of the caliph Uthman, whose assassination in 656 brought Ali to power for half a decade, a period of virtual civil war. In the end, the community's separation was final, between the majority Sunnis (currently over 80 percent) and a minority of Shi'ites who followed Ali's legacy. Both sides continued splitting internally, leading to the kind of complex denominationalism characteristic of most religions.

All Shi'ites share a belief in the divinely ordered status of Ali as the successor to the Prophet (Q 2:124; 21:72–73). The Twelvers, by far the largest and most important Shi'ite denomination, has developed a highly sophisticated genetic line of succession from Ali through his two sons (Hasan and Husayn) all the way to the Twelfth one. Its most distinctive claim has to do with the last imam (after Hasan ibn Ali al-Askari of the ninth century), titled Muhammad b. Hasan, who allegedly went into "occultation" (that is, concealment) and whose return they await. In this interpretation, all imams possess inerrancy in order to be able to prevent the community from being led astray. That said, there are a number of fiercely debated issues among the three main Shi'ite traditions (the Twelvers, the Ishmaelites, and the Zaydis, the first two sharing much more in common concerning the imamate) about the line of succession and related issues.

What is amazing and confusing to the outsider about the global Muslim community is that, despite how much they share in tradition and doctrine, their mutual relationships are so antagonistic and condemnatory. Both parties share the same Qur'an, the same prophethood, and the Five Pillars, including prayers, fasting, and other rituals (albeit somewhat differently nuanced and practiced). Yet it seems that any kind of global ecumenical reconciliation is not on the horizon—although the Qur'an mandates work for unity. "And hold fast to God's bond, together, and do not scatter" (3:103–5).

Spiritual Life and Worship in Islam

Obedience; submission to Allah, including willing service; and honoring *tawhid*, the absolute unity/oneness of God shape Muslim life in all aspects, including what we call devotion and liturgy. Together these constitute the "five pillars"—confession, ritual prayer, fasting, pilgrimage, and alms—routinely preceded by the important rites of purification, both physical and spiritual.

The ritual prayer is the most visible form of piety. Muslims ought to pray five times a day at designated times, regardless of their location. Prayer is preceded by ablution and employs a prescribed form and content. Prayer is also the main activity in the mosque; nowadays the Friday afternoon gathering there includes a sermon. Holy Scripture is highly honored and venerated. Since there is no clergy and no theologically trained priesthood, any male is in principle qualified to lead; he is usually chosen from among those most deeply knowledgeable in the tradition.

Although the Prophet Muhammad was but a human being, particularly in folk Islam and forms of Sufism, his status is elevated to that of a (semi)divine object of veneration. Sufi mysticism also has a number of saints similarly elevated, particularly Ali (even among the Sunnis).

As in other religions, the annual life cycle follows the religious calendar, starting from the honoring of the date when Muhammad migrated from Mecca to Medina. Friday is not considered a holy day, although it is the day of congregation. Instead, a number of other holy days commemorate significant days in the life of the Prophet and early *ummah*. Globalization has caused much diversity in rituals and rites, but not in doctrine and prayers.

Mission to Nonbelievers and Perception of the Religious Other

Like Christianity's, Islam's outlook is universal. Echoing biblical theology, the Qur'an teaches that "'to God belongs the kingdom (*mulk*) of the heavens and earth' (e.g., 2:107)."[51] The Qur'an instructs us that "had God willed, He would have made them one community" (42:8; see also 42:10). The key verse is well known: "God is our Lord and your Lord. Our deeds concern us and your deeds concern you. There is no argument between us and you. God will bring us together, and to Him is the [final] destination" (42:15).

In this light it is understandable that the earliest Qur'anic passages were not calling people to convert to a new religion; rather, the Meccans

---

51. Woodberry, "Kingdom of God," 49.

were called to "worship the Lord of this House [Ka'ba]" (106:3).[52] Only later, with the rising opposition from the worshipers of local deities, was a decisive break announced, and the confession became "There is no god except God" (37:35). We know that in Medina the Prophet with his companions lived among the Jews, and we may safely infer that he assumed that the new faith was in keeping with theirs as well as with the Christian faith (2:40–41). Recall also that at that time the term *muslim* could also be applied to non-Muslims, such as Solomon (27:44) and disciples of Jesus (3:52). Only when the Jews rejected the Prophet was the direction of Muslims's prayer changed from Jerusalem to Mecca (2:142).

In keeping with this is the special status assigned to Abrahamic sister faiths. Between what Muslims call "the Abode of Peace and the Abode of War," a third region was acknowledged, "the Abode of the People of the Book," that is, Jews and Christians. These two traditions enjoy a unique relation to Islam (2:135–36; 5:12, 69), implying that in some real sense the diversity of religions is not only tolerated by Allah but even planned and endorsed, at least when it comes to those who are the "people of the book" (48:29; 5:48; 3:113–15).

This inclusive tendency notwithstanding, Islam retains a unique place in God's eyes, say Muslims. The inclusion is similar to Roman Catholic inclusivism: while other nations might have known God, only Muslims know Allah intimately and are rightly related to God. That is most probably the meaning of the Qur'anic statements that Muslims, in distinction from others, are "God's sincere servants" (37:40), and "they are of the elect, the excellent" (38:47). Therefore, ultimately even Jewish and Christian traditions suffer from corruption and misunderstanding of the final revelation.

At her core, Islam is an active missionary community, based on the Qu'ranic mandate to reach out to nonbelievers (16:125). This is often expressed with the Arabic term *da'wah*, literally "call" or "summons." Combining a universalizing tendency and fervent missionary mandate, Islam's goal of outreach is comprehensive, including ideally social, economic, cultural, and religious spheres. Likewise, ideally it would result in the establishment of Sharia law and the gathering of all peoples under one *ummah*. During various historical eras, *da'wah* has been exercised with the help of military and political means, as Christianity did as well, although the Qur'an prohibits evangelism by force (2:256). Yet alliances with earthly powers, militarism, and economic interests were all employed to spread Islam with force and brutality. In other words, not only Christianity but also Islam bears the long legacy of colonialism.

---

52. The Ka'ba is the holiest place in Islam, in Mecca.

Muslim-Christian Relations: A Brief Assessment

Not only does Judaism stand in a unique position in relation to the Christian church, so does Islam, albeit differently. That said, it is too rarely appreciated how different the Christianity first encountered by the Prophet and the early Muslim *ummah* was from the global Christian church today. In the seventh century, notwithstanding internal differences, there was one undivided church (at least formally). Importantly, the segments of the church that early Islam engaged were either marginal or heretical in the eyes of the mainstream Christianity, namely, advocates of Nestorianism and monophysitism (of various sorts). Most ironically, many of the objections of Muslims against the orthodox Christian doctrine of the Trinity and Christology either stem from or are strongly flavored by these Christian divergences.

On the one hand, the Christian-Muslim encounters throughout history have been characterized by misperceptions, misrepresentations, and even hostility. On the other hand, more often than not there has been more tolerance than would be expected from, say, cultures of the Middle Ages. There was also a shift in Christian perception: whereas for Christian apologists from the seventh century, such as John of Damascus, to the late medieval period, Islam was represented more like a heresy, from the late medieval period onward it was taken as a false religion, apostasy. Nowadays, a number of promising signs indicate that concerted efforts are underway to continue constructive mutual engagement, heal memories, and improve understanding of the two faiths.

Recall the wise words from Vatican II's *Nostra Aetate* (para. 3):

> The Church regards with esteem also the Moslems. They adore the one God, living and subsisting in Himself; merciful and all-powerful, the Creator of heaven and earth, who has spoken to men; they take pains to submit wholeheartedly to even His inscrutable decrees, just as Abraham, with whom the faith of Islam takes pleasure in linking itself, submitted to God. Though they do not acknowledge Jesus as God, they revere Him as a prophet. They also honor Mary, His virgin Mother; at times they even call on her with devotion.

The common basis of these two faiths in monotheism, scriptural heritage, doctrine of creation, theological anthropology, eschatology, and the person of Jesus has been detailed above, and it alone mandates ongoing dialogue. Commonalities and differences also come to the surface in the missional orientation of both traditions.

Mission, Colonialism, and Power: Shared Concerns between Muslims and Christians

Similarly to Judaism, Islam sees "the appropriate way to human fulfillment in obedience to a divinely revealed law," named in that tradition as the Sharia, which differs from Judaism in that it is "given to be followed by all humanity, and not just by one special community."[53] How does Christian mission relate to that claim? Instead of a divinely given law to govern all of life as in a theocracy, Christian mission aims at providing a holistic way of life based on love of God and neighbor, leaving open issues of government (most inclusively understood).

From a Christian perspective, it is highly ironic that the Islamic pursuit of global Sharia has from the beginning been closely allied with a specific ethnicity and language (Arabic) and, in modern and contemporary times, often with nationalism, particularly in the regions of the world colonized by European powers. How would a universal reach to all humanity be reconciled with that? "If Islam is indeed meant to be a global community, then it is self-defeating for Islam to oppose 'the West,' when Westerners should be Muslims too, and when many are."[54]

Both Islam and Christianity carry a legacy of colonialism as part of their mission history. Unbeknownst to many, "[w]hile from the first there were considerable numbers of Christians under Muslim rule, yet until the appearance of European colonialism there were virtually no Muslims under Christian rule except for limited periods."[55] Everywhere Christians lived under Muslim rule, the Sharia law totally forbade Christian sharing of the gospel with Muslims. Indeed, according to Sharia law, the penalty for apostasy—the Islamic perception of converting to Christianity—is death.

Hindu Communities and Christian Church

Who Is a Hindu? And Is There a Defining Community of Hindus?

Both Judaism and Hinduism emerged over a long period of time. Neither one has a human founder. They are also similar in that while one can be a Jew only by birth (through a Jewish mother), the assumption is that to have been born as an Indian, one is Hindu. Doctrine does not determine belonging in either tradition, although holy Scriptures are honored in both.

---

53. Ward, *Religion and Community*, 31.
54. Ward, *Religion and Community*, 32–33, here 33.
55. Watt, *Muslim-Christian Encounters*, 74.

Differently from Abrahamic faiths, community does not play a central role in Hinduism, as the religion's main goal is the spiritual release of the individual, rather than the reform of the society or communal (let alone cosmic) eschatological renewal. By saying this I do not in any way mean to undermine the deeply and widely communal orientation of Indian culture and, as part of that, the celebration of religious rites in communal settings in the family, village, or temple. Rather, I mean by this that the basic orientation of Hinduism lacks an internal and ultimate communal goal. In keeping with this, there is no single term to describe the communal side of Hindu spirituality. Perhaps the term *sampradaya* comes closest to describing its intention, but this term is not widely, let alone universally, used.

The plurality of Hinduism allows a plethora of local deities to be worshiped. That said, the existing diversity does not mean a person can choose which deity to worship, as might be misunderstood by readers more conversant with the hyperindividualism of the Global North. Rather, it is the family and wider community's religion and rites that one follows.

Spiritual Rites and Communal Acts among Hindus

Without claiming any real similarity between Christian sacraments and Hindu life-cycle-related *samskaras*, through which one becomes a full member of the community and society, the Christian interpreter may nonetheless identify them as "Hindu sacraments." Similarly to rites of passage in almost all religions, these rites cover the entire life span from birth to death, as prescribed in the sacred literature.

Among these, the one called "the second birth," which occurs at eight to twelve years of age, is particularly important. The exact time of this rite of initiation is determined by an astrologer, and it marks a person's shift from childhood to the first of the four ashrams, which is studenthood, including religious education.

The final sacrament, that of death, universally practiced by all Hindus, even secular ones, likewise plays a central role. The funeral, in which the body is burned, includes elaborate rites and rituals. Ancestor rites typically continue for years after the funeral to "establish the deceased harmoniously within their appropriate worlds and prevent them from becoming hungry and haunting their living descendants."[56]

As explained in the chapter on soteriology, Hinduism recognizes three paths to liberation: devotion, knowledge, and work. The most typical at the grassroots level is the way of devotion, and for the large majority, this *bhakti*

---

56. Courtright, "Worship and Devotional Life," 9821.

devotion comes in the form of theistic Vaishnavism. Based on the Bhagavad Gita, this loving, intimate devotion is often focused on Krishna.

In India's worship life, "space and time are permeated and filled with the presence of the Supreme."[57] Among artistic manifestations of the supreme, the most profound is *murti*, or image, which can also be called "embodiment," the highest form of manifestation of the divine. In temples, devout Hindus are surrounded and embraced by this divine presence. In that presence, masses of devotees may experience *darsana*, a special kind of spiritual "seeing" or insight. Indeed, this "auspicious seeing" is mutual as, on the one hand, the deity makes herself or himself visible, and, on the other, the god is "seen" by the devotee. Open to all Hindus, regular *pujas*, or acts of worship to the deities, take place daily to celebrate the divine presence.

Closely related to the centrality of divine presence is a special kind of prayer rite, originating in Vedic religion,[58] the mantra "OM," which functions as the representation not only of God (Brahman) but in some sense also of all reality. It is customary for the head of the household to utter this word first thing in the morning after purification rituals.

Similar to other religious traditions, along with rites of passage, a rich and diverse annual festival menu is an essential part of Hindu devotion and worship life. Although the basic structure of festivals may be simple, to outsiders these festivals look extremely complex. They may last several days and exhibit unusually rich local and denominational diversity.

Not unlike in other faiths, there is also the "professional" religious class, the Brahmins, related to the ancient class system of India, formerly a caste society. Whereas ordinary devotees have Puranas (the rich narrative and epic literature) as their holy Scripture, only the Brahmins are experts in Vedic literature. Another related structure of Indian society and culture has to do with the four ashrams. Ideally by the end of life one reaches the final stage of the "renouncer," after studenthood, family life, and the period of forest hermit. Only a tiny minority of Hindus belong to the Brahmin class or reach the stage of renouncer. Along with these two classes, there is a vast group of gurus of various sorts, many highly respected, others less so. A *sampradaya* is formed around the guru, a community for masses of Hindus.

What about Other Religions?

Hinduism embraces diversity in a way that no other major living tradition does. This diversity, however, differs from modernist Western pluralism in

57. Klostermaier, *A Survey of Hinduism*, 263.
58. The classic passage is Rig Veda 3.62.10.

many respects. First of all, although tolerating other rites and deities, Hindus typically take their own beliefs (and no others) as true. Second, Hindu tolerance has much to do with the idea that since God is bigger than any other concept of ours, various ways of approaching God are complementary in that the infinite God is beyond and transcends any particular path.

What about mission and desire to convert others? It is clear that Hinduism is not a missional religion like Buddhism, Christianity, and Islam. In that it considers itself the "original" religion, it tends to assimilate others under its own purview, not necessarily inviting them to change.

Understandably, Hinduism faces grave difficulties when encountering Christian and Islamic types of claims regarding the finality of revelation and the uniqueness of God. In keeping with the assimilationist principle, Hindus resist and oppose any efforts at evangelization by other traditions. In that light it appears inhospitable that some movements, such as Arya Samaj, oppose the conversion of Hindus to Islam and Christianity while at the same time strongly advocating that recent converts to Christianity convert back to Hinduism.

All in all, notwithstanding the hesitancy about conversion, Hinduism not only recognizes the reconversion of their lapsed faithful but also engages in active missionary efforts to convert "pagans." This was certainly the case in the third to fifth centuries during the establishment of Hindu rajas in South India to replace Buddhism. Itinerant "evangelists" played a critical role in that enterprise. More recently, Hare Krishna and a number of other less well-known revival movements in the West have also sought new converts.

The Complexity of Hindu-Christian Engagement

Significant to Hindu-Christian relations is Hinduism's tendency to assimilate others under itself, believing itself to be the "original" and perhaps best revelation, thus making it in some real sense a counterpart to Roman Catholicism. At the same time, the Hindu attitude toward Christian faith is more complicated than that. Consider the well-known spokespersons of Hinduism in the West, Swami Vivekananda, India's delegate to the World Parliament of Religions meeting in Chicago in 1893, and Sarvepalli Radhakrishnan, the former president of India. Known for tolerance and religious coexistence, they are also critics of Christianity.

Indeed, there is no standard, universal Hindu response to the religious other. In light of this complexity, it is important to recall that the roots of Hindu-Christian engagement and coexistence go far back in history. It is probable that there was a Christian presence in India as early as the first century. Syrian Christianity is believed to have reestablished itself beginning in the fourth century. Although Western colonialism helped poison mutual relations between Hindus and Christians in a number of ways, it is significant that, beginning from the end of the nineteenth century, a new wave of interpretations of Christ related to the so-called Indian renaissance or neo-Hindu reform emerged, testing affinities between the two traditions.

Because of the difference of orientations between Hindu and Christian traditions—the former's individualistic pursuit of release and the latter's deeply communal faith—dialogue with Hindus that is focused on ecclesiology yields fewer results and areas of shared concerns than dialogue between the church and the synagogue or the *ummah*.

In many ways Hindu spiritual life and devotion are oriented differently than Judeo-Christian traditions. For example, for the Hindu, rather than petition and pleading, as in the Judeo-Christian tradition, prayer is more about chanting the sacred mantra, linked with the search for *darsana* in the divine presence. There is also what can be called "ritual enhancement," that is, a devotional practice that "aims at sustaining or improving the circumstances of the worshiper," whether in regards to practical life situations like sickness or business or family concerns, or to the spiritual aims of liberation and release. This is, of course, also a common feature of Abrahamic traditions.

What is a foundational difference has to do with another common theme in Hindu devotional life, namely, "negotiation or exchange, in which devotional performances become occasions for giving human resources of food, gifts, and devotion to supernatural entities and powers in exchange for human well-being, which is understood to flow from those persons and powers as a consequence of the rite."[59] Although this kind of exchange mentality is not unknown in Christian spirituality, theologically it is a foreign concept.

Buddhist *Sangha* and the Christian Church

How Did the Buddhist Community Emerge?

Differently from the parent religion of Hinduism, Buddhism has a founder, Siddhartha Gautama. Although historical details of Gautama's life are few, the religion- and community-forming narrative is based on the enlightenment experience of this former noble prince and renouncer. The teaching

---

59. Courtright, "Worship and Devotional Life," 9820.

of the emerging new religion, similarly to Hinduism, is not centered on faith as much as on commitment to pursuing release from attachment to the world of impermanence and the resulting *dukkha*.

The enlightened Sakyamuni (Gautama) established the *sangha* (or *samgha*) community with five initial disciples. Originally it was an inclusive community, open to both male monks and female nuns. The nuns lived separately from the men but belonged to the community. That inclusive vision, however, became limited over the course of centuries, and now it is usual (particularly in Theravada contexts) to have only male monks.

Soon after the founding of *sangha*, Buddha began to send the enlightened monks (*arhats*, "worthy ones") out on missionary trips to preach the Dhamma, the Buddha's teachings. So, unlike Hinduism, but like Christian and Muslim traditions, Buddhism is a missionary religion, and there is scriptural commissioning for such activity. Particularly during the founding centuries, the missionary vision was fervent. Similarly to Christianity, the new religion also proliferated through merchants and other travelers.

Following Buddha's *parinirvana* (complete liberation at death), the First Ecumenical Council was summoned, gathering together five hundred *arhats* to whom Buddha's Dhamma was entrusted, comprising Tipitaka, the "Three Baskets" of teachings, the middle one of which (Vinaya Pitaka) contains all instructions and teachings for the life of the *sangha*. Subsequently, the Second Council, one hundred years later, brought to the surface disagreements and strife. A number of other councils followed, along with deep disagreements and splits.

The most significant split occurred around the beginning of the common era, and resulted in the birth of the Mahayana school.[60] Later, it made a foundational claim to Buddha's own teaching, though so far such a teaching document has not been discovered.

Mahayana advocates much more open access to the pursuit of nirvana for all men and women, not only to a few religious. It also adopted a more theistically oriented cosmology and highlighted the importance of notions of grace and mercy, particularly in its later developments having to do with the Pure Land and related movements. Mahayana has also developed a growing tradition of spiritual exercises in pursuit of liberative insight.

The third major strand is commonly called Vajrayana ("Diamond Vehicle") or Tantrism, and it can be found in Tibet. Broadly related to Mahayana,

---

60. Whereas Theravada is dominant in Thailand, Myanmar, and Sri Lanka, Mahayana is currently present in India, Vietnam, Tibet (mainly in the form of Tantric Buddhism or Vajrayana), China, Taiwan, Korea, and Japan, among other locations. That tradition is also the most familiar form of Buddhism in the Global North.

it has also contextualized itself in rich Tibetan folk religiosity and mysticism with a focus on diverse rituals, mantras, and esoteric rites.

Buddhist Devotion and Rituals

Differently from Jewish-Christian tradition, but in keeping with Hindu traditions, becoming a Buddhist does not usually entail any initiatory rite (whereas joining the *sangha* takes a long period of discipline and teaching, culminating in "ordination" by a legitimate leader). Instead of an initiatory act, it is (almost) universally taught among Buddhists that taking refuge in Buddha, Dhamma, and *sangha* constitutes becoming a Buddhist. This typically entails adhering to the five precepts of abstaining from killing, stealing, adultery, lying, and drinking. At the same time, one commits oneself to the pursuit of liberation from *dukkha* following the Noble Eightfold Path.

Although in Theravada the releasing enlightenment is typically thought to be attained only by monks, and even then only by a few of them, Gautama also included in the sphere of the *sangha* laypersons, regardless of their profession.

Sanghas are supposed to be located near the rest of the society, distinct from it but not so separated as to be isolated. Monks go out every morning to collect gifts and donations, and they also serve the people in the temples and homes in religious rituals.

While in principle there are no mandatory rituals or rites to perform, Buddhist lands are filled with the most elaborate devotional and worship acts and patterns, with liturgy at their center. Furthermore, all denominations, astonishingly even Theravada, are highly "animistic": in everyday religiosity, spirits and spirituality are alive and well.

Furthermore, not unlike most religions, "many Buddhists believe that ritual and devotion are also instrumental in bringing about blessings in life and even inner spiritual transformation."[61] Indeed, notwithstanding wide and deep variety in the Buddhist world, rites related to giving or offering in worship form the basic structure. Giving with the right attitude is the key, and only then is it meritorious. Offerings of candles, water, food, flowers, and so forth are ways of honoring Buddha.

Another defining feature across the varied Buddhist world is meditation, whose aim is to bring about "a state of perfect mental health, equilibrium and tranquility."[62] Unlike in many other contexts, Buddhist meditation is not an exit from ordinary life but, instead, is deeply

---

61. Ludwig, *xSacred Paths*, 158.
62. Rahula, *What the Buddha Taught*, 67.

embedded in it. Its core has to do with mindfulness, an aptitude and skill to be developed throughout one's life.[63]

Because of the nontheistic orientation and nondivine status of Buddha, strictly speaking there is no prayer in original Buddhist devotion; "it is only a way of paying homage to the memory of the Master who showed the way."[64] Similarly, the Scriptures—though they are honored and venerated in many forms of (particularly Mahayana) liturgy—are not regarded as divine revelation but rather as guides to human effort. Furthermore, particularly in folk spirituality, Buddhist devotion, similarly to Islamic religious life, elevates the founder to a (semi-)divine status.

Similarly to all other religions, Buddhism embraces daily rituals and worship patterns as well as holy days and festivals, including rites of passage from birth to initiation into (young) adulthood to death. Counterintuitively, throughout the Buddhist world the worship patterns, rituals, and rites seem to be similar to those of theistic faiths, with a strong focus on devotion.

Meeting the Religious Other

Similarly to Hinduism, among Buddhists the appropriate way to discern the religious other includes both intra- and interfaith dimensions. Yet another shared feature is that it is typical for Buddhist movements to consider other Buddhist movements through the lens of "hierarchical inclusivism." In this, it also resembles Catholicism. All of these three traditions consider their own movement as the "fulfillment," while others are at a lower level and yet belong to the same family. An aspect of that tolerance of sectarian diversity is to lift up one's own Scriptures as superior to the other sister movements' ones (rather than simply denying the worth of the others).

Encounter with the non-Buddhist religious other is not new to the tradition; on the contrary, during Buddhism's rise in India, along with emerging Jainism, it had to negotiate its identity not only in relation to Hinduism and other local religions but also (when moving outside India) in relation to Taoism, Confucianism, Shintoism, and others. Although neither Buddhism's past nor present iteration is without conflicts with the other, occasional campaigns of coercion, and other forms of religious colonialism, by and large Buddhism has sought peaceful coexistence with others. This inclusivist paradigm it has also at times applied, at least to its closest cousin faiths. Yet, as can also be said of Hinduism, one cannot find many clear

---

63. For an explanation of how meditation cultivates mindfulness, see Batchelor, "Meditation and Mindfulness."

64. Rahula, *What the Buddha Taught*, 81.

examples of what we Westerners call religious pluralism. Only recently have a growing number of Buddhists, many of them scholars from or residing in the Global North, begun more systematic work toward Buddhist comparative theology and interfaith engagement.

The Slow Emergence of Buddhist and Christian Engagement

In contrast to Christianity's interaction with Judaism and Islam, Christian and Buddhist communities do not have a long history of dialogue and mutual engagement; indeed, until the nineteenth century, very little exchange took place, notwithstanding some meaningful encounters between Nestorian Christians and Buddhists in India and China from the sixth to the eighth centuries. The best-chronicled friendship-based and intimate knowledge of Buddhism among Christians comes from the sixteenth-century Jesuit Francis Xavier.

Similarly to all other faith traditions, Buddhism in the contemporary world faces massive challenges, many of which have to do with relations to Christianity and the linked colonialist burden. The effects of modernization D. L. McMahan aptly calls "detraditionalization" and "demythologization." Well known also in post-Enlightenment Christianity, these effects of modernization seek to highlight the importance of reason and critique over traditional beliefs and authorities.[65] Part of this process is the coming of Buddhism into the Global North in new contextualized forms, from Zen Buddhism to Buddhist theosophical societies, among others.

For the sake of continuing dialogue, let us register some foundational differences:

- Although the *sangha* is an important part of Buddhist pursuit of spiritual liberation, as in Hinduism, spiritual liberation is ultimately a matter of each individual's effort. Hence, Buddhism is not, ecclesiologically, a religion of "communion."
- Although not atheistic in the Western sense, a deity is marginal to Buddhists. One's salvation depends on one's own effort.
- Although Buddhism does not lack a social ethic or noble examples of working toward peace, reconciliation, and improvement of the society and world, as a religious-ethical system it is not optimistic about the future consummation. Ultimately, as with Hinduism, it is a religion of renunciation.

---

65. McMahan, *Making of Buddhist Modernism*, 42–52.

Despite these radical differences of orientation, what is common to both traditions is their missionary nature. That said, Buddhism's missional nature is nothing like that of the Christian tradition, whose mission is anchored in the sending God. The *sangha*'s mission is to spread the knowledge of the liberating insight of the Buddha for the sake of men and women pursuing a similar path and for the well-being and benefit of all.

Concerning women's status in religion and the religious community, the Christian Church may be in a position to inspire and instruct the Buddhist community. Despite the inclusive vision of Buddha discussed above, almost as a rule throughout the Buddhist world, females are either completely banned from the highest religious calling—full monastic life—or relegated to lower monastic levels. Religious authority is kept firmly in men's hands.

Having engaged the four religious communities and their spiritual life from a Christian perspective, we now do the same with secularisms.

The Christian Church and Ecclesiology in the "Secular City"

The Many Locations and Meanings of Secularism

With the founding of the United States of America in 1789, and the Constitution's endorsement of freedom of religion and its prohibition against privileging any particular faith, a new kind of officially formulated relation between religion and society emerged. The same was reaffirmed with the founding of India and Israel in 1947. The Russian Federation also comes to mind in this connection. Whereas particularly in the United States the desire not to affiliate the state with religion was motivated mostly by the need for tolerance and freedom of choice, in France, Spain, and Italy it was a protest-secularism against the dominant religion, Catholicism. These events testify to a growing desire to ensure freedom of religion, including the choice not to follow any faith tradition.

Globally, there are about 1.5 billion self-designated seculars or those with no religious affirmation, over against over 6 billion adherents of religions. Understandably, secularism is a more robust phenomenon in the Global North. That said, it is not limited to that region.

The meaning and manifestations of secularism, however, are quite different in various contexts of the Global South. Unlike in the West, religion in Africa is not separate from the rest of life. This is not to say that secularism is unknown in Africa, but rather that its appearance and meaning differ vastly from that of European and North American contexts. As one may expect, secularism in the vast continent of Asia comes in various forms. India is a case in point. There are those who allege its absence in that subcontinent while others discern secularism there.

The latest "turn" in secularism discourse owes much to the leading German philosopher Jürgen Habermas and the concept of the postsecular that he helped to launch. He draws attention to the obvious "multifaceted transformation" in the landscape of religions in the Global North and beyond, as a result of which "religious symbols and language games are being transposed into other, not genuinely religious, domains," including literature, the performing arts, and advertising, among others.[66] Counterintuitively, (post-)secularism has not done away with all forms of religiosity as, according to research, many rituals and rites that have religious overtones or forms are found among them. The borderline between religion and the secular is becoming thinner and more complex.

What might or should the Christian church's response look like? Understandably, a number of strategies have been tried, to which we now turn in this last section of the chapter.

Churches Respond to (Post)secularism(s)

Beginning in the nineteenth century, one way the church has sought to encounter the emerging secular age has been through accommodation. That is, it reinterpreted Christian doctrines in ways it thought would appeal to those who rejected religion. This led to a reductionist grab bag of beliefs, excluding the miraculous and transcendent. This same program in various forms continues even now in the third millennium, but in a more radical form. Consider book titles representing "postreligion" such as Diana Butler Bass's *Christianity after Religion* (2012) and Phil Zuckerman's *Faith No More: Why People Reject Religion* (2012).

Not all churches, not even a majority, are excited by these versions of accommodation (or as some might say capitulation) of faith. Briefly put: those strategies would not only mean compromising the identity of the church and her missional calling, but also basically constructing a new "secular religion" not based on any known tradition.

On the other extreme of the spectrum (on the American scene and many other global locations) stands the "Constantinian" project of the Religious Right, which seeks to reestablish a "Christian nation" aligned with political powers. There is no need to elaborate on problems related to it, including eradicating bridges between the church and the secular public.

---

66. As paraphrased by Reder and Schmidt, "Habermas and Religion," 1–2.

Neither one of these two extreme tactics seems to be a constructive way to find common ground with secular people. Instead, the missional calling outlined in this text leads to a robust, hospitable encounter with (post)secularism(s) through the church's missional existence as a worshiping-liturgical and diaconal-charismatic communion, presenting a credible Christian gospel for religionless secularists, the nones, and followers of other religious paths.

10

Eschatology

What Will Happen at the End?

The Winding Road of the Christian Expectation of the End

The Intense Expectation of the End Under Trial

IN ALL LIVING RELIGIONS there are visions of the future and the final "end." But not only among religions: for the expectation—or at times the fear—of the end can also be found in the secular realm. Consider, for example, the growing concern, at times anxiety, in secular culture and scientific study over the impending "end" either of our planet or of human life.

Based on the intense expectation of the final coming of God's kingdom among the earliest followers of Jesus Christ, the patristic church was preparing for the appearance of the world-to-come and for the final resolution or consummation of all things. Although this eschatological hope waned somewhat after the establishment of Christendom, the establishment of Christianity as a state-promoted religion, in no way did it die out. Indeed, more often than not, particularly in the Middle Ages and all way to the Reformation era, eschatological imagination has fueled spirituality.

As with so many other Christian themes, with the dawn of modernity and its critical principle, the whole idea of the world ending in a catastrophic manner and of the ushering in of God's rule on earth became suspect and was totally rejected by many academic theologians. Instead, what mattered to liberal Protestants of the nineteenth century was the this-worldly ethical and moral teaching of Jesus. At the same time, all notions of an "apocalyptic" end-time preacher were dismissed or silently overlooked. A nice, European-type, gentle moral teacher replaced him.

However, some famous biblical scholars and theologians severely criticized this "Quest of the Historical Jesus," as it was named (and briefly discussed in chapter 5), at the turn of the twentieth century, rightly reminding NT readers of the robustly eschatological and apocalyptic nature of Jesus's preaching. We see this orientation particularly clearly in the Gospel of Mark chapter 13 and its parallel passages in Matthew (24–25), for example. Most ironically, however, this valid criticism did not result in anything similar to traditional affirmation of the truthfulness of Jesus's expectation of the end. On the contrary, these critics were just as much children of the Enlightenment as their historical Jesus counterparts, but took the NT eschatology as time-bound and deeply superstitious humbug. Yet, in honesty to the Gospels's portrait of Jesus they acknowledged its presence in Scripture!

The most ironic case is that of Albert Schweitzer, a Swiss-born polymath, medical doctor, musician, and theologian. Though he wrote a devastating critique of the Liberal Quest of the Historical Jesus, he was also deeply influenced by Jesus's radical call to follow him without counting the cost. At the peak of his fame as a academic, doctor, and cultural influencer, he left Europe to practice medicine as a missionary to Africa. But rather than a traditional missionary forsaking everything for Jesus's sake in hopes of heavenly recompense in the afterlife, Schweizer was convinced that unfortunately Jesus, as the child of his times, was absolutely mistaken in his hopes for the divine intervention at the end of the world!

The Rediscovery of Eschatology in Contemporary Theology

Simultaneously—though for different reasons—dismissal or even an aggressive disavowal of Christian eschatological hope was funded by other leading philosophical and cultural figures. As is well known, Ludwig Feuerbach, the leading atheist of the nineteenth century, understood the human desire for life after death as a form of egotism! Sigmund Freud's rejection of religious imagination of the afterlife as a merely neurotic, or at least immature, form of illusion attracted many modern followers. No wonder that the growing number of atheists with a materialist worldview considered the idea of afterlife to be absurd.

In the twentieth century, though in a different form, the well-known American Jesus Seminar, with luminaries such as the late Marcus J. Borg, advocated a totally "non-eschatological" interpretation of Jesus and understood the kingdom of God as a merely this-worldly entity. This radical domestication of the biblical and traditional historical Christian other-worldly hope has continued in much of mainstream academic theology. But that is not the whole picture of where theology stands at the beginning of the third millennium. The road becomes even more winding!

It is not that all twentieth-century theological movements are willing to ignore eschatology. Some leading contemporary theologians have helped rediscover eschatology and even put it at the center of theological conversations. Karl Barth's classic rediscovery of eschatology is routinely considered to be the clarion call for this: he claimed that without eschatology, no theology is worth its salt. The publication of the Reformed theologian Jürgen Moltmann's *Theology of Hope* in the mid-1960s launched a new movement called "theology of hope." For him, eschatology is the "first" chapter of Christian theology; hence, the future matters—and matters a lot. Another German theologian, the Lutheran Wolfhart Pannenberg, has claimed counterintuitively that not only is the future real but that in some real sense it has influence on what happens now because God is in the "future," so to speak. Many others have joined this resurgence of interest in eschatology.

Unrelated to these developments in academic theology, a reinvigoration of eschatological hope and preaching has happened among many conservative and Fundamentalist movements both in the Global North and Global South. While a welcome development, it is also liable to extremes, as will be noted below.

But what is eschatology and what is its task? So far I have used the term as if everyone knows what it is and as if everyone uses it in the same way.

Eschatological Hope Is Bigger than Life!

Eschatology was first called in Latin "the last things" (from Latin *de novissimis*, literally "the newest things"), and it simply referred to what we believed will happen at the end of human life and the world. As every native English speaker knows, the term "end" is a polyvalent term. It can mean both completion (that is, coming or bringing to an end) and fulfillment (as in having reached the destiny). Both these meanings are also present in the Christian eschatological expectation. When put in the wider context of religions, "[i]n its broadest sense the term 'eschatology' includes all concepts of life beyond death and everything connected with it such as heaven and hell, paradise and immortality, resurrection and transmigration of the soul, rebirth and reincarnation, and last judgment and doomsday."[1]

---

1. Schwarz, *Eschatology*, 26.

What makes Christian eschatology distinctive among religions is that it encompasses all of creation, not only humans, nor merely Earth—but the entire vast cosmos. This broadest understanding, however, has not been at the center of Christian eschatology. Indeed, what happened early in Christian theology was that personal eschatology became the focus of the Christian hope and that "the last things" were limited to death, resurrection, judgment, and heaven and hell. Only in recent years has this broader conception of the end been rediscovered.

With this broader vision in mind, I suggest we consider the domain of Christian eschatology under three interrelated rubrics: it encompasses

- personal and communal hope,
- human and cosmic destiny, and
- present and future hope.

Alongside my own personal hope in something beyond my physical death, eschatology also includes the same for the church and, indeed, for the whole of humanity. In fact, counterintuitively to our human way of thinking, it was such communal hope that was at the forefront in the OT (and Jewish faith). The personal emerged only later, and it was connected with the broader hope for the whole community of men and women.

The Christian church adopted this Jewish hope and extended it beyond the individuals and communities already among the people of God to also include gentiles. In comparison, the pagan hope of the immortality of the soul (as in Plato) has no reference to the whole of humanity, only to the individual. Nor is the contemporary secular hope for the completion of human dreams in an ideal society, as expressed particularly in Marxism, satisfactory, as it only deals with those currently living; those who have passed away will miss it entirely. In other words, Christian eschatological hope is superior to secular visions for the future because it integrates the communal and personal aspects.

Another superior feature of Christian eschatology is its integration of the hope for humanity and for the entire cosmos, including nature and the environment, and the whole world. We are not saved "from" but rather "with" the world as we wait for the establishment of the new heaven and new earth. That hope includes both the spiritual and the earthly, as the focus of our hope is the resurrection of body. Too often in the past Christian hope has been divorced from that of the whole world, but it should not be.

Finally, against those who claim that Christian religion is "opium" for the masses (Karl Marx) in that it prompts them to disregard today's responsibilities due to a heightened desire to leave this world in favor of the next, let me remind us all that eschatology integrates the hope for tomorrow with hopeful investment for today. In doing so, on the one hand it saves Christians from otherworldly visions that end up being escapist and dismissive of work toward improving the current world. On the other hand, this is also a corrective to merely this-worldly "eschatologies" mentioned above.

At its deepest core, eschatology is about hope. Christian eschatology is not wishful thinking, nor the desire for a utopia. As with Christian faith at large, eschatology is based on God and God's promises, and this is the source of its superiority to mere human hopefulness.

Christian Hope Is Anchored in the God of Hope

What Happened with the Loss of Hope

Whereas before modernity, belief in God was people's source of hope and confidence, in the post-Enlightenment world, that belief was replaced by self-confidence and trust in human resources. That led to naive optimism about progress, and it only fueled secularization and distance from God. By the latter part of the twentieth century, though, that confidence had encountered dramatic defeats in light of the horrors of world wars and international conflicts, impending natural catastrophes and nuclear threat, as well as other related dangers. No wonder that alongside theologians, philosophers, psychologists, and even psychiatrists are now investigating and propounding the influence, necessity, and nature of hope.

What are the theological implications of the loss of hope? According to the astute analysis of the German Lutheran theologian Hans Schwarz, Christian eschatology helps the confused world discern two vital truths: First, "it shows that the modern idea of progress alienated itself from its Christian foundation ... [as it] deprived history of its God-promised goal." As a result, "we promoted ourselves from God-alienated and God-endowed actors *in history* to deified agents *of history*" (emphasis original). As a remedy to this dilemma, Christian eschatology, second, "provides a hope and a promise that we are unable to attain through our own efforts."[2]

As an alternative and challenge to either pessimism stemming from the loss of hope or optimism derived from naive confidence in human progress, Christian faith proposes a solid, historically based but also history-transcending hope based on the faithfulness of God, who raised from the dead the crucified Son in the power of the Spirit. Rather than

---

2. Schwarz, *Eschatology*, 17–21, here 20.

based on a human utopia, Christian hope intuits history as meaningful based on God's providence.

In the biblical worldview, hope is expressed in terms of promise. Divine promises are radical as they often contradict human expectation. Or what else can be said of Abraham and Sarah to whom a child was promised after they were both way beyond the age of fertility! The promise of Christ's resurrection, the "anchor" of concrete hope, illustrates this best. In the biblical drama, the greatest threat is death—and the greatest promise is deliverance from under the power of death.

Christian Hope Is Guaranteed by Christ's Resurrection from the Dead

According to Saint Paul, Christ's resurrection forms the basis for Christian hope (1 Cor 15:14). Indeed, the apostle goes so far as to claim that had Christ not been raised, Christian faith would be futile and there would be no hope for eternal life (vv. 17–19). Christ was raised to new life by the Father through the Holy Spirit (Rom 1:4). As a result, the indwelling Spirit in believers constantly reminds them of the certainty of their own resurrection by the same Spirit who raised Christ (Rom 8:11).

In order for Christ's resurrection to guarantee eschatological consummation, it has to be historical and factual, a topic widely contested by modernity and contemporary theology (as discussed in chapter 5). Without the validity of Christ's resurrection, we are left with only the possibility of falsification of Christian hope:

> Such a falsification would come in two forms, one looking backward and one looking forward. Looking backward, we could imagine evidence put forward to claim that Jesus hung on the cross, died, and remained dead. . . . Looking forward, we could imagine a future without a consummation, without the new creation promised by the Easter resurrection. . . . The resurrection of Christ, according to Christian faith . . . was the advent of the world's transformation. Without the consummation of this transformatory promise, the Christian faith is in vain.[3]

Theologically, it can be said that resurrection is both an event that happens in history and an event that goes beyond (but not against) history; it is a *"new kind of historical happening"* (emphasis original).[4]

---

3. Peters, "Introduction," viii.
4. Torrance, *Space, Time, and Resurrection*, 88.

What about the challenge from the sciences? The theologian Michael Welker reminds us of the obvious, that "[t]here is perhaps no topic that seems less suited for the dialogue between theology and the so-called exact sciences than the topic of the resurrection."[5] Of course, the reason for this has to do with the current secular naturalist worldview that is dominant among the scientific communities in the Global North, with its aversion to all notions of life after death and the category of the "supernatural." Along with naturalism, the main scientific challenge to the resurrection is that it seems to violate the regularity of natural occurrences, the laws of nature.

Having critiqued and put naturalism in a proper theological perspective (in chapters 3 and 8), suffice it to reaffirm here the possibility of resurrection as the unique event it is. As discussed in the context of Christology (chapter 5), the evidence of the empty tomb and from a large group of contemporary eyewitnesses strongly supports the factuality of the event. Rather than going against nature, the resurrection of Christ—who, himself, in biblical testimonies is the very agent of creation (Col 1:15–17), points to a future when creation "will be set free from its bondage to decay" (Rom 8:21), so much so that, as a result, even death will be defeated (1 Cor 15:55).

Before beginning the actual discussion of Christian eschatology, it is good to scrutinize briefly an alternative to the sound biblical-theological vision of the future, an alternative named "neo-apocalypticism." This harmful way of thinking is fast gaining ground, not only among Christian but also Islamic and some Jewish communities; hence, it has to be contrasted with proper eschatology.

The Dangers of Contemporary Neo-Apocalypticism— Eschatological Hope Gone Awry

Tapping into the long and rich tradition of apocalypticism with its deeply dualistic view of the world and expectation of the imminent catastrophic end of history, contemporary neo-apocalypticism is gaining strongholds not only in conservative and Fundamentalist Christian but also in Jewish and Islamic movements. Although it is easy to dismiss these kinds of movements as harmless or excessive, it is best not to underestimate their importance to the faithful.

Christian neo-apocalypticism is currently quite well known even beyond church walls thanks to the phenomenal sales of writings, movies, and other products. I am thinking of best-selling titles such as *The Late, Great Planet Earth* (1970) by Hal Lindsey and the Left Behind series by Tim LaHaye

---

5. Welker, "Resurrection and Eternal Life," 279.

(and Jerry B. Jenkins), the latter having sold tens of millions of copies. This kind of enthusiastic apocalyptic expectation is also widespread among rapidly growing Christian movements and communities in the Global South, both among the church leaders and the lay folks.

The neo-apocalyptic vision of the world is deeply dualistic, dividing the world into evil and good, them and us, enemies and friends. A common hallmark of the Fundamentalist movements in all Abrahamic traditions is the expectation of the terror of Armageddon. Often the advocates of neo-apocalypticism also consider themselves agents of God's righteous judgment, in extreme cases even believing that God authorizes their violent actions.

The theological and ethical liabilities of neo-apocalypticism are obvious given this deep dualism between us and them, good and evil, and its built-in potential for violence. Neo-apocalypticism reads Scripture ideologically in its attempt to justify its own cause and show the falsehood of the other. The neo-apocalyptic eschatological timetable is deterministic, meaning that it is entirely out of our hands, and this may lead to fatalism, the belief in blind fate rather than in God's caring guidance. Furthermore, adherents of neo-apolocalypticism thwart and deny the need to work for the peace of the world, cleaning and caring for the environment, erasing poverty and injustice, and similar good efforts for the improvement of the world, even saying that such efforts only impede the coming of the Day, as will be discussed below.

Plan of the Chapter

The immediately following section briefly introduces scientific visions of the "end" of the cosmos and human life, including clarifications of what is at stake theologically. The ensuing discussion then considers the "hard" question concerning death and its meaning, as well as resurrection as its defeat. Among others, this discussion will raise the difficult question of how to guarantee that the person who dies physically will be the same person as the one to be resurrected in eternity. Yet another hard question concerns the destiny of men and women after death, namely blessedness or damnation—and what kinds of insights and intimations theologians are entertaining to speculate about this vital issue.

Before delving into many details of the final consummation, it is useful to look at the reasons why for many Christians eschatological hope may stifle their energy to care for justice and equality and for the well-being of nature. Another issue has to do with the hope for overcoming evil, suffering, and injustices in the coming of God's kingdom, or what classical terminology calls "theodicy." Speculations regarding the timing and signs of Christ's return and the final coming of God's righteous rule, a topic of much interest even to the first disciples, are taken up next.

In contemporary theology, the question of how to envision the transition from this world to the "new heaven and new earth"—somewhat parallel to each individual's transition in resurrection from the mortal to heavenly body—is one of the most widely debated topics, not least because of the challenges and opportunities presented by science. That question of transition from this world to the next also raises the topic of the necessity of judgment and purification as the condition for a person's entrance into God's kingdom.

From its beginning, Christian theology has imagined an interim period before the final consummation, which it has called the Millennium. I will explore its possibility, nature, and purpose. Having done that, we will be ready to imagine and envision what might be the meaning of heaven, the final end and desire of Christians. Though we may know little about this hoped-for future, it is uplifting to set our eyes upon this lofty goal. A fitting way to wrap up the chapter is to delve into a careful dialogue with eschatological visions and symbols in Judaism, Islam, Buddhism, and Hinduism. Several small-scale comparisons have already been completed earlier in the chapter; this final section seeks to give a more comprehensive vision of these competing eschatological traditions.

What Are the Sciences Saying about the End of Life and the Cosmos?

Scientific Predictions about the "Future" of the Universe

Scientific conjectures about the future are based on our current best knowledge about the cosmos's origins, evolvement, and workings. Since I presented a detailed discussion of scientific cosmology's views of origins in chapter 3, I am not repeating it here.

Due to an almost infinite future time-span, I divide the question of the future into three interrelated time frames:

- the far-distant future (the "end" of the whole cosmos);
- the distant future (the end of the earth, sun, and our solar system); and
- the near future (the end of life conditions on the earth).

With regard to the most distant future of the cosmos, our best estimates are that in 5 billion years, the sun will become a red giant, and that in 40–50 billion years, star formation in our galaxy will have ended. If the universe is closed, then in 10^{12} (i.e., 1,000,000,000,000) years, the universe will have reached its maximum size and will begin to recollapse, back to a singularity like the original hot big bang. And in 10^{34} years, all carbon-based life-forms will inevitably become extinct. The end result is that, ultimately, after an almost inconceivably long period of time, everything will become—nothing.

But what if there are other forms of "life" or platforms other than carbon-based ones that will enable life to continue? Not surprisingly, a number of such proposals have been put forth, but since all of that is currently mere speculation, the topic does not merit discussion here.

What about the distant future prospects, beyond the conditions of life on this earth and in this solar system? Well known and well documented is the possibility of Earth being hit by a comet or asteroid. A familiar example from history is the extinction of dinosaurs (and their environment) due to a comet hitting Earth about 65 million years ago. Be that as it may, in 5 billion years, Earth will be uninhabitable and eventually lifeless. The sun will come to the end of its available hydrogen fuel supply and will begin to swell up and eventually run out of its energy, as it were.

All the above-mentioned conditions are totally out of our human control, as opposed to the relatively significant human factor concerning the more proximate future of this earth and its life conditions. The impending catastrophes facing the future, which, let us be clear, threaten all life on Earth, are well known and well documented, and include pollution, global warming, and the nuclear threat (chapter 3).

Given these scientific predictions, the all-important question now emerges: What is at stake theologically?

Why Should Theology Be Concerned about What the Sciences Are Saying?

Why bother with scientific predictions about the end, in the distant or the near future? The answer is simple: because both the sciences and theology study the same creation—notwithstanding significant differences in methodology and tools. Recall the recommendation in chapter 3 to pursue mutual critical dialogue between the two.

With that in mind, the main challenge to theology is this: How can we even begin to reconcile Christian eschatology's expectation of the *imminent* return of Christ and the bringing about of the "new heaven and new earth" in light of the extremely, almost infinitely long horizons of the sciences? Add to the equation (and the question) the fact that whereas for the sciences this is a "natural" process without any intervention from outside, for theology the driver, so to speak, is the Triune God.

For sure, there are no easy answers to this foundational question! Perhaps the wisest thing for theology to do is to clearly acknowledge this profound challenge and be willing to live in this dynamic tension—and continue practicing conversation with the sciences. As big a temptation as it might be, merely to ignore the scientific challenge is not sufficient! Happily, a growing number of theologians are doing constructive, critical work in this area.

In the meantime, both sides do well to bear in mind that "the idea of a hope after death and an end that fulfills history as a whole is as intrinsic to the Christian tradition as it is foreign to the projects of science."[6] Indeed, this theological conviction sounds incredible not only to most scientists but also to the wider public. Theology's challenge to scientists is that "an unaided scientific account of the world does not succeed in making complete sense of cosmic history,"[7] and that science has no means of reaching beyond the observed world and empirically verified observations.

Now, to the work of thinking through a number of key eschatological issues in Christian tradition, keeping in mind the contributions from the sciences and, later in the discussion, also the visions and opinions of other faiths.

Death and Resurrection: The "Last Enemy" and the "Blessed Hope"

Is Physical Death "Natural" or the Result of the Fall?

It says something about our modern culture in the Global North that a best-selling book since the 1970s has been *The Denial of Death* by the anthropologist and philosopher Ernst Becker. Its main thesis is that humanity fears death and hence seeks to either ignore or overcome it. Death seems to make null and void all hopes of any lasting value. Not surprisingly, modern society has pushed death out of its purview and does everything in its power to deny its reality. And yet, a new academic field named

---

6. Clayton, "Eschatology as Metaphysics," 134.
7. Polkinghorne, "Eschatology," 38.

thanatology has emerged.[8] Furthermore, debates about what constitutes death have been with us for some time.[9]

What makes death unique to humanity is that, differently from all other creatures, we alone have an awareness of the coming to an end of life. As far as we know, animals (similarly to human infants) do not have that capacity. Even if higher animals may experience an instinctual awareness of impending death in danger, only humans can make it a concern and reflect on it. In that light, it is no surprise that hope for life after death is deeply embedded in human evolution. The custom of burials going back at least to the (Middle) Paleolithic age (300,000 to 50,000 years ago) is an indication of that hope.

Early in Christian theology, building on Paul's teaching, death came to be seen as an enemy and as punishment for sin. It was linked tightly to original sin and the fall in Christian tradition. In modern theology, also related to the rise of evolutionary theory, this belief has been replaced by one in the "naturalness" of death, because of the finitude and decay of all created life.

The traditional position of course claimed biblical support. There is no denying that for Paul, the child of his own times, natural death was in view when he wrote Romans 5:12—"as sin came into the world through one man and death through sin, and so death spread to all men because all men sinned"—and 1 Corinthians 15:44-48. Yet we know now that physical death has been the destiny of all created entities, including of humanity, even ages before the fall. And contemporary theology claims that we hardly have any solid biblical basis for the idea of the immortality of humanity before the fall. In modern theology, a correct terminological distinction is made between "natural" death that is not related to sin but to finite nature, and the death of "judgment" that manifests the intensification of the personal feeling toward death in light of the possibility of being cut off from the life of God. In support of this current interpretation, consider Genesis 3, according to which the first couple did not die but rather was expelled from the Garden for having committed the "fatal" transgression; and Ephesians 2:1, that "you were dead through the trespasses and sins"; here Paul is obviously speaking to those who are still physically alive!

All that said, the idea of death as "natural"—while true in principle—has to be handled with care and qualified theologically. The Catholic catechism puts this seemingly paradoxical statement in perspective: "Even though man's nature is mortal God had destined him not to die" (1.3.11.2, para. 1008).

---

8. For an overview of thanatology, see "Thanatology."
9. Montoya, "What Is Death, Exactly," n.p.

Second, while inevitable, death is nonetheless seen as an "enemy" (1 Cor 15:26). In the OT, death means separation from God (Ps 88:5).

So, Christian theology should "understand death as a necessary companion of life, and its actual presupposition,"[10] yet as something to be defeated because it is the "last enemy" (1 Cor 15:26). Although all created life necessarily comes to an end, Christian faith envisions a world in which death, as the final enemy, will be destroyed, and in which God, as the giver of life, grants eternal life as a gift. Death then is "natural" only in the sense that no creature can avoid it in our kind of world.

A related issue, or set of issues, has to do with what traditional theology names the "intermediate state": that is, what, if anything, happens between my personal physical death and the resurrection of all at the end? It is only because of the limitations of our human minds that we have to take one topic at a time although several of them are part of the same concern, namely how to envision the transition from physical death to God's eternity in resurrected life.

Is There an "Interval" between My Death and the Resurrection of All?

The beginning point for considering what, if anything, awaits us after our physical death is the following dynamic: On the one hand, physical death means nothing less than bringing to an end all of the human person and his or her life. Period. On the other hand, in light of Christian hope, this statement has to be qualified with the equally important thesis that "God is the future of the finite from which it again receives its existence as a whole."[11] In other words, physical death is both the end, and the transition to life eternal.

A related theological concern is that all talk about the completion of one's personal destiny in the eschaton has to be linked tightly with the common destiny of other human beings (and of course, the whole of creation). Recall our definition above of eschatology as encompassing the hope for both each person and the rest of God's creation.

With these two caveats in mind, several guiding principles for thinking about what might come "after" physical death can be outlined. First, the earthly "body," that is, the whole human person, has to undergo a radical change, without losing the person's identity. Second, what makes me the person I am—my human identity—is kept in God's "memory" despite the

10. Schwarz, *Eschatology*, 253.
11. Pannenberg, *Systematic Theology* 3:607.

"gap" between my entrance into eternity and the general resurrection of all. Third, because God in his eternity is on both sides of death whereas we are time-bound, "all individuals go into eternity at the moment of death," and "yet it is only at the end of the age that all those who sleep in Christ receive in common by the Spirit of God the being-for-self of the totality of their existence that is preserved in God, and thus live with all others before God."[12] Fourth, because we are "constituted by relation to God,"[13] even death is not able to separate us from God and God's love (Rom 8:38–39). If there is any meaning to an intermediate state, it is that "God [is] holding us fast until the resurrection."[14]

These wider theological considerations are important guides to our thinking, particularly in light of the fact that the Bible does not give us a coherent picture of what happens after physical death. Passages such as Philippians 1:20–24 merely seem to imply some type of continuation of personal life. Other passages can be read as supporting immediate entrance into blessedness at death (2 Cor 5:8; Phil 1:23; 1 Thess 5:10). The biblical data also include a number of references to what became the "soul-sleep" view in tradition (Dan 12:2; Luke 8:52; 1 Cor 15:51; 2 Pet 3:4). Whereas "sleep" entails inactivity, some passages seem to imply conscious activity (particularly the parable in Luke 16:22–23). It seems as if the focus of all these diverse biblical testimonies and metaphors is, first, to assure us that as final and inevitable as death is, it is not the last word; God is. Similarly, they clearly seem to be saying that, second, in no way does the "intermediate" state usurp the bliss of one's eternal destiny. At its best, the "gap" between personal death and general resurrection is temporary, while we await final consummation.

As long as our contemporary reflection on the nature and mode of the intermediate state is in keeping with these general biblical pointers, there is leeway for diverse interpretations. In the most traditional view, what happens at death is the temporary separation between the decaying body and the living soul, which will be reunited at resurrection. I don't see any conclusive objection as to why there couldn't be a temporary non-embodied personal existence—although on earth we know human existence only as embodied. I also wonder if we could think of this period as time for the beginning of healing, transformation, and change—without in any way taking away from the all-important role of resurrection? Theoretical physicist John Polkinghorne puts it well: "We may expect that God's love

---

12. Pannenberg, *Systematic Theology*, 3:606–7.
13. Johnson, *Friends of God*, 194.
14. Grenz, *Theology for the Community*, 597.

will be at work, through the respectful but powerful operation of divine grace, purifying and transforming the souls awaiting resurrection in ways that respect their integrity."[15] Ecumenically speaking, that insight would make it easier for non-Roman Catholics to understand the possibility of the doctrine of purgatory. Could that intuition also correspond to the traditional idea of paradise (or Abraham's bosom) as the "waiting room" for the blessed? (In the traditional view, however, the souls of those on the way to eternal damnation wait in *Hades*, a gateway to hell.)

Speculatively, one might also consider that, if God keeps us during this intermediate state, then the biblically based intuition of some kind of connection between the living and the dead becomes meaningful. Setting aside some unhelpful—and perhaps heretical—beliefs and customs stemming from the medieval period and even before, theologically it is not only permissible but also appropriate to make space, for example, for prayer for the dead. Similarly, there is no reason to exclude their prayer for us.

As said, speculations about the intermediate state are just that—*speculations*—and one's orthodoxy is not measured by them. On the contrary, Christian theology rests confidently in the hope of bodily resurrection in eternal communion with God. That is not contested. What is debated is how best to imagine the transition from "here" (life on earth) to "there" (bodily resurrection in eternity.)

The Dilemma: The Continuity of Personal Identity in Resurrection—and in This Life

Christian tradition agrees that the belief in the resurrection of the body is hope for defeating death in the new creation. As established above, the resurrection of Jesus Christ on the first Easter morning provided the "first fruit," or an anticipation, of the coming new creation in which the power of entropy, ultimate decay and death, is overcome. Christ's resurrection from the dead signals to humanity not only the overcoming of death; it also serves as the paradigm for the whole of creation, as St. Paul explains so eloquently in Romans 8:19–27. Humanity's hope participates in this cosmic hope.

It is significant that already in early Christian theology, "the resurrection was based on a strong understanding of God as Creator, and this led to a strong sense of God's purposes for this material creation and its goodness."[16] The Church Fathers rightly rejected Gnosticism, which could not embrace an eschatological vision related to bodily and earthly realities

---

15. Polkinghorne, *God of Hope*, 111.
16. Wilkinson, *Christian Eschatology*, 103.

because it considered all material evil and impure and only spiritual reality good and pure. Hope for the resurrection of the body decisively defeated this pagan error.

That said, it is one thing to affirm the theological significance of the bodily resurrection in the Christian eschatological vision; it is another thing to intuit how it might happen. In other words, how might we envision the transition from pre-mortem embodied existence (via physical death as well as general resurrection and judgment) to postmortem "physical" resurrection existence in the new creation—particularly when the person of whom we are speaking has to be the same person? This is a major challenge for all thinking Christians, and understandably more than one solution to this question has been offered. It all boils down to the question of the continuity of personal identity. Ironically, this conundrum is not made easier by the commonsense observation that even in this life continuity is somewhat mysterious. How do we know that I am the same person now at the writing of these lines as I was over sixty-four years ago at the time of my birth? My personal continuity cannot be a matter of material continuity since atoms are in constant flux through wear and tear.

Some of the best human minds have long pondered this problem of identity persistence in this life. The two standard philosophical tactics are the "memory criterion" that, beyond mere memory, points to complex mental functions as the key, and the "bodily criterion," that is, this person can be considered to be identical with that person if and only if they have the same body throughout the person's life. Yet although neither one alone, or both together, suffices because the demand that there be continuous brain activity in order to ensure the psychical structure supporting mental properties cannot be met in resurrection, a related version of this perhaps can point in the right direction. This version we might call "consciousness continuity," or to be more precise, "self-consciousness continuity," that is the ability to have a first-person perspective, in other words, the capacity to be self-reflective. Such a capacity has to be assumed in order for a person to have judgment, experience and offer forgiveness, and feel a sense of responsibility. But even that alone hardly suffices. Hence, something more is needed, and above all that "more" is "character formation." More than mere moral-ethical integrity, such character formation has to do with practices and virtues. By placing individuals in the wider context of communities that shape us and essential relationships, we have now considerably advanced the pursuit of identity continuity in this life.

But, as I hinted earlier, things become even more complex when speaking of the problem of continuity between this life and the hoped-for bodily resurrection. Interestingly enough, the problem was already clearly acknowledged in early theology. What can be conveniently called the "anthropology of composition" became a fairly standard view in patristic theology: once the body decays at death, on the last day God reassembles it from the last constitutive material particles available and rejoins it with the soul that did not die. The Fathers were aware of obvious problems such as death by cannibalism or at sea, instances in which there would be no traces of the deceased person's material body available, and so they sought creative solutions. A more sophisticated solution came from the medieval master Thomas Aquinas in his idea of the "soul as the form of the body." In that model, the soul has a role something like an architect's plan. With the right materials ("body"), the plan ("soul") can be worked out; neither one alone suffices. This is a very helpful idea and a number of contemporary theologians have acknowledged its basically correct intuitions.

Without downplaying any of these insights, something more is needed when considering postmortem continuity. Not surprisingly, a number of sophisticated and competing options have been proposed in contemporary philosophy and philosophical theology, the discussion of which, however, would require philosophical learning way beyond a theological primer. Let us instead seek for some key biblical-theological resources.

The Solution: God's Faithfulness and Creative Power

The starting point for all inquiries into the possibility of the resurrection of the body has to be Paul's note of the "change" (1 Cor 15:51). Change refers neither to total replacement nor to replication. Another critical theological insight is the theology of the human being as the image of God, which signals our relatedness to and contingency on God. The moment the divine life-giving Spirit is taken away, all creaturely life comes to an end (Ps 104:29–30).

The personal identity that defines me as a person cannot be "transferred" from this earthly life to the afterlife with my own innate powers; divine faithfulness and creative power are needed. What will transition from here to there is the "whole package" of what has made me the person I am. The judgment of my life, and its reconciliation, will be based on my capacity to recognize myself as the actor of the deeds attributed to me, and on the quality of my character both at the personal and at the communal level.

What about the physical body in this regard? There is no denying that in this life my body, and more widely myself as an embodied person, is the platform for me as this person, including my mental, social, and other experiences. But because the human being is a "person" rather than a "material object," "there is no reason *in principle* why a body that is numerically distinct but similar in all relevant aspects could not support the same personal characteristics."[17]

In any case, my physical composition changes several times during my lifetime (albeit gradually rather than instantly, as in resurrection). A temporal interval (however that may be understood) does not in principle frustrate the continuity of identity. Indeed, for "new creation" to be *new*, the "matter" (body, physicality) must be different from the earthly body (notwithstanding the continuity to the point that it still makes sense to speak of "body" rather than merely "spirit").

I find very useful the late John Polkinghorne's way of speaking of the "how" of the continuity of identity in the transition from here to there in terms of "the almost infinitely complex, information-bearing pattern in which the matter of the body is organized at any one time." This is basically what the traditional soul-language means to convey.[18] In that regard, Aquinas's hylomorphic account of human nature mentioned above intuited something similar, notwithstanding his vastly different intellectual context. Using the concept of an information-bearing pattern, it can be stated that "the faithful God will remember the pattern that is me and re-embody it in the eschatological act of resurrection." Polkinghorne elaborates: "In making this assertion, I want to affirm the intrinsically embodied character of human being, without supposing that the flesh and blood of this world represents the only possible form that embodiment might take."[19]

Consider also the fact that "what takes place in time can never be lost so far as God's eternity is concerned. To God all things that were are always present, and as what has been they are present in the totality of their existence." The conclusion to this is that "the identity of creatures needs no continuity of their being on the time line but is insured by the fact that their existence is not lost in God's eternal present."[20] Moltmann puts it succinctly: "God's relationship to people is a dimension of their existence which they do not lose even in death."[21]

So far we have talked about resurrection as the anchor of Christian hope. But as is well-known, Christian theology envisions more than one type of religious end for humans. That complicated and sensitive topic we will tackle next.

17. Murphy, "Resurrection Body," 214–15.
18. Polkinghorne, "Anthropology," 98.
19. Polkinghorne, "Anthropology," 99–100.
20. Pannenberg, *Systematic Theology*, 3:606.
21. Moltmann, *Coming of God*, 76.

Who Will Be Saved—and Who Will Not?

Do We Really Still Have to Believe in Hell?

Eternal Damnation in Traditional and Modern Thought

All Abrahamic traditions and even Asiatic faiths engaged in this book, albeit in their own distinctive ways, endorse the doctrine of hell as an unparalleled eschatological suffering and penalty. The mainline Jewish belief is that those who do not obey Yahweh, along with heretics and the like, should prepare for eternal judgment. The destiny of gentiles is disputed. Similarly to modern Christian tradition, among Jews there are diametrically opposed beliefs about the reality of hell—for and against. Islam has unusually rich traditions about hell. Against common misconceptions, even the two Asiatic faiths affirm hell and consider it necessary, if not for other reasons, then because karma/kamma alone makes it so; however, it is not the most ultimate destiny.

Among Christians, both advocates and opponents freely grant strong biblical support for what became the Christian doctrine of hell (Isa 66:15–16; Jer 7:30–34; Joel 3:1–2; Matt 13:42, 49–50; 22:13; and Synoptic parallels; 2 Thess 1:9; Jude 7; Rev 14:10–11).[22]

That said, despite its wide, indeed almost universal attestation, there is no single Christian understanding of hell. What might be called the "traditional" understanding includes the following arguments:

- it is for punishment for sins in earthly life and refusal to receive forgiveness from God;
- it is a final judgment from which there is no escape once executed;
- at least part of humanity will end up there; and
- it is at least in some sense a form of conscious existence.

An important alternative model denies the eternity of hell (in terms of unending existence). That version fits both universalism, according to which after one has suffered for a period of time in hell, one will be saved, and annihilationism, which teaches the ultimate destruction (coming to an end) of those who are not believers.

While the two destinies were almost universally embraced in early theology, hell was not in any way the focus of early Christians' hope for the

---

22. The Greek transliteration *gehenna* comes from the Hebrew *ge hinnom*, a valley south of Jerusalem where garbage was brought and children were sacrificed to Molech in fire (2 Kgs 16:3; 2 Chr 28:3; 33:6).

future. Rather, they "portrayed an optimistic certainty concerning salvation and focused much more on heaven as a desirable state to reach."[23] Early creeds make no mention of hell. Only after the establishment of Christianity as a state religion with unprecedented mass conversions and a rapid increase of nominalism did the need to highlight the reality of perdition give the topic increasing significance. By the Middle Ages, occupation with hell had become an intensive matter.

To no one's surprise, Enlightenment criticism was particularly harsh toward any idea of anyone suffering in hell. What about contemporary theology? The following kinds of broad principles can be discerned: First, physical punishment and suffering are not an integral or necessary part of the doctrine. Metaphors such as the "gnashing of teeth" and similar in the Bible are just that: *metaphors*. Second, punishment does not have to be the primary motif of hell, although it is certainly one aspect of it in biblical testimonies. The logic of hell may be supported by other forms of justice, such as restorative justice and the irrevocability of human freedom. Third, the position that hell will be "densely populated" should not be the default position; rather, our desire and prayer should be that as few as possible be found there. Fourth, making hell an absolutely unending form of damnation to all may not be the only alternative. And finally, although normally one's eternal destiny is sealed at the moment of death, one could also imagine some kind of possibility of purification and preparation before final consummation.

The Logic of Hell—For and Against

Typical objections to hell are concisely listed by the late John Hick:

> [F]or a conscious creature to undergo physical and mental torture through unending time . . . is horrible and disturbing beyond words; and the thought of such torment being deliberately inflicted by divine decree is totally incompatible with the idea of God as infinite love; the absolute contrast of heaven and hell, entered immediately after death, does not correspond to the innumerable gradations of human good and evil; justice could never demand for finite human sins the infinite penalty of eternal pain; such unending torment could never serve any positive or reformative purpose precisely because it never ends; and it renders any coherent christian [sic] theodicy

---

23. Schwarz, *Eschatology*, 399–400.

impossible by giving the evils of sin and suffering an eternal lodgment within God's creation.[24]

As weighty as these and related rebuttals of hell might be, understandably the advocates of hell are not easily convinced by the force of these arguments—if not for other reasons, then for its prevalence in the biblical teaching. But even they who advocate the possibility of hell have to face the obvious biblical dynamic: one can easily find passages that warn us of the possibility of eternal damnation (Matt 18:8–9; 25:41; Mark 9:43–48; Luke 16:26) and passages that carry some kind of a "universalist" orientation (Rom 5:18; 11:32; 1 Cor 15:22, 28; 1 Tim 2:4).

Perhaps the theologically most responsible way to approach this is to affirm both types of passages, rather than pitting them against each other. Yet, it seems to mainstream theology that in the NT "we notice that the tenor is not one of universal homecoming but of a twofold outcome of human history, namely acceptance and rejection." The NT seems to make the human response a condition. Hence, the "universalistic message would contradict the NT's insistence that our response to the gospel determines our final destiny."[25]

Assuming two destinies poses severe philosophical and theological challenges, the most serious of which is perhaps the seeming conflict between hell and divine love and goodness. To negotiate that dilemma, the argument of the Eastern fathers that "God did not create hell: it was created by humans for themselves [is particularly important]. The source of eschatological torment is the will of those humans who are unable to partake in God's love, to feel God's love as a source of joy and blessedness."[26] At the same time, "God does everything he can to save all persons, short of destroying their freedom."[27] With these insights in mind, it is important to attempt to hold in a dynamic tension the love of God and human freedom. A useful insight comes from the Brazilian Catholic theologian Leonardo Boff, who claims that the "human person has absolute value: he can say *no* to God. He can decide alone for his future which centers around himself and his navel" (emphasis original).[28] Along similar lines, Polkinghorne adds that although "God's offer of mercy and forgiveness is not withdrawn at death," because God's love lasts forever, it is also the case

---

24. Hick, *Death and Eternal Life*, 200–201.
25. Schwarz, *Eschatology*, 346.
26. Alfeyev, "Eschatology," 113–14.
27. Walls, *Hell*, 87, 103; also 88, 93.
28. Boff, *Was kommt nachher*, 75, my translation.

that "no one will be carried into the kingdom of heaven against their will by an empowering act of divine power."[29]

The other major alternatives are annihilation/conditional immortality and universalism. These we consider next.

What If, after Some Suffering, the Sinner Simply Ceases to Exist?

An innovative view concerning the destiny of those who chose not to believe in God has emerged in the twentieth century. It is called annihilationism and/or conditional immortality. "Annihilationism" means that after the last judgment—and perhaps after having spent some time in hell (which is not eternal in that outlook)—the person simply ceases to exist. The point of "Conditional Immortality" is that only believers will live eternally in communion with God; in other words, one's eternal life depends on faith.

Annihilationists believe that their view is in keeping with human persons' freedom. The biblical support for annihilationism comes from the numerous allusions in the Bible, both OT and NT, to the effect that the "wicked" face destruction at the end (Ps 37:9-10; Mal 4:1; Matt 3:10-12; Phil 3:19; 2 Thess 1:9; 2 Pet 3:7; Rev 20:14-15). Opponents are of course quick to appeal to other biblical texts that seem to support the idea of the ultimate finality of hell (Matt 25:46; Rev 14:9-11; 20:10; among others).

Much is at stake with the interpretation of the term "eternal" (Greek *aionios*). Although there used to be a strong case for understanding *aionios* to mean less than "eternal," in recent years the tide has turned. The general scholarly consensus no longer supports the idea that rather than being everlasting, eternity means something like "final" [judgment]. Furthermore, some critics have also noted that the idea of simply passing out of existence is not particularly comforting to many people.

What If All Are Saved?

Universalism—aka universal salvation or the restoration of all things (*apokatastasis panton*[30])—is undoubtedly the most vividly and widely disputed concept in Christian eschatology. It did not arise until the third century and is routinely attributed to Origen. His main argument is twofold: that at the end all things will be restored to their original state and all things will be subjected to the lordship of Christ; Origen's most often-cited biblical

---

29. Polkinghorne, *God of Hope*, 136.
30. The noun *apokatastasis* occurs only once in the New Testament: Acts 3:21.

passage in support of this view is 1 Corinthians 15:22–28. At the end, even hell will be destroyed.

Although other noted early theologians proposed ideas that either taught universalism or echoed that orientation, universalism encountered strong opposition—notwithstanding early theology's great interest in and hope for postmortem salvation. Augustine's strict doctrine of predestination led him to assure two destinies and reject universalism, and the latter was officially condemned by the church. Most creeds and confessions all the way through Reformation times ruled against universalism and in favor of two destinies.

Again, not surprisingly, only at the time of the Enlightenment and modernity did universalism gain significant support. Ironically, the strong critic of modernity's theology, Karl Barth, ended up embracing a form of universalism, not for liberal reasons, but due to his robust Christocentrism. Because Christ as our representative has already experienced the judgment of God against sin and, as a result sinful humanity, and has been raised to new life, there will be no more condemnation.

Among contemporary theologians, the most forceful and nuanced defense of universalism comes from Moltmann. He argues that:

- divine grace is more powerful than human sinfulness;
- God's loving and compassionate desire to save is able to overcome the sinner's resistance;
- at stake is "confidence in God: what God wants to do he can do, and will do," that is, salvation rather than condemnation—otherwise ultimately human destiny is left in the hands of the human;[31] and
- "if *the double outcome of judgment* is proclaimed, the question is then: Why did God create human beings if he is going to damn most of them in the end, and will only redeem the least part of them?"[32]

Not surprisingly, religious pluralists support universalism with their own distinctive arguments. Gleaning from the Enlightenment ideals of the common essence of religions that leads to the idea of a "rough parity" of all faiths, any demand to subscribe to a particular kind of tradition as a precondition for salvation is compromised or outright rejected. Hick's pluralistic universalism is well known. On top of rejecting any claims for the unique role of Christ as the door to salvation and similar pluralistic orientations, talk about hell and judgment lost its traditional legacy. He

---

31. Moltmann, *Coming of God*, 244.
32. Moltmann, *Coming of God*, 239.

argues that "since man has been created by God for God, and is basically oriented toward him, there is no final opposition between God's saving will and our human nature acting in freedom."[33]

On the other side, reasons against universalisms include the following, along with numerous biblical references to two destinies:

- the argument from free will cannot imagine that God, the giver of freedom, will overrule the human person who wishes to choose otherwise;
- "the point of no return" argument says that although God is patiently waiting for repentance, physical death constitutes a final boundary mark;
- the argument from justice simply means that if everybody ends up in the same eternal destiny, all demands of justice and fairness may be in danger of compromise; and
- the pastoral and missiological argument opposes universalism for the obvious reason that it has the potential of making Christian outreach and discipline meaningless.

In sum: notwithstanding the rise of universalism in various forms in contemporary theology, it is still a fairly marginal phenomenon as a stated opinion, even if it echoes many sensibilities and intuitions of a large number of contemporary Christians.

The Possibility of Two Destinies Coupled with the "Optimism of Salvation"

Generally speaking, the possibility of two destinies continues to be the standard theological opinion among most churches and theologians. The possibility of hell in some form or another, at least for some who willfully have turned their backs on God, is still the most widely held view. Annihilationism is not widely known and universalism, as said, is a fairly marginal opinion.

At the same time, a growing number of theologians and church leaders are also rediscovering the importance of some glimmers of hope for those who might be considered outsiders to God's kingdom. Notwithstanding the great number of direct and indirect references to hell and eternal damnation, there is also a radical widening in the offer of salvation in NT passages

---

33. Hick, *Death and Eternal Life*, 254.

such as Matthew 8:11–12, in which Jesus says: "I tell you, many will come from east and west and sit at table with Abraham, Isaac, and Jacob in the kingdom of heaven, while the sons of the kingdom will be thrown into the outer darkness; there men will weep and gnash their teeth." The passage seems to be saying that those who take for granted their entrance into God's kingdom—be it Israelites or Christians—may face condemnation, whereas pagans (non-Jews) or non-Christians may be included.

Recall also the Roman Catholic "inclusivistic" attitude (discussed in chapter 2) toward those who for no reasons of their own have never heard the Gospel but might still be saved. In distinction to "exclusivists," to whom only conscious faith in Christ saves and "pluralists" to whom all religions are equally salvific, inclusivists believe that many non-Christians seeking for God and living to the best of their knowledge might be saved because of the universal salvific effects of Christ.

In light of these considerations, it is useful to follow the distinction between "strong" and "hopeful" universalism: whereas the former assumes "universal salvation," the latter hopes that as few as possible will find themselves suffering eternal punishment.[34] The late Canadian Baptist Clark Pinnock coined the term "optimism of salvation." Says Pinnock: "The God we love and trust is not One to be satisfied until there is a healing of the nations and an innumerable host of redeemed people around his throne." This as opposed to the "fewness doctrine," according to which only a small number of people will be saved.[35]

On the basis of biblical teaching and Christian tradition, not much more can be claimed conclusively. The Orthodox bishop Kallistos Ware puts it well: "Our belief in human freedom means that we have no right to categorically affirm, 'All *must* be saved.' But our faith in God's love makes us dare to *hope* that all will be saved. . . . Hell exists as a possibility because free will exists."[36] There is also a further reason to link heaven ("salvation") and hell closely together, one that has to do with the ancient biblical and creedal doctrine of Christ's descent into hell.

---

34. Parry and Partridge, *Universal Salvation*, xx–xxii.

35. Pinnock, *Wideness in God's Mercy*, terms "optimism of salvation" and "fewness doctrine" introduced on 13, quotation from 19.

36. Ware, "Dare We Hope," 215.

What Does Christ's Descent into Hell Have to Do with the Question of Eternal Salvation?

Although the biblical basis for it is scant, Christ's descent into hell became a vibrant topic in patristic theology and Christian spirituality. Except for the two references in 1 Peter (3:18–20; 4:6), which in themselves have stirred a lot of debate, the NT leaves us with fairly little. In that light, it is surprising that the descent of Christ into hell is part of the Apostles' Creed.

Both in Catholic and in Orthodox traditions, the descent into hell was originally related mainly to the deliverance of the OT righteous ones, but it soon became "an expression of the universal significance of Christ's death for salvation," encompassing all deceased before the coming of Christ.[37] It is hard to contest the fact that "the natural reading of 1 Peter . . . is that Jesus's preaching is to the disobedient, and that preaching is meant to lead to penitence."[38]

The late Reformed theologian Donald Bloesch coined the term "divine perseverance," which expresses this hope in contemporary theology. The view

> holds that God in his love does not abandon any of his people to perdition but pursues them into the darkness of sheol or hell, thereby keeping open the opportunity for salvation. . . . God's grace penetrates the barrier of death, thus kindling the hope of conversions beyond the pale of death.[39]

Bloesch is not advocating universalism but instead acknowledges that various kinds of hopeful expectations can be based on this model.

Theologically, Christ's proclamation and releasing work can be seen as dramatic expressions of the victory over death and the underworld in light of the Pauline statement: "Death is swallowed up in victory" (1 Cor 15:54). By the inclusion of this statement in the creed, the church meant "not only to indicate that Christ has triumphed over all possible dimensions, even over that dimension where death usually reigns, but also to express something of the divine compassion."[40]

Before delving into many exciting topics regarding the final consummation of Christian eschatological hope (and after that the visions of afterlife among other religions), let us pause for a short while to wonder whether too much emphasis on hope for an afterlife might be detrimental to our

---

37. Pannenberg, *Systematic Theology*, 3:616.
38. Ward, *Religion and Human Nature*, 273.
39. Bloesch, *Last Things*, 40.
40. Schwarz, *Christology*, 294.

commitment toward our current responsibilities. I raised this question tentatively at the beginning of the chapter—and responded to it negatively. Now, it is time to redeem that promise!

Would Eschatological Hope Stifle Work toward Improvement of This World?

Can Hope for the Future and Work for Justice and Equality Be Integrated?

Some say that eschatology may not be at all helpful when thinking about the huge problems our world is facing right now, from poverty and malnutrition, to wars and conflicts, to impending ecocatastrophes. How helpful is it for the well-being and flourishing of nature to await the final judgment and establishment of a new heaven and new earth? No wonder liberationists do not typically discuss eschatology at any length. Some female theologians have also rejected the idea of personal survival in the resurrected body in eternity on the basis of its alleged anti-liberationist and egoistic tones.

While carefully listening to such viewpoints, it can be argued that the reconciliation of peoples and societies ultimately requires the reconciliation of the basic relationship between the individual and society. Although efforts toward that end should be doggedly pursued, it may only happen finally at the eschaton with the coming of God's righteous rule. In this regard, Christian vision is superior to secular and (merely) political dreams, including atheist Marxism-Leninism. In fact, the Marxist dream of a just society never materialized, based as it was on human resources alone. And more importantly: even if it were to happen by earthly means, it would only relate to that particular generation—never to countless generations that have already passed away.

Knowing that the ultimate reconciliation of peoples and groups can only happen in a new creation does not lead the church into passivity, let alone apathy. The church is participating in the work for liberation and justice precisely because it knows that in so doing it is participating in the work of the Trinitarian God. The missionary church participates in the liberative work for its own sake: after all, helping people in need is a Christian "thing." At the same time, "being aware that all of its efforts are at best patchwork, bandages on the wounds of a hurting world, the church also witnesses with its action to a world that will be without anguish and suffering."[41] In sum:

---

41. Schwarz, *Eschatology*, 371.

rather than fostering passivity and apathy, Christian hope for the future, God's future, inspires commitment to liberation.

Can Eschatological Hope and Care for the Environment Be Integrated?

Those who criticize eschatology for its alleged otherworldly focus and thus for causing Christians to become complacent about the future of the environment certainly have a point to make when listening to statements by Christian Fundamentalists and their ilk:

> Why care about the earth when the droughts, floods, and pestilence brought by ecological collapse are signs of the Apocalypse foretold in the Bible? Why care about global climate change when you and yours will be rescued in the Rapture? And why care about converting from oil to solar when the same God who performed the miracle of the loaves and fishes can whip up a few billion barrels of light crude with a Word?... Natural-resource depletion and overpopulation, then, are not concerns for End-Timers—and nor are other ecological catastrophes.[42]

With these kinds of statements in mind, there is no ignoring "the existence of a powerful, well-financed group of Evangelical Fundamentalist Christians who deny the scientific evidence for global warming, climate change and the consequent need for urgent action."[43]

Speaking not only of these kinds of extreme views but Christian eschatology at large, the critics sought to refocus "eschatology from the distant future ('unrealized eschatology') to the here-and-now ('realised eschatology')." At the same time, they "have shifted the thematic centre from humanity, as the apex of creation, to creation itself, with humanity removed from centre stage to a supporting position."[44]

There is much to be appreciated in this concern about eschatology—and unambiguous rejection of the Fundamentalist misconceptions. Similarly, any form of escapism with reference to what God is doing in the future as the pretext for our ignoring of current efforts to save the environment should be condemned. At the same time, mainstream theology has also much that is

---

42. Scherer, "Christian-Right Views," para. 17.

43. Greene, "Evangelical Fundamentalists," abstract. On the Fundamentalist rejection of science, see Pigliucci, "Science and Fundamentalism."

44. Karras, "Eschatology," 243.

positive to show in defense of a proper eschatological expectation as the way to empower rather than stifle care for God's good creation.

Unfortunately, the critics of eschatology in relation to environment seem to totally ignore—or, even worse: be ignorant of—the growing Christian concern for nature and environment. Developments such as "Green theology," which advocates for robust work to enable nature's flourishing, are promising and far-reaching. Fortunately, in contrast to Fundamentalist-Conservative Christians' desire to abandon the Climate Act and their resistance to climate scientists' unanimous global warnings about an impending natural catastrophe, mainline Protestant and Anglican/Episcopal denominations, as well as the Roman Catholic Church, have strongly denounced any departure from environmental care, such as, for example, President Donald J. Trump's withdrawal of the US from the Paris Agreement; even major Jewish, Muslim, and Hindu organizations joined in condemning that withdrawal. Consider also the Holy Father Francis's "green" encyclical's opening words: "LAUDATO SI', mi' Signore"—"'Praise be to you, my Lord.' In the words of this beautiful canticle, Saint Francis of Assisi reminds us that our common home is like a sister with whom we share our life and a beautiful mother who opens her arms to embrace us."[45] The Pope laments that "this sister"—nature—"now cries out to us because of the harm we have inflicted on her by our irresponsible use and abuse of the goods with which God has endowed her."[46]

Furthermore, it is highly suspicious to claim that building merely a this-worldly, human-made hope for the future of creation would *necessarily* deliver a nature-affirming lifestyle, as many critics of eschatology claim. Recall that in scientific accounts, ultimately, though very slowly, the earth, life, and the entire cosmos will ultimately come to naught. Without eschatological hope, Christian theology has nothing to offer beyond what we know now.

As established, most broadly, a Christian eschatological vision includes not only human and cosmic hope but also hope for nature, the environment. This kind of hope-filled expectation may provide a superior incentive for working toward preservation of the earth in anticipation of the "new heaven and a new earth."

Beyond the injustice and violence in society and the impending ecocatastrophe, Christian eschatology also has to wrestle with the foundational and ancient problem of evil and suffering—and whether there is

---

45. Pope Francis, *Laudato Si*, para. 1.
46. Pope Francis, *Laudato Si*, para. 2.

any solution in view. This is classically named the problem of theodicy, and to this we turn next.

Will Evil and Suffering Ever Be Overcome?
Wrestling with the Problem of Theodicy

Truly, the mystery of evil is not only a pressing philosophical-ethical conundrum; it is also a profound challenge to all theistic faiths, particularly Abrahamic traditions that insist on God's fairness, love, and goodness. Early modern atheists saw this clearly and did not hold back from attacking Christianity for its alleged incapacity to offer a solution—failing to see at the same time that evil and suffering are also problems for atheists, albeit differently.

In Christian understanding, the overcoming of evil can only be fully discussed in the context of the End, although it also has to do with the doctrine of creation. The reason is simple and obvious: until the End, it looks as if there is simply a great deal of innocent, random, and purposeless suffering and evil in the world.

Having discussed suffering and pain in nature when we explored the doctrine of creation in chapter 3 and the flourishing of human life against the horizon of created life as vulnerable and decaying in theological anthropology in chapter 4, we now continue the same themes particularly with regard to eschatology and with a focus on what in classical philosophy and theology is called theodicy. Theodicy refers to attempts to defend the goodness and love of God, the Creator and Provider, in a world full of suffering, pain, and decay.

Theodicy is a highly complex issue, and the basic theological question about it has to do with negotiating three kinds of claims, namely that:

- God is perfectly good,
- God is omnipotent, and
- evil exists.

Negotiating these three claims can result in vastly different solutions; that is the classic dilemma of theodicy. Unless one is willing to pay the price for compromising any of the three—all almost universally assumed to be givens, at least in the Abrahamic traditions—one must tolerate a dynamic tension between them.

In order to make sense and provide a "big picture" of the complex reflections on theodicy in Christian theology, I turn to the helpful template that the late John Hick famously suggested decades ago in naming two ways of interpretation, namely the Augustinian and the Irenaean.[47] For the Augustinian tradition (which basically means the Christian West) evil is merely a "privation," a lack of goodness. It does not really exist—notwithstanding the reality of the *experience* of suffering and pain. Ultimately only good exists. Not only is the world very good because of God's creation, but the principle of plenitude even helps explain the presence of evil (in that it maximizes good's plenitude). Along with privation, the key claim of the Augustinian view is that evil's origin is linked tightly with the human abuse of the God-given (and intrinsically good) capacity for making choices resulting in the fall. Even nature's suffering can be traced to human fall, which caused death (as in Rom 5:21).

The major alternative is the originally Irenaean "world as vale of soul-making" tradition. This Eastern Church's view of humanity can also be called "teleological" or "developmental." Rather than perfected beings, humanity is on a long path of development toward maturity. In that process, evil, suffering, and other troubles help to cultivate humans' character. Thus, negative experiences serve higher teleological purposes. In that sense, as some later followers of the Irenaean model suggest, evil is God-willed in serving as an instrument for testing and maturity.

Hick himself follows the Irenaean way. He rightly critiques the outdated features of the Augustinian model, including a literalist understanding of the fall as a cause for physical death, and particularly its desire to absolve the Creator from responsibility, making evil merely a matter of human disobedience. In so doing Hick significantly advances the discussion.

At the same time, Hick's proposal is problematic in that making *all* evil a matter of maturity can only ever be a partial explanation. Undoubtedly, there is (much?) evil that has little to do with the maturity of any being, evil that is ruthlessly destructive and damaging to persons and communities. Hick's final vision is also too narrow, as he only considers evil and suffering from a human perspective. What about nature and cosmos and the needed coming of the kingdom of God to bring about a new earth and new heaven?

In this regard, what strikes me about the most well-known biblical account of evil, namely Job's narrative, is that human suffering is put in the wider context of nature's beauty and wonder, as well as its suffering (read chapters 38 and 39). The close linking of human destiny—including evil and suffering—to that of the nature and the cosmos helps us correct yet

---

47. Hick, *Evil and the God of Love*.

another major liability in tradition. That is the linking of evil and suffering to human sin, indeed, making the fall the main culprit, as Augustine famously established. Whatever connection there might be between sin and suffering, it seems to me nonsensical to make that in any way the main explanation for earthquakes, floods, and other nature catastrophes, as well as animal suffering. The four billion year-long evolutionary history of our own planet alone would disqualify any proposal which would wait until the last seconds of the timeline, as it were, for the appearance of humankind and its sinfulness as the reason for suffering.

Only at the End Will We Know Everything!

Yes, it will take us until the End to find a resolution to this fundamental challenge facing the lives of humans and the cosmos. From Augustine we could learn that evil is basically not real in itself, but parasitic on good. God created the world good; evil is deviation from it. Evil is a later intrusion into God's world, as the early chapters of the Bible seem to suggest.

Although neither the exercise of human will nor human corruption can be made solely responsible for evil and suffering—not even in human life, as illustrated by rampant innocent suffering not caused by humans, let alone in the life of nature—theology should consider carefully the role of free will, such as the understanding developed by the American philosopher Alvin Plantinga. He rebuts the atheistic charge that it is impossible for God and evil to coexist in any possible world. Simply put, the critics say, a good, omnipotent, omniscient God would want to prevent evil and be able to do so. To counter this objection to theism, Plantinga argues that it is not impossible to think that God would allow evil for a good and honorable purpose, in this case for bringing about independent, conscious beings endowed with freedom of choice. Free choice of course entails its misuse.[48]

Where Plantinga errs is that (following Augustine) he seeks to absolve God of responsibility, assuming that free, independent creatures rather than the Creator are to be held ultimately responsible for allowing evil's presence in God's world. Unless God is held responsible, dualism follows—meaning that ultimately there will be two "powers" or "realities" at the End instead of one, and the question of the ultimate reality of the world will not be resolved even eschatologically. In Christian faith—and more widely speaking, in Abrahamic traditions—God will be all in all at the End! Having decided to create this kind of world and these independent creatures, God assumed the responsibility for suffering and the misuse of

---

48. Plantinga, *God, Freedom, and Evil*.

freedom. The kind of evolutionary world we know entails growth and decline, pain and joy. It is a world filled with death and decay, suffering and pain, as well as violence and cruelty. Happily, we know from the biblical testimonies that God, the Creator, did not shirk responsibility for evil and suffering. Rather, according to the biblical testimony, God, in the suffering of his Son, embraced evil and made sin his own.

Making God responsible for sin, however, should not lead theology to the conclusion that God in any way ordained sin. Nor should we say that God wills sin any more than, say, a medical doctor wishes a car accident in order to undertake surgery. On the contrary, in a world like ours, car accidents—negative and bad events in themselves—happen, and surgery is a way to "redeem" many of their bodily results.

At the same time, we also have to handle with great care the Irenaean-Hickian insistence on the pedagogical and sanctifying role of suffering. Although no one contests the occasional redemptive value of suffering and pain, the limitations of that argument are severe and well known. First of all, it seems that much less (and much less random) suffering and pain would deliver the same results. Furthermore, this reasoning hardly helps explain natural catastrophes and much violence and pain.

Ultimately, the eschatological coming of the kingdom of God also brings about the needed resolution that avoids dualism: Only God remains at the end; evil does not, for it will have been defeated. God will rectify all wrongs and bring about peace and joy.

Christian theodicy also raises questions about how this vision of the overcoming of evil may relate to hope in other faith traditions. To that topic we turn next.

How Other Abrahamic Religions Respond to the Challenges of Evil and Suffering

All religions, as well as secularism, are bound to offer some explanations for the presence of suffering and evil in relation to Ultimate Reality. That said, each religious tradition accounts for its own specific kinds of evil. Particularly pertinent is the challenge of theodicy among Abrahamic traditions. Hence, this brief discussion is limited to them.

As will be discussed below, the rise of Jewish eschatology is widely attributed to the theodicy question, as the conviction arose that final resolution of innocent suffering could only occur in the life to come. The sheer amount and absurdity of suffering, not only at Auschwitz but also throughout Israel's existence, makes the issue a burning one. Although the earlier part of the OT sees evil as the result of disobedience, in the later parts, final retribution and vindication are relegated to the eschatological future and "new covenant." Think merely of the testimony of Job: it offers a decisive rebuttal to the idea that good people will be rewarded and bad people penalized. In the OT, at large, there is a dynamic between the preexilic writings, which see God as the sovereign source of both good and evil, and postexilic writings in which, after the catastrophe of losing the land, God's power and human disobedience each play their roles. At the same time, confidence in the capacity of God to bring good out of evil—as is evident in the life testimonies of Joseph and Job—is maintained.

In later Jewish literature, a view called divine retribution emerges. It does not deny but presupposes divine mercy, but not without punishment in order to maintain God's holy nature. Similarly to the Christian tradition, divine retribution is often linked with eschatological fulfillment. However, at some point, the divine-retribution template turns out to be unsatisfactory to those who suffer too much and too long without seeing any sign of retribution (see Jer 12:1–2; Job 9:24). Not surprisingly, at the time of the Holocaust, retribution theology endured radical scrutiny and revision—to the point that many Jewish theologians saw it as completely useless for the post-Holocaust world. The reason is that "in a monotheistic faith evil as well as good must ultimately be referred back to God."[49]

Concerning contemporary Jewish responses, even when theodicy is not rejected in the first place—for the simple reason that for many the topic does not make sense in light of what happened at Auschwitz—they all refer to the Holocaust.

At the center of Islamic tradition is God's unqualified power rather than divine vindication, as is the case in Judeo-Christian theodicies. As a result, the urgency of theodicy in Islam is far less intense than in Judaism. That said, there is also a long tradition of reflection on suffering and evil. Think of the narrative of Job—"Ayyub" (one of the prophets!)—scattered over several passages in the Holy Qur'an (4:163; 6:84; 21:83; 38:41–44). Although Ayyub stands out as a paragon of patience in the midst of calamities, the focus overall is less on theodicy and more on the instructions God gives Ayyub for him to settle the problems.

Similarly to Judaism, at times suffering may be taken as punishment for sin. That said, in light of divine omnipotence, the idea of suffering as the test of character and faithfulness is more prominent a theme in the Qur'an. Furthermore, similarly to Judaism and Christianity, Islam also invokes the final eschatological resolution.

---

49. Sherwin, "Theodicy," 966.

Having now discussed in some detail what in theological tradition is called "personal" (or "individual") eschatology—issues related mainly, although not exclusively, to each human person—the rest of the chapter focuses more on "cosmic" eschatology. The first question we tackle has to do with the timing of Christ's return and its secrecy.

Do We Know the Timing of Christ's Return or Not?

Why the Long Delay?

It is highly curious that, on the one hand, Jesus's proclamation was thoroughly eschatological, waiting for the final ushering in the kingdom of God and setting up the righteous divine rule over the world ruled by the evil empire, which was oppressing God's people. On the other hand, Jesus curiously did not provide any kind of prophetic timetable for future events, even when his disciples asked him about it (Acts 1:6–7). His reluctance to reveal the timetable illustrates the robust dynamic between the "already" (arrival of the kingdom in Jesus's words and deeds) and the "not yet" (the final consummation) brilliantly reflected in the classic title of the book by the late American NT scholar G. E. Ladd, *The Presence of the Future*.

So, what are we to think about the problem in the Gospel traditions regarding an interim era? Is it the case that the original Gospel writers and Paul were simply mistaken in expecting the coming of God's kingdom during their lifetime? The data in the Synoptic Gospels is far more complex than that. Notwithstanding their internal differences, all writers sought to combat the apocalyptic enthusiasm that set dates, which they know would first have led to disenchantment and then to final disappointment with the overly long delay in meeting people's intense expectation.

All three Synoptic Gospels (Mark, Matthew, and Luke) seem to balance statements that can be interpreted as proposing an immediate eschatological consummation within their lifetime (Mark 9:1; 13:10) with those that postpone its coming to the future, if not necessarily to the distant future. Highly illustrative is the intentional dynamic contained within one and the same saying preserved in all three Gospels: "Truly, I say to you, this generation will not pass away before all these things take place. Heaven and earth will pass away, but my words will not pass away. But of that day or that hour no one knows, not even the angels in heaven, nor the Son, but only the Father" (Mark 13:30–32; par. Matt 24:34–36; Luke 21:32–33). Clearly, the first part is speaking of the imminent end, whereas the latter leaves it open, perhaps even to the distant future.

Whereas the Gospel of Mark, as the earliest account, is closest to the enthusiasm of imminent expectation, he also importantly makes the interim period the time of mission to the world (16:9–20). For Matthew it is important to highlight the continuity in Jesus's ministry with the old covenant and the fulfillment in him of the divine promises. Matthew is also the only one to speak explicitly of the church (16:18), including of its structures and how to cope with practical problems (18:15–17), thus implying a significant interim. Finally, it was given to Luke to move "beyond the notion of a strict interim period by introducing a salvation-historical understanding of history" and place Jesus in the wider context of the history of the whole world (3:23–28; also 2:1–4). Most striking in this respect is the Lukan Jesus saying that "when you hear of wars and tumults, do not be terrified; for this must first take place, but the end will not be at once" (21:9). As is well known, in the Gospel of John, a "realized eschatology"—the belief that with the coming of Jesus the kingdom of God has already arrived in its entirety—seems to take the upper hand, although not exclusively so.[50]

Similarly, Paul intuits the Christian's and church's life between two ages, this age and the age to come. Hence, it was to mission and labor in the service of Christ's gospel that Paul called Christians.

Are We to Discern the Signs of the Return of Christ?

Despite the repeated reservation of Jesus (Matt 24:36; Acts 1:7), the signs of the end have been quite a popular topic among Christians. The same is true—if not more true—of Islam, as will be discussed below.

That said, a cautious and discerning scrutiny of signs is not discouraged in the NT. Among the expected signs, the NT mentions a heightened excitement over the occult, coupled with self-appointed prophets eager to lead astray the faithful (Matt 24:24; 2 Thess 2:3, 9–11). The gathering back to their homeland of the Jews and their restoration is an abiding mark of the coming end in both Testaments (Isa 11:11; Luke 21:24; Acts 15:14–17; Rom 9–11). Dramatic cosmic changes and portents in nature and the heavens (Isa 13:13; Joel 2:30; 3:14–16; Matt 24:29; Luke 21:26; Acts 2:20), including seismic events and famines (Luke 21:10–11; Rev 6:12), as well as intensified wars and conflicts (Mark 13:7; Matt 24:6; Luke 21:9), signal the *Parousia* (from Greek "return") of the Lord. To the end-time signs belongs also the proclamation of the gospel to the whole world (Matt 24:14). A sure sign of the impending end is the appearance of the antichrist, indeed antichrists—or christ counterfeits.

50. This paragraph is based on Schwarz, *Eschatology*, 83–90.

Indeed, a prominent figure in both the Christian and the Islamic imagination of the end times is the antichrist, a human opponent of Christ. In light of the prominence of Jesus in Muslim eschatology, it is not surprising that the picture of the antichrist in Islam is not radically different from that of Christianity. In the biblical testimonies (2 Thess 2:3–12), he is depicted as "a universal ruler whose reign is a time of unprecedented evil and whom Christ will defeat at his parousia." We glean from the Jewish apocalyptic prophecy concerning the Syrian ruler Antiochus Epiphanes, who defiled the temple (Dan 11:29–45), that he is not only a religious but also a political figure, seeking to establish a "counterfeit theocracy."[51]

Jewish apocalypticism also provided cues for corollary adversaries with its depiction of the enticing false prophet (Deut 13:1–5), which lies behind the Christian Apocalypse's (book of Revelation) account of two monsters, the sea beast and land beast (Rev 13:1–18), the former a blasphemous ruler and the latter a false prophet (16:13; 19:20). Similarly to the false prophets of old, these antagonists in the NT perform miracles and seek to entice people away from worship of the true God and to the worship of idols. Chapter 17 of Revelation adds yet another evil figure, the harlot of Babylon, likely representing economic enticement.

Fascination with the figure of antichrist has been intense throughout history. Although the appearance of such an evil figure has been assigned to the future, there has also been constant attention to identifying his appearance in contemporary life. For the Reformers, it was the pope; for twentieth-century Christians, Hitler or Stalin or the European Union. Although modern and contemporary academic theology has virtually dismissed the topic as something mythical and vacuous, the expectation of the antichrist persists vividly in popular apocalypticism, particularly in Christian and Islamic forms. In light of the long history of Christians' failed attempts to identify the antichrist, we should be very cautious. Theologically we have to say that, on the one hand, the God-opposing "mystery of lawlessness is already at work" (2 Thess 2:7) in any given historical time, and that, on the other hand, the final culmination of the growth of evil will happen on the eve of the final consummation.

---

51. Bauckham and Hart, *Hope Against Hope*, 111–12, here 111.

How Are We to Imagine Eternity and the Transition from "Here" to "There"?

Eternity as the Fulfillment of Ultimate Contentment

One of the thorniest puzzles facing everyone who hopes to spend eternity in heaven is the meaning of, well, the term *eternity*! To make the issue even more complicated: How are we to conceive of the transition from "here" to "there," from the earthly space-time to eternity's "space-time"? Recall our investigation into the meanings of "time" and "space" (in chapter 3) (conveniently smashed together in the post-Einsteinian world as "space-time"/time-space). In that investigation we found wanting the popular idea of eternity merely as an infinite extension of time, or of eternity as "canceling out" time. Nor did we find helpful the old idea of God existing "outside" time and space in terms of not being involved in earthly happenings.

The first task in the clarification of the term "eternity," particularly in relation to modern science, is the foundational question of whether, in the first place, it makes sense to speak of a "future." Think about it! "Of course, there is a future as surely as there is a past," you may say; "Why invest time on this ridiculous problem?" Wait a moment before passing judgment! The issue has to do with two radically different notions of time, conveniently named "flowing time" (A-time) and "block time" (B-time). Whereas the former is the common sense idea of time as transition from the past, to the present, to the future, the latter—favored by the majority of natural scientists—does not allow the reality of such distinctions between tenses. The best way to illustrate what B-time means is to compare it to space laid out there completely!

Now, what is at stake for theology? A great deal: for the vision in which the future brings about something new (flowing time) may secure the judgment, reconciliation, and healing of our lives and memories in new creation. Other problems result from the adoption of the block-time view. One of the most serious involves the question of authentic human freedom if the future does not include potentialities. Furthermore, without insistence on the openness of the future, divine freedom is also at stake. Finally, in terms of interfaith engagement, it seems that for Abrahamic faith traditions, a block-time model would be a major theological obstacle, whereas the Asiatic faiths' cyclical worldview of eternal emergence and return points in a different direction from the Abrahamic faiths' emphasis on history and historical time.

Alongside theological considerations, there are also scientific and logical reasons for supporting the flowing-time conception, the details of which will not concern us here. Now we are ready to describe the core meaning of "eternity."

Rather than "outside" time, we should envision God both as deeply engaged in earthly happenings and as transcending space-time in terms of maintaining absolute freedom. Although the almighty Creator cannot be limited in space-time, this understanding allows God to be in time, so to speak. Indeed, both divine omnipresence (that God is present everywhere at all times) and incarnation imply some kind of temporality in divine life. In other words, eternity is neither timelessness nor lack of movement and liveliness. Briefly put: the infinite God is to be imagined to exist in both time and in eternity without any of the limitations pertinent to created realities.

This kind of conception of time gives us the needed resources to imagine the final eschatological redemption that makes possible final reconciliation and peace with the "entry of eternity into time."[52] As I will explain below, God's eternity not only brings fulfillment but also judges all that does not hold up to the standard of eternity.[53] So how might we imagine the transition from "here" to "there"?

How Are We to Conceive of the Transition from the Earthly to the Heavenly Realm?

Would the transition from time to eternity imply total destruction of the world? Or is there a way to think of the transformation in other terms? Biblical symbols, visions, and teachings assume a dynamic tension and interrelationship between continuity and discontinuity. The very term "new creation" implies this twofold dynamic: that it is "new" reflects discontinuity, and "creation" bespeaks continuity. A striking juxtaposition and mutual conditioning can also be found in biblical sayings according to which "flesh and blood" may not enter God's eternity, and yet it is *physical* resurrection that stands at the forefront of that hope! Polkinghorne put it well: "the new creation does not arise from a radically novel creative act *ex nihilo*, but as a redemptive act *ex vetere*, out of the old."[54]

It has taken a long time for Christian theology to reach a dynamic balance in this understanding. On the basis of 2 Peter 3:10—"then the heavens will pass away with a loud noise, and the elements will be dissolved with fire, and the earth and the works that are upon it will be burned up"—and related passages (like Rev 20:11; 21:1), the view of the annihilation of the

---

52. Pannenberg, *Systematic Theology*, 3:603.
53. Russell, *Time in Eternity*, 6.
54. Polkinghorne, *God of Hope*, 116.

world established itself. Following final judgment, the world will be burned to ashes, so to speak. An opposite position is that of transformation, which finds support in passages such as Romans 8:19–25 employing the metaphor of cosmic birth pangs as the manner in which the present reality will transition to the new creation. As painful as birthing may be, it suggests the emergence of new life without destroying the old.

The transformation view highlights God's faithfulness as Creator to creation. Since both visions are in the Holy Scripture, theology's task is not to pit one against the other but to seek to hold to the radical dynamic. That said, the emphasis on the transformation view seems to do better justice to the total picture of biblical revelation. Just consider the vision of Revelation (21:1): "Then I saw a new heaven and a new earth."

Holding together in a dynamic mutual conditioning the interpretations of annihilation and transformation tells us that there is much in the "old creation" to be annihilated, particularly decay and the effects of sin and fall. That said, the final cleansing and sanctification are not unrelated to the "first creation"; in all of God's works, there is continuity, even in discontinuity. Among other things, the bodily resurrection view demands that there is some real correspondence between current conditions that make possible embodied life and new creation in terms of heavenly existence making possible not only "spiritual" but also embodied life.

A proper negotiation of the dynamic tension between annihilation and transformation has tremendous effects on a number of lifestyle and attitudinal issues. Whereas the implications for ecology were discussed above, let us mention here work and its value. If human work (comprehensively understood) is related to the divine purpose of creation that points to new creation, then work gains its ultimate meaning from God's future; understood this way, work is not only a matter of the present world. On the contrary, affirming only the annihilationist vision does not leave much hope for this world.

This model has significant implications for the location of the new creation, the eschatological kingdom of God. While transcending the earth and current cosmos, in order for it to be interesting and desirable, heavenly existence has to have some real correspondence with the laws of nature governing our current existence, or else any talk about resurrected embodied life does not make sense! Let us take a closer look at this crucial issue.

Transformed "Space" and "Time" in the New Creation

So, what does it mean to envision time-space in the new creation as (in some sense) analogous to the current world? What does the biblical idea that "there is no more time (*chronos*)"[55] mean (Rev 10:6; my translation)? In light of the continuity-discontinuity model, temporality as the condition for creaturely life cannot be taken as antagonistic to God and hence, as something to be destroyed. Rather, God is patient, and "acts through temporally unfolding processes in the old creation."[56] Hence, temporality in itself cannot be something to be deleted, because that would mean nothing less than the destruction of creation! Rather, the idea of the "end of time" has to be understood in terms of eternity bringing about the "fufillment of time," a "new" eternal "time" that lacks the potential for sin and entropy and, unlike earthly time, does not denote creaturely limitations characteristic of current space-time. We might term this "finitude beyond transience."[57] Even in heaven, we will be finite, created persons, for only God is infinite.

This, in turn, has to assume a new kind of time-space environment in the new creation. It is built on the assumption that if "[i]n this universe, space, time and matter are all mutually interlinked in the single package deal of general relativity . . . [then it] seems reasonable to suppose that this linkage is a general feature of the Creator's will. If so, the new creation will also have its 'space' and 'time' and 'matter'"[58] but in a new form of existence that bears some real resemblance to the old but that also radically transforms it to make possible life in physical resurrection, which never tastes death. The current life without this divine transformation is not fit for God's eternity (1 Cor 15:50).

This dynamic of continuity and discontinuity also makes it possible for us to conceive rightly the meaning of judgment and purification as the conditions for final reconciliation.

Why Judgment?

While opinions about divine judgment vary, it is self-evident that for the new creation to be "new" there needs to be "redemptive purging and healing of our lives." Sins and omissions need to be confessed and forgiven, good deeds and virtues to be celebrated and honored. This is because eternity "is

---

55. Translated routinely in contemporary English versions as "[no more] delay."
56. Polkinghorne, *God of Hope*, 120.
57. Volf, "Enter into Joy," 273.
58. Polkinghorne, *God of Hope*, 117.

not only a time of endless rejoicing in all that is true and good and beautiful, it is also a time of leaving off and destroying of all that is wrong and false and ugly in this creation."[59] Divine judgment is in keeping with the holiness and purity of God, the Creator.

Judgment is a frequent biblical theme. The agent of judgment in the NT is the Father (Matt 6:4; Rom 3:6; 1 Cor 5:13). Jesus's role as judge is more complicated: it is said, on one hand, that Jesus judges no one (John 3:17), but on the other hand, that he serves as judge (John 5:22). However, at his coming Christ brings grace (1 Pet 1:13), and even now he acts as our advocate (1 John 2:1).

The NT speaks of the standard of judgment in many complementary ways; it calls it God's will (cf. Matt 6:10), the word of Jesus (John 12:48), or more widely, the message of Jesus (see particularly Luke 12:8-9). Pannenberg's reasonable argument is that "the message of Jesus is the norm by which God judges even in the case of those who never meet Jesus personally," not of course in relation to the response to the gospel (which is impossible in that case), but in keeping with the direction in which Jesus's message points.[60]

The way judgment relates to eternity is that "Eternity is judgment... [because it] brings the truth about earthly life to light." That, however, does not mean the annihilation or destruction of creatures, because God, the Judge, is also Creator, who holds fast to his creatures.[61]

Indeed, judgment has begun already in this life, and those who submit their lives to God's purifying and reconciling judgment may hope to be preserved at the last judgment (see Mal 3:2-3). Even if the Christian suffers loss as their lifework "burns up" like wood or stubble, their lives will be saved (1 Cor 3:12-15). This cleansing effect of judgment is the necessary precondition for the bodily resurrection to happen in the new creation as the "perishable puts on the imperishable, and the mortal puts on immortality" (1 Cor 15:54).[62]

Who or what will be judged? According to the NT teaching, it is our works that God will judge (1 Cor 3:12-15), whether as affirmation of their value in God's sight or as condemnation. In that it is fair and thoroughgoing, judgment is not an act of divine wrath or vengeance. For the Judge is also the Creator and the Savior. This Divine Judge is fair and

---

59. Russell, *Time in Eternity*, 6.

60. Pannenberg, *Systematic Theology*, 3:615.

61. Pannenberg, *Systematic Theology*, 3:610. Moltmann (*Coming of God*, 236) also rightly notes that ultimately the question of judgment is "the question about God" and whether he wishes to hold on to his creatures.

62. Pannenberg, *Systematic Theology*, 3:619-20.

his judgment is in proportion to our opportunities and resources (Luke 12:48). Ultimately, we can be confident that "the final judgment is not a judgment of our merits, but of our response to God's grace which he has extended to us in Jesus Christ."[63]

On the Way to the Final Consummation: Will There Be an Earthly Millennium?

There has long been an expectation that there will be a period of the earthly reign of Christ that showers us with unspeakable blessings and peace and, being a thousand years in duration, that is called the "millennium." Although there is only one explicit statement in the NT regarding what became the hope for the millennium in Christian theology, namely Revelation 20:1–15, a number of other biblical references in both Testaments have been linked to it (1 Cor 15:23–25; Isa 2 and 11; Jer 31–33; Ezek 36–37; Dan 7:18, 27; Mic 4). The idea also appears in the Jewish apocalyptic tradition. While in early theology some readers and biblical theologians opted for an allegorical interpretation, the majority went with a more-or-less literal expectation of the thousand-year rule. In hindsight, this was called "premillennialism," and the teaching around it says that following Christ's return to earth, the millennium will be set up for a thousand-year period, after which the new heaven and new earth will be established. That was the default option in the earliest iterations of Christian theology.

Beginning from Augustine, the enthusiasm for an earthly rule of Christ began to wane, undoubtedly because of the new status of Christianity as the official religion of the empire. In its place, the church became the locus and embodiment of God's kingdom. Usually named "amillennialism," this view soon established itself as the normative one. This view concerns the belief that there is no other reign of Christ but that which is already happening in the church. As a result, the church soon condemned the literally understood millennial hopes, which at the time of the Reformation was an understanding held by Lutherans and some others.

Earthly millennial hopes did not, however, die out. Various types of mystical and spiritualist movements took up the importance of the millennial hope. Similarly, premillennialism—according to which the return of Christ happens before the earthly millennial reign of Christ, the millennium—did not disappear, notwithstanding a steady and strong resistance from the establishment. Beginning with various types of revival movements during the Protestant Reformation, such as the Anabaptists, many

63. Schwarz, *Eschatology*, 391.

other Free Churches, including Pentecostal/charismatic groups, adopted premillennialism as a favorite expectation.

The third form of millennialism, which emerged later in history, is named "postmillennialism," according to which Christ's reign is progressing in history through the presence and proclamation of the church and will culminate in a "Christianized" world. Postmillennialists locate "the Second Coming *after* a long period of gradual and incremental 'gospel success' in which the vast majority of humanity is converted to Christ and human society is radically reformed" (emphasis original).[64] Their understanding of the golden era of Christ's rule on earth is consequently less literal than that of the premillennialists. This belief, of course, meshes well with the optimism related to missions movements as expressed particularly in the modern missionary movements.

Although in twentieth-century academic theology the millennium became marginalized and virtually forgotten—except among conservative Protestant traditions—a striking exception is Moltmann. Linking the millennium with the "future" of history, Moltmann places the millennium hope between personal and cosmic expectations. While identifying and critiquing several human-made millennial programs such as political ones, he also strongly affirms the importance of the peaceful and harmonious reign of Christ—without going into any detail as to when it will happen and how.

So, what would the millennium mean to us today? While important, and still debated, we should never take the millennium as the center of Christian hope. For it is temporary, and only a gateway to the final consummation. Rightly understood, the millennial hope's true significance has to do with its "earthly" orientation. It represents the this-worldly part of the eschatological hope. God the Creator is going to show the possibility of peace and reconciliation in the world God has created—something the world has never seen before.

In sum: millennial hopes are penultimate hopes. The ultimate consummation in its fullness in Christian theology has to do with the establishment of a new heaven and a new earth.

---

64. Weber, "Millennialism," 367.

The Ultimate Consummation: "A New Heaven and a New Earth"

Is Heaven This-Worldly or Other-Wordly?

Having broadly discussed a number of topics related to eschatology, we will now imagine what might be the final and ultimate consummation. It may come as a surprise to you that as widely and deeply as the imagination and spirituality of heaven occupied the minds of patristic and medieval theologians, theological reflection on heaven is ominously missing in contemporary academic theology. The omission is so frequent in almost all biblical and systematic theologies that—embarrassingly!—the world's largest (at thirty-six volumes) and most prestigious theological encyclopedia, the *Theologische Realenzyklopädie*, has no entry on "heaven"!

A delightful exception to contemporary theology's lack of discussion about heaven is Moltmann. His *Coming of God* devotes an entire section to the topic of heaven, under the weighty heading "The Cosmic Temple: The Heavenly Jerusalem."[65] That said, Moltmann's discussion of cosmic eschatology under the wider rubric of "New Heaven—New Earth"[66] is so strongly focused on the hope for the "new earth" that at times one is left wondering how much newness he dares to hope for. He repeatedly warns readers not to be too otherworldly minded. While this warning is timely, it makes one wonder what exactly is the meaning and nature of heaven!

A highly important and thoughtful challenge to the traditional notion of future-driven hope for heaven comes from the Scottish NT scholar N. T. Wright with his innovative suggestion that "Heaven, in the Bible, is not a future destiny but the other, hidden, dimension of our ordinary life—God's dimension, if you like."[67] That said, he still acknowledges the future orientation mentioned elsewhere in the NT, although he does so quite minimally. The critical question to Wright is obvious: Why cannot "heaven" be both a future dimension and a hidden dimension of our ordinary life? Where is the newness of eschatological hope?

The main critical theological challenge to the merely this-worldly vision is whether it is able to support a truly cosmic and comprehensive vision of God's making "all things new." How would fixing our globe's conditions of life be a lasting solution to the problems of entropy and decay? In other words, how *cosmic* (in light of our current scientific knowledge)

---

65. Moltmann, *Coming of God*, 308–19.
66. Moltmann, *Coming of God*, part 4.
67. Citations in Wright, *Surprised by Hope*, 19.

is a vision of a "new earth" if "cosmic" (by and large) is understood only as referring to our globe (Earth)?

So, what would be a more balanced view? While it's important that we acknowledge the many pitfalls of being overly spiritual and overly otherworldly, imaginations that are overly this-worldly also seem not to provide much newness. We must hold tightly to the continuity-in-discontinuity template. Whereas contemporary theology has rather one-sidedly opted for the idea of continuity and whereas traditional theology has taken the opposite side, a robust account of the radically new future with the consummation of God's kingdom seeks a radical middle road. Consider the astute assertion of the Christian philosopher J. L. Walls: "Theism [religions believing in God] raises the ceiling on our hopes for happiness for the simple reason that God provides resources for joy that immeasurably outstrip whatever the natural order can offer."[68] With these desiderata in mind, let us piously inquire into the nature of heaven.

Heaven as Communion, Contentment, and Consummation

We are clear that the biblical narrative provides a meager account of the nature of heaven—and when it does engage the topic, the chosen genre tends to be imaginative and poetic. It offers pictures, images, and metaphors rather than definitions, statements, and analyses. It is also noteworthy that none of the classical creeds say anything overt on the nature of heaven and eternal life; such matters they merely assume.

The biblical symbols and metaphors of heaven could be conveniently classified under three linguistic forms: space language, person language, and time language. Space-language-driven metaphors abound, including the "city" and "garden," gleaning from the rich traditions of Jerusalem, the holy city, and the paradise of Genesis 2. The garden stands as "a symbol of innocence and harmony, a place of peace, rest, and fertility."[69] The city speaks of the security and community of people, as well as settlement for a nomadic, wandering people. The new Jerusalem of Revelation is a walled city, denoting protection, but also a city with permanently open gates, implying constant access. Examples of person language are expressions such as "be[ing] with Christ" (Phil 1:22–23), seeing God "face to face" (Matt 5:8; 1 Cor 13:12), and related metaphors such as glorification (John 17:4–5, 22–26). Time language relates to expressions such as "eternal life" and corollary terms.

---

68. Walls, "Heaven," 399.
69. McGrath, *Brief History of Heaven*, 41.

An essential aspect of heaven is the consummation of union with God as expressed in Aquinas's pursuit of the beatific vision; this "seeing" of God is alone what satisfies the endless human thirst for union. Augustine put it memorably: "He shall be the end of our desires who shall be seen without end, loved without cloy, praised without weariness."[70] Even though one has "arrived" in eternity, progress and evolvement do not have to stop, as there might be an endless journey of new explorations.

Because of bodily resurrection, life in heaven is embodied life. In this regard, N. T. Wright's observation is to the point, namely, that Revelation's vision "is not about people leaving 'earth' and going to 'heaven,' but rather about the life of 'heaven,' more specifically the New Jerusalem, coming down from heaven to earth—exactly in line with the Lord's Prayer."[71]

The "new heaven" must be imagined as cosmos-wide: the mere fixing of life conditions in one part of the cosmos would only be a temporary solution. Human knowledge at the moment has very few resources at its disposal for imagining such a cosmic renewal (somewhat similarly to the question of the ultimate origins of the cosmos in the first place).

This much—or, this little—we are able to say of the ultimate consummation. Prayerfully imagining and anticipating it is therefore more important and fitting than analytic rational study. What about other religions and their visions of the future, the end, the consummation? Although the Christian theologian has to be careful when speaking of "eschatology" as a pan-religious theme, it is true that all world religions express a concern about mortality and a vision of life after death, as mentioned at the beginning of this chapter.

Eschatological Visions and Symbols among Religions

Jewish Eschatology

Hope for the Afterlife Emerged Slowly

Interestingly, no OT books are devoted to death or afterlife; indeed, the theme is marginal. As discussed, the OT worldview is very much this-worldly although it is deeply *theo*logical, God-driven. When eschatological themes do occasionally appear, they pertain less to the individual and much more to national hope and to Yahweh's intervention in the world. This-worldly blessings from Yahweh are at the center of the Israelite religion. Yahweh's role

---

70. Augustine, *City of God*, 22.30, in *NPNF¹* 02; I am indebted to Walls, *Heaven*, 37.
71. Wright, *For All the Saints*, 59; cited in Walls, "Heaven," 401.

as judge is also envisioned in relation to earthly affairs, particularly with the establishment of justice and righteousness.

In stark contrast to neighboring lands, particularly Egypt, Israelite culture was definitely not death-driven. The OT describes the condition of the dead as some sort of shadowy existence (Isa 38:18). An eschatological consciousness only arose gradually in the OT. The hope for an afterlife in terms of resurrection evolved slowly toward the end of the OT, although intimations and anticipations appear here and there (Job 19:25–26; Pss 49:15; 73:24; Isa 26:19). Daniel 12:2 is widely taken as the apogee of that development: "And many of those who sleep in the dust of the earth shall awake, some to everlasting life, and some to shame and everlasting contempt."

Only after the return from the Exile did intimations of life beyond slowly emerge, and thus it is the later rabbinic traditions, the standard teaching of Judaism, that delve deeply and widely into eschatological and apocalyptic speculations. Eschatology becomes a defining feature, and against that background it can be said "that no significant movement in the course of Jewish history had lacked an eschatology."[72] Whence the rise of an eschatological orientation? The standard scholarly response is that it had to do with the question of suffering and theodicy, the lot of the Jewish people throughout history. As a result, the hope for the afterlife also became more defined, as death was no longer looked upon as the end.

In very broad strokes, Jews came to believe that, at the end of days,

- the dead will be resurrected and come before God to account for their lives on earth;
- the righteous will be rewarded and the evil punished;
- Jews, free from the yoke of the exile, will return to their homeland, rebuild it, and become masters of their own destiny;
- they will rebuild the temple and reinstitute the temple cult;
- the nations of the world will flock to study Torah with the Jewish people;
- peace and justice will rule;
- all people will come to know and worship the God of Israel; and
- this entire scenario will be brought to pass through the initiative of the Messiah.[73]

---

72. Gillman, *Death of Death*, 12.
73. Gillman, *Death of Death*, 21–22.

Who Will Be Saved—and Who Condemned?

Who then will inherit salvation? As discussed in chapter 8, following the Torah is the key to salvation or condemnation. Rabbinic theology mentions a number of types of people who might end up in hell, including those who deny resurrection or the Torah's heavenly origin, or the heretic, or the one who abuses the divine name, and so forth. This much almost all Jewish traditions agree upon—keeping Torah and doing good deeds. Debated issues include, for example, the balance between good and bad deeds, on which no final agreement exists.

Yet an important and long-standing but unresolved issue of debate relates to the destiny of gentiles. Not surprisingly, no definitive opinion was reached among the different rabbinical schools. This much can be said: while the Christian type of "no salvation outside the church" principle was often held as the normal opinion, there is also undoubtedly a strong prophetic tradition in the OT that envisions some kind of "universal scope of salvation." Rather than leading to ultimate destruction and annihilation, Yahweh's judgment will have shalom as the final word (Amos 9:11–15; Isa 2:2–4). But even then, no unanimity exists about whether "nations" (as opposed to the "people" of Yahweh) are included in this salvation, which by extension would also encompass nature and the whole world.

Broadly speaking, until modernity, the core rabbinic belief in two destinies remained intact. By contrast, the majority of modern and contemporary Jews have left it behind or at least qualified it significantly. This is possible because, as we know, the Torah says little about the nature of judgment and blessedness beyond this world. As is true of Christian theology, particularly difficult for contemporary Jewish theologians is the affirmation of hell.

Do Jews Believe in Resurrection of the Dead?

What about resurrection? The resurrection of the dead is a central belief in classical Judaism. Indeed, those who deny the centrality of this belief are already condemned. Briefly stated, resurrection and the authority of Torah "are the two dogmas the rabbis required, minimally, that no Jew deny and, maximally, that every Jew affirm."[74] That said, there were of course dissenting voices within Jewish orthodoxy: while the Pharisees fully endorsed the doctrine, the Sadducees did not. For rabbinic theology, it was not enough merely to affirm immortality: a *bodily* resurrection also had to

---

74. Novak, "Jewish Eschatology," 123.

be affirmed. When it comes to contemporary theology, as expected, great divergences can be found on the axis from conservative to mainstream to liberal. Leading theologians such as Arthur A. Cohen seek to establish the belief in the bodily resurrection as an indispensable tenet of faith for contemporary Judaism. Another formative scholar, Neil Gillman, finds two powerful reasons for refusing to let the critical mind *alone* dictate one's ultimate vision. On the one hand, along with all other Jews, theologically he is fully convinced of the omnipotence of God, even over death. Yet on the other hand, the anthropological argument also seems convincing: the biblical view of the human as a psycho-physical unity makes him believe that without the body his own self is not complete.

What about the eschatological vision of the youngest Abrahamic tradition? To the consideration of Islamic theology of the end we turn next.

Islamic Eschatology

Why the End-Time Expectation Plays Such a Big Role in Islam

Eschatology plays an extraordinary role in Islam. Recall that the Prophet's first and continuing message was about the coming judgment and the need for everyone to submit to Allah to avoid the hell of judgment. For the Muslim, life on this earth is but preparation for eternity, at the core of which is obedience to and desire to please Allah. Hence, death should be appropriately kept in mind (Q 23:15; 3:185). The Qur'an gives humans a "fixed" time, a stated life span (6:2).

Both the Qur'an and particularly Hadith texts go to great lengths in discussing the afterlife. Eschatological beliefs are also prominent fare in many Muslim creedal statements. Generally speaking, contemporary Muslims tend to take the traditional teaching on eschatology much more seriously than do most Jews and Christians. The eschatological narrative lays claim on everything in the Muslim's faith and life. Similarly to Judaism and Christianity, a rich tradition of apocalypticism can be found in Islam, including radical millenarian and jihadist movements.

As in Christian tradition, in Islam the (final) hour is unknown to all but God (Q 31:34). As the Prophet stated: "Knowledge thereof lies only with God—and what do you know, perhaps the Hour is near" (33:63). Differently from Hadith and apocalyptic traditions, the Qur'an is reticent to talk about signs. That said, eschatological undergirding lies beneath a number of suras such as for example 22 with the opening verse: "O mankind, fear your Lord. Surely the earthquake of the Hour [of Doom] is a tremendous thing."

Understandably, Muslims have not stopped looking for signs. Books, blogs, and talks on "signs of the hour" abound. The search for signs is fueled by the presence in the Hadith of detailed lists of signs. "Geological, moral, social, and cosmic signs . . . [as well as] the erosion of the earth, the spread of immorality, the loss of trust among the people, and the administration of unjust rulers [are perceived] as some signs of the Hour." In distinction from these "minor" signs, the Hadith lists as "major" ones the "emergence of the Antichrist, the descent of Jesus, and the rising of the sun in the west," which all point to the imminence of the end. Quite similarly to the descriptions in the book of Revelation, trumpets, archangels, and cataclysmic changes on earth, including earthquakes, play a role in the final consummation (39:67–69; 81:1–14; 99:1–5); the unfaithful will suffer intensely. The rise of the mysterious nations of Gog and Magog also plays a role in the eschatological scheme of Islam.

Jesus and Mahdi, the Central End-Time Players in Islamic Eschatology

Unbeknownst to most Christians, first, Jesus plays a central role in Islamic eschatology, and second, the main player is the mysterious figure of the Mahdi. The task of the Mahdi is to defeat the antichrist and bring justice and peace to the world and lead people to truth. An ordinary human being rather than a divine figure, the Mahdi is supernaturally endowed to accomplish his task. While affirmed by all major denominations, the role of the Mahdi is particularly important among the Shi'ites. Yet he is not mentioned in the Qur'an nor in the two main Hadith traditions, that of Bukhari and that of Muslim.

The relationship between the Mahdi and Jesus is close yet somewhat undefined. While the Qur'an itself does not directly mention Jesus's "descent" to earth, it is widely attested in the Hadith. As discussed in chapter 5, according to the standard Islamic interpretation, Jesus of Nazareth was not killed on the cross but was instead "taken up" by Allah to heaven to await the return (Q 4:157–58). At that point, he will fight alongside the Mahdi against the antichrist and defeat him. Jesus will slaughter pigs, tear down crosses, and destroy churches and synagogues; most probably he will also kill Christians unwilling to embrace Islamic faith.

The picture of the antichrist in Islam is not radically different from that in Christianity. Obviously an archenemy of Jesus, the antichrist can be seen as the personification of evil (similarly to Satan and Iblis). Although the term *antichrist* itself does not appear in the Qur'an, there is wide agreement in Islamic tradition that allusions and indirect references are found in it,[75] including the saying attributed to Jesus: "Nay, but verily man is [wont to be] rebellious" (96:6).

Understandably, the Hadith traditions greatly expand and elaborate on the description and influence of the antichrist: "The Antichrist is short, hen-toed, woolly-haired, one-eyed, an eye-sightless, and neither protruding nor deep-seated. If you are confused about him, know that your Lord is not one-eyed" (Abu Dawud 32, para. 4306). The antichrist will fight against the believers until the Mahdi and Jesus come and help defeat his power.

Visions of Death, Judgment, and Resurrection

Although the Qur'an provides precious few details about what happens between death and resurrection, later traditions have produced fairly detailed accounts. Similarly to Christian tradition, those accounts say that whereas the body decays, the "soul" (or "spirit") continues to exist (see 39:42). According to a major Muslim tradition, the deceased person meets two angels—named Munkar and Nakir—who test the faith of the person and help determine that person's final destiny. In all Muslim accounts of the afterlife, there is thus an intermediate state that, according to some Muslim theologians, is similar to the Roman Catholic idea of purgatory. Muslims also believe in the resurrection of the body, as well as in (eternal) retribution (Q 75; 36:77–79; and so forth).

The main theological debate about the resurrection is whether it entails a total annihilation of the person before re-creation or a reconstitution and renewal. The lack of unanimity is understandable in light of two kinds of directions in Scripture itself. Compare 28:88, "Everything will perish except His Countenance," which clearly assumes the annihilationist view, with 10:4, "To Him is the return of all of you. . . . Truly He originates creation, then recreates it," which teaches the other option.

Final judgment is of great concern to Islam. Consider that a typical list of the basic beliefs includes "belief in one God, His messengers, His books, His angels, and the day of judgment."[76] The final accounting happens when in the hereafter men and women "return" to their God (32:7–11). Numerous chapters of the Qur'an speaks of or refers to the theme of judgment.[77] Similarly to the NT, even the evil spirits (*jinn*) will be judged on that day.

The general picture of the day of judgment is very similar to that given in the Bible. Great earthquakes will rock the earth, setting mountains in

---

75. McGinn, *Antichrist*, 111.
76. Haleem, "Qur'an and Hadith," 25.
77. Fromherz, "Judgment, Final," n.p.

motion (Q 99). The sky will split open and heaven will be "stripped off," rolled up like a parchment scroll. The sun will cease to shine; the stars will be scattered and fall upon the earth. The oceans will boil over. Graves will be opened, the earth bringing forth its burdens (Q 82). All will bow, willingly or not, before God. After resurrection, each human person is given a "book" that indicates their final destiny (18:49), either heaven or hell.

A debated issue among the Muslim schools is the lot of the (gravely) sinning believer, and no agreement has been reached about this. A related debate asks: How do the person's good and bad deeds account for the final judgment received? Common to all opinions is the centrality of obedience to Allah or lack thereof; furthermore, it is widely agreed that only grave sins bring about judgment (4:31).

What is not debated is that there are two destinies taught in the Scripture (9:100–102; 7:37–51; and so forth). Hell is a place of great pain and torture. What about heaven? Often depicted in the Qur'an with garden images (Q 37), paradise is a place of great enjoyment, peace, and reunion. The Qur'an offers sensual descriptions, including the pleasures of exquisitely delicious food and drink, as well as of sexual relations with divine maidens (often interpreted metaphorically). Particularly splendid and elaborate accounts of paradise ("Garden") can be found in the Hadith. Similarly to the Bible, there are also various levels of rewards for the blessed ones.

"End-Time" Visions and Symbols in Hindu Traditions

Unlike Abrahamic traditions with a linear and historical view of history, "Hinduism has no last day or end time, nor any completion of history, resurrection of the dead, and universal last judgment."[78] Instead, its focus is on "the deliverance of the individual from the unreal realm of the empirical and temporal to the timeless realm of the spirit."[79] Even the role of the deities is ambiguous, as a number of them undergo death and even rebirth in another form.

"Cosmic eschatology" is usually described in terms of *kalpas*. Each *kalpa* encompasses the life span from origination to dissolution. At the end of a *kalpa*, a great dissolution occurs, "which coincides with the end of the life of Brahma. The world will be reabsorbed into Brahma by involution and remain in that state until the hatching of a new cosmic age."[80] And so on, ad infinitum.

78. Knipe, "Hindu Eschatology," 171.
79. Dhavamony, "Death and Immortality," 100–101, here 100.
80. Dhavamony, "Death and Immortality," 100–101, here 101.

ESCHATOLOGY

The last two books (the ninth and tenth) of the oldest Vedic Scripture, Rig Veda, speak extensively of death. The Funeral Hymn (10.14), dedicated to Yama, the god of death—the first one to die and thus to show the rest of mortals the way to go—speaks of death in terms of meeting Yama and the "Fathers" (the honored ancestors). Yama is assisted by two messenger dogs, the guardians of death's pathway. Yama and the Fathers prepare a wonderful place for the deceased (10.14.8–11). The last part of the Vedas, the Upanishads, further develops the view of death and the afterlife.

The most innovative and theologically significant Upanishadic development has to do with the evolvement of the doctrines of karma and the transmigration of the soul (rebirth). The soul continues its afterlife journey from one state to another conditioned by the deeds of one's lifetime. Until one is ready to be absorbed into "Reality" (*satya*), the migration continues.

Known as karmic samsara, continuous rebirths are believed by adherents of all Hindu movements, both theistic and otherwise. It is essential to note that samsara is a "universal" law concerning "the conditioned and ever changing universe as contrasted to an unconditioned, eternal, and transcendent state (*moksa* or *nirvāna*)." The liberated one is no longer under karma.[81]

Karma evolves from moral and immoral actions from the past lives to their consequences and one's actions in subsequent lives. While personal, both good and bad karma may also be transferred to another person. At death, "the various component parts of [the deceased person's] body unite with their corresponding counterparts in nature, while the sum total of his karma remains attached to his self (*atman*). The force of this karma decides the nature of his next birth where he reaps the fruit of what he merits."[82]

That teaching helps put death in a different perspective: as aversive as it may appear to human desire to cling to life, death is not the ultimate reality and has only relative significance. Death is an "earthly" matter and hence belongs to the "appearance" aspect of reality. "The knowing (Self) is not born, it dies not; it sprang from nothing, nothing sprang from it. The Ancient is unborn, eternal, everlasting; he is not killed, though the body is killed" (Katha Upanishad 1.2.18). That said, however, reverence for the dead and the obligation of the relatives to the deceased are an integral part of Hindu cultures, and sophisticated funeral rites have evolved to help the deceased begin the journey in the afterlife.

The Bhagavad Gita affirms the basic Upanishadic teachings: the inevitability of death, its transitory nature because of transmigration, and

---

81. Smith, "*Samsāra*," 8098.
82. Dhavamony, "Death and Immortality," 94.

the two destinies (at least as long as one has not yet achieved the ultimate goal). As is well known, the Gita (chapter 8) pays special attention to one's last thoughts, that is, whether one is totally devoted to one's deity or to some earthly goal.

Similarly to the doctrine of resurrection, rebirth raises the question of the constitution of human nature and the corollary question of what continues beyond physical death. Although the Vedanta Hindu philosophical schools do not typically lean toward the Hellenistic type of body-soul dualism (or if they do, they frame it differently), there is a dualism of "true" (real) and "not-self." As long as one does not grasp the single most important insight that "Self [*atman*] is indeed Brahman [the eternal Self]" (Brihadaranyaka Upanishad 4.4.5), one remains at a distance from the real self. Only with the removal of "ignorance" (*avidya*) can the effects of karma be overcome and final release (*moksa*) be attained (see chapter 4).

Only vaguely intuited in the Vedic literature, a fairly clearly defined picture of heaven and hell does not appear until the great epics, particularly the *Mahabharata*. Because of rebirth, their meaning is obviously different from those of Abrahamic traditions. Neither one is the ultimate destiny.

Buddhist Visions of End and "Release"

Although Buddhism, similarly to Hinduism, does not recognize any final closure, already during the time of Gautama himself a diversity of views of the "end" of human life had emerged, although Buddha himself showed great reticence toward such speculations. Somewhat similarly to Hindu tradition, Buddhism speaks of the "history" of the cosmos in terms of exceedingly long ages, called "great eons," and divides them into four periods, beginning with the destruction of the cosmos and extending to various durations of renovation when the universe again reemerges.

To be liberated from the illusion of being permanent and hence clinging to anything conditioned, the "salvific" insight into the true nature of reality, leading to *nibbana* (or nirvana) as "ultimate release," is needed as a way of release from samsara, the cycle of rebirths. Lest one conceive of the karmic samsara cycle of rebirths along the lines of Hinduism—and common sense—that is, that the deceased self will be reborn, Buddhism imagines only some kind of "a flux of becoming in which successive lives are linked together by causal transmission of influence rather than by substantial identity."[83]

---

83. Bodhi, "Introduction," 45.

What, if anything, can then be said of the nature of *nibbana*? Recall that this is the only non-conditioned aspect of reality and therefore free from change and decay. The main logical challenge to such a vision is well known among both Buddhists and its critics: If everything is non-permanent, how can nirvana then be the "final" goal? I am not aware of satisfactory solutions to this conundrum.

The end result of reaching *nibbana* in the Theravada tradition is the *arahant*, the enlightened one who has attained final release. In the Mahayana tradition, this original concept of *arahant* was revised into Boddhisattva, the Enlightened One who for the sake of others postpones stepping into *nibbana*.

Having now briefly surveyed the eschatological profiles of the four chosen religions, let us take a look at the competing vision of afterlife between them and Christian theology, and even beyond.

Religious Visions of Personal Consummation: Resurrection, Immortality, Reincarnation

Much older than the belief in bodily resurrection is the belief in immortality and reincarnation (rebirth) among ancient and living faith traditions. With all their differences, the Greek and Hindu versions of immortality share some common "ground beliefs" that differ significantly from those of the Abrahamic faiths. First, rather than the soul possessing inherent powers in itself, in the Abrahamic view life eternal is a gift from God. Second, rather than the soul being the person itself, let alone the "true" person, the resurrection doctrine considers the whole human being as the human person. Third, rather than the soul having its endless journey and history through incarnations, the person, after once-for-all earthly life, looks forward to eternal life in communion with the Creator. Finally, for Abrahamic faiths, each human life and human personality (individuality) is unique and nonrepeatable.

With the Abrahamic faiths' doctrine of bodily resurrection, Asiatic faiths' teaching on reincarnation/transmigration shares the problem of identity constitution, though in the latter that is of course differently framed, namely, "how to preserve the identity of the soul in the mutability of the forms which the soul assumes." The problem of identity continuation from one human life to another is a huge challenge. But it becomes hugely more challenging when we think of a sequence of lives from human to animal and back to human. Is the "soul" still the carrier of the identity in such instances?[84]

A common and persistent misunderstanding among Christian observers of Hinduism is that rebirth signifies a "second chance." That is a fatal mistake. Belief in rebirth has nothing to do with yet another potential opportunity to fix one's life. Rebirth is rather the result of the karmic law of cause and effect. Even gods cannot break the power of karma. As a result, Hinduism (and Buddhism) in general seeks a way to defeat the possibility of having to be born again. Rather than a positive possibility, rebirth is more like a curse.

A standard question to both Hindu and Buddhist eschatologies has to do with the assignment of this-worldly fortunes or ills to previous lives. Morally, it seems highly questionable to refer the sufferings of the poor, sick, those with disabilities, and other unfortunate people to their past deeds. Nor does it seem morally fair to count the fortunes of the rich, famous, and healthy as their personal accomplishments. Rather, in our kind of world evil and good seem to be mixed together.

Provided (for the sake of the argument) that the karmic cause-and-effect logic were to work, a problem arises with regard to memory. How many persons recall their former lives in order to see the logic and learn from them? Hindu philosophy has so far failed to offer a reasonable explanation. It is merely assumed that one recalls something from one's past lives and that this in some way or another guides one's life choices. But even if those memories do not appear, the person is claimed to have lived his or her life in the "shadow" of past lives' experiences and memories.

An even more difficult question has to do with the capacities of the "soul" of nonhuman entities in the samsaric cycle. Rebirth (or transmigration) of course assumes some kind of "animating principle, however defined, from one more or less physical, terrestrial body to another."[85] Now, believing that karma may lead the human being not only upward but also downward in the evolutionary tree results in a highly problematic assumption: namely, that all souls must know and understand, make choices; in other words, they must have self-consciousness and advanced intellectual skills. While that is not a problem with most humans—unless they die as infants or are mentally impaired—with subhuman entities it is a problem, beginning even with the "highest" animals. For example: How could the "soul" of an insect or a dog have these capacities in its way

---

84. Moltmann, *Coming of God*, 112–13.
85. Goldman, "Karma, Guilt, and Buried Memories," 414.

"upward" in the cycle of rebirths? Again, no satisfactory and reasonable account comes to mind.

To the outsider, belief in reincarnation seems highly individualistic. Obviously, it neglects the effects on each person's behavior and attitudes of environmental, social, cultural, sociopolitical, and economic factors, to name a few. However, we know that much of what we are is the result of effects from the milieu in which we evolve and live. Of course, the counterargument could be that we are put in this place of suffering because of our previous deeds, but even in such a case, the effects of the community and human relatedness are not to be appropriately addressed. A corollary problem is that if another person—or even a divine being—seeks to alleviate my suffering, then it must lead to the postponement of my final release. Is that charitable act then really charitable, or rather an unintentional way of adding to my suffering?[86]

Hindu and Buddhist visions of afterlife also seem to defeat any permanent meaning of embodiment, and this is a major difference from Abrahamic faith traditions' focus on the resurrection of the body. The latter understand final release in terms of liberation *from* all bodily life, not a renewal of it. Likewise, the Buddhist vision of no-self in particular seems to block any fruitful notion of personal self or individuality. And that carries over to eschatology. No wonder that a Christian commentator is so deeply troubled by any kind of possibility of a "rebirth" of something that does not exist. Indeed, in the absence of self, it is impossible—at least for the Western mind—to imagine a person who clings to life due to desire, suffers from the effects of karma, and comes to the enlightening realization. Doesn't all of that require a person, a self? Related to this is the question of how we affirm the dignity of human personhood if there is nothing "permanent." Finally, how should we conceive the principle of karma in the absence of the "self" whose destiny it should determine? Further dialogue between Christian (Abrahamic) theology and Asiatic faiths is needed to clear up these kinds of specific questions.

Moving away from personal questions related to the end, to the cosmic ones, let us briefly consider diverse faiths' vision of consummation.

Religious Visions of Cosmic Consummation among Religions

The Jewish tradition has not spilled much ink trying to describe the final consummation because of its this-worldly orientation. Similarly to Christian tradition, post-Enlightenment nontraditional Jewish movements virtually

---

86. Ward, *Religion and Human Nature*, 66–67.

ignore any mention of heaven. Even in the rabbinic writings, reservation in speaking about the future is the norm. Somewhat similarly to the Christian vision, various stages on the way to the final messianic consummation can be seen in Judaism; the Christian counterparts are the intermediate state and the millennium. Although the cosmic eschatological vision is not totally foreign to Judaism, neither is it at the heart of that tradition.

Islam's vision of heaven is the most transcendent, rich with elaborate descriptions of the final consummation, which take their departure from the beauties and enjoyment of this world but also develop them into highly sophisticated accounts of otherworldly bliss. In that sense, the danger of escapism looms large in many forms of Muslim spirituality, not least in Sufi traditions.

A radical difference concerning consummation can be found between Asiatic and Abrahamic faiths. The Asiatic traditions reject any final resolution in their cyclical and ever-repeating cosmologies (even if the individual person's cycle may come to an end in nirvana). A major difference also has to do with the decidedly theo-centric vision of Abrahamic faiths in their expectations of consummation. Even in theistic Hinduism as well as Buddhism's Mahayana traditions, which freely acknowledge deities, their role is ambiguous or at least marginal. Particularly for Buddhism, any talk about "eschatology" in reference to a doctrine of "last things" or "consummation" with any sense of closure is highly problematic in principle. For the sake of interfaith hospitality, these dramatic differences have to be highlighted and respected.

Epilogue

THE POPULAR VERSION OF Moltmann's massive eschatology, *The Coming of God*, is wittily titled *In the End—the Beginning*. It is a wonderful way of wrapping up this brief presentation on Christian doctrine for the sake of the religiously pluralistic and secular world of the third millennium. The title reminds us that any attempt to summarize Christian beliefs is a task without end. It is an ongoing labor.

This primer has reminded us over and over again that at the heart of Christian vision of faith and the world is what the Triune God—Father, Son, and Spirit—has done in the past, is doing in the now, and will be doing at the end. What a grand vision it is! What an occasion for praise and glory!

The most a fallible and limited human mind can do is to sketch an outline, a picture, a vision of the incredible work of the Triune God. The Father, having revealed himself to us in the Son through the power of the Spirit, acts jointly with them to create the world and human beings in his image. The Son, sent by his Father in tandem with the Spirit, lives, ministers, dies on the cross, and rises to new life for us and our salvation, to be seated on the Father's right hand as coruler. The life-giving Spirit, who sustains all life in this cosmos, is also the One who, with the Father, raises the Son from the dead, brings about faith in Christ, and empowers the Christian walk in obedience to Christ's teaching. The triune God's salvific gifts are donated by the Spirit to us as persons and members of the Christian community. The church/temple of the Spirit, body of Christ, people of God, images the triune God by being a sent community and an agent of reconciliation toward the unity of all people in God. The eschatological consummation, the joint work of Father, Son, and Spirit, brings to realization the eternal promises of God for men and women, as well as this whole cosmos created by the same God.

This is the Christian vision, based on the biblical revelation, and it has to be put in dialogue with other faith traditions' visions as well as the rest of human knowledge as discovered in the sciences. If the triune God is the Creator, Provider, and Consummator of all things, then nothing in the world—including religions as ways of pursuing God's truth—escapes the theologian's notice. Hence, constant dialogue with living faiths (Jewish, Muslim, Buddhist, and Hindu) as well as secular knowledge are hallmarks of this new way of doing Christian theology.

While faith and reason should not be juxtaposed, ultimately theological convictions and beliefs are just that: *convictions* and *beliefs*. They are person-related. The American philosopher William James's classic essay "The Will to Believe" sets forth some characteristics of a commitment to believe when one is faced with a lack of conclusive evidence. The three basic conditions James outlines are that, first, the decision to believe does not leave any choices ("belief is forced") because of its urgency; second, that it makes a vital difference in life; and third, that it presents itself as a plausible or realistic option.[1] It is easy to see the application of James's reasoning to the discussion of certainty with regard to revelation and faith. Although there is no conclusive evidence available—and in this sense, to quote Kierkegaard, the believer lives in "objective uncertainty"—the call of the gospel comes to one's life as a total call for surrender. Even when the intellectual and rational homework is done, that alone will persuade no one to surrender, particularly when the Christian gospel also calls for moral obedience, similarly to Jewish and Islamic traditions.

In his discussion James refers to French philosopher Blaise Pascal's famous wager metaphor, which introduces the concept of risk as well—but risk worth taking. Advises the French philosopher: "Let us weigh the gain and the loss in wagering that God is. Let us estimate these two chances. If you gain, you gain all; if you lose, you lose nothing. Wager, then, without hesitation that He is."[2] The recommendation to take up this wager is another fitting way of repeating the message of this epilogue: *In the End—the Beginning.*

---

1. James, "Will to Believe," 1–31 (see esp. 1–4 for a brief presentation and discussion of these conditions). I am indebted to Ward, *Religion and Revelation*, 26–27, for turning my attention to this essay for the consideration of this topic.

2. Pascal, "Of the Necessity of the Wager," section 3, citation in para. 233.

Bibliography

Abe, Masao. "Kenotic God and Dynamic Sunyata." In *Divine Emptiness and Historical Fullness: A Buddhist-Jewish-Christian Conversation with Masao Abe*, edited by Christopher Ives, 25–90. Valley Forge, PA: Trinity, 1995.
Abrahams, Israel. "Belief: The Bible." In *Encyclopedia Judaica*, edited by Fred Skolnik and Michael Berenbaum, 3:290–91. 2nd ed. Detroit: Macmillan Reference USA, 2007.
Adiswarananda, Swami. "Hinduism (Part 2)." Ramakrishna-Vivekananda Center of New York, 1996. https://www.ramakrishna.org/hinduism2.html.
Al-Baghawi, ed. *Mishkat al-Masabih*. Translated by James Robinson. 4 vols. Lahore: Sh. Muhammad Ashraft, 1965–66.
Alfeyev, Bishop Hilarion. "Eschatology." In *The Cambridge Companion to Orthodox Christian Theology*, edited by Mary B. Cunningham and Elizabeth Theokritoff, 107–20. New York: Cambridge University Press, 2008.
al-Ghazali [al-Ghazzali], Abu Hamid Muhammad. *Al-Ghazzali on Repentance*. Translated by M. S. Stern. New Delhi: Sterling, 1990. http://www.ghazali.org/books/gz-repent.pdf.
Anselm of Canterbury. *Proslogion*. In *Anslem of Canterbury: The Major Works*, edited by Brian Davies and G. R. Evans, 82–104. Oxford: Oxford University Press, 1998.
Aquinas, Thomas. *Summa contra Gentiles*. Edited by Joseph Kenny OP. Translated by Anton C. Pegis et al. New York: Hanover, 1955–57.
———. *The Summa Theologica of St. Thomas Aquinas*. 2nd and rev. ed., 1920. Literally translated by Fathers of the English Dominican Province. Online Edition, 2017, by Kevin Knight. http://www.newadvent.org/summa/.
Aristotle. *Nicomachean Ethics*. In *The Complete Works of Aristotle*, edited by Jonathan Barnes, 1729–1867. Vol. 2. Princeton: Princeton University Press, 1984.
Attwood, Jayarava Michael. "Did King Ajātasattu Confess to the Buddha, and Did the Buddha Forgive Him?" *Journal of Buddhist Ethics* 15 (2008) 279–307.
Augustine. *Confessions*. Translated by Vernon J. Bourke. The Fathers of the Church: A New Translation 21. Washington, DC: The Catholic University of America Press, 1953.

———. *The Literal Meaning of Genesis*. Translated and annotated by John Hammond Taylor SJ. 2 vols. Ancient Christian Writers 41–42. Edited by Johannes Quasten, Walter J. Burghardt, and Thomas Comerford Lawler. New York: Newman, 1982.

———. *On Free Choice of the Will*. Translated by Thomas Williams. Indianapolis: Hackett, 1993.

Aune, David E. "Repentance." In vol. 11 of *Encyclopedia of Religion*, edited by Lindsay Jones, 7755–59. 2nd ed. Detroit: Macmillan Reference USA, 2005.

Ayoub, Mahmoud Mustafa. "Towards an Islamic Christology, II: The Death of Jesus, Reality or Delusion (a Study in the Death of Jesus in Tafsīr Literature)." *The Muslim World* 70.2 (1980) 91–121.

Baker-Fletcher, Garth Kasimu. *Xodus: An African American Male Journey*. Minneapolis: Fortress, 1996.

Bales, Kevin. *Disposable People: New Slavery in the Global Economy*. Rev. ed. with a new preface. Berkeley: University of California Press, 2004.

Barker, Gregory A. "Muslim Perceptions of Jesus: Key Issues." In *Jesus beyond Christianity: The Classic Texts*, edited by Gregory A. Barker and Stephen E. Gregg, 83–86. New York: Oxford University Press, 2010.

Barth, Karl. *Church Dogmatics*. Edited by Geoffrey William Bromiley and Thomas Forsyth Torrance. Translated by G. W. Bromiley. Edinburgh: T&T Clark, 1956–75. Online edition by Alexander Street Press, 1975.

Batchelor, Martine. "Meditation and Mindfulness." *Contemporary Buddhism* 12.1 (2011) 157–64.

Bauckham, Richard, and Trevor A. Hart. *Hope against Hope: Christian Eschatology at the Turn of the Millennium*. Grand Rapids: Eerdmans, 1999.

Bauman, Zygmunt. *Globalization: The Human Consequences*. New York: Columbia University Press, 1998.

Bebawi, George H. "Atonement and Mercy: Islam between Athanasius and Anselm." In *Atonement Today*, edited by John Goldingay, 185–202. London: SPCK, 1995.

Bennett, Clinton. *Understanding Christian-Muslim Relations: Past and Present*. London: Continuum, 2008.

Bergen, Jeremy M. "The Holy Spirit in the World." *Vision: A Journal for Church and Theology* 13.1 (Spring 2012) 84–92.

Berger, Peter L. *A Rumor of Angels: Modern Society and the Rediscovery of the Supernatural*. Garden City, NY: Doubleday, 1969.

Berkhof, Hendrikus. *Christ and the Powers*. Translated by John Howard Yoder. Scottdale, PA: Herald, 1962.

Berkhof, Louis. *Systematic Theology*. Rev. and enlarged ed. Grand Rapids: Eerdmans, 1953 [1941].

Bharat, Sandy. "Hindu Perspectives on Jesus." In *The Blackwell Companion to Jesus*, edited by Delbert Burkett, 250–66. Malden, MA: Wiley-Blackwell, 2011.

Bloesch, Donald G. *The Last Things: Resurrection, Judgment, Glory*. Christian Foundations. Downers Grove, IL: IVP Academic, 2004.

Bloom, Dov. "What Is the Amidah? Understanding the Shemoneh Esrei." Chabad.org, n.d. https://www.chabad.org/library/article_cdo/aid/3834226/jewish/What-Is-the-Amidah.htm.

Blue, Ken. *Authority to Heal*. Downers Grove, IL: InterVarsity, 1987.

BIBLIOGRAPHY

Bodhi, Bhikkhu. "Introduction." In *The Middle Length Discourses of the Buddha: A Translation of the Majjhima Nikāya*, original translation by Bhikkhu Ñāṇamoli, translation edited and revised by Bhikku Bodhi, 19–60. 4th ed. Somerville, MA: Wisdom, 2015 [1995].

Boff, Leonardo. *Was kommt nachher? Das Leben nach dem Tode*. Translated from Portuguese to German by Horst Goldstein. Salzburg: Otto Müller Verlag, 1982.

Brannan, Rick, ed. *Historic Creeds and Confessions*. Grand Rapids: Christian Classics Ethereal Library. https://ccel.org/ccel/brannan/hstcrcon/hstcrcon?queryID=2308 1851&resultID=985.

Browning, George. "Sabbath Reflections 5: Capitalism and Inequity versus a Gospel Mandate." Anglican Communion Environmental Network, 2012. https://acen.anglicancommunion.org/media/61249/Sabbath-Study-5.pdf.

Brueggemann, Walter. *The Covenanted Self: Explorations in Law and Covenant*. Edited by Patrick D. Miller. Minneapolis: Augsburg Fortress, 1999.

———. *Theology of the Old Testament: Testimony, Dispute, Advocacy*. Minneapolis: Augsburg Fortress, 1997.

Cabezón, José Ignacio. "Buddhism and Science: On the Nature of the Dialogue." In *Buddhism and Science: Breaking New Ground*, edited by B. Alan Wallace, 35–68. New York: Columbia University Press, 2003.

———. "Buddhist Views of Jesus." In *Jesus in the World's Faiths: Leading Thinkers from Five Religions Reflect on His Meaning*, edited by Gregory A. Barker, 15–24. Maryknoll, NY: Orbis, 2005.

Cahill, Lisa Sowle. *Sex, Gender, and Christian Ethics*. New York: Cambridge University Press, 1996.

Calvin, John. *Institutes of the Christian Religion*. Translated by Henry Beveridge. 1845. https://ccel.org/ccel/calvin/institutes/institutes.

———. *Commentary on the Epistle of Paul the Apostle to the Romans*. Translated by John Owen. Grand Rapids: Christian Classics Ethereal Library. https://ccel.org/ccel/calvin/calcom38/calcom38?queryID=23035169&resultID=1116.

Carman, John B. *Majesty and Meekness: A Comparative Study of Contrast and Harmony in the Concept of God*. Grand Rapids: Eerdmans, 1994.

Chan, Simon. "Sanctification." In *Global Dictionary of Theology*, edited by William A. Dyrness and Veli-Matti Kärkkäinen, associate editors Juan Francisco Martinez and Simon Chan, 789–91. Downer's Grove, IL: IVP Academic, 2008.

Chishti, Saadia Khawar Khan. "*Fiṭra*: An Islamic Model for Humans and the Environment." In *Islam and Ecology: A Bestowed Trust*, edited by Richard C. Foltz et al., 67–82. Cambridge: Harvard University Press, 2003.

Clayton, Philip C. "Eschatology as Metaphysics under the Guise of Hope." In *World without End: Christian Eschatology from a Process Perspective*, edited by Joseph A. Bracken, SJ, 128–49. Grand Rapids: Eerdmans, 2005.

———. "The Impossible Possibility: Divine Causes in the World of Nature." In *God, Life, and the Cosmos: Christian and Islamic Perspectives*, edited by Ted Peters, Muzaffar Iqbal, and Syed Nomanul Haq, 249–80. Burlington, VT: Ashgate, 2002.

———. *Mind and Emergence: From Quantum to Consciousness*. Oxford: Oxford University Press, 2004.

Clifford, Anne M. "Creation." In *Systematic Theology: Roman Catholic Perspectives*, edited by Francis Schüssler Fiorenza and John P. Galvin, 1:193–248. Minneapolis: Fortress, 1991.

BIBLIOGRAPHY

Clooney, Francis X., SJ. "Trinity and Hinduism." In *Cambridge Companion to the Trinity*, edited by Peter C. Phan, 309–24. Cambridge: Cambridge University Press, 2011.

Cohon, Samuel S. *Essays in Jewish Theology*. Cincinnati: Hebrew Union College Press, 1987.

———. *Jewish Theology: A Historical and Systematic Interpretation of Judaism and Its Foundations*. Assen: Royal VanGorcum, 1971.

Collins, Robin. "Evolution and Original Sin." In *Perspectives on Evolving Creation*, edited by K. B. Miller, 469–501. Grand Rapids: Eerdmans, 2003.

Cone, James H. *A Black Theology of Liberation*. 2nd ed. 20th anniversary ed. Maryknoll, NY: Orbis, 1986.

———. *God of the Oppressed*. Rev. ed. Maryknoll, NY: Orbis, 1997.

International Health Conference. "Constitution of the World Health Organization." New York, June 19–July 22, 1946. https://apps.who.int/gb/bd/PDF/bd47/EN/constitution-en.pdf?ua=1.

Cornell, Vincent. "Listening to God through the Qur'an." In *Scriptures in Dialogue: Christians and Muslims Studying the Bible and the Qur'an Together*, edited by Michael Ipgrave, 36–43. London: Church House, 2004.

Couenhoven, Jesse. "Forgiveness and Restoration: A Theological Exploration." *Journal of Religion* 90.2 (2010) 148–70.

Courtright, Paul B. "Worship and Devotional Life: Hindu Devotional Life." In vol. 14 of *Encyclopedia of Religion*, edited by Lindsay Jones, 9820–26. 2nd ed. Detroit: Macmillan Reference USA, 2005.

Coward, Harold G. *Sacred Word and Sacred Text: Scripture in World Religions*. Maryknoll, NY: Orbis, 1988.

Culpepper, Robert H. *Interpreting the Atonement*. Grand Rapids: Eerdmans, 1966.

Darwin, Charles. *The Origin of Species by Means of Natural Selection*. With additions and corrections from the sixth and last English edition. New York: D. Appleton, 1896. In vol. 49 of *Great Books of the Western World*, edited by Robert Maynard Hutchins. Chicago: Encyclopaedia Britannica, 1952.

Davary, Bahar. "Forgiveness in Islam: Is It an Ultimate Reality?" *Ultimate Reality and Meaning* 27.2 (June 2004) 127–41.

Dawkins, Richard. *The Blind Watchmaker: Why the Evidence of Evolution Reveals a Universe Without Design*. New York: Norton, 1996.

D'Costa, Gavin. *The Meeting of Religions and the Trinity*. Faith Meets Faith. Maryknoll, NY: Orbis, 2000.

de Lange, Nicholas. *An Introduction to Judaism*. New York: Cambridge University Press, 2000.

de Mesa, José M. "Making Salvation Concrete and Jesus Real: Trends in Asian Christology." *Exchange* 30.1 (2001) 1–17.

"Deoxyribonucleic Acid (DNA) Fact Sheet." National Human Genome Research Institute, n.d. https://www.genome.gov/about-genomics/fact-sheets/Deoxyribonucleic-Acid-Fact-Sheet.

Dhavamony, Mariasusai. "Death and Immortality in Hinduism." In *Death and Immortality in the Religions of the World*, edited by Paul Badham and Linda Badham, 93–108. New York: Paragon, 1987.

Dickson, John. "Quest for the Historical Jesus," Parts 1 and 2. Center for Public Christianity, March 16, 2008. https://www.publicchristianity.org/quest-for-the-historical-jesus-part-i/; https://www.publicchristianity.org/quest-for-the-historical-jesus-part-ii/.

BIBLIOGRAPHY

"DNA: Chemical Compound." Britannica, n.d. https://www.britannica.com/science/DNA.

Dufault-Hunter, Erin Elizabeth. *The Transformative Power of Faith: A Narrative Approach to Conversion*. Lanham, MD: Lexington, 2012.

Dyson, Freeman J. *Disturbing the Universe*. New York: Harper & Row, 1979.

Dwivedi, O. P. "Dharmic Ecology." In *Hinduism and Ecology: The Intersection of Earth, Sky, and Water*, edited by Christopher Key Chapple and Mary Evelyn Tucker, 3–22. Religions of the World and Ecology. Cambridge: Harvard University Press, 2000.

Eckel, Malcolm David. "A Buddhist Approach to Repentance." In *Repentance: A Comparative Perspective*, edited by Amitai Etzioni and David E. Carney, 122–42. Lanham, MD: Rowman & Littlefield, 1997

"Emerging Church." Theopedia, n.d. https://www.theopedia.com/Emerging_Church.

Enns, Peter. *The Evolution of Adam: What the Bible Does and Doesn't Say about Human Origins*. Grand Rapids: Brazos, 2012.

Fergusson, David. "Reclaiming the Doctrine of Sanctification." *Interpretation* 53.4 (1999) 380–90.

Feuerbach, Ludwig. *The Essence of Christianity*. Translated by Marian Evans [George Eliot]. Cambridge Library Collection—Philosophy. Cambridge: Cambridge University Press, 2012.

Fischer, John Martin. "Putting Molinism in Its Place." In *Molinism: The Contemporary Debate*, edited by Kenneth Perszyk, 208–26. New York: Oxford University Press, 2011.

Flood, Gavid D. "Jesus in Hinduism: Closing Reflection." In *Jesus Beyond Christianity: The Classic Texts*, edited by Gregory A. Barker and Stephen E. Gregg, 201–6. New York: Oxford University Press, 2010.

Francis, Pope. *Laudato Si'. Encyclical Letter, On Care for Our Common Home*. Vatican, May 24, 2015. https://www.vatican.va/content/francesco/en/encyclicals/documents/papa-francesco_20150524_enciclica-laudato-si.html.

Fromherz, Allen. "Judgment, Final." In *The Oxford Encyclopedia of the Islamic World*, edited by John L. Esposito. Oxford: Oxford University Press, 2009. http://www.oxfordislamicstudies.com/article/opr/t236/e1107.

Gaiser, Frederik J. *Healing in the Bible: Theological Insight for Christian Ministry*. Grand Rapids: Baker Academic, 2010.

Garrett, James Leo. *Systematic Theology: Biblical, Historical, and Evangelical*. 2 vols. Grand Rapids: Eerdmans, 1990–95.

Gertel, Elliot B. "The Holy Spirit in the Zohar." *CCAR Journal: A Reform Jewish Quarterly* 56.4 (Fall 2009) 80–102.

Gibbs, Eddie, and Ryan K. Bolger. *The Emerging Churches: Creating Christian Community in Postmodern Cultures*. Grand Rapids: Baker Academic, 2005.

Gillman, Neil. *The Death of Death: Resurrection and Immortality in Jewish Thought*. Woodstock, VT: Jewish Lights, 1997.

Goldingay, John, and David Payne. *A Critical and Exegetical Commentary on Isaiah 40–55*. Vol. 2. The International Critical Commentary. London: T&T Clark International, 2006.

Goldman, Robert P. "Karma, Guilt, and Buried Memories: Public Fantasy and Private Reality in Traditional India." *Journal of the American Oriental Society* 105.3 (1985) 413–25.

Grant, Jacquelyn. "Womanist Theology: Black Women's Experience as a Source for Doing Theology, with Special Reference to Christology." In *Constructive Christian Theology in the Worldwide Church*, edited by William R. Barr, 337–54. Grand Rapids: Eerdmans, 1997.

Green, Joel B. "Luke, Gospel of." In *Dictionary of Jesus and the Gospels*, edited by Joel B. Green, Jeannine K. Brown, and Nicholas Perrin, 540–52. 2nd ed. Downers Grove, IL: IVP Academic, 2013.

Greene, Sidney L. "Evangelical Fundamentalists and the Science of Climate Change." ISCAST, September 30, 2014. https://iscast.org/uncategorized/evangelical-fundamentalists-and-the-science-of-climate-change/.

Grenz, Stanley J. *The Social God and Relational Self: A Trinitarian Theology of the* Imago Dei. Louisville: Westminster John Knox, 2001.

———. *Theology for the Community of God*. Grand Rapids: Eerdmans, 1994.

Gross, Rita M. "Meditating on Jesus." In *Buddhists Talk about Jesus, Christians Talk about the Buddha*, edited by Rita M. Gross and Terry C. Muck, 32–51. New York: Continuum, 2005 [1999].

Gutiérrez, Gustavo. *The Power of the Poor in History*. Translated by Robert R. Barr. Maryknoll, NY: Orbis, 1983.

———. *A Theology of Liberation: History, Politics, and Salvation*. Translated and edited by Sister Caridad Inda and John Eagleson. Maryknoll, NY: Orbis, 1986 [1973]; rev. ed. with a new introduction, 1988.

Haitch, Russell. *From Exorcism to Ecstasy: Eight Views of Baptism*. Louisville: Westminster John Knox, 2007.

Haleem, M. A. S. Abdel. "Qur'an and Hadith." In *The Cambridge Companion to Classical Islamic Theology*, edited by Tim Winter, 19–32. New York: Cambridge University Press, 2008.

Harris, Sam. *Free Will*. New York: Free Press, 2012.

Haught, John F. *Is Nature Enough? Meaning and Truth in the Age of Science*. New York: Cambridge University Press, 2006.

Hawking, Stephen. *A Brief History of Time*. Updated and expanded 10th anniversary ed. New York: Bantam, 1998 [1988].

Hejzlar, Pavel. *Two Paradigms for Divine Healing: Fred F. Bosworth, Kenneth E. Hagin, Agnes Sanford, and Francis MacNutt in Dialogue*. Global Pentecostal and Charismatic Studies 4. Boston: Brill, 2010.

Heschel, Susannah. "Jewish Views of Jesus." In *Jesus in the World's Faiths: Leading Thinkers from Five Religions Reflect on His Meaning*, edited by Gregory A. Barker, 149–60. Maryknoll, NY: Orbis, 2005.

Hick, John. *Death and Eternal Life: With a New Preface by the Author*. Louisville: Westminster John Knox, 1994 [1976].

———. *Evil and the God of Love*. 2nd reissued ed. New York: Palgrave Macmillan, 2010.

———. *God and the Universe of Faiths: Essays in the Philosophy of Religion*. Reissued with a new preface. London: Macmillan, 1988.

Hiebert, Paul G. "Conversion in Hinduism and Buddhism." In *Handbook of Religious Conversion*, edited by H. Newton Malony and Samuel Southard, 9–21. Birmingham, AL: Religious Education Press, 1992.

———. "Discerning the Work of God." In *Charismatic Experiences in History*, edited by Cecil M. Robeck, Jr., 147–63. Peabody, MA: Hendrickson, 1985.

Hodge, Charles. *Systematic Theology.* Vol. 3. Grand Rapids: Eerdmans, 1952 [1871–1872].

"Hominid." Science Direct, n.d. https://www.sciencedirect.com/topics/pharmacology-toxicology-and-pharmaceutical-science/hominid.

Howell, Elizabeth, and Daisy Dobrijevic. "What Is the Cosmic Microwave Background?" Space, January 28, 2022. https://www.space.com/33892-cosmic-microwave-background.html.

Hunter, Harold D. "Ordinances." In *The New International Dictionary of Pentecostal and Charismatic Movements*, edited by Stanley M. Burgess and Eduard M. van der Maas, 948–49. Rev. and exp. ed. Grand Rapids: Zondervan, 2002.

Hyun, Younghak, "Three Talks on Minjung Theology." *Inter-Religion* 7 (Spring 1985) 2–40. https://nirc.nanzan-u.ac.jp/journal/7/issue/209/article/1571.

Iqbal, Muzaffar. "In the Beginning: Islamic Perspectives on Cosmological Origins." *Islam and Science* 4.1 (Summer 2006) 61–78.

James, William. "The Will to Believe." In *"The Will to Believe" and Other Essays in Popular Philosophy and Human Immortality*, by William James, 1–31. Mineola, NY: Dover, 1956.

Jeffery, Arthur. *The Foreign Vocabulary of the Qurʾān.* Leiden: Brill, 2007.

Jewett, Paul King. *Election and Predestination.* Grand Rapids: Eerdmans, 1985.

Jewett, Paul King, with Marguerite Shuster. *Who We Are: Our Dignity as Human; A Neo-Evangelical Theology.* Grand Rapids: Eerdmans, 1996.

Jewish Virtual Center. "Kabbalah: The Zohar." n.d. https://www.jewishvirtuallibrary.org/the-zohar.

Joh, Wonhee Anne. *Heart of the Cross: A Postcolonial Christology.* Louisville: Westminster John Knox, 2006.

Johnson, Elizabeth. *Friends of God and Prophets: A Feminist Theological Reading of the Communion of Saints.* New York: Continuum, 1998.

———. *She Who Is: The Mystery of God in Feminist Theological Discourse.* New York: Crossroad, 1992.

———. *Women, Earth, and Creator Spirit.* Mahwah, NJ: Paulist, 1993.

Jones, L. Gregory. *Embodying Forgiveness: A Theological Analysis.* Grand Rapids: Eerdmans, 1995.

Kant, Immanuel. *The Critique of Practical Reason* [1788]. Translated by Thomas Kingsmill Abbott. Auckland: Floating Press, 2009.

Kärkkäinen, Veli-Matti. *Christology: A Global Introduction.* 2nd ed. Grand Rapids: Baker Academic, 2016.

———. *A Constructive Christian Theology for the Pluralistic World.* 5 vols. *Christ and Reconciliation* (2013), *Trinity and Revelation* (2014), *Creation and Humanity* (2015), *Spirit and Salvation* (2016), *Community and Hope* (2017). Grand Rapids: Eerdmans, 2013–17.

———. *An Introduction to Ecclesiology: Historical, Global, and Interreligious Perspectives.* 2nd ed. Downer's Grove, IL: IVP Academic, 2021.

———. *Trinity and Revelation: A Constructive Christian Theology for the Pluralistic World.* Grand Rapids: Eerdmans, 2014.

Karras, Valerie A. "Eschatology." In *Cambridge Companion to Feminist Theology*, edited by Susan Frank Parsons, 243–60. New York: Cambridge University Press, 2002.

BIBLIOGRAPHY

Kelly, J. N. D. *Early Christian Doctrines*. London: Bloomsbury Academic, 2014. Online edition. https://www.bloomsburycollections.com/book/early-christian-doctrines/.

Kelsey, David H. *Eccentric Existence: A Theological Anthropology*. 2 vols. Louisville: Westminster John Knox, 2009.

Khalidi, Tarif, ed. and trans. *The Muslim Jesus: Sayings and Stories in Islamic Literature*. Cambridge: Harvard University Press, 2001.

Klausner, Joseph. *Jesus of Nazareth: His Life, Times, and Teaching*. Translated by Herbert Danby. New York: Macmillan, 1925.

Klostermaier, Klaus K. *A Survey of Hinduism*. 3rd ed. Albany: State University of New York Press, 2007.

Knipe, David M. "Hindu Eschatology." In *Oxford Handbook of Eschatology*, edited by Jerry L. Walls, 170–90. New York: Oxford University Press, 2009. Online edition.

Knitter, Paul F. *One Earth, Many Religions: Multifaith Dialogue and Global Responsibility*. Maryknoll, NY: Orbis, 1995.

Kogan, Michael S. *Opening the Covenant: A Jewish Theology of Christianity*. New York: Oxford University Press, 2008.

Kritzeck, James. "Holy Spirit in Islam." In *Perspectives on Charismatic Renewal*, edited by Edward D. O'Connor, 101–11. Notre Dame: University of Notre Dame Press, 1975.

Kulandran, Sabapathy. *Grace in Christianity and Hinduism*. Cambridge: James Clarke, 2004 [1964].

Kumar, B. J. Christie. "An Indian Appreciation of the Doctrine of the Holy Spirit: A Search into the Religious Heritage of the Indian Christian." *Indian Journal of Theology* 30 (1981) 29–35.

Küng, Hans. "A Christian Response [to Josef van Ess, "Islam and the Other Religions: Jesus in the Qur'an; Islamic Perspectives"]." In *Christianity and the World Religions: Paths of Dialogue with Islam, Hinduism, and Buddhism*, by Hans Küng et al., translated by Peter Heinegg, 109–30. New York: Doubleday, 1986.

———. *The Church*. Translated by Ray and Rosaleen Ockenden. London: Burns & Oates, 1968.

LaCugna, Catherine Mowry. *God for Us: The Trinity and Christian Life*. San Francisco: HarperSanFrancisco, 1991.

Langmead, Ross. "Transformed Relationships: Reconciliation as the Central Model for Mission." *Mission Studies* 25.1 (2008) 5–20.

Lapide, Pinchas. *Israelis, Jews, and Jesus*. Translated by Peter Heinegg. Garden City, NY: Doubleday, 1979.

———. *The Resurrection of Jesus: A Jewish Perspective*. Translated by Wilhelm C. Linss. Minneapolis: Augsburg, 1983.

Ledgerwood, Elaine C. "The Hope of Forgiveness." *Compass* 47.1 (Autumn 2013) 14–20.

Lee, Jung Young. *The Trinity in Asian Perspective*. Nashville: Abingdon, 1996.

Leirvik, Oddbjørn. *Images of Jesus Christ in Islam*. 2nd ed. New York: Continuum, 2010.

Graetz, Michael J. "Redemption: Modern Jewish Thought." In *Encyclopedia Judaica*, 17:154–55. 2nd ed. Detroit: Macmillan Reference, USA, 2007.

Ludwig, Theodore M. *The Sacred Paths: Understanding the Religions of the World*. 4th ed. Upper Saddle River, NJ: Pearson, 2006.

BIBLIOGRAPHY

Luther, Martin. *The Large Catechism of Martin Luther*. Translated by Robert H. Fischer. Philadelphia: Fortress, 1959.

———. *Luther's Works*. American ed. Libronix Digital Library. Edited by Jaroslav Pelikan and Helmut T. Lehman. 55 vols. Minneapolis: Fortress, 2002.

Lutheran World Federation and the Catholic Church. "Joint Declaration on the Doctrine of Justification." Dicastery for Promoting Christian Unity, 1999. http://www.christianunity.va/content/unitacristiani/en/dialoghi/sezione-occidentale/luterani/dialogo/documenti-di-dialogo/1999-dichiarazione-congiunta-sulla-dottrina-della-giustificazion/en.html.

Lyden, John C. "Atonement in Judaism and Christianity: Towards a Rapprochement." *Journal of Ecumenical Studies* 29.1 (Winter 1992) 47–54.

Maguire, Daniel. *The Moral Core of Judaism and Christianity: Reclaiming the Revolution*. Minneapolis: Fortress, 1993.

Maimonides, Moses. *The Guide for the Perplexed*. Translated by M. Friedländer [1903]. http://www.sacred-texts.com/jud/gfp/index.htm#contents.

Marks, Jonathan. *What It Means to Be 98% Chimpanzee: Apes, People, and Their Genes*. Berkeley: University of California Press, 2002.

Marouscelo, Ileana. "Free Will and Determinism." In vol. 5 of *Encyclopedia of Religion*, edited by Lindsay Jones, 3200–3202. 2nd ed. Detroit: Macmillan Reference USA, 2005.

McGinn, Bernard. *Antichrist: Two Thousand Years of the Human Fascination with Evil*. San Francisco: HaperSanFrancisco, 1994.

McGrath, Alister E. *A Brief History of Heaven*. Malden, MA: Blackwell, 2003.

———. *Dawkins' God: Genes, Memes, and the Meaning of Life*. Malden, MA: Blackwell, 2005.

McLellan, Don. "Justice, Forgiveness, and Reconciliation: Essential Elements in Atonement Theology." *Evangelical Review of Theology* 29.1 (2005) 4–15.

McClendon, James Wm., Jr. *Doctrine*. Vol. 2 of *Systematic Theology*. Nahsville: Abingdon, 1994.

McMahan, David L. *The Making of Buddhist Modernism*. New York: Oxford University Press, 2008.

McMullin, Ernan. "How Should Cosmology Relate to Theology?" In *The Sciences and Theology in the Twentieth Century*, edited by A. R. Peacocke, 17–57. Notre Dame: University of Notre Dame Press, 1981.

Meeks, M. Douglas. "The Economy of Grace: Human Dignity in Market System." In *God and Human Dignity*, edited by R. K. Soulen and L. Woodhead, 196–214. Grand Rapids: Eerdmans, 2006.

Melanchthon, Philipp. *Loci Communes Theologici*. Translated by Lowell J. Sartre and Wilhelm Pauck. In *Melanchthon and Bucer*, edited by Wilhelm Pauck, 18–154. Philadelphia: Westminster, 1969.

Merriam-Webster. "Worship." n.d. https://www.merriam-webster.com/dictionary/worship.

Meyer, Harding. *That All May Be One: Perceptions and Models of Ecumenicity*. Translated by William G. Rusch. Grand Rapids: Eerdmans, 1999.

Misner, Charles W., et al. *Gravitation*. San Francisco: W. H. Freeman and Company, 1973.

Miyahira, Nozomu. *Towards a Theology of the Concord of God: A Japanese Perspective on the Trinity*. Carlisle, UK: Paternoster, 2000.

Mohamed, Yasien. *Fitrah: The Islamic Concept of Human Nature.* London: Ta-Ha, 1996.

Moltmann, Jürgen. *The Church in the Power of the Spirit: A Contribution to Messianic Ecclesiology.* Translated by Margaret Kohl. Minneapolis: Fortress, 1993 [1977].

———. *The Coming of God: Christian Eschatology.* Translated by Margaret Kohl. Minneapolis: Fortress, 1996.

———. *The Crucified God: The Cross of Christ as the Foundation and Criticism of Christian Theology.* Translated by R. A. Wilson and John Bowden. Preface to the paperback edition translated by Margaret Kohl. Minneapolis: Fortress, 1993 [1974].

———. *Experiences in Theology: Ways and Forms of Christian Theology.* Translated by Margaret Kohl. Minneapolis: Fortress, 2000.

———. *God in Creation: A New Theology of Creation and the Spirit of God.* Translated by Margaret Kohl. Minneapolis: Fortress, 1993 [1985].

———. *In the End—the Beginning: The Life of Hope.* Translated by Margaret Kohl. Minneapolis: Fortress, 2004.

———. *The Spirit of Life: A Universal Affirmation.* Translated by Margaret Kohl. Minneapolis: Fortress, 2001.

———. *Theology of Hope: On the Ground and the Implications of a Christian Eschatology.* London: SCM, 1967 [1964].

———. *The Trinity and the Kingdom: The Doctrine of God.* Translated by Margaret Kohl. San Francisco: Harper & Row; London: SCM, 1981.

———. *The Way of Jesus Christ: Christology in Messianic Dimensions.* Translated by Margaret Kohl. Minneapolis: Fortress, 1993 [1989].

Montoya, Ryan. "What Is Death, Exactly?" *Scientific American*, October 18, 2019. https://blogs.scientificamerican.com/observations/what-is-death-exactly/.

Müller, Max, trans. *Sacred Books of the East.* 50 vols. Oxford: Oxford University Press, 1879–1910. www.sacred-texts.com.

Murphy, Nancey. "The Resurrection Body and Personal Identity: Possibilities and Limits of Eschatological Knowledge." In *Resurrection: Theological and Scientific Assessments*, edited by T. Peters, R. J. Russell, and M. Welker, 202–18. Grand Rapids: Eerdmans, 2002.

Nalunnakkal, George Mathew. "Come Holy Spirit, Heal and Reconcile: Called in Christ to Be Reconciling and Healing Communities." *International Review of Mission* 94.372 (2005) 7–19.

Nanda, Meera. "Vedic Science and Hindu Nationalism: Arguments against a Premature Synthesis of Religion and Science." In *Science and Religion in a Post-colonial World: Interfaith Perspectives*, edited by Zainal Abidin Bagir, 27–36. Adelaide: ATF, 2005.

NASA. "Discoveries—Highlights: Discovering a Runaway Universe." NASA, Hubble, n.d. https://www.nasa.gov/content/discoveries-highlights-discovering-a-runaway-universe.

———. "What Is the Big Bang?" NASA Science: Space Place, last modified March 17, 2021. https://spaceplace.nasa.gov/big-bang/en/.

———. "What Is the Inflation Theory?" Universe 101. Accessed January 2, 2023. https://wmap.gsfc.nasa.gov/universe/bb_cosmo_infl.html.

———. "What Is the Universe Made Of?" Wilkinson Microwave Anisotropy Probe, last modified April 16, 2010. https://map.gsfc.nasa.gov/universe/WMAP_Universe.pdf.

BIBLIOGRAPHY

Neusner, Jacob. "Repentance in Judaism." In *Repentance: A Comparative Perspective*, edited by Amitai Etzioni and David E. Carney, 60–75. Lanham, MD: Rowman & Littlefield, 1997.

Newbigin, Lesslie. *The Light Has Come: An Exposition of the Fourth Gospel*. Grand Rapids: Eerdmans, 1982.

Newlands, George, and Allen Smith. *Hospitable God: The Transformative Dream*. Surrey, UK: Ashgate, 2010.

Niebuhr, Reinhold. "Sin." In *A Handbook of Christian Theology*, edited by Marvin Halverson and Arthur A. Cohen, 348–51. New York: Meridian, 1958.

Novak, David. "Jewish Eschatology." In *Oxford Handbook of Eschatology*, edited by Jerry L. Walls, 113–31. New York: Oxford University Press, 2009. Online edition.

O'Brien, Glen. *Christian Worship: A Theological and Historical Introduction*. Eugene, OR: Wipf & Stock, 2015.

O'Shaughnessy, Thomas, SJ. *The Development of the Meaning of Spirit in the Koran*. Rome: Pont. Institutum Orientalium Studiorum, 1953.

Orthodox Presbyterian Church. *Larger Catechism*. n.d. https://www.opc.org/lc.html.

"Our Story." Fresh Expressions, n.d. https://freshexpressions.org.uk/what-is-fx/our-story/.

Panikkar, Raimundo. *The Unknown Christ of Hinduism: Towards an Ecumenical Christophany*. Rev. and enlarged ed. London: Darton, Longman & Todd, 1981.

Pannenberg, Wolfhart. *Systematic Theology*. Translated by Geoffrey W. Bromiley. 3 vols. Grand Rapids: Eerdmans, 1991, 1994, 1998.

Park, Andrew Sung. *The Wounded Heart of God: The Asian Concept of Han and the Christian Doctrine of Sin*. Nashville: Abingdon, 1993.

Parry, Robin A., and Christopher H. Partridge, eds. *Universal Salvation? The Current Debate*. Waynesboro, GA: Paternoster, 2003.

Pascal, Blaise. "Of the Necessity of the Wager." In *Pensées*, translated by W. F. Trotter, section 3. 1944 [1690]. ccel.org.

Pathrapankal, Joseph. "Editorial." *Journal of Dharma* 23.3 (1998) 299–302.

Paul, Pope, VI. *Dei Verbum*. Dogmatic Constitution on Divine Revelation. Vatican, November 18, 1965. https://www.vatican.va/archive/hist_councils/ii_vatican_council/documents/vat-ii_const_19651118_dei-verbum_en.html.

———. *Gaudium et Spes*. Pastoral Constitution on the Church in the Modern World. Vatican, December 7, 1965. https://www.vatican.va/archive/hist_councils/ii_vatican_council/documents/vat-ii_const_19651207_gaudium-et-spes_en.html.

Peters, Ted. "Introduction: What Is to Come." In *Resurrection: Theological and Scientific Assessments*, edited by T. Peters, R. J. Russell, and M. Welker, viii–xvii. Grand Rapids: Eerdmans, 2002.

Pew Research Center. "Summary of Key Findings." In *Pew Forum on Religion & Public Life / U.S. Religious Landscape Survey*, 3–20. Washington, DC: Pew Research Center, 2008.

Pieris, Aloysius, SJ. *An Asian Theology of Liberation*. Maryknoll, NY: Orbis, 1988.

Pigliucci, Massimo. "Science and Fundamentalism: A Strategy on How to Deal with Anti-science Fundamentalism." *Embo Reports* 6.12 (2005) 1106–9. http://www.ncbi.nlm.nih.gov/pmc/articles/PMC1369219.

Pinnock, Clark H. *A Wideness in God's Mercy: The Finality of Jesus Christ in a World of Religions*. Grand Rapids: Zondervan, 1992.

Plantinga, Alvin. *God, Freedom, and Evil*. London: Allen & Unwin, 1975.

Polkinghorne, John. "Anthropology in an Evolutionary Context." In *God and Human Dignity*, edited by R. Kendall Soulen and Linda Woodhead, 89–103. Grand Rapids: Eerdmans, 2006.

———. "Eschatology: Some Questions and Some Insights from Science." In *The End of the World and the Ends of God: Science and Theology on Eschatology*, edited by John Polkinghorne and Michael Welker, 29–41. Harrisburg, PA: Trinity, 2000.

———. *The God of Hope and the End of the World*. New Haven: Yale University Press, 2002.

Purcell, Brendan. *From Big Bang to Big Mystery: Human Origins in the Light of Creation and Evolution*. Hyde Park, NY: New City, 2012.

Rahner, Karl. *The Trinity*. Translated by Joseph Donceel. London: Burns & Oates, 1970.

Rahula, Walpola. *What the Buddha Taught*. Rev. ed. New York: Grove, 1974.

Rambo, Lewis R., and Charles E. Farhadian. "Conversion." In vol. 3 of *Encyclopedia of Religion*, edited by Lindsay Jones, 3200–3202. 2nd ed. Detroit: Macmillan Reference USA, 2005.

Ray, Reginald A. "Buddhism: Sacred Text Written and Realized." In *The Holy Book in Comparative Perspective*, edited by Frederick M. Denny and Rodney L. Taylor, 148–80. Columbia: University of South Carolina Press, 1985.

Reder, Michael, and Josef Schmidt, SJ. "Habermas and Religion." In *An Awareness of What Is Missing: Faith and Reason in a Post-secular Age*, by Jürgen Habermas et al., translated by Ciaran Cronin, 1–14. Cambridge: Polity, 2010 [2008].

Rivera, Mayra. *The Touch of Transcendence: A Postcolonial Theology of God*. Louisville: Westminster John Knox, 2007.

Roberts, Alexander, and James Donaldson, et al., eds. *The Ante-Nicene Fathers: Translations of the Writings of the Fathers down to A.D. 325*. 9 vols. Edinburgh, 1885–97. www.ccel.org.

Robinson, John A. T. *The Human Face of God*. Philadelphia: Westminster, 1973.

Robinson, Neil. *Christ in Islam and Christianity*. New York: State University of New York Press, 1991.

Rogers, Eugene F., Jr. *After the Spirit: A Constructive Pneumatology from Resources Outside the Modern West*. Grand Rapids: Eerdmans, 2005.

Ruether, Rosemary Radford. *Introducing Redemption in Christian Feminism*. Introductions in Feminist Theology 1. Sheffield: Sheffield Academic, 1998.

———. *Sexism and God-Talk: Toward a Feminist Theology*. Boston: Beacon, 1983.

———. *To Change the World: Christology and Cultural Criticism*. New York: Crossroad, 1981.

Ruse, Michael. *The Evolution-Creation Struggle*. Cambridge: Harvard University Press, 2005.

Russell, Letty M. *Just Hospitality: God's Welcome in the World of Difference*. Edited by J. Shannon Clarkson and Kate M. Ott. Louisville: Westminster John Knox, 2009.

Russell, Robert J. *Cosmology: From Alpha to Omega; The Creative Mutual Interaction of Theology and Science*. Minneapolis: Fortress, 2008.

———. *Time in Eternity: Pannenberg, Physics, and Eschatology in Creative Mutual Interaction*. Notre Dame: University of Notre Dame Press, 2012.

Samartha, Stanley J. *Courage for Dialogue: Ecumenical Issues in Inter-Religious Relationships*. Geneva: WCC, 1981.

———. "The Holy Spirit and People of Other Faiths." *Ecumenical Review* 42.3–4 (July 1990) 250–63.

BIBLIOGRAPHY

Sanneh, Lamin. *Translating the Message: The Missionary Impact on Culture*. Maryknoll, NY: Orbis, 1989.

Schaff, Philip, ed. *The Creeds of Christendom*. 3 vols. New York: Harper & Row, 1877. 6th ed., 1931. Reprint, Grand Rapids: Baker, 1990. www.ccel.org.

———. *A Select Library of the Nicene and Post-Nicene Fathers of the Christian Church*. 1st ser. 14 vols. Edited by Philip Schaff. Edinburgh, 1886-90. www.ccel.org.

Schaff, Philip, and Henry Wace, eds. *A Select Library of the Nicene and Post-Nicene Fathers of the Christian Church*. 2nd ser. 14 vols. Edinburgh, 1890-1900. www.ccel.org.

Sen, Keshub Chunder. "Lectures in India." In *Jesus beyond Christianity: The Classic Texts*, edited by Gregory A. Barker and Stephen E. Gregg, 165-66. New York: Oxford University Press, 2010.

Scherer, Glenn. "Christian-Right Views Are Swaying Politicians and Threatening the Environment." *Grist*, October 28, 2004. https://grist.org/politics/scherer-christian/.

Schombert, James. "Anthropic Principle." University of Oregon, Physics Department, lecture 28. June 2, 2004. http://www.welchco.com/02/14/01/60/04/03/1228.HTM.

Schumm, Darla, and Michael Stoltzfus. "Chronic Illness and Disability: Narratives of Suffering and Healing in Buddhism and Christianity." In *Disability and Religious Diversity: Cross-Cultural and Interreligious Perspectives*, edited by Darla Schumm and Michael Stoltzfus, 159-75. New York: Palgrave Macmillan, 2011.

Schwarz, Hans. *Christology*. Grand Rapids: Eerdmans, 1998.

———. *Eschatology*. Grand Rapids: Eerdmans, 2000.

Schweizer, Eduard. "Pneuma: The New Testament." In *Theological Dictionary of the New Testament*, edited by Gerhard Friedrich, translated and edited by Geoffrey W. Bromiley, 6:396-451. 10 vols. Grand Rapids: Eerdmans, 1964-76.

Sharma, Arvind. *Classical Hindu Thought: An Introduction*. New York: Oxford University Press, 2000.

Shatz, David. "A Jewish Perspective." In *The Oxford Handbook of Religious Diversity*, edited by Chad Meister, 365-80. New York: Oxford University Press, 2011.

Sherwin, Byron L. "Theodicy." In *Contemporary Jewish Religious Thought: Original Essays on Critical Concepts, Movements, and Beliefs*, edited by Arthur A. Cohen and Paul Mendes-Flohr, 959-70. New York: Charles Scribner's Sons, 1987.

Smedes, Lewis B. *Forgive and Forget: Healing the Hurts We Don't Deserve*. New York: Harper & Row, 1984.

Soskice, Janet M. "*Creatio Ex Nihilo*: Its Jewish and Christian Foundations." In *Creation and the God of Abraham*, edited by David B. Burrell et al., 24-39. New York: Cambridge University Press, 2010.

Smith, Brian K. "*Samsāra*." In vol. 12 of *Encyclopedia of Religion*, edited by Lindsay Jones, 8097-99. 2nd ed. Detroit: Macmillan Reference USA, 2005.

Smith, Gordon T. *Transforming Conversion: Rethinking the Language and Contours of Christian Initiation*. Grand Rapids: Baker Academic, 2010.

Spitzer, Robert J., SJ. *New Proofs for the Existence of God: Contributions of Contemporary Physics and Philosophy*. Grand Rapids: Eerdmans, 2010.

Steenwyk, Carrie Titcombe, and John D. Witvliet, eds. *The Worship Sourcebook*. 2nd ed. Grand Rapids: Baker, 2013.

Sugirtharajah, R. S., ed. *Asian Faces of Jesus*. Maryknoll, NY: Orbis, 1993.

Tappert, Theodore G., ed. and trans. *The Book of Concord: The Confessions of the Evangelical Lutheran Church*. Philadelphia: Fortress, 1959.

Tattersall, Ian. *The World from Beginnings to 4000 BCE*. New York: Oxford University Press, 2008.

Tattersall, Ian, and Jeffrey H. Schwartz. *Extinct Humans*. Boulder, CO: Westview, 2000.

Taylor, Charles. *A Secular Age*. Cambridge, MA: Belknap Press of Harvard University Press, 2007.

Taylor, Mark Lewis. *The Executed God: The Way of the Cross in Lockdown America*. Minneapolis: Fortress, 2001.

Terrell, JoAnne Marie. *Power in the Blood? The Cross in the African American Experience*. Maryknoll, NY: Orbis, 1998.

Terry, Justyn. "The Forgiveness of Sins and the Work of Christ: A Case for Substitutionary Atonement." *Anglican Theological Review* 95.1 (Winter 2013) 9–24.

"Thanatology." Wikipedia, n.d. https://en.wikipedia.org/wiki/Thanatology.

Thanh, Minh, and P. D. Leigh. *Sutra of the Medicine Buddha*. Translated by Dharma Master Hsuan Jung. 2nd ed. North Hills, CA: International Buddhist Monastic Institute, 2001. https://www.buddhanet.net/pdf_file/medbudsutra.pdf.

Timoner, Rachel. *Breath of Life: God as Spirit in Judaism*. Brewster, MA: Paraclete, 2011.

Torrance, Thomas F. *Space, Time and Resurrection*. New York: T&T Clark, 2019 [1976].

Van Huyssteen, J. Wentzel. *Alone in the World? Human Uniqueness in Science and Theology*. Grand Rapids: Eerdmans, 2006.

Volf, Miroslav. *After Our Likeness: The Church as the Image of the Trinity*. Grand Rapids: Eerdmans, 1998.

———. *The End of Memory: Remembering Rightly in a Violent World*. Grand Rapids: Eerdmans, 2006.

———. "Enter into Joy! Sin, Death, and the Life of the World to Come." In *The End of the World and the Ends of God: Science and Theology on Eschatology*, edited by John Polkinghorne and Michael Welker, 256–78. Harrisburg, PA: Trinity, 2000.

———. *Exclusion and Embrace: A Theological Exploration of Identity, Otherness, and Reconciliation*. Nashville: Abingdon, 1996.

———. *Work in the Spirit: Toward a Theology of Work*. Eugene, OR: Wipf & Stock, 2001 [1991].

Vroom, Hendrik. *No Other Gods: Christian Belief in Dialogue with Buddhism, Hinduism, and Islam*. Translated by Lucy Jansen. Grand Rapids: Eerdmans, 1996.

Wagner, C. Peter, and Rebecca Greenwood. "The Strategic-Level Deliverance Model." In *Understanding Spiritual Warfare: Four Views*, edited by James K. Beilby and Paul Rhodes Eddy, 173–98. Grand Rapids: Baker Academic, 2012.

Wallace, B. Alan. "A Buddhist View of Free Will: Beyond Determinism and Indeterminism." *Journal of Consciousness Studies* 18.3–4 (2011) 217–33.

Wallace, Dewey D. "Free Will and Predestination: An Overview." In vol. 5 of *Encyclopedia of Religion*, edited by Lindsay Jones, 3202–6. 2nd ed. Detroit: Macmillan Reference USA, 2005.

Wallace, Mark I. *Finding God in the Singing River: Christianity, Spirit, Nature*. Minneapolis: Fortress, 2005.

Walls, Jerry L. "Heaven." In *Oxford Handbook of Eschatology*, edited by Jerry L. Walls, 399–412. New York: Oxford University Press, 2009. Online edition.

———. *Heaven: The Logic of Eternal Joy*. New York: Oxford University Press, 2002.

———. *Hell: The Logic of Damnation.* Library of Religious Philosophy 9. Notre Dame: University of Notre Dame Press, 1992.

Ward, Keith. *Is Religion Dangerous?* Oxford: Lion, 2006.

———. "Personhood, Spirit, and the Supernatural." In *All That Is: A Naturalistic Faith for the Twenty-First Century*, by Arthur Peacocke, edited by Philip Clayton, 152–62. Minneapolis: Fortress, 2007.

———. *Religion and Community.* New York: Oxford University Press, 1999.

———. *Religion and Human Nature.* New York: Oxford University Press, 1998.

———. *Religion and Revelation: A Theology of Revelation in the World's Religions.* New York: Oxford University Press, 1994.

Ware, Bishop Kallistos. "Dare We Hope for the Salvation of All? Origen, St. Gregory of Nyssa and St. Isaac the Syrian." In *The Inner Kingdom, The Collected Works 1*, 193–215. Crestwood, NY: St. Vladimir's Seminary Press, 2001.

———. "The Holy Trinity: Model for Personhood-in-Relation." In *The Trinity and the Entangled World: Relationality in Physical Science and Theology*, edited by John Polkinghorne, 107–29. Grand Rapids: Eerdmans, 2010.

Watt, William Montgomery. *Muslim-Christian Encounters: Perceptions and Misperceptions.* London: Routledge, 1991.

Weaver, J. Denny. *The Nonviolent Atonement.* Grand Rapids: Eerdmans, 2001.

Weber, Timothy P. "Millennialism." In *Oxford Handbook of Eschatology*, edited by Jerry L. Walls, 365–83. New York: Oxford University Press, 2009. Online edition.

Welker, Michael. "Resurrection and Eternal Life: The Canonic Memory of the Resurrected Christ, His Reality, and His Glory." In *The End of the World and the Ends of God: Science and Theology on Eschatology*, edited by John Polkinghorne and Michael Welker, 279–90. Harrisburg, PA: Trinity, 2000.

Wessels, Anton. *Images of Jesus: How Jesus Is Perceived and Portrayed in Non-European Cultures.* Translated by John Vriend. Grand Rapids: Eerdmans, 1990.

"What Is DNA?" Medline Plus, n.d. https://medlineplus.gov/genetics/understanding/basics/dna/.

Wheeler, Brannon. "Ummah." In vol. 14 of *Encyclopedia of Religion*, edited by Lindsay Jones, 9446–48. 2nd ed. Detroit: Macmillan Reference USA, 2005.

Wilkinson, David. *Christian Eschatology and the Physical Universe.* New York: T&T Clark, 2010.

Wink, Walter. *The Powers That Be: Theology for a New Millennium.* New York: Doubleday, 1998.

Woodberry, J. Dudley. "The Kingdom of God in Islam and the Gospel." In *Anabaptists Meeting Muslims: A Calling for Presence in the Way of Christ*, edited by James R. Krabill et al., 48–58. Scottdale, PA: Herald, 2005.

World Council of Churches [WCC]. *Baptism, Eucharist and Ministry.* Faith and Order Paper 111. Geneva, WCC, 1982.

———. *Mission and Evangelism: An Ecumenical Affirmation.* Geneva: WCC, 1982. In *The Ecumenical Movement: An Anthology of Key Texts and Voices*, edited by Michael Kinnamon and Brian E. Cope, #25, 372–83. Geneva: WCC, 1997.

———. *The Nature and Mission of the Church—A Stage on the Way to a Common Statement.* Faith and Order Paper 198. Geneva: WCC, December 15, 2005. https://www.oikoumene.org/en/resources/documents/commissions/faith-and-order/i-unity-the-church-and-its-mission/the-nature-and-mission-of-the-church-a-stage-on-the-way-to-a-common-statement.

———, Commission on World Mission and Evangelism. *Together towards Life: Mission and Evangelism in Changing Landscapes.* September 6, 2012. https://www.oikoumene.org/resources/documents/together-towards-life-mission-and-evangelism-in-changing-landscapes.

———. "Towards Common Witness." September 19, 1997. https://www.oikoumene.org/resources/documents/towards-common-witness.

———. "What is the World Council of Churches?" n.d. https://www.oikoumene.org/about-the-wcc.

Wright, N. T. *For All the Saints?: Remembering the Christian Departed.* Harrisburg, PA: Morehouse, 2003.

———. *Jesus and the Victory of God.* Vol. 2 of *Christian Origins and the Question of God.* Minneapolis: Fortress, 1996.

———. *Surprised by Hope: Rethinking Heaven, the Resurrection, and the Mission of the Church.* New York: HarperOne, 2008.

Yogananda, Paramahansa. *Man's Eternal Quest.* Los Angeles: Self-Realization Fellowship, 1975.

Yong, Amos. *The Cosmic Breath: Spirit and Nature in the Christianity-Buddhism-Science Trialogue.* Philosophical Studies in Science and Religion 4. Boston: Brill, 2012.

———. *Pneumatology and the Christian-Buddhist Dialogue: Does the Spirit Blow through the Middle Way?* Studies in Systematic Theology 11. Boston: Brill, 2012.

———. *The Spirit of Creation: Modern Science and Divine Action in the Pentecostal-Charismatic Imagination.* Pentecostal Manifestos. Grand Rapids: Eerdmans, 2011.

———. *Theology and Down Syndrome: Reimagining Disability in Late Modernity.* Waco: Baylor University Press, 2007.

Author Index

Abe, Masao, 75
Abelard, Peter, 201-2
Adiswarananda, Swami, 132
Al-Hallajah, Husayn ibn Mansur, 236
Anselm of Canterbury, 42, 178, 201, 203-204
Apollinarius of Laodicea, 172-73
Aquinas, Thomas, 2-3, 10, 42, 58, 121, 126, 130, 137, 177, 202, 225, 285-86, 372, 373, 402
Aristotle 80, 121, 130, 260
Arius 52-53, 170-71
Athanasius of Alexandria, 171, 177-78, 224, 266
Atkins, Peter, 40
Augustine, 9, 93, 94-95, 100, 126, 136, 137, 165, 182, 221, 247-48, 267-68, 270, 275, 296, 316-17, 319-20, 321, 322, 378, 387, 398, 402
Averroes, 130
Avicenna (Ibn Sina), 130

Baker-Fletcher, Garth Kasimu, 139, 210
Barth, Karl, 8-9, 10-11, 16, 49, 79, 176, 180, 184, 202, 216, 228, 248, 358, 378
Basil the Great, 82-83, 221
Bauman, Zygmunt, 154
Becker, Ernst, 366

Berger, Peter, 43
Berkhof, Hendrikus, 229
Biel, Gabriel, 268
Bloesch, Donald, 381
Boethius, 127
Boff, Leonardo, 376
Borg, Marcus J., 357
Brueggemann, Walter, 45-46, 332
Buddhaghosa, 28

Cabezón, José Ignacio, 82, 192
Calvin, John, 10, 13, 23, 126, 137, 226, 248, 269-70
Clifford, Anne M., 85
Clooney, F. X., 73
Cohen, Arthur A., 405
Cohen, Hermann, 235
Cohon, Samuel S., 129
Cone, James H., 18, 58-59, 157-58, 166
Cornell, Vincent, 32-33
Cyprian, 165, 296

Darwin, Charles, 39, 97, 98
Dawkins, Richard, 40
D'Costa, Gavin, 332
de Molina, Luis, 127
Deedat, Ahmed, 215
Diana Butler Bass, 354
Dufault-Hunter, Erin, 254
Dyson, Freeman, 95-96

AUTHOR INDEX

Einstein, Albert, 80, 89, 91, 94
Enns, Peter, 141
Erasmus, 248
Evodius, 126

Feuerbach, Ludwig, 38, 39, 43, 84, 357
Francis, Pope, 384
Freud, Sigmund, 38, 43, 357

Gaiser, Frederick J., 279
Ghandi, Mahatma, 195, 246, 252
Giggs, Eddie, 291
Gillman, Neil 405
Grant, Jacquelyn, 162
Gregory of Nanzianzen, 173
Gregory of Nyssa, 68, 201, 203
Gregory of Palamas, 267
Grenz, Stanley J., 229
Gross, Rita M., 192
Guessoum, Nidhal, 81
Gutiérrez, Gustavo, 139, 165

Habermas, Jürgen, 354
Hartle, James, 92, 93, 94
Hawking, Stephen, 92, 93, 94
Hick, John 64–65, 185, 375–76, 378–79, 386
Hitchens, Christopher, 40
Hodge, Charles, 202
Hubmaier, Balthasar, 270

Ibn Gabirol, Solomon (Avicebron), 128
Irenaeus, 9, 11, 137, 200, 201, 266

James, William, 255, 416
Jenkins, Jerry B., 363
John of Damascus, 68, 343
Johnon, Elizabeth, 223
Juergensmeyer, Mark, 60

Kant, Immanuel, 42, 43, 202
Kierkegaard, Søren, 138, 416
Klausner, Joseph, 162
Klostermaier, Klaus, 252
Knitter, Paul F., 186
Kogan, Michael S., 213
Küng, Hans, 191

LaCugna, C. M., 53
Lahaye, Tim, 362
Ladd, G. E., 390
Lapide, Pinchas, 186
Lee, Jung Young, 224
Lemaître, Georges, 91
Libet, Benjamin, 125
Lindsey, Hal, 362
Locke, John, 13
Luther, Martin, 23, 58, 59, 68, 155, 202, 223, 248, 268, 269, 272, 273, 307, 321

Maimonides, Moses, 80, 128–29, 251
Martyr, Justin, 169, 221
Marx, Karl, 1, 38, 39, 43, 359
McMahan, D. L., 352
Melanchton, Philip, 155
Mendelssohn, Moses, 187
Miyahira, Nozomu, 56
Moltmann, Jürgen, 17, 18–19, 45, 49, 57, 118, 122, 157, 161, 178, 187, 188, 197, 207–8, 210, 219, 223, 260, 275, 358, 373, 378, 397n61, 399, 400, 415
Müller, Max, 24
Murphy, Nancey, 101

Nalunnakkal, George M., 275
Nasr, N. H., 108
Nestorius, 173
Neusner, Jacob, 262
Newbigin, Lesslie, 239
Newlands, George, 59
Newton, Isaac, 89, 95
Nicholas of Cusa, 68
Niebuhr, Reinhold, 134
Nietzsche, Friedrich, 39
Nyamiti, Charles, 165

Origen 169, 225, 377–78

Panenberg, Wolfhart, 3, 17, 55, 156, 322, 358, 397
Panikkar, Raimundo, 194, 238
Paramahansa, Ramakrishna, 194
Park, Andrew Sung, 209
Pascal, Blaise, 416

AUTHOR INDEX

Pathrapankal, Joseph, 234
Pelagius, 136, 247–48
Philo of Alexandria, 128
Pieris, Aloysius, 208
Pinnock, Clark, 48, 380
Plantinga, Alvin, 387
Plato, 121, 128, 130, 359
Polanyi, Michael, 2
Polkinghorne, John, 369–70, 373, 376–77, 394
Pseudo-Dionysius, 225

Rahner, Karl, 50
Rahula, Walpola, 133
Ramanuja, 71–73, 120, 131
Rivera, Mayra, 85
Robinson, J. A. T., 183, 184, 185
Rogers, Eugene F., 224
Rosenzweig, Franz, 211
Ruether, Rosemary Radford, 165–66
Russell, Letty M., 60, 311
Russell, Robert J., 101

Sadra, Mulla, 130
Samartha, Stanley J., 65, 194, 220
Sankara, 71–73, 120, 131, 246
Sartre, Jean-Paul, 83
Schleiermacher, F. D. E., 13–14, 138
Schwartz, Jeffrey H., 113
Schwarz, Hanz, 360
Schweitzer, Albert, 357
Sen, Keshub Chunder, 195
Smith, Adam, 152

Smith, Allen, 59
Socrates, 39

Tattersall, Ian, 113
Taylor, Charles, 38
Tertullian, 165, 170
Thomas, M. M., 194
Timoner, Rachel, 235

Upadhyay, Brahmabandhab, 73

Vivekananda, Swami, 194, 195, 347
Volf, Miroslav, 152, 206, 259, 295, 307

Wallace, M. I., 224
Walls, J. L., 401
Ward, Keith, 133
Ward, Peter, 291
Ware, Kallistos, 49, 380
Warfield, B. B., 276
Welker, Michel, 362
Wesley, John, 270–71, 273
Wheeler, John, 89
Wink, Walter, 229
Wright, N. T., 400, 402

Xavier, Francis, 352

Yong, Amos, 232–33, 239

Zuckerman, Phil, 354
Zwingli, Ulrich, 23

Subject Index

adharma, 144, 145, 245
advaita, 71, 120, 131–32, 246
Aditi, 70
Agni, 70
ahimsa, 150, 195
Allah, 32, 66–67, 69, 108, 119, 129, 130, 189, 190, 214, 230, 235, 236, 244, 245, 251, 263, 341, 342, 405, 406, 408
Allah, ancient Christian approaches to, 68
amillennialism, 398
Ananda, 73, 238
angels, 128, 225–26, 228, 229. *See also* spiritual powers
angels, biblical testimony. *See* spiritual powers, biblical testimony
annihilationism, 374, 377, 379
antaryamin, 237
anthropic principle, 95–96
antichrist, 391–92
antichrist, in Islam, 392, 406–7
anti-Semitism, 35, 187, 336
Apollinarism, 172
apostolicity. *See* church, marks of
Arianism, 52, 167, 170–71
aseity, 54
atheism, 37, 38, 39–40, 43, 101, 255; in Judaism, 334. *See also* New Atheists

atman, 70, 71, 75, 131, 237, 409, 410
atonement: 197–98, and ascension 210; and healing, 277–78; and resurrection, 209–10; and violence, 205–6; biblical metaphors for, 198–200, suffering of God and Christ, 207–8, Trinitarian shape of, 207
atonement theories: Christus Victor, 200, 202; moral example, 201, 202, 205, penal substitution, 202, 204, 205; ransom, 200–201, 203; recapitulation, 200, 202–3; satisfaction, 201, 202, 203–4, 205
atonement, among religions: Buddhism, 215–16; Hinduism, 144–45, 196, 216–17, 264; Islam, 214–15; Judaism, 187, 211–13, 262
avatar, 132, 194, 195, 196, 246
avidya, 71, 131, 145, 245, 410

baptism: 317–18, 320–22; and forgiveness, 258; believers' 312, 322–23; biblical testimony, 318–19; infant, 319–20, 322, 323. *See also* Spirit baptism
beatific vision, 285, 402
believers' baptism. *See* baptism, believers'

437

SUBJECT INDEX

bhakti, 25, 72, 246, 264, 345–46
big bang theory, 91–92, 93–94
binitarianism, 51
biology, 84, 110
body-soul dualism, 121, 130, 132
Brahma, 70, 73, 196, 408
Brahman, 26, 70, 71, 72, 75, 88, 131, 196, 237, 346, 410
Brahman-*atman* relationship, 71
Buddha, Guatama, 24, 27, 28, 74, 87, 106, 133, 144, 147, 231, 252, 349, 353, 410
Buddha, Guatama, role of in Buddhism, 28, 74, 75, 191–94, 215, 246
Buddhism, historical development, of 348–50

caste system, 145, 147
catholicity. *See* church, marks of
cessationism, 275–76
chaos theory, 90, 102
charisms, 232, 276, 307, 308–9
Christ: as healer, 163–164, 276–77; descent to hell, 381–82; gospel narratives, 159–60; humanity and divinity of, 168–69, 172, 174–75, 178–79; incarnation of, 177–78; Jewishness of, 187; life and ministry of, 160–63; preexistence of, 182–83; resurrection of, 175, 176; second coming, signs of, 391; self-emptying of 178–79; sinlessness of, 180–82; two natures of, 178–79; uniqueness of, 185–86, virgin birth, 183–84
Christ, among other religions: Buddhism, 162, 191–94; Hinduism, 194–96; Islam, 163, 189–91, 406; Judaism, 186–87
Christ, views of his miracles in other religions: Buddhism, 164; Hinduism, 164; Islam, 164; Judaism, 164–65
Christian–Buddhist relations, 352–53
Christian–Hindu relations, 347–48
Christian–Jewish relations, 336–38
Christian–Muslim relations, 343

Christology: 155; and race, 166; African, 165; Alexandrian School, 172–73; Antiochean School, 172, 173; colonialism 166–67; feminist, 165–66; from above, 156; from below, 156; liberation, 157, 165; logos, 169; orthodox, 173–75
church governance: forms of, 305–6; historical development of, 304–5
church: as sign of God's reign, 295; biblical metaphors for, 293–94; diversification of, 290–91; marks of, 295–98; missional existence of, 298, 300
Cit, 73
classical theism, 48
colonialism, 148, 167, 299–300, 342, 344, 348, 351
compatibilism, 126
confirmation, 316, 323–24
conversion, 253–57
conversion, among other faiths: Buddhism, 265–66, Hinduism, 264–65, in Islam, 262–63; Judaism, 261–62
cosmic consummation, among other religions: Buddhism; 414, Hinduism, 414; Islam, 414; Judaism, 413–14
cosmic eschatology, Hindu, 408
Council of Chalcedon, 174, 175
Council of Nicaea, 173, 222, 327
creation: 45; *ex nihilo*, 93; narratives, 111, 121–22, 151: Trinitarian, 82–83
creation, among other religions: Abrahamic traditions, 86–87, 93; Buddhist, 87–88; Hindu, 88–89
creative explosion, 113
cultural big bang, 113

dark energy, 95
dark matter, 95
da'wah, 342
death, 105, 121, 136, 366–68, 381, 386

438

death, among other religions:
    Buddhism, 410; Hinduism, 409;
    Islam, 405, 407; Judaism, 404
dehumanization, 148
deification, 137, 266-67, 271, 273, 285
demons, 225, 226. See also spiritual
    powers
demons, biblical testimony. See spiritual
    powers, biblical testimony
denominations, 4, 288, 289
determinism, 126-28
devas, 70, 231
Dhamma, 29, 30, 144, 193, 196, 349,
    350
Dharma, 144, 147, 150, 196, 245,
dialogue, among religions: 333
dialogue, Christian-Buddhist, 74.
    See also Christian-Buddhist
    relations
dialogue, Christian-Jewish, 188. See also
    Christian-Jewish relations
dispensationalism. See Israel, Christian
    views of
diversity of religions. See religious
    plurality
divine action, 101-2
divinization, 266
doctrine, 3, 15
Donatism, 296
double predestination, 126, 248, 249
dukkha, 74, 106, 132, 144, 280, 349, 350

ecclesiology, 287-88
ecological pneumatology. See green
    pneumatology
ecology, 108-9
ecology, among other religions:
    Buddhist, 106-7; Hindu, 107;
    Islamic, 108, Judaism, 107-8
economics, 152-54
ecumenism: 327-31; dialogues, 329
Eightfold Path, 147, 247, 350
election: 242, 249-50; doctrinal
    development of, 247-48
election, among other religions. See
    human freedom, among other
    religions
emergence, 90-91

emerging church, 291-292
enlightenment, 28, 29, 30, 191, 192, 193,
    216, 231, 246-47, 348, 350
epistemology, 2
eschatology: and liberation, 382; and the
    created order; consummation,
    delay of, 390-91 383-85;
    contemporary approaches to,
    357-58; historical development
    of, 356-57; in light of science,
    364-66
eschatology, among other religions:
    Buddhism, 410-11; Hinduism,
    408-10; Islam, 405-8; Judaism,
    402-4
eternity, 54-55, 94, 393, 394, 396, 397
eternity solution, 127
ethnocentrism, 148
Eucharist, 253, 294, 305, 310, 316,
    324-26
Evangelicalism, 15
evangelism, 301-2
evil, 104-6, 387. See also theodicy
evolution, 41, 97-99, 110, 114-15,
    140-41, 388
evolution, among other religions:
    Buddhism, Hinduism, Islam,
    Judaism, 99
exclusivism. See religious pluralism,
    approaches to
exorcism, 232-33, 275, 319

fall: 134; contemporary views of, 137-
    39; historical views of, 135-37
fine-tuning argument, 95-96
fitrah, 119, 129
five pillars of Islam, 67, 245, 340, 341
forgiveness, 257-61
forgiveness, among other religions:
    Buddhism, 265; Hinduism, 264;
    Islam, 263; Judaism, 262
Free Church, 297
freedom, human, 124, 125, 126, 127,
    136, 250, 267, 375, 376, 380, 393
freedom, human, among other religions:
    Islam, 141, 251; Judaism, 141
fundamentalism, 14, 15, 16, 41, 79, 106,
    183, 358, 363, 383, 384

SUBJECT INDEX

Gage, Phineas, 123
gender relations, 117
gender relations, Islamic view of, 147
general relativity theory, 89
Global South, 3, 24, 37, 44, 157, 163, 165, 218, 219, 234, 275, 289, 292, 303, 353, 358, 363
globalization, 151, 288, 289, 292, 330, 341
glorification, 242, 284–86, 401
glossolalia. See tongues
God: as eternal, 54; as Father of Jesus, 46; faithfulness/constancy of, 54–55; freedom of, 48; goodness of, 57–58; hiddenness of, 47–48; holiness of, 54; hospitality of, 59–60; immutability of, 57; impassibility of, 58; inclusive language for, 61–62; loving compassion of, 56–57; names of, 44–45; nearness of, 47–48; omniscience of, 55; omnipotence of, 55; patience of 59; 58–59; proofs for, 41–43; righteousness of, 58; Spirit of, 55; works of, 45–46
God-of-the-gaps, 102
green pneumatology, 224

Hadith, 30, 31, 81, 130, 191, 263, 280, 405–6, 407, 408
han, 57, 209
Hawking-Hartle proposal, 92, 93, 94
healing, 209, 227, 243, 274–78, 302–3
healing, among other religions: Buddhism, 280–81; Hinduism, 280; Islam, 280, Judaism, 279–80
heaven, 400–402
hell, 374–77
herem, 149
Hindu deities: conception of, 69–71; female, 71
Holy Spirit: and Jesus, 222; discernment of, 239–40; presence in creation, 223–24
Holy Spirit, among other faiths: Buddhism, 238–39; Hinduism, 237–38; Islam 235–37; Judaism, 234–35
holy war: in Islam, 149–150; in Judaism, 149
hope, 360–61
hospitality, 59–60, 151, 259, 311, 331
human dignity, 148
human dignity, Islamic view of, 146–47
human flourishing, 117, 146
human freedom. *See* election
human freedom, among other religions: Buddhism, 252; Hinduism, 252; Islam; 251, Judaism, 250–51
human nature, 120–21
human nature among other religions: Buddhism, 132–34; Hinduism, 130–32; Islam, 129–30; Judaism, 128–29
humanity: consciousness, 114; development of, 112–13; gender relations, 117–18; genetics, 114; image of God in, 117; in relation to creation, 110–11; language, 115; relationality of, 117; self-transcendence, 113–14; uniqueness of, 113–14
humanity, Islamic understanding of, 118–19
hypostatic union, 175, 182

image of God (*imago Dei*): 9, 43, 110, 111, 116–17, 122, 125, 136, 138, 148, 149, 153, 154, 181, 372; views of, 116
image of God, in Islam, 118–19, 130
incarnation: 20, 50, 94, 163, 166, 168, 169, 173, 177–78, 179, 180, 182, 183, 200, 201, 202, 203, 209, 224, 394; revisionist views of, 184–85
incarnation, in Hinduism. *See* avatar
inclusivism. *See* religious plurality, approaches to
incompatibilism, 126
Indra, 70
inerrancy, 15
inerrancy, in Islam, 340
infant baptism. *See* baptism, infant

SUBJECT INDEX

integrated duality, 121
intermediate state, 368–70
intermediate state, in Islam, 407
isa, isvara, 70, 72
Islam, Sunni/Shi'ite division, 339–40
Israel, Christian views of, 337

Jesus. *See* Christ
jihad, 149–50
jinn, 230–31, 407
jnana, 246
Joint Declaration on Justification, 271
judgment, divine, 396–97
judgment, in other religions: Islam, 407–8; Judaism, 402–3
justice, 58, 112, 146, 148, 233, 260, 262, 300, 302–3, 363, 382
justification, 242, 267–71, 273

Kabbalistic traditions, 234, 262
kamma (karma), 147, 215, 246, 265, 374
karma, 72, 107, 133, 145, 150, 216, 246, 252, 264, 280, 374, 409, 410, 412, 413,
karmic samsara, 409, 410
kingdom of God, 46–47, 162, 164, 227, 294–95, 357, 388, 390, 391, 395
koinonia, 294, 327
Krishna, 131–32, 150, 194, 195, 196, 246, 346

liberation, 18, 58, 139, 146, 186, 200, 203, 382–83
liberation, in other religions: Buddhism, 27, 88, 106, 246–47, 252, 413; Hinduism, 27, 217, 246, 345, 348, 350, 413
liberation, potential for in other religions: Abrahamic traditions, 146; Buddhism 147; Hinduism, 147; Islam, 147
Lord's Supper. *See* Eucharist

Mahdi, 406–7
Mahayana Buddhism 24, 28–29, 74, 75, 76, 87, 164, 191, 192, 193, 215, 231, 246, 247, 252, 265–66, 280, 349, 351, 411, 414

materialism, 226, 276
maya, 131, 145, 245
Messiah, Jewish conception of, 211–13
migration, 112, 151, 154
millennialism, 398–99
mind–body relationship, 123–24
minister, status of, 306–7
ministry, diaconal-charismatic, 307–8
miracles, 103–4, 163
mission, among other religions, Buddhism, 349; Hinduism, 264; Islam, 342; Judaism, 335
mission, to Jews, 338–39
moksa, 27, 245–46, 409, 410
Molinism, 127, 128
monarchianism, 51–52, 169–70
monotheism, 44
Muhammad, 31, 164, 190, 191, 230, 237, 251, 263, 339–40, 341
Muhammad, role of in Islam, 31, 32, 190, 341
murti, 346
mutual conditioning, 121

naturalism, 101, 226, 362
neo-apocalypticism, 362–63
Nestorianism, 172, 343
neuroscience, 125
New Atheists, 40–41
new creation, 370, 394–95, 396
Newtonian theory, 89
nibbana, 215, 410–11
Nicene-Constantinopolitan Creed, 171, 174, 182, 222
Nirguna, 72
nirvana, 215, 266, 349, 411, 414
nondualism, Hindu, 71–72, 131
Non-interventionist Objective Divine Action, 101, 102

Open Theism, 127, 128
open universe, 90
order of salvation (ordo salutis), 241–42
ordination: 310; of women, 311–12
ordinances, 316
origin-of-life studies, 96–97

panentheism, 48–49

SUBJECT INDEX

pantheism, 48, 55, 76, 83, 267
pantheism, among other religions: Buddhism, 76; Hinduism, 132
Parvati, 71
Pentecostal-Charismatic movements, 289–90
People of the Book, 342
perseverance, 284–85
pluralism, 64–66. *See also* religious plurality, approaches to
pneumatology: 218–20; historical development of, 220–22; Indian Christian approaches to, 238. *See also* Holy Spirit
powers, structural, 229
priesthood of all believers, 307
progressive revelation, 61
prophetic Judaism, 34
proselytism, 256–57, 301–2,
providence, 100, 101, 103, 226, 228, 361
Pure Land Buddhism, 193, 215–16, 247, 265, 349

qualified nondualism, Hindu, 71–72, 131
quantum entanglement, 90
quantum theory, 90, 102
Qur'an, 30–33, 81, 86–87, 118, 130, 142, 143, 146, 150, 163, 164, 189–90, 230, 236, 245, 251, 262, 263, 339, 341, 342, 389, 405, 406, 407, 408

Rabbinic Judaism, 34, 335
racism, 148–49, 299, 324
rebirth, 72, 88, 150, 408, 409–10, 411, 412, 413. *See also* reincarnation, transmigration
reductionism, 124
reincarnation, 231, 411–13. *See also* rebirth, transmigration
religious plurality, approaches to, 63
religious plurality, among other religions: Buddhism, 351–52; Hinduism, 347; Islam, 341–42; Judaism, 336
repentance, 253, 258

repentance, among other religions: Buddhism, 265; Hinduism, 264; Islam, 263; Judaism, 262
resurrection, 370–73. *See also* Christ, resurrection of
resurrection, among other religions: Islam, 407–8; Judaism, 404–5
reunionism. *See* Israel, Christian views of
revelation: as promise, 17; as history, 17; as human awareness/capacity, 12; 13–14; as liberation, 18–19; as testimony, 16; biblical, 12; general, 8–10; in Christ, 11; "revised" theology of, 12; special, 8–9; traditional view of, 12, 15
revisionism. *See* Israel, Christian views of
revivalism, 254–255
rita, 216, 264
ruach, 219, 235
Ruah ha-Kodesh, 234
ruh, 235, 236

saccidananda, 73, 238
sacraments, 316–17
saguna, 72
Saivism, 217
Sakti, 71
Salvation, among other religions: Buddhism, 120, 246–47; Hinduism, 245–46; Islam, 244–45; Judaism 243–44
sampradaya, 345
sanctification, 243, 269, 270–71, 272–74
Sat, 73
Satan, 203, 227, 230
satyagraha, 195
Savitri, 70
science, approaches to, 78–80
science, approaches among other religions: Buddhism, 82; Hinduism, 81–82; Islam, 80–81; Judaism, 80
Scripture: and tradition, 22–23; inspiration of, 20–21

Scripture, among other religions: Buddhism, 28–30; Hinduism, 25–27; Islam, 30–32; Judaism, 335
secularism, 4–5, 37–39, 288, 292, 353–55
Shaivism, 71
shakti, 194, 237, 238
Sharia, 342, 344
Shema, 44, 335
shirk, 67, 68, 118, 189
Shiva, 70, 71, 196
sin: biblical testimony, 134–35; contemporary views of, 137–39; historical views of, 135–37; original, 140, 141; structural, 139
sin, among other religions: Buddhism, 144; Hinduism, 144–45; Islam, 142–43; Judaism, 142
slavery, 112, 148, 151, 154
sola Scriptura, 23
special relativity theory, 89
Spirit baptism, 281–83
Spirit Christology, 222
spiritual gifts. *See* charisms
spiritual powers: 225, 226, 229; biblical testimony, 227–28
spiritual powers, among other religions: Buddhism, 231; Hinduism, 231; Islam, 230–31; Judaism, 230
spiritual warfare, 225, 232–34
Sri (Lakshmi), 71
stewardship principle, 153
suffering. *See* theodicy
suffering, nonhuman, 105–6
Sufism, 30, 236, 245, 263, 280, 341, 414
sunyata, 29, 74, 75, 76, 239
supercessionism. *See* Israel, Christian views of
synagogue, 335

theodicy, 105, 385–88
theodicy, among other religions: Islam, 389; Judaism, 388–89
theological anthropology, 3, 111
theology: 2; contextual nature of, 4; dialogical, 5

Theravada Buddhism, 28, 29, 63, 74, 87, 133, 147, 191, 192, 193, 215, 231, 238, 265, 280, 349, 350, 411
time, 93, 94–95, 393–94
Tipitaka, 28, 29, 349
tongues, 282, 284
Torah, 33–34, 212, 244, 262, 335, 403, 404
tradition. *See* scripture, and tradition
transmigration, 131, 358, 409, 411, 412. *See also* rebirth, reincarnation
Trimurti, 73
Trinity: 53; biblical testimony, 50–51; communion within, 53; economic, 50; immanent, 50; love of, 56; Muslim objections to, 68; relationality, 60

ultimate reality: Buddhist, 74, 75, 76, 339; Hindu, 70, 71, 237
ummah, 251, 339, 340, 342
unity, 327. *See also* ecumenism
universalism. *See* religious plurality, approaches to

Vaishnavism, 71, 217, 246, 346
Vedanta, 26, 71, 88, 120, 131, 410
Vedas, 25–26, 70, 409
vice-regency, 120
violence: 60–61, 112, 140, 148, 151, 198, 205–6, 299, 303, 363, 388
violence, among other religions; Abrahamic faiths, 149–50; Buddhism, 150; Hinduism, 150
Vishnu, 25, 70, 71, 73, 132, 150, 194, 195, 196, 217, 231, 246

work, theology of, 151–52
World Council of Churches, 329
worship, 314–16
worship, among other religions: Buddhism, 350–51; Hinduism, 345–46; Islam, 341; Judaism, 335–36

Zoharic literature, 234

www.ingramcontent.com/pod-product-compliance
Lightning Source LLC
Chambersburg PA
CBHW021927290426
44108CB00012B/746